D0281781

THE TREATY OF LISBON IN PERSPECTIVE

The European Reform Treaty:
Consolidated Treaty on European Union and
the Consolidated Treaty on the Functioning of the European Union

The full text with all Protocols and Declarations as signed in Lisbon on 13 December 2007 together with supplementary key papers, a detailed analysis and a comprehensive index

BRITISH MANAGEMENT DATA FOUNDATION

'The Treaty of Lisbon in Perspective'

© Anthony Cowgill and Andrew Cowgill, 2008

The authors have asserted their right to be identified as the authors of **the analyses, tables and summaries** of this work in accordance with the Copyright, Designs and Patents Act 1988.

All rights reserved. No part of **analyses, annotations, tables and summaries** of this publication may be reproduced, stored in a retrieval system, copied or transmitted, in any form or by any means, save with written permission of the publisher or in accordance with the provisions of the Copyright, Designs and Patents Act 1988, or under the terms of any licence permitting limited copying issued by the Copyright Licencing Agency, 90 Tottenham Court Road, London W1P 0LP.

Published by:

British Management Data Foundation
Highfield
Longridge
Sheepscombe
STROUD
Gloucestershire, England
GL6 7QU

Tel: (01452) 812837 Fax: (01452) 812527
E-mail: bmdfstroud@aol.com
Web-sites: www.bmdf.co.uk
www.eurotreaties.com

7 February 2008

ISBN: 978-0-9558262-0-7

Previous publications in this series:

The European Constitution in Perspective

Published : December 2004 ISBN 0 9520366 7 3

The Treaty of Nice in Perspective - Consolidated Treaty on European Union

Volume One : *Analysis* ISBN No: 0 9520366 4 9
Volume Two : *Consolidated Treaty on European Union* ISBN No: 0 9520366 5 7

Published : July 2001

The Treaty of Amsterdam in Perspective - Consolidated Treaty on European Union

Second Edition : October 1999 ISBN No: 0 9520366 3 0

The Maastricht Treaty in Perspective – Consolidated Treaty on European Union

Third Edition : October 1996 ISBN 0 9520366 1 4

CONTENTS

		Page
Foreword		vii
Notes on the Text		ix
Background to the Treaty of Lisbon		xv
Principal Issues and Key Points		xxvii
Pertinent Articles		xlvii
British Business Concerns		lxiii
Voting in the Institutions		lxv
Legislative Procedures		lxxi
Changes from Unanimity to Qualified Majority		lxxxvii
THE TREATY ON EUROPEAN UNION		1
Preamble		1
Title I:	**Common Provisions**	3
Title II:	**Provisions on Democratic Principles**	6
Title III:	**Provisions on the Institutions**	7
Title IV:	**Provisions on Enhanced Co-operation**	11
Title V:	**General Provisions on the Union's External Action and specific provisions on the Common Foreign and Security Policy**	12
	Chapter 1: General Provisions on the Union's External Action	12
	Chapter 2: Specific Provisions of the Common Foreign and Security Policy	13
	Section 1: Common Provisions	13
	Section 2: Provisions of the Common Security and Defence Policy	18
Title VI:	**Final Provisions**	21
THE TREATY ON THE FUNCTIONING OF THE EUROPEAN UNION		25
Preamble		25
Part One:	**Principles**	26
Title I:	Categories and Areas of Union Competence	26
Title II:	Provisions having General Application	28
Part Two:	**Non-Discrimination and Citizenship**	30

			Page
Part Three:	**Union Policies and Internal Actions**		32
Title I:	The Internal Market		32
Title Ia:	Free Movement of Goods		32
	Chapter 1:	The Customs Union	33
	Chapter 1a:	Customs co-operation	33
	Chapter 2:	Prohibition of quantitative restrictions between Member States	33
Title II:	Agriculture and Fisheries		34
Title III:	Free Movement of Persons, Services and Capital		36
	Chapter 1:	Workers	36
	Chapter 2:	Right of Establishment	37
	Chapter 3:	Services	39
	Chapter 4:	Capital and Payments	40
Title IV:	Area of Freedom, Security and Justice		41
	Chapter 1:	General Provisions	41
	Chapter 2:	Policies on border checks, asylum and immigration	42
	Chapter 3:	Judicial co-operation in civil matters	44
	Chapter 4:	Judicial co-operation in criminal matters	45
	Chapter 5:	Police co-operation	47
Title V:	Transport		48
Title VI:	Common Rules on Competition, Taxation and Approximation of Laws		50
	Chapter 1:	Rules on Competition	50
	Chapter 2:	Tax Provisions	53
	Chapter 3:	Approximation of laws	54
Title VII:	Economic and Monetary Policy		55
	Chapter 1:	Economic Policy	56
	Chapter 2:	Monetary Policy	59
	Chapter 3:	Institutional Provisions	61
	Chapter 3a:	Provisions specific to Member States whose currency is the Euro	62
	Chapter 4:	Transitional Provisions	63
Title VIII:	Employment		66
Title IX:	Social Policy		67
Title X:	The European Social Fund		70
Title XI:	Education, Vocational Training, Youth and Sport		71
Title XII:	Culture		72
Title XIII:	Public Health		72
Title XIV:	Consumer Protection		73
Title XV:	Trans-European Networks		74
Title XVI:	Industry		75
Title XVII:	Economic, Social and Territorial Cohesion		75
Title XVIII:	Research and Technological Development and Space		76
Title XIX:	Environment		78
Title XX:	Energy		80
Title XXI:	Tourism		80
Title XXII:	Civil Protection		81
Title XXIII:	Administrative Co-operation		81
Part Four:	**Association of the Overseas Countries and Territories**		82
Part Five:	**The Union's External Action in areas other than the Common Foreign and Security Policy**		83
Title I:	General Provisions on the Union's External Action		83
Title II:	Common Commercial Policy		83
Title III:	Co-operation with Third Countries and Humanitarian Aid		84
	Chapter 1:	Development Co-operation	84
	Chapter 2:	Economic, Financial and Technical Co-operation with Third Countries	85

			Page
	Chapter 3:	Humanitarian Aid	86
Title IV:	Restrictive Measures		86
Title V:	International Agreements		87
Title VI:	The Union's relations with international organisations and Third Countries and Union delegations		89
Title VII:	Solidarity Clause		89
Part Six:	**Institutional and Budgetary Provisions**		90
Title I:	Provisions governing the Institutions		90
	Chapter 1:	The Institutions	90
		The European Parliament	90
		The European Council	92
		The Council	93
		The Commission	94
		The Court of Justice of the European Union	95
		The European Central Bank	101
		The Court of Auditors	102
	Chapter 2:	Legal Acts of the Union, adoption procedures and other provisions	104
		The legal acts of the Union	104
		Procedures for the adoption of Acts and other provisions	105
	Chapter 3:	The Union's Advisory Bodies	108
		The Economic and Social Committee	108
		The Committee of the Regions	109
		European Investment Bank	109
Title II:	Financial Provisions		110
	Chapter 1:	The Union's Own Resources	111
	Chapter 2:	The Multiannual Financial Framework	111
	Chapter 3:	The Union's Annual Budget	112
	Chapter 4:	Implementation of the Budget and discharge	113
	Chapter 5:	Common Provisions	114
	Chapter 6:	Combating Fraud	115
Title III:	Provisions on Enhanced Co-operation		116
Part Seven:	**General and Final Provisions**		118
Annexes to the Treaty			123
Protocols:			
Index			127
Protocols annexed to the Treaty			129
Declarations:			
Index			207
Declarations of the Conference			211
Additional Papers			231
Treaty of Lisbon:			
Text of Treaty of Lisbon			233
Final Act			239
Annex: Tables of Equivalences			243
Charter of Fundamental Rights			269
Explanations relating to the Charter of Fundamental Rights			277

Page

Additional Papers:

Berlin Declaration of 25 March 2007 291

Speeches:

The European Union after the Lisbon Treaty – José Barroso, 4 December 2007 293

Debate on the informal Council in Lisbon - José Barroso, 23 October 2007 297

Report on the Lisbon informal Summit - José Sócrates, 23 October 2007 299

European Parliament Decision on the Charter of Fundamental Rights 303

European Parliament Resolution on the convening of the IGC 305

Commission Opinion: 'Reforming Europe for the 21st Century' 309

Council Decision on cross-border co-operation (the Prüm Treaty) 315

The Laeken Declaration on the future of the European Union, 15 December 2001 327

Tables of Equivalences - Tables from the Constitution to the TEU and TFEU 333

General Index 339

FOREWORD

The Treaty of Lisbon, or the Reform Treaty, has come about through the failure of the Constitutional Treaty to be ratified by the Member States, owing to the results of the referendums held in France and The Netherlands. After a period of 'reflection' lasting two years, it was agreed by the Heads of Government that a new treaty should be drawn up, and at the European Council of 26 June 2007, an Inter-Governmental Conference (IGC) Mandate was adopted that set out the basis and framework of the provisions that would be adopted.

As such, the Treaty of Lisbon is not a treaty in its own right, but is composed of a series of amendments to the existing treaties, '*The Treaty on European Union*', introduced by the Maastricht Treaty in 1992, and *'The Treaty establishing the European Community'*, introduced by the Treaty of Rome in 1957, and is the successor to the Treaties of Amsterdam and Nice.

The new Treaty incorporates many of the provisions of the draft Constitution, as well as introducing new ones of its own. As each treaty becomes law, it is incorporated into the existing treaties; as a result, the changes and amendments made by each successive treaty become increasingly difficult to follow. This BMDF book places these amendments in context by highlighting the changes made by the Treaty of Lisbon and the changes made by the draft Constitution which have been included into the Treaty of Lisbon.

A provision was included in the Treaty of Nice for the Treaties to be revised once the number of Member States reached twenty-seven; with the accession of Bulgaria and Romania in January 2007, this number was reached. The purpose of this provision was to enable a review to take place to access the state of the institutions of the Union and how the Union should proceed with a far larger number of Member States than the original six members. The Treaty is a continuation of the process begun in the Treaty of Amsterdam and the Treaty of Nice in reforming the Union and its institutions in preparation for enlargement of the Union; as part of this process, the Treaty incorporates the amendments made by the draft Constitution to the institutional structure.

In the IGC Mandate, the concept of a constitution was stated as being a single text that replaced the existing treaties, implying that the main difference between the Constitutional Treaty and the Treaty of Lisbon is that with the Treaty of Lisbon, the existing treaties will continue to be in force with the text being modified by the new amendments. The IGC Mandate makes it clear that the consequences of the Treaty of Lisbon are that the European Community will be replaced and succeeded by the new European Union and that the two treaties, the Treaty on the European Union and the Treaty on the Functioning of the European Union, will constitute the basis and framework on which the Union is based.

In an open letter published in *Le Monde* on 26 October 2007, Valéry Giscard d'Estaing, the President of the Convention that drew up the text of the draft Constitution, said:

> *"If one looks at the content, the result is that the institutional proposals of the Constitutional Treaty ... are found complete in the Treaty of Lisbon, only in a different order, and inserted in the preceding treaties."*
>
> *"In the Treaty of Lisbon, drawn up exclusively from the Constitutional Treaty, the tools are exactly the same. Only the order has been changed in the tool box. The box itself has been redecorated, using an old model, which has three compartments in which you have to rifle around to find what you are looking for."*

During the debates leading up to the agreement of the text on 18 October 2007, there had been considerable discussion among the Member States, each of which had put forward requests and expectations on what they would wish to be in the Treaty, and what they would consider to be essential for them to agree. In the event, there was the inevitable compromise and a consensus was reached. The President of the Commission, José Barroso, in a speech to the European Parliament on 23 October 2007 said:

"I know that some committed Europeans are not happy with the number of opt-outs. Myself and the Commission, we would also have preferred to avoid them. However, diversity is a central feature of the European Union and sometimes it requires political and institutional compromises. I prefer to have specific opt-outs for specific countries than to be forced to lower the level of overall ambition of the Treaty."

As a consequence, the Treaty of Lisbon is a compromise and reflects the tension arising from the conflicting interests of the small and large states, the balance between the social, economic and environmental policies, which together represent the three principal objectives of the Union, and the two principal views in which direction the European Union might follow: that of the inter-governmental view of separate nation states acting together where appropriate and in a free market and that of the European Union being a single political entity operating under the principles of a European social market with the Member States having a subordinate role.

It is noticeable that the draft Constitution and the Treaty of Lisbon are the first treaties to be signed by the Heads of State or of Government, rather than being delegated to the Foreign Ministries of each Member State, signifying the increased importance of the new treaties and the European Union as a whole.

As with the previous European treaties, all of the Member States must ratify the Treaty before it can come into force. In the ratification process that takes place within the national parliaments, the Treaty can only be accepted or rejected as a whole and amendments cannot be made.

The aim of this book is to identify the principal important areas in the Treaty and to give the reader sufficient information to interpret the provisions of the Treaty of Lisbon in the context of the consolidated Treaties. The consolidation of the texts has been done to show the amendments made by the draft Constitution, which have been brought forward to the Treaty of Lisbon, and the amendments made by Lisbon in its own right. These are described more fully in the chapter 'Notes to the Text'.

This is the fifth major book by the BMDF on the European Treaties and follows the same layout as the previous texts in the series.

The analysis is in the front of the book, in Roman numerals:

- There are summaries on the background the Treaties and some notes on the text of the Treaties, to explain the layout and the annotations that the BMDF has added to the text;
- The main part of the analysis covers the principal issues and key points in the Treaties and the changes to the legislative procedure;
- there is a summary of the changes in the voting by the Council from unanimity to qualified majority voting and a summary of the areas that are still under unanimity;

The complete consolidated texts of the Treaties, together with all of the Protocols and Declarations, are shown in Arabic numerals.

There are a number of additional papers including the text of the Treaty of Lisbon, the Charter of Fundamental Rights, the Berlin Declaration, three speeches given at the time of the signing of the Treaty, and the opinions of the Commission and the European Parliament relating to the Treaty of Lisbon. In addition, there are the texts of the Prüm Treaty, concerning the sharing of information on DNA, and the Leaken Declaration of 2001.

In addition, the BMDF has prepared a fourteen-page index to the Treaty and a Table of Equivalences to enable the reader to trace individual articles in the Constitution to the corresponding article in the existing Treaties as amended by the Treaty of Lisbon.

* * * * *

NOTES ON THE TEXT

Introduction

This book is a working document to aid a proper understanding of the provisions of the Treaty of Lisbon that amend the existing Treaty on European Union and the Treaty establishing the European Community. The texts of the Treaties in this book have been consolidated by including the amendments of the Accession Treaties of 2003 and 2005 and the amendments of the Treaty of Lisbon in the text of the treaties as they stood after the Treaty of Nice. The text of the Treaty of Lisbon has been taken from the *Official Journal of the European Union* on 17 December 2007, 2007/C 306/01.

The proposals of the Treaty of Lisbon comprise amendments and additions to the two main treaties forming the European Union, updated at Nice on 26 February 2001, i.e. the 'Treaty on European Union' and the 'Treaty Establishing the European Community' (now renamed 'Treaty on the Functioning of the European Union'). In addition, there is a Protocol attached to the Treaty of Lisbon amending the Treaty establishing the European Atomic Energy Community.

In order to clarify and put into perspective all the changes now introduced by the Treaty of Lisbon, the changes have been integrated into the text of the existing treaties as follows:

- amendments to the text of the existing treaties are in bold type:
  - what has been transferred from the draft Constitution is in **normal bold**,
  - what is new as introduced by the Treaty of Lisbon is in ***bold italics***;

  This system is used for the amendments to the protocols, declarations and the Charter of Fundamental Rights;
- the numbering system used in the text of the main treaties, the protocols and declarations, as well as the analysis , is the new numbering system introduced by the Treaty of Lisbon;
- each article is annotated to clarify the origin of key additions and charges and the change in numbering system and reference is also made to relevant protocols and declarations. More details on these annotations are shown below;
- Abbreviations used in the text:

  'TEU' - Treaty on European Union;

  'TEC' - Treaty establishing the European Community;

  'TFEU' - Treaty on the Functioning of the European Union;

  '2004 IGC' - draft Constitutional Treaty.

Annotations in the Text

The numbering system in both of the main treaties has changed with the development of the text through the amendments introduced by successive treaties. This led to complications in the numbering system, with gaps in the numbering through deletions of certain articles and additional articles being given numbers and letters to identify them. The first change in the numbering sequence took place in the Treaty of Amsterdam and this system consolidated the numbering of the articles in both the Treaty on European Union and the Treaty establishing the European Community. This numbering was used in the Treaty of Nice and in the consolidated texts as of 1 January 2007.

The draft Constitution used an entirely different system, with the four Parts being designated by the Part number and an article number. The Treaty of Lisbon has one system for the text of the Treaty itself and introduces another system for the main Treaties. As there are now four systems of numbering, it is difficult to trace the origin of a particular article back from the new numbering system introduced by the Treaty of Lisbon.

The articles in the official text of the Treaty of Lisbon do not have any references to the old article numbers from the existing Treaties. There are Tables of Equivalences attached to the Treaty of Lisbon as an annex to show the article numbers in the existing treaties and the new numbering resulting from the changes made by the new Treaty.

Where appropriate, the BMDF has included references to this old article numbering to show the origin of the articles from both the draft Constitution and the existing treaties. New articles introduced by the draft Constitution and the Treaty of Lisbon are indicated as such.

An example of the numbering used in the title of each article in the main treaties is shown below:

ARTICLE 12 [6a] *[Article III-120 (ex Article 153(2) TEC)]*

- the main Article number is in bold italic type and follows the new numbering system;
- the second number is the article number as used in the text of the Treaty of Lisbon and is in square brackets in normal type;
- the third article number is in square brackets and in italics, it refers to the equivalent number of the draft Constitution;
- the final reference is to the original article in the earlier Treaty, as amended by the Treaty of Nice;
- where the article was introduced in the draft Constitution, reference is made to it being '*new article in 2004 IGC*'.

In particular cases, such as Article 4(2) TFEU [Article I-14(2)], ex-article numbers are shown against individual provisions i.e. - Tourism *(new)*; - Environment (*ex Article 174 TEC*). Where the source the text of the article is more complicated, notes are appended to the article, showing the source of each paragraph.

The ex-article numbers refer to the article numbers in the Treaty on European Union (TEU) and the Treaty establishing the European Community (TEC), as renumbered by the Treaty of Amsterdam and included in the consolidated treaties as modified by the Treaty of Nice.

The new Treaty extensively rewrites and reorders the articles from the earlier Treaties, and so in some cases the references to the old article numbers can only give an indication of their origin. This particularly applies to Title I of the Treaty on European Union and to the areas in Part Three of the Treaty on the Functioning of the European Union concerning 'the Area of Freedom, Security and Justice' (starting at Article 67 TFEU) and 'The Union's External Action' (starting at Article 205 TFEU).

In Economic and Monetary Policy, Article 139(2) TFEU defines the provisions that do not apply to the United Kingdom, owing to the opt-out from the Euro. This opt-out is also described in Protocol 18. BMDF notes are attached at the end of each individual article or provision to indicate the articles that do not apply to the UK.

The United Kingdom has an opt-out in the areas of border controls, asylum and immigration judicial co-operation in civil matters and police co-operation; the opt-out is described in two Protocols (Protocols 21 and 22). BMDF notes are attached at the end of each individual article or provision in the main text of the Treaties to indicate where the opt-out applies.

Structure of the Treaties

The Treaty of Lisbon comprises of a series of amendments to the text of the two main European treaties. This book incorporates the amendments in the Treaty of Lisbon into the current texts of the Treaty on European Union and the Treaty establishing the European Community, which has been re-titled 'Treaty on the Functioning of the European Union', as they are after the Treaty of Nice and the Accession Treaty of Bulgaria and Romania.

The texts of the amendments introduced by the Treaty of Lisbon in this book are taken from the text published in the *Official Journal of the European Union* on 17 December 2007, 2007/C 306/01 and the text of the Charter of Fundamental Rights is taken from the text published in the Official Journal of the European Union on 14 December 2007, 2007/C 306/02.

The base text of the existing Treaties is taken from the 'Consolidated versions of the Treaty on European Union and of the Treaty establishing the European Community', OJ C 321 29.12.2006; this has been modified to take into account the amendments made by the Act of Accession relating to Bulgaria and Romania joining the European Union on 1 January 2007.

Each of the two main European treaties is broken into several sections:

Preamble

The Preamble lays out the philosophical aspirations of each of the Treaties and of the European Union and refers both to the Member States governments and to the peoples of the Union;

Main Text

The main text of each Treaty provides the detailed provisions on specific areas and is separated into several parts. There are fifty-five articles in the Treaty on European Union and three hundred and fifty eight articles in the Treaty on the Functioning of the European Union;

The *Treaty on European Union* is split into six Titles:

Title I:	Common Provisions, covering the values and objectives of the Union and fundamental rights;
Title II:	Provisions on Democratic Principles, covering the principles of democracy in the European Union and the role of national parliaments;
Title III:	Provisions on the Institutions, covering the roles of each of the institutions of the Union;
Title IV:	Provisions on Enhanced Co-operation;
Title V:	General Provisions on the Union's External Action and specific provisions on the Common Foreign and Security Policy;
Title VI:	Final Provisions, including legal personality, the scope of the Treaty and the revision procedure.

The *Treaty on the Functioning of the European Union* is split into seven Parts:

Part One:	Principles, including the areas of Union competence;
Part Two:	Non-Discrimination and Citizenship;
Part Three:	Union Policies and Internal Actions, including provisions on the internal market, the four freedoms (workers, right of establishment, services and capital), agriculture, area of freedom, security and justice, competition, economic and monetary policy, and other areas concerning the functioning of the Union;
Part Four:	Association of the Overseas Countries and Territories;
Part Five:	The Union's External Action in areas other than the Common Foreign and Security Policy;
Part Six:	Institutional and Budgetary Provisions;
Part Seven:	General and Final Provisions, including the rights and obligations of the institutions and servants of the Union and the Member States, the flexibility clause, the scope of the Treaty and the suspension of rights of Member States.
Annexes:	There are two Annexes attached to the Treaty on the Functioning of the European Union. Annex I lists the products that come under the provisions of the common agricultural and fisheries policies in Article 38(3). Annex II lists the non-European overseas countries and territories that have special relationships with some of the Member States and are subject to the provisions in Articles 198 and 355(2).

In addition to the main texts, there are two other groups of documents attached to the treaties:

Protocols

These provide detailed provisions on specific areas that have been more generally described in the main text of the Treaty. There are thirty-nine Protocols attached to the treaties, of which they form an integral part and they are legally binding;

Declarations

These give supporting statements and interpretation to the provisions in the main text of the treaties and in the protocols. They are not legally binding but they are intended to give a clear indication of the political will behind the statements. The declarations are made either by the institutions of the Union and agreed by all of the Member States or they are made by individual or groups of Member States. There are sixty-five declarations attached to the Treaty of Lisbon and they are also form part of the consolidated treaties;

The Treaty of Lisbon

The Treaty is split into three parts: the first contains the main text and comprises the amendments to the Treaties and is signed by the heads of State or Government and government ministers of each of the Member States. The second part is the Final Act, this states that the Member States have signed and thus formally adopted the text of the Treaty of Lisbon and the amendments made to the treaties together with the associated protocols and declarations. This is also signed by the heads of State or Government and government ministers of each of the Member States. In addition, there is an annex, which contains tables of equivalences, referred to in Article 5 of the Treaty, comparing the old numbering of articles in the treaties to the new numbering in the treaties as a consequence of the Treaty of Lisbon.

The Charter of Fundamental Rights

The Charter is not in the text of the treaties and is a separate document; it forms part of the primary law of the Union. In the draft Constitutional Treaty, the Charter was an integral part of the text and was included in Part II of that treaty. The Charter was signed in Strasbourg on 12 December 2007 and incorporates the amendments made to the text by the draft Constitution; these amendments are shown in the text in bold type. Adjustments made to the text of the Charter, and to the explanations to the Charter, resulting from the Treaty of Lisbon are shown in bold italics.

Numbering of the Articles

A new numbering system for the Treaty on European Union and the Treaty on the Functioning of the European Union has been introduced by the Treaty of Lisbon. This replaces the existing numbering system used in the Treaties as amended by the Treaty of Nice. This system follows the numbering system introduced by the Treaty of Amsterdam, which consolidated and renumbered both the Treaty of European Union and the Treaty establishing the European Community; these had become difficult to read through successive amendments that had either repealed some articles, leaving gaps in the numbering or had introduced articles with letters as well as numbers to identify them.

In the draft Constitution, the articles were renumbered to be consecutive for ease of identification. In the text of the Treaty of Lisbon, the numbering of the articles has been revised for both of the main treaties; however, the numbering is not consecutive and a new numbering system has been introduced, where new or redrafted articles are identified using capital letters, e.g. 188 A TFEU, 188 B TFEU, to distinguish these new articles from the old articles in the TEU and TEC, such as 118a TFEU.

In the initial drafts of the Treaty of Lisbon, the old numbering was retained for the two main treaties as amended by the Treaty of Nice. The amendments in the Treaty of Lisbon meant that a large number of the articles were either repealed or moved and this led to the articles being numbered by letters as well as numbers, e.g. 188a, 188b etc. In addition, the numbering of the two treaties is not consecutive and there are large gaps in the numbering, where old articles have been repealed or moved, e.g. Articles 300 to 305 TFEU. In Article 5 of the Treaty of Lisbon, it is stated that that the two treaties would be renumbered once the amendments had been agreed.

The final numbering of the two main Treaties was completed during the final revisions of the Treaty in preparation of the signing on 13 December 2007 and the new numbering system is shown in the Annex to the Treaty of Lisbon. This revised numbering system is used throughout this book, including the analysis and the cross references in the text of the main treaties, the protocols and the declarations, following the new numbering system in the annex attached to the Treaty of Lisbon published in the Official Journal (2007/C 306/01 (C 306/01-C 306/230) 17.12.2007).

A detailed set of Tables of Equivalences, comparing the numbering of the articles in the draft Constitution to the revised numbering of the two main treaties after the Treaty of Lisbon, has been prepared by the BMDF and is shown at the back of this book.

Table of Equivalences and General Index

The BMDF has prepared a Table of Equivalences to enable the reader to trace articles from the Constitution to the two main treaties (the Treaty on European Union and the Treaty on the Functioning of the European Union), using the new numbering system introduced by the Treaty of Lisbon. A fourteen-page subject index has been included, prepared by the BMDF, covering the Treaties and the principal Protocols and Declarations. In addition there are separate indices for the Protocols and for the Declarations.

Sources and References

The analysis and the texts of the Treaties have been prepared using a number of different documents.

* Official Journal of the European Union 2007/C 306/01 (C 306/01-C 306/230) 17.12.2007: Treaty of Lisbon amending the Treaty on European Union and the Treaty establishing the European Community;
* Official Journal of the European Union 2007/C 306/02 (C 306/231-C 306/271) 17.12.2007: Final Act;
* CIG 15/07 Brussels, 3 December 2007, Final Act;
* CIG 14/07 Brussels, 3 December 2007, Treaty of Lisbon amending the Treaty on European Union and the Treaty establishing the European Community;
* CIG 1/1/07 REV 1 IGC 2007 Brussels, 5 October 2007: Draft Treaty amending the Treaty on European Union and the Treaty establishing the European Community;
* CIG 2/1/07 REV 1 IGC 2007 Brussels, 5 October 2007: Draft Treaty amending the Treaty on European Union and the Treaty establishing the European Community – Protocols;
* CIG 3/1/07 REV 1 IGC 2007 Brussels, 5 October 2007: Draft Declarations;
* CIG 4/1/07 REV 1 IGC 2007 Brussels, 5 October 2007: Draft Treaty amending the Treaty on European Union and the Treaty establishing the European Community – Draft Preamble;
* CIG 1/07 IGC 2007 Brussels, 23 July 2007 (30.07): Draft Treaty amending the Treaty on European Union and the Treaty establishing the European Community;
* CIG 2/07 IGC 2007 Brussels, 23 July 2007 (31.07): Draft Treaty amending the Treaty on European Union and the Treaty establishing the European Community – Protocols;
* CIG 3/07 IGC 2007 Brussels, 23 July 2007 (26.07): Draft Declarations;
* CIG 4/07 IGC 2007 Brussels, 24 July 2007 (26.07): Draft Treaty amending the Treaty on European Union and the Treaty establishing the European Community – Draft Preamble;
* IGC 2007 Mandate, Council Document 11218/07 POLGEN 74, Brussels 26 June 2007;

Other Documents:

* Official Journal of the European Union 2007/C 303/01 (C 303/01-C 303/16) 14.12.2007: Charter of Fundamental Rights;
* Official Journal of the European Union 2007/C 303/02 (C 303/17-C 303/35) 14.12.2007: Explanations relating to the Charter of Fundamental Rights;
* Official Journal of the European Union C 310 16.12.2004: Treaty establishing a Constitution for Europe;
* Official Journal of the European Union C 321 29.12.2006: Consolidated versions of the Treaty on European Union and of the Treaty establishing the European Community;
* Official Journal of the European Union L 157/203 21.6.2005: Act concerning the conditions of accession of the Republic of Bulgaria and Romania and the adjustments to the treaties on which the European Union is founded;
* European Parliament resolution of 11 October 2007 on the composition of the European Parliament (2007/2169(INI)), 13875/07, Brussels, 12 October 2007;
* Internet Blog of Valéry Giscard d'Estaing on the nine essential points between the Constitution and the Treaty of Lisbon: http://vge-europe.eu/index.php?q=neuf+points+essentiels http://vge-europe.eu/index.php?post/2007/12/02/Les-9-avancees-essentielles-%3A-comparaison-Traite-constitutionnel-/-Traite-de-Lisbonne

Reference has also been made to the following UK Government documents:

* "Treaty of Lisbon amending the Treaty establishing the European Union and the Treaty Establishing the European Community, including the Protocols and Annexes, and Final Act with Declarations, Lisbon 13 December 2007" Command Paper Cm 7294, European Communities no. 13 (2007), 17 December 2007;
* 'The Treaty of Lisbon: The British Approach to the European Union Intergovernmental Conference, July 2007', FCO Cm 7174, 7 July 2007;
* 'White Paper on the Treaty establishing a Constitution for Europe', FCO Cm 6309, September 2004;
* 'The Draft Constitutional Treaty for the European Union', FCO Cm 5897, August 2003.

* * *

BACKGROUND TO THE TREATY OF LISBON

The Treaty of Lisbon, or the Reform Treaty, is the culmination of a process to prepare the European Union for enlargement, in particular that the institutions of the Union would be organised to be able to operate on a more efficient basis with a Union of twenty-seven Member States. An additional aim was to enable the Union to enhance the efficiency of it external action.

During the discussions that led to the Treaty of Nice in 2001, there was a general agreement among the heads of government and within the European institutions that the legislation and the institutional arrangements that had been drawn up under the existing European Treaties had become increasingly incapable of allowing the Union to function. In particular, the arrangements for qualified majority voting in the Council agreed in the Treaty of Nice, did not resolve the concerns over the ability of the European institutions to be able to operate after further enlargement. The initial treaties were drafted in 1957 to accommodate a European Community of six Member States and were not designed to accommodate twenty-five or twenty-seven countries.

Currently, there are three major Treaties forming the primary law of the European Union: the Treaty on European Union (TEU), introduced by the Maastricht Treaty, the Treaty establishing the European Community (TEC) and the Treaty establishing the European Atomic Energy Community. A fourth Treaty, the Treaty establishing the European Coal and Steel Community, expired on 23 July 2002, fifty years after it came into force. In addition to the three principal Treaties, there have been a number of acts and treaties that have supplemented and amended these major treaties, including the four accession treaties.

The Treaty of Amsterdam began the process towards preparing the Union for enlargement, by including a Protocol containing provisions for the size of the Commission and the weighting of votes in the Council, which included the concept of dual majority (i.e. votes and size of population in each Member State). The Protocol did not contain any details on these provisions and also included a provision that at least one year before the membership of the European Union enlarged to twenty Member States, there would be another inter-governmental conference.

In the negotiations leading up to the Treaty of Amsterdam, the issue of enlargement was addressed but no conclusion could be reached. A protocol was agreed on the size of the Commission and the modification of the voting in the Council. In addition, a declaration was attached to the Treaty by Belgium, France and Italy, stating that they considered that the Treaty of Amsterdam did not properly address the changes of the institutions for enlargement. This view formed the basis of the discussions at the successive inter-governmental conferences leading up to the Treaty of Nice.

The issues left in Amsterdam were reconsidered at Nice and the Treaty of Nice attempted to prepare and adjust the operations of the Community institutions for enlargement. Nice was an uncomfortable compromise which satisfied none of the Member States and it was recognised that the Treaty would not properly prepare the Union for enlargement. It was agreed that there should be a further Treaty to resolve the problems of enlargement on the institutions of the Union. A Declaration was attached to the Treaty of Nice instigating the process that continued with the Laeken Declaration in December 2001 and the Convention on the future of Europe and culminated in the agreement of the Constitutional Treaty on 18 July 2004.

Under the terms of the Declaration attached to the Treaty of Nice, the review of the future of the Union was intended to cover the following major points:

- how to establish and monitor a more precise delimitation of powers between the European Union and the Member States, reflecting the principle of subsidiarity;
- the status of the Charter of Fundamental Rights of the European Union, proclaimed in Nice, in accordance with the conclusions of the European Council in Cologne;
- a simplification of the Treaties with a view to making them clearer and better understood without changing their meaning;
- the role of national parliaments in the European architecture.

The Laeken Declaration set out the arrangements for a Convention on the future of the European Union to be formed to review these points and to reach a conclusion that would in turn be the basis for discussion by the heads of government to produce a new treaty.

The Convention was formed in March 2002 and after eighteen months of discussion, the text of the concluding draft Constitutional Treaty was presented by the Convention to the European Council on 18 July 2003. There was then a review by the European Union's Legal experts, which was followed by the Inter-Governmental Conference under the Italian Presidency.

The text had a number of irreconcilable issues in it, principally a dispute between France and Germany on the one hand, and Spain and Poland on the other, over the distribution of the number of weighted votes in the Council, and in December 2003 it was agreed by the Heads of Government that the issues were so difficult to resolve that the discussions on the Constitution should be stopped.

The Irish Government took over the Presidency of the European Council in January 2004 and decided to attempt to reinstate the negotiations. They were successful in reconciling the concerns of the Member States and the Treaty was agreed in Brussels on 18 June 2004. The formal signing took place in Rome on 29 October 2004.

Owing to the radical change in the nature and structure of the Constitutional Treaty, a number of Member States decided to hold referenda. These changes included combining the texts of the Treaty on European Union, the Treaty establishing the European Community and the Charter of Fundamental Rights into one document, the change in the nature of the Union from one of being essentially inter-governmental to being a new and legally separate European Union and the nature of some of the provisions included in the text (described more fully below). France and the Netherlands held their referenda on 29 May 2005 and 1 June 2005 respectively and the negative results in both referenda (France: 'No' vote 54.68%; Netherlands: 'No' vote 61.6%) meant that the completion of the ratification process did not take place. A total of eighteen countries ratified the Treaty, including Bulgaria and Romania as part of their accession to the European Union.

With the failure of the Constitution to be ratified, there was a period of 'reflection' in the Union which lasted for two years. At the end of this period, it was agreed by the European Council June 2006 that the possibility of a new treaty should be examined and 25 March 2007 the Berlin Declaration was signed. This gave an increased impetus to the development of the new treaty and a mandate, setting out the detailed amendments, was adopted at the European Council meeting of 21 June 2007. The Inter-governmental Conference (IGC) Mandate provided the exclusive basis and framework for the discussions which started on 23 July 2007.

As in the case of the previous treaty negotiations, each Member State had issues and principles that were considered to be essential to be accepted in order that the Treaty could be agreed. The British had four specific 'red lines', including protection of the UK's common law system, police and judicial processes, existing labour and social legislation and tax and social security system, the maintenance of the UK's independent foreign and security policy and the impact of the Charter of Fundamental Rights. Other countries had their concerns, including France, references to competition to be removed from the main text of the Treaty, and Poland, on the size of the blocking minority in the Council. Despite these concerns, the negotiations were completed quickly so that the Treaty of Lisbon was agreed by the heads of state and government in Lisbon on 18 October 2007.

Ratification and entry into force of the Treaty of Lisbon

The procedure of ratification of the Treaty of Lisbon follows the approach of the existing Treaties, in that each Member State must ratify the Treaty under its own constitutional methods and all of the Member States have to ratify the treaty in order for it to come into force.

There has been one modification to this procedure, which has been brought forward from the draft Constitution, where if after two years of the signing of the Treaty, two-thirds of the Member States have ratified the new Treaty, and the remaining Member States have difficulties in ratification, the matter will be passed to the European Council, Article 48(5) TEU [Article IV-443(4)]. This provision suggests that the European Council would attempt to reach a compromise, by introducing derogations and additional Protocols or Declarations to ensure that all the Member States would be able to ratify the Treaty.

Given the difficulties that the Member States had in attempting to ratify the Constitution, it is expected that only one Member State will hold a referendum on the Treaty of Lisbon; this is Ireland, as it is required to hold a referendum under its national constitution. The other Member States are likely to ratify the Treaty through their national parliaments. If the ratification process is completed in the anticipated time-scale, the Treaty will come into force on 1 January 2009 (Treaty of Lisbon, Article 6).

Development of the provisions of the European Treaties

The competences of the European Union have developed over time, from the Treaty of Rome in 1957, which was essentially a Treaty concerned with the economic aspects of the European Community, to the much more clearly-defined political ambitions of the later Treaties that amended the Treaty of Rome. The Treaty of Rome formed the European Economic Community and competences were conferred by the Member States to the Community, and the Community was given legal personality.

The European Court of Justice confirmed that the Community had primacy of law over the Member States in *Costa v. ENEL*, described more fully in the next chapter. With the creation of the European Union by the Maastricht Treaty, competences began to be transferred to the Union. In the Treaty of Lisbon, which follows the terms of the draft Constitution, it is made explicit in the main text that the competences are transferred to the European Union, and not to the Communities (Articles 2 to 6 TFEU). Under the terms of the Treaty of Lisbon, the European Community ceases to exist and is replaced and succeeded by the European Union (Article 1 TEU) and this completes the transfer of competences and the primacy of law from the European Community to the European Union.

In addition to the European Economic Community, the European Atomic Energy Community and the European Coal and Steel Community were also granted legal personality on their formation. Under the terms of the Treaty of Lisbon, the Treaty on European Union and the Treaty on the Functioning of the European Union form the basis of the European Union while the European Atomic Energy Community remains a separate entity.

The Treaty of Rome

The Treaty of Rome was signed on 25 March 1957 and came into force on 1 January 1958. It established the European Economic Community and was the second of the three treaties that established the European Communities; the others were the Treaty establishing the Coal and Steel Community (now no longer in force) and the Treaty establishing the European Atomic Energy Community (signed on 25 March 1957 in Rome).

The Treaty of Rome laid down the overall structure together with the principal terms and initial provisions for the economic community, including the development of the internal market and the common agricultural policy, and the structure of the Community institutions. In this treaty, the concept of qualified majority voting was introduced, although the majority of areas were under unanimity. There were provisions drawn up in this Treaty that would pass to qualified majority voting from unanimity after an initial period lasting until 31 December 1971.

The Treaty of Rome introduced:

- the legal personality of the European Economic Community;
- the four fundamental freedoms of the Community (freedom of movement of services, capital and workers and the freedom of establishment);
- a customs union - elimination of restrictions on trade, including quotas;
- competition policy and taxation, state aid and anti-dumping provisions;
- harmonisation of laws to create the common market;
- economic policy - general requirement of the Member States to operate and co-ordinate, and treat their economic policy as a common concern;
- common commercial policy;
- the role of the European Parliament was restricted to consent and opinion.

- budget provisions;
- the process of the revision and ratification of the Treaties.

The Single European Act

The Single European Act (SEA) was signed on 28 February 1986 and came into force on 1 July 1987; it was signed by Lynda Chalker, Minister to the Foreign Office, on behalf of the United Kingdom. The main purpose of the Treaty was to speed up the process of the introduction of the Single European Market so that it would be completed by 31 December 1992. The Market was intended to comprise an area without restrictions on the four basic 'freedoms' of the European Community, i.e. persons, goods, capital and services.

This Treaty was essentially brought about owing to the Luxembourg Compromise of 1966, which required the Community to take into account an individual member state's concerns that its vital national interests would be damaged if a certain policy were adopted. Under this agreement, little progress in the formation of the internal market was made and changes to the voting system to allow qualified majority voting was considered vital to improve the decision-making to enable the common market to develop.

Another aspect of the Single European Act was the introduction of the concept of a common foreign policy, termed 'European co-operation in the sphere of foreign policy' and was the forerunner of the provisions introduced by the Maastricht Treaty. In the Single European Act, the emphasis was placed on initiative of the Member States so that they will endeavour to implement a foreign policy and give due consideration to other Member States. They would ensure that common principles and objectives are gradually developed. The role of the Community institutions was restricted to being informed of the decisions of the Member States.

The Treaty extended qualified majority voting to eight areas that had been stated in the Treaty of Rome that these should change from unanimity to qualified majority after the end of the initial period on 31 December 1971 (by the time of the Single European Act, it was already sixteen years after this should have happened). In addition, four other areas were introduced with qualified majority voting and the Treaty provided for the European Parliament to have an increased role in decision-making.

The Treaty also introduced measures concerning:

- the harmonisation of legislation concerned with the functioning of the Internal Market was changed to qualified majority voting;
- environment;
- research and technological research;
- the Court of First Instance, to assist the Court of Justice;
- the concept of economic and monetary union. This was drafted in general terms and the text stated that the Member States should co-operate to ensure the convergence of economic and monetary policies necessary for the further development of the Community (Article 20.1 SEA).

The Maastricht Treaty

The Maastricht Treaty was signed on 7 February 1992 and came into force in 1 November 1993; it was signed by Douglas Hurd, Foreign Secretary, and Francis Maude, Financial Secretary to the Treasury, on behalf of the United Kingdom. The Treaty introduced the concept of the European Union by the *Treaty on European Union* and reinforced the irreversibility of the progress of the integration of the Member Sates towards 'ever-closer' political union. The Treaty introduced the concept of the three pillars - the Economic Community, the Common Foreign and Security Policy, and Justice and Home Affairs. In the case of the last two areas, the role of the Court of Justice was clearly defined and restricted.

The most important aspect of the *Treaty establishing the European Community* was the introduction of the provisions for the introduction of the Single Currency and economic union. In addition, the voting process for co-decision was introduced. Finally, a small but important change was to remove the word Economic from the title, indicating the fundamental change in the Community's approach to the Treaty and the ideals of the European Union as a whole. Importantly, it did not give legal personality to the Union.

Some of the principal changes introduced by the Treaty were:

- the Treaty introduced more social provisions, including the 'Social Chapter', from which the UK Government gained an opt-out;
- establishment of 'citizenship of the Union' to enjoy the rights confirmed by the Treaty and be subject to the duties imposed thereby;
- strengthening economic and social cohesion by structural and other aid to the poorer EC countries;
- widening the scope of the competence of the European Communities into new areas, such as education, public health, culture, consumer protection, trans-European networks, industry and development co-operation;
- introducing the concepts of subsidiarity and proportionality into the Treaties;
- the Treaty repealed the provisions of the Single European Act concerned with foreign policy and introduced the Common Foreign and Security Policy, with an increased role of the Union to implement a common policy, with clearly defined objectives, and a defined role for the European Council, although the area still remained essentially an inter-governmental one;
- the environment given greater prominence in all EC acts and became the third principal objective of the European Community, with the economic and social objectives.
- the concept of co-decision with the Council acting with the European Parliament to pass acts of the Community, hence increasing the role of the European Parliament.
- thirty articles were moved or introduced subject to qualified majority voting.

The Treaty of Amsterdam

The Treaty of Amsterdam was signed on 2 October 1997 and came into force in 1 May 1999; it was signed by Douglas Henderson, Minister in the Foreign Office, on behalf of the United Kingdom. The aim of the Treaty was to prepare the Union for enlargement and to develop the decision-making of the Community institutions through the extension of co-decision and strengthening the involvement of the European Parliament and introducing more qualified majority voting.

The Treaty introduced:

- the concepts of the fundamental principles of the European Union: liberty, democracy, respect for human rights and fundamental freedoms and the rule of law;
- moved the provisions concerned with asylum and immigration from the TEU, and therefore inter-governmental in nature, to the TEC, and therefore justiciable by the Court of Justice, though there were qualifications to the extent of the role of the Court of Justice, and a passerelle clause was introduced to allow the Council to change the method of voting from unanimity to qualified majority voting after five years from the date of entry into force of the Treaty;
- incorporation of the Schengen *acquis* into the Treaties, through a Protocol, the UK secured an opt-out from this;
- change of name of 'Justice and Home Affairs' to 'Police and Judicial co-operation in Criminal Matters', following the guidance of the European Council meeting in Vienna to develop a single geographical area of freedom, security and justice.
- introduced the concept of 'closer co-operation' into the TEU, which was open to all Member States;
- the concepts of subsidiarity and proportionality were developed by the introduction of a Protocol;
- Social policy was developed, through the inclusion of the Social Chapter in the main text of the Treaty, as the UK had given up its opt-out;

- the Articles of the Treaty on European Union and the Treaty establishing the European Community were renumbered and twenty-four areas were moved from unanimity to qualified majority voting.

The Treaty of Nice

The Treaty of Nice was signed on 26 February 2001 and came into force on 1 February 2003; it was signed by Robin Cook, Foreign Secretary, on behalf of the United Kingdom. The Treaty continued the process of preparation of the Union for enlargement started at Amsterdam, including dealing with areas that had not been concluded at Amsterdam. These were the size and composition of the Commission, the reweighting of votes in the Council and the possible extension of qualified majority voting.

Some of the principal changes introduced by the Treaty were:

- forty-six articles were either moved from unanimity to qualified majority voting, or were introduced into the Treaty and subject to qualified majority voting;
- changes to the weighting of votes in the Council and the number of seats in the European Parliament (from 1 January 2005);
- extension of powers of the President of the Commission;
- reduction in the number of Commissioners from two to one for France, Germany, Italy and the United Kingdom (from 1 January 2005)
- a declaration was attached to the Treaty on the Future of the Union, which led to the Laeken Declaration and the draft Constitution;
- closer co-operation was renamed as 'enhanced co-operation' and extended to cover the common foreign and security policy;
- the common commercial policy was extended to cover intellectual property;
- Eurojust was incorporated into the treaties;
- judicial panels attached to the Court of Justice were introduced in order to free up the main courts for more important cases.

The Draft Treaty establishing The European Union (draft Spinelli Treaty)

This draft Treaty is otherwise known as the Spinelli Treaty, named after the Italian socialist MEP and European Commissioner Altiero Spinelli, who is regarded as one of the principal architects of the European Union, to the extent that one of the buildings of the European Parliament in Brussels is named after him. This draft treaty is essentially a draft constitution and is arguably one of the most influential documents concerned with the development of the European Union.

It was drafted in 1984 and was presented to the European Parliament, where it was overwhelmingly passed on 14 February 1984, by 237 votes for, 32 against and 34 abstentions. Although it never became law, as the Council did not approve it, it did form the basis of the negotiations of the Single European Act in 1986 and it had considerable influence on the Maastricht Treaty of 1992. It has also formed one of the guidelines for the later treaties; with the provisions of the Treaty of Lisbon, the majority of its ideas and principles have now been included in the Treaty on European Union and the Treaty establishing the European Community.

The principal provisions of the Spinelli Treaty which have been included in the Treaties leading up to and including the Treaty of Nice concern:

- the creation of the European Union and Union citizenship;
- the principle of subsidiarity;
- the institutionalisation of the European Council;
- the investiture of the Commission by the European Parliament;
- the principle of legislative co-decision between the European Parliament and the Council;

- co-operation in foreign and security policy and justice and home affairs;
- the European monetary system;
- social, health, environment, consumer, culture, and development aid policies;
- the multi-annual programming of expenditure.

The main provisions which had not been included in the Treaties to the Treaty of Nice are shown below, with the corresponding articles from the Treaty of Lisbon and the draft Constitution attached to show how these provisions are now incorporated into the text of the Treaties:

- revision of the Treaty through the use of the co-decision procedure (Article 48(6)and (7) TEU) [Articles IV-444 and IV-445];
- the Union having legal personality (Article 47 TEU) [Article I-7];
- formal acknowledgement of the primacy of Union law over that of the Member States (Declaration 52) [Article I-6];
- the formal inclusion into the text of the Treaties of the European Council as an institution of the Union (Article 15 TEU) [Articles I-21 and I-22];
- abolition of unanimity in the Council (Article 23 of the Spinelli Treaty provided for abolition of the veto within ten years) (Article 288 TFEU) [Article I-34];
- the designation of Commission members by the Commission President (Article 17(6) TEU) [Article I-27];
- the Council being composed of ministers entrusted with the Union's affairs;
- the suspension of the rights of Member States in the event of serious and permanent violation of the Treaty provisions (this is partially covered by Article 7 TEU, pre-Lisbon) (Article 354 TFEU) [Article 309 TFEU];
- the formal inclusion of the designation of exclusive competences of the Union and shared competences between the Union and the Member States (Articles 3 and 4 TFEU) [Articles I-13 and I-14];
- the Union's shared competence in the area of energy (Articles 4 and 194 TFEU) [Articles I-14 and III-256];
- financial autonomy of the Union (partially covered by Article 311 TFEU) [Article I-54];
- the introduction of a hierarchy of Union legislation (basic law, laws, budgetary laws, regulations and decisions) (Articles 288 to 292 TFEU) [Articles I-33 to I-37];
- the Union having exclusive competence over competition policy (partially covered by Articles 2 and 119 TFEU) [Articles I-12 and III-177].

It is very noticeable that the majority of these provisions were introduced by the draft Constitution and are included in the Treaty of Lisbon, in particular acknowledgement of the primacy of Union law and legal personality, although the primacy of Union law has been placed in a declaration and not in the main text, as it had been in the draft Constitution. The normal form of voting in the Council will be by qualified majority. The Union is still not a completely separate entity from the Member States, as they have conferred competences to it and therefore retain a certain control over the Union (Article 1 TEU).

The draft Treaty establishing the Constitution

The draft Constitution was signed on 29 October 2004; Tony Blair, Prime Minister and Jack Straw, Foreign Secretary, signed on behalf of the United Kingdom. The Constitutional Treaty has not been ratified, owing to the negative votes in the French and Dutch referenda. The principal intention of the Constitution was to prepare and re-design the European institutions for enlargement, while not affecting the *acquis communautaire* of the European Union. In addition, the opportunity was taken to repeal the existing treaties and to codify and consolidate the disparate parts of the European legislation into a single document, which would incorporate the two principal Treaties, the Treaty on European Union and the Treaty establishing the European Community, and the five Treaties of Accession.

Under the Constitution:

- all of the existing Treaties would be repealed and replaced by the Constitution, combing the Treaty on European Union and the Treaty establishing the European Community into one text and the 'three pillars' would be replaced by a single treaty structure;
- the Constitution would redefine and form the basis of a new European Union, replacing the existing European Union and the European Community. The new European Union would be a separate entity in its own right;
- the Union would have legal personality;
- stated that the Constitution and European Union law would have primacy over the Member States;
- included the Charter of Fundamental Rights in the main text of the Treaty and gave it legal status;
- included the explanations to the Charter of Fundamental Rights as a Declaration;
- drew together into two protocols all of the Treaties of Accession, including the recent accession of the ten new Member States;
- formally introduced the symbols of the Union, including the description of the Union flag, the currency, anthem and motto of the Union, and Europe Day,
- introduced a Union Minister for Foreign Affairs;
- the Union would accede to the European Convention on Human Rights;
- introduced an appointed President of the European Council, who would be in post for two-and-a-half years;
- laid out the distribution of powers between the Union and the Member States and defined the areas of exclusive competence of the Union and the areas of shared competence with the Member States;
- laid out the revised inter-institutional relationship for the Commission, the Council and the European Parliament and redefined the co-decision process as the 'ordinary legislative procedure' and described other methods of voting in the Council as 'special legislative procedures'.
- extended qualified majority voting under the ordinary legislative procedure (co-decision) to forty-four areas, of which nineteen were new areas. Sixteen areas were extended to qualified majority voting in the Council through the special legislative procedures, with five new areas.

The Treaty of Lisbon– the Reform Treaty

The Treaty of Lisbon was agreed by the Heads of Government on 18 October 2007 and signed on 13 December 2007; Gordon Brown, Prime Minister, and David Miliband, Foreign Secretary, signed on behalf of the United Kingdom. The process of ratification is intended to be completed in such time that the Treaty can enter force on 1 January 2009 (Treaty of Lisbon, Article 6).

The purpose of the Treaty has been to continue the process started in the Treaties of Amsterdam and Nice and in the debates leading to the draft Constitution, in preparing the Union for enlargement, to reorganise the institutions of the Union to act more efficiently and effectively and to organise the coherence of the Union's external action.

The Treaty retains the structure of the Treaties introduced in the Maastricht Treaty, i.e. the separate nature of the two main treaties, the Treaty on European Union and the Treaty establishing the European Community, and re-names the latter as the *Treaty on the Functioning of the European Union*. The Treaty establishing the European Atomic Energy Community (Euratom) is amended by a Protocol attached to the Treaty of Lisbon, and Euratom remains a separate community with its own legal personality.

The three pillar structure, introduced by the Maastricht Treaty, is removed and all of the provisions come under the legislative procedures of the Union, except in the case of the second pillar, the Common Foreign and Security Policy. This remains in the TEU, where the form of decision-making is clearly differentiated and the jurisdiction of the Court of Justice is restricted; the third pillar, Justice and Home

Affairs, is now absorbed fully into the Treaty on the Functioning of the European Union and is justiciable, with certain restrictions, in the European Court of Justice. This area has been renamed 'Area of Freedom, Security and Justice'.

The following summary lists the major amendments introduced by the Treaty of Lisbon. The summary is in three parts; the first part shows the principal changes introduced by the Treaty, including amendments to the provisions introduced by the draft Constitution; the second part lists the major areas introduced by the draft Constitution and included in the Treaty of Lisbon; the final part lists the principal areas of the draft Constitution which have *not* been included in the Treaty of Lisbon, and this last list indicates the extent of the provisions in the Constitution that are in the Treaty of Lisbon.

The principal new provisions introduced by the Treaty of Lisbon are:

- the Treaty on European Union and the Treaty on the Functioning of the European Union have the same legal value and the Union replaces and succeeds the European Community (Article 1 TEU and Article 1 TFEU);
- objectives of the Union changed to remove the term 'free and undistorted competition', the reference to the area of freedom, security and justice adjusted to include measures concerning border controls, asylum, immigration and crime (Article 3(2) TEU); the phrase 'protection of its citizens' inserted (Article 3(5) TEU).
- national security is stated as remaining the sole responsibility of the Member States (Article 4 TEU);
- national security is defined as a responsibility of the Member States, including co-operation and co-ordination between them (Article 4(2) TEU and Article 73 TFEU);
- The Charter of Fundamental Rights is given legal force and becomes part of the primary law of the Union, with equal status to the Treaties (Article 6 TEU) but is not in the text of the Treaty;
- provisions on democratic principles introduced into the TEU (Articles 9 to 12 TEU);
- new articles listing the increased role of national parliaments in the functioning of the Union (Article 12 TEU);
- the European Central Bank and the Court of Auditors included as institutions of the Union (Article 13 TEU);
- the role, structure and arrangements of the institutions included in the TEU (originally in the TEC) (Articles 13 to 19 TEU);
- composition of the European Parliament agreed at 750 plus the president (Article 14 TEU, Declarations 4 and 57);
- transitional provisions introduced for voting in the Council until 31 October 2014 and proposals for qualified majority voting in the Council from 1 November 2014 (Article 16 TEU and Article 238 TFEU);
- transitional provisions for the appointment of the Commission until 31 October 2014 (Article 17(4) TEU);
- introduces a High Representative of the Union for Foreign Affairs and Security Policy (Article 18 TEU);
- the competence of the Union and the Member States is more clearly defined in the Common Foreign and Security Policy (Article 23 TEU);
- Common Foreign and Security Policy: specific procedures for decision-making in the Council and the limits of the jurisdiction of the Court of Justice defined; the Union will define and implement a CFSP based on the development of mutual political solidarity and an ever-increasing degree of convergence of Member States' actions (Article 24 TEU);
- the High Representative and the Member States will put the CFSP into effect, using national and Union resources (Article 26(3) TEU);
- protection of personal data relating to the CFSP under the decision-making of the Council, to exclude the Court of Justice from having jurisdiction (Article 39 TEU);

- Justice and Home Affairs (renamed 'Area of Freedom, Security and Justice') moved fully from Treaty on European Union to Treaty on the Functioning of the European Union and becomes justiciable in the Court of Justice (Articles 67 to 89 TFEU);
- national security: it will be open to Member States to organise the co-operation and co-ordination of their administrations amongst themselves (Article 73 TFEU);
- Capital and payments restrictions on terrorists moved to freedom, security and justice, thus bringing this under the terms of the Protocol defining the UK opt-out (Article 75 TFEU);
- authority for the Council to be able to adopt measures relating to passports, identity cards, residence permits relating to citizens' rights to move freely in the Union moved to the Area of Freedom, Security and Justice, thus bringing this under the terms of the Protocol defining the UK opt-out (Article 77(3) TFEU);
- specific emergency brake and enhanced co-operation provisions introduced into the 'Area of Freedom, Security and Justice': European Public Prosecutor's Office and police co-operation (Articles 86 and 87 TFEU);
- provisions for enhanced co-operation moved from the TEU to the TFEU (Articles 326 to 334 TFEU);
- the general and final provisions cover the TEU and the TFEU (Articles 335 to 358 TFEU);
- flexibility clause amended to include the new provisions that where the Council is required by the Treaties to act by a special legislative procedure, it must vote by unanimity, the flexibility clause does not apply to the Common Foreign and Security Policy or to the revision procedures of the Treaties (Article 352(1) and (4), and Article 353 TFEU);
- protocol on subsidiarity amended to allow a simple majority of votes allocated to national parliaments to require the Commission to review any proposal for compliance with subsidiarity under the ordinary legislative procedure (Protocol 2, Article 7(3));
- new protocol on the internal market and competition stating that the Union will use the flexibility clause to ensure that competition in the internal market is not distorted (Protocol 6);
- new protocols on exercise of shared competence, services of general interest and transitional voting arrangements (Protocols 8 – 11);
- new protocol relating to the United Kingdom concerning the application of the Charter of Fundamental Rights (Protocol 7);
- blocking minority in the Council more clearly defined through the Ioannina clause (Protocol 10);
- transitional provisions applying to 31 October 2014 and from 1 November 2014 to 31 March 2017 concerning voting in the Council are laid out in a Protocol (Protocol 11). Protocol amended to include articles on provisions relating to the UK prior to the Treaty of Lisbon coming into force (Protocol 11, Articles 9 and 10);
- new declarations on the responsibilities of Member States over areas of the Common Foreign and Security Policy (Declarations 13 and 14);
- European Union law would have primacy over the Member States included as a declaration (Declaration no. 17);
- delimitation of competences between the Union and the Member States laid out, including method for returning competences to the Member States (Declaration 18);
- number of advocate-generals to be increased from eight to eleven (Declaration 38);
- new declaration on the restriction of the scope of the flexibility clause (Declaration 42);
- new declarations on the Schengen *acquis* being integrated into the framework of the European Union, including financial implications (Declarations 44 to 47);
- symbols of the Union acknowledged by sixteen Member States (Declaration no. 52);
- new declaration by the United Kingdom on opting into provisions concerning the area of freedom, security and justice regarding financial measures regarding terrorism (Declaration 65).

Provisions introduced by the draft Constitution and also included in the Treaty of Lisbon:

- the first indent of the preamble of the Constitution is included as the second indent in the preamble to the Treaty on European Union;
- the explicit statement that the Member States confer competences to the Union (Article 1 TEU);
- values and objectives of the Union redrafted and revised (Articles 2 and 3 TEU);
- the Union would accede to the European Convention for the Protection of Human Rights and Fundamental Freedoms (Article 6 TEU, Protocol 5);
- provisions on democratic principles introduced, involving democratic equality and democratic and participatory democracy, which includes the provisions for initiatives for proposals for legislation of one million citizens from a significant number of Member States (Articles 9 to 12 TEU);
- the role, structure and arrangements of the institutions redefined and revised (Articles 13 to 19 TEU);
- the number of MEPs in the Parliament defined and a minimum of six and a maximum of ninety-six MEPS from each Member State (Article 14 TEU);
- the role, responsibilities and organisation of the European Council are formally set out in the Treaties (Article 15 TEU);
- introduces an appointed President of the European Council, who would be in post for two-and-a-half years, renewable for one term (Article 15(5) TEU);
- the voting system for a qualified majority in the Council is defined as at least 55% of the Members, representing at least 65% of the population of the Union (Article 16 TEU);
- reduction in the number of Commissioners from one Commissioner for each Member State to two-thirds of the number of Member States to take place from 1 November 2014 (Article 17(5) TEU);
- the Common Foreign and Security Policy redrafted and introduces the provisions on the common security and defence policy, including permanent structured co-operation among the Member States with appropriate military capabilities (Articles 21 to 46 TEU);
- the Union will have legal personality and becomes a separate legal entity (Article 47 TEU);
- sets out the methods by which the Treaties may be revised, including the ordinary and simplified revision procedures and the provision that if four-fifths of the Member States have ratified a new treaty amending the treaties as they stand *after* the Treaty of Lisbon and the remaining States have problems in ratification, the matter will pass to the European Council (Article 48 TEU);
- voluntary withdrawal of Member States from the Union is defined (Article 50 TEU);
- lays out the distribution of competences, or powers, between the Union and the Member States and the areas of competence conferred on the Union by the Member States (Article 2 TFEU);
- defines the areas of exclusive competence of the Union and the areas of shared competence with the Member States (Articles 3 and 4 TFEU);
- citizenship of the Union more clearly defined (Article 20 TFEU);
- 'emergency brake' mechanism introduced for social security provisions (Article 48 TFEU);
- intellectual property rights introduced (Article 118 TFEU);
- provisions specific to the members of the Eurozone introduced (Articles 136 to 138);
- transitional provisions for the Member States outside the Eurozone redrafted (Article 139 TFEU);
- role of the social partners (employer and employee organisations) emphasised and the tripartite Social Summit to be involved in discussions (Article 152 TFEU);
- measures introduced for cross-border health issues (Article 168(5) TFEU), space policy (Article 189 TFEU), energy policy (Article 194 TFEU), tourism (Article 195 TFEU), civil protection (Article 196 TFEU), and administrative co-operation (Article 197 TFEU);

- external action by the Union defined and reorganised in the TFEU, including humanitarian aid (Article 214 TFEU), international agreements (Articles 216 to 221 TFEU), and a solidarity clause (Article 222 TFEU);
- lays out the revised inter-institutional relationship for the Commission, the Council and the European Parliament and redefines the co-decision process as the 'ordinary legislative procedure' and describes other methods of voting in the Council as 'special legislative procedures' (Articles 288 to 299 TFEU)
- increase in the power of the European Parliament in passing legislation through the co-decision procedure (Article 294 TFEU);
- extends qualified majority voting under the ordinary legislative procedure (co-decision) to forty-six areas, of which nineteen are new areas. Sixteen areas are extended to qualified majority voting in the Council through the special legislative procedures, of which five are new areas.
- budgetary process redrawn, with the increased role of the European Parliament and conciliation committee (Article 314 TFEU);
- new protocols, including protocols on the role of national parliaments, on the application of subsidiarity and proportionality, the Euro Group (Protocols no. 1, 2 and 3);
- ten protocols repealed by the Constitution and by the Treaty of Lisbon (Protocol B.1, attached to the Treaty of Lisbon);
- majority of declarations brought forward to the Treaty of Lisbon;

Provisions introduced by the draft Constitution but not included in the Treaty of Lisbon:

- the preamble, with the exception of the first indent, has not been brought forward;
- primacy of Union law: article stating that European Union law would have primacy over that of the Member States is removed from the main text of the Treaty [Article I-6];
- symbols of the Union, introduced by the draft Constitution, are removed from the main text of the Treaties [Article I-8];
- new structure of laws, incorporating European laws and European framework laws, introduced by the draft Constitution, are withdrawn [Article I-33].
- the Court of Justice having jurisdiction over the protection of personal data relating to the CFSP is withdrawn [Article I-51(2)];
- the Charter of Fundamental Rights not included in the main text of the Treaty [Part II];
- Accession to the European Convention for the Protection of Human Rights would have been by qualified majority voting [Article III-325(80], under the Treaty of Lisbon voting will be by unanimity;
- the concept of the "Constitution", in which the existing treaties would be repealed and replaced by a single text, has been removed [Article IV-437];
- the concept of a new European Union being formed, succeeding and replacing the old European Union represented by the existing treaties, is removed [Article IV-438];
- the term 'Union Minster for Foreign Affairs' is removed;
- protocols on the Treaties and Acts of Accession and a protocol on the repeal of other protocols not included in the Treaty of Lisbon.
- declaration on ratification of the Constitution not brought forward to the Treaty of Lisbon (where if four fifths of the Member States ratify and there are problems for the other states, the matter is taken to the European Council).

PRINCIPAL ISSUES AND KEY POINTS

The European Treaties as a Constitution

In the IGC Mandate of 26 June 2007, the term 'Constitution' was defined as being a single document that repealed and replaced the existing treaties. In order that the constitutional process was recognised as having been abandoned and not used in the Treaty of Lisbon, the term "Constitution" would not mentioned in the amendments to the existing treaties.

The draft Constitution repealed the existing Treaty on European Union [TEU] and the Treaty establishing the European Community [TEC] and replaced them with a single document [Article IV-437] and in so doing, the existing European Union ceased to exist and a new European Union was created [Article IV-438]. It was on this basis that the changes made by the Constitution to the European Treaties were considered to be sufficiently important that the governments of a large number of Member States decided that a referendum was required for ratification.

A fundamental difference between the draft Constitution and the Treaty of Lisbon is that the Treaty of Lisbon does not repeal the existing treaties but makes amendments to them, and as a consequence, it is considered by the Member States' governments that referenda are not required.

However, the concept of a constitution is perhaps wider than this approach would suggest. A constitution could be described as a legal document defining the framework of how a state is organised and how the divisions of sovereign powers are regulated. Hence, it is the body of fundamental principles and rules of a state from which stem the duties and powers of the government and the duties and rights of the people.

In the United Kingdom, the constitution does not consist of a single formal document but is composed of a number of separate documents, being a combination of statute, common law and convention; as such, the constitution is considered to be unwritten. In the same way, the European treaties are separate documents that represent the primary law of the European Union and therefore, by providing the legal framework for the organisation of the Union, they fulfil the role of a constitution for the European Union even though they are not consolidated into a single document.

The 'Three Pillars' and consolidation of the Treaties

Under the existing Treaty on European Union and the Treaty establishing the European Community, the Union has a 'three Pillar' structure, comprising the European Community, Common Foreign and Security Policy and Justice and Home Affairs [renamed 'Area of Freedom, Security and Justice' in the Treaty of Lisbon].

The three-pillar structure was introduced in the Maastricht Treaty as an informal description of the three principal parts of the European Union, but this structure was not formally or explicitly stated as such in the text of the Treaty on European Union or the Treaty establishing the European Community. It was a general political interpretation of the manner in which the delineation of the competences in these areas was agreed at Maastricht.

The second and third pillars were included in the Treaty on European Union and under the terms of the Maastricht Treaty were principally based on inter-governmental agreements, while the provisions in the European Community were justiciable under the Court of Justice. The role of the Court of Justice was restricted in relation to the second and third pillars, and Article 46 of the existing Treaty on European Union defined the extent of the powers of the Court.

Under the Treaty of Amsterdam, parts of Justice and Home Affairs were moved to the Treaty establishing the European Community and certain parts of police co-operation (rulings on guidelines and on visas, asylum and immigration) became justiciable in the Court of Justice. In the draft Constitution, the pillar system was removed and the three policies were consolidated into a unified text. The whole of the Constitutional Treaty became justiciable under the Court of

Justice, with certain exceptions in the foreign and security policy and police and judicial co-operation.

The amendments in the Treaty of Lisbon have incorporated the changes proposed by the draft Constitution and the pillar system has been removed entirely from the Treaties. The Common Foreign and Security Policy remains in the Treaty on European Union, except for the provisions on enhanced co-operation and international agreements which are moved to the Treaty on the Functioning of the European Union, and has separate voting procedures; the Court of Justice does not have jurisdiction, except in the detailed provisions of the Foreign and Security Policy where the Court can review the legality of the decisions of the Council concerning restrictive measures (Article 275 TFEU).

The Area of Freedom, Security and Justice has been moved into Title IV of the Treaty on the Functioning of the European Union and becomes completely justiciable and the Court of Justice will be able to act in all areas of the policy, except in the specific areas of judicial co-operation in criminal matters and police co-operation or for matters relating to the maintenance of law and order and the safeguarding of the internal security of the Member States (Article 276 TFEU). There is a new provision in the Treaty of Lisbon that states that internal security remains the sole responsibility of the Member States together with any co-operation and co-ordination between them (Article 4(2) TEU).

The Treaty on European Union and the Treaty establishing the European Community were separate and distinct in the structure initially set out in the Treaty of Rome and maintained up to the Treaty of Nice, so that each Treaty could be read on its own with little cross-referencing of the articles or provisions. Under the draft Constitution, the Treaties were combined into one document and the provisions of the two treaties became interlinked so that the text of the Constitution had to be read as a whole.

Under the Treaty of Lisbon, the two treaties remain distinct entities, but they have a much closer relationship and have equal legal status (Article 1 TEU and Article 1 TFEU); the Treaty on European Union contains the provisions on the organisation of the Union and the Treaty on the Functioning of the European Union contains the details of how the Union will operate. Thus the provisions of the two treaties on any area are much more inter-related and reference will have to be made to both treaties for the provisions to be understood. Examples are the competences of the Union and the Member States (Articles 4 and 5 TEU and Articles 2 to 6 TFEU), enhanced co-operation (Article 20 TEU and Articles 326 to 334 TFEU), and external action of the Union (Articles 21 and 22 TEU and Articles 205 to 222 TFEU).

General comparison of the Treaty of Lisbon to the draft Constitution

As described above, the overall structure of the Treaties is retained by the amendments in the Treaty of Lisbon, and this contrasts with the draft Constitution, which fundamentally altered the arrangement of the provisions. In the Constitution, there were four parts; Part I contained the general principles under which the Union would operate, Part II contained the text of the Charter of Fundamental Rights, Part III contained the detailed provisions of the policies and functioning of the Union, including the voting mechanisms and the implementation of the principles in Part I and in general terms contained the text of the Foreign and Security Policy and the Treaty establishing the European Community, Part IV contained the general provisions on the Constitution including the revision of the Constitution.

The intention of the Constitution was that Part I would be able to stand-alone and be read as a single document without any reference being needed to the other Parts. However, by the end of the final discussions, the texts of the different Parts became more interconnected, so that the different Parts of the Constitution had to be referred to in order to understand the implications of a particular clause. An example of this were the provisions for enhanced co-operation, as this area was sufficiently complicated that the provisions in Part III had to be referred to in order to understand the application of the provisions in Part I.

With the structure of the treaties reverting back to the two separate treaties under the Treaty of Lisbon, the Charter of Fundamental Rights is not now part of the text of the treaties and the articles that had been in Parts I and IV of the Constitution are now generally contained in the

Treaty on European Union, while the text of Part III is mostly contained in the Treaty on the Functioning of the European Union. The main exceptions are that the provisions on the Foreign and Security Policy are in the Treaty on European Union.

The title of the Treaty establishing the European Community has been altered to The Treaty on the Functioning of the European Union, indicating that the European Community no longer exists, since the Union replaces and succeeds the European Community (Article 1 TEU). The new title reflects the title of Part III of the draft Constitution, 'The Policies and Functioning of the Union'.

One of the most important aspects of the constitutional process and the one that fundamentally differentiates the Treaty of Lisbon from the draft Constitution is that the Constitution repealed the existing treaties and replaced tem by a single text. In so doing, the Constitution would have created a new European Union that would have replaced and succeeded the existing Union. In contrast, the Treaty of Lisbon retains the existing treaty structure and makes amendments to the existing treaties.

Other major areas are as follows:

- legal personality of the Union has been brought forward from the draft Constitution to the Treaty of Lisbon (Article 47 TEU);
- the changes to the inter-relationship between the two treaties and the changes to the three pillar system is discussed above;
- primacy of Union law is removed from the main text of the treaties and included as a declaration (Declaration 17);
- the symbols of the Union are removed from the main text and included as a declaration by sixteen Member States (Declaration 52);
- the Charter of Fundamental Rights was included in main text of the draft Constitution the explanations to the Charter were included as a declaration. Under the Treaty of Lisbon, the Charter has been removed from the text of the treaties to a separate document and the explanations; although the Charter is given legal status by the Treaty on European Union (Article 6 TEU);
- the concept of free and undistorted competition in the internal market has been removed from the objectives of the Union (Article 3(2) TEU) [Article I-3(2)] and has been replaced by a protocol that states that competition should not be distorted and that the flexibility clause (Article 352 TFEU) should be used to ensure this (Protocol 6). However, the Protocol does not include the term 'free' competition, only that competition should be undistorted.
- other changes to the objectives of the Union include a reference to the area of freedom, security and justice, in particular to border controls, asylum, immigration and crime (Article 3(2) TEU); an additional reference is made in the objectives to economic and monetary union and the currency of the Union (Article 3(4) TEU) and that the Union will contribute to the protection of its citizens (Article 3(5) TEU);
- other principal differences and similarities between the draft Constitution and the Treaty of Lisbon are listed above in the section covering the background to the Treaty of Lisbon and discussed more fully in each area below.

In his internet blog of 23 November 2007, Valéry Giscard d'Estaing, the President of the Convention that drew up the text of the draft Constitution, described the nine essential points that he had incorporated into the draft Constitution and that were brought forward into the Treaty of Lisbon:

> *"I have given myself the task of comparing the new Lisbon treaty with the Constitution on the 'nine essential points' published on this blog. To my surprise and in truth, to my great satisfaction, these nine points are repeated word for word in the new project. There is not a single comma that has changed".*

He noted that there was one aspect that had changed, in that the reduction in the number of Commissioners and the voting procedure would change on 1 November 2014 in the Treaty of

Lisbon, whereas in the draft Constitution the change would have taken place on ratification. The reference to the blog is shown in 'Notes on the Text', above.

The nine points are as follows:

- legal personality, Article 47 TEU [Article I-7];
- the fixed presidency for the period of two and a half years, as opposed to the current system of six monthly rotating presidencies among the Member States, Article 15 TEU [Article I-22];
- creation of the role of the Union Minister for Foreign Affairs, renamed the 'High Representative for the Union for Foreign Affairs and Security Policy', Article 18 TEU [Article I-28];
- definition and separation of competences, Articles 2 to 6 TFEU [Articles I-12 to I-17];
- the legislative procedure for the ordinary and special legislative procedures, Article 294 TFEU [Article III-396];
- role of the national parliaments under the principles of subsidiarity and proportionality, Article 5 TEU [Article I-11];
- number of commissioners to be reduced to two thirds of the number of Member States, Article 17(5) TEU [Article I-26(6)] ;
- confirmation of the Commission's sole right to initiate legislation Article 17(2) TEU [Article I-26(2)];
- the definition of the voting procedures for qualified majority voting, Article 238(2) TFEU [Article III-343].

Ratification, entry into force and revision of the Treaty of Lisbon (Article 48 TEU)

Each Member State has to ratify the Treaty of Lisbon in order for it to become law under the existing legislation of the Treaty on European Union (old Article 48 TEU). It is intended that the ratification process should take two years from the date of signature, through the ratification processes of each country. This will either take the form of a parliamentary system or by referendum. The Treaty should enter into force on 1 January 2009, or failing that, the first day of the second month after the last Member State has ratified the Treaty (Treaty of Lisbon, Article 6).

In the case of future treaties, there is an additional qualification, that if two years after the signature of any future treaty, four-fifths of the Member States have ratified that treaty and one or more Member States have difficulties, the matter will be referred to the European Council. (Article 48(5) TEU). This is a modification of the provisions in the draft Constitution, which stated in a declaration that the ratification of the Constitution would be subject to this. The declaration has not been included in the Treaty of Lisbon. In theory, this provision has no effect as in order for a treaty to become law, it has to be ratified by all of the Member States; this article is therefore a statement of intent, indicating the political will to ensure that future treaties will pass into law.

Preamble

The preamble at the beginning of each treaty contains resolutions and affirmations by the Heads of State and serves to describe, in general terms, the aspirations for the treaty. The preamble refers both to the Member States and to the peoples of the European Union. Although it is not binding, the preamble is important in that it is intended to express the clear common political will among the contracting parties and to define the intentions of the Union.

The term "ever closer union" was deleted the draft Constitution in order to remove the suggestion of the Union becoming more federal and was redrafted to read "united ever more closely". In the Treaty of Lisbon, the wording in the first paragraph of the Preamble to the Treaty on the Functioning of the European Union has retained the phrase "ever closer union" which has been brought forward from the Treaty of Rome.

One clause has been brought forward from the draft Constitution into the preamble of the Treaty on European Union and this refers to the cultural, religious and humanist inheritance of Europe; the remainder of the preamble in the Constitution has not been included. In the Preamble to the Treaty of Lisbon, references are made to the process started by the Treaties of Amsterdam and Nice, referring to the issue of enlargement and how the Union is organised to prepare for an increase in the number of Member States form an original six to accommodate twenty-seven Member States.

Primacy of Union law (Declaration no.27)

The principle of European law having primacy of over that of the Member States was established by a Court of Justice case, *Costa v. ENEL*, Case 6/64. The ruling by the Court concerned the provisions of the European Community and stated that the Member States and individuals are bound by Community law and in addition, Community law must be applied by the national courts. It was not stated in the text of the treaties that the provisions of the Treaties, which make up the primary law of the Union, do have primacy.

When the Treaty of European Union was introduced by the Maastricht Treaty in 1992, nearly twenty years after the Court's ruling, the extent of the Court's authority was clearly defined in the Treaty and the Union had an inter-governmental structure whereby the Member States organised between themselves any co-operation. In several Member States, the national courts have queried the extent of European law over national law, and the conclusions of these courts have been that European law only has force because the Member States confer that authority.

Primacy was introduced into the draft Constitution as an article in the main text, with the intention that this would remove any ambivalence and formally extended the primacy of law from Community law to cover European Union law. By doing so, it established the concept that European Union law has primacy over that of the Member States in both international and internal law, which is the national law inside the Member States themselves. In addition, the Article was explicit in stating that the Constitution itself would have primacy over the law of the Member States.

In the Treaty of Lisbon, the article has been withdrawn form the text of the Treaty and included as a declaration, which includes the opinion of the Council Legal Service on the principle that Community law has primacy over the law of the Member States. The opinion states that primacy was established in *Costa* and although primacy has not been stated in the treaties, it does not alter the existence of the principle (Declaration 17).

One of the major amendments made to the treaties by the Treaty of Lisbon was that the Union will replace and succeed the Community (Article 1 TEU) and one of the consequences of this is that primacy of Community law established by *Costa* will be replaced by Union law having primacy.

Legal personality (Article 47 TEU)

Under the existing treaties, the European Union does not have legal personality while the separate Communities (the European Community and the European Atomic Energy Community) do; as a result, the Union has been unable to act in its own right and has only been able to act through the Community institutions; the jurisdiction of the Court of Justice has been restricted under Article 46 TEU (provisions as in the Treaty of Nice) to certain areas, including preliminary rulings on framework decisions on police and judicial co-operation and rulings on enhanced co-operation.

Legal personality for the Union was first discussed during the negotiations for the Maastricht Treaty when the Union was being formed; it was considered inappropriate at that time, so that the Union was created as an essentially intergovernmental or multi-national organisation and was an extension of the Member States and an extension of their sovereignty. The concept of legal personality was included as an article in the main text of the draft Constitution and this has been carried forward to the Treaty of Lisbon. The granting of legal personality to the Union is perhaps the most important provision in the Treaty of Lisbon, as it fundamentally alters the relationship between the Member States and the Union, since the Union will become a separate legal entity, albeit based on the conferral of competences to it from the Member States.

The reasons for giving legal personality to the Union is ostensibly to enable it to act in making international agreements, for example under Article 3(2) TFEU [Article I-13], Articles 216 to 219 TFEU [Articles III-323 to III-326] and Articles 220 and 221 TFEU [Articles III-327 and III-328], but this is not defined or limited as such in the Treaty of Lisbon and therefore has wider implications. Under the existing Treaties, the Union has not had a budget of its own and has depended on that of the Community (e.g. in the Common Foreign and Security Policy). In the amendments made by the Treaty of Lisbon, following on from the draft Constitution, the Union will have its own budget, allowing it to become financially independent from the Member States (Articles 313 and 314 TFEU) [Articles III-403 and III-404].

Symbols of the Union

The symbols of the Union, which are the flag with a circle of twelve golden stars on a blue background, the anthem based on the "Ode to Joy" from the Ninth Symphony by Ludwig van Beethoven, the motto "United in diversity", the euro as the currency of the European Union and Europe Day on 9 May, were listed in the text of the draft Constitution [Article I-8].

The date of the public holiday, 9 May, commemorates the date in 1950 when Robert Schumann, the then French Foreign Minister, gave a speech describing plans for France and Germany to pool their coal and steel production; this led to the formation of the European Coal and Steel Community in 1951and the European Community in 1957.

In the process of references to the constitutional process being excluded from the Treaty of Lisbon, the article relating to these symbols was not included in the main text, although all of the symbols will continue to be used. In a Declaration which was added to the Treaty in December 2007, sixteen Member States, including Germany, Italy and Spain, declared that they would acknowledge the symbols of the Union to 'express the sense of community of the people in the European Union and their allegiance to it' (Declaration no. 52).

'Passerelle' or 'Escalator' Clauses

'*Passerelle*' means a footbridge or gangway and these provisions allow either the European Council or the Council, deciding by unanimity, to change the method of voting of the Council from unanimity to qualified majority voting in a particular area or case. This would mean that areas that have been negotiated in the Treaty revision procedure as being under unanimity could be changed without the matter passing through the normal Treaty ratification process.

There are eight passerelle clauses in the Treaty, of which six are new in the Treaty of Lisbon and have been brought forward from the draft Constitution.

The general passerelle article (Article 48(6) TEU) allows the European Council, acting by unanimity, to amend the provisions in Part Three of the Treaty on the Functioning of the European Union, so that the Council may act by qualified majority in that particular area. The details are discussed more fully below and in the chapter on 'Legislative Procedures'.

One passerelle clause in the existing Treaties has been superseded by the provisions of the Treaty of Lisbon and has been removed; this concerns asylum and immigration (Article 67 TEC). Under this Article, the Council could amend the provisions to be voted on by qualified majority voting five years after the Treaty of Amsterdam had come into force (i.e. May 2004).

Objectives of the Union (Article 3 TEU and Protocol no. 6))

The Treaty of Lisbon lays out the objectives of the Union, redrafting the articles from the existing Treaty on European Union and the Treaty establishing the European Community; this follows the changes introduced by the draft Constitution.

There are some alterations from that text, in particular the phrase that the Union shall offer '*an internal market where competition is free and undistorted*' has been replaced by the simple statement that the Union '*shall establish an internal market*' (Article 3(3) TEU); another change was to add the phrase '*and contribute to the protection of its citizens*' in relation to dealings with the wider world (Article 3(5) TEU). These two changes were at the request of the French government, and a Protocol has been introduced on competition, stating that competition is not distorted and the Union will take appropriate action on this (Protocol no. 3).

Other changes are that the Union will establish an economic and monetary union whose currency is the euro and that the free movement of persons is related to the external border controls, asylum, immigration and the prevention and combating of crime, stressing the importance of Justice and Home Affairs (Article 3(2) and (4) TEU).

Competences (Articles 4 and 5 TEU and Articles 2 to 6 TFEU)

The Treaty of Lisbon explicitly lays out the concept of conferral, in that the Member States grant, or confer, authority to the Union and so the Union only has competence, or powers, to act in particular areas through the authority granted to it by the Member States. The Treaty also lays down the extent and nature of the competences of the Union, which have been conferred to it and that these competences shall be subject to the principles of subsidiarity and proportionality (Article 5 TEU). Although conferral are mentioned in the existing treaties (Article 5 TEC), it has not been described in such detail and these changes were first set out in the draft Constitution [Articles I-11 to I-18]

The amendments made by the Treaty of Lisbon closely follow those made by the draft Constitution and there are only a small number of changes. It is made explicit that competences not conferred to the Union remain with the Member States, and that in particular national security remains the sole responsibility of the Member States (Article 4 TEU). The other change from the text of the draft Constitution is that the Member States will exercise their competence where the Union has decided to cease exercising its competence, and therefore it is the Union's decision as to whether the Member States can exercise competence in a particular area (Article 2(2) TFEU).

Competences fall into three distinct groups. The first is exclusive competence, where only the Union may act, the second is shared competence, where the Union and the Member States will share competence in areas which are not exclusive to the Union, the third group is where the Union can carry out actions to support and co-ordinate the actions of the Member States.

Where the Union has exclusive competence, the Member States can only act where the Union gives them the authority. The areas of exclusive competence, which include the customs union, establishing the competition rules for the functioning of the internal market and conservation of marine biological resources, have been defined in the judgements of the Court of Justice but have not been laid out in the Treaties until now (Article 3(1) TFEU). The Union will also have the exclusive competence to conclude international agreements that affect the Union's internal competence (Article 3(2) TFEU).

Social and employment policies and the common foreign and security policy will be co-ordinated by the Union, which will have the competence to define and implement guidelines for these areas (Article 2(3) and (4) and Article 5 TFEU).

The Member States will co-ordinate their economic policies (Articles 2(3) and Article 5 TFEU), but the Union will have the competence to define guidelines and the arrangements for co-ordination. The Union has exclusive competence over the monetary policy of the Member States in the euro. In the earlier drafts of the Constitution, the Union would co-ordinate the economic policy of the Member States; this was changed in the final text of the draft Constitution reflecting the concerns of the national governments that they should be able to preserve their ability to conduct their own economic policy. This change has been included in the Treaty of Lisbon.

Shared competencies (Article 4 TFEU)

The addition of areas of '*shared competence*' (Articles 2(2) and 4 TFEU) [Articles I-12 and I-14] to those in which the Union has exclusive competence (Article I-13) widens the powers of the

Union. The term '*shared'* is misleading as Member States can only exercise their competence when and to the extent that the Union has not exercised or has decided to cease exercising its competence. Member States have to respect the primacy of law of the Union and cannot enact laws that conflict with existing European law and principles.

Energy is the one new area where there is shared competence between the Union and the Member States, and this was included in the draft Constitution (Article 194 TFEU).

The phrase, '*the Union ... has decided to cease exercising the competence*' (Article 2(2) TFEU) is the only mention in the Treaty of the concept that part of the *acquis*, or competences, might be returned to the Member States. There is no explanation of the mechanism in the main text of the Treaty for this procedure; therefore it is likely that the European Council would act under the general voting provisions to act by unanimity or for the governments to meet in an intergovernmental conference to alter the treaties. However, a new Declaration has been attached to the Treaty of Lisbon which sets out the understanding of the delimitation of competences between the Member States and the Union and states that the competences that the Member States have not conferred to the Union remain with the Member States. The Declaration also describes how the Union can cease to exercise its competence. The mechanism outlined is that the Council may, on the initiative of one or more of its members, request the Commission to propose the repeal of a piece of legislation (Declaration 18).

Flexibility (Article 352 TFEU)

The general flexibility clause provides the Union institutions with the ability to adopt measures to achieve one of the objectives set out in the Treaties, where the Treaties do not provide the necessary powers. The Council will act by unanimity in adopting these measures, and therefore there is the possibility of a member using the national veto (Article 352(1) TFEU). The flexibility of the clause is more to do with competence and implied powers of the Union, rather than the flexibility of either the interpretation of the Treaty articles or the flexibility of Member States to opt in or out of the provisions.

There have been a number of changes made to the Article; in particular, the phrase that the objective of a measure is in relation to the internal market has been removed and so the potential application of the Article is much wider and that the Council will act with the consent of the European Parliament. In the Treaty of Nice, the Council only had to consult the Parliament (Article 352(1) TFEU).

The Article has been expanded, to state that national parliaments will be informed of the proposals, any measures will not lead to harmonisation of the laws of the Member States and that the Article cannot serve as a basis for legislation in relation to the Common and Foreign and Security Policy (Article 352(2), (3)and (4) TFEU).

Flexibility in the European Union is intended to provide a pragmatic method to solve any irreconcilable opinions between the Member States, and to allow certain countries to opt-out of various Union projects, such as the Single Currency and border control co-ordination in the Schengen *acquis*. It is expected that these derogations are only temporary, and that all Member States will join EMU and Schengen; in relation to this, there is a new paragraph in the objectives of the Union that states that the Union will establish an economic and monetary union and the currency is the euro (Article 3(4) TEU).

Enhanced Co-operation (Article 20 TEU and Articles 326 to 334 TFEU)

One of the principal aspects of flexibility in the Treaties is the enhanced co-operation provisions (Article 20 TEU and Articles 326 to 334 TFEU). The concept of enhanced co-operation provides the opportunity of a small group of Member States to act together more closely in a particular area than the rest of the Member States and is a solution to a situation where some of the Member States do not wish to be involved in certain proposals.

The provisions for enhanced co-operation were introduced in the Treaty of Amsterdam and then given more depth and detail in the Treaty of Nice. The provisions have been reorganised and redrafted in the Treaty of Lisbon, and follows the wording in the draft Constitution. There is now a single article in the Treaty on European Union and the general provisions, including the separate rules relating to the Common Foreign and Security Policy and Justice and Home Affairs, have been brought together in the Treaty on the Functioning of the European Union and will apply to all provisions in the Treaties. There are specific rules for enhanced co-operation introduced by the Treaty of Lisbon concerning the establishment of a European Public Prosecutor's Office (Article 86 TFEU) and police co-operation (Article 87(3) TFEU).

Member States that wish to join in with an arrangement under enhanced co-operation have to demonstrate to the Commission that they are willing and able to fulfil the conditions of entry (Article 328 TFEU). This means that Member States can be excluded from the opportunity to participate in the enhanced co-operation.

Since the Union institutions are involved, these provisions can only be applied where the Union does not have exclusive competence and legislation relating to enhanced co-operation becomes Union law and will be justiciable in the Court of Justice. The minimum number of States that can be involved is nine, or one-third, of the number of Member States. All of the Member States will be involved in the discussions but only those which will be part of the co-operation will vote in the Council (Article 330 TFEU). The European Parliament must give its consent and the entire Parliament will be able to vote, including the MEPs from the countries that are not involved, as these might be in the majority, they might prevent the proposals for enhanced co-operation from being passed (Article 329(1) TFEU). Details of the specific areas where enhanced co-operation may be applied are discussed more fully in the chapter on 'Legislative Procedures'.

Although the enhanced co-operation provisions have been in the Treaties since the Treaty of Amsterdam, they have not yet been implemented. They have tended to have been used as a mechanism to encourage Member States to negotiate any difficulties they have had over certain policies, rather than a principled disagreement. This might change as a result of the increase in the number of areas where Member States can invoke the 'emergency brake' provisions and in specific policy areas, such as corporate taxation.

National Parliaments (Article 12 TEU and Protocols nos. 1 and 2)

National parliaments have been brought into the legislative process, in that they can review all prospective legislation, other than that which is under the exclusive competence of the Union (Article 5(3) TEU).

Two new protocols have been included in the Treaty, which has the intention of involving the national parliaments in the legislative procedure (Protocols no. 1 and no. 2). All legislative proposals will be sent to the national parliaments and the parliaments may send an opinion on whether the proposals comply with the principles of subsidiarity and proportionality. There is an eight-week time limit for the parliaments to reply. This time has been extended in the Treaty of Lisbon from the time limit of six weeks in the draft Constitution. More details are shown in the chapter on 'Legislative procedures'.

National parliaments are involved in the evaluation procedures on Eurojust and Europol, and the extent of implementation by Member States in the area of freedom, security and justice (Article 70 TFEU and Articles 85 and 88 TFEU).

The national parliaments are involved in the general 'passerelle' clause, in that they have the availability of an 'emergency brake' provision in Article 48(3) TEU. Where the European Council intends to amend the voting procedure of provisions in Part Three of the Treaty on the Functioning of the European Union from unanimity to qualified majority voting, the national parliaments will be informed and if one national parliament opposes the decision, that decision will not be adopted.

European Parliament (Article 14 TEU and Articles 223 to 234 TFEU)

The role and the importance of the European Parliament within the Union institutions have been greatly expanded by the Treaty of Lisbon, through the increase in the number of policy areas in which the Parliament will be involved in. An important new area where the Parliament will now act is in justice and home affairs; see the chapter on 'Changes from Unanimity to qualified majority'. In particular, the Parliament will act as the co-legislator with the Council in the ordinary legislative procedure.

The Treaty of Lisbon does not make any major changes to the articles in the TFEU compared to the TEC, but there is a new article in the Treaty on European Union. This Article defines the role and the numbers of the Parliament; the text is taken from the draft Constitution and has one change, in the number of members of the Parliament will be increased by one, which will be the President (Article 14(2) TEU). The numbers and the voting arrangements for the Parliament are discussed more fully in the chapter on 'Voting in the Institutions'.

The Parliament will act jointly with the Council both the budgetary and the legislative processes (Article 14 TEU). It will have political control and consultation, as defined in the Treaties; this will include electing the European Ombudsman (Article 228 TFEU) and a temporary Committee of Inquiry (Article 226 TFEU), and vote on motions of censure against the Commission (Article 234 TFEU). The Parliament will elect the President of the Commission and give its consent to the Commission as a whole (Article 17(7) TEU).

European Council (Article 15 TEU and Articles 235 to 236 TFEU)

The European Council is formally made an institution of the Union by the Treaty of Lisbon (Article 13 TEU). Its role and position are more clearly defined than they have been in the Treaty of Nice and are in a new article (Article 15 TEU), which is taken from the draft Constitution without any significant changes.

The European Council will consist of the Heads of Government of the Member States, the President of the European Council and the President of the Commission; in addition, the High Representative for Foreign Affairs and Security Policy is included as a member. In a new provision, a member of the European Council may act on behalf of one other member as well as himself and any abstentions will not prevent the Council from adopting a measure either by unanimity or by a simple majority.

The role of the European Council is to provide the general political impetus for the development of the Union, define the priorities and give general political guidance for the Union; it will not have any legislative function. In addition, the European Council acts as an unofficial final court of appeal where differences of opinion between the other institutions of the Union can be discussed and agreement reached.

The Treaty provides for specific tasks of the European Council; these include electing the President of each of the Council configurations (Article 236 TFEU), and defining the strategic interests and objectives of the Union in the common foreign and security policy (Articles 22, 26 and 31 TEU) and justice and home affairs (Article 68 TFEU). The voting arrangements for the European Council are discussed more fully in the chapter on 'Voting in the Institutions'.

President of the European Council (Article 15 TEU)

The system in the current Treaties provides for equal rotation of the presidency every six months among the Member States, which in an enlarged Union means that each country would have the presidency once every 13½ years. Under the terms of the Treaty of Lisbon, which have not changed from the text of the draft Constitution, the President of the European Council will be elected and hold the post for a term of two and a half years, renewable once.

The European Council will elect the President by qualified majority and therefore a Member State will not have a veto over the appointment. There is concern in the smaller States that the larger countries will vote for their chosen candidate and the smaller countries are unlikely to have a President.

A clause in the earlier drafts of the draft Constitution specifically excluded the President of the Commission from becoming the President of the European Council. However, this clause was removed from the final draft, and there is nothing in the text of the Treaty of Lisbon to prevent the President of the Commission also becoming the President of the European Council, though the President cannot hold a national office.

The role of the President of the European Council will include chairing the European Council and representing the Union on issues concerning the Common Foreign and Security Policy (Article 15 TEU); in addition the President may convene an extraordinary meeting of the European Council to define the strategic policy of the Union in foreign and security policy (Article 26 TEU).

The Treaty of Lisbon does not set out details on the limits on the role of the President of the European Council in foreign affairs, and on how this role will be co-ordinated with the roles of the High Representative for Foreign Affairs or the President of the Commission, or on the relationship between the President and the governments of the Member States.

The Council (Article 16 TEU and Articles 237 to 243 TFEU)

The role and formation of the Council has been redrafted and a new article included in the Treaty on European Union; the text has been brought forward from the draft Constitution without any changes except for the provisions on voting. The principal role of the Council is to act jointly with the European Parliament in both the budgetary and the legislative processes; in addition, it will make policy and co-ordinate action by the Union and the Member States.

The Treaty of Lisbon has delayed the introduction of the new arrangements for qualified majority voting and they will take effect from 1 November 2014 (Article 16 TEU and Article 238 TFEU); the detailed voting arrangements are the same as those in the draft Constitution and are described in the chapter on 'Voting in the Institutions'. The role of the General Affairs Council and the Foreign Affairs Council are formally set out (Article 16 TEU).

The presidency of the Council formations will be held by the Member States under a system of equal rotation which will be decided by the European Council, acting by qualified majority (Article 16(9) TEU).

The Council will meet in public as part of the process of ensuring openness of the activities of the Union institutions; each Council meeting will be split into two parts, dealing with legislative acts and non-legislative acts (Article 16(8) TEU).

The Commission (Article 17 TEU and Articles 244 to 250 TFEU)

The responsibilities of the Commission have been laid out for the first time in the treaties in a new article taken from the draft Constitution (Article 17 TEU). These responsibilities include:

i. the promotion of the general interest of the Union, to take appropriate initiatives to that end, ensuring the application of the Treaties, and Union law under the control of the Court of Justice, and the exercise of co-ordinating, executive and management functions;

ii the sole right to initiate and prepare proposals for Union legislative acts, except in specific cases;

iii. the initiation of the Union's annual and multi-annual programmes and execution of the budget and programme management;

iv. representing the Union in external relations, except for the Common Foreign and Security Policy.

The Commission has been given new powers in the Treaty of Lisbon, so that it may impose competition regulations concerning the detailed rules for agreements that are exceptions to the general prohibitions and that improve trade (Article 105(3) TFEU). In the Treaty establishing the European Community, the Commission could only make proposals in this area.

Selection and number of Commissioners (Article 17 TEU and Article 244 TFEU)

The President of the Commission will be appointed by the European Parliament on a proposal from the European Council; if the candidate is not elected by the Parliament, the European Council will propose a new candidate with one month to be elected by the same procedure (Article 17(7) TEU). The President of the Commission will be able to request a member of the Commission to resign; previously, the President would have to seek the approval of the whole Commission. The President can also request the resignation of the High Representative for Foreign Affairs (Article 17(6) TEU).

Under the provisions introduced by the Treaty of Lisbon, there will one Commissioner from each Member State for the Commission for the period between the date the Treaty has entered into force and 31 October 2014; this will include the Commission appointed for the five-year period starting on 1 November 2009.

From 1 November 2014, the number of members of the Commission will be restricted to two-thirds of the number of Member States, including the President of the Commission and the High Representative of the Union for Foreign Affairs. With the current number of Member States, the total number of Commissioners will be 19, with 17 coming from the Member States. The purpose of these changes is to prevent the Commission from becoming too unwieldy and to ensure that there is no discrimination against the medium and smaller-sized Member States.

The Commissioners will be selected on a strict equal rotational basis regarding the sequence and the time spent by each the nationality; the difference of the terms spent will never be more than one. Each successive Commission will be composed to reflect the demographic and geographical range of all the Member States (Article 244 TFEU). The system will be established by the European Council acting by unanimity (Article 17(5) TEU).

Initially, it was intended that the changes to the Commission would take place once the Treaty of Lisbon entered into force. However, this system provoked a great deal of criticism from the Member States during the IGC and a compromise was reached and there will be a transitional period of seven years before the changes take place.

This new system has raised concerns on whether the Commission will be able to function effectively, in particular over the varying abilities of the Commissioners and the validity of a Commission that does not include members from the largest Member States and this could potentially cause problems in the operation of the Commission. The European Council can, by unanimity, alter the size of the Commission and the system of rotation (Article 244 TFEU).

High Representative for Foreign Affairs and Security Policy (Article 18 TEU)

The title of High Representative for Foreign Affairs and Security Policy has been used in the Treaty of Lisbon and is a change from the title of the Union Minister for Foreign Affairs, which had been the title in the draft Constitution. The High Representative will be appointed by the European Council, acting by qualified majority, and will conduct the Union's common foreign policy and act as the president of the Foreign Affairs Council.

There is a potential conflict in the position, as it will combine two existing appointments in the Council and in the Commission, and the High Representative will be both a Vice-President of the Commission and at the same time a member of the Council. The new title reflects the name in the existing treaties, the 'High Representative for the Common Foreign and Security Policy'; this post has been attached to the Council, while the position in the Commission has been a separate appointment.

Although in general the European Council and the Council will vote by unanimity in the CFSP, the Council will vote by qualified majority on proposals made by the High Representative (Article 31(2) TEU).

The High Representative will be assisted by a secretariat, created by the Treaty of Lisbon, entitled the European External Action Service, which will be a form of a common foreign office. It will be composed of staff from the national diplomatic services as well as staff from the

Commission and the Council (Article 27 TEU). Its role will be to assist the High Representative for Foreign Affairs and to provide the staff for the Union's delegation in third countries and international organisations (Article 221 TFEU). This gives an indication that the Union intends to establish a separate body that is the equivalent to the foreign ministries of the Member States.

The external action of the Union also includes the common commercial policy and development aid (Articles 206 to 207 and Articles 208 to 214 TFEU). There is no indication in the Treaties on the distribution of responsibilities between the Commission, the Council and the Member States the operation of these areas or of the organisation or role of the Action Service; more generally, there is no indication on how the President of the Commission, the President of the European Council or the High Representative, as President of the Foreign Affairs Council, will co-ordinate their differing roles and activities in the Union's external action.

The Union's External Action – Common Foreign and Security Policy (Articles 21 to 46 TEU and Articles 206 to 222 TFEU)

External action includes the common foreign and security policy, the common security and defence policy, the common commercial policy, humanitarian aid and international agreements, where through its newly acquired legal personality, the Union will be able to conclude agreements with third countries (Articles 209 and 216 TFEU).

The Common Foreign and Security Policy, which was the second pillar in the existing Treaties, remains in the Treaty on European Union and as discussed above, the pillar system no longer exists. The text has been extensively rewritten and reorganised, in general following the provisions of the draft Constitution; the general principles are set out in Article 21 TEU and the main changes are to introduce provisions for the High Representative and for the Common Security and Defence Policy.

The voting arrangements are set out in Article 24(1) TEU; the European Council and the Council will act unanimously, except in certain circumstances and the High Representative will be responsible for enacting the policy with the Member States. The areas where the Council will vote by qualified majority are on the Union's strategic interests, on proposals from the High Representative, adopting decisions defining Union action, and appointing a special representative (Article 31(2) TEU).

The European Parliament and the Commission will have limited and specific roles and the Court of Justice will not have jurisdiction over this area; the limitations on its actions are defined in Article 275 TFEU. There is a passerelle clause, allowing the European Council to change its method of voting to qualified majority, except in areas having military or defence implications (Article 31(3) TEU).

There has been a change in emphasis in the text: under the current provisions, the Common Foreign and Security Policy **might** lead to a common defence (Article 17 TEU and Article 2 TEU, existing Treaties). In the new text, the policy **will** lead to a common defence (Article 42(2) TEU).

A European Defence Agency is introduced, to be involved with defence capabilities development, research, acquisition and armaments (Articles 42(3) and 45 TEU, and Protocol no. 4).

There are two new declarations stating that the provisions of the CFSP and the creation of the High Representative and the External Action Service do not affect the responsibilities of the Member States, as they currently exist, to conduct their foreign policy or its membership of the UN Security Council, nor does it give the Commission new powers to initiate decisions or to increase the role of the European Parliament (Declarations 13 and 14).

The concept of permanent structured co-operation for Member States that have the appropriate capability is introduced (Articles 42(6) TEU and 46 TEU, and Protocol no. 4); this is not the same as enhanced co-operation and concerns specific military issues. The intention is that the structured co-operation will take effect by 2010, with combat units available within a period of 5 to 30 days and sustained for at least 120 days. The Member States involved are expected to harmonise their defence as much as possible, while remaining autonomous and commitments to this co-operation will be consistent with the Member States' obligations to NATO (Article 42(7) TEU).

The Treaty of Lisbon introduces solidarity (mutual defence) clauses, where if a Member State suffers a terrorist attack or a major disaster, the other Member States will be obliged to come to its assistance (Articles 42(7) TEU and Article 222 TFEU).

Area of freedom, Security and Justice (Articles 67 to 89 TFEU and Protocol no. 11)

This area is the successor to the provisions under the heading of 'Justice and Home Affairs' introduced by the Maastricht Treaty and modified by the Treaty of Amsterdam. The whole policy has been extensively redrafted and moved from the Treaty on European Union to the Treaty on the Functioning of the European Union. The intention is to consolidate all of the disparate parts of the provisions spread throughout the Treaties into a single co-ordinated policy for the whole of the geographical area of the European Union. This follows from the policy of removing the internal borders within the European Union, to allow the freedom of movement for European citizens throughout the European Union.

At present, this area is one of the three pillars and is generally inter-governmental, and the Court of Justice has a limited jurisdiction. In the Treaty of Amsterdam, the areas of asylum and immigration were removed from the inter-governmental procedures to the European Community, and so came under the jurisdiction of the European Court (with a limited amount of inter-governmental co-operation and voting in the Council by unanimity).

Under the new Treaty, this area comes under the legislative authority of the Union and the area, including the provisions on Eurojust and Europol, is justiciable by the Court of Justice. There is an exception to this, in that the Court has no jurisdiction to review the validity or proportionality of operations carries out by the police or other law-enforcement services of a Member State or the safeguarding of internal security (Article 276 TFEU).

The term 'area of freedom, security and justice' was introduced into the text of the Treaties by the Treaty of Amsterdam. At the European Council meeting in Tampere in 1999, the principles of the area of freedom, security and justice were developed to give more structure and to include the roles of Europol and Eurojust, and establish a European Police College for senior law enforcement officials.

The policy areas include external border controls, asylum and immigration, cross-border crime including money laundering and taxation matters, and a genuine European area of justice, including the mutual recognition of judicial decisions. The external border control matters include the provisions of the Schengen *acquis*. The policy also includes the provisions of the Charter of Fundamental Rights, to ensure the right of freedom of movement and security of individuals within the borders of the European Union.

The Commission will have the right of initiative to present proposals in this area, and in judicial co-operation in criminal matters and police co-operation, the right of initiative will be shared between the Commission and a quarter of the Member States (Article 76 TFEU).

There is a five-year transitional period from the date of entry into force of the Treaty of Lisbon, where the existing restrictions on the Court of Justice will still apply for legislative acts that have become law before the Treaty has entered into force, unless these measures are amended in that period (Protocol no. 11 on Transitional Provisions, Articles 9 and 10).

The final legal issue to be resolved in the negotiations on the Treaty of Lisbon was the way in which the United Kingdom and Ireland would be involved in changes to the Schengen *acquis*. Both countries have an opt-out but are able to take part in certain parts of the agreement. The Protocol on Schengen has been amended to describe the mechanism for the situation where the United Kingdom or Ireland opts into and then opts out of a provision (Protocol on the Schengen *acquis*, Article 5); in addition, if the consequences of the opt-out affect the operability of the action or there is a financial cost to the other Member States, the Council can urge the United Kingdom or Ireland to opt into the provision or they will have to bear the financial costs

(Protocol on the position of the UK and Ireland, Article 4a). A similar procedure will apply to the five year transitional period (Protocol no. 11 on Transitional Provisions, Article 10).

Provisions relating to capital and payments (Article 75 TFEU) and to passports, identity cards and other documents (Article 77(3) TFEU), have been moved into the Area of Freedom, Security and Justice and therefore are covered by the general opt-outs of the United Kingdom and Ireland (Protocol no. 22). The UK has attached a declaration stating that it will opt into the provisions on capital (Declaration 65).

National parliaments will be involved in this area, in judicial co-operation in criminal matters and police co-operation (Articles 82 to 89 TFEU) and they will be able to review proposed legislation under the terms of the Protocol on Subsidiarity (Articles 69 and 81 TFEU and Protocol no.2).

Member States have the use of an 'emergency brake' in judicial co-operation in civil and criminal matters, concerning mutual recognition of judgements and criminal offences (Articles 81, 82(3) and 83(3) TFEU), the establishment of the European Public Prosecutor (Article 86 TFEU) and police co-operation (Article 87 TFEU), so that the Member State is able to oppose a draft framework law and the matter will be passed to the European Council for further discussion.

Democratic Principles (Articles 9 to 11 TEU, Article 24 TFEU)

The Treaty of Lisbon formalises a number of principles under which the Union will operate and are effectively rights of the individual citizen. As a result, they have links to the Charter of Fundamental Rights, particularly Titles III and V of the Charter on equality and citizens' rights. The principles are democratic equality, representative democracy and participatory democracy and are in addition to the concepts of subsidiarity and proportionality.

The principle of participatory democracy enables citizens and representative associations to have the opportunity to explain their views on any area of Union policy. In Article 11(4) TEU, there is provision for individuals to petition the Commission to make proposals on any Union policy. In order that this can take place, there has to be at least one million people involved from a significant number of Member States. The Treaty of Lisbon does not give any details on how this might operate, but the European Parliament and the Council will act by the ordinary legislative procedure to adopt regulations to define the terms (Article 24 TFEU). This system could be used by a single-issue pressure group, on an area such as the environment, to initiate legislation.

Simplified revision procedure (Article 48(6) – (7) TEU)

The general *passerelle* clause concerns the '*simplified revision procedure*'; this approach was first suggested during the debates leading up to the Treaty of Nice concerning the policies and action of the Union to introduce a certain amount of flexibility in revision in the Treaty. This concept was developed in the draft Constitution and brought forward to the Treaty of Lisbon.

The general clause covers internal Union policies and internal action in Part Three of the Treaty on the Functioning of the European Union (Article 48(6) TEU) and includes provisions on the internal market, free movement of persons, services and capital, EMU and the area of freedom security and justice. The provisions will not apply to decisions concerning defence or military matters.

The European Council, acting by unanimity, may adopt a decision amending all or part of these provisions, but the Member States must approve the revisions by their respective constitutional procedures. This process avoids the need to have an Inter-Governmental Council meeting to agree the changes and is discussed more fully in the chapter on 'Legislative Procedures'.

In an amendment to the Treaty, an 'emergency brake' provision was added to the general passerelle procedure to include the national parliaments, so that a single national parliament can veto a European Council decision under the passerelle clause to change from unanimity to qualified majority voting, if the parliament notifies its opposition within six months of being notified of the proposed change; Article 48(7) TEU.

Voluntary withdrawal from the Union (Article 50 TEU)

Any Member State may decide to withdraw from the Union and the process of withdrawal would be expected to take up to two years. Before the Treaty comes into force, Member States are in theory able to withdraw under the terms of the Vienna Convention on the Law of Treaties of 27 January 1980.

The new provisions appear to make the process of withdrawing from the Union a difficult process and would involve a complicated combination of national law, European law, and international law, together with a lengthy negotiation period. The process of withdrawal would itself need a Treaty to define the terms of both the separation and the new relationship.

Under the terms of the Article, which is not changed from the draft Constitution, the Council is able to act by qualified majority on the conditions of the agreement with the Member State leaving the Union. There are no provisions laid down on how the negotiations for withdrawal would take place and over what time-period, or what the nature of the relationship would be after withdrawal. In addition, there are no provisions for withdrawal from the Single Currency in the Article.

Charter of Fundamental Rights

The intention behind the creation of the Charter of Fundamental Rights was to bring together all of the rights of European citizens in the Union into a single clearly drafted document, which includes the rights relating to dignity, freedoms, equality, solidarity and justice.

In order to reinforce the importance of the Charter, a revised version was signed by the Presidents of the Commission, the European Parliament and the Council on 12 December 2007. Article 6 TEU concerns fundamental rights and makes specific reference to the Charter to link the Charter to the Treaty on European Union; the Article refers to the signing and states that the text will have the same legal value as the Treaties. Hence the Charter will be legally-binding and become part of the primary law of the Union once the Treaty of Lisbon enters into force; as a result, it will come under the jurisdiction of the Court of Justice (Charter, Article 52).

The provisions in the Charter will not extend the competences of the Union as defined in the Treaties and the rights and freedoms in the Charter will be interpreted in accordance with the explanations relating to the Charter (Article 6(1) TEU).

The concepts in the Charter have been drawn from the European Treaties (particularly Article 6 TEU (from the Treaty of Nice), which concern discrimination, fundamental freedoms and the obligations of the Member States to their citizens), rulings by the European Court of Justice and the European Convention of Human Rights of 1950.

The principle of fundamental rights was introduced into the formal treaty structure in the Maastricht Treaty of 1992, where Article 6(2) TEU stated that 'the Union shall respect fundamental rights.' The intention is that the Charter should apply primarily to the institutions and bodies of the Union and to the Member States when they are applying Union law (Charter, Article 51).

In 1999, the European Council of Cologne agreed to establish a Charter and the presidents of the European Parliament, the Council and the Commission proclaimed the Charter at Nice on 7 December 2000. A set of explanations for the interpretation of the Charter, including a commentary on the scope of the Charter, was attached to the Charter to provide further understanding of the provisions. The explanations state that the Charter will not extend the rights already included in national law and that it will only apply to issues affected by Union law.

At this stage, the Charter did not have legal status and it was included as one of the four main areas for consideration identified in the Declaration on the future of the Union attached to the Treaty of Nice. The Charter was incorporated into the draft Constitution, as Part II, and given binding legal force. In the negotiations for the Treaty of Lisbon, it was agreed by the Member States that the Charter should not be in the text of the treaties.

There have not been any major changes to the text of the Charter from Nice to the version in the Treaty of Lisbon, except in incorporating the legally-binding nature of the Charter, so that it comes under the jurisdiction of the Court of Justice. In addition, updated explanations for the interpretation of the Charter are attached to the new Charter signed on 12 December 2007. The introduction to the explanations states that the explanations do not have the status of law, but that they are "a valuable tool of interpretation".

There is one protocol and four declarations attached to the Treaty of Lisbon relating to the Charter. The protocol concerns the application of the Charter to the United Kingdom and Poland and states that the Charter does not extend the ability of the Court of Justice to find that the laws of the two countries are inconsistent with the Charter and that nothing in Title IV of the Charter (relating to 'solidarity', in particular workers' rights) will create rights other than those already granted by the countries (Protocol 7, Articles 2 and 3). The declarations reaffirm that the Charter does not extend the powers of the Union and the Czech Republic and Poland make specific statements concerning their interpretation of the Charter (Declarations 1, 53, 61 and 62).

Any revision of the Charter will be made by the institutions of the Union since the Charter is a separate document and not part of the Treaty structure. This is different to the situation in the draft Constitution, where the Charter was in the main text of the Treaty and it would have been revised following the normal procedure for revision of the Treaties, in an intergovernmental conference with the heads of government.

There are concerns over the structure of the Charter, in that it has some contradictions and uncertainties, in particular the potential conflict between individual rights and the common good, which would need to be decided by the national and European courts. For example, the right to strike is included in Article 28 and this could lead to the Court of Justice overruling the UK's industrial legislation. The impact of the Charter will only be properly assessed when test cases are brought before the Court of Justice.

The Court of Justice has already begun to refer to the Charter in its judgements, in a supportive and non-contentious role, even though the Charter only has legal effect once the Treaty of Lisbon enters into force. The Court has used the Charter in a wide range of issues, such as cartels, in *JFE Engineering v Commission* (T-67/00), disclosure of insider information, in *Grøngaard and Bang* (C-384-/02), persons unable to be tried twice, in *Tokai Carbon v Commission* (T-236/01), the legality of Community measures, in *Commission v. Jégo-Quéré* (C-263/02P), conflicting rights, in *Varec V État belge* (C-450/06), abuse of a dominant position, *Alrosa Company Ltd v Commission* (T-170/06) and rights of trade unions to defend collective agreements against the rights of employers, *The International Transport Workers' Federation and The Finnish Seamen's Union v. Viking Line ABP and OÜ Viking Line Eesti* (C-438/05) and *Laval un Partneri Ltd v Svenska Byggnadsarbetareförbundet and Others* (C-341/05).

European Public Prosecutor (Article 86 TFEU)

A European Public Prosecutor will be formed from Eurojust to investigate and prosecute people involved in crimes affecting the financial interests of the Union and it will be able to act as prosecutor in the national courts of the Member States.

The provisions have been brought forward from the draft Constitution; at the time of the negotiations for the Constitution, the UK government was opposed to the post on the grounds that it was unnecessary. This argument was over-ruled and at the moment the remit is restricted to financial interests, however, there are concerns that this will be extended to cover other offences, and this is made possible by Article 86(4) TFEU, giving the European Council the ability to extend the powers to cover any crime of a cross-border dimension.

There is a new amendment to the Article which allows a minimum of nine Member States that do not wish the public prosecutor to be established to appeal to the European Council. In addition, there is specific provision for enhanced co-operation to be available for a minimum of nine Member States to establish a public prosecutor (Article 86(1) TFEU).

Euro Group (Articles 136 to 138 TFEU, Protocol no. 3)

This is a new policy taken from the draft Constitution and the group consists of the Member States in the Single Currency and is intended to co-ordinate the economic guidelines and the budgetary discipline of these Member States (Article 136 TFEU). The President of the Eurogroup will be appointed by the members of the group by qualified majority for a period of two and a half years (Protocol no. 3).

Space Policy (Article 189 TFEU)

This is a new policy area and has been introduced as space is considered to be of vital importance to the economic and political security of the European Union. The area includes the guarantee of European independent access to space, covering defence policy needs, as well as weather forecasts, observation and satellite navigation services, as well as transport and agriculture.

Environmental and Energy provisions (Articles 191 to 194 TFEU and Declaration no.35)

The provisions relating to the environment have been amended with the addition of combating of climate change to the objectives of Union policy (Article 191(1) TFEU); there is a new *passerelle* clause where the Council can change the method of voting to the ordinary legislative procedure from unanimity; this could have an impact on the environmental policy on Member States' choice of energy sources and the general structure of its energy supply (Article 192(2)(c) TFEU).

The energy provisions in the Treaty of Lisbon have been brought forward from the draft Constitution and are new to the European treaties; although there are references to energy in the Treaty establishing the European Community, it was considered appropriate in the IGC to have a specific article on energy given the increasing importance of energy to the European Union.

Energy matters are referred to specifically in the existing treaties in three articles: Article 3(1)(u) TEC, on the activities of the Community, Article 154(1) TEC on trans-European networks, concerning energy infra-structure and open and competitive markets, and in relation to environment, Article 175(2)(c) TEC. These and more general articles have been interpreted as being relevant to energy matters, for example the right of establishment and the freedom to provide services (Articles 47(2) and 55 TEC) has been used for the liberalisation of competition in the internal market for electricity and gas, and the provisions on environment have been used for the directive on the emissions trading scheme (Directive 2003/87/EC referred to Article 175 TEC).

In these cases, the Council was required to act by unanimity in order to adopt measures relating to energy, and so all decisions on regulations and directives had to be reached by consensus.

The terms of reference in the energy article in the Treaty of Lisbon have been broadly drawn, and there are a number of concerns, including whether the Member States have competence over boundary issues, nuclear energy and specific treaty negotiations with countries outside the European Union.

The new article introduces energy as a shared competence (Article 4 TFEU) and the Council may act by qualified majority on ensuring the functioning of the energy market, security of supply and energy efficiency (Article 194(1) TFEU). There are two provisions that are new in the Treaty of Lisbon and are changes from the text in the draft Constitution: the energy policy will be conducted in a spirit of solidarity between Member States and a new objective is introduced to promote the interconnection of energy networks (Article 194(1) TFEU).

The Council will act by unanimity to establish measures covering duties and taxation on energy, giving the Member States the right of veto and to be able to retain control over fiscal policy (Article 194(3) TFEU).

There has been an amendment to the provisions relating to economic policy: measures that can be adopted by the Council in response to severe difficulties in the supply to certain products now include a specific reference to energy and to solidarity between Member States (Article 122(1) TFEU).

Other provisions in the Treaties that will continue to have an impact on energy matters include the provisions on trans-European networks, concerning pipelines (Articles 170 to 172 TFEU), competition rules (Articles 101 to 106 TFEU), state aid (Articles 107 to 109 TFEU), approximation of laws (Articles 104 to 118 TFEU) and finally the flexibility clause which allows the Union to act where the objectives of the Treaties so require (Article 352 TFEU).

A Declaration (Declaration no. 35) has been attached to the Treaty to indicate that the Member States could protect their energy supplies for the essential interests of their internal security, but this should not impact on the internal market, as described in Article 347 TFEU. This declaration was also attached to the draft Constitution.

The Union's Own Resources (Article 311 TFEU)

The Union's method of financing the budget comes from duties, tariffs, VAT and payments from the Member States, termed 'own resources' and the UK negotiated a rebate of VAT in the 1980s. Under the existing treaties, the Council votes by unanimity for the whole of the area, but the Treaty of Lisbon will enable the Council to act by qualified majority in order to provide sufficient funds to fulfil the Union's objectives laying down the method of procedure in Article 311(4) TFEU and this could enable the Council to withdraw the UK rebate.

'Red Lines' of the British Government

During the debates leading up to the agreement of the text of the Treaty of Lisbon on 18 October 2007, the Member States had put forward their requests and expectations on what they would wish to be in the Treaty; the UK Government set out its position on the principles, or 'red lines', that it would consider to be essential to be respected as part of the negotiations on the Treaty in order to agree to the text and sign it.

The red lines have been narrowly drawn and tend to refer to specific articles and specific points. However, all the provisions in the particular area, and more broadly all the articles in the treaties, need to be referred to in order to understand the extent of the Union's competence and how strong the red-lines actually are. Ultimately, the red lines have to be tested in the Court of Justice.

Given the similarity in the draft Constitution and the Treaty of Lisbon, there is considerable overlap in the areas that the UK Government defined as red lines in each Treaty and the issues are briefly summarised below, with references to the appropriate Article or Protocol.

- *Representation in international organisations including NATO and permanent membership of the UN Security Council together with the rights associated with it;*
    * The concerns over NATO are covered by Article 42(7) TEU [Article I-41(7), which states that NATO will remain the foundation of the defence of the Member States who are members. Permanent membership of the UN Security Council is covered by Article 34(1) TEU [Article III-305(2)], which retained from the text in the existing treaties. These areas are also covered by Protocol no. 4 on Permanent Structured Co-operation [Protocol 23 in the draft Constitution];

- *Role of national parliaments in treaty change*;
    * National parliaments will be involved in the ordinary revision procedure (Article 48(2) TEU [Article IV-(3)] and in the simplified revision procedure (Article 48(6) and (7) TEU) [Articles IV-444 and IV-445].

- *European Regional Development Fund to remain intergovernmental*
    * The first provisions under the Constitution would have been under unanimity; Lisbon has removed this and the vote will be by QMV under the ordinary legislative procedure (Articles 177 and 178 TFEU).

- *European Public Prosecutor;*
    * The establishment of the European Public prosecutor will be by unanimity; there a are additional provisions added by the Treaty of Lisbon, where nine Member States

can request the matter to go to the European Council, and there is an enhanced co-operation provision (Article 86 TFEU).

- *Charter of Fundamental Rights.*
  - * There is a Protocol in the Treaty of Lisbon relating to the UK on the restrictions of the Charter, in particular concerning Title IV on solidarity, where the Charter will not create rights that are not already recognised in the UK (Protocol 7).

- *National veto retained on the following areas*:

1. *Treaty change*;

* Any changes in the Treaties, under the ordinary revision procedure, has to be agreed by all of the Member States; this has not altered since the Treaty of Rome in 1957 (Article 48(4) TEU) [Article IV-443(3)]. However, there is a passerelle clause, which allows the European Council to act by qualified majority to change the method of voting to qualified majority for areas in the TFEU [Part III of the Constitution] (Article 48(7) TEU) [Article IV-444(2)].

2. *Tax policy*;

* The issue of introducing provisions on direct tax and to change the method of voting to qualified majority were discussed but ultimately removed from the draft Constitution in order for it to be agreed. The national veto is very narrowly drawn in that the issue is whether voting on the provisions on tax in the Treaty are by unanimity or by qualified majority. It does not take into account decisions by the Court of Justice or proposals by the Commission that will be agreed by consensus. The issue of making any changes to this did not arise in the negotiations for the Treaty of Lisbon (Articles 110 to 113 TFEU) [Articles III-170 to III-171].

3. *Social security rights for workers including working conditions and employment relations and discrimination*;

* An 'emergency brake' was introduced in the draft Constitution to prevent provisions affecting fundamental issues on social security from being voted on by qualified majority (Article 48 TFEU) [Article III-136]. The emergency brake has been brought forward to the Treaty of Lisbon, with the term 'fundamental' changed to 'important'.

4. *Common foreign and security policy, including defence*;

* Decisions on the CFSP will by unanimity, except in certain circumstances. An emergency brake was introduced into the draft Constitution, together with a passerelle clause and these arrangements have been brought forward to the Treaty of Lisbon. Proposals by the High Representative will be voted on by qualified majority (Article 31(2) TEU) [Article III-300(2)]. The areas that can be voted ion by QMV do not apply to military or defence issues (Article 31(4) TEU).

  In the Treaty of Lisbon, there has been an additional sentence added to state that national security remains the sole responsibility of the member States and a paragraph has been added to state that the Council will act by unanimity (Articles 4(2), 24 and 30 TEU) [Article III-300].

5. *Protection of the UK's common law system, frontier controls and our police and judicial processes and criminal procedural law;*

* There is a general opt-out of the JHA, summarised in a Protocol (Protocol 22), and there are opt-ins for specific measures, e.g. on the Schengen *acquis* (Protocols 20 and 22).

6. *Own resources;*

* The Council will vote by unanimity, under a special legislative procedure, to adopt measures on own resources, including establishing any new categories (Article 311 TFEU).

PERTINENT ARTICLES

The following articles, and extracts from articles, are intended to summarise the most important provisions in the Treaties as amended by the Treaty of Lisbon. Where the articles were first introduced in the draft Constitution, the reference is highlighted and the Article in the Constitution is shown in square brackets.

The text in normal type is from the treaties as amended by the treaty of Nice, the text in bold is from the draft Constitution and the text in bold italics is new in the Treaty of Lisbon.

TREATY ON EUROPEAN UNION

- **Preamble:** *Second recital (new in 2004 IGC – first recital)*
  - **DRAWING INSPIRATION from the cultural, religious and humanist inheritance of Europe, from which have developed the universal values of the inviolable and inalienable rights of the human person, freedom, democracy, equality and the rule of law,**

- **Article 1 TEU:** *['Establishment of the Union' Article I-1 (new Article in 2004 IGC)]*
  - By this Treaty, the HIGH CONTRACTING PARTIES establish among themselves a EUROPEAN UNION, hereinafter called 'the Union', **on which the Member States confer competences to attain objectives they have in common.**
    This Treaty marks a new stage in the process of creating an ever closer union among the peoples of Europe, in which decisions are taken as openly as possible and closely as possible to the citizen.
    The Union shall be founded on the present Treaty and on the Treaty on the functioning of the European Union (hereinafter referred to as "the Treaties"). Those two Treaties shall have the same legal value. The Union shall replace and succeed the European Community.

- **Article 3 TEU:** *['The Union's Objectives', Article I-3] (ex Article 2 TEC and Article 2 TEU)*
  - **2. The Union shall offer its citizens an area of freedom, security and justice without internal frontiers *in which the free movement of persons is ensured in conjunction with appropriate measures with respect to external border controls, asylum, immigration and the prevention and combating of crime.***

- **Article 4 TEU:** *['Relations between the Union and the Member States', Article I-5] (ex Article 10 TEC and Article 6(3) TEU)*
  - ***1. In accordance with Article 3b, competences not conferred upon the Union in the Treaties remain with the Member States.***

    2. In particular, national security remains the sole responsibility of each Member State.

- **Article 6 TEU:** *['Fundamental Rights' Article I-9] (ex Article 6(2) TEU)*
  - **1. *The Union recognises* the rights, freedoms and principles set out in the Charter of Fundamental Rights *of 7 December 2000, as adapted at Strasbourg, on 12 December 2007, which shall have the same legal value as the Treaties.***
    The provisions of the Charter shall not extend in any way the competences of the Union as defined in the Treaties.

- **Article 12 TEU:** *['The role of national Parliaments', new Article in Treaty of Lisbon 2007]*
  - ***National parliaments shall contribute actively to the good functioning of the Union:***

a) ***through being informed by the institutions of the Union and having draft legislative acts forwarded to them in accordance with the Protocol on the role of national parliaments in the European Union;***

b) ***by seeing to it that the principle of subsidiarity is respected in accordance with the procedures provided for in the Protocol on the application of the principles of subsidiarity and proportionality;***

- **Article 15 TEU** *[Article I-21 and Article I-22 'The European Council and its President'(new Article in 2004 IGC)]*

    - **1. The European Council shall provide the Union with the necessary impetus for its development and shall define the general political directions and priorities thereof. It shall not exercise legislative functions.**

      5. **The European Council shall elect its President, by a qualified majority, for a term of two and a half years, renewable once. In the event of an impediment or serious misconduct, the European Council can end his or her term of office in accordance with the same procedure.**

      6. The President of the European Council shall not hold a national office.

- **Article 16 TEU** *['The Council, its Presidency and the definition of a qualified majority', Articles I-23 to I-25]*

    - ***4. As from 1 November 2014*****, a qualified majority shall be defined as at least 55% of the members of the Council, comprising at least fifteen of them and representing Member States comprising at least 65% of the population of the Union.**
      A blocking minority must include at least four Council members, failing which the qualified majority shall be deemed attained.

- **Article 17 TEU** *['The European Commission and its President', Articles I-26 and I-27 (new Article in 2004 IGC)]*

    - ***5.*** **As from 1 November 2014, the Commission shall consist of a number of members, including its President and the *High Representative of the Union for Foreign Affairs and Security Policy*, corresponding to two thirds of the number of Member States, unless the European Council, acting unanimously, decides to alter this number.**
      The members of the Commission shall be selected from among the nationals of the Member States on the basis of a system of equal rotation between the Member States. This system shall be established unanimously by the European Council *in accordance with Article 244 of the Treaty on the Functioning of the European Union.*

- **Article 18 TEU** *['The High Representative of the Union for Foreign Affairs and Security Policy', Article I-28 'The Union Minister for Foreign Affairs' (new Article in IGC 2004)]*

    - **1. The European Council, acting by a qualified majority, with the agreement of the President of the Commission, shall appoint the *High Representative of the Union for Foreign Affairs and Security Policy.* The European Council may end his term of office by the same procedure.**

      2. The *High Representative* shall conduct the Union's common foreign and security policy. He shall contribute by his proposals to the development of that policy, which he shall carry out as mandated by the Council. The same shall apply to the common security and defence policy.

- **Article 20 TEU:** *['Enhanced Co-operation' Article I-44 (ex Article 11 TEC and Articles 43 – 45 TEU)]*

    - **1. Member States which wish to establish enhanced co-operation between themselves within the framework of the Union's non-exclusive competences may make use of its Institutions and exercise those competences by applying the relevant provisions of the *Treaty*. . . . .**

      Enhanced co-operation shall aim to further the objectives of the Union, protect its interests and reinforce its integration process.

4. **Acts adopted in the framework of enhanced co-operation shall bind only participating States. They shall not be regarded as an *acquis* which has to be accepted by candidates for accession to the Union.**

- **Article 24 TEU:** *[Article I-16 'The common foreign and security policy' (ex Articles 17 TEU and 11(2) TEU)]*

  - *1.* **The Union's competence in matters of common foreign and security policy shall cover all areas of foreign policy and all questions relating to the Union's security, including the progressive framing of a common defence policy that might lead to a common defence.**
    The adoption of legislative acts shall be excluded. The common foreign and security policy shall be put into effect by the High Representative of the Union for Foreign Affairs and Security Policy and by Member States, in accordance with the Treaties.

    2. ***Within the framework*** **of the principles and objectives of its external action, the Union shall** ***conduct,*** **define and implement a common foreign and security policy,** ***based on the development of mutual political solidarity among Member States, the identification of questions of general interest and the achievement of an ever-increasing degree of convergence of Member States' actions.***

    3. The Member States shall support the common foreign and security policy actively and unreservedly in a spirit of loyalty and mutual solidarity **and shall comply with the Union's actions in this area.**

- **Article 27 TEU:** *[Article III-296 'The Union Minister for Foreign Affairs'* (*new Article in 2004 IGC)]*

  - **1. The** ***High Representative for the Union for Foreign Affairs and Security Policy,*** **who shall chair the Foreign Affairs Council, shall contribute through his or her proposals towards the preparation of the common foreign and security policy and shall ensure implementation of the decisions adopted by the European Council and the Council.**

    2. The ***High Representative*** **shall represent the Union for matters relating to the common foreign and security policy. He shall conduct political dialogue with third parties on the Union's behalf and shall express the Union's position in international organisations and at international conferences.**

    3. In fulfilling his mandate, the ***High Representative*** **shall be assisted by a European External Action Service. This service shall work in co-operation with the diplomatic services of the Member States and shall comprise officials from relevant departments of the General Secretariat of the Council and of the Commission as well as staff seconded from national diplomatic services of the Member States. The organisation and functioning of the European External Action Service shall be established by a decision of the Council. The Council shall act on a proposal from the** ***High Representative*** **after consulting the European Parliament and after obtaining the consent of the Commission.**

- **Article 34 TEU:** *[Article III-305 'International organisations and at international conferences'* (*ex Article 19 TEU*)]

  - 1. Member States shall co-ordinate their action in international organisations and at international conferences. They shall uphold the **Union's** positions in such fora. The ***High Representative for the Union for Foreign Affairs and Security Policy*** **shall organise this co-ordination.**
    In international organisations and at international conferences where not all the Member States participate, those which do take part shall uphold the Union's positions.

    2. **When the Union has defined a position on a subject which is on the United Nations Security Council agenda, those Member States which sit on the Security Council shall request that the** ***High Representative*** **be** ***invited*** **to present the Union's position.**

- **Article 42 TEU** *[Article I-41 (new Article in 2004 IGC)]*

  - **1. The common security and defence policy shall be an integral part of the common foreign and security policy. It shall provide the Union with an operational capacity drawing on civil and military assets. The performance of these tasks shall be undertaken using capabilities provided by the Member States.**

    2. The common foreign and security policy shall include **the progressive framing of a common Union defence policy. This will** lead to a common defence, **when** the European Council**, acting unanimously,** so decides.

- **Article 46 TEU**: [*'Common Security and defence policy' Article III-312 (new Article in 2004 IGC*)]

  - **1. Those Member States which wish to participate in the permanent structured co-operation referred to in *Article 42(6)*, which fulfil the criteria and have made the commitments on military capabilities set out in the Protocol on permanent structured co-operation shall notify their intention to the Council and to the *High Representative for the Union for Foreign Affairs and Security Policy.***

    2. Within three months following the notification referred to in paragraph 1 the Council shall adopt a decision establishing permanent structured co-operation and determining the list of participating Member States. The Council shall act by a qualified majority after consulting the *High Representative.*

- **Article 47 TEU**: [*'Legal personality', Article I-7 (new Article in 2004 IGC)]*

  - **The Union shall have legal personality.**

- **Article 48 TEU:** *['Treaty revision procedures', Articles IV-443, IV-444 and IV-445 (ex-Article 48 TEU and new Article in 2004 IGC)]*

  - ***1. The Treaties may be amended in accordance with an ordinary revision procedure. They may also be amended in accordance with simplified revision procedures.***

    5. If, two years after the signature of *a* treaty amending *the Treaties*, four fifths of the Member States have ratified it and one or more Member States have encountered difficulties in proceeding with ratification, the matter shall be referred to the European Council.

    7. ***Where the Treaty on the Functioning of the European Union or Title V of this Treaty* provides for the Council to act by unanimity in a given area or case, the European Council may adopt a decision authorising the Council to act by a qualified majority in that area or in that case. This *sub*paragraph shall not apply to decisions with military implications or those in the area of defence.**
    ***Where the Treaty on the Functioning of the European Union* provides for *legislative acts* to be adopted by the Council in accordance with a special legislative procedure, the European Council may adopt a decision allowing for the adoption of such *acts* in accordance with the ordinary legislative procedure.**
    Any initiative taken by the European Council on the basis of *the first or second subparagraph* shall be notified to the national Parliaments. If a national Parliament makes known its opposition within six months of the date of such notification, the decision referred to in *the first or second subparagraph* shall not be adopted. In the absence of opposition, the European Council may adopt the decision.
    For the adoption of the decisions referred to in *the first or second subparagraphs*, the European Council shall act by unanimity after obtaining the consent of the European Parliament, which shall be given by a majority of its component members.

- **Article 50 TEU:** *['Voluntary withdrawal from the Union', Article I-60 (new Article in IGC 2004)]*

  - **1. Any Member State may decide to withdraw from the European Union in accordance with its own constitutional requirements.**

2. A Member State which decides to withdraw shall notify the European Council of its intention. … [T]he Union shall conclude an agreement with that State, setting out the arrangements for its withdrawal, taking account of the framework for its future relationship with the Union. That agreement shall be negotiated in accordance with *Article 218(3) TFEU*; it shall be concluded by the Council acting by a qualified majority on behalf of the Union, after obtaining the consent of the European Parliament.

TREATY ON THE FUNCTIONING OF THE EUROPEAN UNION

- **Article 2 TFEU:** *[Categories of competence' Article I-12 (new Article in 2004 IGC)]*

  - **2. When the *Treaties* confer on the Union a competence shared with the Member States in a specific area, the Union and the Member States may legislate and adopt legally binding acts in that area. *The Member States shall again exercise their competence to the extent that the Union has decided to cease exercising its competence.***

    3. The Member States shall co-ordinate their economic and employment policies within arrangements as determined by *the Treaties*, which the Union shall have competence to provide.

    4. The Union shall have competence … to define and implement a common foreign and security policy, including the progressive framing of a common defence policy.

- **Article 3 TFEU:** *[Areas of exclusive competence Article I-13 (new Article in 2004 IGC)]*

  - **1. The Union shall have exclusive competence in the following areas:**
    (a) customs union,
    (b) the establishing of the competition rules necessary for the functioning of the internal market,
    (c) monetary policy, for the Member States whose currency is the euro,
    (d) the conservation of marine biological resources under the common fisheries policy,
    (e) common commercial policy.

    2. The Union shall also have exclusive competence for the conclusion of an international agreement when its conclusion is provided for in a legislative act of the Union or is necessary to enable the Union to exercise its internal competence, or insofar as its conclusion may affect common rules or alter their scope.

- **Article 3 TFEU:** *['Areas of shared competence' Article I-14 (new Article in 2004 IGC)]*

  - **1. The Union shall share competence with the Members States where the *Treaties confer* on it a competence which does not relate to the areas referred to in *Articles 3 and 6.***

    2. Shared competence between the Union and the Member States applies in the following principal areas:
    (a) internal market,
    (b) social policy, for aspects defined in *this Treaty*,
    (c) economic, social and territorial cohesion,
    (d) agriculture and fisheries, excluding the conservation of marine biological resources,
    (e) environment,
    (f) consumer protection,
    (g) transport,
    (h) trans-European networks,
    (i) energy,
    (j) area of freedom, security and justice,

(k) **common safety concerns in public health matters, for aspects defined in *this Treaty*.**

- **Article 5 TFEU:** *['The co-ordination of economic and employment policies' Article I-15 (new Article in 2004 IGC)]*

    - **1. The Member States shall co-ordinate their economic policies within the Union. To this end, the Council of Ministers shall adopt measures, in particular broad guidelines for these policies.**
    Specific provisions shall apply to those Member States whose currency is the euro.

    2. The Union shall take measures to ensure co-ordination of the employment policies of the Member States, in particular by defining guidelines for these policies.

    3. The Union may take initiatives to ensure co-ordination of Member States' social policies.

- **Article 6 TFEU** *[Article I-17: Area of supporting, co-ordinating or complementary action (new article in 2004 IGC)]*

    - **1. The Union shall have competence to carry out *actions to support, co-ordinate or supplement the actions of the Member States. The areas of such* action shall, at European level, be**
    (a) protection and improvement of human health;
    (b) industry;
    (c) culture;
    (d) tourism; *(new Article in 2004 IGC)*
    (e) education, youth, sport and vocational training; *(sport - new Article in 2004 IGC)*
    (f) civil protection; *(new Article in 2004 IGC)*
    (g) administrative co-operation. *(new Article in 2004 IGC)*

- **Article 7 TFEU:** *['General' Article III-115 (new Article in 2004 IGC)]*

    - **The Union shall ensure consistency between *its* policies and activities, taking all of its objectives into account and in accordance with the principle of conferral of powers.**

- **Article 10 TFEU:** *['Discrimination' Article III-118 (new Article in 2004 IGC)]*

    - **In defining and implementing *its* policies and activities, the Union shall aim to combat discrimination based on sex, race or ethnic origin, religion or belief, disability, age or sexual orientation.**

- **Article 26 TFEU:** *['Establishment and functioning of the internal market' Article III-130 (ex Articles 14 & 15 TEC)]*

    - 1. The **Union** shall adopt measures with the aim of establishing **or ensuring the functioning of** the internal market, in accordance with **the relevant** provisions of ***the Treaties.***

- **Article 38 TFEU:** *['Common agriculture and fisheries policy' Article III-225 (new Article in 2004 IGC)]*

    - 1. **The Union shall define and implement a common agriculture and fisheries policy.**
    The **internal** market shall extend to agriculture, ***fisheries*** and trade in agricultural products. "Agricultural products" means the products of the soil, of stock-farming and of fisheries and products of first-stage processing directly related to these products. **References to the common agricultural policy or to agriculture, and the use of the term "agricultural", shall be understood as also referring to fisheries, having regard to the specific characteristics of this sector.**

- **Article 48 TFEU:** *['Social security' Article III-136 (ex Article 42 TEC)]*
    - **Where a member of the Council considers that a draft *legislative act* referred to in the first subparagraph would affect *important* aspects of its social security system, including**

its scope, cost or financial structure, or would affect the financial balance of that system, it may request that the matter be referred to the European Council. In that case, the *ordinary legislative procedure* shall be suspended. After discussion, the European Council shall, within four months of this suspension, either:

(a) refer the draft back to the Council, which shall terminate the suspension of the *ordinary legislative procedure*, or

(b) request the Commission to submit a new proposal; in that case, the act originally proposed shall be deemed not to have been adopted.

- **Article 67 TFEU:** *['Specific provisions relating to the area of freedom, security and justice' Article I-42 (ex Article 61 TEC)*
  - **1. The Union shall constitute an area of freedom, security and justice with respect for fundamental rights and the different legal systems and traditions of the Member States.**

    2. It shall ensure the absence of internal border controls for persons and shall frame a common policy on asylum, immigration and external border control, based on solidarity between Member States, which is fair towards third-country nationals. For the purpose of this *Title*, stateless persons shall be treated as third-country nationals.

    3. The Union shall endeavour to ensure a high level of security through measures to prevent and combat crime, racism and xenophobia, and through measures for co-ordination and co-operation between police and judicial authorities and other competent authorities, as well as through the mutual recognition of judgments in criminal matters and, if necessary, through the approximation of criminal laws.

    4. The Union shall facilitate access to justice, in particular through the principle of mutual recognition of judicial and extra-judicial decisions in civil matters.

- **Article 68 TFEU:** *[Article III-258 (new provision in 2004 IGC)]*
  - **The European Council shall define the strategic guidelines for legislative and operational planning within the area of freedom, security and justice.**

- **Article 75 TFEU:** *['Capital and payments' Article III-160 (new Article in 2004 IGC)]*
  - **Where necessary to achieve the objectives set out in *Article 61*, as regards preventing and combating terrorism and related activities, *the European Parliament and the Council, acting by means of regulations in accordance with the ordinary legislative procedure,* shall define a framework for administrative measures with regard to capital movements and payments, such as the freezing of funds, financial assets or economic gains belonging to, or owned or held by, natural or legal persons, groups or non-State entities.**
    The Council, on a proposal from the Commission, shall adopt *measures* to implement the *framework* referred to in the first paragraph.

- **Article 78 TFEU:** *['Policy on border checks, asylum and immigration' Article III-266 (ex Article 63, points 1 and 2, and ex Article 64(2) TEC)]*
  - **1. The Union shall develop a common policy on asylum, subsidiary protection and temporary protection with a view to offering appropriate status to any third-country national requiring international protection and ensuring compliance with the principle of *non-refoulement.***

- **Article 79 TFEU:** *['Policy on border checks, asylum and immigration' Article III-267 (ex Articles 29 and 31(1)(e) TEU and points 3 and 4 of ex Article 63 TEC)]*
  - **1. The Union shall develop a common immigration policy aimed at ensuring, at all stages, the efficient management of migration flows, fair treatment of third-country nationals residing legally in Member States, and the prevention of, and enhanced measure to combat, illegal immigration and trafficking in human beings.**

- **Article 81 TFEU:** *['Judicial co-operation in civil matters' Article 65 TFEU (ex Article 65 TEC)]*

  - **1. The Union shall develop judicial co-operation in civil matters having cross-border implications, based on the principle of mutual recognition of judgments and decisions in extra-judicial cases. Such co-operation shall include the adoption of measures for the approximation of the laws and regulations of the Member States.**

    3. Notwithstanding paragraph 2, measures concerning family law with cross-border implications *shall be established by the Council, acting in accordance with a special legislative procedure.* The Council shall act unanimously after consulting the European Parliament.
    The Council, on a proposal from the Commission, may adopt a European decision determining those aspects of family law with cross-border implications which may be the subject of acts adopted by the ordinary legislative procedure. The Council shall act unanimously after consulting the European Parliament.

- **Article 82 TFEU:** *['Judicial co-operation in criminal matters' Article III-270 (ex Article 31(1) TEU)]*

  - **1. Judicial co-operation in criminal matters in the Union shall be based on the principle of mutual recognition of judgments and judicial decisions and shall include the approximation of the laws and regulations of the Member States in the areas referred to in paragraph 2 and in *Article 83*.**

    3. Where a member of the Council considers that a draft *directive* as referred to in paragraph 2 would affect fundamental aspects of its criminal justice system, it may request that the draft *directive* be referred to the European Council. In that case, the *ordinary legislative procedure* shall be suspended. After discussion, *and in case of a consensus,* the European Council shall, within four months of this suspension, refer the draft back to the Council, which shall terminate the suspension of the *ordinary legislative procedure.*

- **Article 83 TFEU:** *['Serious crime with a cross-border dimension' Article III-271 TFEU (new Article in 2004 IGC)]*

  - **1. *The European Parliament and the Council may, by means of directives adopted in accordance with the ordinary legislative procedure* establish minimum rules concerning the definition of criminal offences and sanctions in the areas of particularly resulting from the nature or impact of such offences or from a special need to combat them on a common basis.**
    These areas of crime are the following: terrorism, trafficking in human beings and sexual exploitation of women and children, illicit drug trafficking, illicit arms trafficking, money laundering, corruption, counterfeiting of means of payment, computer crime and organised crime.

    3. Where a member of the Council considers that a draft *directive* as referred to in paragraph 1 or 2 would affect fundamental aspects of its criminal justice system, it may request that the draft *directive* be referred to the European Council. In that case, the *ordinary legislative procedure* shall be suspended. After discussion, *and in case of a consensus,* the European Council shall, within four months of this suspension, refer the draft back to the Council, which shall terminate the suspension of the *ordinary legislative procedure.*

- **Article 86 TFEU:** *['European Public Prosecutor's Office' Article III-274 (new Article in 2004 IGC)]*
  - **1. In order to combat crimes affecting the financial interests of the Union, the Council, *by means of a regulation adopted in accordance with a special legislative procedure,* may establish a European Public Prosecutor's Office from Eurojust. The Council shall act unanimously after obtaining the consent of the European Parliament.**
    In case of absence of unanimity in the Council, a group of at least nine Member States may request that the draft regulation be referred to the European Council. In that case, the procedure in the Council shall be suspended. After discussion, and in case of a

consensus, the European Council shall, within four months of this suspension, refer the draft back to the Council for adoption.

4. The European Council may, at the same time or subsequently, adopt a European decision amending paragraph 1 in order to extend the powers of the European Public Prosecutor's Office to include serious crime having a cross-border dimension.... The European Council shall act unanimously after obtaining the consent of the European Parliament and after consulting the Commission.

- **Article 118 TFEU:** *['Intellectual property rights' Article III-176 (new Article in 2004 IGC)]*
  - **In the context of the establishment and functioning of the internal market, *the European Parliament and the Council, acting in accordance with the ordinary legislative procedure,* shall establish measures for the creation of European intellectual property rights to provide uniform intellectual property rights protection throughout the Union and for the setting up of centralised Union-wide authorisation, co-ordination and supervision arrangements.**
    The Council, acting unanimously in accordance with a special legislative procedure, shall by means of regulations **establish language arrangements for the European intellectual property rights. The Council shall act unanimously after consulting the European Parliament.**

- **Article 152 TFEU:** *['The social partners and autonomous social dialogue' Article I-48 (ex Article 138 TEC)]*
  - **The Union recognises and promotes the role of the social partners at its level, taking into account the diversity of national systems; it shall facilitate dialogue between the social partners, respecting their autonomy.**

- **Article 189 TFEU:** *['Space policy' Article III-254 (new Article in 2004 IGC)]*
  - **1. To promote scientific and technical progress, industrial competitiveness and the implementation of its policies, the Union shall draw up a European space policy. To this end, it may promote joint initiatives, support research and technological development and co-ordinate the efforts needed for the exploration and exploitation of space.**

    2. To contribute to attaining the objectives referred to in paragraph 1, *the European Parliament and the Council, acting in accordance with the ordinary legislative procedure,* shall establish the necessary measures, which may take the form of a European space programme, *excluding any harmonisation of the laws and regulations of the Member States.*

- **Article 194 TFEU:** *['Energy' Article III-256 (new Article in 2004 IGC)]*
  - **1. In the context of the establishment and functioning of the internal market and with regard for the need to preserve and improve the environment, Union policy on energy shall aim, *in a spirit of solidarity between Member States,* to:**
    (a) ensure the functioning of the energy market;
    (b) ensure security of energy supply in the Union, and
    (c) promote energy efficiency and energy saving and the development of new and renewable forms of energy;
    (d) promote the interconnection of energy networks.

    2. Without prejudice to the application of other provisions of the *Treaties, the European Parliament and the Council, acting in accordance with the ordinary legislative procedure, shall establish the measures necessary to achieve* the objectives in paragraph 1. Such *measures* shall be adopted after consultation of the Economic and Social Committee and the Committee of the Regions.
    Such *measures* shall not affect a Member State's right to determine the conditions for exploiting its energy resources, its choice between different energy sources and the general structure of its energy supply, without prejudice to *Article 192(2)(c).*

    3. By way of derogation from paragraph 2, *the Council, acting in accordance with a special legislative procedure, shall unanimously and after consulting the European*

Parliament, **establish the measures referred to therein when they are primarily of a fiscal nature.**

- **Article 196 TFEU:** *['Civil protection' Article III-284 (new Article in 2004 IGC)]*

  - **1. The Union shall encourage co-operation between Member States in order to improve the effectiveness of systems for preventing and protecting against natural or man-made disasters.**
    Union action shall aim to:
    (a) support and supplement Member States' action at national, regional and local level in risk prevention, in preparing their civil-protection personnel and in responding to natural or man-made disasters within the Union;
    (b) promote swift, effective operational co-operation within the Union between national civil-protection services;
    (c) promote consistency in international civil-protection work.

    2. ***The European Parliament and the Council, acting in accordance with the ordinary legislative procedure,*** **shall establish the measures necessary to help achieve the objectives referred to in paragraph 1, excluding any harmonisation of the laws and regulations of the Member States.**

- **Article 197 TFEU:** *['Administrative co-operation' Article III-285 (new Article in 2004 IGC)]*

  - **1. Effective implementation of Union law by the Member States, which is essential for the proper functioning of the Union, shall be regarded as a matter of common interest.**

    2. The Union may support the efforts of Member States to improve their administrative capacity to implement Union law. Such action may include facilitating the exchange of information and of civil servants as well as supporting training schemes. No Member State shall be obliged to avail itself of such support. ***The European Parliament and the Council, acting by means of regulations in accordance with the ordinary legislative procedure,*** **shall establish the necessary measures to this end, excluding any harmonisation of the laws and regulations of the Member States.**

    3. This Article shall be without prejudice to the obligations of the Member States to implement Union law or to the prerogatives and duties of the Commission. It shall also be without prejudice to other provisions of the ***Treaties*** **providing for administrative co-operation among the Member States and between them and the Union.**

- **Article 222(1) TFEU:** *['Solidarity clause' Article I-43 (new Article in 2004 IGC)]*

  - **1. The Union and its Member States shall act jointly in a spirit of solidarity if a Member State is the object of a terrorist attack or the victim of a natural or man-made disaster. The Union shall mobilise all the instruments at its disposal, including the military resources made available by the Member States, to:**
    (a) – prevent the terrorist threat in the territory of the Member States;
    – protect democratic institutions and the civilian population from any terrorist attack;
    – assist a Member State in its territory, at the request of its political authorities, in the event of a terrorist attack;
    (b) assist a Member State in its territory, at the request of its political authorities, in the event of a natural or man-made disaster.

- **Article 289 TFEU:** *['Legislative acts' Article I-34 (new Article in 2004 IGC)]*

  - **1.** ***The ordinary legislative procedure shall consist in the joint adoption by the European Parliament and the Council of a regulation, directive or decision on a proposal from the Commission. This procedure is defined in Article 294.***

- **Article 290 TFEU:** *['Delegated regulations' Article I-36 (new Article in 2004 IGC redrafted from Article 202 TEC)*
  - **1. *A legislative act* may delegate to the Commission the power to adopt *non-legislative acts* to supplement or amend certain non-essential elements of the *legislative act.***

- **Article 311 TFEU:** *['The Union's own resources' Article I-54 (ex Article 269 TEC)]*
  - **The Union shall provide itself with the means necessary to attain its objectives and carry through its policies.**
    Without prejudice to other revenue, the budget shall be financed wholly from own resources.
    The Council, acting ***in accordance with a special legislative procedure, shall unanimously*** and after consulting the European Parliament ***adopt a decision laying*** down **the** provisions relating to the system of own resources of the **Union. In this context it may establish new categories of own resources or abolish an existing category. That *decision* shall not enter into force until it is approved by** the Member States in accordance with their respective constitutional requirements.
    ***The Council, acting by means of regulations in accordance with a special legislative procedure,* shall lay down implementing measures of the Union's own resources system insofar as this is provided for in the *regulation* adopted on the basis of the *first paragraph.* The Council shall act after obtaining the consent of the European Parliament.**

- **Article 312 TFEU:** *['The multiannual financial framework' Article I-55 (new Article in 2004 IGC)]*
  - **1. The multiannual financial framework shall ensure that Union expenditure develops in an orderly manner and within the limits of its own resources.**
    ***It* shall be established for a period of at least five years.**
    The annual budget of the Union shall comply with the multiannual financial framework.

    2. *The Council, acting in accordance with a special legislative procedure, shall adopt a regulation laying* down the multiannual financial framework. The Council shall act unanimously after obtaining the consent of the European Parliament, which shall be given by a majority of its component members.
    The European Council may, unanimously, adopt a decision authorising the Council to act by a qualified majority when adopting the *regulation* referred to in the *first paragraph.*

- **Article 333 TFEU:** *['Enhanced co-operation 'passerelle' clause' Article III-422 (new Article in 2004 IGC)]*
  - **1. Where a provision of the *Treaties* which may be applied in the context of enhanced co-operation stipulates that the Council shall act unanimously, the Council, acting unanimously in accordance with the arrangements laid down in Article 330, may adopt a European decision stipulating that it will act by a qualified majority.**

    2. Where a provision of the *Treaties* which may be applied in the context of enhanced co-operation stipulates that the Council shall adopt European laws or framework laws under a special legislative procedure, the Council, acting unanimously in accordance with the arrangements laid down in Article 330, may adopt a European decision stipulating that it will act under the ordinary legislative procedure. The Council shall act after consulting the European Parliament.

    3. Paragraphs 1 and 2 shall not apply to decisions having military or defence implications.

- **Article 352 TFEU:** *['Flexibility clause', Article I-18]*
  - **1.** If action by the **Union** should prove necessary, **within the framework of the policies defined *by the Treaties,*** to attain one of the objectives **set out in the *Treaties,***

and the Treaties have not provided the necessary powers, the Council, **acting unanimously on a proposal from the Commission and after obtaining the consent of the European Parliament,** shall, **adopt** the appropriate measures. ***Where the measures in question are adopted by the Council in accordance with a special legislative procedure, it shall also act unanimously on a proposal from the Commission and after obtaining the consent of the European Parliament.***

2. Using the procedure for monitoring the subsidiarity principle referred to in *Article 3b(3) of the Treaty on European Union*, the Commission shall draw national Parliaments' attention to proposals based on this Article.

3. Measures based on this Article shall not entail harmonisation of Member States' laws or regulations in cases where the *Treaties* exclude such harmonisation.

4. This Article cannot serve as a basis for attaining objectives pertaining to the common foreign and security policy and any acts adopted pursuant to this Article shall respect the limits set out in Article 40, second paragraph, of the Treaty on European Union.

PROTOCOLS

Protocol no. 1 on the Role of National Parliaments in the European Union

- **Article 1**
  Commission consultation documents (green and white papers and communications) shall be forwarded directly by the Commission to national Parliaments upon publication. The Commission shall also forward the annual legislative programme as well as any other instrument of legislative planning or policy to national Parliaments, at the same time as to the European Parliament and the Council.

- **Article 3**
  National Parliaments may send to the Presidents of the European Parliament, the Council and the Commission a reasoned opinion on whether a draft European legislative act complies with the principle of subsidiarity, in accordance with the procedure laid down in the Protocol on the application of the principles of subsidiarity and proportionality.

- **Article 9**
  The European Parliament and national Parliaments shall together determine the organisation and promotion of effective and regular inter-parliamentary co-operation within the Union.

Protocol no. 2 on the application of the principles of subsidiarity and proportionality

- **Article 2**
  Before proposing European legislative acts, the Commission shall consult widely. Such consultations shall, where appropriate, take into account the regional and local dimension of the action envisaged. In cases of exceptional urgency, the Commission shall not conduct such consultations. It shall give reasons for the decision in its proposal.

- **Article 6**
  The European Parliament, the Council of Ministers and the Commission, and, where appropriate, the group of Member States, the Court of Justice, the European Central Bank or the European Investment Bank if the draft legislative act comes from them, shall take account of the reasoned opinions issued by national Parliaments or by a chamber of a national Parliament.

- **Article 7**
  1. The European Parliament, the Council and the Commission, and, where appropriate, the group of Member States, the Court of Justice, the European Central Bank or the European Investment Bank, if the draft legislative act originates from them, shall

take account of the reasoned opinions issued by national Parliaments or by a chamber of a national Parliament.

2. **Where reasoned opinions on a draft legislative act's non-compliance with the principle of subsidiarity represent at least one third of all the votes allocated to the national Parliaments in accordance with the second *sub*paragraph *of paragraph 1*, the draft must be reviewed. This threshold shall be a quarter in the case of a draft legislative act submitted on the basis of *Article 76 of the Treaty on the Functioning of the European Union* on the area of freedom, security and justice.**
After such review, the Commission or, where appropriate, the group of Member States, the European Parliament, the Court of Justice, the European Central Bank or the European Investment Bank, if the draft European legislative act originates from them, may decide to maintain, amend or withdraw the draft. Reasons must be given for this decision.

3. Furthermore, under the ordinary legislative procedure, where reasoned opinions on the non-compliance of a proposal for a legislative act with the principle of subsidiarity represent at least a simple majority of the votes allocated to the national Parliaments in accordance with the second subparagraph of paragraph 1, the proposal must be reviewed. After such review, the Commission may decide to maintain, amend or withdraw the proposal.

Protocol no. 3 on the Euro Group

- **Article 1**
  The Ministers of the Member States whose currency is the euro shall meet informally.

- **Article 2**
  The Ministers of the Member States whose currency is the euro shall elect a president for two and a half years, by a majority of those Member States.

Protocol no. 4 on permanent structured co-operation established by Article 42 TEU

- **Article 1**
  The permanent structured co-operation referred to in *Article 42(6) of the Treaty on European Union* shall be open to any Member State which undertakes, from the date of entry into force of the *Treaty of Lisbon*, to:
  - **(a) proceed more intensively to develop its defence capacities through the development of its national contributions and participation, where appropriate, in multinational forces, in the main European equipment programmes, and in the activity of the Agency in the field of defence capabilities development, research, acquisition and armaments (European Defence Agency), and**
  - **(b) have the capacity to supply by *2010* at the latest, either at national level or as a component of multinational force groups, targeted combat units for the missions planned, structured at a tactical level as a battle group, with support elements including transport and logistics, capable of carrying out the tasks referred to in *Article 43 of the Treaty on European Union*, within a period of 5 to 30 days, in particular in response to requests from the United Nations Organisation, and which can be sustained for an initial period of 30 days and be extended up to at least 120 days.**

Protocol no. 6 on the Internal Market and Competition

CONSIDERING that the internal market as set out in Article 3 of the Treaty on European Union includes a system ensuring that competition is not distorted,
HAVE AGREED that to this end, the Union shall, if necessary, take action under the provisions of the Treaties, including under Article 308 of the Treaty on the Functioning of the European Union.

Protocol no. 7 on the application of the Charter of Fundamental Rights to Poland and to the United Kingdom

- *ARTICLE 1*

  1. The Charter does not extend the ability of the Court of Justice of the European Union, or any court or tribunal of Poland or of the United Kingdom, to find that the laws, regulations or administrative provisions, practices or action of Poland or of the United Kingdom are inconsistent with the fundamental rights, freedoms and principles that it reaffirms.

  2. In particular, and for the avoidance of doubt, nothing in Title IV of the Charter creates justiciable rights applicable to Poland or the United Kingdom except in so far as Poland or the United Kingdom has provided for such rights in its national law.

Protocol no. 11 on transitional provisions

- **Article 3**

  1. ***In accordance with Article 16(4) of the Treaty on European Union, the provisions of that paragraph and of Article 238(2) of the Treaty on the Functioning of the European Union relating* to** the definition of the qualified majority in the European Council and the Council shall take effect on 1 November ***2014***.

  2. Between 1 November 2014 and 31 March 2017, when an act is to be adopted by qualified majority, a member of the Council may request that it be adopted in accordance with the qualified majority as defined in paragraph 3. In that case, paragraph 3 shall apply.

DECLARATIONS

Declaration no. 1 concerning the Charter of Fundamental Rights of the European Union

The Charter of Fundamental Rights, which has legally binding force, confirms the fundamental rights guaranteed by the European Convention on Human Rights and Fundamental Freedoms and as they result from the constitutional traditions common to the Member States.
The Charter does not extend the field of application of Union law beyond the powers of the Union or establish any new power or task for the Union, or modify powers and tasks as defined by the Treaties.

Declaration no. 7 on Article 16(4) TEU and Article 238(2) TFEU

- Whereas:

  (1) Provisions should be adopted allowing for a smooth transition from the system for decision-making in the Council by a qualified majority as defined in ***Article 3(3)*** of the Protocol on the transitional provisions, which will continue to apply until 31 October 2014, to the voting system provided for in ***Article 16(4) of the Treaty on European Union and Article 238(2) of the Treaty on the Functioning of the European Union***, which will apply with effect from 1 November 2014, including, during a transitional period until 31 March 2017, specific provisions laid down in ***Article 3(2)*** of that Protocol.

- **Article 1**

  From 1 November 2014 to 31 March 2017, if members of the Council, representing:

  (a) at least three quarters of the population, or

  (b) at least three quarters of the number of Member States

  necessary to constitute a blocking minority resulting from the application of ***Article 16(4), first subparagraph, of the Treaty on European Union or Article 238(2) of the Treaty on the Functioning of the European Union***, indicate their opposition to the Council adopting an act by a qualified majority, the Council shall discuss the issue.

- **Article 4**

  As from 1 April 2017, if members of the Council, representing:

(a) at least 55 % of the population, or
(b) at least 55 % of the number of Member States
necessary to constitute a blocking minority resulting from the application of ***Article 16(4), first subparagraph, of the Treaty on European Union or Article 238(2) of the Treaty on the Functioning of the European Union***, indicate their opposition to the Council adopting an act by a qualified majority, the Council shall discuss the issue.

Declaration no. 9 on Article 16(9) TEU concerning the European Council Decision on the exercise of the Presidency of the Council

- **Article 1**

  1. The Presidency of the Council, with the exception of the Foreign Affairs configuration, shall be held by pre-established groups of three Member States for a period of 18 months. The groups shall be made up on a basis of equal rotation among the Member States, taking into account their diversity and geographical balance within the Union.

  2. Each member of the group shall in turn chair for a six-month period all configurations of the Council, with the exception of the Foreign Affairs configuration. The other members of the group shall assist the Chair in all its responsibilities on the basis of a common programme. Members of the team may decide alternative arrangements among themselves.

Declaration no. 17: *Union Law (new in the Treaty of Lisbon)*

- ***The Conference recalls that, in accordance with well settled case law of the EU Court of Justice, the Treaties and the law adopted by the Union on the basis of the Treaties have primacy over the law of Member States, under the conditions laid down by the said case law.***
The Conference has also decided to attach as an Annex to this Final Act the Opinion of the Council Legal Service on the primacy of EC law as set out in 11197/07 (JUR 260):

"Opinion of the Council Legal Service
of 22 June 2007

It results from the case-law of the Court of Justice that primacy of EC law is a cornerstone principle of Community law. According to the Court, this principle is inherent to the specific nature of the European Community. At the time of the first judgment of this established case law (Costa/ENEL, 15 July 1964, Case 6/64[1]) there was no mention of primacy in the treaty. It is still the case today. The fact that the principle of primacy will not be included in the future treaty shall not in any way change the existence of the principle and the existing case-law of the Court of Justice."

1. *Extract from the Judgement in Costa/ENEL*: "It follows (…) that the law stemming from the treaty, an independent source of law, could not, because of its special and original nature, be overridden by domestic legal provisions, however framed, without being deprived of its character as Community law and without the legal basis of the Community itself being called into question."

Declaration no 18 in relation to the delimitation of competences

- ***The Conference underlines that, in accordance with the system of division of competences between the Union and the Member States as provided for in the Treaty on European Union and the Treaty on the Functioning of the European Union, competences not conferred upon the Union in the Treaties remain with the Member States.***
  When the Treaties confer on the Union a competence shared with the Member States in a specific area, the Member States shall exercise their competence to the extent that the Union has not exercised, or has decided to cease exercising, its competence. The latter situation arises when the relevant EU institutions decide to repeal a legislative act, in particular better to ensure constant respect for the principles of subsidiarity and proportionality. The Council may … request the Commission to submit proposals for repealing a legislative act. The Conference welcomes the Commission's declaration that it shall devote particular attention to those requests.
  Equally, the representatives of the governments of the Member States, meeting in an Intergovernmental Conference, in accordance with the ordinary revision procedure provided

for in Article 48(2) to (5) of the Treaty on European Union, may decide to amend the Treaties, including either to increase or to reduce the competences conferred on the Union in the said Treaties.

Declaration no. 24 on legal personality of the Union

- ***The Conference confirms that the fact that the European Union has a legal personality will not in any way authorise the Union to legislate or to act beyond the competences conferred upon it by the Member States in the Treaties.***

Declaration no. 35 on Article 194 TFEU

- The Conference believes that **Article 194** does not affect the right of the Member States to take the necessary measures to ensure their energy supply under the conditions provided for in **Article 297**.

Declaration no. 65 by the United Kingdom on Article 75 TFEU

- ***The United Kingdom fully supports robust action with regard to adopting financial sanctions designed to prevent and combat terrorism and related activities. Therefore, the United Kingdom declares that it intends to exercise its right under Article 3 of the Protocol on the position of the United Kingdom and Ireland in respect of the area of freedom, security and justice to take part in the adoption of all proposals made under Article 75 of the Treaty on the Functioning of the European Union.***

CHARTER OF FUNDAMENTAL RIGHTS

- **Preamble** *to the Charter of Fundamental Rights*

  The peoples of Europe, in creating an ever closer union among them, are resolved to share a peaceful future based on common values.

  To this end, it is necessary to strengthen the protection of fundamental rights. . . . by making those rights more visible in a Charter.

  This charter reaffirms . . . . the rights as they result from . . . . the social charters adopted by the Union and the case law of the Court of Justice of the European Union and of the European Court of Human Rights. In this context the Charter will be interpreted by the courts of the Union and the Member States with due regard to the explanations prepared under the authority of the Praesidium of the Convention which drafted the Charter and updated under the responsibility of the Praesidium of the European Convention.
  The Union therefore recognises the rights, freedoms and principles set out hereafter.

Explanations relating to the Charter of Fundamental Rights

- The Conference takes note of the explanations relating to the Charter of Fundamental Rights prepared under the authority of the Praesidium of the Convention which drafted the Charter and updated under the responsibility of the Praesidium of the European Convention, as set out below.

EXPLANATIONS RELATING TO THE CHARTER OF FUNDAMENTAL RIGHTS

These explanations were originally prepared under the authority of the Praesidium of the Convention which drafted the Charter of Fundamental Rights of the European Union. They have been updated under the responsibility of the Praesidium of the European Convention, in the light of the drafting adjustments made to the text of the Charter by that Convention (notably to Articles 51 and 52) and of further developments of Union law. Although they do not as such have the status of law, they are a valuable tool of interpretation intended to clarify the provisions of the Charter.

BRITISH BUSINESS CONCERNS

Increased Regulatory Burden

Although the Government has retained a number of 'opt outs' to meet expressed concerns on some key points, all sections of British industry still have serious reservations about the Treaty of Lisbon - particularly its centralising approach with the prospect of a further increase in detailed regulatory burden.

This is contrary to the spirit of the Laeken Declaration which required the division of power between Brussels and Member States to be clarified and reviewed to see, *inter alia,* whether significant powers could be repatriated to Member States under the subsidiarity principle.

In the event, although the importance of subsidiarity is underlined, there is no mechanism in the Treaty of Lisbon for reviewing the current 100,000 pages of the *acquis communautaire*, many of which are unduly prescriptive.

Underlying the general concerns on 'over regulation' expressed strongly by the British Chambers of Commerce, by the CBI and by the IoD is the progressive increase in 'micro management' from Brussels ('one size fits all') reflecting the fundamental flaw of the command structure of the Soviet Union.

Some specific concerns are listed below.

Increase in Regulatory Burden

Rather than reducing the current burden of detailed regulations and directives emanating from Brussels this burden is likely to be significantly increased with the wider powers being granted to the Commission.

Concreting in the '*Acquis Communautaire'*.

There are now over 100,000 regulations encompassed in the *acquis communautaire* which the Treaty will concrete in.

It is not only the number of regulations that causes concern but the difficulty of amending such regulations if the circumstances change or if it can be seen they do not fit particular situations in some countries.

Deletion of the 'Sunset Clause'

The proposal by the Better Regulation Task Force to insert a *'sunset clause'* (so that regulations would lapse after a certain period of time and only be extended after reconsideration) into the draft Constitutional Treaty of 2004 was included in an earlier draft of that Treaty.

It was removed subsequently on the grounds that this clause *'could be a source of uncertainty and problems for legal security'*, which would impact on the nature of the direct effect of legislation. This view has prevailed in the drafting of the Treaty of Lisbon and so no mention of withdrawal of either proposed or formalised legislation is made in the Treaty.

Subsidiarity

Subsidiarity is a 'top down' concept making the principle difficult to apply in practice. Once the competence has been given to the Union the power firmly rests in the centre. To get a consensus for amendment with so many different countries with varying interests is difficult.

There is much misunderstanding about this concept. When John Major agreed to Maastricht he was confident that the new clauses on **subsidiarity** would enable perhaps 25% of the then current regulations to be repatriated to member states. In the event not one was able to be repatriated.

Competence acquired by the European Union has never been returned to Member States. Disputes about subsidiarity only really arise in those areas of competence not yet acquired by the European Union.

Shared Competencies

The addition of areas of *'shared competence'* Article 5 TEU and Article 4 TFEU [Articles 1-11 and 1-14] to those in which the Union has exclusive competence Articles 2 and 3 TFEU [Articles 1-12 and I-13] further widens the powers of the Union (perhaps to over 70% of Government fields).

The term *'shared'* is misleading as the power has been shifted fully to the Union. Member states can only exercise their competence when and to the extent *'that the Union has not exercised or has decided to cease exercising the competence'*.

Increasing Impotence

If this shift of power is coupled with the proposed considerable **extension of QMV to more than sixty new areas** (shown below) it will be seen that the areas in which individual countries can take action in their own right on matters of particular concern or worry are being **progressively** eroded.

With the increased areas which will come under **the jurisdiction of the European Court of Justice** there are grounds to be considerably worried about the tightening bureaucratic network on business.

Social Partners

The potential strengthening of the position of unions (see Article 152 TFEU [Article 1-48] on the social partners) adds to the possibility of further problems to good management. These problems include the **right to strike** included in the Charter of Fundamental Rights, which could impact on the UK's industrial law.

Legal Uncertainty

In addition to some loose language, the Treaty of Lisbon leaves much open to future interpretation. This problem is greatly enhanced by the **Charter of Fundamental Rights**, being given legally binding force under Article 6 TEU, to add to that of the **Charter of Human Rights**. There are particularly serious and damaging implications for restrictive employment practices – and time wasting and expensive legal arguments.

Although there is a Protocol (Protocol no. 7) defining the restrictions and scope of the application of the Charter for the United Kingdom, there is some doubt on how robust this will be in the European Court of Justice.

* * * * * *

VOTING IN THE INSTITUTIONS

Weighting of Votes in the European Council and the Council (Article 16 TEU, Article 238 TFEU and Protocol no. 11)

The preferred method of adopting decisions in the European Council and the Council is by consensus, where there will be some compromise but all the members agree on the resulting legislation. In the cases where there is a vote, the method of reaching a qualified majority has changed in the course of the development of the European Union.

One of the main issues in the negotiations of the Treaty of Lisbon was the change in the weighting of the votes in the European Council and the Council to more accurately reflect the size of population of each Member State; a majority vote will be dependent on the percentage of votes of the members of the Council and the percentage that vote represents in the size of the population of the Union (Article 16 TEU and Article 238 TFEU).

There was a compromise agreement so that the current voting structure, as agreed in the Treaty of Nice, will continue until 31 October 2014 and the changes in the voting arrangements will start on 1 November 2014. The agreement is further complicated by a transitional arrangement which will apply between 1 November 2014 and 31 March 2017.

The Treaty of Nice introduced a new and more complicated system of voting in the European Council and the Council, where the voting would be based on the number of votes and the proportion of the members. In addition, a member of the Council could request that the qualified majority must represent at least 62% of the population.

This system was introduced as part of the process of the enlargement of the Union and was intended to take effect for the 2004 – 2009 session. However, this new procedure did not satisfy many Member States, and there were disagreements over the different weighting of seats and populations.

There were certain anomalies in the allocation of the weightings introduced in the Treaty of Nice, such as between Portugal and the Czech Republic, where Portugal has a smaller population but more seats in the European Parliament. Spain had negotiated a higher number of votes relative to its population, to the disapproval of Germany.

The number of weighted votes in the European Council and the Council has been changed in the Treaty of Lisbon in recognition of the disagreements which had arisen in Nice. However, the concerns of the smaller countries remain over the relative voting weights, since the six largest counties have 70.3% of the population, which in the new voting system from 1 November 2014 would potentially give them greater influence over the result of Council votes than the small countries could have.

Number of representatives in each Institution (Article 14 to 16 TEU)

The Treaty of Nice laid down the size of the European Parliament and the number of votes allocated for the weighting of votes in the Council for the period 2004 to 2009, in the cases where the Council would act by qualified majority. These provisions have been adjusted for the accession of Bulgaria and Romania and the arrangements for the allocation of votes for the Council will now continue until 31 October 2014. The arrangements for the allocation of votes under the Treaty of Lisbon will apply from 1 November 2014.

The European Parliament (Article 14 TEU)

The Treaty of Lisbon stipulates that there will be a maximum of 750 members in the European Parliament plus the President. This last point was introduced at the behest of the Italian government, which wanted to have the same number of MEPs as the United Kingdom; there are two declarations on this issue (Declarations nos. 4 and 57).

The changes to the number of members of the European Parliament are intended to take effect from the elections in June 2009, dependent on whether the Treaty of Lisbon is ratified in time. The European Council will act by unanimity to establish the composition of the Parliament, regarding the allocation of seats. The European Parliament passed a resolution (2007/2169(INI)) on the composition of the Parliament for the 2009 – 2014 session, which has formed the basis of the allocation of seats; Table 1 shows the allocation of members.

The Treaty of Lisbon also introduces minimum and maximum numbers of MEPs from each Member State: a maximum of ninety-six members and a minimum of six members per Member State (Article 14(2) TEU). The changes in the voting and the number of seats in the European Parliament have been based on the size of the populations, so that the larger states have more seats and the smaller states fewer seats (i.e. degressively proportional). The detailed numbers are shown in Protocol no. 11 and in Table 1, below.

The European Council (Article 15 TEU)

The European Council consists of the Heads of State or Government of the Member States, together with the Presidents of the European Council and the Commission and the High Representative of the Union for Foreign Affairs and Security Policy; in addition, the members of the European Council can choose to be assisted by a minister.

The Council (Article 16 TEU)

The Council consists of one representative from each Member State, who will have ministerial rank have the authority to act and to vote in the Council.

Voting arrangement in the Institutions (Articles 15 and 16 TEU, Articles 235 and 238 TFEU and Protocol 11)

The ***European Parliament*** will continue to vote by a majority of its members (Article 231 TFEU).

In general, the ***European Council*** will take decisions by unanimity, or consensus, and this is the preferred method of reaching agreement. The Treaties provide for certain situations where the vote will be by qualified majority, and in these cases the voting arrangements will be the same as for the Council (Article 15(4) TEU and Article 235 TFEU).

The ***Council*** either vote by a simple majority or by qualified majority under the following system of 'double majority' from **1 November 2014** (Article 16 TEU and Article 238 TFEU):

1. On a proposal from the Commission, or acting on the initiative of the High Representative of the Union for Foreign Affairs, there has to be at least 55% of the Member States in favour for the act to be passed (a minimum of 15 Member States), representing at least 65% of the population of the Union (i.e. 320.43 m.)
2. In other cases, there must be 72% of the Member States in favour (a minimum of 20 Member States), representing at least 65% of the population of the Union.

The request by a member that the votes in favour represent at least 62% of the population of the Union, introduced by the Treaty of Nice, will longer apply.

Complexities of the voting system until 31 March 2017

The intention of the review of the voting system agreed at Nice was to simplify the procedure from the double majority requirement to a more straightforward one. The compromise arrangements that have been finally agreed will actually make the voting more complicated.

The arrangements for the period **until 31 October 2014** will be that the Council will vote by the weighting system set out in the Declaration on Enlargement in the Treaty of Nice (though the actual number of votes has changed), and the voting arrangements are shown in Table 3, below. In the cases where the Commission proposes the legislation, there have to be a minimum of 255 votes out of a total of 345 votes in favour representing a majority of the Member States (i.e. 73.91%).

In other cases, the majority will be 255 votes representing three-quarters of the members (i.e. 21 Member States). A member can request that the votes in favour represent at least 62% of the population of the Union; this provision was introduced by the Treaty of Nice and included in the draft Constitution (Protocol on transitional provisions, Article 3(3)).

As a comparison, under the terms of the Treaty of Nice, the number of votes for a qualified majority in the cases where the Commission would propose the legislation was 258 votes out of a total of 345 votes (i.e. 74.78%) and under the draft Constitution, it was 232 votes out of 321 total votes (72.27%).

For the period from **1 November 2014**, the principal method of voting in the Council will follow the arrangements set out in Article 16 TEU and Article 238 TFEU, described above. However, for the period of 1 November 2014 to 31 March 2017, a member can request that the vote follows the arrangements for the period until 31 October 2014.

Blocking Minority and the Ioannina Compromise

A **blocking minority** is defined as a minimum of four members where the Council votes by qualified majority (Article 16(4) TEU) and at least the minimum Council members to represent more than 35% of the population of the Member States involved in the vote plus one member (Article 238 TFEU); if this number is not reached, a qualified majority is deemed to have been attained.

If all of the Council members are involved in the vote, the representative population necessary for a blocking minority would be more than 172.54 million. The arrangements for the blocking minority are intended to prevent the three largest Member States to block any proposal they object to, as they have 41.75% of the total EU population; the four largest Member States have 264.58 m. people or 53.67% of the population.

Another complexity is that there is no adjustment for abstentions in the Treaty, hence if one Member State abstains, requirements for a blocking minority of four Member States remains, as does the requirement of the majority being 55% of the remaining Member States with 65% of the population.

During the final negotiations leading up to both the draft Constitution and the Treaty of Lisbon, there were disagreements among the Member States over the size of the blocking minority and the ability of the smaller Member States to block a piece of legislation.

The solution to this issue was to attach a Decision to the Treaty (Declaration 7), which was also in the draft Constitution. This proposes a voting system based on the **Ioannina Compromise**, which had been arranged at a Council meeting on 29 March 1994 to recognise the concerns of the existing Member States over the changes in voting weights resulting from the accession of Austria, Finland and Sweden.

The compromise in the Treaty of Lisbon is that for the period from 1 November 2014 to 31 March 2017, if Council members representing at least three-quarters of the population (i.e. 26.25%) or at least three-quarters of the number of Member States required to form a blocking minority (i.e. 3 Member States) state their opposition to a proposed act, the Council will continue discussions within a reasonable time-scale to reach a satisfactory solution, without affecting the time limits laid down by Union law (Declaration 7, Articles 1 and 2). In addition, a member of the Council may request that the vote in the Council should be held using the arrangements in operation until 31 October 2014 (Protocol on transitional provisions, Article 3(2)).

The arrangements that will apply from 1 April 2017 are that if Council members representing at least 55% of the population (i.e. 19.25%) or at least 55% of the number of Member States required to form a blocking minority (i.e. 3 Member States) state their opposition to a proposed act, the Council will continue discussions within a reasonable time-scale to reach a satisfactory solution, without affecting the time limits laid down by Union law (Declaration 7, Articles 4 and 5).

Table 1: Number of seats in the European Parliament

Member States	Seats in European Parliament To 2009 *	From 2009 Nice Treaty*	From 2009 Proposed	Population (million) 2006	Population %
Germany	99	99	96	82.44	16.72
France	78	72	74	63.00	12.78
United Kingdom	78	72	73	60.39	12.25
Italy	78	72	73	58.75	11.92
Spain	54	50	54	43.76	8.88
Poland	54	50	51	38.16	7.74
Romania	35	33	33	21.61	4.38
Netherlands	27	25	26	16.33	3.31
Greece	24	22	22	11.13	2.26
Portugal	24	22	22	10.57	2.14
Belgium	24	22	22	10.51	2.13
Czech Republic	24	22	22	10.25	2.08
Hungary	24	22	22	10.10	2.05
Sweden	19	18	20	9.05	1.83
Austria	18	17	19	8.27	1.68
Bulgaria	18	17	18	7.72	1.57
Slovakia	14	13	13	5.39	1.09
Denmark	14	13	13	5.43	1.10
Finland	14	13	13	5.26	1.07
Ireland	13	12	12	4.21	0.85
Lithuania	13	12	12	3.40	0.69
Latvia	9	8	9	2.29	0.46
Slovenia	7	7	8	2.00	0.41
Estonia	6	6	6	1.34	0.27
Cyprus	6	6	6	0.77	0.16
Luxembourg	6	6	6	0.47	0.10
Malta	5	5	6	0.41	0.08
Total:	**785**	**736**	**751**	**492.97**	**100**

* Votes per TEC, modified by Treaties of Accession   Table by BMDF Population Source: Eurostat

Table 1 sets out the voting arrangements for the European Parliament, calculated on the relative size of population of each Member State (i.e. degressively proportional – Article 14(2) TEU).

The Table shows the number of seats in the Parliament in three columns: until June 2009, the proposed number of seats listed in the Declaration on enlargement on the Treaty of Nice, and the proposed number of seats for 2009 to 2014, as calculated in the European Parliament Resolution (2007/2169(INI)) on the composition of the Parliament for the 2009 – 2014 session.

The number of MEPs for the period 2009 to 2014 includes the adjustment for the President of the Parliament (Article 14(1) TEU) to increase the number of members from 750 to 751.

Since the numbers of MEPs are not shown in the Treaties, the calculation of the number of seats will be done by secondary legislation.

Table 2: Weighting of Votes and number of seats in the European Parliament

Member States	Votes To 2009 % (a)	Votes From 2009 Proposed % (b)	Votes % Change (b) - (a)/(a)	Population %	No of Voters per MEP To 2009	No of Voters per MEP From 2009 Proposed
Germany	12.61	12.78	1.36	16.72	832,727	858,750
France	9.94	9.85	- 0.83	12.78	807,692	851,351
United Kingdom	9.94	9.72	- 2.17	12.25	774,231	827,260
Italy	9.94	9.72	- 2.17	11.92	753,205	804,795
Spain	6.88	7.19	4.53	8.88	810,370	810,370
Poland	6.88	6.79	- 1.28	7.74	706,667	748,235
Romania	4.46	4.39	- 1.45	4.38	617,429	654,848
Netherlands	3.44	3.46	0.66	3.31	604,815	628,077
Greece	3.06	2.93	- 4.18	2.26	463,750	505,909
Portugal	3.06	2.93	- 4.18	2.14	440,417	480,455
Belgium	3.06	2.93	- 4.18	2.13	437,917	477,727
Czech Republic	3.06	2.93	- 4.18	2.08	427,083	465,909
Hungary	3.06	2.93	- 4.18	2.05	420,833	459,091
Sweden	2.42	2.66	10.03	1.83	474,211	450,500
Austria	2.29	2.53	10.33	1.68	459,444	435,263
Bulgaria	2.29	2.40	4.53	1.57	428,889	428,889
Slovakia	1.78	1.73	- 2.94	1.09	385,000	414,615
Denmark	1.78	1.73	- 2.94	1.10	387,857	417,692
Finland	1.78	1.73	- 2.94	1.07	375,714	404,615
Ireland	1.66	1.60	- 3.51	0.85	323,846	350,833
Lithuania	1.66	1.60	- 3.51	0.69	261,538	283,333
Latvia	1.15	1.20	4.53	0.46	254,444	254,444
Slovenia	0.89	1.07	19.46	0.41	285,714	250,000
Estonia	0.76	0.80	4.53	0.27	223,333	223,333
Cyprus	0.76	0.80	4.53	0.16	128,333	128,333
Luxembourg	0.76	0.80	4.53	0.10	78,333	78,333
Malta	0.64	0.80	25.43	0.08	82,000	68,333
Total:	**100**	**100**		**100**	*** 453,548**	*** 472,641**

Table by BMDF * = Average number of voters per MEP

Table 2 shows the weighting of votes in the European Parliament, based on the proposed numbers shown in the European Parliament Resolution (2007/2169(INI)).

The table shows the change in the voting share of each Member State compared to the number of MEPs in the Treaty of Nice and the change in the average number of voters per MEP.

Table 3: Weighting of Votes in the Council (2009 to 2014)

Member States	**Council Votes *** **(a)**	**Votes %** **(b)**	**Population %** **(c)**	**Council votes pro-rata population** **(c)/(b) x (a)**
Germany	29	8.41	16.72	58
France	29	8.41	12.78	44
United Kingdom	29	8.41	12.25	42
Italy	29	8.41	11.92	41
Spain	27	7.83	8.88	31
Poland	27	7.83	7.74	27
Romania	14	4.06	4.38	15
Netherlands	13	3.77	3.31	11
Greece	12	3.48	2.26	8
Portugal	12	3.48	2.14	7
Belgium	12	3.48	2.13	7
Czech Republic	12	3.48	2.08	7
Hungary	12	3.48	2.05	7
Sweden	10	2.90	1.83	6
Austria	10	2.90	1.68	6
Bulgaria	10	2.90	1.57	5
Slovakia	7	2.03	1.09	4
Denmark	7	2.03	1.10	4
Finland	7	2.03	1.07	4
Ireland	7	2.03	0.85	3
Lithuania	7	2.03	0.69	2
Latvia	4	1.16	0.46	2
Slovenia	4	1.16	0.41	1
Estonia	4	1.16	0.27	1
Cyprus	4	1.16	0.16	1
Luxembourg	4	1.16	0.10	0
Malta	3	0.87	0.08	0
Total:	**345**	**100**	**100**	**345**

* Council votes per TEC, modified by Treaties of Accession

Table by BMDF

Table 3 shows the weighting of votes in the European Council and the Council when a vote is taken by qualified majority; these are the current weightings and they will continue to apply until 31 October 2014.

The number of votes are based on the relative size of population (i.e. degressively proportional) and has been brought forward from the Treaty of Nice, as modified by Treaties of Accession of Bulgaria and Romania, and the draft Constitution to the Treaty of Lisbon without any changes.

The numbers are listed in the Protocol on Transitional Provisions, Article 3(3) and will operate between 31 October 2014 and 31 March 2017 if a member of the Council so requests. From 1 November 2014, the European Council and the Council will vote under the new system of 55% of the members and 65% of the population (Article 238 TFEU).

LEGISLATIVE PROCEDURES

Introduction

The Treaties comprise the primary legislation of the European Union and these define the relationship between the Union and the Member States, the powers of the Union and the fundamental structure of the Union and its institutions. The powers are granted, or conferred, by the Member States to the Union through the Treaties and these are negotiated directly by the governments of the Member States. The Treaties provide the outline or framework of the law of the Union and as such lay down the principles of the areas in which the Union may act. The secondary legislation is the detailed legislative procedures by which the Union will act and consists of regulations, directives and decisions.

In the early stages of the European Community, the legislative procedure laid down in the Treaty of Rome followed a clearly defined pattern for any prospective legislation, where the Commission would have the right of initiative to produce a draft of the legislation and the Council would vote on the proposals in order that the legislation became law. The voting process did not directly involve the European Parliament, beyond its being informed of any prospective legislation and its opinion being sought.

As the Community, and latterly the Union, has developed, the European Parliament's role in the legislative procedure has grown. Over successive Treaties, the Parliament has been able to vote on more areas. The changes on the voting arrangements introduced by the draft Constitution have been included in the Treaty of Lisbon, so that the Parliament is now directly involved in the legislative procedure on an equal basis as the Council in more areas. The intention is that the Parliament will become the main legislature of the Union.

Primacy and application of European legislation: direct application and direct effect

The concept of Community law having precedence, or primacy, over the national law of Member States defined in a European Court of Justice case, *Costa v. ENEL* in 1964 (Case 6/64) The principle is that where there is a conflict between national law and Union law, Union law will take precedence.

The concept of primacy was first introduced into the main text of the Treaties in the draft Constitution [Article I-6], and so confirming the principle in Union law; by doing so, it established that the Constitution would also have primacy over the laws of the Member States. In addition, there was a declaration which briefly referred to the case law of the European Court of Justice.

The concept of primacy has been removed from the main text of the Treaties by the Treaty of Lisbon and a Declaration has been attached to the Treaty, as part of the changes made to incorporate the concerns over the draft Constitution. The Declaration (Declaration 27) includes more details than the corresponding declaration in the draft Constitution and reproduces the opinion of the Council Legal Service, which states that the "*primacy of EC law is a cornerstone principle of Community law*", and emphasises the nature of the primacy of EU law over that of the Member States and includes an extract from the judgement of the European Court on *Costa.*

A second principle of European Union law is that of direct effect. Direct effect is not defined in the Treaties, and it was formulated in the European Court of Justice case *Van Gend en Loos* v. *Nederlandse Administratie der Belastingen* (Case 26/62). In this case, direct effect was defined as the Treaties conferring rights on individuals which they could invoke before both the national and Union courts. In its judgement, the Court stated:

> *"Community law not only imposes obligations on individuals but is also intended to confer upon them rights which become part of their legal heritage ... and Article 12 (of the Treaty) must be interpreted as creating individual rights which national courts must protect".*

In order for direct effect to apply, the provision must be sufficiently clear and precisely stated, it must be unconditional or non-dependent and it must confer a specific right for the citizen to base his claim in the national or European courts. If these criteria are met, the provision has direct effect both from the citizen to the state (vertical effect) and between citizens (horizontal effect). However, the European Court has stated that if a Member State has any discretion in the manner in which European legislation is interpreted, then the provision in the Treaty does not have direct effect, *Ursula Becker v Finanzamt Münster-Innenstadt* (Case 8/81).

The situation for direct effect of secondary law (regulations, directives and decisions) is more complicated. In Article 288 TFEU, regulations and decisions are described as effectively being directly applicable both on a vertical and horizontal basis, but directives are not necessarily directly applicable as they are directed to Member States and not to individuals and have to transposed into national legislation to have vertical direct effect.

The definition of regulations in Article 288 TFEU ['European laws' in the draft Constitution - Article I-33] describes them as being of general application. This indicates the nature of their legislative character in that they are the principle mechanism to ensure the uniformity of Union law throughout the European Union.

Regulations are described as being '**directly applicable**', hence they must be directly entered into the national law of the Member States, without any need for implementing measures by the national authorities. Once the legislation is in force, and provided that the provisions are clear and unconditional, it creates rights for individuals that can be claimed against the Member States in national and European courts, giving the legislation direct effect.

Directives are binding as to the result to be achieved, but leave the individual Member States freedom in how they implement the legislation. If the legislation is not implemented correctly or by the time stated, then individuals affected by the legislation may acquire rights, and as a result, these types of legislation can have direct effect.

Decisions are binding in their entirety on the individuals they are addressed to and there is no discretion in the manner of implementation. As a result, individuals can acquire rights from the provisions of the decisions and therefore the legislation can have direct effect.

Vertical and horizontal provisions

Once direct effect is established, individuals can rely on the legislation in national and European courts in actions brought against other individuals (**horizontal** provisions) and against a state or the Union (**vertical** provisions).

Co-Decision - Ordinary Legislative Procedure

The concept of the normal procedure to adopt legislation in the European Union is to directly involve the three principal Union institutions, the Commission, the Council and the European Parliament. The role of the Commission is to initiate and submit draft proposals to the European Parliament and the Council, which together have the power to jointly adopt the legislation. This process has been termed the 'Community method' or 'co-decision' and this structure was introduced in the Maastricht Treaty and covers regulations and directives. The title of this process was changed to the 'ordinary legislative procedure' in the draft Constitution, and this term has been incorporated into the Treaty of Lisbon (Article 294 TFEU) [Article III-396]. One of the aspects of the Treaty of Lisbon is that the European Community will no longer exist once the Treaty has been ratified, and so the term 'Community Method' will become redundant, and this is one of the reasons for changing the name to the 'ordinary legislative procedure'.

One of the consequences of the Community method of voting is that the Member States have a reduced role in the process of legislation, since the legislative process is confined to the Community bodies. The significance of the change of voting in the Council from qualified majority to the ordinary legislative procedure is that it indicates the progressive movement towards having the Community method operate in all proposed legislation. As a form of a check and balance to this, the national parliaments have an increased role in the prospective legislation, in that they can review the proposals for adherence to the principles of subsidiarity and proportionality (Protocol 1).

Forms of Secondary Legislation

In the current Treaties, as amended by the Treaty of Nice, regulations and directives are the principal forms of instruments used; in addition, there are decisions, which are binding, and recommendations and opinions, which are for guidance and do not have binding force. Overall, there are fifteen different types of legal instruments, including 'joint actions' and 'common positions'. These two legal instruments relate to the common foreign and security policy and police and judicial co-operation in criminal matters and are adopted by the Council on an inter-governmental basis and are binding on the Member States.

In the discussions held by the Convention that led to the draft Constitution, it was decided that the legal instruments should be simplified and reduced in number, so that there would be a more clearly defined distinction between the various types of legislation. As a result, a number of changes were introduced in the draft Constitution to the types of legislative instruments, and these changes have been brought forward into the Treaty of Lisbon, so that the legislative procedures are simplified to the instruments described in Articles 289 to 292 TFEU [Articles I-34 to I-37], i.e. regulations, directives, decisions, recommendations and opinions. The terms 'joint actions' and 'common positions' have been removed from the Treaties, except for the term 'common positions' in relation to relations with international organisations (Articles 34 TEU and Articles 138 and 139 (2)(i) TFEU) [Article III-305 and Articles III-196 and III-197].

The draft Constitution introduced two principal classes of legislative instruments: 'legislative acts' and 'non-legislative acts'. Legislative acts consisted of European laws and European framework laws. These two types of laws corresponded to regulations and directives respectively in the Treaties (Article 288 TEC) and would have been jointly adopted by the European Parliament and the Council. These two terms have not been used in the Treaty of Lisbon as part of the process of removing any aspect of the constitutional approach from the Treaties. Non-legislative acts consisted of European regulations and European decisions. The new type of regulation would have taken over the definition of the existing regulations and the existing directives; the term 'directive' would no longer be used. Non-legislative acts would have been adopted by the Commission and the Council.

The Treaty of Lisbon uses the terms 'legislative acts' and 'non-legislative acts' from the draft Constitution, but has retained the terms for the principal different types of instrument from the existing Treaties:

Legislative Acts

These are the principal forms of legislative instrument in the European Union and are adopted by the ordinary legislative procedure. The types of legislative acts are defined in Articles 288 and 289 TFEU [Articles I-33 and I-34] as follows:

- **Regulations** shall be legislative acts of general application. They shall be binding in their entirety and directly applicable in all Member States. In the draft Constitution, the term was 'European Law'.
- **Directives** shall be legislative acts binding, as to the result to be achieved, on the Member States to which they are addressed, but leaving the national authorities entirely free to choose the form and means of achieving those results. In the draft Constitution, the term was 'European Framework Law'.
- **Decisions** shall be legislative acts binding in its entirety. In the draft Constitution, the term was 'European Decisions'. The definition of a decision has been revised in the Treaty of Lisbon to be more precise, so that a decision that specifies those to whom it is addressed is binding only on those specific individuals.

Non-legislative Acts

Non-legislative acts are used to supplement or amend certain non-essential elements of the legislative acts. The authority to adopt the non-legislative act will be delegated to the Commission and the terms and conditions will be defined in the legislative act Article 290 TFEU [Article I-36].

Other Acts

In addition to the legislative and non-legislative acts, there are two other forms of legal instruments, defined in Articles 291 and 292 TFEU [Articles I-37 and I-35]:

- **Implementing acts:** Member States are required to adopt national legislation to implement legally-binding acts of the Union. Where uniform conditions are required for the implementation of the acts, the Commission will be given authority to implement the acts, except in the case of the Common Foreign and Security Policy, where the Council will have the authority.
- **Recommendations** are non-binding instruments for the attention of the Member States and will be adopted by the Council on a proposal from the Commission, except where the Treaties state that the Commission or the European Central Bank can adopt recommendations. The principal areas concern the functioning of the internal market in relation to the Commission (Services - Article 60 TFEU, transport – Article 97 TFEU and competition – Article 117 TFEU) and the general authority of the ECB (Article 132 TFEU).

The procedure for the adoption of the legal acts of the Union is laid down in Article 294 TFEU [Article III-396]. Legislative acts will be adopted by the ordinary legislative procedure, unless specified in the text of the Treaty, where the process will be by a special legislative procedure (Article 289(2) TFEU) [Article I-34(2)].

Methods of voting

The two principal types of voting used by the Council are retained in the Treaty of Lisbon. *Unanimity* is used in areas of sensitive national interests; the other form of voting is by **qualified majority voting** and this is increasingly becoming the standard method. This has evolved as a way of avoiding the difficulties of passing Community legislation where there had been unanimity and a individual Member State could invoke the national veto and prevent a piece of legislation becoming law.

Voting by Unanimity

In the Treaty of Rome, the principal form of voting in the Council was by unanimity, reflecting the inter-governmental structure of the European Community, and only a minority of areas were subject to qualified majority voting. The use of unanimity in the European Council and the Council meant that a Member State could block legislation by voting against the proposals, and thus have a veto over legislation. In the circumstances where the members of the Council do not agree on a proposal, and as a result the European Union does not act, the Member States are free to pursue their own policies and this is a guarantee of national sovereignty.

In each successive Treaty, more areas have been moved away from unanimity to qualified majority in order to reduce the areas where the national veto could be used. There are still a number of areas where the Council will act by unanimity, since these are especially important for national interest.

The principal areas where the Council or the European Council will act by unanimity are:

- revision of the Treaties and changes in voting through the use of the passerelle clauses (Article 48 TEU), *see below for details of the passerelle clauses,*
- membership of the Union, including suspension of rights (Article 7 TEU), accession (Article 49 TEU) and voluntary withdrawal from the Union (Article 50 TEU),
- institutional matters, including the composition of the European Parliament (Article 14 TEU), the Commission (Article 17 TEU), the Economic and Social Committee and the Committee of the Regions (Articles 301 and 305 TFEU), amendment of the Statute of the European Investment Bank (Article 308 TFEU), the seats of the Institutions (Article 341 TFEU) and the languages of the union (Article 342 TFEU),
- the common foreign and security policy, including defining strategic interests, implementation and the budget (Articles 22, 24 and 41 TEU),
- common security and defence policy, including permanent structured co-operation (Article 46 TEU),
- justice and home affairs, including border checks (Article 77 TFEU), judicial co-operation in civil matters regarding family law (Article 81 TFEU), formation of a European Protection Office (Article 86 TFEU) and police co-operation (Articles 87 and 89 TFEU),

- social policy, including social security and social protection (Article 21 TFEU) discrimination and citizens' rights (Articles 19 and 25 TFEU), and arrangements for voting in municipal and European elections (Article 22 TFEU),
- taxation, including general tax provisions (Article 113 TFEU) and restrictions to capital payments (Article 65 TFEU),
- finances of the Union, including own resources (Article 311 TFEU) and the multi-annual framework (Article 312 TFEU),
- enhanced co-operation provisions (Articles 329 to 333 TFEU),
- the flexibility clause (Article 352 TFEU).

Voting by Qualified Majority

The procedure of qualified majority voting takes two forms. The first, and principal method, is where the Commission initiates and proposes legislative acts, and the Council, in conjunction with the European Parliament, adopts the legislation, which in the current treaties is termed the 'Community Method' or **co-decision**.

The other procedure is where the Council acts on its own and the involvement of the European Parliament is limited to giving its consent or its opinion. In certain cases, it will only be informed of the actions of the Council. In the current Treaties, the involvement of the European Parliament can be by consent and using the co-operation method, which is a modified version of co-decision. Under the Treaty of Lisbon, following the changes made by the draft Constitution, the co-operation method has been discarded and replaced by the ordinary legislative procedure. This is discussed more fully below.

The co-decision procedure was introduced in the Maastricht Treaty in 1993 and has been progressively applied to more areas in the Treaties of Amsterdam and Nice; the intention is that the co-decision procedure will become the principal method of enacting legislation in the Union, with fewer areas subject to adoption by the Council acting on its own. As the Council consists of the Heads of Government or senior ministers representing their national interests, it acts in an intergovernmental manner. The move towards co-decision, with the increased involvement (and therefore importance) of the European Parliament, is intended to enable the Union to move away from a inter-governmental structure to one where the Union acts in its own right.

Ordinary legislative procedure

The Treaty of Lisbon renames the co-decision method as the '**ordinary legislative procedure**' to indicate that this is intended to become the normal procedure to enact legislation in the Union. This is described in Article 289 TFEU [Article I-34]. This method can either be under unanimity or qualified majority voting. The detailed provisions were introduced by the draft Constitution and they have been brought forward into the Treaty of Lisbon without any amendments.

The detailed process for the adoption of legislation by the ordinary legislative procedure is laid out in Article 294 TFEU [Article III-396]. The Commission will submit a proposal to both the Council and to the European Parliament. The European Parliament will vote on the proposal and pass its decision to the Council, which will make its own assessment. If the two bodies agree, the proposal is adopted as law. If there is no agreement, a conciliation committee is formed to attempt to reach an agreement. If there is no agreement within six weeks of the Committee being convened, the proposal will not be adopted. If there is agreement in the Committee within the six week period, the Council and the European Parliament will have a further six weeks to adopt the legislation.

Special legislative procedure

Where the Council acts in any manner other than by the ordinary legislative procedure, the method of enacting legislation is termed the '**special legislative procedure**'; this follows the terminology introduced in the draft Constitutional Treaty. In this procedure, the European Parliament is not directly involved in the legislative process. It is intended to be the exception to the usual method of enacting legislation and is described in Article 289(2) TFEU [Article I-34(2)]. There is a general passerelle clause where the Council may vote to change the method of voting from the special procedure to the ordinary procedure Article 48(7) TEU [Article IV-444(2)] and this is described more fully below.

The co-operation method in the current Treaties has been removed and the voting method used under this system has been changed so that the provisions are now either adopted under the ordinary legislative procedure or with the consent of the European Parliament. This is described more fully below.

The method of voting in the Council has been changed in the Treaty of Lisbon in a number of areas from unanimity to qualified majority voting, which follows the changes made in the draft Constitution. The summary below shows the principal areas where the procedure of voting in the Council has been changed from unanimity, together with an indication of where the method of qualified majority voting has changed to the ordinary legislative procedure.

Role of the European Parliament

In the legislative structure created by the original Treaty of Rome, signed in 1957, the Community primarily acted on an inter-governmental basis and the principal role of adopting legislation was held by the Council. The involvement of the European Parliament was restricted to being a reviewing chamber with the ability to give opinions and consent to proposed legislation.

As the nature of the Community has changed, the legislative process has changed so that the Community institutions act independently from the Member States. An increasing number of areas of legislation have been progressively changed to be adopted by the Council acting in conjunction with the European Parliament using co-decision. As the Community has acquired new competences, these new areas have also been made subject to co-decision. The role of the European Parliament has become more important and the intention is that the Parliament should be the main legislature of the Union.

The Treaty of Lisbon incorporates the changes made by the draft Constitution and continues this process of moving the legislative process to co-decision and increases the number of areas where the Parliament acts in conjunction with the Council and as a consequence, the power and influence of the Parliament has been substantially increased. The areas where the Parliament is involved in the ordinary legislative procedure, on an equal basis with the Council, are shown below.

Role of national parliaments

One of the issues raised in the Laeken Declaration of 2001 was the importance of bringing the European Union closer to European citizens. In the draft Constitution, national parliaments were given an increased role in the legislative procedure and these amendments have been brought forward into the Treaty of Lisbon. There are a number of instances in the main text of the Treaties, where the Union institutions are required to consult the national parliaments. The consultation procedure is part of the application of the principle of subsidiarity and therefore does not apply where the Union has exclusive competence, Article 2 TFEU [Article I-12].

There is a new provision introduced into the Treaty of Lisbon, and not in the draft Constitution, which sets out the general conditions for the involvement of national parliaments in the functioning of the Union, Article 12 TEU.

In particular, this provision enables the national parliaments to be involved in the agreements for legislation procedures to be changed from unanimity to qualified majority voting or from a special legislative procedure to the ordinary legislative procedure under the passerelle clauses. In the United Kingdom, the European Union (Amendment) Act 2008 introducing the Treaty of Lisbon specifically identifies the passerelle clauses where the Houses of Parliament will be required to give approval before the government can vote in the Council. These are described more fully in a later section below.

The principal areas where the national parliaments are consulted are:

- ensuring compliance by the Union institutions of the principle of representative democracy and the concept of subsidiarity, particularly in relation to the flexibility clause, Articles 5 and 10 TEU and Article 352(2) TFEU [Articles I-11, I-18 and I-46];
- ordinary revision of the Treaties, Article 48 TEU [Article IV-443];
- revision procedure through the general passerelle clause of the Treaty on the Functioning of the European Union and the Common Foreign and Security Policy in Title V of the Treaty on European Union, Article 48(7) TEU [Article IV-444];

- accession of a European state to the Union, Article 49 TEU [Article I-58(2)];
- revision of rights of citizens of the Union, Article 25 TFEU [Article III-129];
- review of activities in the area of freedom, security and justice: to ensure that proposals comply with the principles of subsidiarity, Article 70 TFEU [Article III-260]; the national parliaments will be informed of evaluations made by the Council on the implementation of Union policies by the Member States, Article 70 TFEU [Articles I-42 and III-260];
- judicial co-operation in civil matters: decisions concerning family law with cross-border implications will be subject to an emergency brake provision, where a national parliament may oppose the proposal and the decision will not be adopted, Article 81 TFEU [Article III-269 (ex Article 65 TEC)];
- evaluation of the activities of Eurojust, Article 85(1) TFEU [Article III-273] and Europol, Article 88(2) TFEU [Article III-276];
- evaluation of new categories of the Union's own resources, Article 269 TFEU [Article I-54].

In addition, two protocols (Protocols no. 1 and 2) on the role of national parliaments and the application of subsidiarity have been attached to the Treaties setting out the extent of the involvement of the national parliaments.

Under the terms of the Protocols, all legislative proposals will be sent to the national parliaments and they may send an opinion on whether the proposals comply with the principles of subsidiarity and proportionality within a eight-week time limit. This is a change from the draft Constitution, where the time-limit was six weeks.

Under the terms of the Protocol on subsidiarity (Protocol no. 2, Articles 5 and 6), if one third of the parliaments consider that there has not been compliance with the principle of subsidiarity, the Commission is required to review its proposal. The threshold will be reduced to one quarter where the proposed legislation originates from the Commission and if it proposal concerns the area of freedom, security and justice. The Commission may decide to maintain, amend or withdraw its proposal. Although there is no obligation for the Commission to change its proposal, there is the possibility under the voting procedures in the Council that the proposal could be rejected at that stage, depending on which Member States disagree with the proposed legislation.

There is a new provision added by the Treaty of Lisbon in Protocol 2, where the Commission is required to review a proposal for legislation with the principle of subsidiarity under the ordinary legislative procedure if there is a simple majority of votes of the national parliaments. After the review, the Commission may decide to maintain, amend or withdraw the proposal; if it chooses to maintain the proposal, the Commission must explain why it is doing so. This opinion, together with the opinions of the national parliaments would then be submitted to the Council and the European Parliament for a decision. If 55% of the Council votes and a simple majority of the European Parliament considers that the proposal is not compatible with the principle of subsidiarity, the proposal will not be adopted. This provision was introduced at the request of the Dutch government as part of the negotiations of the Treaty and is termed 'the Orange card', Protocol 2, Article 7(3).

Revision of the Treaties

The method used to revise the Treaties has been to convene an Intergovernmental Conference of the Heads of Government, who agree a text that is signed and then ratified by each Member State and is described in the current Treaty on European Union, as amended by the Treaty of Nice, in Article 48. This system has been used for all of the Treaties and is used for the Treaty of Lisbon.

In the case of the draft Constitution, it was agreed by the Heads of Government, described in the Laeken Declaration of 15 December 2001, to form a Convention to discuss and formulate the text before the Heads of Government met in an Intergovernmental Conference. The Convention consisted of representatives of the national and European Parliaments, the national governments and the Commission. This approach was incorporated into the text of the draft Constitution as the ordinary revision procedure [Article IV-443] for the revision of future Treaties.

This approach has been incorporated into the Treaty of Lisbon, which has replaced the procedure in Article 48 TEU with a new system, comprising of two distinct procedures. The first is the 'Ordinary Revision Procedure', outlined above, which involves the convening of a Convention to examine the proposed amendments before the Intergovernmental Conference agrees to the new text. If four-fifths of the Member States have ratified the new Treaty after two years from the date of the signing by the Heads of Government and one or more Member States have problems ratifying the Treaty, then the matter will be passed to the European Council (Article 48 (2) to (5) TEU).

The second approach to revising the Treaties is termed the 'Simplified Revision Procedure', and this was also introduced by the draft Constitution [Article IV-444]. There are two forms of this procedure. The first is that any amendments to all or some of the provisions of Part Three of the Treaty on the Functioning of the European Union, concerning Union policies and internal actions, may be proposed to the European Council by the Member States, the European Parliament or the Commission. The European Council shall adopt a decision by unanimity to amend the Treaties and will come into effect once the Member States have all approved the changes in accordance with their constitutional requirements.

The other form of the simplified revision procedure is the general passerelle clause and this enables the European Council to change the method of voting in the Council in the provisions of Part Three of the Treaty on the Functioning of the European Union, concerning Union policies and internal actions, and the Common Foreign and Security Policy (excluding provisions on defence or with military implications). These changes can be made without the need to have the formality of a new Treaty, with the large amount of time necessary for the negotiations and for all of the Member States to ratify the new text. There are two aspects to this:

- Where the Council acts by unanimity, the European Council can adopt a decision to authorise the Council to act by qualified majority;
- Where provisions in the Treaty on the Functioning of the European Union are adopted by a special legislative procedure, the European Council can adopt a decision for the ordinary legislative procedure to apply (Article 48(7) TEU).

There is an emergency brake provision, where a national parliament can oppose the proposals, if it notifies the European Council within six months of being informed of the proposed changes. In this case, the proposals will not be adopted (Article 48(7) TEU).

ORDINARY LEGISLATIVE PROCEDURE (Article 294 TFEU)

I. CHANGES FROM UNANIMITY

Details are given in the chapter on ***'Changes from Unanimity to Qualified Majority'.***

II. CHANGES FROM QUALIFIED MAJORITY

Freedom of movement of establishment

- Exclusion of certain activities in a Member State from the scope of the provisions on freedom of establishment relating to the official authority of that State; Article 51 TFEU, second paragraph [Article III-139, second paragraph] *(ex Article 45(2) TEC)*

Free movement of capital and payments

- Extension of the provisions on services to third-country nationals established within the Community; Article 56 TFEU, second paragraph [Article III-144, second paragraph] *(ex Article 49(2) TEC)*
- Liberalisation of services; Article 59 TFEU [Article III-147] (*ex Article 52(1) TEC*)
- Adoption of measures on movement of capital to or from third countries. Where measures constitute a step back in the liberalisation process under EU law, these will be adopted

unanimously, after consulting the European Parliament; Article 64 TFEU(2) and (3) [Article III-157] *(ex Article 57(2) TEC)*

- Adoption of other measures on movement of capital to or from third countries; Article 64(2) TFEU [Article III-157(2)] *(ex Article 57(2) TEC)*

Economic and Monetary Policy

- Co-ordination of economic policies – the Council can make recommendations to Member States where the national policies are inconsistent with the broad economic policy guidelines of the Union. Voting in the Council excludes the Member State concerned. *[UK Opt-out]*; Article 121(4) TFEU [Article III-179] *(ex Article 99(4) TEC)*

- Multilateral surveillance of Member States' economic policies by the Commission; Article 121(6) TFEU [Article III-179(6)] *(ex Article 99(5) TEC).*
  This has changed from the co-operation procedure (see below).

- Excessive government deficits – procedure where an excessive deficit develops in a Member State. Voting in the Council excludes the Member State concerned. *[UK Opt-out]*; Article 126(13) TFEU [Article III-184 (7)] *(ex Article 104(13) TEC)*

Economic and social cohesion

- Structural Funds and Cohesion Fund: tasks, priority objectives and organisation. Under the Constitution, the first provisions to take effect once the new Treaty comes into force to be adopted by unanimity and consent of the European Parliament, after this by QMV under the ordinary legislative procedure; this provision has been excluded in the Treaty of Lisbon. Article 177 TFEU [Article III-223] *(ex Article 161 TEC) This has changed from QMV with assent of the European Parliament, under the provisions introduced by the Treaty of Nice, which would have come into effect on 1 January 2007.*

Monetary policy

- Amendment of the Protocol on the Statute of the ESCB and of the ECB, on a recommendation from the ECB after consulting the Commission; Article 129(3) TFEU [Article III-187(5)] *(ex Article 107(5) TEC)*

Agriculture and fisheries

- Application of competition rules to the common agricultural policy; Article 43(2) TFEU [Article III-231(1)] *(ex Article 37(2) TEC)*

- Common agricultural policy legislation – common organisation of markets; Article 43(3) TFEU [Article III-231(2)] *(ex Article 37(2) TEC)*

Common commercial policy

- Commercial policy – implementing measures; Article 207(2) TFEU [Article III-315(2)] *(ex Article 133 TEC)*

Environment

- Cohesion Fund: financial support for transport infrastructure. Article 177 TFEU [Article III-223] *(ex Article 161 TEC) This has changed from QMV with assent of the European Parliament, under the provisions introduced by the Treaty of Nice, which would have come into effect on 1January 2007.*

Trans-European Networks

- Cohesion Fund: financial support for transport infrastructure. Article 177 TFEU [Article III-223] *(ex Article 161 TEC) This has changed from QMV with assent of the European Parliament, under the provisions introduced by the Treaty of Nice, which would have come into effect on 1 January 2007.*

Economic, financial and technical co-operation with third countries

- Economic, financial and technical co-operation with third countries; Article 212(2) TFEU [Article III-319(2)] *(ex Article 181a TEC)*

Financial provisions

- Adoption of financial regulations for the budget and rules for responsibilities of financial actors; Article 322(1) TFEU [Article III-412] *(ex Article 279(1) TEC)*
- Enactment of Staff Regulations for officials of the European Community and Conditions of Employment of other servants of the Union; Article 336 TFEU [Article III-427] *(ex Article 283 TEC)*

III. CHANGES FROM QUALIFIED MAJORITY [CO-OPERATION PROCEDURE]

Under the co-operation procedure, introduced in the Maastricht Treaty in Article 252 TEC, the European Parliament was involved in the legislative process by being able to present amendments to any proposed legislation. The Commission could decide which of the proposals it would accept, but was not obliged to incorporate any of the European Parliament's suggestions.

The Treaty of Lisbon has incorporated the changes introduced by the Constitutional Treaty and repeals the co-operation procedure. The four areas covered by this procedure now come under the consultation procedure (Article 295 TFEU), except for the multilateral surveillance of Member States' economic policies by the Commission (Article 121 TFEU), which is now under the ordinary legislative procedure.

In the consultation procedure, the European Parliament is not directly involved in the legislative process, but the Council will now obtain the consent of the European Parliament before voting on a particular proposal from the Commission.

Economic policy

- Rules for the multi-lateral surveillance procedure; Article 121(3), (4) and (6) TFEU [Article III-179(3), (4) and (6)] *(ex Article 99(3)-(5) TEC)*
- Application of the ban on privileged access; Articles 124 and 125 TFEU [Articles III-182 and III-183(2)] *(ex Article 102(2) TEC)*
- Application of the ban on assuming commitments or granting overdraft facilities; Article 125 TFEU [Article III-183(2)] *(ex Article 103(2) TEC)*

Monetary policy

- Measures to harmonise the denominations and technical specifications of coins; Article 128(2) TFEU [Article III-186(2)] *(ex Article 106(2) TEC)*

SPECIAL LEGISLATIVE PROCEDURE

A special legislative procedure is the process by which a legislative act (regulation, directive or decision) is adopted by either by the European Parliament (acting with the participation of the Council), or the Council (acting with the participation of the European Parliament). The texts of the Treaties do not provide details on how the procedure will operate. As a result, the process will depend on the circumstances and legal bases of each specific case.

There is a general passerelle clause (Article 48(7) TEU) which allows the European Council (by unanimity) to change the voting arrangements for all of the areas under the special legislative procedure to the ordinary legislative procedure.

This procedure concerns particular areas in the Treaties and primarily applies to the following areas:

- Citizens rights (Articles 19 to 22 TFEU) [Article III-124 to III-126];

- Justice and home affairs (Articles 77 to 89 TFEU) [Articles III-265 to III-277];
- Harmonisation of indirect taxes (Article 113 TFEU) [Article III-171];
- Social security and certain provisions for workers rights (Article 153 TFEU) [Article III-210];
- Research and development programmes (Article 182 TFEU) [Article III-251];
- Environment – fiscal measures (Article 192(2) TFEU) [Article III-234(2)];
- Energy – fiscal measures (Article 194(3) TFEU) [Article III-256];
- Functioning of the European Parliament (Articles 223, 226 and 228 TFEU) [Articles III-330, III-333 and III-335];
- EU budget (Articles 312 and 314 TFEU) [Article III-402 to III-404].

I. CHANGES FROM UNANIMITY

Details are given in the chapter on ***'Changes from Unanimity to Qualified Majority'.***

II. CHANGES FROM QUALIFIED MAJORITY

European Parliament

- Arrangements for exercising the right to set up a Committee of Inquiry to investigate mal-administration in the implementation of Union law: legislation by the European Parliament by a special legislative procedure, with the consent of the Council and the Commission; Article 226 TFEU [Article III-333] *(ex Article 193 TEC)*

Financial provisions

- Annual budget; law adopted under a special procedure; Article 314(5) TFEU [Article III-404] *(ex Article 272(5) TEC)*

NEW PROVISIONS UNDER UNANIMITY

There are a number of provisions introduced by the Treaty of Lisbon that are adopted under voting by unanimity.

Accession to the European Convention for the Protection of Human Rights

- The Union will accede to the European Convention (Article 6 TEU [Article I-9]). In the draft Constitution, the Union would accede by qualified majority voting [Article III-325(8) (extensively redrafted from Article 300 TEC)]. In the Treaty of Lisbon, the method of voting has been changed to unanimity and the decision to accede to the European Convention will only happen once all of the Member States have given their approval (Article 216(8) TFEU).

Selection of members of the Commission

- Members of the Commission shall be selected on the basis of equal rotation between the Member States; the number of members of the Commission will be two-thirds of the number of Member States (i.e. 18 members). The European Council acting by unanimity, with the provisions taking effect from 1 November 2014; Article 17(5) TEU and Article 244 TFEU [Article I-26(6)]. ***New provision in 2004 IGC.***

Area of Freedom, Security and Justice

- Judicial co-operation in civil matters: European decision on family law having cross-border implications. This is also subject to a passerelle clause; Article 81(3)(4) TFEU [Article III-269(3)]. ***New provision in 2004 IGC.***

- Judicial co-operation in criminal matters: extension of the definition of criminal offences and sanctions concerning serious crimes to other areas of crime that meet the criteria; Article 83(1) TFEU [Article III-271(1)]. ***New provision in 2004 IGC***.
- Public Prosecutor's Office to be established by a regulation, with the Council acting *unanimously*. This will initially cover the general rules of operation, but may be extended to cover serious cross-border crime; Article 86 TFEU [Article III-274]. ***New provision in 2004 IGC.***

Energy

- Fiscal measures, relating to duties and taxation of energy policy, will be established by unanimity; Article 194 TFEU [Article III-256(3)]. ***New provision in 2004 IGC***.

European Intellectual Property Rights

- Jurisdiction to enable the Court of Justice to decide on disputes over the application of acts creating European intellectual property rights; Article 262 TFEU [Article III-364]. ***New provision in 2004 IGC***.

Multi-annual financial framework

- Terms of the multi-annual financial framework. Council acting by unanimity, with the consent of the European Parliament; Article 312 TFEU [Article I-55]. ***New provision in 2004 IGC.***

PASSERELLE OR BRIDGING CLAUSES

'*Passerelle'* is French for a footbridge or gangway and is used in the Treaties as a term to mean a bridging or an escalator clause. The passerelle clauses are provisions in the text of the Treaties that allow the Council, or the European Council, to change the method of voting on a particular area, as set out in the Treaties, without having to introduce a new treaty that would otherwise be required to make amendments to the voting method. The intention of the clause is to make changing the method of voting more efficient, since this would be easier than the drawn-out process of negotiating a new treaty.

The passerelle clause allows the Council to change the method of voting from unanimity either to qualified majority or to the ordinary voting procedure.

An important aspect of the passerelle clauses are that they allow the European Parliament to become involved in the legislative process under the co-decision process, and therefore on an equal basis to the Council, in areas where previously the Parliament could only act by giving consent or an opinion. Article 48(7) TEU [Article IV-444] ***New provision in 2004 IGC***.

The national parliaments of the Member States are involved in the agreement to the changes in the voting procedure, Article 12 TEU and Protocol 1. The changes are subject to each Member State's constitutional requirements and parliamentary approval will be required in order that the changes can take place.

The passerelle clauses are closely connected to the 'emergency brake' provisions and the enhanced co-operation provisions, where a Member State is able to prevent changes to QMV if there are serious reasons to do so. In this case, the matter is passed o the European Council. However in these circumstances, a minimum of nine Member States can then decide to continue with the proposals under the enhanced co-operation clauses. This is discussed below.

There are eight 'passerelle' clauses in the Treaty of Lisbon, of which two were also present in the Treaty establishing the European Community.

These areas are:

- **General passerelle clause**, where the European Council may decide by unanimity to change the method of voting in the Treaty on the Functioning of the European Union and the Common and

Security Policy, excluding defence or military matters. This procedure avoids the need to have the formality of negotiating a new Treaty; Article 48(7) TEU [Article IV-444] ***New provision in 2004 IGC.***
Where the legislative acts in the Treaty on the Functioning of the European Union are adopted by a special legislative procedure, the European Council can adopt a decision by unanimity to allow the acts to be adopted by the ordinary legislative procedure. Article 48(7) TEU [Article IV-444] ***New provision in 2004 IGC.***
An 'emergency brake' provision is attached to allow a national parliament to veto a European Council decision under the passerelle clause, if the parliament notifies its opposition within six months of being notified of the proposed change; Article 48(7) TEU [Article IV-444(3)] ***New Provision in 2004 IGC***;

- **Simplified revision procedures of the Treaties**, where the government of any Member State, the European Parliament or the Commission may present proposals to the European Council to amend all or part of Part Three of the Treaty on the Functioning of the European Union, concerned with Union policies and internal actions. The European Council shall decide by unanimity; Article 48(6) TEU [Article IV-445] ***New provision in 2004 IGC.***

  An 'emergency brake' provision is attached so that the amendments must be agreed by all of the Member States in order for the changes to be adopted; Article 48(6) TEU [Article IV-445(2)] (ex Article 48 TEU).

- **Common Foreign and Security Policy**: European decisions on CFSP, other than military or defence matters; Article 31(3) TEU [Article III-300(3)] ***New provision in 2004 IGC***;

- **Judicial co-operation in civil matters** – family law with cross-border implications, where the Council may decide to change the method of voting; Article 81(3) TFEU [Article III-269] *New provision in 2004 IGC, but adapted from Articles 65 and 67 TEC, introduced by the Treaty of Amsterdam*;

- **Social policy**, protection of workers' rights, where the Council may decide to change the method of voting; Article 153(2) TFEU [Article III-210(3)] (*ex Article 137 TEC*);

- **Environmental protection**, where the Council may decide to change the method of voting; Article 192(2) TFEU [Article III-234(2)] (*ex Article 175 TEC*);

- **Multi-annual financial framework** where the European Council may decide to change the voting; Article 312(2) TFEU [Articles I-55(4), III-402] ***New provision in 2004 IGC***;

- **Enhanced co-operation**, excluding defence implications, where the Council acts by unanimity, it may decide to change the method of voting to qualified majority; Article 333(1) TFEU [Article III-422(1)] ***New provision in 2004 IGC.***
  Where the legislative acts are adopted by a special legislative procedure, the European Council can adopt a decision by unanimity to allow the acts to be adopted by the ordinary legislative procedure. Article 333(2) TFEU [Article III-422(2)] ***New provision in 2004 IGC.***

EMERGENCY BRAKE PROVISIONS

The emergency brake is a method by which a Member State can prevent legislation from being adopted if the proposed law would affect fundamental aspects of its law or vital aspects of national policy. In this case, a vote would not be taken in the Council and the matter would be referred to the European Council, which would then attempt to reach consensus on the issue.

The emergency brake provisions apply where the Council would be voting on the proposals by qualified majority or where the intention is to change the voting from unanimity to qualified majority under the passerelle clauses. When the matter is passed to the European Council, the voting would be by unanimity.

The national parliaments are involved in this legislative procedure, so that the parliaments must give their approval for the changes in voting to take place, so the emergency brake will apply where the national parliament do not approve changes in the voting procedure. The involvement of the national parliaments is either described in the text of the article, or is in the general Article (Article 12 TEU) or in Protocols 1 and 2.

The involvement of the parliaments applies to all of the areas listed below, except for decisions under the common foreign and security policy, in Article 31 TFEU. In the case of the United Kingdom, the European Union (Amendment) Act 2008 specifically requires approval by the Houses of Parliament for the Government to vote on this measure.

The emergency brake provisions were first introduced in the Maastricht Treaty and concerned the Common Foreign and Security Policy. The number of provisions where the emergency brake applies has been extended over successive treaties, to cover areas which include passerelle clauses, where the Council can change the method of voting from unanimity to qualified majority. The braking mechanism allows Member States to retain their national veto over these particular areas.

- **Ordinary Revision Procedure of the Treaties**: An 'emergency brake' provision is attached so that the amendments must be agreed by all of the Member States in order for the changes to be adopted; Article 48(4) TEU [Article IV-445(3)] (ex Article 48 TEU);

- **Simplified revision procedures**: an 'emergency brake' provision is attached so that amendments to all or part of Part Three of the Treaty on the Functioning of the European Union, concerning Union policies and internal actions, must be agreed by all Member States in order for the changes to be adopted; Article 48(6) TEU [Article IV-445(2)] ***New Provision in 2004 IGC***;

- **General passerelle clause**: an 'emergency brake' provision is attached to enable a national parliament to veto a European Council decision concerning the Treaty on the Functioning of the European Union and the Common Foreign and Security Policy, when either the change of voting is from unanimity to qualified majority, or from a special legislative procedure to the ordinary legislative procedure. The national parliament must notify its opposition within six months of being informed of the proposed change; Article 48(7) TEU [Article IV-444(3)] ***New Provision in 2004 IGC***;

- **Common Foreign and Security Policy**: the Council may act by qualified majority on adopting measures concerning the strategic interests and objectives, decisions on Union action or appointing a special representative. Member States can oppose on the grounds of national policy. Article 31(2) TFEU [Article III-300] (ex Article 23 TEU)

- **Free movement of workers**: the Council can adopt provisions on the benefits to workers by qualified majority. Member States can oppose these proposals on the grounds of important aspects of the social security system, including the scope, cost or financial structure; Article 48 TFEU [Article III-136] ***New Provision in 2004 IGC***;

- **Judicial co-operation in civil matters**: the Council may decide to change the method of voting, by means of a passerelle clause, on measures concerning family law with cross-border implications; a national parliament may oppose the measure and prevent it from being adopted, but the parliament must notify its opposition within six months of being informed of the proposed change; Article 81(3) TFEU [Article III-269] ***New provision in Treaty of Lisbon***;

- **Judicial co-operation in criminal matters**: the Council may adopt proposals on judicial co-operation by qualified majority and a Member State can oppose these proposals on the grounds of their affecting the fundamental aspects of its criminal justice system:
  - the Council can adopt measures to establish minimum rules for the mutual recognition of judgements and judicial decisions.; Article 82 TFEU [Article III-270] ***New Provision in 2004 IGC;***
  - minimum rules on the definition of criminal offences and sanctions concerning particularly serious cross-border crime and the harmonisation of criminal laws and regulations in certain areas of criminal law; Article 83 TFEU [Article III-271] ***New Provision in 2004 IGC.***

A minimum of nine Member States can oppose the following proposals on the grounds of their affecting the fundamental aspects of its criminal justice system:

- European Prosecutor's Office to combat crimes affecting the financial interests of the Union; Article 86(1) TFEU ***New Provision in Treaty of Lisbon.***
- Police co-operation, particularly operational co-operation between the authorities in matters relating to the exchange of data, training of staff and common investigative techniques in relation to organised crime; Article 87(3) TFEU ***New Provision in Treaty of Lisbon.***

ENHANCED CO-OPERATION PROVISIONS

Enhanced co-operation, or flexibility, enables a group of Member States to develop closer relationships with one another, in situations where the other Member States do not want to participate. Examples of this are the Single Currency and the Schengen *acquis*. The importance of these arrangements is that if a Member State invokes the emergency brake provisions in a particular area, the other Member States have the possibility of using the flexibility clauses to proceed with the activity without that Member State.

This possibility is drafted into the Treaty of Lisbon, where a group of member States can make arrangements in minimum rules for judicial co-operation in criminal matters (Article 82(4) and 83(4) TFEU), the formation of a European Public Prosecutor's Office from Eurojust (Article 86 TFEU) and police co-operation (Article 87(3) TFEU).

The general provisions on enhanced co-operation were first introduced in the Treaty of Amsterdam and placed in the Treaty on European Union as a separate Title, where the provisions were called 'closer co-operation'. The title was extensively rewritten and expanded by the Treaty of Nice, which also changed the name to 'enhanced co-operation'. The provisions were redrafted for the Constitution and these have been brought forward into the Treaty of Lisbon with only a small number of adjustments. The majority of the articles have been moved into Part Six of the Treaty on the Functioning of the European Union, which deals with institutional and budgetary provisions, as a separate Title.

The changes from the draft Constitution concern the more specific definition of the minimum number of Member States that can be involved in enhanced co-operation. In the Constitution, the number is one third of Member States, while the Treaty of Lisbon states the number to be nine, which results in the same number with the current size of the Union. The other change is the voting arrangements, where the Council will act under the terms of Article 238 TFEU.

The general article describing the outline of the provisions consists of one article and is in the Treaty on European Union (Article 20 TEU). This article sets out the concept that:

- enhanced co-operation should be among a minimum of nine Member States (i.e. one third of the Member States);
- cannot be applied where the Union has exclusive competence in a particular area;
- should only be adopted as a last resort when other means of agreement among the Member States cannot be reached;
- the institutions of the Union will be involved and the competences described in the Treaties;
- the arrangements do not undermine the internal market or distort competition within the Union;
- all the Member States can be involved in the discussions but only those that are part of the co-operation may vote on these matters, and legislative acts will be binding on the Member States concerned.

The main Articles relating to enhanced co-operation are in Articles 326 to 334 TFEU, and these give the detailed arrangements on how the co-operation will operate. The principal aspects of enhanced co-operation are as follows:

- Member States that wish to establish enhanced co-operation should make a request to the Commission which will assess the proposal and present the request to the Council; the Council will decide on the proposal by qualified majority after obtaining the consent of the European Parliament (Article 329(1) TFEU);
- in the case of the common foreign and security policy, the request will be addressed to the Council, which will ask for opinions from the High Representative of the Union for Foreign Affairs and Security Policy and the Commission. The Council will act by unanimity. The European Parliament will not be involved, except to be informed (Article 329(2) TFEU);
- the High Representative of the Union for Foreign Affairs and Security Policy will be involved in all matters involving enhanced co-operation which relate to the common foreign and security policy (Articles 327, 329(2) and 331(2) TFEU);
- if a Member State wishes to participate in an area already arranged as enhanced co-operation, it must notify the Commission and the Council, and in the case of the common foreign and security policy, it must also inform the High Representative of the Union for Foreign Affairs and Security Policy. The Commission will assess the acceptability of the Member State and inform that Member State within four months whether it has been accepted to participate. The Council may decide not to allow the Member State to participate and give reasons for the decision (Article 331 TFEU);
- there is a *passerelle* clause, where if the terms of the Treaties require voting by unanimity or by a special legislative procedure, the participating Member States can agree to change the method of voting in the Council from unanimity to qualified majority or from a special legislative procedure to the ordinary legislative procedure. This excludes decisions with military or defence implications (Article 333 TFEU).

These provisions are different to those of the Treaty of Nice, where all Member States would be encouraged to participate and participation would be deemed to have been accepted unless the Council took the decision to hold the application in abeyance. The provisions in the Treaty of Lisbon have been expanded, and follow and the emphasis has changed so that the Council will review the acceptability of the Member State joining and form an opinion on whether the State can participate.

Three specific areas where enhanced co-operation may take place are included in the text of the Treaties by the Treaty of Lisbon:

- draft directives on mutual recognition of judgements and judicial decisions and police and judicial co-operation in criminal matters having a cross-border dimension. This is related to the emergency brake provisions where a Member State can request the matter to go to the European Council (Article 82(3) and (4) TFEU). This provision was introduced in the draft Constitution;
- draft directives concerning the definition of criminal offences and sanctions in the areas of serious crime with a cross-border dimension, including terrorism, illegal drug and arms trafficking and organised crime. This is related to the emergency brake provisions where a Member State can request the matter to go to the European Council (Article 83(3) and (4) TFEU). This provision was introduced in the draft Constitution;
- the establishment of a European Public Prosecutor's Office from Eurojust to deal with crimes affecting financial issues affecting the Union. This is related to the emergency brake provisions where a minimum of nine Member States can request the matter to go to the European Council (Article 86(1) TFEU). This is a new provision in the Treaty of Lisbon and was not in the draft Constitution;
- measures concerning operational co-operation between the authorities, including collection, storage and exchange of data, under police co-operation. This is related to the emergency brake provisions where a minimum of nine Member States can request the matter to go to the European Council (Article 87(3) TFEU). This is a new provision in the Treaty of Lisbon and was not in the draft Constitution.

* * * * *

CHANGES FROM UNANIMITY TO QUALIFIED MAJORITY

The Treaty of Lisbon has changed the method of voting in the European Council and the Council in a significant number of areas from unanimity to qualified majority voting. These tables show the principal areas where the procedure of voting in the Council has been changed from unanimity, with an indication of which are under the ordinary or special legislative procedures. Reference is made to changes introduced by the draft Constitutional Treaty (2004 IGC) and brought forward into the Treaty of Lisbon.

European Council

- Election of the President of the European Council, by the members of the European Council;
  Article 15(5) TEU [Article I-22(1)] ***New provision in 2004 IGC***

- Configurations of the European Council, other than the Foreign Affairs Council;
  Article 16 TEU and Article 236(a) TFEU [Article I-24(4)] ***New provision in 2004 IGC***

- Conditions and rotation of presidencies of the European Council configurations;
  Article 16 TEU and Article 236(b) TFEU [Article I-24(6)] *(ex Article 203 TEC)*

- Appointment of the High Representative of the Union for Foreign Affairs and Security Policy; Article 17(8) TEU [Article I-27(1)] ***New provision in 2004 IGC***

- Appointment of ECB President, Vice-President and executive board *[UK opt-out]*;
  Article 283(2b) TFEU [Article III-382(2)] *(ex Article 112 and 113 TEC)*

The Council

Ordinary Legislative Procedure

Exercise of Union competence: Implementing acts

- Arrangements for control of implementing powers (comitology);
  Article 291(3) TFEU [Article I-37(3)] *(ex Article 202 TEC)*

Participation of EU Citizens in Union democracy

- Determination of the procedures and conditions for Citizens' initiative for legislation;
  Article 11(4) TEU and Article 24 TFEU [Article I-47(4)] ***New provision in 2004 IGC***

Free movement of workers

- Internal market: **social security** measures, principally benefits, for Community migrant workers; Article 48 (para. 1) TFEU [Article III-136(1)]
  Where a Member State considers that a draft legislative act would affect fundamental aspects of its social security system, it may request a referral to the European Council, which may refer back to the Council or request the Commission to submit a new proposal ('*Emergency brake provision*').
  Article 48 (para. 2) TFEU [Article III-136(2)] ***New Provision in 2004 IGC***

Freedom of Establishment

- **Self-employed persons**: co-ordination of provisions laid down by law, regulation or administrative action in Member States concerning the taking-up and pursuit of activities as self-employed persons. Change from unanimity to QMV in the case of co-ordination of existing principles laid down by law governing the professions with respect to training and conditions of access for natural persons; Article 53(1) TFEU [Article III-141(1)(b)]

Cont'd....

Areas where the Union may take co-ordinating, complementary or supporting action

- **Sport** - promotion of sporting issues, including sport's social and educational function; Article 165 TFEU, [Article III-282(1)] ***New provision in 2004 IGC***
- **Culture**, including education, conservation, cultural exchanges and artistic creation (except for recommendations) - incentive measures; Article 167 TFEU [Article III-280]*(ex Article 151 TEC)*
- **Tourism**; Article 195 TFEU, [Article III-281] ***New provision in 2004 IGC***
- **Civil protection** against natural and man-made disasters; Article 196 TFEU, [Article III-284] ***New provision in 2004 IGC***
- **Administrative co-ordination** to help Member States administrative capacity to implement Union law; Article 197 TFEU [Article III-285] ***New provision in 2004 IGC***

Policies in specific areas:

- **Common Security and Defence Policy**
  Measures for drawing up **permanent structured co-operation,** including selection of participating Member States, confirmation of fulfilment of criteria and suspension from this co-operation;
  Article 46 TEU [Article III-312] ***New provision in 2004 IGC***
- **Services of General Economic Interest**
  Public services: establishment of the principles and conditions, especially economic and financial conditions, to provide, commission and to fund the services, to promote social and territorial cohesion. The Council acts after consultation with the European Parliament; Article 14 TFEU [Article III-122] (*ex Article 16 TEC*)
- **Transport**
  Measures for drawing up a policy for transport across Member States, where there is serious effect on the standard of living and employment, and air and sea transport; Articles 91(1) and 100(2) TFEU [Articles III-236 and III-245]
- **Intellectual Property Rights**
  Measures to provide uniform intellectual property rights protection throughout the Union and setting up of the centralised Union-wide authorisation, co-ordination and supervision arrangements;
  Article 118 TFEU [Article III-176] ***New provision in 2004 IGC***
- **European Research Area**
  Research area where researchers, scientific knowledge and technology can circulate freely; Article 179(1) and 182(5) TFEU [Articles III-248 and III-251]
  New provision in 2004 IGC
- **Space**
  Measures for drawing up a European space policy;
  Article 189 TFEU [Article III-254] ***New provision in 2004 IGC***
- **Energy**
  Measures to ensure the functioning of the energy market, the security of supply of energy in the Union and energy efficiency and saving;
  Article 194 TFEU [Article III-256] ***New provision in 2004 IGC***
- **Common Commercial Policy**
  Measures for negotiation and conclusion of international agreements, including intellectual property and foreign direct investment (FDI is a new provision). Previously, the Union could act by unanimity on intellectual property matters and for internal rules or where there were no conferred powers;
  Article 207 TFEU [Article III-315] *(ex Article 133 TEC)*

Cont'd....

- **Economic, financial and technical co-operation with third countries**
  Measures to implement association and accession agreements concerned with economic, financial and technical co-operation;
  Article 212 TFEU [Article III-319] (*ex Article 181a TEC*)
- **Humanitarian Aid**
  Measures for drawing up a framework for humanitarian aid operations, including the formation of European Voluntary Humanitarian Aid Corps;
  Article 214 TFEU [Article III-321(3)] ***New provision in 2004 IGC***
- **European Union Administration**
  Measures for drawing up an open, efficient and independent European administration, or 'civil service' to support the EU institutions, including conditions of employment for the staff;
  Article 298 TFEU [Article III-398] ***New provision in 2004 IGC***

Area of Freedom, Security and Justice

- **Border controls, visa and short-term residence policy**, freedom of travel of third country nationals, gradual integration of integrated external border management, absence of internal border controls *[UK opt-in]*;
  Article 77 TFEU [Article III-265] *(ex Articles 62, 64 and 67 TEC)*
- **Asylum** - uniform status of asylum and subsidiary status for nationals of third countries, common system of temporary protection, common procedures for granting and withdrawing uniform asylum or subsidiary protection status, standards for conditions for reception of applicants, co-operation with third countries to manage inflows of people; Article 78 TFEU [Article III-266] *(ex Articles 63, 64 and 67 TEC)*
- **Immigration** - conditions of entry and residence and standards on issue of long-term visas, definition of rights of third-country nationals living legally in the EU, illegal immigration and residence in the EU, combating trafficking in people, especially women and children *[UK opt-in]*;
  Article 79 TFEU [Article III-267(2) *(ex Articles 63, 64 and 67 TEC)*
- **Integration of third country nationals** - measures to provide incentives and support for Member States' actions;
  Article 79(4) TFEU [Article III-267(4)] (*ex Articles 63, 64 and 67 TEC*)
- **Judicial co-operation in civil matters** - mutual recognition and enforcement of judgements and decisions and **cross-border co-operation**;
  Article 81 TFEU [Article III-269(2)] (*ex Articles 65 and 67 TEC*).

Under the TEC, the Union could act by unanimity for the above areas until May 2004 (five-year transitional period after the entry into force of the Amsterdam Treaty). Through the use of a passerelle clause, the Union could vote by unanimity to act by QMV after May 2004 (*Article 67 TEC*).

The UK has an opt-in to these Articles, under Protocol no. 21, Article 1, and Protocol no. 22, Articles 1 and 2.

- **Judicial co-operation in criminal matters** - procedures, co-operation, training and minimum rules; an 'emergency brake' has been introduced *[UK opt-in]*;
  Article 82 TFEU [Article III-270] *(ex Article 31 TEU)*
- Minimum rules on establishing definitions of criminal offences and sanctions for serious crime with a **cross-border** dimension; also applies to areas subject to harmonisation measures; an 'emergency brake' has been introduced *[UK opt-in]*; Article 83 TFEU [Article III-271] ***New provision in 2004 IGC***

Cont'd….

- **Crime prevention** - promotion and supporting measures *[UK opt-in]*; Article 84 TFEU [Article III-272] ***New provision in 2004 IGC***
- **Eurojust** - determination of structure, operation, field of action and tasks, together with arrangements for involvement of the European Parliament and national parliaments *[UK opt-in]*; Article 85 TFEU [Article III-273(1)] *(ex Article 31(2) TEU)*
- **Police co-operation** - some aspects, including analysis and exchange of information and staff training *[UK opt-in]*; Article 87 TFEU [Article III-275(2)] *(ex Article 30 TEU)*
- **Europol** - determination of structure, operation, field of action and tasks, together with arrangements for involvement of the European Parliament and national parliaments *[UK opt-in]*; Article 88 TFEU [Article III-276] *(ex Article 30(2) TEU)*

Provisions affecting Germany

- Two articles, concerning transport and state aid, affecting the division of Germany and no longer relevant, to be repealed five years after the entry into force of the Reform Treaty. Article 98 and 107 TFEU [Articles III-243 and III-167(2)(c)] *(ex Articles 78 and 87 TEC)*

Economic and Monetary Policy

- Amendment of articles in the Protocol on the Statute of the ESCB and of the ECB on a proposal from the Commission. The articles concern collection of statistical information, and the functioning and operation of the ESCB and the ECB; Article 129 TFEU [Article III-187(3) *(ex Article 107(5) TEC)*
- Measures required for use of the euro *[UK Opt-out]*; Article 132 TFEU [Article III-190] ***New provision in 2004 IGC***
- Recommendations by Eurozone members to the Council for Member States to join the euro; Article 140(2) TFEU [Article III-198(2)] ***New provision in 2004 IGC***

Economic and social cohesion

- Structural Funds and Cohesion Fund: tasks, priority objectives and organisation. The first provisions to take effect once the new Treaty comes into force to be adopted by unanimity, after this by QMV; Article 177 TFEU [Article III-223] *(ex Article 161 TEC)*

Environment

- Cohesion Fund: financial support for transport infrastructure. The first provisions to take effect once the new Treaty comes into force to be adopted by unanimity and consent of the European Parliament, after this by QMV under the ordinary legislative procedure; Article 177 TFEU [Article III-223] *(ex Article 161 TEC)*

Trans-European networks

- Cohesion Fund: financial support for transport infrastructure. The first provisions to take effect once the new Treaty comes into force to be adopted by unanimity and consent of the European Parliament, after this by QMV under the ordinary legislative procedure; Article 177 TFEU [Article III-223] *(ex Article 161 TEC)*

Court of Justice

- Establishment of **specialist courts** [judicial panels] attached to General Court (previously, the Court of First Instance), rules on organisation and extent of jurisdiction; Article 257 TFEU [Article III-359] *(ex Article 225a TEC)*
- Amendment of the Statute of the Court of Justice (except for Title I); Article 281 TFEU [Article III-381] *(ex Article 245 TEC)*

Cont'd....

The Union's advisory bodies

- Review of the nature and composition of the advisory bodies, including the Committee of the Regions and the Economic and Social Committee; Article 300(5) TFEU [Article I-32(2)] *(ex Articles 257 - 265 TEC)*

Special Legislative Procedure

Voluntary withdrawal from the Union

- Agreement with the Member State wishing to leave the Union: Council acts by qualified majority; Article 50 TEU [Article I-60(2)] ***New provision in 2004 IGC***

The Union's finances and resources

- Arrangements for the budget funds provided from **own resources** being made available to the Commission: regulation by the Council; Article 310 and 322 TFEU [Articles I-53(3) and (4) and III-412(2)] *(ex Article 279(2) TEC)*
- **Own resources** arrangements:
  Implementing measures on the system of own resources by European law adopted by the Council by a qualified majority, with the consent of the European Parliament ***(the UK rebate is covered by unanimity under Article 311(3) TFEU)***;
  Article 311 TFEU [Article I-54(4)] *(ex Article 269 TEC)*

Area of Freedom, Security and Justice

- Arrangements for how the **Member States conduct evaluation** of the implementation of Union policies in the area of freedom, security and justice (in particular, mutual recognition). European Parliament and national parliaments to be informed of the results. [*UK opt-in*]; Article 70 TFEU [Article III-260] ***New provision in 2004 IGC***
- **Administrative co-operation**; Article 74 TFEU [Article III-263]*(ex Articles 66 TEC and Articles 30-31 TEU)*

Culture

- Recommendations on cultural matters: Council shall act by majority;
  Article 167(5) TFEU [Article III-280(5)(b)] *(ex Article 151(5), second indent, TEC)*

Common foreign and security policy

- The Council acts by a qualified majority under the CFSP when adopting a decision on the **initiative of the High Representative for Foreign Affairs**, further to a request from the European Council; Article 31 TEU [Article III-300(2)(b)] ***New provision in 2004 IGC***
- Urgent financing for initiatives in the framework of the common foreign and security policy, particularly preparatory activities for the 'Petersberg tasks', from the Union budget or from a **Start-up Fund** from Member States;
  Article 41(3) TEU [Article III-313(3)] ***New provision in 2004 IGC***
- **European Defence Agency** – statute, seat and operational rules; by qualified majority;
  Article 45 TEU [Article III-311] ***New provision in 2004 IGC***

Economic, financial and technical co-operation with third countries

- **Emergency aid**: Urgent financial assistance for third countries: European decision by the Council; Article 213 TFEU [Article III-320] ***New provision in 2004 IGC***

Cont'd....

Economic and Monetary Union

- Establishment of common positions among the members of EMU on matters concerning the **Euro in the international monetary system** and to ensure unified representation. The Council will act after consulting the ECB *[UK opt-out]*;
Article 138 TFEU [Article III-196(1) and (2)] ***New provision in 2004 IGC***

Financial provisions

- Establishment of the **EU budget** by the Council and the European Parliament, by the production of a European law; Article 314 TFEU [Article III-404] (*ex Article 272 TEC*)

Diplomatic and consular protection

- **Protection of citizens in third countries**, following the right defined in Article I-10(2). The Council will act after consulting the European Parliament; Article 23 TFEU [Article III-127] (*ex Article 20 TEC*)

Solidarity clause

- Arrangements for the implementation of the solidarity clause, in the case of a Member State suffering a terrorist attack or a natural or man-made disaster. The Council will act on the initiative of the Commission and the Union Minister for Foreign Affairs, the European Parliament will be informed; Article 222 TFEU [Article III-329] ***New provision in 2004 IGC***

Court of Justice

- Establishment of a **panel to select judges and advocate-generals**, including appointment of the panel and the panel's operating rules. The Council will act on the initiative of the President of the Court of Justice; Article 255 TFEU [Article III-357] ***New provision in 2004 IGC***
- Jurisdiction for the Court of Justice in **intellectual property** matters;
Article 262 TFEU [Article III-364] *(ex Article 229a TEC)*

* * *

THE

CONSOLIDATED

TREATY ON EUROPEAN UNION

AND

THE

CONSOLIDATED

TREATY ON THE FUNCTIONING OF

THE EUROPEAN UNION

THE TREATY ON EUROPEAN UNION

HIS MAJESTY THE KING OF THE BELGIANS *,

THE PRESIDENT OF THE REPUBLIC OF BULGARIA,

THE PRESIDENT OF THE CZECH REPUBLIC,

HER MAJESTY THE QUEEN OF DENMARK *,

THE PRESIDENT OF THE FEDERAL REPUBLIC OF GERMANY *,

THE PRESIDENT OF THE REPUBLIC OF ESTONIA,

THE PRESIDENT OF IRELAND *,

THE PRESIDENT OF THE HELLENIC REPUBLIC *,

HIS MAJESTY THE KING OF SPAIN *,

THE PRESIDENT OF THE FRENCH REPUBLIC *,

THE PRESIDENT OF THE ITALIAN REPUBLIC *,

THE PRESIDENT OF THE REPUBLIC OF CYPRUS,

THE PRESIDENT OF THE REPUBLIC OF LATVIA,

THE PRESIDENT OF THE REPUBLIC OF LITHUANIA,

HIS ROYAL HIGHNESS THE GRAND DUKE OF LUXEMBOURG *,

THE PRESIDENT OF THE REPUBLIC OF HUNGARY,

THE PRESIDENT OF MALTA,

HER MAJESTY THE QUEEN OF THE NETHERLANDS *,

THE FEDERAL PRESIDENT OF THE REPUBLIC OF AUSTRIA,

THE PRESIDENT OF THE REPUBLIC OF POLAND,

THE PRESIDENT OF THE PORTUGUESE REPUBLIC *,

THE PRESIDENT OF ROMANIA,

THE PRESIDENT OF THE REPUBLIC OF SLOVENIA,

THE PRESIDENT OF THE SLOVAK REPUBLIC,

THE PRESIDENT OF THE REPUBLIC OF FINLAND,

THE GOVERNMENT OF THE KINGDOM OF SWEDEN,

HER MAJESTY THE QUEEN OF THE UNITED KINGDOM OF GREAT BRITAIN AND NORTHERN IRELAND *,

* *BMDF Note: Heads of State at the time of signature of the Treaty on European Union at Maastricht, 7 February 1992.*

RESOLVED to mark a new stage in the process of European integration undertaken with the establishment of the European Communities,

DRAWING INSPIRATION from the cultural, religious and humanist inheritance of Europe, from which have developed the universal values of the inviolable and inalienable rights of the human person, freedom, democracy, equality and the rule of law,
[BMDF Note: Recital taken from 2004 IGC – First Recital of Preamble]

RECALLING the historic importance of the ending of the division of the European continent and the need to create firm bases for the construction of the future Europe,

CONFIRMING their attachment to the principles of liberty, democracy and respect for human rights and fundamental freedoms and of the rule of law,

CONFIRMING their attachment to fundamental social rights as defined in the European Social Charter signed at Turin on 18 October 1961 and in the 1989 Community Charter of the Fundamental Social Rights of Workers,

DESIRING to deepen the solidarity between their peoples while respecting their history, their culture and their traditions,

DESIRING to enhance further the democratic and efficient functioning of the institutions so as to enable them better to carry out, within a single institutional framework, the tasks entrusted to them,

RESOLVED to achieve the strengthening and the convergence of their economies and to establish an economic and monetary union, in accordance with the provisions of ***this Treaty and the Treaty on the Functioning of the European Union***, a single and stable currency,

DETERMINED to promote economic and social progress for their peoples, taking into account the principle of sustainable development and within the context of the accomplishment of the internal market and of reinforced cohesion and environmental protection, and to implement policies ensuring that advances in economic integration are accompanied by parallel progress in other fields,

RESOLVED to establish a citizenship common to nationals of their countries,

RESOLVED to implement a common foreign and security policy including the progressive framing of a common defence policy, which might lead to a common defence in accordance with the provisions of Article 17 [*BMDF Note: now Article 42*], thereby reinforcing the European identity and its independence in order to promote peace, security and progress in Europe and in the world,

RESOLVED to facilitate the free movement of persons, while ensuring the safety and security of their peoples, by establishing an area of freedom, security and justice, in accordance with the provisions of ***this Treaty and the Treaty on the Functioning of the European Union***,

RESOLVED to continue the process of creating an ever closer union among the peoples of Europe, in which decisions are taken as closely as possible to the citizen in accordance with the principle of subsidiarity,

IN VIEW of further steps to be taken in order to advance European integration,

HAVE DECIDED to establish a European Union and to this end have designated as their plenipotentiaries:

WHO, having exchanged their full powers, found in good and due form, have agreed as follows.

TITLE I

COMMON PROVISIONS

ARTICLE 1 [1] *['Establishment of the Union' Article I-1 (new Article in 2004 IGC)]*
By this Treaty, the HIGH CONTRACTING PARTIES establish among themselves a EUROPEAN UNION, hereinafter called 'the Union', **on which the Member States confer competences to attain objectives they have in common.**
This Treaty marks a new stage in the process of creating an ever closer union among the peoples of Europe, in which decisions are taken as openly as possible and closely as possible to the citizen.
The Union shall be founded on the present Treaty and on the Treaty on the functioning of the European Union (hereinafter referred to as "the Treaties"). Those two Treaties shall have the same legal value. The Union shall replace and succeed the European Community.

ARTICLE 2 [1a] *['The Union's Values', Article I-2 (ex Article 6(1) TEU)]*
The Union is founded on the values of respect for human dignity, freedom, democracy, equality, the rule of law and respect for human rights, including the rights of persons belonging to minorities. These values are common to the Member States in a society in which pluralism, non-discrimination, tolerance, justice, solidarity and equality between women and men prevail.
[BMDF Note: Original text moved from Article 6 TEU]

ARTICLE *3* [2] *['The Union's Objectives', Article I-3 (ex Article 2 TEC and Article 2 TEU)]*
1. The Union's aim is to promote peace, its values and the well-being of its peoples.

2. The Union shall offer its citizens an area of freedom, security and justice without internal frontiers *in which the free movement of persons is ensured in conjunction with appropriate measures with respect to external border controls, asylum, immigration and the prevention and combating of crime.*

3. *The Union shall establish an internal market. It* shall work for the sustainable development of Europe based on balanced economic growth and price stability, a highly competitive social market economy, aiming at full employment and social progress, and a high level of protection and improvement of the quality of the environment. It shall promote scientific and technological advance.
It shall combat social exclusion and discrimination, and shall promote social justice and protection, equality between women and men, solidarity between generations and protection of the rights of the child.
It shall promote economic, social and territorial cohesion, and solidarity among Member States.
It shall respect its rich cultural and linguistic diversity, and shall ensure that Europe's cultural heritage is safeguarded and enhanced.

4. The Union shall establish an economic and monetary union whose currency is the euro.

***5.* In its relations with the wider world, the Union shall uphold and promote its values and interests *and contribute to the protection of its citizens.* It shall contribute to peace, security, the sustainable development of the Earth, solidarity and mutual respect among peoples, free and fair trade, eradication of poverty and the protection of human rights, in particular the rights of the child, as well as to the strict observance and the development of international law, including respect for the principles of the United Nations Charter.**

6.* The Union shall pursue its objectives by appropriate means commensurate with the competences which are conferred upon it in the *Treaties.

[BMDF Note: Article 3 TEU shall be repealed]

ARTICLE 4 [3a] *['Relations between the Union and the Member States', Article I-5 (ex Article 10 TEC and Article 6(3) TEU)]*
1. ***In accordance with Article 5, competences not conferred upon the Union in the Treaties remain with the Member States.***

2. **The Union shall respect the equality of Member States before the *Treaties* as well as their national identities, inherent in their fundamental structures, political and constitutional, inclusive of regional and local self-government. It shall respect their essential State functions, including ensuring the territorial integrity of the State, maintaining law and order and safeguarding national security. *In particular, national security remains the sole responsibility of each Member State.***

3. **Pursuant to the principle of sincere co-operation, the Union and the Member States shall, in full mutual respect, assist each other in carrying out tasks which flow from the *Treaties.***
The Member States shall take any appropriate measure, general or particular, to ensure fulfilment of the obligations arising out of the *Treaties* or resulting from the acts of the institutions of the Union.
The Member States shall facilitate the achievement of the Union's tasks and refrain from any measure which could jeopardise the attainment of the Union's objectives.

ARTICLE 5 [3b] *['Fundamental principles relating to competences', Article I-11 (Paragraphs 3 and 4 ex Article 5 TEC)]*
1. The limits of Union competences are governed by the principle of conferral. The use of Union competences is governed by the principles of subsidiarity and proportionality.

2. Under the principle of conferral, the Union shall act within the limits of the competences conferred upon it by the Member States in the *Treaties* to attain the objectives set out *therein.* Competences not conferred upon the Union in the *Treaties* remain with the Member States.

3. Under the principle of subsidiarity, in areas which do not fall within its exclusive competence, the Union shall act only if and insofar as the objectives of the proposed action cannot be sufficiently achieved by the Member States, either at central level or at regional and local level, but can rather, by reason of the scale or effects of the proposed action, be better achieved at Union level. *[BMDF Note: Paragraph taken from Article 5 TEC]*
The institutions of the Union shall apply the principle of subsidiarity as laid down in the Protocol on the application of the principles of subsidiarity and proportionality. National Parliaments shall ensure compliance with that principle in accordance with the procedure set out in that Protocol.

4. Under the principle of proportionality, the content and form of Union action shall not exceed what is necessary to achieve the objectives of the *Treaties.*
The institutions of the Union shall apply the principle of proportionality as laid down in the Protocol on the application of the principles of subsidiarity and proportionality.

[BMDF Note: Article 4 TEU shall be repealed.]

[BMDF Note: Article 5 TEU shall be repealed.]

ARTICLE 6 [6] *['Fundamental Rights', Article I-9 (ex Article 6 TEU)]*
[BMDF Note: Original text moved to Article 2 TEU]
1. *The Union recognises* the rights, freedoms and principles set out in the Charter of Fundamental Rights *of 7 December 2000, as adapted at Strasbourg, on 12 December 2007, which shall have the same legal value as the Treaties.*
The provisions of the Charter shall not extend in any way the competences of the Union as defined in the Treaties.
The rights, freedoms and principles in the Charter shall be interpreted in accordance with the general provisions in Title VII of the Charter governing its interpretation and application and with due regard to the explanations referred to in the Charter, that set out the sources of those provisions.
[BMDF Note: Paragraph redrafted to reflect the UK's opt-out, Protocol No. 7]

2. **The Union shall accede to the European Convention for the Protection of Human Rights and Fundamental Freedoms. Such accession shall not affect the Union's competences as defined in the *Treaties*.**

3. Fundamental rights, as guaranteed by the European Convention for the Protection of Human Rights and Fundamental Freedoms and as they result from the constitutional traditions common to the Member States, shall constitute general principles of the Union's law.
[BMDF Note: See also Protocols nos. 5 and 7 and Declarations nos. 1, 2, 53, 61 and 62]

ARTICLE 7 [7] *['Suspension of certain rights resulting from Union membership', Article I-59 (ex Article 49 TEU)]*
1. On a reasoned proposal by one third of the Member States, by the European Parliament or by the ***European*** Commission, the Council, acting by a majority of four-fifths of its members after obtaining the ***consent*** of the European Parliament, may determine that there is a clear risk of a serious breach by a Member State of ***the values referred to in Article 2***. Before making such a determination, the Council shall hear the Member State in question ***and may address recommendations to it, acting in accordance with the same procedure***.
The Council shall regularly verify that the grounds on which such a determination was made continue to apply.

2. ***The European Council, acting by unanimity*** on a proposal by one-third of the Member States or by the ***European*** Commission and after obtaining the ***consent*** of the European Parliament, may determine the existence of a serious and persistent breach by a Member State of ***the values referred to in Article 2***, after inviting the Member State in question to submit its observations.

3. Where a determination under paragraph 2 has been made, the Council, acting by a qualified majority, may decide to suspend certain of the rights deriving from the application of ***the Treaties*** to the Member State in question, including the voting rights of the representative of the government of that Member State in the Council. In doing so, the Council shall take into account the possible consequences of such a suspension on the rights and obligations of natural and legal persons.
The obligations of the Member State in question under ***the Treaties*** shall in any case continue to be binding on that State.

4. The Council, acting by a qualified majority, may decide subsequently to vary or revoke measures taken under paragraph 3 in response to changes in the situation which led to their being imposed.

5. The voting arrangements applying to the European Parliament, the European Council and the Council for the purposes of this Article are laid down in Article 354 of the Treaty on the Functioning of the European Union.

ARTICLE 8 [7a] *['The Union and its neighbours', Article I-57 (ex Article 300 TEC)]*
1. The Union shall develop a special relationship with neighbouring countries, aiming to establish an area of prosperity and good neighbourliness, founded on the values of the Union and characterised by close and peaceful relations based on co-operation.

2. For the purposes of paragraph 1, the Union may conclude specific agreements with the countries concerned. These agreements may contain reciprocal rights and obligations as well as the possibility of undertaking activities jointly. Their implementation shall be the subject of periodic consultation.
[BMDF Note: See also Declaration no. 3]

[BMDF Note: The Provisions of Title II and Article 8 (amending the Treaty establishing the European Economic Community), Title III and Article 9 (amending the Treaty establishing the European Coal and Steel Community) and Title IV and Article 10 (amending the Treaty establishing the European Atomic Energy Community), which formed part of the Treaty on European Union and contained provisions from the Maastricht Treaty, the Treaty of Amsterdam and the Treaty of Nice are repealed under the terms of Article 1(11), Article 1(13) and Article 1(21) of the Treaty of Lisbon.]

TITLE II

PROVISIONS ON DEMOCRATIC PRINCIPLES

ARTICLE ***9*** [8] *['The principle of democratic equality', Articles I-45 (new Article in 2004 IGC) and I-10 (ex Article 17 TEC)]*
In all its activities, the Union shall observe the principle of the equality of its citizens, who shall receive equal attention from its institutions, bodies, offices and agencies. Every national of a Member State shall be a citizen of the Union. Citizenship of the Union shall be additional to national citizenship and shall not replace it.

ARTICLE ***10*** [8A] *['The principle of representative democracy', Article I-46 (new Article in 2004 IGC)]*
1. The functioning of the Union shall be founded on representative democracy.

2. Citizens are directly represented at Union level in the European Parliament.
Member States are represented in the European Council by their Heads of State or Government and in the Council by their governments, themselves democratically accountable either to their national Parliaments, or to their citizens.

3. Every citizen shall have the right to participate in the democratic life of the Union. Decisions shall be taken as openly and as closely as possible to the citizen.

4. Political parties at European level contribute to forming European political awareness and to expressing the will of citizens of the Union.

ARTICLE ***11*** [8B] *['The principle of participatory democracy', Article I-47 (new Article in 2004 IGC)]*
1. The institutions shall, by appropriate means, give citizens and representative associations the opportunity to make known and publicly exchange their views in all areas of Union action.

2. The institutions shall maintain an open, transparent and regular dialogue with representative associations and civil society.

3. The *European* Commission shall carry out broad consultations with parties concerned in order to ensure that the Union's actions are coherent and transparent.

4. Not less than one million citizens who are nationals of a significant number of Member States may take the initiative of inviting the Commission, within the framework of its powers, to submit any appropriate proposal on matters where citizens consider that a legal act of the Union is required for the purpose of implementing the *Treaties*.
The* procedures and conditions required for such a citizens' initiative *shall be determined in accordance with Article 24 of the Treaty on the Functioning of the European Union.

ARTICLE 12 [8C] *['The role of national Parliaments', new Article in Treaty of Lisbon 2007]*
National parliaments shall contribute actively to the good functioning of the Union:

a) through being informed by the institutions of the Union and having draft legislative acts forwarded to them in accordance with the Protocol on the role of national parliaments in the European Union;
b) by seeing to it that the principle of subsidiarity is respected in accordance with the procedures provided for in the Protocol on the application of the principles of subsidiarity and proportionality;
c) by taking part, within the framework of the area of freedom, security and justice, in the evaluation mechanisms for the implementation of the Union policies in that area, in accordance with Article 70 of the Treaty on the Functioning of the European Union, and through being involved in the political monitoring of Europol and the evaluation of Eurojust's activities in accordance with Articles 88 and 85 of that Treaty;
d) by taking part in the revision procedures of the Treaties, in accordance with Article 48 of this Treaty;

e) ***by being notified of applications for accession to the Union, in accordance with Article 49 of this Treaty;***

f) ***by taking part in the inter-parliamentary co-operation between national Parliaments and with the European Parliament, in accordance with the Protocol on the role of national Parliaments in the European Union.***

[BMDF Note: See also Protocol no. 2 and Declaration no. 51]

TITLE III

PROVISIONS ON THE INSTITUTIONS

ARTICLE *13* [9] *['The Union's institutions', Article I-19 (ex Article 7 TEC and Article 3 TEU)]*

1. The Union shall have an institutional framework which shall aim to promote its values, advance its objectives, serve its interests, those of its citizens and those of the Member States, *and* ensure the consistency, effectiveness and continuity of its policies and actions.

The Union's institutions shall be:

- **the European Parliament,**
- **the European Council,**
- **the Council,**
- **the European Commission (hereinafter referred to as the "Commission"),**
- **the Court of Justice of the European Union,**
- ***the European Central Bank,***
- ***the Court of Auditors.***

2. Each institution shall act within the limits of the powers conferred on it in the *Treaties*, and in conformity with the procedures and conditions set out in *them*. The institutions shall practise mutual sincere co-operation.

3. The provisions relating to the European Central Bank and the Court of Auditors and detailed provisions on the other institutions are set out in the Treaty on the Functioning of the European Union.

4. The European Parliament, the Council and the Commission shall be assisted by an Economic and Social Committee and a Committee of the Regions acting in an advisory capacity.

ARTICLE *14* [9A] *['The European Parliament', Article I-20 (new article in 2004 IGC)]*

1. The European Parliament shall, jointly with the Council, exercise legislative and budgetary functions. It shall exercise functions of political control and consultation as laid down in the *Treaties*. It shall elect the President of the Commission.

2. The European Parliament shall be composed of representatives of the Union's citizens. They shall not exceed seven hundred and fifty in number, *plus the President*. Representation of citizens shall be degressively proportional, with a minimum threshold of six members per Member State. No Member State shall be allocated more than ninety-six seats.

The European Council shall adopt by unanimity, on the initiative of the European Parliament and with its consent, a decision establishing the composition of the European Parliament, respecting the principles referred to in the first subparagraph.

3. The members of the European Parliament shall be elected for a term of five years by direct universal suffrage in a free and secret ballot.

4. The European Parliament shall elect its President and its officers from among its members.

[BMDF Note: See also Declarations nos. 4, 5 and 57. Paragraph 2 amended on 19 October 2007 at the Lisbon summit.]

ARTICLE *15* [9B] *['The European Council and its President', Article I-21 and Article I-22]*
1. The European Council shall provide the Union with the necessary impetus for its development and shall define the general political directions and priorities thereof. It shall not exercise legislative functions.

2. The European Council shall consist of the Heads of State or Government of the Member States, together with its President and the President of the Commission. The *High Representative of the Union for Foreign Affairs and Security Policy* shall take part in its work.

3. The European Council shall meet quarterly, convened by its President. When the agenda so requires, the members of the European Council may decide each to be assisted by a minister and, in the case of the President of the Commission, by a member of the Commission. When the situation so requires, the President shall convene a special meeting of the European Council.

4. Except where the *Treaties* provide otherwise, decisions of the European Council shall be taken by consensus.

5. **The European Council shall elect its President, by a qualified majority, for a term of two and a half years, renewable once. In the event of an impediment or serious misconduct, the European Council can end his or her term of office in accordance with the same procedure.**

6. **The President of the European Council:**
(a) shall chair it and drive forward its work;
(b) shall ensure the preparation and continuity of the work of the European Council in co-operation with the President of the Commission, and on the basis of the work of the General Affairs Council;
(c) shall endeavour to facilitate cohesion and consensus within the European Council;
(d) shall present a report to the European Parliament after each of the meetings of the European Council.
The President of the European Council shall, at his level and in that capacity, ensure the external representation of the Union on issues concerning its common foreign and security policy, without prejudice to the powers of the *High Representative of the Union for Foreign Affairs and Security Policy*.
The President of the European Council shall not hold a national office.
[BMDF Note: See also Declarations nos. 6 and 8. Paragraphs 1-4 taken from 2004 IGC - Article I-21 'The European Council' (ex Article 4 TEU); Paragraphs 5 and 6 taken from 2004 IGC - Article I-22 'The European Council President' (new article in the 2004 IGC)]

ARTICLE *16* [9C] *['The Council, its Presidency and the definition of a qualified majority', Articles I-23 to I-25]*
1. The Council shall, jointly with the European Parliament, exercise legislative and budgetary functions. It shall carry out policy-making and co-ordinating functions as laid down in the *Treaties*.

2. The Council shall consist of a representative of each Member State at ministerial level, who may commit the government of the Member State in question and cast its vote.

3. The Council shall act by a qualified majority except where the *Treaties* provide otherwise.
[BMDF Note: Paragraphs 1-3 taken from 2004 IGC - Article I-23 'The Council of Ministers' (ex Articles 202, 203 and 205 TEC)]

4. ***As from 1 November 2014*, a qualified majority shall be defined as at least 55% of the members of the Council, comprising at least fifteen of them and representing Member States comprising at least 65% of the population of the Union.**
A blocking minority must include at least four Council members, failing which the qualified majority shall be deemed attained.
The other arrangements governing the qualified majority are laid down in Article 238(2) of the Treaty on the Functioning of the European Union.
[BMDF Note: See also Protocols no. 5 and 10 and Declaration no. 7. Paragraph 4 taken from Article I-25 paragraph 1, 'Definition of qualified majority within the European Council and the Council' (new Article in 2004 IGC)

5. *The transitional provisions relating to the definition of the qualified majority which shall be applicable until 31 October 2014 and those which shall be applicable from 1 November 2014 to 31 March 2017 are laid down in the Protocol on transitional provisions.*

6. **The Council shall meet in different configurations,** ***the list of which shall be adopted in accordance with Article 236 of the Treaty on the Functioning of the European Union.***
The General Affairs Council shall ensure consistency in the work of the different Council configurations. It shall prepare and ensure the follow-up to meetings of the European Council, in liaison with the President of the European Council and the Commission.
The Foreign Affairs Council shall elaborate the Union's external action on the basis of strategic guidelines laid down by the European Council and ensure that the Union's action is consistent.

7. **A Committee of Permanent Representatives of the Governments of the Member States shall be responsible for preparing the work of the Council.**

8. **The Council shall meet in public when it deliberates and votes on a draft legislative act. To this end, each Council meeting shall be divided into two parts, dealing respectively with deliberations on Union legislative acts and non-legislative activities.**

9. **The Presidency of Council configurations, other than that of Foreign Affairs, shall be held by Member State representatives in the Council on the basis of equal rotation, in accordance with the conditions established** ***in accordance with Article 236 of the Treaty on the Functioning of the European Union.*** *[BMDF Note: See also Declaration no. 9]*
[BMDF Note: Paragraphs 6-9 taken from Article I-24 'Configurations of the Council of Ministers' (new Article in 2004 IGC, except Paragraph 9 ex Article 203 TEC)]

ARTICLE *17* [9D] *['The European Commission and its President', Articles I-26 and I-27 (new Article in 2004 IGC)]*
1. The Commission shall promote the general interest of the Union and take appropriate initiatives to that end. It shall ensure the application of the ***Treaties,*** **and measures adopted by the institutions pursuant to** ***them.*** **It shall oversee the application of Union law under the control of the Court of Justice of the European Union. It shall execute the budget and manage programmes. It shall exercise co-ordinating, executive and management functions, as laid down in the** ***Treaties.***
With the exception of the common foreign and security policy, and other cases provided for in the ***Treaties,*** **it shall ensure the Union's external representation. It shall initiate the Union's annual and multiannual programming with a view to achieving inter-institutional agreements.**

2. Union legislative acts may be adopted only on the basis of a Commission proposal, except where the ***Treaties*** **provide otherwise. Other acts shall be adopted on the basis of a Commission proposal where the** ***Treaties*** **so provide.**

3. The Commission's term of office shall be five years.
The members of the Commission shall be chosen on the ground of their general competence and European commitment from persons whose independence is beyond doubt.
In carrying out its responsibilities, the Commission shall be completely independent. Without prejudice to Article 18(2), the members of the Commission shall neither seek nor take instructions from any government or other institution, body, office or entity. They shall refrain from any action incompatible with their duties or the performance of their tasks.

4. **The Commission appointed** ***between the date of entry into force of the Treaty of Lisbon and 31 October 2014*** **shall consist of one national of each Member State, including its President and the** ***High Representative of the Union for Foreign Affairs and Security Policy*** **who shall be one of its Vice-Presidents.**

5. **As from 1 November 2014, the Commission shall consist of a number of members, including its President and the** ***High Representative of the Union for Foreign Affairs and Security Policy,*** **corresponding to two thirds of the number of Member States, unless the European Council, acting unanimously, decides to alter this number.**
The members of the Commission shall be selected from among the nationals of the Member States on the basis of a system of equal rotation between the Member States. This system shall be

established unanimously by the European Council *in accordance with Article 244 of the Treaty on the Functioning of the European Union.*

6. **The President of the Commission shall:**
(a) lay down guidelines within which the Commission is to work;
(b) decide on the internal organisation of the Commission, ensuring that it acts consistently, efficiently and as a collegiate body;
(c) appoint Vice-Presidents, other than the *High Representative of the Union for Foreign Affairs and Security Policy*, from among the members of the Commission.
A member of the Commission shall resign if the President so requests.
The *High Representative of the Union for Foreign Affairs and Security Policy* shall resign, in accordance with the procedure set out in *Article 18(1)*, if the President so requests.

7. **Taking into account the elections to the European Parliament and after having held the appropriate consultations, the European Council, acting by a qualified majority, shall propose to the European Parliament a candidate for President of the Commission. This candidate shall be elected by the European Parliament by a majority of its component members. If he or she does not obtain the required majority, the European Council, acting by a qualified majority, shall within one month propose a new candidate who shall be elected by the European Parliament following the same procedure.**
The Council, by common accord with the President-elect, shall adopt the list of the other persons whom it proposes for appointment as members of the Commission. They shall be selected, on the basis of the suggestions made by Member States, in accordance with the criteria set out in *paragraph 3*, second subparagraph *and paragraph 5, second paragraph.*
The President, the *High Representative of the Union for Foreign Affairs and Security Policy* and the other members of the Commission shall be subject as a body to a vote of consent by the European Parliament. On the basis of this consent the Commission shall be appointed by the European Council, acting by a qualified majority.

8. The Commission, as a body, shall be responsible to the European Parliament. In accordance with *Article 234 of the Treaty on the Functioning of the European Union*, the European Parliament may vote on a censure motion on the Commission. If such a motion is carried, the members of the Commission shall resign as a body and the *High Representative of the Union for Foreign Affairs and Security Policy* shall resign from the duties that he carries out in the Commission.
[BMDF Notes: See also Declarations nos.6, 10 and 11. Paragraphs 1-5 and 8 taken from 2004 IGC - Article I-26 'The European Commission' (new Article in 2004 IGC); Paragraph 6 taken from 2004 IGC - Article I-27, paragraphs 1 and 2 'The President of the European Commission' (new Article in 2004 IGC);
Paragraph 7 taken from 2004 IGC - Article I-27, paragraph 3 'The President of the European Commission' (new Article in 2004 IGC)]

ARTICLE *18* [9E] *['The High Representative of the Union for Foreign Affairs and Security Policy', Article I-28 'The Union Minister for Foreign Affairs' (new Article in 2004 IGC)]*
1. The European Council, acting by a qualified majority, with the agreement of the President of the Commission, shall appoint the *High Representative of the Union for Foreign Affairs and Security Policy*. The European Council may end his term of office by the same procedure.

2. The *High Representative* shall conduct the Union's common foreign and security policy. He shall contribute by his proposals to the development of that policy, which he shall carry out as mandated by the Council. The same shall apply to the common security and defence policy.

3. The *High Representative* shall preside over the Foreign Affairs Council.

4. The *High Representative* shall be one of the Vice-Presidents of the Commission. He shall ensure the consistency of the Union's external action. He shall be responsible within the Commission for responsibilities incumbent on it in external relations and for co-ordinating other aspects of the Union's external action. In exercising these responsibilities within the Commission, and only for these responsibilities, the *High Representative* shall be bound by Commission procedures to the extent that this is consistent with paragraphs 2 and 3.
[BMDF Note: See also Declarations nos. 6, 12, 13 and 14]

ARTICLE *19* [9F] *['The Court of Justice of the European Union', Article I-29 (ex Articles 220, 221, 222 and 234 TEC)]*

1. The Court of Justice of the European Union shall include the Court of Justice, the General Court and specialised courts. It shall ensure that in the interpretation and application of the *Treaties* the law is observed.

Member States shall provide remedies sufficient to ensure effective legal protection in the fields covered by Union law.

2. The Court of Justice shall consist of one judge from each Member State. It shall be assisted by Advocates-General.

The General Court shall include at least one judge per Member State.

The judges and the Advocates-General of the Court of Justice and the judges of the General Court shall be chosen from persons whose independence is beyond doubt and who satisfy the conditions set out in *Articles 253 and 254 of the Treaty on the Functioning of the European Union.* They shall be appointed by common accord of the governments of the Member States for six years. Retiring judges and Advocates-General may be reappointed.

3. The Court of Justice of the European Union shall in accordance with *the Treaties*:

(a) rule on actions brought by a Member State, an institution or a natural or legal person;

(b) give preliminary rulings, at the request of courts or tribunals of the Member States, on the interpretation of Union law or the validity of acts adopted by the institutions;

(c) rule in other cases provided for in the *Treaties.*

TITLE IV

PROVISIONS ON ENHANCED CO-OPERATION

[BMDF Note: Articles 43 to 45 TEC are replaced by new Article 20]

ARTICLE *20* [10] *['Enhanced co-operation', Article I-44 (ex Article 11 TEC and Articles 43 - 45 TEU)]*

1. Member States which wish to establish enhanced co-operation between themselves within the framework of the Union's non-exclusive competences may make use of its institutions and exercise those competences by applying the relevant provisions of the *Treaty,* subject to the limits and in accordance with the *detailed arrangements* laid down in this Article and in *Articles 326 to 334 of the Treaty on the Functioning of the European Union.*

Enhanced co-operation shall aim to further the objectives of the Union, protect its interests and reinforce its integration process. Such co-operation shall be open at any time to all Member States, in accordance with *Article 328 of the Treaty on the Functioning of the European Union.*

2. The decision authorising enhanced co-operation shall be adopted by the Council as a last resort, when it has established that the objectives of such co-operation cannot be attained within a reasonable period by the Union as a whole, and provided that at least *nine* of the Member States participate in it. The Council shall act in accordance with the procedure laid down in *Article 328 of the Treaty on the Functioning of the European Union.*

3. All members of the Council may participate in its deliberations, but only members of the Council representing the Member States participating in enhanced co-operation shall take part in the vote. *The voting rules are set out in Article 330 of the Treaty on the Functioning of the European Union.*

4. Acts adopted in the framework of enhanced co-operation shall bind only participating Member States. They shall not be regarded as part of the *acquis* which has to be accepted by candidate States for accession to the Union.

TITLE V

GENERAL PROVISIONS ON THE UNION'S EXTERNAL ACTION AND SPECIFIC PROVISIONS ON THE COMMON FOREIGN AND SECURITY POLICY

CHAPTER 1

GENERAL PROVISIONS ON THE UNION'S EXTERNAL ACTION

ARTICLE *21* [10A] *[Article III-292 (Article 3, second paragraph, TEU and ex Article 11 TEU)]*

1. The Union's action on the international scene shall be guided by the principles which have inspired its own creation, development and enlargement, and which it seeks to advance in the wider world: democracy, the rule of law, the universality and indivisibility of human rights and fundamental freedoms, respect for human dignity, the principles of equality and solidarity, and respect for the principles of the United Nations Charter and international law.

The Union shall seek to develop relations and build partnerships with third countries, and international, regional or global organisations which share the principles referred to in the first subparagraph. It shall promote multilateral solutions to common problems, in particular in the framework of the United Nations.

2. The Union shall define and pursue common policies and actions, and shall work for a high degree of co-operation in all fields of international relations, in order to:

(a) safeguard its values, fundamental interests, security, independence and integrity;

(b) consolidate and support democracy, the rule of law, human rights and the principles of international law;

(c) preserve peace, prevent conflicts and strengthen international security, in accordance with the purposes and principles of the United Nations Charter, with the principles of the Helsinki Final Act and with the aims of the Charter of Paris, including those relating to external borders;

(d) foster the sustainable economic, social and environmental development of developing countries, with the primary aim of eradicating poverty;

(e) encourage the integration of all countries into the world economy, including through the progressive abolition of restrictions on international trade;

(f) help develop international measures to preserve and improve the quality of the environment and the sustainable management of global natural resources, in order to ensure sustainable development;

(g) assist populations, countries and regions confronting natural or man-made disasters;

(h) promote an international system based on stronger multilateral co-operation and good global governance.

3. The Union shall respect the principles and pursue the objectives set out in paragraphs 1 and 2 in the development and implementation of the different areas of the Union's external action covered by this Title *and Part Five of the Treaty on the Functioning of the European Union,* and the external aspects of its other policies.

The Union shall ensure consistency between the different areas of its external action and between these and its other policies. The Council and the Commission, assisted by the *High Representative of the Union for Foreign Affairs and Security Policy*, shall ensure that consistency and shall co-operate to that effect.

ARTICLE *22* [10B] *[Article III-293 (new Article in 2004 IGC)]*

1. On the basis of the principles and objectives set out in *Article 21*, the European Council shall identify the strategic interests and objectives of the Union.

***D*ecisions of the European Council on the strategic interests and objectives of the Union shall relate to the common foreign and security policy and to other areas of the external action of the Union. Such decisions may concern the relations of the Union with a specific country or region or may be thematic in approach. They shall define their duration, and the means to be made available by the Union and the Member States.**

The European Council shall act unanimously on a recommendation from the Council, adopted by the latter under the arrangements laid down for each area. *D*ecisions of the European Council shall be implemented in accordance with the procedures provided for in the *Treaties*.

2. The *High Representative of the Union for Foreign Affairs and Security Policy*, for the area of common foreign and security policy, and the Commission, for other areas of external action, may submit joint proposals to the Council.

CHAPTER 2

SPECIFIC PROVISIONS OF THE COMMON FOREIGN AND SECURITY POLICY

SECTION 1

COMMON PROVISIONS

ARTICLE 23 [10C] *[New Article in Treaty of Lisbon]*
The Union's action on the international scene, pursuant to this Chapter, shall be guided by the principles, shall pursue the objectives of, and be conducted in accordance with, the general provisions laid down in Chapter 1.

ARTICLE ***24*** [11] *[Article I-16 and Article III-294 paragraphs 1 and 2 (ex Articles 11 and 12 TEU)]*
1. **The Union's competence in matters of common foreign and security policy shall cover all areas of foreign policy and all questions relating to the Union's security, including the progressive framing of a common defence policy that might lead to a common defence.** *[Article I-16(1)]*
The common foreign and security policy is subject to specific procedures. It shall be defined and implemented by the European Council and the Council acting unanimously, except where the Treaties provide otherwise. The adoption of legislative acts shall be excluded. The common foreign and security policy shall be put into effect by the High Representative of the Union for Foreign Affairs and Security Policy and by Member States, in accordance with the Treaties. The specific role of the European Parliament and of the Commission in this area is defined by the Treaties. The Court of Justice of the European Union shall not have jurisdiction with respect to these provisions, with the exception of its jurisdiction to monitor the compliance with Article 40 of this Treaty and to review the legality of certain decisions as provided for by Article 275 of the Treaty on the Functioning of the European Union.

2. ***Within the framework* of the principles and objectives of its external action, the Union shall *conduct,* define and implement a common foreign and security policy, *based on the development of mutual political solidarity among Member States, the identification of questions of general interest and the achievement of an ever-increasing degree of convergence of Member States' actions.*** *[Article III-294(1)] [BMDF Note: This paragraph added after the 2007 Mandate.]*

3. The Member States shall support the common foreign and security policy actively and unreservedly in a spirit of loyalty and mutual solidarity **and shall comply with the Union's actions in this area.**
The Member States shall work together to enhance and develop their mutual political solidarity. They shall refrain from any action which is contrary to the interests of the Union or likely to impair its effectiveness as a cohesive force in international relations.
The Council **and the *High Representative*** shall ensure ***compliance with*** these principles.
[BMDF Note: See also Declarations nos. 13 and 14]

ARTICLE ***25*** [12] *[Article III-294 paragraph 3 (ex Articles 11 and 12 TEU)]*
The Union shall conduct the common foreign and security policy by:
(a) defining the general guidelines;
(b) adopting decisions defining:
- **(i) actions to be undertaken by the Union;**
- **(ii) positions to be taken by the Union;**
- **(iii) arrangements for the implementation of the decisions referred to in points (i) and (ii);**

and by

(c) strengthening systematic co-operation between Member States in the conduct of policy.

ARTICLE *26* [13] *[Article III-295 (ex Article 13 TEU)]*
1. The European Council shall ***identify the Union's strategic interests, determine the objectives of and define*** general guidelines for the common foreign and security policy, including for matters with defence implications. ***It shall adopt the necessary decisions.***
If international developments so require, the President of the European Council shall convene an extraordinary meeting of the European Council in order to define the strategic lines of the Union's policy in the face of such developments.
[BMDF Note: Sub-paragraph taken from 2004 IGC – Article III-295 paragraph 1 (ex Article 13 TEU)]

2. ***The Council shall frame the common foreign and security policy and take the decisions*** **necessary for defining and implementing *it* on the basis of the general guidelines and strategic lines defined by the European Council.**
The Council ***and the High Representative of the Union for Foreign Affairs and Security Policy*** shall ensure the unity, consistency and effectiveness of action by the Union.
[BMDF Note: Second sub-paragraph taken from 2004 IGC – Article III-295 paragraph 2 (ex Article 13 TEU)]

3. ***The common foreign and security policy shall be put into effect by the High Representative and by the Member States, using national and Union resources.***

ARTICLE *27* [13a] *[Article III-296 (new Article in 2004 IGC)]*
1. The *High Representative of the Union for Foreign Affairs and Security Policy*, who shall chair the Foreign Affairs Council, shall contribute through his proposals towards the preparation of the common foreign and security policy and shall ensure implementation of the decisions adopted by the European Council and the Council.

2. The *High Representative* shall represent the Union for matters relating to the common foreign and security policy. He shall conduct political dialogue with third parties on the Union's behalf and shall express the Union's position in international organisations and at international conferences.

3. In fulfilling his mandate, the *High Representative* shall be assisted by a European External Action Service. This service shall work in co-operation with the diplomatic services of the Member States and shall comprise officials from relevant departments of the General Secretariat of the Council and of the Commission as well as staff seconded from national diplomatic services of the Member States. The organisation and functioning of the European External Action Service shall be established by a decision of the Council. The Council shall act on a proposal from the *High Representative* after consulting the European Parliament and after obtaining the consent of the Commission.
[BMDF Note: See also Declaration no. 15]

ARTICLE *28* [14] *[Article III-297 (ex Article 14 TEU)]*
1. **Where the international situation requires operational action by the Union, the Council shall adopt the necessary decisions.** They shall lay down their objectives, scope, the means to be made available to the Union, if necessary their duration, and the conditions for their implementation.
If there is a change in circumstances having a substantial effect on a question subject to **such a decision**, the Council shall review the principles and objectives of that **decision** and take the necessary decisions.

2. ***D*ecisions referred to in paragraph 1** shall commit the Member States in the positions they adopt and in the conduct of their activity.

3. Whenever there is any plan to adopt a national position or take national action pursuant to a **decision as referred to in paragraph 1**, information shall be provided **by the Member State concerned** in time to allow, if necessary, for prior consultations within the Council. The obligation to provide prior information shall not apply to measures which are merely a national transposition of Council decisions.

4. In cases of imperative need arising from changes in the situation and failing a **review of the** Council decision ***as referred to in paragraph 1***, Member States may take the necessary measures as a matter of urgency having regard to the general objectives of **that decision**. The Member State concerned shall inform the Council immediately of any such measures.

5. Should there be any major difficulties in implementing a **decision as referred to in this Article**, a Member State shall refer them to the Council which shall discuss them and seek appropriate solutions. Such solutions shall not run counter to the objectives of the ***decision as referred to in paragraph 1*** or impair its effectiveness.

ARTICLE ***29*** [15] *[Article III-298 (ex Article 15 TEU)]*
The Council shall adopt **decisions which** shall define the approach of the Union to a particular matter of a geographical or thematic nature. Member States shall ensure that their national policies conform to the ***Union*** positions.

ARTICLE ***30*** [15a] *[Article III-299 (ex Article 22 TEU)]*
1. Any Member State**, the *High Representative of the Union for Foreign Affairs and Security Policy*, or *the High Representative* with the Commission's support, may refer any question relating to the common foreign and security policy** to the Council and may submit **to it initiatives or proposals as appropriate**.

2. In cases requiring a rapid decision, the ***High Representative***, of ***his*** own motion, or at the request of a Member State, shall convene an extraordinary Council meeting within forty-eight hours or, in an emergency, within a shorter period.

ARTICLE ***31*** [15b] *[Article III-300 (ex Article 23 TEU)]*
1. Decisions under this ***Chapter*** shall be taken by the ***European Council and the*** Council acting unanimously***, except where this Chapter provides otherwise. The adoption of legislative acts shall be excluded.***
When abstaining in a vote, any member of the Council may qualify its abstention by making a formal declaration under the present sub-paragraph. In that case, it shall not be obliged to apply the decision, but shall accept that the decision commits the Union. In a spirit of mutual solidarity, the Member State concerned shall refrain from any action likely to conflict with or impede Union action based on that decision and the other Member States shall respect its position. If the members of the Council qualifying their abstention in this way represent ***at*** **least** one-third **of the Member States comprising at least one-third of the population of the Union,** the decision shall not be adopted.

2. By derogation from the provisions of paragraph 1, the Council shall act by qualified majority:
- **when adopting *a* decision defining a Union action or position on the basis of a decision of the European Council relating to the Union's strategic interests and objectives, as referred to in *Article 22(1)*;**
- **when adopting a decision defining a Union action or position, on a proposal which the *High Representative of the Union for Foreign Affairs and Security Policy* has presented following a specific request to him or her from the European Council, made on its own initiative or that of the *High Representative*;**
- when adopting any decision implementing a **decision defining a Union action or position;**
- when appointing a special representative in accordance with ***Article 33***.

If a member of the Council declares that, for **vital** and stated reasons of national policy, it intends to oppose the adoption of a decision to be taken by qualified majority, a vote shall not be taken. **The *High Representative* will, in close consultation with the Member State involved, search for a solution acceptable to it. If he or she does not succeed,** *t*he Council may, acting by a qualified majority, request that the matter be referred to the European Council for decision by unanimity.

3. The European Council may unanimously adopt a decision stipulating that the Council shall act by a qualified majority in cases other than those referred to in paragraph 2.

4. **Paragraphs 2 and 3** shall not apply to decisions having military or defence implications.

5. For procedural questions, the Council shall act by a majority of its members.

ARTICLE ***32*** [16] *[Article III-301 (new Article in 2004 IGC)]*
Member States shall consult one another within ***the European Council and*** the Council on any matter of foreign and security policy of general interest in order to ***determine a common approach***.

Before undertaking any action on the international scene or any commitment which could affect the Union's interests, each Member State shall consult the others within the European Council or the Council. Member States shall ensure, through the convergence of their actions, that the Union is able to assert its interests and values on the international scene. Member States shall show mutual solidarity.

When the European Council or the Council has defined a common approach of the Union within the meaning *of the first paragraph, the High Representative of the Union for Foreign Affairs and Security Policy* and the Ministers for Foreign Affairs of the Member States shall co-ordinate their activities within the Council.

The diplomatic missions of the Member States and the Union delegations in third countries and at international organisations shall co-operate and shall contribute to formulating and implementing the common approach.

[BMDF Note: Last two paragraphs taken from 2004 IGC - Article III-301 (new article in 2004 IGC)]

ARTICLE 17 (old numbering) *[BMDF Note: Article moved to Article 42 TEU]*
[BMDF Note: See also Protocol no. 29]

ARTICLE ***33*** [18] *[Article III-302 (ex Article 18(5) TEU)]*

The Council may, **on a proposal from the *High Representative of the Union for Foreign Affairs and Security Policy*,** appoint a special representative with a mandate in relation to particular policy issues. **The special representative shall carry out his mandate under the authority *of the High Representative.***

ARTICLE ***34*** [19] *[Article III-305(ex Article 19 TEU)]*

1. Member States shall co-ordinate their action in international organisations and at international conferences. They shall uphold the **Union's** positions in such fora. **The *High Representative of the Union for Foreign Affairs and Security Policy* shall organise this co-ordination.**

In international organisations and at international conferences where not all the Member States participate, those which do take part shall uphold the common positions.

2. **In accordance with *Article 24(3)*,** Member States represented in international organisations or international conferences where not all the Member States participate shall keep ***the other Member States and the High Representative***, informed of any matter of common interest.

Member States which are also members of the United Nations Security Council will concert and keep the other Member States **and the *High Representative*** fully informed. Member States which are members of the Security Council will, in the execution of their functions, **defend** the positions and the interests of the Union, without prejudice to their responsibilities under the provisions of the United Nations Charter.

When the Union has defined a position on a subject which is on the United Nations Security Council agenda, those Member States which sit on the Security Council shall request that the *High Representative* be *invited* to present the Union's position.

ARTICLE ***35*** [20] *[Article III-306 (ex Article 20 TEU)]*

The diplomatic and consular missions of the Member States and the **Union** delegations in third countries and international conferences, and their representations to international organisations, shall co-operate in ensuring that **decisions defining Union positions and actions adopted pursuant to this Chapter** are complied with and implemented.

They shall step up co-operation by exchanging information **and** carrying out joint assessments.

They shall contribute to the implementation of the right of European citizens to protection in the territory of third countries as referred to in *Article 20(2)(c) of the Treaty on the Functioning of the European Union* and the measures adopted pursuant to *Article 23 of that Treaty.*

ARTICLE ***36*** [21] *[Article III-304 (ex Article 21 TEU)]*

The ***High Representative of the Union for Foreign Affairs and Security Policy*** shall ***regularly*** consult the European Parliament on the main aspects and the basic choices of the common foreign and security policy ***and the common security and defence policy and inform it of how those policies evolve. He*** shall ensure that the views of the European Parliament are duly taken into consideration. **Special representatives may be involved in briefing the European Parliament.**

The European Parliament may ask questions of the Council or make recommendations to it ***and to the High Representative.*** **Twice a year it shall hold a** debate on progress in implementing the common foreign and security policy, **including the common security and defence policy.**

[BMDF Note: Articles 22 and 23 TEU (old numbering) moved to Articles 30 and 31 above]

ARTICLE *37* [24] *[Article III-303 (ex Article 24 TEU and Article 300 TEC)]*
The Union may conclude agreements with one or more States or international organisations in areas covered by this Chapter.

ARTICLE *38* [25] *[Article III-307 (ex Article 25 TEU)]*
Without prejudice to ***Article 240*** of the Treaty ***on the Functioning of the European Union***, a Political and Security Committee shall monitor the international situation in the areas covered by common foreign and security policy and contribute to the definition of policies by delivering opinions to the Council at the request of the Council **or of the *High Representative of the Union for Foreign Affairs and Security Policy*** or on its own initiative. It shall also monitor the implementation of agreed policies, without prejudice to the **powers of the *High Representative***.
Within the scope of this **Chapter**, **the Political and Security** Committee shall exercise, under the responsibility of the Council **and of the *High Representative*, the** political control and strategic direction of **the** crisis management operations **referred to in *Article 43***.
The Council may authorise the Committee, for the purpose and for the duration of a crisis management operation, as determined by the Council, to take the relevant decisions concerning the political control and strategic direction of the operation.

ARTICLE 39 [25a] *[Article I-51(2) Protection of personal data (ex Article 286 TEC, paragraph 1)]*
***In accordance with Article 16 of the Treaty on the Functioning of the European Union and by way of derogation from paragraph 2 thereof, the Council* shall lay down the rules relating to the protection of individuals with regard to the processing of personal data by the Member States when carrying out activities which fall within the scope of *this Chapter,* and the rules relating to the free movement of such data. Compliance with these rules shall be subject to the control of independent authorities.**

ARTICLE 40 [25b] *[Article III-308 (ex Articles 46(f) and 47 TEU)]*
The implementation of the common foreign and security policy shall not affect the application of the procedures and the extent of the powers of the institutions laid down by the *Treaties* for the exercise of the Union competences referred to in Articles *3 to 6 of the Treaty on the Functioning of the European Union.*
Similarly, the implementation of the policies listed in those Articles shall not affect the application of the procedures and the extent of the powers of the institutions laid down by the *Treaties* for the exercise of the Union competences under this Chapter.
[BMDF Note: Court of Justice has jurisdiction on this Article under Article 275 TFEU]

[BMDF Note: Articles 26 and 27 TEU (old numbering) shall be repealed]

[BMDF Note: Articles 27a to 27e TEU (renumbered 27 A to 27 E by the Treaty of Lisbon) are replaced by new Article 20, shown above in Title VII on 'Enhanced Co-operation'.]

ARTICLE *41* [28] *[Article III-313 (ex Article 28 TEU)]*
1. Administrative expenditure **to which the implementation of this Chapter gives rise** for the institutions shall be charged to the **Union budget**.

2. Operational expenditure to which the implementation of **this Chapter** gives rise shall also be charged to the **Union budget**, except for such expenditure arising from operations having military or defence implications and cases where the Council acting unanimously decides otherwise.
In cases where expenditure is not charged to the **Union budget** it shall be charged to the Member States in accordance with the gross national product scale, unless the Council acting unanimously decides otherwise. As for expenditure arising from operations having military or defence implications, Member States whose representatives in the Council have made a formal declaration under ***Article 31(1)***, second sub-paragraph, shall not be obliged to contribute to the financing thereof.

3. The Council shall adopt a decision establishing the specific procedures for guaranteeing rapid access to appropriations in the Union budget for urgent financing of initiatives in the framework of the common foreign and security policy, and in particular for preparatory activities for the tasks referred to in *Article 42(1)* and *Article 43*. It shall act after consulting the European Parliament.

Preparatory activities for the tasks referred to in *Article 42(1)* and *Article 43* which are not charged to the Union budget shall be financed by a start-up fund made up of Member States' contributions.
The Council shall adopt by a qualified majority, on a proposal from the *High Representative of the Union for Foreign Affairs and Security Policy*, decisions establishing:
(a) the procedures for setting up and financing the start-up fund, in particular the amounts allocated to the fund;
(b) the procedures for administering the start-up fund;
(c) the financial control procedures.
When the task planned in accordance with *Article 42(1)* and *Article 43* cannot be charged to the Union budget, the Council shall authorise the *High Representative* to use the fund. The *High Representative* shall report to the Council on the implementation of this remit.

SECTION 2

PROVISIONS ON THE COMMON SECURITY AND DEFENCE POLICY

ARTICLE *42* [28A] *[Article I-41 (new Article in 2004 IGC)]*
1. The common security and defence policy shall be an integral part of the common foreign and security policy. It shall provide the Union with an operational capacity drawing on civil and military assets. The Union may use them on missions outside the Union for peace-keeping, conflict prevention and strengthening international security in accordance with the principles of the United Nations Charter. The performance of these tasks shall be undertaken using capabilities provided by the Member States.

2. The common foreign and security policy shall include **the progressive framing of a common Union defence policy. This will** lead to a common defence, **when** the European Council, **acting unanimously,** so decides. It shall in that case recommend to the Member States the adoption of such a decision in accordance with their respective constitutional requirements.
The policy of the Union in accordance with this ***Section*** shall not prejudice the specific character of the security and defence policy of certain Member States and shall respect the obligations of certain Member States, which see their common defence realised in the North Atlantic Treaty Organisation (NATO), under the North Atlantic Treaty and be compatible with the common security and defence policy established within that framework.

3. Member States shall make civilian and military capabilities available to the Union for the implementation of the common security and defence policy, to contribute to the objectives defined by the Council. Those Member States which together establish multinational forces may also make them available to the common security and defence policy.
Member States shall undertake progressively to improve their military capabilities. The Agency in the field of defence capabilities development, research, acquisition and armaments (*hereinafter referred to as "the* European Defence Agency") shall identify operational requirements, *shall* promote measures to satisfy those requirements, *shall* contribute to identifying and, where appropriate, implementing any measure needed to strengthen the industrial and technological base of the defence sector, *shall* participate in defining a European capabilities and armaments policy, and *shall* assist the Council in evaluating the improvement of military capabilities.

4. *D*ecisions relating to the common security and defence policy, including those initiating a mission as referred to in this Article, shall be adopted by the Council acting unanimously on a proposal from the *High Representative of the Union for Foreign Affairs and Security Policy* or an initiative from a Member State. The *High Representative* may propose the use of both national resources and Union instruments, together with the Commission where appropriate.

5. The Council may entrust the execution of a task, within the Union framework, to a group of Member States in order to protect the Union's values and serve its interests. The execution of such a task shall be governed by *Article 44.*

6. Those Member States whose military capabilities fulfil higher criteria and which have made more binding commitments to one another in this area with a view to the most demanding missions shall establish permanent structured co-operation within the Union framework. Such co-operation shall be governed by *Article 46*. It shall not affect the provisions of *Article 43*.

7. If a Member State is the victim of armed aggression on its territory, the other Member States shall have towards it an obligation of aid and assistance by all the means in their power, in accordance with Article 51 of the United Nations Charter. This shall not prejudice the specific character of the security and defence policy of certain Member States.
Commitments and co-operation in this area shall be consistent with commitments under the North Atlantic Treaty Organisation, which, for those States which are members of it, remains the foundation of their collective defence and the forum for its implementation.
[BMDF Note: See also Protocols nos. 4 and 29]

ARTICLE *43* [28B] *[Article III-309 (ex Article 17(2) TEU)]*
1. The tasks referred to in *Article 42(1)*, in the course of which the Union may use civilian and military means, shall include joint disarmament operations, humanitarian and rescue tasks, military advice and assistance tasks, conflict prevention and peace-keeping tasks, tasks of combat forces in crisis management, including peace-making and post-conflict stabilisation. All these tasks may contribute to the fight against terrorism, including by supporting third countries in combating terrorism in their territories.

2. The Council shall adopt decisions relating to the tasks referred to in paragraph 1, defining their objectives and scope and the general conditions for their implementation. The *High Representative of the Union for Foreign Affairs and Security Policy*, acting under the authority of the Council and in close and constant contact with the Political and Security Committee, shall ensure co-ordination of the civilian and military aspects of such tasks.

ARTICLE *44* [28C] *[Article III-310 (new Article in 2004 IGC)]*
1. Within the framework of the decisions adopted in accordance with *Article 43*, the Council may entrust the implementation of a task to a group of Member States which are willing and have the necessary capability for such a task. Those Member States, in association with the *High Representative of the Union for Foreign Affairs and Security Policy*, shall agree among themselves on the management of the task.

2. Member States participating in the task shall keep the Council regularly informed of its progress on their own initiative or at the request of another Member State. Those States shall inform the Council immediately should the completion of the task entail major consequences or require amendment of the objective, scope and conditions determined for the task in the decisions referred to in paragraph 1. In such cases, the Council shall adopt the necessary decisions.

ARTICLE *45* [28D] *[Article III-311 (new Article in 2004 IGC)]*
1. *The European Defence Agency referred to in Article 42(3)* subject to the authority of the Council, shall have as its task to:
(a) contribute to identifying the Member States' military capability objectives and evaluating observance of the capability commitments given by the Member States;
(b) promote harmonisation of operational needs and adoption of effective, compatible procurement methods;
(c) propose multilateral projects to fulfil the objectives in terms of military capabilities, ensure co-ordination of the programmes implemented by the Member States and management of specific co-operation programmes;
(d) support defence technology research, and co-ordinate and plan joint research activities and the study of technical solutions meeting future operational needs;
(e) contribute to identifying and, if necessary, implementing any useful measure for strengthening the industrial and technological base of the defence sector and for improving the effectiveness of military expenditure.

2. The European Defence Agency shall be open to all Member States wishing to be part of it. The Council, acting by a qualified majority, shall adopt a decision defining the Agency's statute, seat and operational rules. That decision should take account of the level of effective participation in the Agency's activities. Specific groups shall be set up within the Agency bringing together

Member States engaged in joint projects. The Agency shall carry out its tasks in liaison with the Commission where necessary.

ARTICLE *46* [28E] *[Article III-312 (new Article in 2004 IGC)]*

1. Those Member States which wish to participate in the permanent structured co-operation referred to in *Article 42(6)*, which fulfil the criteria and have made the commitments on military capabilities set out in the Protocol on permanent structured co-operation shall notify their intention to the Council and to the *High Representative of the Union for Foreign Affairs and Security Policy.*

2. Within three months following the notification referred to in paragraph 1 the Council shall adopt a decision establishing permanent structured co-operation and determining the list of participating Member States. The Council shall act by a qualified majority after consulting the *High Representative.*

3. Any Member State which, at a later stage, wishes to participate in the permanent structured co-operation shall notify its intention to the Council and to the *High Representative.*
The Council shall adopt a decision confirming the participation of the Member State concerned which fulfils the criteria and makes the commitments referred to in Articles 1 and 2 of the Protocol on permanent structured co-operation. The Council shall act by a qualified majority after consulting the *High Representative.* Only members of the Council representing the participating Member States shall take part in the vote.
A qualified majority shall be defined in accordance with Article 238(3)(a) of the Treaty on the Functioning of the European Union.

4. If a participating Member State no longer fulfils the criteria or is no longer able to meet the commitments referred to in Articles 1 and 2 of the Protocol on permanent structured co-operation, the Council may adopt a decision suspending the participation of the Member State concerned.
The Council shall act by a qualified majority. Only members of the Council representing the participating Member States, with the exception of the Member State in question, shall take part in the vote.
A qualified majority shall be defined in accordance with Article 238(3)(a) of the Treaty on the Functioning of the European Union.

5. Any participating Member State which wishes to withdraw from permanent structured co-operation shall notify its intention to the Council, which shall take note that the Member State in question has ceased to participate.

6. The decisions and recommendations of the Council within the framework of permanent structured co-operation, other than those provided for in paragraphs 2 to 5, shall be adopted by unanimity. For the purposes of this paragraph, unanimity shall be constituted by the votes of the representatives of the participating Member States only.

*[BMDF Note: The provisions of **Title VI, Police and Judicial Co-operation in Criminal Matters** (Articles 29 to 39 TEU), shall be replaced by Articles 67 to 76 and Articles 82 to 89 [Articles III-257 to III-264 and III-270 to III-277] of the Treaty on the Functioning of the European Union, under the Title on the Area of Freedom, Security and Justice, i.e. Chapters 1, 4 and 5 of Title IV of Part Three.]*

[BMDF Note: Articles 40 to 40b (renumbered 40 to 40B by the Treaty of Lisbon) of Title VI of the Treaty on European Union relating to enhanced co-operation, shall be replaced by Article 20 TEU [Article I-44] in Title VII shown above.]

[BMDF Note: Articles 41 and 42 TEU (old numbering) shall be repealed]

[*BMDF Note: **Title VII, 'Provisions on Enhanced Co-operation'**, is moved to Title IV and Articles 43 to 45 TEU (old numbering) are replaced by Article 20 TEU, shown above*]

TITLE VI

FINAL PROVISIONS

***ARTICLE** 47* [46a] *['Legal personality', Article I-7 (new Article in 2004 IGC)]*
The Union shall have legal personality.
[BMDF Note: See also Declaration no. 24]

[BMDF Note: Article 46 TEU shall be repealed; paragraph (e) moved to Article 269 TFEU]

[BMDF Note: Article 47 TEU replaced by new Article 40 in Title V]

[BMDF Note: Article 48 is amended by the Treaty of Lisbon to draw together the procedures for revising the Treaties, including the ability to increase or reduce the competences conferred upon the Union. The three relevant articles from the 2004 IGC are Articles III-443, III-444 and III-445. These articles will be combined to form the replacement article to Article 48 TEU.]

ARTICLE *48* [48] *['Treaty revision procedures', Articles IV-443, IV-444 and IV-445 (ex-Article 48 TEU and new Article in 2004 IGC)]*
1. ***The Treaties may be amended in accordance with an ordinary revision procedure. They may also be amended in accordance with simplified revision procedures.***

Ordinary revision procedure

2. The government of any Member State, the European Parliament or the Commission may submit to the Council proposals for the amendment of *the Treaties. These proposals may, inter alia, serve either to increase or to reduce the competences conferred on the Union in the Treaties.* These proposals shall be submitted to the European Council by the Council and the national Parliaments shall be notified.

3. If the European Council, after consulting the European Parliament and the Commission, adopts by a simple majority a decision in favour of examining the proposed amendments, the President of the European Council shall convene a Convention composed of representatives of the national Parliaments, of the Heads of State or Government of the Member States, of the European Parliament and of the Commission. The European Central Bank shall also be consulted in the case of institutional changes in the monetary area. The Convention shall examine the proposals for amendments and shall adopt by consensus a recommendation to a conference of representatives of the governments of the Member States as provided for in paragraph 4.
The European Council may decide by a simple majority, after obtaining the consent of the European Parliament, not to convene a Convention should this not be justified by the extent of the proposed amendments. In the latter case, the European Council shall define the terms of reference for a conference of representatives of the governments of the Member States.

4. A conference of representatives of the governments of the Member States shall be convened by the President of the Council for the purpose of determining by common accord the amendments to be made to *the Treaties.*
The amendments shall enter into force after being ratified by all the Member States in accordance with their respective constitutional requirements.

5. If, two years after the signature of *a* treaty amending *the Treaties*, four fifths of the Member States have ratified it and one or more Member States have encountered difficulties in proceeding with ratification, the matter shall be referred to the European Council.
[BMDF Note: Article from 2004 IGC - Article IV-443 'Ordinary revision procedure' (ex-Article 48 TEU)]

Simplified revision procedures

6. The Government of any Member State, the European Parliament or the Commission may submit to the European Council proposals for revising all or part of the provisions of Part Three

***of the Treaty on the Functioning of the European Union relating to* the internal policies and action of the Union.**
The European Council may adopt a decision amending all or part of the provisions of Part Three *of the Treaty on the Functioning of the European Union.* The European Council shall act by unanimity after consulting the European Parliament and the Commission, and the European Central Bank in the case of institutional changes in the monetary area. *That* decision shall not *enter* into force until it is approved by the Member States in accordance with their respective constitutional requirements.
The decision referred to in *the second subparagraph* shall not increase the competences conferred on the Union in *the Treaties.*
[BMDF Note: Article from 2004 IGC - Article IV-445 'Simplified revision procedure concerning internal Union policies and action' (new Article in 2004 IGC)]

***7. Where the Treaty on the Functioning of the European Union or Title V of this Treaty* provides for the Council to act by unanimity in a given area or case, the European Council may adopt a decision authorising the Council to act by a qualified majority in that area or in that case. This *sub*paragraph shall not apply to decisions with military implications or those in the area of defence.**
***Where the Treaty on the Functioning of the European Union* provides for *legislative acts* to be adopted by the Council in accordance with a special legislative procedure, the European Council may adopt a decision allowing for the adoption of such *acts* in accordance with the ordinary legislative procedure.**
Any initiative taken by the European Council on the basis of *the first or second subparagraph* shall be notified to the national Parliaments. If a national Parliament makes known its opposition within six months of the date of such notification, the decision referred to in *the first or second subparagraph* shall not be adopted. In the absence of opposition, the European Council may adopt the decision.
For the adoption of the decisions referred to in *the first or second subparagraphs*, the European Council shall act by unanimity after obtaining the consent of the European Parliament, which shall be given by a majority of its component members.
[BMDF Note: Article from 2004 IGC - Article IV-444 'Simplified revision procedure' (new Article in 2004 IGC)]

ARTICLE ***49*** [49] *['Conditions of eligibility and procedure for accession to the Union', Article I-58(2) (ex Article 49 TEU)]*
Any European State which respects the ***values referred to*** in ***Article 2 and is committed to promoting them*** may apply to become a member of the Union. ***The European Parliament and national Parliaments shall be notified of this application. The applicant State*** shall address its application to the Council, which shall act unanimously after consulting the Commission and after receiving the ***consent*** of the European Parliament, which shall act by an majority of its component members. ***The conditions of eligibility agreed upon by the European Council shall be taken into account.***
[BMDF Note: Sub-paragraph from 2004 IGC - Article I-58(2) Conditions of eligibility and procedure for accession to the Union (ex Article 49 TEU)]
The conditions of admission and the adjustments to the Treaties on which the Union is founded which such admission entails shall be the subject of an agreement between the Member States and the applicant State. This agreement shall be submitted for ratification by all the contracting States in accordance with their respective constitutional requirements.

ARTICLE *50* [49A] *['Voluntary withdrawal from the Union', Article I-60 (new Article in 2004 IGC)]*
1. Any Member State may decide to withdraw from the Union in accordance with its own constitutional requirements.

2. A Member State which decides to withdraw shall notify the European Council of its intention. In the light of the guidelines provided by the European Council, the Union shall negotiate and conclude an agreement with that State, setting out the arrangements for its withdrawal, taking account of the framework for its future relationship with the Union. That agreement shall be negotiated in accordance with *Article 218(3) of the Treaty on the Functioning of the European Union.* It shall be concluded by the Council, acting by a qualified majority, after obtaining the consent of the European Parliament.

3. The *Treaties* shall cease to apply to the State in question from the date of entry into force of the withdrawal agreement or, failing that, two years after the notification referred to in paragraph 2, unless the European Council, in agreement with the Member State concerned, unanimously decides to extend this period.

4. For the purposes of paragraphs 2 and 3, the member of the European Council or of the Council representing the withdrawing Member State shall not participate in the discussions of the European Council or Council or in decisions concerning it.
A qualified majority shall be defined in accordance with Article 238(3)(b) of the Treaty on the Functioning of the European Union.

5. If a State which has withdrawn from the Union asks to rejoin, its request shall be subject to the procedure referred to in *Article 49.*

ARTICLE 51 [49B] *['Protocols and Annexes', Article IV-442 (ex Article 311 TEC)]*
The Protocols and Annexes to the Treaties shall form an integral part thereof.

ARTICLE 52 [49C] *['Territorial scope', Article IV-440, paragraph 1, 'Scope' (ex Article 299 TEC)]*
1. The Treaties shall apply to the Kingdom of Belgium, *Republic of Bulgaria*, the Czech Republic, the Kingdom of Denmark, the Federal Republic of Germany, the Republic of Estonia, the Hellenic Republic, the Kingdom of Spain, the French Republic, Ireland, the Italian Republic, the Republic of Cyprus, the Republic of Latvia, the Republic of Lithuania, the Grand Duchy of Luxembourg, the Republic of Hungary, the Republic of Malta, the Kingdom of the Netherlands, the Republic of Austria, the Republic of Poland, the Portuguese Republic, *Romania*, the Republic of Slovenia, the Slovak Republic, the Republic of Finland, the Kingdom of Sweden and the United Kingdom of Great Britain and Northern Ireland.

2. ***The territorial scope of the Treaties is specified in Article 355 of the Treaty on the Functioning of the European Union.***

[BMDF Note: Article 50 TEU shall be repealed]

ARTICLE ***53*** [51] *['Duration', Article IV-446 (ex Articles 51 TEU and 312 TEC)]*
This Treaty is concluded for an unlimited period.

ARTICLE ***54*** [52] *['Ratification and entry into force', Article IV-447 (ex Articles 52 TEU and 313 TEC)]*
1. This Treaty shall be ratified by the High Contracting Parties in accordance with their respective constitutional requirements. The instruments of ratification shall be deposited with the government of the Italian Republic.

2. This Treaty shall enter into force on 1 January 1993, provided that all the instruments of ratification have been deposited, or, failing that, on the first day of the month following the deposit of the instrument of ratification by the last signatory State to take this step.

ARTICLE ***55*** [53] *['Authentic texts and translations', Article IV-448 (ex Articles 53 TEU and 314 TEC)]*
1. This Treaty, drawn up in a single original in the ***Bulgarian*, Czech**, Danish, Dutch, English, **Estonian, Finnish,** French, German, Greek, **Hungarian,** Irish, Italian, **Latvian, Lithuanian, Maltese, Polish,** Portuguese, ***Romanian*, Slovak, Slovenian,** Spanish **and Swedish** languages, the texts in each of these languages being equally authentic, shall be deposited in the archives of the government of the Italian Republic, which will transmit a certified copy to each of the governments of the other signatory States.

2. This Treaty may also be translated into any other languages as determined by Member States among those which, in accordance with their constitutional order, enjoy official status in all or part of their territory. A certified copy of such translations shall be provided by the Member States concerned to be deposited in the archives of the Council.
[BMDF Note: See also Declaration no. 16]

IN WITNESS WHEREOF the undersigned Plenipotentiaries have signed this Treaty.

Done at Maastricht on the seventh day of February in the year one thousand nine hundred and ninety-two.

[*BMDF Note: For each Member State, the names and the signatures of the Plenipotentiaries follow here.*]

* * * * *

TREATY ON
THE FUNCTIONING OF THE EUROPEAN UNION

[*BMDF Note: Title changed from "Title II: The Treaty Establishing The European Community" . The Title of Part III of the draft Constitution was 'The Policies and Functioning of the Union'.*]

His Majesty the King of the Belgians*, the President of the Republic of Bulgaria,

the President of the Czech Republic, Her Majesty the Queen of Denmark,

the President of the Federal Republic of Germany*, the President of the Republic of Estonia,

the President of Ireland, the President of the Hellenic Republic, His Majesty the King of Spain,

the President of the French Republic*, the President of the Italian Republic*,

the President of the Republic of Cyprus, the President of the Republic of Latvia,

the President of the Republic of Lithuania, His Royal Highness the Grand Duke of Luxembourg*,

the President of the Republic of Hungary, the President of Malta,

Her Majesty the Queen of the Netherlands*, the Federal President of the Republic of Austria,

the President of the Republic of Poland, the President of the Portuguese Republic,

the President of Romania, the President of the Republic of Slovenia,

the President of the Slovak Republic, the President of the Republic of Finland,

the Government of the Kingdom of Sweden,

Her Majesty the Queen of the United Kingdom of Great Britain and Northern Ireland,

DETERMINED to lay the foundations of an ever-closer union among the peoples of Europe,

RESOLVED to ensure the economic and social progress of their ***States*** by common action to eliminate the barriers which divide Europe,

AFFIRMING as the essential objective of their efforts the constant improvement of the living and working conditions of their peoples,

RECOGNISING that the removal of existing obstacles calls for concerted action in order to guarantee steady expansion, balanced trade and fair competition,

ANXIOUS to strengthen the unity of their economies and to ensure their harmonious development by reducing the differences existing between the various regions and the backwardness of the less-favoured regions,

DESIRING to contribute, by means of a common commercial policy, to the progressive abolition of restrictions on international trade,

INTENDING to confirm the solidarity which binds Europe and the overseas countries and desiring to ensure the development of their prosperity, in accordance with the principles of the Charter of the United Nations,

RESOLVED by thus pooling their resources to preserve and strengthen peace and liberty, and calling upon the other peoples of Europe who share their ideal to join in their efforts,

DETERMINED to promote the development of the highest possible level of knowledge for their peoples through a wide access to education and its continuous updating,
and to this end ***HAVE DESIGNATED*** their Plenipotentiaries,

WHO, having exchanged their Full Powers, found in good and due form, have agreed as follows.

---

* *BMDF Note: Heads of State at the time of signature of the Treaty establishing the European Economic Community at Rome, 25 March 1957.*

PART ONE

PRINCIPLES

[BMDF Note: Article 1 shall be repealed]

ARTICLE 1 [1a] *[New Article in 2007 Treaty of Lisbon]*
1. This Treaty organises the functioning of the Union and determines the areas, the scope of, and arrangements for exercising its competences.

2. This Treaty and the Treaty on European Union constitute the Treaties on which the Union is founded. These two Treaties, which have the same legal value, shall be referred to as "the Treaties".

TITLE I

CATEGORIES AND AREAS OF UNION COMPETENCE

[BMDF Note: Article 2 shall be repealed]

ARTICLE 2 [2A] *[Article I-12 'Categories of competence' (new article in 2004 IGC)]*
1. When *the Treaties* confer on the Union exclusive competence in a specific area, only the Union may legislate and adopt legally binding acts, the Member States being able to do so themselves only if so empowered by the Union or for the implementation of Union acts.

2. **When *the Treaties* confer on the Union a competence shared with the Member States in a specific area, the Union and the Member States may legislate and adopt legally binding acts in that area. The Member States shall exercise their competence to the extent that the Union has not exercised its competence. *The Member States shall again exercise their competence to the extent that the Union has decided to cease exercising its competence.***

3. The Member States shall co-ordinate their economic and employment policies within arrangements as determined by *the Treaties,* which the Union shall have competence to provide.

4. The Union shall have competence, *in accordance with the provisions of the Treaty on European Union,* to define and implement a common foreign and security policy, including the progressive framing of a common defence policy.

5. In certain areas and under the conditions laid down in the *Treaties*, the Union shall have competence to carry out actions to support, co-ordinate or supplement the actions of the Member States, without thereby superseding their competence in these areas.
Legally binding acts of the Union adopted on the basis of the provisions *of the Treaties* relating to these areas shall not entail harmonisation of Member States' laws or regulations.

6. The scope of and arrangements for exercising the Union's competences shall be determined by the provisions *of the Treaties relating to each area.*
[BMDF Note: See also Declaration no. 18]

ARTICLE 3 [2B] *[Article I-13 'Areas of exclusive competence' (new article in 2004 IGC)]*
1. The Union shall have exclusive competence in the following areas:
(a) customs union;
(b) the establishing of the competition rules necessary for the functioning of the internal market;
(c) monetary policy for the Member States whose currency is the euro;
(d) the conservation of marine biological resources under the common fisheries policy;
(e) common commercial policy.

2. The Union shall also have exclusive competence for the conclusion of an international agreement when its conclusion is provided for in a legislative act of the Union or is necessary to enable the Union to exercise its internal competence, or insofar as its conclusion may affect common rules or alter their scope.

ARTICLE 4 [2C] *[Article I-14 'Areas of shared competence' (new article in 2004 IGC, specified TEC articles)]*
1. The Union shall share competence with the Member States where the *Treaties confer* on it a competence which does not relate to the areas referred to in *Articles 3 and 6.*

2. Shared competence between the Union and the Member States applies in the following principal areas:
(a) internal market; *(ex Articles 14, 15 and 95 TEC)*
(b) social policy, for the aspects defined in *this Treaty*; *(ex Article 137 TEC)*
(c) economic, social and territorial cohesion; *(ex Article 159 TEC)*
(d) agriculture and fisheries, excluding the conservation of marine biological resources; *(ex Article 37 TEC)*
(e) environment; *(ex Article 174 TEC)*
(f) consumer protection; *(ex Article 153 TEC)*
(g) transport; *(ex Article 154 TEC)*
(h) trans-European networks; *(ex Article 154 TEC)*
(i) energy; *(new Article in 2004 IGC)*
(j) area of freedom, security and justice; *(ex Articles 61 - 64 TEC)*
(k) common safety concerns in public health matters, for the aspects defined in *this Treaty*. *(ex Article 152 TEC)*

3. In the areas of research, technological development and space, the Union shall have competence to carry out activities, in particular to define and implement programmes; however, the exercise of that competence shall not result in Member States being prevented from exercising theirs.

4. In the areas of development co-operation and humanitarian aid, the Union shall have competence to carry out activities and conduct a common policy; however, the exercise of that competence shall not result in Member States being prevented from exercising theirs.

ARTICLE 5 [2D] *[Article I-15 'The co-ordination of economic and employment policies' (new article in 2004 IGC)]*
1. The Member States shall co-ordinate their economic policies within the Union. To this end, the Council shall adopt measures, in particular broad guidelines for these policies.
Specific provisions shall apply to those Member States whose currency is the euro.

2. The Union shall take measures to ensure co-ordination of the employment policies of the Member States, in particular by defining guidelines for these policies.

3. The Union may take initiatives to ensure co-ordination of Member States' social policies.

ARTICLE 6 [2E] *[Article I-17 'Areas of supporting, co-ordinating or complementary action' (new Article in 2004 IGC, drawing on specified TEC articles)]*
The Union shall have competence to carry out *actions to support, co-ordinate or supplement the actions of the Member States. The areas of such* action shall, at European level, be:
(a) protection and improvement of human health; *(ex Article 152 TEC)*
(b) industry; *(ex Article 157 TEC)*
(c) culture; *(ex Article 151 TEC)*
(d) tourism; *(new in 2004 IGC)*
(e) education, vocational training, youth and sport; *(ex Article 149 TEC, sport new in 2004 IGC)*
(f) civil protection; *(new in 2004 IGC)*
(g) administrative co-operation. *(new in 2004 IGC)*

TITLE II

PROVISIONS HAVING GENERAL APPLICATION

ARTICLE 7 [2F] *[Article III-115 (new Article in 2004 IGC)]*
The Union shall ensure consistency between *its* policies and activities, taking all of its objectives into account and in accordance with the principle of conferral of powers.

ARTICLE ***8*** [3] *[Article III-116 (ex Article 3(2) TEC)]*
In ***its activities***, the **Union** shall aim to eliminate inequalities, and to promote equality, between men and women. *[BMDF Note: See also Declaration no. 19]*

[BMDF Note: Article 4 TEC moved to Article 119]

[BMDF Note: Article 5 TEC moved to and replaced by Article 5 TEU]

ARTICLE 9 [5a] *[Article III-117 (new Article in 2004 IGC)]*
In defining and implementing its policies and actions, the Union shall take into account requirements linked to the promotion of a high level of employment, the guarantee of adequate social protection, the fight against social exclusion, and a high level of education, training and protection of human health.

ARTICLE 10 [5b] *[Article III-118 (new Article in 2004 IGC)]*
In defining and implementing *its* policies and activities, the Union shall aim to combat discrimination based on sex, racial or ethnic origin, religion or belief, disability, age or sexual orientation.

ARTICLE ***11*** [6] *[Article III-119 (ex Article 6 TEC)]*
Environmental protection requirements must be integrated into the definition and implementation of the ***Union*** policies and activities, in particular with a view to promoting sustainable development.

ARTICLE 12 [6a] *[Article III-120 (ex Article 153(2) TEC)]*
Consumer protection requirements shall be taken into account in defining and implementing other **Union** policies and activities.
[BMDF Note: Article moved from Article 153(2) TEC]

ARTICLE 13 [6b] *[Article III-121 (new Article in 2004 IGC)]*
In formulating and implementing the Union's agriculture, fisheries, transport, internal market, research and technological development and space policies, the Union and the Member States shall, since animals are sentient beings, pay full regard to the requirements of animal welfare, while respecting the legislative or administrative provisions and customs of Member States relating in particular to religious rites, cultural traditions and regional heritage.
[BMDF Note: Article taken from Protocol on the protection and welfare of animals, introduced by the Treaty of Amsterdam]

[BMDF Note: Articles 7 to 10 TEC shall be repealed]

[BMDF Note: Articles 11 and 11a TEC shall be repealed and replaced by Article 20 TEU and Articles 326 to 334 TFEU]

[BMDF Note: Article 12 TEC moved to Article 18 TFEU]

[BMDF Note: Article 13 TEC moved to new Article 19 TFEU]

[BMDF Note: Article 14 TEC moved to Article 26 TFEU]

[BMDF Note: Article 15 TEC moved to Article 27 TFEU]

ARTICLE ***14*** [16] *[Article III-122 (ex Article 16 TEC)]*
Without prejudice to ***Article 4 of Treaty on European Union and*** Articles ***93, 106*** and ***107 of this Treaty***, and given the place occupied by services of general economic interest in the shared values of the Union as well as their role in promoting social and territorial cohesion, the ***Union*** and the Member States, each within their respective **competences** and within the scope of application of ***the Treaties***, shall take care that such services operate on the basis of principles and conditions, **particularly economic and financial conditions,** which enable them to fulfil their missions. ***The European Parliament and the Council, acting by means of regulations in accordance with the ordinary legislative procedure,*** **shall establish these principles and set these conditions without prejudice to the competence of Member States, in compliance with the *Treaties*, to provide, to commission and to fund such services.**
[BMDF Note: See Protocol no. 9]

ARTICLE 15 [16A] *[Article I-50 and Article III-399(2) (ex Article 255 TEC)]*
1. In order to promote good governance and ensure the participation of civil society, the Union institutions, bodies, offices and agencies shall conduct their work as openly as possible.

2. The European Parliament shall meet in public, as shall the Council when considering and voting on a draft legislative act.

3. Any citizen of the Union, and any natural or legal person residing or having its registered office in a Member State, shall have a right of access to **documents of the Union institutions, bodies, offices and agencies, whatever their medium,** subject to the principles and the conditions to be defined in accordance with ***this paragraph***.
General principles and limits on grounds of public or private interest governing this right of access to documents shall be determined by ***the European Parliament and*** the Council ***by means of regulations***, acting in accordance with the ***ordinary legislative procedure***.
Each institution, **body, office or agency** shall ***ensure that its proceedings are transparent and shall elaborate*** in its own Rules of Procedure specific provisions regarding access to its documents, ***in accordance with the legislative act referred to in the second subparagraph.***
The Court of Justice of the European Union, the European Central Bank and the European Investment Bank shall be subject to this paragraph only when exercising their administrative tasks.
The European Parliament and the Council shall ensure publication of the documents relating to the legislative procedures *under the terms laid down by the legislative act* referred to in *the second sub-paragraph.*
[BMDF Note: Article moved from Article 255 TEC. New paragraphs 1 and 2 and amendments to new paragraph 3 taken from 2004 IGC Article I-50 'Transparency of the proceedings of Union institutions, bodies, offices and agencies' (ex Article 255 TEC). Article also from Article III-399(2) (ex Article 255 TEC)]

ARTICLE 16 [16B] *[Article I-51 'Protection of personal data' (ex Article 286 TEC)]*
1. Everyone has the right to the protection of personal data concerning *them.*

2. ***The European Parliament and the Council, acting in accordance with the ordinary legislative procedure, shall*** **lay down the rules relating to the protection of individuals with regard to the processing of personal data by Union institutions, bodies, offices and agencies, and by the Member States when carrying out activities which fall within the scope of Union law, and the rules relating to the free movement of such data. Compliance with these rules shall be subject to the control of independent authorities.**
The rules adopted on the basis of this Article shall be without prejudice to the specific rules laid down in Article 39 of the Treaty on European Union.
[BMDF Note: See also Declarations nos. 20 and 21. This Article replaces Article 286 TEC]

ARTICLE 17 [16C] *[Article I-52 Status of churches and non-confessional organisations (new Article in 2004 IGC)]*
1. The Union respects and does not prejudice the status under national law of churches and religious associations or communities in the Member States.

2. The Union equally respects the status under national law of philosophical and non-confessional organisations.

3. Recognising their identity and their specific contribution, the Union shall maintain an open, transparent and regular dialogue with these churches and organisations.

PART TWO

NON-DISCRIMINATION AND CITIZENSHIP

ARTICLE 18 [16D] *[Article I-4(2) and Article III-123 (ex Article 12 TEC)]*
Within the scope of application of ***the Treaties***, and without prejudice to any special provisions contained therein, any discrimination on grounds of nationality shall be prohibited.
The European Parliament and the Council, acting in accordance with the ***ordinary legislative procedure***, may adopt rules designed to prohibit such discrimination.
[BMDF Note: Article moved from Article 12 TEC]

ARTICLE 19 [16E] *[Article III-124 (ex Article 13 TEC)]*
1. Without prejudice to the other provisions of ***the Treaties*** and within the limits of the powers conferred by it upon the ***Union***, the Council, acting unanimously ***in accordance with a special legislative procedure*** and after ***obtaining the consent of*** the European Parliament, may take appropriate action to combat discrimination based on sex, racial or ethnic origin, religion or belief, disability, age or sexual orientation.

2. By way of derogation from paragraph 1, ***the European Parliament and*** the ***Council, acting in accordance with the ordinary legislative procedure may adopt the*** **basic principles for *Union*** incentive measures, excluding any harmonisation of the laws and regulations of the Member States, to support action taken by the Member States in order to contribute to the achievement of the objectives referred to in paragraph 1. *[BMDF Note: Article moved from Article 13 TEC]*

ARTICLE ***20*** [17] *[Article I-10 Citizenship of the Union (ex Articles 17 to 21 TEC)]*
1. Citizenship of the Union is hereby established. Every person holding the nationality of a Member State shall be a citizen of the Union. Citizenship of the Union shall ***be additional to*** and not replace national citizenship.

2. Citizens of the Union shall enjoy the rights and be subject to the duties **provided for in the Treaties. They shall have, *inter alia*:**
(a) the right to move and reside freely within the territory of the Member States;
(b) the right to vote and to stand as candidates in elections to the European Parliament and in municipal elections in their Member State of residence, under the same conditions as nationals of that State;
(c) the right to enjoy, in the territory of a third country in which the Member State of which they are nationals is not represented, the protection of the diplomatic and consular authorities of any Member State on the same conditions as the nationals of that State;
(d) the right to petition the European Parliament, to apply to the European Ombudsman, and to address the institutions and advisory bodies of the Union in any of the *Treaty* languages and to obtain a reply in the same language.
These rights shall be exercised in accordance with the conditions and limits defined by the *Treaties* and by the measures adopted thereunder.
[BMDF Note: Article moved from Article 17 TEC]

ARTICLE ***21*** [18] *[Paragraph 2 and 3 taken from 2004 IGC – Article III-125 (ex Article 18 TEC)]*
1. Every citizen of the Union shall have the right to move and reside freely within the territory of the Member States, subject to the limitations and conditions laid down in ***the Treaties*** and by the measures adopted to give it effect.

2. If action by the ***Union*** should prove necessary to attain this objective and ***the Treaties have*** not provided the necessary powers, ***the European Parliament and*** the Council***, acting in accordance with***

the ordinary legislative procedure, may adopt provisions with a view to facilitating the exercise of the rights referred to in paragraph 1.

3. **For the same purposes as those referred to in paragraph 1 and if *the Treaties have not provided the necessary powers, the Council, acting in accordance with a special legislative procedure, may adopt* measures concerning social security or social protection. The Council shall act unanimously after consulting the European Parliament.**

ARTICLE *22* [19] *[Article III-126 (ex Article 19 TEC)]*
1. Every citizen of the Union residing in a Member State of which he is not a national shall have the right to vote and to stand as a candidate at municipal elections in the Member State in which he resides, under the same conditions as nationals of that State. This right shall be exercised subject to detailed arrangements adopted by the Council, acting unanimously ***in accordance with a special legislative procedure*** and after consulting the European Parliament; these arrangements may provide for derogations where warranted by problems specific to a Member State.

2. Without prejudice to Article *223*(4) and to the provisions adopted for its implementation, every citizen of the Union residing in a Member State of which he is not a national shall have the right to vote and to stand as a candidate in elections to the European Parliament in the Member State in which he resides, under the same conditions as nationals of that State. This right shall be exercised subject to detailed arrangements adopted by the Council, acting unanimously ***in accordance with a special legislative procedure*** and after consulting the European Parliament; these arrangements may provide for derogations where warranted by problems specific to a Member State.

ARTICLE *23* [20] *[Article III-127 (ex Article 20 TEC)]*
Every citizen of the Union shall, in the territory of a third country in which the Member State of which he is a national is not represented, be entitled to protection by the diplomatic or consular authorities of any Member State, on the same conditions as the nationals of that State. Member States shall **adopt the necessary provisions and** start the international negotiations required to secure this protection.
***The Council, acting in accordance with a special legislative procedure and after consulting the European Parliament, may adopt directives establishing the co-ordination and co-operation* measures necessary to facilitate such protection.**
[BMDF Note: The text of the second paragraph is new in the Treaty of Lisbon, but has been adapted from the text introduced by the 2004 IGC]

ARTICLE *24* [21] *[Article I-47, paragraph 4 and Articles I-10(2d) and III-128 (ex Article 21 TEC)]*
The European Parliament and the Council, acting by means of regulations in accordance with the ordinary legislative procedure, shall adopt the provisions for the procedures and conditions required for a citizens' initiative within the meaning of Article 11 of the Treaty on European Union, including the minimum number of Member States from which such citizens must come.
Every citizen of the Union shall have the right to petition the European Parliament in accordance with Article *227*.
Every citizen of the Union may apply to the Ombudsman established in accordance with Article ***228***.
Every citizen of the Union may write to any of the ***institutions, bodies, offices or agencies*** referred to in this Article or in ***Article 13 of the Treaty on European Union*** in one of the languages mentioned in ***Article 55(1) of the Treaty on European Union*** and have an answer in the same language.
[BMDF Note: Paragraph 1 added by Treaty of Lisbon with the text modified from 2004 IGC]

ARTICLE *25* [22] *[Article III-129 (ex Article 22 TEC)]*
The Commission shall report to the European Parliament, to the Council and to the Economic and Social Committee every three years on the application of the provisions of this Part. This report shall take account of the development of the Union.
On this basis, and without prejudice to the other provisions of ***the Treaties***, the Council, acting unanimously ***in accordance with a special legislative procedure*** and after ***obtaining the consent of*** the European Parliament, may adopt provisions to strengthen or to add to **the rights *listed in Article 20(2).* *These provisions* shall enter into force *after their approval* by the Member States in accordance with their respective constitutional requirements.**

PART THREE

UNION POLICIES *AND INTERNAL ACTIONS*

TITLE I

THE INTERNAL MARKET

ARTICLE ***26*** [22a] *[Article III-130(1)-(3) (ex Article 14 TEC)]*
1. The **Union** shall adopt measures with the aim of establishing **or ensuring** the **functioning of** the internal market in accordance with the **relevant** provisions of ***the Treaties***.

2. The internal market shall comprise an area without internal frontiers in which the free movement of goods, persons, services and capital is ensured in accordance with the provisions of ***the Treaties***.

3. The Council, on a proposal from the Commission, shall determine the guidelines and conditions necessary to ensure balanced progress in all the sectors concerned.
[BMDF Note: Article moved from Article 14 TEC. See also Protocol no. 21]

ARTICLE ***27*** [22b] *[Article III-130(4) (ex Article 15 TEC)]*
When drawing up its proposals with a view to achieving the objectives set out in Article ***26***, the Commission shall take into account the extent of the effort that certain economies showing differences in development will have to sustain **for the establishment** of the internal market and it may propose appropriate provisions.
If these provisions take the form of derogations, they must be of a temporary nature and must cause the least possible disturbance to the functioning of the **internal** market.
[BMDF Note: Article moved from Article 15 TEC. The UK has an opt-out from the provisions of these two Articles in relation to border controls, under Protocol No. 25, Article 1.]

TITLE I *a*

FREE MOVEMENT OF GOODS

ARTICLE ***28*** [23] *[Article III-151(1)and (2) (ex Article 23 TEC)]*
1. The ***Union*** **shall comprise** a customs union which shall cover all trade in goods and which shall involve the prohibition between Member States of customs duties on imports and exports and of all charges having equivalent effect, and the adoption of a common customs tariff in their relations with third countries.

2. The provisions of Article ***30*** and of Chapter 2 of this Title shall apply to products originating in Member States and to products coming from third countries which are in free circulation in Member States.

ARTICLE ***29*** [24] *[Article III-151(3) (ex Article 24 TEC)]*
Products coming from a third country shall be considered to be in free circulation in a Member State if the import formalities have been complied with and any customs duties or charges having equivalent effect which are payable have been levied in that Member State, and if they have not benefited from a total or partial drawback of such duties or charges.

CHAPTER 1

THE CUSTOMS UNION

ARTICLE ***30*** [25] *[Article III-151(4) (ex Article 25 TEC)]*
Customs duties on imports and exports and charges having equivalent effect shall be prohibited between Member States. This prohibition shall also apply to customs duties of a fiscal nature.

ARTICLE ***31*** [26] *[Article III-151(5) (ex Article 26 TEC)]*
Common Customs Tariff duties shall be fixed by the Council on a proposal from the Commission.

ARTICLE ***32*** [27] *[Article III-151(6) (ex Article 27 TEC)]*
In carrying out the tasks entrusted to it under this Chapter the Commission shall be guided by:
(a) the need to promote trade between Member States and third countries;
(b) developments in conditions of competition within the **Union** in so far as they lead to an improvement in the competitive capacity of undertakings;
(c) the requirements of the **Union** as regards the supply of raw materials and semi-finished goods; in this connection the Commission shall take care to avoid distorting conditions of competition between Member States in respect of finished goods;
(d) the need to avoid serious disturbances in the economies of Member States and to ensure rational development of production and an expansion of consumption within the **Union**.

CHAPTER 1 a

CUSTOMS CO-OPERATION

ARTICLE ***33*** [27a] *[Article III-152(ex Article 135 TEC)]*
Within the scope of application of ***the Treaties***, ***the European Parliament and*** the Council, acting in accordance with the ***ordinary legislative procedure***, shall take measures in order to strengthen customs co-operation between Member States and between the latter and the Commission.
[BMDF Note: Title and Article moved from Article 135 TEC]

CHAPTER 2

PROHIBITION OF QUANTITATIVE RESTRICTIONS BETWEEN MEMBER STATES

ARTICLE ***34*** [28] *[Article III-153 (ex Article 28 TEC)]*
Quantitative restrictions on imports and all measures having equivalent effect shall be prohibited between Member States.

ARTICLE ***35*** [29] *[Article III-153 (ex Article 29 TEC)]*
Quantitative restrictions on exports, and all measures having equivalent effect, shall be prohibited between Member States.

ARTICLE ***36*** [30] *[Article III-154 (ex Article 30 TEC)]*
The provisions of Articles ***34*** and ***35*** shall not preclude prohibitions or restrictions on imports, exports or goods in transit justified on grounds of public morality, public policy or public security; the protection of health and life of humans, animals or plants; the protection of national treasures possessing artistic, historic or archaeological value; or the protection of industrial and commercial property. Such prohibitions or restrictions shall not, however, constitute a means of arbitrary discrimination or a disguised restriction on trade between Member States.

ARTICLE *37* [31] *[Article III-155 (ex Article 31 TEC)]*
1. Member States shall adjust any State monopolies of a commercial character so as to ensure that no discrimination regarding the conditions under which goods are procured and marketed exists between nationals of Member States.

The provisions of this Article shall apply to any body through which a Member State, in law or in fact, either directly or indirectly supervises, determines or appreciably influences imports or exports between Member States. These provisions shall likewise apply to monopolies delegated by the State to others.

2. Member States shall refrain from introducing any new measure which is contrary to the principles laid down in paragraph 1 or which restricts the scope of the Articles dealing with the prohibition of customs duties and quantitative restrictions between Member States.

3. If a State monopoly of a commercial character has rules which are designed to make it easier to dispose of agricultural products or obtain for them the best return, steps should be taken in applying the rules contained in this Article to ensure equivalent safeguards for the employment and standard of living of the producers concerned.

TITLE II

AGRICULTURE ***AND FISHERIES***

ARTICLE ***38*** [32] *[Paragraph 1 - Article III-225 (new Article in 2004 IGC) and Article III-226 (ex Article 32 TEC)]*

1. **The Union shall define and implement a common agriculture and fisheries policy.**
The **internal** market shall extend to agriculture***, fisheries*** and trade in agricultural products. 'Agricultural products' means the products of the soil, of stock farming and of fisheries and products of first-stage processing directly related to these products. **References to the common agricultural policy or to agriculture, and the use of the term "agricultural", shall be understood as also referring to fisheries, having regard to the specific characteristics of this sector**.

2. Save as otherwise provided in Articles ***39*** to ***44***, the rules laid down for the establishment **and functioning** of the **internal** market shall apply to agricultural products.

3. The products subject to the provisions of Articles ***39*** to ***44*** are listed in Annex I.

4. The operation and development of the **internal** market for agricultural products must be accompanied by the establishment of a common agricultural policy.

ARTICLE ***39*** [33] *[Article III-227 (ex Article 33 TEC)]*

1. The objectives of the common agricultural policy shall be:
(a) to increase agricultural productivity by promoting technical progress and by ensuring the rational development of agricultural production and the optimum utilisation of the factors of production, in particular labour;
(b) thus to ensure a fair standard of living for the agricultural community, in particular by increasing the individual earnings of persons engaged in agriculture;
(c) to stabilise markets;
(d) to assure the availability of supplies;
(e) to ensure that supplies reach consumers at reasonable prices.

2. In working out the common agricultural policy and the special methods for its application, account shall be taken of:
(a) the particular nature of agricultural activity, which results from the social structure of agriculture and from structural and natural disparities between the various agricultural regions;
(b) the need to effect the appropriate adjustments by degrees;
(c) the fact that in the Member States agriculture constitutes a sector closely linked with the economy as a whole.

ARTICLE ***40*** [34] *[Article III-228 (ex Article 34 TEC)]*

1. In order to attain the objectives set out in Article ***39***, a common organisation of agricultural markets shall be established.
This organisation shall take one of the following forms, depending on the product concerned:

(a) common rules on competition;
(b) compulsory co-ordination of the various national market organisations;
(c) a European market organisation.

2. The common organisation established in accordance with paragraph 1 may include all measures required to attain the objectives set out in Article ***39***, in particular regulation of prices, aids for the production and marketing of the various products, storage and carryover arrangements and common machinery for stabilising imports or exports.
The common organisation shall be limited to pursuit of the objectives set out in Article ***39*** and shall exclude any discrimination between producers or consumers within the **Union**.
Any common price policy shall be based on common criteria and uniform methods of calculation.

3. In order to enable the common organisation referred to in paragraph 1 to attain its objectives, one or more agricultural guidance and guarantee funds may be set up.

ARTICLE ***41*** [35] *[Article III-229 (ex Article 35 TEC)]*
To enable the objectives set out in Article ***39*** to be attained, provision may be made within the framework of the common agricultural policy for measures such as:
(a) an effective co-ordination of efforts in the spheres of vocational training, of research and of the dissemination of agricultural knowledge; this may include joint financing of projects or institutions;
(b) joint measures to promote consumption of certain products.

ARTICLE ***42*** [36] *[Article III-230 (ex Article 36 TEC)]*
The provisions of the Chapter relating to rules on competition shall apply to production of and trade in agricultural products only to the extent determined by ***the European Parliament and*** the Council within the framework of Article ***43*(2)** and in accordance with the procedure laid down therein, account being taken of the objectives set out in Article ***39***.
The Council**, on a proposal from the Commission,** may authorise the granting of aid:
(a) for the protection of enterprises handicapped by structural or natural conditions;
(b) within the framework of economic development programmes.

ARTICLE ***43*** [37] *[Article III-231 (ex Article 37 TEC)]*
1. The Commission shall submit proposals for working out and implementing the common agricultural policy, including the replacement of the national organisations by one of the forms of common organisation provided for in Article ***40(1)***, and for implementing the measures specified in this Title.
These proposals shall take account of the interdependence of the agricultural matters mentioned in this Title.

2. *The European Parliament and the Council, acting in accordance with the ordinary legislative procedure and after consulting the Economic and Social Committee,* shall establish the common organisation of *agricultural markets* provided for in *Article 40(1)* and the other provisions necessary for the pursuit of the objectives of the common agricultural policy and the common fisheries policy.

3. The Council, on a proposal from the Commission, shall adopt *measures* on fixing prices, levies, aid and quantitative limitations and on the fixing and allocation of fishing opportunities.

4. In accordance with paragraph 2, the national market organisations may be replaced by the common organisation provided for in Article ***40(1)*** if:
(a) the common organisation offers Member States which are opposed to this measure and which have an organisation of their own for the production in question equivalent safeguards for the employment and standard of living of the producers concerned, account being taken of the adjustments that will be possible and the specialisation that will be needed with the passage of time;
(b) such an organisation ensures conditions for trade within the **Union** similar to those existing in a national market.

5. If a common organisation for certain raw materials is established before a common organisation exists for the corresponding processed products, such raw materials as are used for processed products intended for export to third countries may be imported from outside the **Union**.

ARTICLE ***44*** [38] *[Article III-232 (ex Article 38 TEC)]*
Where in a Member State a product is subject to a national market organisation or to internal rules having equivalent effect which affect the competitive position of similar production in another Member State, a countervailing charge shall be applied by Member States to imports of this product coming from the Member State where such organisation or rules exist, unless that State applies a countervailing charge on export.
The Commission shall fix the amount of these charges at the level required to redress the balance; it may also authorise other measures, the conditions and details of which it shall determine.

TITLE III

FREE MOVEMENT OF PERSONS, SERVICES AND CAPITAL

CHAPTER 1

WORKERS

ARTICLE ***45*** [39] *[Article III-133 (ex Article 39 TEC)]*
1. Freedom of movement for workers shall be secured within the ***Union***.

2. Such freedom of movement shall entail the abolition of any discrimination based on nationality between workers of the Member States as regards employment, remuneration and other conditions of work and employment.

3. It shall entail the right, subject to limitations justified on grounds of public policy, public security or public health:
(a) to accept offers of employment actually made;
(b) to move freely within the territory of Member States for this purpose;
(c) to stay in a Member State for the purpose of employment in accordance with the provisions governing the employment of nationals of that State laid down by law, regulation or administrative action;
(d) to remain in the territory of a Member State after having been employed in that State, subject to conditions which shall be embodied in regulations to be drawn up by the Commission.

4. The provisions of this Article shall not apply to employment in the public service.

ARTICLE ***46*** [40] *[Article III-134 (ex Article 40 TEC)]*
The European Parliament and the Council, acting in accordance with the ***ordinary legislative procedure*** and after consulting the Economic and Social Committee, issue directives or make regulations setting out the measures required to bring about freedom of movement for workers, as defined in Article 39, in particular:
(a) by ensuring close co-operation between national employment services;
(b) by abolishing those administrative procedures and practices and those qualifying periods in respect of eligibility for available employment, whether resulting from national legislation or from agreements previously concluded between Member States, the maintenance of which would form an obstacle to liberalisation of the movement of workers;
(c) by abolishing all such qualifying periods and other restrictions provided for either under national legislation or under agreements previously concluded between Member States as imposed on workers of other Member States conditions regarding the free choice of employment other than those imposed on workers of the State concerned;
(d) by setting up appropriate machinery to bring offers of employment into touch with applications for employment and to facilitate the achievement of a balance between supply and demand in the employment market in such a way as to avoid serious threats to the standard of living and level of employment in the various regions and industries.

ARTICLE *47* [41] *[Article III-135 (ex Article 41 TEC)]*
Member States shall, within the framework of a joint programme, encourage the exchange of young workers.

ARTICLE *48* [42] *[Article III-136 (ex Article 42 TEC)]*
The European Parliament and the Council, acting in accordance with the ***ordinary legislative procedure***, adopt such measures in the field of social security as are necessary to provide freedom of movement for workers; to this end, it shall make arrangements to secure for **employed and self-employed** migrant workers and their dependants :
(a) aggregation, for the purpose of acquiring and retaining the right to benefit and of calculating the amount of benefit, of all periods taken into account under the laws of the several countries;
(b) payment of benefits to persons resident in the territories of Member States.
Where a member of the Council considers that a draft *legislative act* referred to in *the first subparagraph* would affect *important* aspects of its social security system, including its scope, cost or financial structure, or would affect the financial balance of that system, it may request that the matter be referred to the European Council. In that case, the *ordinary legislative procedure* shall be suspended. After discussion, the European Council shall, within four months of this suspension, either:
(a) refer the draft back to the Council, which shall terminate the suspension of the *ordinary legislative procedure*, or
(b) *take no action or* request the Commission to submit a new proposal; in that case, the act originally proposed shall be deemed not to have been adopted.
[BMDF Note: See also Declarations nos. 22 and 23]

CHAPTER 2

RIGHT OF ESTABLISHMENT

ARTICLE *49* [43] *[Article III-137 (ex Article 43 TEC)]*
Within the framework of the provisions set out below, restrictions on the freedom of establishment of nationals of a Member State in the territory of another Member State shall be prohibited. Such prohibition shall also apply to restrictions on the setting up of agencies, branches or subsidiaries by nationals of any Member State established in the territory of any Member State.
Freedom of establishment shall include the right to take up and pursue activities as self-employed persons and to set up and manage undertakings, in particular companies or firms within the meaning of the second paragraph of Article ***54***, under the conditions laid down for its own nationals by the law of the country where such establishment is effected, subject to the provisions of the Chapter relating to capital.

ARTICLE *50* [44] *[Article III-138]*
1. In order to attain freedom of establishment as regards a particular activity, ***the European Parliament and*** the Council, acting in accordance with the ***ordinary legislative procedure*** and after consulting the Economic and Social Committee, shall act by means of directives.

2. **The European Parliament,** the Council and the Commission shall carry out the duties devolving upon them under the preceding provisions, in particular:
(a) by according, as a general rule, priority treatment to activities where freedom of establishment makes a particularly valuable contribution to the development of production and trade;
(b) by ensuring close co-operation between the competent authorities in the Member States in order to ascertain the particular situation within the **Union** of the various activities concerned;
(c) by abolishing those administrative procedures and practices, whether resulting from national legislation or from agreements previously concluded between Member States, the maintenance of which would form an obstacle to freedom of establishment;
(d) by ensuring that workers of one Member State employed in the territory of another Member State may remain in that territory for the purpose of taking up activities therein as self-employed persons, where they satisfy the conditions which they would be required to satisfy if they were entering that State at the time when they intended to take up such activities;

(e) by enabling a national of one Member State to acquire and use land and building situated in the territory of another Member State, insofar as this does not conflict with the principles laid down in Article ***39(2);***

(f) by effecting the progressive abolition of restrictions on freedom of establishment in every branch of activity under consideration, both as regards the conditions for setting up agencies, branches or subsidiaries in the territory of a Member State and as regards the subsidiaries in the territory of a Member State and as regards the conditions governing the entry of personnel belonging to the main establishment into managerial or supervisory posts in such agencies, branches or subsidiaries;

(g) by co-ordinating to the necessary extent the safeguards which, for the protection of the interests of members and others, are required by Member States of companies or firms within the meaning of the second paragraph of Article ***54*** with a view to making such safeguards equivalent throughout the **Union**;

(h) by satisfying themselves that the conditions of establishment are not distorted by aids granted by Member States.

ARTICLE ***51*** [45] *[Article III-139 (ex Article 45 TEC)]*
The provisions of this Chapter shall not apply, so far as any given Member State is concerned, to activities which in that State are connected, even occasionally, with the exercise of official authority.
The European Parliament and the Council, ***acting in accordance with the ordinary legislative procedure*** may, rule that the provisions of this Chapter shall not apply to certain activities.

ARTICLE ***52*** [46] *[Article III-140 (ex Article 46 TEC)]*
1. The provisions of this Chapter and measures taken in pursuance thereof shall not prejudice the applicability of provisions laid down by law, regulation or administrative action providing for special treatment for foreign nationals on grounds of public policy, public security or public health.

2. ***The European Parliament and*** the Council, acting in accordance with the ***ordinary legislative procedure***, issue directives for the co-ordination of the above-mentioned provisions.

ARTICLE ***53*** [47] *[Article III-141 (ex Article 47 TEC)]*
1. In order to make it easier for persons to take up and pursue activities as self-employed persons, ***the European Parliament and*** the Council, acting in accordance with the ***ordinary legislative procedure***, issue directives for the mutual recognition of diplomas, certificates and other evidence of formal qualifications **and for the co-ordination of the provisions laid down by law, regulation or administrative action in Member States concerning the taking-up and pursuit of activities as self-employed persons**.

2. In the case of the medical and allied and pharmaceutical professions, the progressive abolition of restrictions shall be dependent upon co-ordination of the conditions for their exercise in the various Member States.

ARTICLE ***54*** [48] *[Article III-142 (ex Article 48 TEC)]*
Companies or firms formed in accordance with the law of a Member State and having their registered office, central administration or principal place of business within the ***Union*** shall, for the purposes of this Chapter, be treated in the same way as natural persons who are nationals of the Member States.
'Companies or firms' means companies or firms constituted under civil or commercial law, including co-operative societies, and other legal persons governed by public or private law, save for those which are non-profit-making.

ARTICLE ***55*** [48a] *[Article III-143 (ex Article 294 TEC)]*
Member States shall accord nationals of the other Member States the same treatment as their own nationals as regards participation in the capital of companies or firms within the meaning of Article 48, without prejudice to the application of the other provisions of ***the Treaties***.
[BMDF Note: Article moved from Article 294 TEC]

CHAPTER 3

SERVICES

ARTICLE ***56*** [49] *[Article III-144 (ex Article 49 TEC)]*
Within the framework of the provisions set out below, restrictions on freedom to provide services within the **Union** shall be prohibited in respect of nationals of Member States who are established in a **Member State** other than that of the person for whom the services are intended.
The European Parliament and the Council, ***acting in accordance with the ordinary legislative procedure*** may extend the provisions of the Chapter to nationals of a third country who provide services and who are established within the **Union**.

ARTICLE ***57*** [50] *[Article III-145 (ex Article 50 TEC)]*
Services shall be considered to be 'services' within the meaning of ***the Treaties*** where they are normally provided for remuneration, insofar as they are not governed by the provisions relating to freedom of movement for goods, capital and persons.
'Services' shall in particular include:
(a) activities of an industrial character;
(b) activities of a commercial character;
(c) activities of craftsmen;
(d) activities of the professions.
Without prejudice to the provisions of the Chapter relating to the right of establishment, the person providing a service may, in order to do so, temporarily pursue his activity in the **Member** State where the service is provided, under the same conditions as are imposed by that State on its own nationals.

ARTICLE ***58*** [51] *[Article III-146(ex Article 51 TEC)]*
1. Freedom to provide services in the field of transport shall be governed by the provisions of the Title relating to transport.

2. The liberalisation of banking and insurance services connected with movements of capital shall be effected in step with the liberalisation of movement of capital.

ARTICLE ***59*** [52] *[Article III-147 (ex Article 52 TEC)]*
1. In order to achieve the liberalisation of a specific service, ***the European Parliament and*** the Council, ***acting in accordance with the ordinary legislative procedure*** and after consulting the Economic and Social Committee ***shall*** issue directives.

2. As regards the directives referred to in paragraph 1, priority shall as a general rule be given to those services which directly affect production costs or the liberalisation of which helps to promote trade in goods.

ARTICLE ***60*** [53] *[Article III-148 (ex Article 53 TEC)]*
The Member States **shall endeavour** to undertake the liberalisation of services beyond the extent required by the directives issued pursuant to Article ***59(1)***, if their general economic situation and the situation of the economic sector concerned so permit.
To this end, the Commission shall make recommendations to the Member States concerned.

ARTICLE ***61*** [54] *[Article III-149 (ex Article 54 TEC)]*
As long as restrictions on freedom to provide services have not been abolished, each Member State shall apply such restrictions without distinction on grounds of nationality or residence to all persons providing services within the meaning of the first paragraph of Article ***56***.

ARTICLE ***62*** [55] *[Article III-150]*
The provisions of Articles ***51*** to ***54*** shall apply to the matters covered by this Chapter.

CHAPTER 4

CAPITAL AND PAYMENTS

ARTICLE ***63*** [56] *[Article III-156 (ex Article 56 TEC)]*
1. Within the framework of the provisions set out in this Chapter, all restrictions on the movement of capital between Member States and between Member States and third countries shall be prohibited.

2. Within the framework of the provisions set out in this Chapter, all restrictions on payments between Member States and between Member States and third countries shall be prohibited.

ARTICLE ***64*** [57] *[Article III-157 (ex Article 57 TEC)]*
1. The provisions of Article ***63*** shall be without prejudice to the application to third countries of any restrictions which exist on 31 December 1993 under national or **Union** law adopted in respect of the movement of capital to or from third countries involving direct investment - including in real estate - establishment, the provision of financial services or the admission of securities to capital markets. In respect of restrictions existing under national law in Bulgaria, Estonia and Hungary, the relevant date shall be 31 December 1999.

2. Whilst endeavouring to achieve the objective of free movement of capital between Member States and third countries to the greatest extent possible and without prejudice to the other Chapters of ***the Treaties***, ***the European Parliament and*** the Council, ***acting in accordance with the ordinary legislative procedure***, ***shall*** adopt ***the*** measures on the movement of capital to or from third countries involving direct investment - including investment in real estate - establishment, the provision of financial services or the admission of securities to capital markets.

3. Notwithstanding paragraph 2, only the Council, ***acting in accordance with a special legislative procedure, may unanimously, and after consulting the European Parliament, adopt*** **measures** which constitute a step back in **Union** law as regards the liberalisation of the movement of capital to or from third countries.

ARTICLE ***65*** [58] *[Article III-158 (ex Article 58 TEC)]*
1. The provisions of Article ***63*** shall be without prejudice to the right of Member States:
(a) to apply the relevant provisions of their tax law which distinguish between taxpayers who are not in the same situation with regard to their place of residence or with regard to the place where their capital is invested;
(b) to take all requisite measures to prevent infringements of national law and regulations, in particular in the field of taxation and the prudential supervision of financial institutions, or to lay down procedures for the declaration of capital movements for purposes of administrative or statistical information, or to take measures which are justified on grounds of public policy or public security.

2. The provisions of this Chapter shall be without prejudice to the applicability of restrictions on the right of establishment which are compatible with ***the Treaties***.

3. The measures and procedures referred to in paragraphs 1 and 2 shall not constitute a means of arbitrary discrimination or a disguised restriction on the free movement of capital and payments as defined in Article ***63***.

4. In the absence of *measures pursuant to Article 64(3)*, the Commission or, in the absence of a Commission *decision* within three months from the request of the Member State concerned, the Council, may adopt a decision stating that restrictive tax measures adopted by a Member State concerning one or more third countries are to be considered compatible with the *Treaties* insofar as they are justified by one of the objectives of the Union and compatible with the proper functioning of the internal market. The Council shall act unanimously on application by a Member State.

ARTICLE ***66*** [59] *[Article III-159 (ex Article 59 TEC)]*
Where, in exceptional circumstances, movements of capital to or from third countries cause, or threaten to cause, serious difficulties for the operation of economic and monetary union, the Council, on a proposal from the Commission and after consulting the European Central Bank, may take safeguard

measures with regard to third countries for a period not exceeding six months if such measures are strictly necessary.

[BMDF Note: Article 60 TEC, as redrafted and amended by Article III-160 of the draft Constitution, is moved to Article 75 TFEU in the Title on Chapter on general provisions in the Title on the Area of freedom, security and justice]

TITLE IV

AREA OF FREEDOM, SECURITY AND JUSTICE

CHAPTER 1

GENERAL PROVISIONS

[BMDF Note: See also Declaration no. 26]

ARTICLE 67 [61] *[Article III-257 (ex Articles 29 TEU and 61 TEC)]*
1. The Union shall constitute an area of freedom, security and justice with respect for fundamental rights and the different legal systems and traditions of the Member States.

2. It shall ensure the absence of internal border controls for persons and shall frame a common policy on asylum, immigration and external border control, based on solidarity between Member States, which is fair towards third-country nationals. For the purpose of this *Title*, stateless persons shall be treated as third-country nationals.

3. The Union shall endeavour to ensure a high level of security through measures to prevent and combat crime, racism and xenophobia, and through measures for co-ordination and co-operation between police and judicial authorities and other competent authorities, as well as through the mutual recognition of judgments in criminal matters and, if necessary, through the approximation of criminal laws.

4. The Union shall facilitate access to justice, in particular through the principle of mutual recognition of judicial and extra-judicial decisions in civil matters.
[BMDF Note: This Article replaces Article 29 TEU]

ARTICLE 68 [61A] *[Article III-258 (new provision in 2004 IGC)]*
The European Council shall define the strategic guidelines for legislative and operational planning within the area of freedom, security and justice.

ARTICLE 69 [61B] *[Article III-259 (new provision in 2004 IGC)]*
National Parliaments shall ensure that the proposals and legislative initiatives submitted under *Chapters* 4 and 5 comply with the principle of subsidiarity, in accordance with the arrangements laid down by the Protocol on the application of the principles of subsidiarity and proportionality.

ARTICLE 70 [61C] *[Article III-260 (new provision in 2004 IGC)]*
Without prejudice to *Articles 258, 259 and 260*, the Council may, on a proposal from the Commission, adopt *measures* laying down the arrangements whereby Member States, in collaboration with the Commission, conduct objective and impartial evaluation of the implementation of the Union policies referred to in this *Title* by Member States' authorities, in particular in order to facilitate full application of the principle of mutual recognition. The European Parliament and national Parliaments shall be informed of the content and results of the evaluation.

ARTICLE 71 [61D] *[Article III-261 (ex Article 36 TEU)]*
A standing committee shall be set up within the Council in order to ensure that operational co-operation on internal security is promoted and strengthened within the Union. Without prejudice to *Article 240*, it shall facilitate co-ordination of the action of Member States' competent authorities. Representatives of the Union bodies, offices and agencies concerned may be involved

in the proceedings of this committee. The European Parliament and national Parliaments shall be kept informed of the proceedings.
[BMDF Note: This Article replaces Article 36 TEU]

ARTICLE 72 [61E] *[Article III-262 (ex Article 33 TEU and ex Article 64(1) TEC)]*
This *Title* shall not affect the exercise of the responsibilities incumbent upon Member States with regard to the maintenance of law and order and the safeguarding of internal security.
[BMDF Note: This Article replaces Article 33 TEU and Article 64(1) TEC]

ARTICLE 73 [61F] *[New Article in Treaty of Lisbon]*
It shall be open to Member States to organise between themselves and under their responsibility such forms of co-operation and co-ordination as they deem appropriate between the competent departments of their administrations responsible for safeguarding national security.
[BMDF Note: This Article introduced by the second draft of the Reform Treaty, 5 October 2007]

ARTICLE 74 [61G] *[Article III-263 (ex Article 66 TEC)]*
The Council shall adopt *measures* to ensure administrative co-operation between the relevant departments of the Member States in the areas covered by this *Title*, as well as between those departments and the Commission. It shall act on a Commission proposal, subject to *Article 76*, and after consulting the European Parliament.

ARTICLE 75 [61H] *[Article III-160 (new provision in 2004 IGC)]*
Where necessary to achieve the objectives set out in *Article 67*, as regards preventing and combating terrorism and related activities, *the European Parliament and the Council, acting by means of regulations in accordance with the ordinary legislative procedure,* shall define a framework for administrative measures with regard to capital movements and payments, such as the freezing of funds, financial assets or economic gains belonging to, or owned or held by, natural or legal persons, groups or non-State entities.
The Council, on a proposal from the Commission, shall adopt *measures* to implement the *framework* referred to in the first paragraph.
The acts referred to in this Article shall include necessary provisions on legal safeguards.
[BMDF Note: See also Declarations nos.25 and 65. This Article has been redrafted, moved from and replaces Article 60 TEC]

ARTICLE 76 [61I] *[Article III-264 (new provision in 2004 IGC)]*
The acts referred to in *Chapters* 4 and 5, together with the *measures* referred to in *Article 74* which ensure administrative co-operation in the areas covered by these Sections, shall be adopted:
(a) on a proposal from the Commission, or
(b) on the initiative of a quarter of the Member States.

CHAPTER 2

POLICIES ON BORDER CHECKS, ASYLUM AND IMMIGRATION

ARTICLE 77 [62] *[Article III-125 and Article III-265 (ex Articles 62 TEC and 64(1) TEC)]*
1. The Union shall develop a policy with a view to:
(a) ensuring the absence of any controls on persons, whatever their nationality, when crossing internal borders;
(b) carrying out checks on persons and efficient monitoring of the crossing of external borders;
(c) the gradual introduction of an integrated management system for external borders.

2. For the purposes of paragraph 1, *the European Parliament and the Council, acting in accordance with the ordinary legislative procedure, shall adopt* measures concerning:
(a) the common policy on visas and other short-stay residence permits;
(b) the checks to which persons crossing external borders are subject;

(c) **the conditions under which nationals of third countries shall have the freedom to travel within the Union for a short period;**
(d) **any measure necessary for the gradual establishment of an integrated management system for external borders;**
(e) **the absence of any controls on persons, whatever their nationality, when crossing internal borders.**

3. If action by the Union should prove necessary to facilitate the exercise of the right referred to in Article 20(2)(a), **and if the** *Treaties have* **not provided the necessary powers,** *the Council, acting in accordance with a special legislative procedure, may adopt provisions* **concerning passports, identity cards, residence permits or any other such document. The Council shall act unanimously after consulting the European Parliament.**
[BMDF Note: This paragraph comes from Article III-125 paragraph 2 (ex Article 18 TEC)]

4. **This Article shall not affect the competence of the Member States concerning the geographical demarcation of their borders, in accordance with international law.**
[BMDF Note: This paragraph comes from Article III-265, paragraph 3 (ex Article 18 TEC). The UK has an opt-out from this Article, under Protocol no. 25, Article 1.]

ARTICLE 78 [63] *[Article III-266 (ex Article 63, points 1 and 2, and ex Article 64(2) TEC)]*
1. The Union shall develop a common policy on asylum, subsidiary protection and temporary protection with a view to offering appropriate status to any third-country national requiring international protection and ensuring compliance with the principle of *non-refoulement.* This policy must be in accordance with the Geneva Convention of 28 July 1951 and the Protocol of 31 January 1967 relating to the status of refugees, and other relevant treaties.

2. For the purposes of paragraph 1, *the European Parliament and the Council, acting in accordance with the ordinary legislative procedure, shall adopt* measures for a common European asylum system comprising:
(a) **a uniform status of asylum for nationals of third countries, valid throughout the Union;**
(b) **a uniform status of subsidiary protection for nationals of third countries who, without obtaining European asylum, are in need of international protection;**
(c) **a common system of temporary protection for displaced persons in the event of a massive inflow;**
(d) **common procedures for the granting and withdrawing of uniform asylum or subsidiary protection status;**
(e) **criteria and mechanisms for determining which Member State is responsible for considering an application for asylum or subsidiary protection;**
(f) **standards concerning the conditions for the reception of applicants for asylum or subsidiary protection;**
(g) **partnership and co-operation with third countries for the purpose of managing inflows of people applying for asylum or subsidiary or temporary protection.**

3. In the event of one or more Member States being confronted by an emergency situation characterised by a sudden inflow of nationals of third countries, the Council, on a proposal from the Commission, may adopt provisional measures for the benefit of the Member State(s) concerned. It shall act after consulting the European Parliament.

ARTICLE 79 [63a] *[Article III-267 (ex Articles 29 and 31(1)(e) TEU, ex Article 63 TEC (points 3 and 4) and new provisions in the 2004 IGC)]*
1. The Union shall develop a common immigration policy aimed at ensuring, at all stages, the efficient management of migration flows, fair treatment of third-country nationals residing legally in Member States, and the prevention of, and enhanced measures to combat, illegal immigration and trafficking in human beings.

2. For the purposes of paragraph 1, *the European Parliament and the Council, acting in accordance with the ordinary legislative procedure, shall adopt* measures in the following areas:
(a) **the conditions of entry and residence, and standards on the issue by Member States of long-term visas and residence permits, including those for the purpose of family reunion;**

(b) the definition of the rights of third-country nationals residing legally in a Member State, including the conditions governing freedom of movement and of residence in other Member States;
(c) illegal immigration and unauthorised residence, including removal and repatriation of persons residing without authorisation;
(d) combating trafficking in persons, in particular women and children.

3. The Union may conclude agreements with third countries for the readmission to their countries of origin or provenance of third-country nationals who do not or who no longer fulfil the conditions for entry, presence or residence in the territory of one of the Member States.

4. ***The European Parliament and the Council, acting in accordance with the ordinary legislative procedure,*** **may establish measures to provide incentives and support for the action of Member States with a view to promoting the integration of third-country nationals residing legally in their territories, excluding any harmonisation of the laws and regulations of the Member States.**

5. This Article shall not affect the right of Member States to determine volumes of admission of third-country nationals coming from third countries to their territory in order to seek work, whether employed or self-employed.
[BMDF Note: See also Declaration no. 22]

ARTICLE 80 [63b] *[Article III-268 (new provision in 2004 IGC)]*
The policies of the Union set out in this ***Chapter*** **and their implementation shall be governed by the principle of solidarity and fair sharing of responsibility, including its financial implications, between the Member States. Whenever necessary, the Union acts adopted pursuant to this** ***Chapter*** **shall contain appropriate measures to give effect to this principle.**
[BMDF Note: The UK has an opt-out from the provisions of this Section, under Protocol no.26, Article 1.]

[BMDF Note: Article 64 TEC shall be repealed]

CHAPTER 3

JUDICIAL CO-OPERATION IN CIVIL MATTERS

ARTICLE 81 [65] *[Article III-269 (ex Article 65 TEC)]*
1. The Union shall develop judicial co-operation in civil matters having cross-border implications, based on the principle of mutual recognition of judgments and decisions in extra-judicial cases. Such co-operation may include the adoption of measures for the approximation of the laws and regulations of the Member States.

2. For the purposes of paragraph 1, ***the European Parliament and the Council, acting in accordance with the ordinary legislative procedure, shall adopt*** **measures, particularly when necessary for the proper functioning of the internal market, aimed at ensuring:**
(a) the mutual recognition and enforcement between Member States of judgments and decisions in extra-judicial cases;
(b) the cross-border service of judicial and extra-judicial documents;
(c) the compatibility of the rules applicable in the Member States concerning conflict of laws and of jurisdiction;
(d) co-operation in the taking of evidence;
(e) effective access to justice;
(f) the elimination of obstacles to the proper functioning of civil proceedings, if necessary by promoting the compatibility of the rules on civil procedure applicable in the Member States;
(g) the development of alternative methods of dispute settlement;
(h) support for the training of the judiciary and judicial staff.

3. Notwithstanding paragraph 2, measures concerning family law with cross-border implications ***shall be established by the Council, acting in accordance with a special legislative procedure.*** **The Council shall act unanimously after consulting the European Parliament.**

The Council, on a proposal from the Commission, may adopt a decision determining those aspects of family law with cross-border implications which may be the subject of acts adopted by the ordinary legislative procedure. The Council shall act unanimously after consulting the European Parliament.
This proposal shall be notified to the national Parliaments. If a national Parliament makes known its opposition within six months of the date of such notification, the decision shall not be adopted. In the absence of opposition, the Council may adopt the decision.

CHAPTER 4

JUDICIAL CO-OPERATION IN CRIMINAL MATTERS

[*BMDF Note: Article 66 TEC is repealed and replaced by Article 74 TFEU, shown above*]

[BMDF Note: Articles 67, 68 and 69 TEC shall be repealed]

ARTICLE 82 [69A] *[Article III-270 (ex Article 31(1) TEU)]*
1. Judicial co-operation in criminal matters in the Union shall be based on the principle of mutual recognition of judgments and judicial decisions and shall include the approximation of the laws and regulations of the Member States in the areas referred to in paragraph 2 and in *Article 83.*
***The European Parliament and the Council, acting in accordance with the ordinary legislative procedure, shall adopt* measures to:**
(a) lay down rules and procedures for ensuring recognition throughout the Union of all forms of judgments and judicial decisions;
(b) prevent and settle conflicts of jurisdiction between Member States;
(c) support the training of the judiciary and judicial staff;
(d) facilitate co-operation between judicial or equivalent authorities of the Member States in relation to proceedings in criminal matters and the enforcement of decisions.

2. To the extent necessary to facilitate mutual recognition of judgments and judicial decisions and police and judicial co-operation in criminal matters having a cross-border dimension, *the European Parliament and the Council may, by means of directives adopted in accordance with the ordinary legislative procedure,* establish minimum rules. Such rules shall take into account the differences between the legal traditions and systems of the Member States.
They shall concern:
(a) mutual admissibility of evidence between Member States;
(b) the rights of individuals in criminal procedure;
(c) the rights of victims of crime;
(d) any other specific aspects of criminal procedure which the Council has identified in advance by a decision; for the adoption of such a decision, the Council shall act unanimously after obtaining the consent of the European Parliament.
Adoption of the minimum rules referred to in this paragraph shall not prevent Member States from maintaining or introducing a higher level of protection for individuals.

3. Where a member of the Council considers that a draft *directive* as referred to in paragraph 2 would affect fundamental aspects of its criminal justice system, it may request that the draft *directive* be referred to the European Council. In that case, the *ordinary legislative procedure* shall be suspended. After discussion, *and in case of a consensus,* the European Council shall, within four months of this suspension, refer the draft back to the Council, which shall terminate the suspension of the *ordinary legislative procedure.*

4. *Within the same timeframe, in case of disagreement,* and *if* at least *nine* Member States wish to establish enhanced co-operation on the basis of the draft *directive* concerned, they shall notify the European Parliament, the Council and the Commission accordingly. In such a case, the authorisation to proceed with enhanced co-operation referred to in *Article 20(2) of the Treaty on European Union* and *Article 329(1) of this Treaty* shall be deemed to be granted and the provisions on enhanced co-operation shall apply.
[BMDF Note: This Article, together with Articles 83 and 85 TFEU, replaces Article 31 TEU]

ARTICLE 83 [69B] *[Article III-271 (new provision in 2004 IGC)]*
1. ***The European Parliament and the Council may, by means of directives adopted in accordance with the ordinary legislative procedure,*** **establish minimum rules concerning the definition of criminal offences and sanctions in the areas of particularly serious crime with a cross-border dimension resulting from the nature or impact of such offences or from a special need to combat them on a common basis.**
These areas of crime are the following: terrorism, trafficking in human beings and sexual exploitation of women and children, illicit drug trafficking, illicit arms trafficking, money laundering, corruption, counterfeiting of means of payment, computer crime and organised crime.
On the basis of developments in crime, the Council may adopt a decision identifying other areas of crime that meet the criteria specified in this paragraph. It shall act unanimously after obtaining the consent of the European Parliament.

2. **If the approximation of criminal laws and regulations of the Member States proves essential to ensure the effective implementation of a Union policy in an area which has been subject to harmonisation measures, *directives* may establish minimum rules with regard to the definition of criminal offences and sanctions in the area concerned. Such *directives* shall be adopted by the same *ordinary or special legislative* procedure as was followed for the adoption of the harmonisation measures in question, without prejudice to *Article 76.***

3. **Where a member of the Council considers that a draft *directive* as referred to in paragraph 1 or 2 would affect fundamental aspects of its criminal justice system, it may request that the draft *directive* be referred to the European Council. In that case, *the ordinary legislative procedure* shall be suspended. After discussion, *and in case of a consensus,* the European Council shall, within four months of this suspension, refer the draft back to the Council, which shall terminate the suspension of the *ordinary legislative procedure.***

4. ***Within the same timeframe, in case of disagreement,* and *if* at least *nine* Member States wish to establish enhanced co-operation on the basis of the draft *directive* concerned, they shall notify the European Parliament, the Council and the Commission accordingly. In such a case, the authorisation to proceed with enhanced co-operation referred to in *Article 20(2) of the Treaty on European Union and Article 329(1) of this Treaty* shall be deemed to be granted and the provisions on enhanced co-operation shall apply.**
[BMDF Note: This Article, together with Articles 82 and 85, replaces Article 31 TEU]

ARTICLE 84 [69C] *[Article III-272 (new provision in 2004 IGC)]*
The European Parliament and the Council, acting in accordance with the ordinary legislative procedure, **may establish measures to promote and support the action of Member States in the field of crime prevention, excluding any harmonisation of the laws and regulations of the Member States.**

ARTICLE 85 [69D] *[Article III-273 (ex Article 31(2) TEU)]*
1. **Eurojust's mission shall be to support and strengthen co-ordination and co-operation between national investigating and prosecuting authorities in relation to serious crime affecting two or more Member States or requiring a prosecution on common bases, on the basis of operations conducted and information supplied by the Member States' authorities and by Europol.**
In this context, *the European Parliament and the Council, by means of regulations adopted in accordance with the ordinary legislative procedure,* shall determine Eurojust's structure, operation, field of action and tasks. Those tasks may include:
(a) **the initiation of criminal investigations, as well as proposing the initiation of prosecutions, conducted by competent national authorities, particularly those relating to offences against the financial interests of the Union;**
(b) **the co-ordination of investigations and prosecutions referred to in point (a);**
(c) **the strengthening of judicial co-operation, including by resolution of conflicts of jurisdiction and by close co-operation with the European Judicial Network.**

***These regulations* shall also determine arrangements for involving the European Parliament and national Parliaments in the evaluation of Eurojust's activities.**

2. In the prosecutions referred to in paragraph 1, and without prejudice to *Article 86* formal acts of judicial procedure shall be carried out by the competent national officials.
[BMDF Note: See also Declaration no. 27. This Article, together with Articles 82 and 83, replaces Article 31 TEU]

ARTICLE 86 [69E] *[Article III-274 (new provision in 2004 IGC)]*
1. In order to combat crimes affecting the financial interests of the Union, the Council, *by means of a regulation adopted in accordance with a special legislative procedure,* may establish a European Public Prosecutor's Office from Eurojust. The Council shall act unanimously after obtaining the consent of the European Parliament.
In case of absence of unanimity in the Council, a group of at least nine Member States may request that the draft regulation be referred to the European Council. In that case, the procedure in the Council shall be suspended. After discussion, and in case of a consensus, the European Council shall, within four months of this suspension, refer the draft back to the Council for adoption.
Within the same timeframe, in case of disagreement, and if at least nine Member States wish to establish enhanced co-operation on the basis of the draft regulation concerned, they shall notify the European Parliament, the Council and the Commission accordingly. In such a case, the authorisation to proceed with enhanced co-operation referred to in Article 20(2) of the Treaty on European Union and Article 329(1)of this Treaty shall be deemed to be granted and the provisions on enhanced co-operation shall apply.
[BMDF Note: This third sub-paragraph has been introduced subsequent to the 2007 Reform Mandate.]

2. The European Public Prosecutor's Office shall be responsible for investigating, prosecuting and bringing to judgment, where appropriate in liaison with Europol, the perpetrators of, and accomplices in, offences against the Union's financial interests, as determined by the *regulation* provided for in paragraph 1. It shall exercise the functions of prosecutor in the competent courts of the Member States in relation to such offences.

3. The *regulation* referred to in paragraph 1 shall determine the general rules applicable to the European Public Prosecutor's Office, the conditions governing the performance of its functions, the rules of procedure applicable to its activities, as well as those governing the admissibility of evidence, and the rules applicable to the judicial review of procedural measures taken by it in the performance of its functions.

4. The European Council may, at the same time or subsequently, adopt a decision amending paragraph 1 in order to extend the powers of the European Public Prosecutor's Office to include serious crime having a cross-border dimension and amending accordingly paragraph 2 as regards the perpetrators of, and accomplices in, serious crimes affecting more than one Member State. The European Council shall act unanimously after obtaining the consent of the European Parliament and after consulting the Commission.

CHAPTER 5

POLICE CO-OPERATION

ARTICLE 87 [69F] *[Article III-275 (ex Article 30(1) TEU)]*
1. The Union shall establish police co-operation involving all the Member States' competent authorities, including police, customs and other specialised law enforcement services in relation to the prevention, detection and investigation of criminal offences.

2. For the purposes of paragraph 1, *the European Parliament and the Council, acting in accordance with the ordinary legislative procedure,* may establish measures concerning:
(a) the collection, storage, processing, analysis and exchange of relevant information;
(b) support for the training of staff, and co-operation on the exchange of staff, on equipment and on research into crime-detection;
(c) common investigative techniques in relation to the detection of serious forms of organised crime.

3. **The Council,** ***acting in accordance with a special legislative procedure,*** **may establish measures concerning operational co-operation between the authorities referred to in this Article. The Council shall act unanimously after consulting the European Parliament.**
In case of the absence of unanimity in the Council, a group of at least nine Member States may request that the draft measures be referred to the European Council. In that case, the procedure in the Council shall be suspended. After discussion, and in case of a consensus, the European Council shall, within four months of this suspension, refer the draft back to the Council for adoption.
Within the same timeframe, in case of disagreement, and if at least nine Member States wish to establish enhanced co-operation on the basis of the draft measures concerned, they shall notify the European Parliament, the Council and the Commission accordingly. In such a case, the authorisation to proceed with enhanced co-operation referred to in Article 20(2) of the Treaty on European Union and Article 329(1) of this Treaty shall be deemed to be granted and the provisions on enhanced co-operation shall apply.
The specific procedure provided in the second and third sub-paragraphs shall not apply to acts which constitute a development of the Schengen acquis.
[BMDF Note: This Article, together with Article 88, replaces Article 30 TEU. The second sub-paragraph of paragraph 3 has been introduced subsequent to the 2007 Reform Mandate]

ARTICLE 88 [69G] *[Article III-276 (ex Article 30(2) TEU)]*
1. Europol's mission shall be to support and strengthen action by the Member States' police authorities and other law enforcement services and their mutual co-operation in preventing and combating serious crime affecting two or more Member States, terrorism and forms of crime which affect a common interest covered by a Union policy.

2. ***The European Parliament and the Council, by means of regulations adopted in accordance with the ordinary legislative procedure,*** **shall determine Europol's structure, operation, field of action and tasks. These tasks may include:**
(a) the collection, storage, processing, analysis and exchange of information forwarded particularly by the authorities of the Member States or third countries or bodies;
(b) the co-ordination, organisation and implementation of investigative and operational action carried out jointly with the Member States' competent authorities or in the context of joint investigative teams, where appropriate in liaison with Eurojust.
These regulations **shall also lay down the procedures for scrutiny of Europol's activities by the European Parliament, together with national Parliaments.**

3. Any operational action by Europol must be carried out in liaison and in agreement with the authorities of the Member State or States whose territory is concerned. The application of coercive measures shall be the exclusive responsibility of the competent national authorities.
[BMDF Note: This Article, together with Article 69F, replaces Article 30 TEU]

ARTICLE 89 [69H] *[Article III-277 (ex Article 32 TEU)]*
The Council, ***acting in accordance with a special legislative procedure,*** **shall lay down the conditions and limitations under which the competent authorities of the Member States referred to in** ***Articles 82 and 87*** **may operate in the territory of another Member State in liaison and in agreement with the authorities of that State. The Council shall act unanimously after consulting the European Parliament.**
[BMDF Note: This Article replaces Article 32 TEU]

TITLE V

TRANSPORT

ARTICLE ***90*** [70] *[Article III-236 (ex Articles 70 and 71 TEC)]*
The objectives of ***the Treaties*** shall, in matters governed by this Title, be pursued within the framework of a common transport policy.

ARTICLE ***91*** [71] *[Article III-236 (ex Articles 70 and 71 TEC)]*

1. For the purpose of implementing Article ***90***, and taking into account the distinctive features of transport, ***the European Parliament and*** the Council, acting in accordance with the ***ordinary legislative procedure*** and after consulting the Economic and Social Committee and the Committee of the Regions, lay down:

(a) common rules applicable to international transport to or from the territory of a Member State or passing across the territory of one or more Member States;

(b) the conditions under which non-resident carriers may operate transport services within a Member State;

(c) measures to improve transport safety;

(d) any other appropriate provisions.

2. **When the *measures* referred to in paragraph 1 are adopted, account shall be taken of cases where their application might seriously affect** the standard of living and **level of** employment in certain **regions,** and on the operation of transport facilities.

ARTICLE ***92*** [72] *[Article III-237 (ex Article 72 TEC)]*

Until the provisions referred to in Article ***91(1)*** have been laid down, no Member State may, **unless the Council has unanimously adopted a *measure* granting a derogation,** make the various provisions governing the subject on 1 January 1958 or, for acceding States, the date of their accession, less favourable in their direct or indirect effect on carriers of other Member States as compared with carriers who are nationals of that State.

ARTICLE ***93*** [73] *[Article III-238 (ex Article 73 TEC)]*

Aids shall be compatible with ***the Treaties*** if they meet the needs of co-ordination of transport or if they represent reimbursement for the discharge of certain obligations inherent in the concept of a public service.

ARTICLE ***94*** [74] *[Article III-239 (ex Article 74 TEC)]*

Any measures taken within the framework of ***the Treaties*** in respect of transport rates and conditions shall take account of the economic circumstances of carriers.

ARTICLE ***95*** [75] *[Article III-240 (ex Article 75 TEC)]*

1. In the case of transport within the ***Union***, discrimination which takes the form of carriers charging different rates and imposing different conditions for the carriage of the same goods over the same transport links on grounds of the country of origin or of destination of the goods in question shall be **prohibited**.

2. Paragraph 1 shall not prevent ***the European Parliament and*** the Council from adopting other measures in pursuance of Article ***91(1)***.

3. The Council shall, on a proposal from the Commission and after consulting **the European Parliament and** the Economic and Social Committee, lay down rules for implementing the provisions of paragraph 1.

The Council may in particular lay down the provisions needed to enable the institutions of the ***Union*** to secure compliance with the rule laid down in paragraph 1 and to ensure that users benefit from it to the full.

4. The Commission shall, acting on its own initiative or on application by a Member State, investigate any cases of discrimination falling within paragraph 1 and after consulting any Member State concerned, shall take the necessary decisions within the framework of the rules laid down in accordance with the provisions of paragraph 3.

ARTICLE ***96*** [76] *[Article III-241 (ex Article 76 TEC)]*

1. The imposition by a Member State, in respect of transport operations carried out within the ***Union***, of rates and conditions involving any element of support or protection in the interest of one or more particular undertakings or industries shall be prohibited, unless authorised by the Commission.

2. The Commission shall, acting on its own initiative or on application by a Member State, examine the rates and conditions referred to in paragraph 1, taking account in particular of the requirements of an appropriate regional economic policy, the needs of underdeveloped areas and the problems of areas

seriously affected by political circumstances on the one hand, and of the effects of such rates and conditions on competition between the different modes of transport on the other.
After consulting each Member State concerned, the Commission shall take the necessary decisions.

3. The prohibition provided for in paragraph 1 shall not apply to tariffs fixed to meet competition.

ARTICLE ***97*** [77] *[Article III-242 (ex Article 77 TEC)]*
Charges or dues in respect of the crossing of frontiers which are charged by a carrier in addition to the transport rates shall not exceed a reasonable level after taking the costs actually incurred thereby into account.
Member States shall endeavour to reduce these costs progressively.
The Commission may make recommendations to Member States for the application of this Article.

ARTICLE ***98*** [78] *[Article III-243 (ex Article 78 TEC)]*
The provisions of this Title shall not form an obstacle to the application of measures taken in the Federal Republic of Germany to the extent that such measures are required in order to compensate for the economic disadvantages caused by the division of Germany to the economy of certain areas of the Federal Republic affected by that division. **Five years after the entry into force of *the Treaty of Lisbon*, the Council, acting on a proposal from the Commission, may adopt a decision repealing this Article.**
[BMDF Note: See also Declaration no. 78]

ARTICLE ***99*** [79] *[Article III-244 (ex Article 79 TEC)]*
An Advisory Committee consisting of experts designated by the Governments of Member States, shall be attached to the Commission. The Commission, whenever it considers it desirable, shall consult the Committee on transport matters.

ARTICLE ***100*** [80] *[Article III-245 (ex Article 80 TEC)]*
1. The provisions of this Title shall apply to transport by rail, road and inland waterway.

2. ***The European Parliament and the Council, acting in accordance with the ordinary legislative procedure,*** **may lay down appropriate provisions** for sea and air transport. ***They shall act after consulting*** **the Committee of the Regions and the Economic and Social Committee.**

TITLE VI

COMMON RULES ON COMPETITION, TAXATION AND APPROXIMATION OF LAWS

CHAPTER 1

RULES ON COMPETITION

SECTION 1

RULES APPLYING TO UNDERTAKINGS

ARTICLE ***101*** [81] *[Article III-161 (ex Article 81 TEC)]*
1. The following shall be prohibited as incompatible with the **internal** market: all agreements between undertakings, decisions by associations of undertakings and concerted practices which may affect trade between Member States and which have as their object or effect the prevention, restriction or distortion of competition within the **internal** market, and in particular those which:
(a) directly or indirectly fix purchase or selling prices or any other trading conditions;
(b) limit or control production, markets, technical development, or investment;
(c) share markets or sources of supply;
(d) apply dissimilar conditions to equivalent transactions with other trading parties, thereby placing them at a competitive disadvantage;

(e) make the conclusion of contracts subject to acceptance by the other parties of supplementary obligations which, by their nature or according to commercial usage, have no connection with the subject of such contracts.

2. Any agreements or decisions prohibited pursuant to this Article shall be automatically void.

3. The provisions of paragraph 1 may, however, be declared inapplicable in the case of:
- any agreement or category of agreements between undertakings;
- any decision or category of decisions by associations of undertakings;
- any concerted practice or category of concerted practices;

which contributes to improving the production or distribution of goods or to promoting technical or economic progress, while allowing consumers a fair share of the resulting benefit, and which does not:
(a) impose on the undertakings concerned restrictions which are not indispensable to the attainment of these objectives;
(b) afford such undertakings the possibility of eliminating competition in respect of a substantial part of the products in question.

ARTICLE ***102*** [82] *[Article III-162 (ex Article 82 TEC)]*
Any abuse by one or more undertakings of a dominant position within the **internal** market or in a substantial part of it shall be prohibited as incompatible with the **internal** market insofar as it may affect trade between Member States.
Such abuse may, in particular, consist in:
(a) directly or indirectly imposing unfair purchase or selling prices or other unfair trading conditions;
(b) limiting production, markets or technical development to the prejudice of consumers;
(c) applying dissimilar conditions to equivalent transactions with other trading parties, thereby placing them at a competitive disadvantage;
(d) making the conclusion of contracts subject to acceptance by the other parties of supplementary obligations which, by their nature or according to commercial usage, have no connection with the subject of such contracts.

ARTICLE ***103*** [83] [*Article III-163 (ex Article 83 TEC)]*
1. The appropriate regulations or directives to give effect to the principles set out in Articles ***101*** and ***102*** shall be laid down by the Council, on a proposal from the Commission and after consulting the European Parliament.

2. The regulations or directives referred to in paragraph 1 shall be designed in particular:
(a) to ensure compliance with the prohibitions laid down in Article ***101(1)*** and in Article ***102*** by making provision for fines and periodic penalty payments;
(b) to lay down detailed rules for the application of Article ***101(3)***, taking into account the need to ensure effective supervision on the one hand, and to simplify administration to the greatest possible extent on the other;
(c) to define, if need be, in the various branches of the economy, the scope of the provisions of Articles ***101*** and ***102***;
(d) to define the respective functions of the Commission and of the Court of Justice **of the European Union** in applying the provisions laid down in this paragraph;
(e) to determine the relationship between national laws and the provisions contained in this Section or adopted pursuant to this Article.

ARTICLE ***104*** [84] [*Article III-164 (ex Article 84 TEC)]*
Until the entry into force of the provisions adopted in pursuance of Article ***103***, the authorities in Member States shall rule on the admissibility of agreements, decisions and concerted practices and on abuse of a dominant position in the **internal** market in accordance with the law of their country and with the provisions of Article ***101***, in particular paragraph 3, and of Article ***102***.

ARTICLE ***105*** [85] *[Article III-165 (Paragraph 3 new in 2004 IGC)]*
1. Without prejudice to Article ***104***, the Commission shall ensure the application of the principles laid down in Articles ***101*** and ***102***. On application by a Member State or on its own initiative, and in co-operation with the competent authorities in the Member States, who shall give it their assistance, the Commission shall investigate cases of suspected infringement of these principles. If it finds that there has been an infringement, it shall propose appropriate measures to bring it to an end.

2. If the infringement is not brought to an end, the Commission shall record such infringement of the principles in a reasoned decision. The Commission may publish its decision and authorise Member States to take the measures, the conditions and details of which it shall determine, needed to remedy the situation.

3. The Commission may adopt regulations relating to the categories of agreement in respect of which the Council has adopted a regulation or a directive pursuant to *Article 103(2)(b).*

ARTICLE ***106*** [86] [*Article III-166 (ex Article 86 TEC)]*

1. In the case of public undertakings and undertakings to which Member States grant special or exclusive rights, Member States shall neither enact nor maintain in force any measure contrary to the rules contained in ***the Treaties***, in particular to those rules provided for in Article ***18*** and Articles ***101*** to ***109.***

2. Undertakings entrusted with the operation of services of general economic interest or having the character of a revenue-producing monopoly shall be subject to the rules contained in ***the Treaties***, in particular to the rules on competition, insofar as the application of such rules does not obstruct the performance, in law or in fact, of the particular tasks assigned to them. The development of trade must not be affected to such an extent as would be contrary to the interests of the ***Union***.

3. The Commission shall ensure the application of the provisions of this Article and shall, where necessary, address appropriate directives or decisions to Member States.

SECTION 2

AIDS GRANTED BY STATES

ARTICLE ***107*** [87] *[Article III-167 (ex Article 87 TEC)]*

1. Save as otherwise provided in ***the Treaties***, any aid granted by a Member State or through State resources in any form whatsoever which distorts or threatens to distort competition by favouring certain undertakings or the production of certain goods shall, in so far as it affects trade between Member States, be incompatible with the **internal** market.

2. The following shall be compatible with the **internal** market:
(a) aid having a social character, granted to individual consumers, provided that such aid is granted without discrimination related to the origin of the products concerned;
(b) aid to make good the damage caused by natural disasters or exceptional occurrences;
(c) aid granted to the economy of certain areas of the Federal Republic of Germany affected by the division of Germany, insofar as such aid is required in order to compensate for the economic disadvantages caused by that division. **Five years after the entry into force of the *Treaty of Lisbon,* the Council, acting on a proposal from the Commission, may adopt a decision repealing this point.**

3. The following may be considered to be compatible with the **internal** market:
(a) aid to promote the economic development of areas where the standard of living is abnormally low or where there is serious underemployment, **and of the regions referred to in *Article 349,* in view of their structural, economic and social situation**;
(b) aid to promote the execution of an important project of common European interest or to remedy a serious disturbance in the economy of a Member State;
(c) aid to facilitate the development of certain economic activities or of certain economic areas, where such aid does not adversely affect trading conditions to an extent contrary to the common interest;
(d) aid to promote culture and heritage conservation where such aid does not affect trading conditions and competition in the **Union** to an extent that is contrary to the common interest;
(e) such other categories of aid as may be specified by decision of the Council on a proposal from the Commission.

[BMDF Note: See also Declaration no. 29]

ARTICLE ***108*** [88] *[Article III-168 (Paragraph 4 new in 2004 IGC)]*
1. The Commission shall, in co-operation with Member States, keep under constant review all systems of aid existing in those States. It shall propose to the latter any appropriate measures required by the progressive development or by the functioning of the **internal** market.

2. If, after giving notice to the parties concerned to submit their comments, the Commission finds that aid granted by a State or through State resources is not compatible with the **internal** market having regard to Article ***107***, or that such aid is being misused, it shall decide that the State concerned shall abolish or alter such aid within a period of time to be determined by the Commission.
If the State concerned does not comply with this decision within the prescribed time, the Commission or any other interested State may, in derogation from the provisions of Articles ***258*** and ***259***, refer the matter to the Court of Justice **of the European Union** direct.
On application by a Member State, the Council, may acting unanimously, decide that aid which that State is granting or intends to grant shall be considered to be compatible with the **internal** market, in derogation from the provisions of Article ***107*** or from the regulations provided for in Article ***109***, if such a decision is justified by exceptional circumstances. If, as regards the aid in question, the Commission has already initiated the procedure provided for in the first sub-paragraph of this paragraph, the fact that the State concerned has made its application to the Council shall have the effect of suspending that procedure until the Council has made its attitude known.
If, however, the Council has not made its attitude known within three months of the said application being made, the Commission shall give its decision on the case.

3. The Commission shall be informed, in sufficient time to enable it to submit its comments, of any plans to grant or alter aid. If it considers that any such plan is not compatible with the **internal** market having regard to Article ***107***, it shall without delay initiate the procedure provided for in paragraph 2. The Member State concerned shall not put its proposed measures into effect until this procedure has resulted in a final decision.

4. The Commission may adopt regulations relating to the categories of State aid that the Council has, pursuant to *Article 109*, determined may be exempted from the procedure provided for by paragraph 3 of this Article.

ARTICLE ***109*** [89] *[Article III-169 (ex Article 89 TEC)]*
The Council, on a proposal from the Commission and after consulting the European Parliament, make any appropriate regulations for the application of Articles ***107*** and ***108*** and may in particular determine the conditions in which Article ***108(3)*** shall apply and the categories of aid exempted from this procedure.

CHAPTER 2

TAX PROVISIONS

ARTICLE ***110*** [90] *[Article III-170 (ex Article 90 TEC)]*
No Member State shall impose, directly or indirectly, on the products of other Member States any internal taxation of any kind in excess of that imposed directly or indirectly on similar domestic products.
Furthermore, no Member State shall impose on the products of other Member States any internal taxation of such a nature as to afford indirect protection to other products.

ARTICLE ***111*** [91] *[Article III-170 (ex Article 91 TEC)]*
Where products are exported to the territory of any Member State, any repayment of internal taxation shall not exceed the internal taxation imposed on them whether directly or indirectly.

ARTICLE ***112*** [92] [*Article III-170 (ex Article 92 TEC)]*
In the case of charges other than turnover taxes, excise duties and other forms of indirect taxation, remissions and repayments in respect of exports to other Member States may not be granted and countervailing charges in respect of imports from Member States may not be imposed unless the measures contemplated have been previously approved for a limited period by the Council on a proposal from the Commission.

ARTICLE ***113*** [93] *[Article III-171 (ex Article 93 TEC)]*
The Council shall, acting unanimously ***in accordance with a special legislative procedure*** and after consulting the European Parliament and the Economic and Social Committee, adopt provisions for the harmonisation of legislation concerning turnover taxes, excise duties and other forms of indirect taxation to the extent that such harmonisation is necessary to ensure the establishment and the functioning of the internal market **and to avoid distortion of competition**.

CHAPTER 3

APPROXIMATION OF LAWS

ARTICLE ***114*** [94] *[Article III-172 (ex Article 94 TEC)]*
1. Save where otherwise provided in ***the Treaties***, the following provisions shall apply for the achievement of the objectives set out in Article ***26***. ***The European Parliament and*** the Council, acting in accordance with the ***ordinary legislative procedure*** and after consulting the Economic and Social Committee, adopt the measures for the approximation of the provisions laid down by law, regulation or administrative action in Member States which have as their object the establishment and functioning of the internal market.

2. Paragraph 1 shall not apply to fiscal provisions, to those relating to the free movement of persons nor to those relating to the rights and interests of employed persons.

3. The Commission, in its proposals envisaged in paragraph 1 concerning health, safety, environmental protection and consumer protection, will take as a base a high level of protection, taking account in particular of any new development based on scientific facts. Within their respective powers, the European Parliament and the Council will also seek to achieve this objective.

4. If, after the adoption of a harmonisation measure ***by the European Parliament and the Council, by the Council or by the Commission,*** a Member State deems it necessary to maintain national provisions on grounds of major needs referred to in Article ***36***, or relating to the protection of the environment or the working environment, it shall notify the Commission of these provisions as well as the grounds for maintaining them.

5. Moreover, without prejudice to paragraph 4, if, after the adoption of a harmonisation measure ***by the European Parliament and the Council, by the Council or by the Commission***, a Member State deems it necessary to introduce national provisions based on new scientific evidence relating to the protection of the environment or the working environment on grounds of a problem specific to that Member State arising after the adoption of the harmonisation measure, it shall notify the Commission of the envisaged provisions as well as the grounds for introducing them.

6. The Commission shall, within six months of the notifications as referred to in paragraphs 4 and 5, approve or reject the national provisions involved after having verified whether or not they are not a means of arbitrary discrimination or a disguised restriction on trade between Member States and whether or not they shall constitute an obstacle to the functioning of the internal market.
In the absence of a decision by the Commission within this period the national provisions referred to in paragraphs 4 and 5 shall be deemed to have been approved.
When justified by the complexity of the matter and in the absence of danger for human health, the Commission may notify the Member State concerned that the period referred to in this paragraph may be extended for a further period of up to six months.

7. When, pursuant to paragraph 6, a Member State is authorised to maintain or introduce national provisions derogating from a harmonisation measure, the Commission shall immediately examine whether to propose an adaptation to that measure.

8. When a Member State raises a specific problem on public health in a field which has been the subject of prior harmonisation measures, it shall bring it to the attention of the Commission which shall immediately examine whether to propose appropriate measures to the Council.

9. By way of derogation from the procedure laid down in Articles ***258*** and ***259***, the Commission and any Member State may bring the matter directly before the Court of Justice **of the European Union** if it considers that another Member State is making improper use of the powers provided for in this Article.

10. The harmonisation measures referred to above shall, in appropriate cases, include a safeguard clause authorising the Member States to take, for one or more of the non-economic reasons referred to in Article ***36***, provisional measures subject to a **Union** control procedure.
[BMDF Note: Order of Articles 94 and 95 TEC reversed, following the order of 2004 IGC.]

ARTICLE ***115*** [95] *[Article III-173 (ex Article 95 TEC)]*
Without prejudice to *Article 114*, the Council shall, acting unanimously ***in accordance with a special legislative procedure*** and after consulting the European Parliament and the Economic and Social Committee, issue directives for the approximation of such laws, regulations or administrative provisions of the Member States as directly affect the establishment or functioning of the **internal** market.
[BMDF Note: Order of Articles 94 and 95 TEC reversed, following the order of 2004 IGC.]

ARTICLE ***116*** [96] *[Article III-174 (ex Article 96 TEC)]*
Where the Commission finds that a difference between the provisions laid down by law, regulation or administrative action in Member States is distorting the conditions of competition in the ***internal*** market and that the resultant distortion needs to be eliminated, it shall consult the Member States concerned.
If such consultation does not result in an agreement eliminating the distortion in question, ***the European Parliament and*** the Council, ***acting in accordance with the ordinary legislative procedure, shall*** issue the necessary directives. ***A***ny other appropriate measures provided for in ***the Treaties*** **may be adopted**.

ARTICLE ***117*** [97] *[Article III-175 (ex Article 97 TEC)]*
1. Where there is reason to fear that the adoption or amendment of a provision laid down by law, regulation or administrative action may cause distortion within the meaning of Article ***116***, a Member State desiring to proceed therewith shall consult the Commission. After consulting the Member States, the Commission shall recommend to the States concerned such measures as may be appropriate to avoid the distortion in question.

2. If a State desiring to introduce or amend its own provisions does not comply with the recommendation addressed to it by the Commission, other Member States shall not be required, in pursuance of Article ***116***, to amend their own provisions in order to eliminate such distortion. If the Member State which has ignored the recommendation of the Commission causes distortion detrimental only to itself, the provisions of Article ***116*** shall not apply.

ARTICLE 118 [97a] *[Article III-176 (new Article in 2004 IGC)]*
In the context of the establishment and functioning of the internal market, *the European Parliament and the Council, acting in accordance with the ordinary legislative procedure,* shall establish measures for the creation of European intellectual property rights to provide uniform intellectual property rights protection throughout the Union and for the setting up of centralised Union-wide authorisation, co-ordination and supervision arrangements.
***The Council, acting unanimously in accordance with a special legislative procedure, shall by means of regulations* establish language arrangements for the European intellectual property rights. The Council shall act unanimously after consulting the European Parliament.**

TITLE VII

ECONOMIC AND MONETARY POLICY

ARTICLE 119 [97b] *[Article III-177 (ex Article 4 TEC)]*
1. For the purposes set out in ***Article 3 of the Treaty on European Union***, the activities of the Member States and the **Union** shall include, as provided in ***the Treaties***, the adoption of an economic policy which is based on the close co-ordination of Member States' economic policies, on the internal market and on the definition of common objectives, and conducted in accordance with the principle of an open market economy with free competition.

2. Concurrently with the foregoing, and as provided in ***the Treaties*** and in accordance with the procedures set out therein, these activities shall include a single currency, the **euro**, and the definition and conduct of a single monetary policy and exchange rate policy the primary objective of both of which shall be to maintain price stability and, without prejudice to this objective, to support the general economic policies in the **Union**, in accordance with the principle of an open market economy with free competition.
[BMDF Note: Article moved from Article 4 TEC; Paragraph does not apply to the UK: Protocol 22, Article 4].

3. These activities of the Member States and the **Union** shall entail compliance with the following guiding principles: stable prices, sound public finances and monetary conditions and a sustainable balance of payments.

CHAPTER 1

ECONOMIC POLICY

ARTICLE ***120*** [98] *[Article III-178 (ex Article 98 TEC)]*
Member States shall conduct their economic policies with a view to contributing to the achievement of the objectives of the ***Union***, as defined in ***Article 3 of the Treaty on European Union***, and in the context of the broad guidelines referred to in Article ***121(2).*** The Member States and the ***Union*** shall act in accordance with the principle of an open market economy with free competition, favouring an efficient allocation of resources, and in compliance with the principles set out in Article ***119***.

ARTICLE ***121*** [99] *[Article III-179 (ex Article 99 TEC)]*
1. Member States shall regard their economic policies as a matter of common concern and shall co-ordinate them within the Council, in accordance with the provisions of Article ***120***.

2. The Council shall, on a recommendation from the Commission, formulate a draft for the broad guidelines of the economic policies of the Member States and of the ***Union***, and shall report its findings to the European Council.
The European Council shall, acting on the basis of the report from the Council, discuss a conclusion on the broad guidelines of the economic policies of the Member States and of the ***Union***.
On the basis of this conclusion, the Council shall, adopt a recommendation setting out these broad guidelines. The Council shall inform the European Parliament of its recommendation.
[BMDF Note: Paragraph does not apply to the United Kingdom, Article 139(2) TFEU]

3. In order to ensure closer co-ordination of economic policies and sustained convergence of the economic performances of the Member States, the Council shall, on the basis of reports submitted by the Commission, monitor economic developments in each of the Member States and in the ***Union*** as well as the consistency of economic policies with the broad guidelines referred to in paragraph 2, and regularly carry out an overall assessment.
For the purpose of this multilateral surveillance, Member States shall forward information to the Commission about important measures taken by them in the field of their economic policy and such other information as they deem necessary.

4. Where it is established, under the procedure referred to in paragraph 3, that the economic policies of a Member State are not consistent with the broad guidelines referred to in paragraph 2 or that they risk jeopardising the proper functioning of economic and monetary union, **the Commission may address a warning to the Member State concerned.** The Council**, on a recommendation from the Commission, may address** the necessary recommendations to the Member State concerned. The Council may, on a proposal from the Commission, decide to make its recommendations public.
Within the scope of this paragraph, the Council shall act without taking into account the vote of the member of the Council representing the Member State concerned.
A qualified majority of the other members of the Council shall be defined in accordance with Article 238(3)(a).
[BMDF Note: Voting rights of the United Kingdom suspended, Article 139(4) TFEU]

5. The President of the Council and the Commission shall report to the European Parliament on the results of multilateral surveillance. The President of the Council may be invited to appear before the competent Committee of the European Parliament if the Council has made its recommendations public.

6. ***The European Parliament and the Council, acting by means of regulations in accordance with the ordinary legislative procedure,*** may adopt detailed rules for the multilateral surveillance procedure referred to in paragraphs 3 and 4.

ARTICLE ***122*** [100] *[Article III-180(ex Article 100 TEC)]*
1. Without prejudice to any other procedures provided for in ***the Treaties***, the Council, on a proposal from the Commission, may decide***, in a spirit of solidarity between Member States,*** upon the measures appropriate to the economic situation, in particular if severe difficulties arise in the supply of certain products***, notably in the area of energy***.

2. Where a Member State is in difficulties or is seriously threatened with severe difficulties caused by natural disasters or exceptional occurrences beyond its control, the Council, on a proposal from the Commission, may grant, under certain conditions, ***Union*** financial assistance to the Member State concerned. The President of the Council shall inform the European Parliament of the decision taken.

ARTICLE ***123*** [101] *[Article III-181 (ex Article 101 TEC)]*
1. Overdraft facilities or any other type of credit facility with the European Central Bank or with the central banks of the Member States (hereinafter referred to as 'national central banks') in favour of ***Union institutions, bodies, offices or agencies***, central governments, regional, local or other public authorities, other bodies governed by public law, or public undertakings of Member States shall be prohibited, as shall the purchase directly from them by the ECB or national central banks of debt instruments.

2. Paragraph 1 shall not apply to publicly-owned credit institutions which, in the context of the supply of reserves by central banks, shall be given the same treatment by national central banks and the European Central Bank as private credit institutions.

ARTICLE ***124*** [102] *[Article III-182 (ex Article 102 TEC)]*
Any measure, not based on prudential considerations, establishing privileged access by ***Union institutions, bodies, offices or agencies***, central governments, regional, local or other public authorities, other bodies governed by public law, or public undertakings of Member States to financial institutions shall be prohibited.

ARTICLE ***125*** [103] *[Article III-183(ex Article 103 TEC)]*
1. The **Union** shall not be liable for or assume the commitments of central governments, regional, local or other public authorities, other bodies governed by public law, or public undertakings of any Member State, without prejudice to mutual financial guarantees for the joint execution of a specific project. A Member State shall not be liable for or assume the commitments of central governments, regional, local or other public authorities, other bodies governed by public law or public undertakings of another Member State, without prejudice to mutual financial guarantees for the joint execution of a specific project.

2. The Council, **on a proposal from the Commission** ***and after consulting the European Parliament,*** may***, as required,*** specify definitions for the application of the prohibitions referred to in Article*s* ***123 and 124*** and in this Article.

ARTICLE ***126*** [104] *[Article III-184 (ex Article 104 TEC)]*
1. Member States shall avoid excessive government deficits.
[BMDF Note: Paragraph does not apply to the UK:, Protocol 18(4)]

2. The Commission shall monitor the development of the budgetary situation and of the stock of government debt in the Member States with a view to identifying gross errors. In particular it shall examine compliance with budgetary discipline on the basis of the following two criteria:
(a) whether the ratio of the planned or actual government deficit to gross domestic product exceeds a reference value, unless:

- either the ratio has declined substantially and continuously and reached a level that comes close to the reference value;
- or, alternatively, the excess over the reference value is only exceptional and temporary and the ratio remains close to the reference value;

(b) whether the ratio of government debt to gross domestic product exceeds a reference value, unless the ratio is sufficiently diminishing and approaching the reference value at a satisfactory pace.

The reference values are specified in the Protocol on the excessive deficit procedure annexed to ***the Treaties***.

3. If a Member State does not fulfil the requirements under one or both of these criteria, the Commission shall prepare a report. The report of the Commission shall also take into account whether the government deficit exceeds government investment expenditure and take into account all other relevant factors, including the medium-term economic and budgetary position of the Member State.
The Commission may also prepare a report if, notwithstanding the fulfilment of the requirements under the criteria, it is of the opinion that there is a risk of an excessive deficit in a Member State.

4. The ***Economic and Financial Committee*** shall formulate an opinion on the report of the Commission.

5. If the Commission considers that an excessive deficit in a Member State exists or may occur, the Commission shall address an opinion to the **Member State concerned and shall inform the Council accordingly.**

6. The Council shall, on a ***proposal*** from the Commission, and having considered any observations which the Member State concerned may wish to make, decide after an overall assessment whether an excessive deficit exists.
[BMDF Note: The voting rights of the United Kingdom suspended, Article 139(4) TFEU]

7. ***Where the Council decides, in accordance with paragraph 6, that an excessive deficit exists, it shall adopt,*** **without undue delay, on a recommendation from the Commission,** recommendations **addressed** to the Member State concerned with a view to bringing that situation to an end within a given period. Subject to the provisions of paragraph 8, these recommendations shall not be made public.
[BMDF Note: The voting rights of the United Kingdom suspended, Article 139(4) TFEU]

8. Where it establishes that there has been no effective action in response to its recommendations within the period laid down, the Council may make its recommendations public.
[BMDF Note: The voting rights of the United Kingdom suspended, Article 139(4) TFEU]

9. If a Member State persists in failing to put into practice the recommendations of the Council, the Council may decide to give notice to the Member State to take, within a specified time limit, measures for the deficit reduction which is judged necessary by the Council in order to remedy the situation.
In such a case, the Council may request the Member State concerned to submit reports in accordance with a specific timetable in order to examine the adjustment efforts of that Member State.
[BMDF Note: Paragraph does not apply to the UK: Article 139(2) TFEU and Protocol 18(4)]

10. The rights to bring actions provided for in Articles ***258*** and ***259*** may not be exercised within the framework of paragraphs 1 to 9 of this Article.

11. As long as a Member State fails to comply with a decision taken in accordance with paragraph 9, the Council may decide to apply or, as the case may be, intensify one or more of the following measures:

- to require the Member State concerned to publish additional information, to be specified by the Council, before issuing bonds and securities;
- to invite the European Investment Bank to reconsider its lending policy towards the Member State concerned;
- to require the Member State concerned to make a non-interest-bearing deposit of an appropriate size with the ***Union*** until the excessive deficit has, in the view of the Council, been corrected;
- to impose fines of an appropriate size.

The President of the Council shall inform the European Parliament of the decisions taken.
[BMDF Note: Paragraph does not apply to the UK: Article 139(2) TFEU and Protocol 18(4)]

12. The Council shall abrogate some or all of its decisions ***or recommendations*** referred to in paragraphs 6 to 9 and 11 to the extent that the excessive deficit in the Member State concerned has, in the view of the Council, been corrected. If the Council has previously made public recommendations, it shall, as soon as the decision under paragraph 8 has been abrogated, make a public statement that an excessive deficit in the Member State concerned no longer exists.
[BMDF Note: Paragraph does not apply to the UK: Article 139(4) TFEU]

13. When taking the decisions referred to in paragraphs ***8,*** 9, 11 and 12, the Council shall act on a recommendation from the Commission.
When the Council adopts the measures referred to in paragraphs 6 to 9 and 11 and 12, it shall act without taking into account the vote of the member of the Council representing the Member State concerned.
A qualified majority of the other members of the Council shall be defined in accordance with Article 238(3)(a).

14. Further provisions relating to the implementation of the procedure described in this Article are set out in the Protocol on the excessive deficit procedure annexed to ***the Treaties***.
The Council shall, acting unanimously on a proposal from the Commission and after consulting the European Parliament and the European Central Bank, adopt the appropriate provisions which shall then replace the said Protocol.
Subject to the other provisions of this paragraph the Council shall, ***in accordance with a special legislative procedure*** and after consulting the European Parliament, lay down detailed rules and definitions for the application of the provisions of the said Protocol.
[BMDF Note: See also Declarations nos. 15 and 30]

CHAPTER 2

MONETARY POLICY

ARTICLE *127* [105] *[Article III-185(ex Article 105 TEC)]*
1. The primary objective of the **European System of Central Banks,** ***hereinafter referred to as*** "ESCB" shall be to maintain price stability. Without prejudice to the objective of price stability, the ESCB shall support the general economic policies in the **Union** with a view to contributing to the achievement of the objectives of the ***Union*** as laid down in Article ***3 of the Treaty on European Union***. The ESCB shall act in accordance with the principle of an open market economy with free competition, favouring an efficient allocation of resources, and in compliance with the principles set out in Article 4.
[BMDF Note: Paragraph does not apply to the UK: Article 39(2) TFEU and Protocol 18(4)]

2. The basic tasks to be carried out through the ESCB shall be:
- to define and implement the monetary policy of the ***Union***;
- to conduct foreign exchange operations consistent with the provisions of ***Article 219***;
- to hold and manage the official foreign reserves of the Member States;
- to promote the smooth operation of payment systems.

[BMDF Note: Paragraph does not apply to the UK: Article 139(2) TFEU and Protocol 18(4)]

3. The third indent of paragraph 2 shall be without prejudice to the holding and management by the governments of Member States of foreign exchange working balances.
[BMDF Note: Paragraph does not apply to the UK: Article 139(2) TFEU and Protocol 18(4)]

4. The European Central Bank shall be consulted:
- on any proposed **Union** act in its fields of competence;
- by national authorities regarding any draft legislative provision in its fields of competence, but within the limits and under the conditions set out by the Council in accordance with the procedure laid down in Article ***129(6).***

The European Central Bank may submit opinions to the appropriate **Union institutions, bodies, offices or agencies** or to national authorities on matters in its fields of competence.
[BMDF Note: Paragraph does not apply to the UK: Article 139(2) TFEU and Protocol 18(4)]

5. The ESCB shall contribute to the smooth conduct of policies pursued by the competent authorities relating to the prudential supervision of credit institutions and the stability of the Financial system.
[BMDF Note: Paragraph does not apply to the UK: Article 139(2) TFEU and Protocol 18(4)]

6. The Council, ***acting by means of regulations in accordance with a special legislative procedure, may unanimously, and after consulting the European Parliament and the European Central Bank,*** confer **specific tasks** upon the European Central Bank concerning policies relating to the prudential supervision of credit institutions and other financial institutions with the exception of insurance undertakings.

ARTICLE ***128*** [106] *[Article III-186 (ex Article 106 TEC)]*
1. The ECB shall have the exclusive right to authorise the issue of **euro** bank notes within the ***Union***. The European Central Bank and the national central banks may issue such notes. The bank notes issued by the European Central Bank and the national central banks shall be the only such notes to have the status of legal tender within the ***Union***.

2. Member States may issue **euro** coins subject to approval by the European Central Bank of the volume of the issue. The Council **on a proposal from the Commission** and after consulting ***the European Parliament and*** the European Central Bank, ***may*** adopt measures to harmonise the denominations and technical specifications of all coins intended for circulation to the extent necessary to permit their smooth circulation within the **Union**.
[BMDF Note: Article does not apply to the UK: Article 139(2) TFEU and Protocol 18(4)]

ARTICLE ***129*** [107] *[Article III-187 (ex Article 107 TEC)]*
1. The **European System of Central Banks,** ***hereinafter referred to as*** **'**ESCB**'** shall be governed by the decision-making bodies of the European Central Bank**,** which shall be the Governing Council and the Executive Board.

2. The **Statute of the European System of Central Banks** ***and of the European Central Bank, hereinafter referred to as*** 'Statute of the ESCB ***and of the ECB'*** is laid down in a Protocol annexed to ***the Treaties***.

3. Articles 5.1, 5.2, 5.3, 17, 18, 19.1, 22, 23, 24, 26, 32.2, 32.3, 32.4, 32.6, 33.1(a) and 36 of the Statute of the ESCB ***and of the ECB*** may be amended by ***the European Parliament and*** the Council, acting ***in accordance with the ordinary legislative procedure. They shall act either on a recommendation from the European Central Bank and after consulting the Commission or on a proposal from the Commission and after consulting the European Central Bank.***

4. The Council, either on a proposal from the Commission and after consulting the European Parliament and the European Central Bank or on a recommendation from the European Central Bank and after consulting the European Parliament and the Commission, shall adopt the provisions referred to in Articles 4, 5.4, 19.2, 20, 28.1, 29.2, 30.4 and 34.3 of the Statute of the ESCB ***and of the ECB***.

ARTICLE ***130*** [108] *[Article III-188(ex Article 108 TEC)]*
When exercising the powers and carrying out the tasks and duties conferred upon them by ***the Treaties*** and the Statute of the ESCB ***and of the ECB***, neither the European Central Bank, nor a national central bank, nor any member of their decision-making bodies shall seek or take instructions from ***Union institutions, bodies, offices or agencies***, from any government of a Member State or from any other body. The ***Union*** institutions and bodies and the governments of the Member States undertake to respect this principle and not to seek to influence the members of the decision-making bodies of the European Central Bank or of the national central banks in the performance of their tasks.
[BMDF Note: Paragraph does not apply to the UK: Protocol 18(4)]

ARTICLE ***131*** [109] *[Article III-189 (ex Article 109 TEC)]*
Each Member State shall ensure that its national legislation including the statutes of its national central bank is compatible with this Treaty ***the Treaties*** and the Statute of the ESCB ***and of the ECB***.
[BMDF Note: Article does not apply to the UK: Protocol 18(4)]

ARTICLE ***132*** [110] *[Article III-190 (ex Article 110 TEC)]*
1. In order to carry out the tasks entrusted to the ESCB, the European Central Bank shall, in accordance with the provisions of ***the Treaties*** and under the conditions laid down in the Statute of the ESCB ***and of the ECB***:
- make regulations to the extent necessary to implement the tasks defined in Article 3.1, first indent, Articles 19.1, 22 and 25.2 of the Statute of the ESCB ***and of the ECB*** and in cases which shall be laid down in the acts of the Council referred to in Article ***129(4)***;
- take decisions necessary for carrying out the tasks entrusted to the ESCB under ***the Treaties*** and the Statute of the ESCB ***and of the ECB***;
- make recommendations and deliver opinions.

2. The European Central Bank may decide to publish its decisions, recommendations and opinions.

3. Within the limits and under the conditions adopted by the Council under the procedure laid down in Article ***129(4)***, the European Central Bank shall be entitled to impose fines or periodic penalty payments on undertakings for failure to comply with obligations under its regulations and decisions.
[BMDF Note: Article does not apply to the UK: Article 139(2) TFEU and Protocol 18(4)]

[BMDF Note: Article 111 TEC: paragraphs 1-3 and 5 moved to Article 219 TFEU, paragraph 4 moved to Article 138 TFEU]

ARTICLE 133 [111a] *[Article III-191 (ex Article 123(4) TEC)]*
Without prejudice to the powers of the European Central Bank *the European Parliament and the Council, acting in accordance with the ordinary legislative procedure*, shall lay down the measures necessary for use of the euro as the single currency. Such *measures* shall be adopted after consultation of the European Central Bank.
[BMDF Note: Article does not apply to the UK: Article 139(2) TFEU and Protocol 18(4)]

CHAPTER 3

INSTITUTIONAL PROVISIONS

[BMDF Note: Article 112 TEC moved to Article 283 TFEU]

[BMDF Note: Article 113 TEC moved to Article 284 TFEU]

ARTICLE ***134*** [114] *[Article III-192 (ex Article 114 TEC)]*
1. In order to promote co-ordination of the policies of Member States to the full extent needed for the functioning of the internal market, a **Economic and Finance Committee** is hereby set up.

2. The Economic and Financial Committee shall have the following tasks:
- to deliver opinions at the request of the Council or of the Commission, or on its own initiative for submission to those institutions;
- to keep under review the economic and financial situation of the Member States and of the **Union** and to report regularly thereon to the Council and to the Commission, in particular on financial relations with third countries and international institutions;
- without prejudice to Article ***240***, to contribute to the preparation of the work of the Council referred to in Articles ***66, 75, 121(2), (3), (4) and (6), 122, 124, 125, 126, 127(6), 128(2), 129(5) and (6), 138, 140(2) and (3), 143, 144(2) and (3) and 219*** and to carry out other advisory and preparatory tasks assigned to it by the Council;
- to examine, at least once a year, the situation regarding the movement of capital and the freedom of payments, as they result from the application of ***the Treaties*** and of measures adopted by the Council; the examination shall cover all measures relating to capital movements and payments; the Committee shall report to the Commission and to the Council on the outcome of this examination.

The Member States, the Commission and the European Central Bank shall each appoint no more than two members of the Committee.

3. The Council shall, on a proposal from the Commission and after consulting the European Central Bank and the Committee referred to in this Article, lay down detailed provisions concerning the composition of the Economic and Financial Committee. The President of the Council shall inform the European Parliament of such a decision.

4. In addition to the tasks set out in paragraph 2, if and as long as there are Member States with a derogation as referred to in ***Article 139***, the Committee shall keep under review the monetary and financial situation and the general payments system of those Member States and report regularly thereon to the Council and to the Commission.
[BMDF Note: Paragraph applies to the UK as if it had a derogation: Protocol 18(5)]

ARTICLE ***135*** [115] *[Article III-193 (ex Article 115 TEC)]*
For matters within the scope of Articles ***121(4), 126*** with the exception of paragraph 14, ***140(1), (2) and (3) and 219*** the Council or a Member State may request the Commission to make a recommendation or a proposal, as appropriate. The Commission shall examine this request and submit its conclusions to the Council without delay.

CHAPTER 3 a

PROVISIONS SPECIFIC TO MEMBER STATES WHOSE CURRENCY IS THE EURO

ARTICLE 136 [115A] *[Article III-194 (new Article in 2004 IGC)]*
1. In order to ensure the proper functioning of economic and monetary union, and in accordance with the relevant provisions of the *Treaties*, the Council shall, in accordance with the relevant procedure from among those referred to in *Articles 121 and 126*, with the exception of the procedure set out in *Article 126(14)*, adopt measures specific to those Member States whose currency is the euro:
(a) to strengthen the co-ordination and surveillance of their budgetary discipline;
(b) to set out economic policy guidelines for them, while ensuring that they are compatible with those adopted for the whole of the Union and are kept under surveillance.

2. For those measures set out in paragraph 1, only members of the Council representing Member States whose currency is the euro shall take part in the vote.
A qualified majority of the said members shall be defined in accordance with Article 238(3)(a).

ARTICLE 137 [115B] *[Article III-195 (new Article in 2004 IGC)]*
Arrangements for meetings between ministers of those Member States whose currency is the euro are laid down by the Protocol on the Euro Group. *[BMDF Note: See also Protocol no.3]*

ARTICLE 138 [115C] *[Article III-196 (new Article in 2004 IGC)]*
1. In order to secure the euro's place in the international monetary system, the Council, on a proposal from the Commission, shall adopt a decision establishing common positions on matters of particular interest for economic and monetary union within the competent international financial institutions and conferences. The Council shall act after consulting the European Central Bank.

2. The Council, on a proposal from the Commission, may adopt appropriate measures to ensure unified representation within the international financial institutions and conferences. The Council shall act after consulting the European Central Bank.
[BMDF Note: Paragraph does not apply to the UK: Article 139(2) TFEU]

3. For the measures referred to in paragraphs 1 and 2, only members of the Council representing Member States whose currency is the euro shall take part in the vote.
A qualified majority of the said members shall be defined in accordance with Article 238(3)(a).
[BMDF Note: Article does not apply to the UK: Protocol 18(4)]

CHAPTER 4

TRANSITIONAL PROVISIONS

[BMDF Note: Article 116 TEC shall be repealed]

ARTICLE 139 [116a] *[Article III-197 (ex Article 122(1) and (3) to (5) TEC)]*
1. Member States in respect of which the Council has not decided that they fulfil the necessary conditions for the adoption of the euro shall hereinafter be referred to as "Member States with a derogation".

2. The following provisions of the *Treaties* shall not apply to Member States with a derogation:
(a) adoption of the parts of the broad economic policy guidelines which concern the euro area generally (*Article 121(2)*);
(b) coercive means of remedying excessive deficits (*Article 126(9) and (11)*);
(c) the objectives and tasks of the European System of Central Banks (*Article 127(1), (2), (3) and (5)*);
(d) issue of the euro (*Article 128*);
(e) acts of the European Central Bank (*Article 132)*;
(f) measures governing the use of the euro (*Article 133*);
(g) monetary agreements and other measures relating to exchange-rate policy (*Article 219*);
(h) appointment of members of the Executive Board of the European Central Bank (*Article 283(2)*);
(i) decisions establishing common positions on issues of particular relevance for economic and monetary union within the competent international financial institutions and conferences (*Article 138(1)*);
(j) measures to ensure unified representation within the international financial institutions and conferences (*Article 138(2)*).
In the Articles referred to in points (a) to (j), "Member States" shall therefore mean Member States whose currency is the euro.

3. Under Chapter IX of the Statute of the ESCB and of the ECB, Member States with a derogation and their national central banks are excluded from rights and obligations within the SCB.

4. The voting rights of members of the Council representing Member States with a derogation shall be suspended for the adoption by the Council of the measures referred to in the Articles listed in paragraph 2, and in the following instances:
(a) recommendations made to those Member States whose currency is the euro in the framework of multilateral surveillance, including on stability programmes and warnings (*Article 121(4)*);
(b) measures relating to excessive deficits concerning those Member States whose currency is the euro (*Article 126(6), (7), (8), (12) and (13)*).
A qualified majority of the other members of the Council shall be defined in accordance with Article 238(3)(a).

[BMDF Note: Article 117 TEC: paragraph 2 (first five indents) moved to Article 141(2), sixth indent shall be repealed, paragraph 3 moved to Article140(3), paragraphs 4 to 9 shall be repealed]

ARTICLE 140 [117a] *[Article III-198 (ex Articles 121, 122(2) and 123(5) TEC)]*
1. **At least once every two years, or at the request of a Member State with a derogation,** the Commission and the **European Central Bank** shall report to the Council on the progress made by the Member States **with a derogation in fulfilling** their obligations regarding the achievement of economic and monetary union. These reports shall include an examination of the compatibility between **the national legislation of each of these Member States,** including the statutes of its national central bank, and Articles 108 and 109 of the Statute of the ESCB ***and of the ECB***.
The reports shall also examine the achievement of a high degree of sustainable convergence by reference to the fulfilment by each Member State of the following criteria:

- the achievement of a high degree of price stability; this will be apparent from a rate of inflation which is close to that of, at most, the three best performing Member States in terms of price stability;
- the sustainability of the government financial position; this will be apparent from having achieved a government budgetary position without a deficit that is excessive as determined in accordance with Article ***126(6)***;
- the observance of the normal fluctuation margins provided for by the Exchange Rate Mechanism of the European Monetary System, for at least two years, without devaluing against the **euro**;
- the durability of convergence achieved by the Member State **with a derogation** and of its participation in the Exchange Rate Mechanism being reflected in the long-term interest rate levels.

The four criteria mentioned in this paragraph and the relevant periods over which they are to be respected are developed further in a Protocol annexed to ***the Treaties***. The reports of the Commission and the **European Central Bank** shall also take account of the results of the integration of markets, the situation and development of the balances of payments on current account and an examination of the development of unit labour costs and other price indices.
[BMDF Note: Paragraph moved from Article 121(1) TEC]

2. After consulting the European Parliament and after discussion in the **European Council**, the Council shall, on a proposal from the Commission, decide which Member States with a derogation fulfil the necessary conditions on the basis of the criteria **laid down in paragraph 1**, and abrogate the derogations of the Member States concerned.
The Council shall act having received a recommendation of a qualified majority of those among its members representing Member States whose currency is the euro. These members shall act within six months of the Council receiving the Commission's proposal.
The qualified majority of the said members, as referred to in the second sub-paragraph, shall be defined in accordance with Article 238(3)(a).
[BMDF Note: First sub-paragraph moved from Article 122(2) TEC, second sentence]

3. If it is decided, **in accordance with the procedure set out in paragraph 2**, to abrogate a derogation, the Council shall, acting with the unanimity of the ***Member States whose currency is the euro*** and the Member State concerned, on a proposal from the Commission and after consulting the European Central Bank, **irrevocably fix** the rate at which the **euro** shall be substituted for the currency of the Member State concerned, and take the other measures necessary for the introduction of the **euro** as the single currency in the Member State concerned.
[BMDF Note: Paragraph moved from Article 123(5) TEC. Paragraph does not apply to the UK: Protocol 18(4)]

[BMDF Note: Article 118 TEC shall be repealed]

ARTICLE 141 [118a] *[Article III-199 (ex Articles 123(3) and 117(2) TEC)]*
1. If and as long as there are Member States with a derogation, and without prejudice to Article ***129(3)***, the General Council of the European Central Bank referred to in Article 45 of the Statute of the ESCB ***and of the ECB*** shall be constituted as a third decision-making body of the European Central Bank. *[BMDF Note: Paragraph moved from Article 123(3) TEC]*

2. **If and as long as there are Member States with a derogation, the European Central Bank shall, as regards those Member States**:
- strengthen co-operation between the national central banks;
- strengthen the co-ordination of the monetary policies of the Member States, with the aim of ensuring price stability;
- monitor the functioning of the **exchange-rate mechanism**;
- hold consultations concerning issues falling within the competence of the national central banks and affecting the stability of financial institutions and markets;
- **carry out the former** tasks of the European Monetary Co-operation Fund, **which had subsequently been taken over by the European Monetary Institute.**

[BMDF Note: Paragraph moved from Article 117(2) TEC]

ARTICLE 142 [118b] *[Article III-200 (ex Article 124(1) TEC)]*
Each Member State **with a derogation** shall treat its exchange rate policy as a matter of common interest. In so doing, Member States shall take account of the experience acquired in co-operation within the framework of the **exchange-rate mechanism**.
[BMDF Note: Article moved from Article 124(1) TEC. Article applies to the UK under Protocol 18(5)]

ARTICLE ***143*** [119] *[Article III-201 (ex Article 119 TEC)]*
1. Where a Member State **with a derogation** is in difficulties or is seriously threatened with difficulties as regards its balance of payments either as a result of an overall disequilibrium in its balance of payments, or as a result of the type of currency at its disposal, and where such difficulties are liable in particular to jeopardise the functioning of the **internal** market or the implementation of the common commercial policy, the Commission shall immediately investigate the position of the State in question and the action which, making use of all the means at its disposal, that State has taken or may take in accordance with the provisions of ***the Treaties***. The Commission shall state what measures it recommends the State concerned to take.
If the action taken by a Member State **with a derogation** and the measures suggested by the Commission do not prove sufficient to overcome the difficulties which have arisen or which threaten, the Commission shall, after consulting the **Economic and Financial Committee**, recommend to the Council the granting of mutual assistance and appropriate methods therefor.
The Commission shall keep the Council regularly informed of the situation and of how it is developing.

2. The Council, shall grant such mutual assistance; it shall adopt directives or decisions laying down the conditions and details of such assistance, which may take such forms as:
(a) a concerted approach to or within any other international organisations to which Member States **with a derogation** may have recourse;
(b) measures needed to avoid deflection of trade where the **Member** State **with a derogation** which is in difficulties maintains or reintroduces quantitative restrictions against third countries;
(c) the granting of limited credits by other Member States, subject to their agreement.

3. If the mutual assistance recommended by the Commission is not granted by the Council or if the mutual assistance granted and the measures taken are insufficient, the Commission shall authorise the **Member** State **with a derogation,** which is in difficulties to take protective measures, the conditions and details of which the Commission shall determine.
Such authorisation may be revoked and such conditions and details may be changed by the Council.

ARTICLE ***144*** [120] *[Article III-202 (ex Article 120 TEC)]*
1. Where a sudden crisis in the balance of payments occurs and a decision within the meaning of Article ***143(2)*** is not immediately taken, the Member State **with a derogation** may, as a precaution, take the necessary protective measures. Such measures must cause the least possible disturbance in the functioning of the ***internal*** market and must not be wider in scope than is strictly necessary to remedy the sudden difficulties which have arisen.

2. The Commission and the other Member States shall be informed of such protective measures not later than when they enter into force. The Commission may recommend to the Council the granting of mutual assistance under Article ***143***.

3. After the Commission has delivered **a recommendation** and the ***Economic and Financial Committee*** has been consulted, the Council may, decide that the **Member** State concerned shall amend, suspend or abolish the protective measures referred to above.

[BMDF Note: Article 121 TEC: Paragraph 1 moved to Article 140(1), Paragraphs 2 to 4 shall be repealed]

[BMDF Note: Article 122 TEC: Paragraph 1 and paragraphs 3 to 6 shall be repealed, paragraph 2 moved to Article 140(2)]

[BMDF Note: Article 123 TEC: Paragraphs 1, 2 and 4 shall be repealed; Paragraph 3 moved to Article 141(1), Paragraph 5 moved to Article 140(3)]

[BMDF Note: Article 124 TEC: Paragraph 1 moved to Article 142, Paragraph 2 shall be repealed]

TITLE VIII

EMPLOYMENT

ARTICLE ***145*** [125] *[Article III-203 (ex Article 125 TEC)]*
Member States and the ***Union*** shall, in accordance with this Title, work towards developing a co-ordinated strategy for employment and particularly for promoting a skilled, trained and adaptable workforce and labour markets responsive to economic change with a view to achieving the objectives defined in ***Article 3*** of the Treaty on European Union.

ARTICLE ***146*** [126] *[Article III-204 (ex Article 126 TEC)]*
1. Member States, through their employment policies, shall contribute to the achievement of the objectives referred to in Article ***145*** in a way consistent with the broad guidelines of the economic policies of the Member States and of the **Union** adopted pursuant to Article ***121(2).***

2. Member States, having regard to the national practices related to the responsibilities of management and labour, shall regard promoting employment as a matter of common concern and shall co-ordinate their action in this respect within the Council, in accordance with the provisions of Article ***147***.

ARTICLE ***147*** [127] *[Article III-205 (ex Article 127 TEC)]*
1. The **Union** shall contribute to a high level of employment by encouraging co-operation between Member States and by supporting and, if necessary, complementing their action. In doing so, the competences of the Member States shall be respected.

2. The objective of a high level of employment shall be taken into consideration in the formulation and implementation of **Union** policies and activities.

ARTICLE ***148*** [128] *[Article III-206 (ex Article 128 TEC)]*
1. The European Council shall each year consider the employment situation in the **Union** and adopt conclusions thereon, on the basis of a joint annual report by the Council and the Commission.

2. On the basis of the conclusions of the European Council, the Council, on a proposal from the Commission and after consulting the European Parliament, the Economic and Social Committee, the Committee of the Regions and the Employment Committee referred to in Article ***150***, shall each year draw up guidelines which the Member States shall take into account in their employment policies. These guidelines shall be consistent with the broad guidelines adopted pursuant to Article ***121(2)***.

3. Each Member State shall provide the Council and the Commission with an annual report on the principal measures taken to implement its employment policy in the light of the guidelines for employment as referred to in paragraph 2.

4. The Council, on the basis of the reports referred to in paragraph 3 and having received the views of the Employment Committee shall each year carry out an examination of the implementation of the employment policies of the Member States in the light of the guidelines for employment. The Council, on a recommendation from the Commission, may, if it considers it appropriate in the light of that examination, make recommendations to Member States.

5. On the basis of the results of that examination, the Council and the Commission shall make a joint annual report to the European Council on the employment situation in the **Union** and on the implementation of the guidelines for employment.

ARTICLE ***149*** [129] *[Article III-207 (ex Article 129 TEC)]*
The European Parliament and the Council, acting in accordance with the ***ordinary legislative procedure*** and after consulting the Economic and Social Committee and the Committee of the Regions, may adopt incentive measures designed to encourage co-operation between Member States and to support their action in the field of employment through initiatives aimed at developing exchanges of information and best practices, providing comparative analysis and advice as well as promoting innovative approaches and evaluating experiences, in particular by recourse to pilot projects.

Those measures shall not include harmonisation of the laws and regulations of the Member States.

ARTICLE ***150*** [130] *[Article III-208 (ex Article 130 TEC)]*
The Council, ***acting*** **by a simple majority** after consulting the European Parliament, shall establish an Employment Committee with advisory status to promote co-ordination between Member States on employment and labour market policies. The tasks of the Committee shall be:
- to monitor the employment situation and employment policies in the Member States and the ***Union***;
- without prejudice to Article ***240***, to formulate opinions at the request of either the Council or the Commission or on its oven initiative, and to contribute to the preparation of the Council proceedings referred to in Article ***148***.

In fulfilling its mandate, the Committee shall consult management and labour.
Each Member State and the Commission shall appoint two members of the Committee.

[BMDF Note: Article 131 TEC moved to Article 206 TFEU]

[BMDF Note: Article 132 TEC shall be repealed]

[BMDF Note: Article 133 TEC moved to Article 207 TFEU]

[BMDF Note: Article 134 TEC shall be repealed]

[BMDF Note: Article 135 TEC moved to Article 33 TFEU]

TITLE IX

SOCIAL POLICY

ARTICLE ***151*** [136] *[Article III-209 (ex Article 136 TEC)]*
The **Union** and the Member States, having in mind fundamental social rights such as those set out in the European Charter signed at Turin on 18 October 1961 and in the 1989 Community Charter of the Fundamental Social Rights of Workers, shall have as their objectives the promotion of employment, improved living and working conditions, so as to make possible their harmonisation while the improvement is being maintained, proper social protection, dialogue between management and labour, the development of human resources with a view to lasting high employment and the combating of exclusion.
To this end the **Union** and the Member States shall implement measures which take account of the diverse forms of national practices, in particular in the field of contractual relations, and the need to maintain the competitiveness of the **Union** economy.
They believe that such a development will ensue not only from the functioning of the **internal** market, which will favour the harmonisation of social systems, but also from the procedures provided for in ***the Treaties*** and from the approximation of provisions laid down by law, regulation or administrative action.

ARTICLE 152 [136a] *[Article I-48 The social partners and autonomous social dialogue (new Article in 2004 IGC)]*
The Union recognises and promotes the role of the social partners at its level, taking into account the diversity of national systems. It shall facilitate dialogue between the social partners, respecting their autonomy.
The Tripartite Social Summit for Growth and Employment shall contribute to social dialogue.

ARTICLE ***153*** [137] *[Article III-210 (ex Article 137 TEC)]*
1. With a view to achieving the objectives of Article ***151***, the **Union** shall support and complement the activities of the Member States in the following fields:
(a) improvement in particular of the working environment to protect workers' health and safety;
(b) working conditions;
(c) social security and social protection of workers;
(d) protection of workers where their employment contract is terminated;

(e) the information and consultation of workers;
(f) representation and collective defence of the interests of workers and employers, including co-determination, subject to paragraph 5;
(g) conditions of employment for third-country nationals legally residing in **Union** territory;
(h) the integration of persons excluded from the labour market, without prejudice to Article ***166***;
(i) equality between men and women with regard to labour market opportunities and treatment at work;
(j) the combating of social exclusion;
(k) the modernisation of social protection systems without prejudice to point (c).

2. To this end, ***the European Parliament and*** the Council:
(a) may adopt measures designed to encourage co-operation between Member States through initiatives aimed at improving knowledge, developing exchanges of information and best practices, promoting innovative approaches and evaluating experiences, excluding any harmonisation of the laws and regulations of the Member States;
(b) may adopt, in the fields referred to in paragraph 1(a) to (i), by means of directives, minimum requirements for gradual implementation, having regard to the conditions and technical rules obtaining in each of the Member States. Such directives shall avoid imposing administrative, financial and legal constraints in a way which would hold back the creation and development of small and medium-sized undertakings.
The European Parliament and the Council shall act in accordance with the ***ordinary legislative procedure*** after consulting the Economic and Social Committee and the Committee of the Regions.
In the fields referred to in paragraph 1(c), (d), (f) and (g) of this Article, the Council shall act unanimously ***in accordance with a special legislative procedure***, after consulting the European Parliament and the said Committees.
The Council, acting unanimously on a proposal from the Commission, after consulting the European Parliament, may decide to render the ***ordinary legislative procedure*** applicable to paragraph 1(d), (f) and (g).

3. A Member State may entrust management and labour, at their joint request, with the implementation of directives adopted pursuant to paragraph 2 **or, where appropriate, with the implementation of *a Council decision* adopted in accordance with *Article 155***.
In this case, it shall ensure that, no later than the date on which a directive **or decision** must be transposed **or implemented**, management and labour have introduced the necessary measures by agreement, the Member State concerned being required to take any necessary measure enabling it at any time to be in a position to guarantee the results imposed by that directive **or *that* decision**.

4. The provisions adopted pursuant to this Article:
- shall not affect the right of Member States to define the fundamental principles of their social security systems and must not significantly affect the financial equilibrium thereof;
- shall not prevent any Member State from maintaining or introducing more stringent protective measures compatible with ***the Treaties***.

5. The provisions of this Article shall not apply to pay, the right of association, the right to strike or the right to impose lock-outs.

ARTICLE ***154*** [138] *[Article III-211 (ex Article 138 TEC)]*
1. The Commission shall have the task of promoting the consultation of management and labour at ***Union*** level and shall take any relevant measure to facilitate their dialogue by ensuring balanced support for the parties.

2. To this end, before submitting proposals in the social policy field, the Commission shall consult management and labour on the possible direction of ***Union*** action.

3. If, after such consultation, the Commission considers ***Union*** action advisable, it shall consult management and labour on the content of the envisaged proposal. Management and labour shall forward to the Commission an opinion or, where appropriate, a recommendation.

4. On the occasion of **the** consultation **referred to in paragraphs 2 and 3**, management and labour may inform the Commission of their wish to initiate the process provided for in Article ***155***. The

duration of the **process** shall not exceed nine months, unless the management and labour concerned and the Commission decide jointly to extend it.

ARTICLE ***155*** [139] *[Article III-212 (ex Article 139 TEC)]*
1. Should management and labour so desire, the dialogue between them at ***Union*** level may lead to contractual relations, including agreements.

2. Agreements concluded at ***Union*** level shall be implemented either in accordance with the procedures and practices specific to management and labour and the Member States or, in matters covered by Article ***153***, at the joint request of the signatory parties, by a Council decision on a proposal from the Commission. **The European Parliament shall be informed.**
The Council shall act ***unanimously*** where the agreement in question contains one or more provisions relating to one of the areas for which unanimity is required pursuant to in Article ***153(2)***.

ARTICLE ***156*** [140] *[Article III-213 (ex Article 140 TEC)]*
With a view to achieving the objectives of Article ***151*** and without prejudice to the other provisions of ***the Treaties***, the Commission shall encourage co-operation between the Member States and facilitate the co-ordination of their action in all social policy fields under this chapter, particularly in matters relating to:
- employment;
- labour law and working conditions;
- basic and advanced vocational training;
- social security;
- prevention of occupational accidents and diseases;
- occupational hygiene;
- the rights of association and collective bargaining between employers and workers.

To this end, the Commission shall act in close contact with Member States by making studies, delivering opinions and arranging consultations both on problems arising at national level and on those of concern to international organizations**, in particular initiatives aiming at the establishment of guidelines and indicators, the organisation of exchange of best practice, and the preparation of the necessary elements for periodic monitoring and evaluation. The European Parliament shall be kept fully informed.**
Before delivering the opinions provided for in this Article, the Commission shall consult the Economic and Social Committee.
[BMDF Note: See also Declaration no. 31]

ARTICLE ***157*** [141] *[Article III-214 (ex Article 141 TEC)]*
1. Each Member State shall ensure that the principle of equal pay for male and female workers for equal work or work of equal value is applied.

2. For the purpose of this Article, 'pay' means the ordinary basic or minimum wage or salary and any other consideration, whether in cash or in kind, which the worker receives directly or indirectly, in respect of his employment, from his employer.
Equal pay without discrimination based on sex means:
(a) that pay for the same work at piece rates shall be calculated on the basis of the same unit of measurement;
(b) that pay for work at time rates shall be the same for the same job.

3. ***The European Parliament and*** the Council, acting in accordance with the ***ordinary legislative procedure***, and after consulting the Economic and Social Committee, shall adopt measures to ensure the application of the principle of equal opportunities and equal treatment of men and women in matters of employment and occupation, including the principle of equal pay for equal work or work of equal value.

4. With a view to ensuring full equality in practice between men and women in working life, the principle of equal treatment shall not prevent any Member State from maintaining or adopting measures providing for specific advantages in order to make it easier for the under-represented sex to pursue a vocational activity or to prevent or compensate for disadvantages in professional careers.
[BMDF Note: See also Protocol no. 32]

ARTICLE ***158*** [142] *[Article III-215 (ex Article 142 TEC)]*
Member States shall endeavour to maintain the existing equivalence between paid holiday schemes.

ARTICLE ***159*** [143] *[Article III-216 (ex Article 143 TEC)]*
The Commission shall draw up a report each year on progress in achieving the objectives of Article ***151***, including the demographic situation in the **Union**. It shall forward the report to the European Parliament, the Council and the Economic and Social Committee.

ARTICLE ***160*** [144] *[Article III-217 (ex Article 144 TEC)]*
The Council, ***acting*** **by a simple majority** after consulting the European Parliament, shall establish a Social Protection Committee with advisory status to promote co-operation on social protection policies between Member States and with the Commission. The tasks of the Committee shall be:

- to monitor the social situation and the development of social protection policies in the Member States and the **Union**;
- to promote exchanges of information, experience and good practice between Member States and with the Commission;
- without prejudice to Article ***240***, to prepare reports, formulate opinions or undertake other work within its fields of competence, at the request of either the Council or the Commission or on its own initiative.

In fulfilling its mandate, the Committee shall establish appropriate contacts with management and labour.
Each Member State and the Commission shall appoint two members of the Committee.

ARTICLE ***161*** [145] *[Article III-218 (ex Article 145 TEC)]*
The Commission shall include a separate chapter on social developments within the **Union** in its annual report to the European Parliament.
The European Parliament may invite the Commission to draw up reports on any particular problems concerning social conditions.

TITLE X

THE EUROPEAN SOCIAL FUND

ARTICLE ***162*** [146] *[Article III-219(1) (ex Article 146 TEC)]*
In order to improve employment opportunities for workers in the internal market and to contribute thereby to raising the standard of living, a European Social Fund is hereby established in accordance with the provisions set out below; it shall aim to render the employment of workers easier and to increase their geographical and occupational mobility within the **Union**, and to facilitate their adaptation to industrial changes and to changes in production systems, in particular through vocational training and retraining.

ARTICLE ***163*** [147] *[Article III-219(2) (ex Article 147 TEC)]*
The Fund shall be administered by the Commission.
The Commission shall be assisted in this task by a Committee presided over by a member of the Commission and composed of representatives of Governments, trade unions and employers' organisations.

ARTICLE ***164*** [148] *[Article III-219(3) (ex Article 148 TEC)]*
The European Parliament and the Council, acting in accordance with the ***ordinary legislative procedure*** and after consulting the Economic and Social Committee and the Committee of the Regions, shall adopt implementing ***regulations*** relating to the European Social Fund.

TITLE XI

EDUCATION, VOCATIONAL TRAINING, YOUTH **AND SPORT**

ARTICLE ***165*** [149] *[Article III-282 (ex Article 149 TEC)]*
1. The **Union** shall contribute to the development of quality education by encouraging co-operation between Member States and, if necessary, by supporting and supplementing their action, while fully respecting the responsibility of the Member States for the content of teaching and the organisation of education systems and their cultural and linguistic diversity.
The Union shall contribute to the promotion of European sporting issues, while taking account of the specific nature of sport, its structures based on voluntary activity and its social and educational function.

2. ***Union*** action shall be aimed at:
- developing the European dimension in education, particularly through the teaching and dissemination of the languages of the Member States;
- encouraging mobility of students and teachers, *inter alia* by encouraging the academic recognition of diplomas and periods of study;
- promoting co-operation between educational establishments;
- developing exchanges of information and experience on issues common to the education systems of the Member States;
- encouraging the development of youth exchanges and of exchanges of socio-educational instructors **and encouraging the participation of young people in democratic life in Europe**;
- encouraging the development of distance education**;**
- **developing the European dimension in sport, by promoting fairness and openness in sporting competitions and co-operation between bodies responsible for sports, and by protecting the physical and moral integrity of sportsmen and sportswomen, especially young sportsmen and sportswomen.**

3. The **Union** and the Member States shall foster co-operation with third countries and the competent international organisations in the field of education **and sport**, in particular the Council of Europe.

4. In order to contribute to the achievement of the objectives referred to in this Article:
- ***the European Parliament and the Council,*** acting in accordance with the ***ordinary legislative procedure***, after consulting the Economic and Social Committee and the Committee of the Regions, shall adopt incentive measures, excluding any harmonisation of the laws and regulations of the Member States;
- **the Council,** on a proposal from the Commission, shall adopt recommendations.

ARTICLE ***166*** [150] *[Article III-283 (ex Article 150 TEC)]*
1. The **Union** shall implement a vocational training policy which shall support and supplement the action of the Member States, while fully respecting the responsibility of the Member States for the content and organisation of vocational training.

2. **Union** action shall aim to:
- facilitate adaptation to industrial changes, in particular through vocational training and retraining;
- improve initial and continuing vocational training in order to facilitate vocational integration and reintegration into the labour market;
- facilitate access to vocational training and encourage mobility of instructors and trainees and particularly young people;
- stimulate co-operation on training between educational or training establishments and firms;
- develop exchanges of information and experience on issues common to the training systems of the Member States.

3. The **Union** and the Member States shall foster co-operation with third countries and the competent international organisations in the sphere of vocational training.

4. The Council, acting in accordance with the procedure referred to in Article ***294*** and after consulting the Economic and Social Committee and the Committee of the Regions, shall adopt measures to contribute to the achievement of the objectives referred to in this Article, excluding any harmonisation of the laws and regulations of the Member States ***and*** **the Council, on a proposal from the Commission, shall adopt recommendations.**

TITLE XII

CULTURE

ARTICLE ***167*** [151] *[Article III-280 (ex Article 151 TEC)]*

1. The **Union** shall contribute to the flowering of the cultures of the Member States, while respecting their national and regional diversity and at the same time bringing the common cultural heritage to the fore.

2. Action by the **Union** shall be aimed at encouraging co-operation between Member States and, if necessary, supporting and supplementing their action in the following areas:
- improvement of the knowledge and dissemination of the culture and history of the European peoples;
- conservation and safeguarding of cultural heritage of European significance;
- non-commercial cultural exchanges;
- artistic and literary creation, including in the audio-visual sector.

3. The **Union** and the Member States shall foster co-operation with third countries and the competent international organisations in the sphere of culture, in particular the Council of Europe.

4. The **Union** shall take cultural aspects into account in its action under other provisions of ***the Treaties***, in particular in order to respect and to promote the diversity of its cultures.

5. In order to contribute to the achievement of the objectives referred to in this Article:
- ***the European Parliament and the Council,*** acting in accordance with the ***ordinary legislative procedure*** and after consulting the Committee of the Regions, shall adopt incentive measures, excluding any harmonisation of the laws and regulations of the Member States;
- **the Council,** on a proposal from the Commission, shall adopt recommendations.

TITLE XIII

PUBLIC HEALTH

ARTICLE ***168*** [152] *[Article III-278 (ex Article 152 TEC)]*

1. A high level of human health protection shall be ensured in the definition and implementation of all ***Union*** policies and activities.

Union action, which shall complement national policies, shall be directed towards improving public health, preventing human illness and diseases, and obviating sources of danger to **physical and mental** health***, and*** **monitoring, early warning of and combating serious cross-border threats to health.**

Such action shall cover the fight against the major health scourges, by promoting research into their causes, their transmission and their prevention, as well as health information and education.

The ***Union*** shall complement the Member States' action in reducing drugs-related health damage, including information and prevention.

2. The ***Union*** shall encourage co-operation between the Member States in the areas referred to in this Article and, if necessary, lend support to their action. **It shall in particular encourage co-operation between the Member States to improve the complementarity of their health services in cross-border areas.**

Member States shall, in liaison with the Commission, co-ordinate among themselves their policies and programmes in the areas referred to in paragraph 1. The Commission may, in close contact with the Member States, take any useful initiative to promote such co-ordination, **in particular initiatives aiming at the establishment of guidelines and indicators, the organisation of exchange of best practice, and the preparation of the necessary elements for periodic monitoring and evaluation. The European Parliament shall be kept fully informed.**

3. The **Union** and the Member States shall foster co-operation with third countries and the competent international organisations in the sphere of public health.

4. **By way of derogation from *Article 2(5)* and *Article 6(a)* and in accordance with *Article 4(2)(k), the European Parliament and the Council,*** acting in accordance with the ***ordinary legislative procedure*** after consulting the Social and Economic Committee and the Committee of the Regions, shall contribute to the achievement of the objectives referred to in this Article through adopting **in order to meet common safety concerns**:

(a) measures setting high standards of quality and safety of organs and substances of human origin, blood and blood derivatives; these measures shall not prevent any Member State from maintaining or introducing more stringent protective measures;

(b) measures in the veterinary and phytosanitary fields which have as their direct objective the protection of public health,

(c) measures setting high standards of quality and safety for medicinal products and devices for medical use.

5. ***The European Parliament and the Council, acting in accordance with the ordinary legislative procedure and after consulting the Committee of the Regions and the Economic and Social Committee,*** **may also** ***adopt*** **incentive measures designed to protect and improve human health and in particular to combat the major cross-border health scourges,** ***measures concerning monitoring, early warning of and combating serious cross-border threats to health, and*** **measures which have as their direct objective the protection of public health regarding tobacco and the abuse of alcohol, excluding any harmonisation of the laws and regulations of the Member States.**

6. The Council, on a proposal from the Commission, may also adopt recommendations for the purposes set out in this Article.

7. ***Union*** action in the field of public health shall fully respect the responsibilities of the Member States **for the definition of their health policy and** for the organisation and delivery of health services and medical care. **The responsibilities of the Member States shall include the management of health services and medical care and the allocation of the resources assigned to them. The** measures referred to in paragraph 4(a) shall not affect national provisions on the donation or medical use of organs and blood.

[BMDF Note: See also Declaration no. 32]

TITLE XIV

CONSUMER PROTECTION

ARTICLE ***169*** [153] *[Article III-235 (ex Article 153 TEC)]*

1. In order to promote the interests of consumers and to ensure a high level of consumer protection, the **Union** shall contribute to protecting the health, safety and economic interests of consumers, as well as to promoting their right to information, education and to organise themselves in order to safeguard their interests.

2. The **Union** shall contribute to the attainment of the objectives referred to in paragraph 1 through:

(a) measures adopted pursuant to Article ***115*** in the context of the completion of the internal market;

(b) measures which support, supplement and monitor the policy pursued by the Member States.

3. ***The European Parliament and*** the Council, acting in accordance with the ***ordinary legislative procedure*** and after consulting the Economic and Social Committee, shall adopt the measures referred to in paragraph 3(b).

4. Measures adopted pursuant to paragraph 4 shall not prevent any Member State from maintaining or introducing more stringent protective measures. Such measures must be compatible with ***the Treaties***. The Commission shall be notified of them.

TITLE XV

TRANS-EUROPEAN NETWORKS

ARTICLE ***170*** [154] *[Article III-246 (ex Article 154 TEC)]*

1. To help achieve the objectives referred to in Articles ***26*** and ***174*** and to enable citizens of the Union, economic operators and regional and local communities to derive full benefit from the setting up of an area without internal frontiers, the **Union** shall contribute to the establishment and development of trans-European networks in the areas of transport, telecommunications and energy infrastructures.

2. Within the framework of a system of open and competitive markets, action by the **Union** shall aim at promoting the interconnection and inter-operability of national networks as well as access to such networks. It shall take account in particular of the need to link island, landlocked and peripheral regions with the central regions of the **Union**.

ARTICLE ***171*** [155] *[Article III-247(1), (3) and (4) (ex Article 155 TEC)]*

1. In order to achieve the objectives referred to in Article ***170***, the **Union**:

- shall establish a series of guidelines covering the objectives, priorities and broad lines of measures envisaged in the sphere of trans-European networks; these guidelines shall identify projects of common interest;
- shall implement any measures that may prove necessary to ensure the inter-operability of the networks, in particular in the field of technical standardisation;
- may support projects of common interest supported by Member States, which are identified in the framework of guidelines referred to in the first indent, particularly through feasibility studies, loan guarantees or interest rate subsidies; the **Union** may also contribute, through the Cohesion Fund set up pursuant to Article ***177***, to the financing of specific projects in Member States in the area of transport infrastructure.

The **Union**'s activities shall take into account the potential economic viability of the projects.

2. Member States shall, in liaison with the Commission, co-ordinate among themselves the policies pursued at national level which may have a significant impact on the achievement of the objectives referred to in Article ***170***. The Commission may, in close co-operation with the Member States, take any useful initiative to promote such co-ordination.

3. The ***Union*** may decide to co-operate with third countries to promote projects of mutual interest and to ensure the inter-operability of networks.

ARTICLE ***172*** [156] *[Article III-247(2) (ex Article 156 TEC)]*

The guidelines and other measures referred to in Article ***171(1)*** shall be adopted by ***the European Parliament and*** the Council, acting in accordance with the ***ordinary legislative procedure*** and after consulting the Economic and Social Committee and the Committee of the Regions.

Guidelines and projects of common interest which relate to the territory of a Member State shall require the approval of the Member State concerned.

TITLE XVI

INDUSTRY

ARTICLE ***173*** [157] *[Article III-279 (ex Article 157 TEC)]*
1. The **Union** and the Member States shall ensure that the conditions necessary for the competitiveness of the **Union**'s industry exist.
For that purpose, in accordance with a system of open and competitive markets, their action shall be aimed at:
- speeding up the adjustment of industry to structural changes;
- encouraging an environment favourable to initiative and to the development of undertakings throughout the **Union**, particularly small and medium-sized undertakings;
- encouraging an environment favourable to co-operation between undertakings;
- fostering better exploitation of the industrial potential of policies of innovation, research and technological development.

2. The Member States shall consult each other in liaison with the Commission and, where necessary, shall co-ordinate their action. The Commission may take any useful initiative to promote such co-ordination**, in particular initiatives aiming at the establishment of guidelines and indicators, the organisation of exchange of best practice, and the preparation of the necessary elements for periodic monitoring and evaluation. The European Parliament shall be kept fully informed**.

3. The **Union** shall contribute to the achievement of the objectives set out in paragraph 1 through the policies and activities it pursues under other provisions of ***the Treaties***. ***The European Parliament and*** the Council, acting in accordance with the ***ordinary legislative procedure*** and after consulting the Economic and Social Committee, may decide on specific measures in support of action taken in the Member States to achieve the objectives set out in paragraph 1**, excluding any harmonisation of the laws and regulations of the Member States**.
This Title shall not provide a basis for the introduction by the ***Union*** of any measure which could lead to a distortion of competition or contains tax provisions or provisions relating to the rights and interests of employed persons.

TITLE XVII

ECONOMIC, SOCIAL ***AND TERRITORIAL*** COHESION

ARTICLE ***174*** [158] *[Article III-220 (ex Article 158 TEC)]*
In order to promote its overall harmonious development, the ***Union*** shall develop and pursue its actions leading to the strengthening of its economic, social **and territorial** cohesion.
In particular, the ***Union*** shall aim at reducing disparities between the levels of development of the various regions and the backwardness of the least-favoured regions.
Among the regions concerned, particular attention shall be paid to rural areas, areas affected by industrial transition, and regions which suffer from severe and permanent natural or demographic handicaps such as the northernmost regions with very low population density and island, cross-border and mountain regions.
[BMDF Note: See also Declaration no. 33]

ARTICLE ***175*** [159] *[Article III-221 (ex Article 159 TEC)]*
Member States shall conduct their economic policies and shall co-ordinate them in such a way as, in addition, to attain the objectives set out in Article ***174***. The formulation and implementation of the **Union**'s policies and actions and the implementation of the internal market shall take into account the objectives set out in Article ***174*** and shall contribute to their achievement. The **Union** shall also support the achievement of these objectives by the action it takes through the Structural Funds (European Agricultural Guidance and Guarantee Fund, Guidance Section; European Social Fund; European

Regional Development Fund), the European Investment Bank and the other existing financial instruments.
The Commission shall submit a report to the European Parliament, the Council, the Economic and Social Committee and the Committee of the Regions every three years on the progress made towards achieving economic, social **and territorial** cohesion and on the manner in which the various means provided for in this Article have contributed to it. This report shall, if necessary, be accompanied by appropriate proposals.
If specific actions prove necessary outside the Funds and without prejudice to the measures decided upon within the framework of the other **Union** policies, such actions may be adopted by ***the European Parliament and*** the Council, acting in accordance with the ***ordinary legislative procedure*** and after consulting the Economic and Social Committee and the Committee of the Regions.

ARTICLE ***176*** [160] *[Article III-222 (ex Article 160 TEC)]*
The European Regional Development Fund is intended to help to redress the main regional imbalances in the **Union** through participation in the development and structural adjustment of regions whose development is lagging behind and in the conversion of declining industrial regions.

ARTICLE ***177*** [161] *[Article III-223 (ex Article 161 TEC)]*
Without prejudice to Article ***178***, ***the European Parliament and*** the Council, acting ***by means of regulations in accordance with the ordinary legislative procedure*** and consulting the Economic and Social Committee and the Committee of the Regions, shall define the tasks, priority objectives and the organisation of the Structural Funds, which may involve grouping the Funds. ***T***he general rules applicable to them and the provisions necessary to ensure their effectiveness and the co-ordination of the Funds with one another and with the other existing financial instruments ***shall also be defined by the same procedure***.
A Cohesion Fund set up in accordance with the same procedure, shall provide a financial contribution to projects in the fields of environment and trans-European networks in the area of transport infrastructure.

ARTICLE ***178*** [162] *[Article III-224 (ex Article 162 TEC)]*
Implementing ***regulations*** relating to the European Regional Development Fund shall be taken by ***the European Parliament and*** the Council, acting in accordance with the ***ordinary legislative procedure*** and after consulting the Economic and Social Committee and the Committee of the Regions.
With regard to the European Agricultural Guidance and Guarantee Fund, Guidance Section, and the European Social Fund, Articles ***43*** and ***164*** respectively shall continue to apply.

TITLE XVIII

RESEARCH AND TECHNOLOGICAL DEVELOPMENT **AND SPACE**

ARTICLE ***179*** [163] *[Article III-248 (ex Article 163 TEC)]*
1. The ***Union*** shall have the objective of strengthening the scientific and technological bases **by achieving a European research area in which researchers, scientific knowledge and technology circulate freely,** and encouraging it to become more competitive, **including in its industry**, while promoting all the research activities deemed necessary by virtue of other Chapters of ***the Treaties***.

2. For this purpose the ***Union*** shall, throughout the ***Union***, encourage undertakings, including small and medium-sized undertakings, research centres and universities in their research and technological development activities of high quality; it shall support their efforts to co-operate with one another, aiming, notably, **at permitting researchers to co-operate freely across borders and** at enabling undertakings to exploit the internal market potential to the full, in particular through the opening up of national public contracts, the definition of common standards and the removal of legal and fiscal obstacles to that co-operation.

3. All ***Union*** activities under ***the Treaties*** in the area of research and technological development, including demonstration projects, shall be decided on and implemented in accordance with the provisions of this Title. *[BMDF Note: See also Declaration no. 34]*

ARTICLE ***180*** [164] *[Article III-249 (ex Article 164 TEC)]*
In pursuing these objectives, the **Union** shall carry out the following activities, complementing the activities carried out in the Member States:
(a) implementation of research, technological development and demonstration programmes, by promoting co-operation with and between undertakings, research centres and universities;
(b) promotion of co-operation in the field of ***Union*** research, technological development and demonstration with third countries and international organisations;
(c) dissemination and optimisation of the results of activities in ***Union*** research, technological development and demonstration;
(d) stimulation of the training and mobility of researchers in the **Union**.

ARTICLE ***181*** [165] *[Article III-250 (ex Article 165 TEC)]*
1. The **Union** and the Member States shall co-ordinate their research and technological development activities so as to ensure that national policies and ***Union*** policy are mutually consistent.

2. In close co-operation with the Member States, the Commission may take any useful initiative to promote the co-ordination referred to in paragraph 1**, in particular initiatives aiming at the establishment of guidelines and indicators, the organisation of exchange of best practice, and the preparation of the necessary elements for periodic monitoring and evaluation. The European Parliament shall be kept fully informed**.

ARTICLE ***182*** [166] *[Article III-251 (ex Article 166 TEC)]*
1. A multiannual framework programme, setting out all the activities of the ***Union***, shall be adopted by ***the European Parliament and*** the Council, acting in accordance with the ***ordinary legislative procedure*** after consulting the Economic and Social Committee.
The framework programme shall:
- establish the scientific and technological objectives to be achieved by the activities provided for in Article ***180*** and fix the relevant priorities;
- indicate the broad lines of such activities;
- fix the maximum overall amount and the detailed rules for ***Union*** financial participation in the framework programme and the respective shares in each of the activities provided for.

2. The framework programme shall be adapted or supplemented as the situation changes.

3. The framework programme shall be implemented through specific programmes developed within each activity. Each specific programme shall define the detailed rules for implementing it, fix its duration and provide for the means deemed necessary. The sum of the amounts deemed necessary, fixed in the specific programmes, may not exceed the overall maximum amount fixed for the framework programme and each activity.

4. The Council, acting ***in accordance with a special legislative procedure*** and after consulting the European Parliament and the Economic and Social Committee, shall adopt the specific programmes.

5. As a complement to the activities planned in the multiannual framework programme, *the European Parliament and the Council, acting in accordance with the ordinary legislative procedure and after consulting the Economic and Social Committee,* shall establish the measures necessary for the implementation of the European research area.

ARTICLE ***183*** [167] *[Article III-252(1) (ex Article 167 TEC)]*
For the implementation of the multiannual framework programme the ***Union*** shall:
- determine the rules for the participation of undertakings, research centres and universities;
- lay down the rules governing the dissemination of research results.

ARTICLE ***184*** [168] *[Article III-252(2) (ex Article 168 TEC)]*
In implementing the multiannual framework programme, supplementary programmes may be decided on involving the participation of certain Member States only, which shall finance them subject to possible ***Union*** participation.
The ***Union*** shall adopt the rules applicable to supplementary programmes, particularly as regards the dissemination of knowledge and access by other Member States.

ARTICLE ***185*** [169] *[Article III-252(3) (ex Article 169 TEC)]*
In implementing the multiannual framework programme the ***Union*** may make provision, in agreement with the Member States concerned, for participation in research and development programmes undertaken by several Member States, including participation in the structures created for the execution of those programmes.

ARTICLE ***186*** [170] *[Article III-252(4) (ex Article 170 TEC)]*
In implementing the multiannual framework programme the ***Union*** may make provision for co-operation in ***Union*** research, technological development and demonstration with third countries or international organisations.
The detailed arrangements for such co-operation may be the subject of agreements between the ***Union*** and the third parties concerned.

ARTICLE ***187*** [171] *[Article III-253 (ex Article 171 TEC)]*
The ***Union*** may set up joint undertakings or any other structure necessary for the efficient execution of ***Union*** research, technological development and demonstration programmes.

ARTICLE ***188*** [172] *[Paragraph 1 from III-253 and Paragraph 2 from Article III-252(2)]*
The Council, acting by qualified majority on a proposal from the Commission and after consulting the European Parliament and the Economic and Social Committee, shall adopt the provisions referred to in Article ***187***.
The European Parliament and the Council, acting in accordance with the ***ordinary legislative procedure*** and after consulting the Economic and Social Committee, shall adopt the provisions referred to in Articles ***183***, ***184*** and ***185***. Adoption of the supplementary programmes shall require the agreement of the Member States concerned.

ARTICLE 189 [172a] *[Article III-254 (new Article in 2004 IGC)]*
1. To promote scientific and technical progress, industrial competitiveness and the implementation of its policies, the Union shall draw up a European space policy. To this end, it may promote joint initiatives, support research and technological development and co-ordinate the efforts needed for the exploration and exploitation of space.

2. To contribute to attaining the objectives referred to in paragraph 1, *the European Parliament and the Council, acting in accordance with the ordinary legislative procedure,* shall establish the necessary measures, which may take the form of a European space programme, *excluding any harmonisation of the laws and regulations of the Member States.*

3. The Union shall establish any appropriate relations with the European Space Agency.

4. This Article shall be without prejudice to the other provisions of this Title.

ARTICLE ***190*** [173] *[Article III-255 (ex Article 173 TEC)]*
At the beginning of each year the Commission shall send a report to the European Parliament and the Council. The report shall include information on research and technological development activities and the dissemination of results during the previous year, and the work programme for the current year.

TITLE XIX

ENVIRONMENT

ARTICLE ***191*** [174] *[Article III-233 (ex Article 174 TEC)]*
1. ***Union*** policy on the environment shall contribute to pursuit of the following objectives:
- preserving, protecting and improving the quality of the environment;
- protecting human health;
- prudent and rational utilisation of natural resources;
- promoting measures at international level to deal with regional or world-wide environmental problems, ***and in particular combating climate change***.

2. ***Union*** policy on the environment shall aim at a high level of protection taking into account the diversity of situations in the various regions of the ***Union***. It shall be based on the precautionary principle and on the principles that preventive action should be taken, that environmental damage should as a priority be rectified at source and that the polluter should pay.
In this context, harmonisation measures answering environmental protection requirements shall include, where appropriate, a safeguard clause allowing Member States to take provisional measures, for non-economic environmental reasons, subject to a **procedure of inspection by the Union**.

3. In preparing its policy on the environment, the ***Union*** shall take account of:
- available scientific and technical data;
- environmental conditions in the various regions of the ***Union***;
- the potential benefits and costs of action or lack of action;
- the economic and social development of the ***Union*** as a whole and the balanced development of its regions.

4. Within their respective spheres of competence, the ***Union*** and the Member States shall co-operate with third countries and with the competent international organisations. The arrangements for ***Union*** co-operation may be the subject of agreements between the ***Union*** and the third parties concerned.
The previous sub-paragraph shall be without prejudice to Member States' competence to negotiate in international bodies and to conclude international agreements.

ARTICLE ***192*** [175] *[Article III-234(1)-(5) (ex Article 175 TEC)]*
1. The Council, acting in accordance with the procedure referred to in Article ***294*** and after consulting the Economic and Social Committee and the Committee of the Regions, shall decide what action is to be taken by the ***Union*** in order to achieve the objectives referred to in Article ***191***.

2. By way of derogation from the decision-making procedure provided for in paragraph 1 and without prejudice to Article ***115***, the Council, acting unanimously ***in accordance with a special legislative procedure*** and after consulting the European Parliament, the Economic and Social Committee and the Committee of the Regions, shall adopt:
(a) provisions primarily of a fiscal nature;
(b) measures affecting:
  - town and country planning;
  - quantitative management of water resources or affecting, directly or indirectly, the availability of those resources;
  - land use, with the exception of waste management;
(c) measures significantly affecting a Member State's choice between different energy sources and the general structure of its energy supply.
The Council ***acting unanimously on a proposal from the Commission and after consulting the European Parliament, the Economic and Social Committee and the Committee of the Regions, may make*** **the ordinary legislative procedure applicable to the matters referred to in the first sub-paragraph.**

3. ***G***eneral action programmes setting out priority objectives to be attained shall be adopted by the Council, acting in accordance with the ***ordinary legislative procedure*** and after consulting the Economic and Social Committee and the Committee of the Regions.
The measures necessary for the implementation of these programmes shall be adopted under the terms of paragraph 1 or 2, as the case may be.

4. Without prejudice to certain measures **adopted by the Union**, the Member States shall finance and implement the environment policy.

5. Without prejudice to the principle that the polluter should pay, if a measure based on the provisions of paragraph 1 involves costs deemed disproportionate for the public authorities of a Member State, **such measure shall *lay down*** in the form of:
- temporary derogations and/or
- financial support from the Cohesion Fund set up pursuant to Article **177**.

ARTICLE ***193*** [176] *[Article III-234(6) (ex Article 176 TEC)]*
The protective measures adopted pursuant to Article ***192*** shall not prevent any Member State from maintaining or introducing more stringent protective measures. Such measures must be compatible with ***the Treaties***. They shall be notified to the Commission.

TITLE XX

ENERGY

ARTICLE 194 [176A] *[Article III-256 (new article in 2004 IGC)]*
1. In the context of the establishment and functioning of the internal market and with regard for the need to preserve and improve the environment, Union policy on energy shall aim, *in a spirit of solidarity between Member States,* to:
(a) ensure the functioning of the energy market;
(b) ensure security of energy supply in the Union, and
(c) promote energy efficiency and energy saving and the development of new and renewable forms of energy;
(d) promote the interconnection of energy networks.

2. Without prejudice to the application of other provisions of the *Treaties*, *the European Parliament and the Council, acting in accordance with the ordinary legislative procedure, shall establish the measures necessary to achieve* the objectives in paragraph 1. Such *measures* shall be adopted after consultation of the Economic and Social Committee and the Committee of the Regions.
Such *measures* shall not affect a Member State's right to determine the conditions for exploiting its energy resources, its choice between different energy sources and the general structure of its energy supply, without prejudice to *Article 192(2)(c).*

3. By way of derogation from paragraph 2, *the Council, acting in accordance with a special legislative procedure, shall unanimously and after consulting the European Parliament,* establish the measures referred to therein when they are primarily of a fiscal nature.
[BMDF Note: See also Declaration no. 35]

TITLE XXI

TOURISM

ARTICLE 195 [176B] *[Article III-281 (new article in 2004 IGC)]*
1. The Union shall complement the action of the Member States in the tourism sector, in particular by promoting the competitiveness of Union undertakings in that sector.
To that end, Union action shall be aimed at:
(a) encouraging the creation of a favourable environment for the development of undertakings in this sector;
(b) promoting co-operation between the Member States, particularly by the exchange of good practice;

2. *The European Parliament and the Council, acting in accordance with the ordinary legislative procedure,* shall establish specific measures to complement actions within the Member States to achieve the objectives referred to in this Article, excluding any harmonisation of the laws and regulations of the Member States.

TITLE XXII

CIVIL PROTECTION

ARTICLE 196 [176C] *[Article III-284 (new article in 2004 IGC)]*
1. The Union shall encourage co-operation between Member States in order to improve the effectiveness of systems for preventing and protecting against natural or man-made disasters.
Union action shall aim to:
(a) support and complement Member States' action at national, regional and local level in risk prevention, in preparing their civil-protection personnel and in responding to natural or man-made disasters within the Union;
(b) promote swift, effective operational co-operation within the Union between national civil-protection services;
(c) promote consistency in international civil-protection work.

2. ***The European Parliament and the Council, acting in accordance with the ordinary legislative procedure,*** **shall establish the measures necessary to help achieve the objectives referred to in paragraph 1, excluding any harmonisation of the laws and regulations of the Member States.**

TITLE XXIII

ADMINISTRATIVE CO-OPERATION

ARTICLE 197 [176D] *[Article III-285 (new article in 2004 IGC)]*
1. Effective implementation of Union law by the Member States, which is essential for the proper functioning of the Union, shall be regarded as a matter of common interest.

2. The Union may support the efforts of Member States to improve their administrative capacity to implement Union law. Such action may include facilitating the exchange of information and of civil servants as well as supporting training schemes. No Member State shall be obliged to avail itself of such support. ***The European Parliament and the Council, acting by means of regulations in accordance with the ordinary legislative procedure,*** **shall establish the necessary measures to this end, excluding any harmonisation of the laws and regulations of the Member States.**

3. This Article shall be without prejudice to the obligations of the Member States to implement Union law or to the prerogatives and duties of the Commission. It shall also be without prejudice to other provisions of the ***Treaties*** **providing for administrative co-operation among the Member States and between them and the Union.**

[BMDF Note: Articles 177 and 179 to 181a TEC moved to Part Five, 'External Action', Article 178 TEC shall be repealed]

PART FOUR

ASSOCIATION OF THE OVERSEAS COUNTRIES AND TERRITORIES

ARTICLE ***198*** [182] *[Article III-286 (ex Article 182 TEC)]*
The Member States agree to associate with the ***Union*** the non-European countries and territories which have special relations with Denmark, France, the Netherlands and the United Kingdom. These countries and territories (hereinafter called the 'countries and territories') are listed in Annex II.
The purpose of association shall be to promote the economic and social development of the countries and territories and to establish close economic relations between them and the ***Union*** as a whole.
In accordance with the principles set out in the Preamble to this Treaty, association shall serve primarily to further the interests and prosperity of the inhabitants of these countries and territories in order to lead them to the economic, social and cultural development to which they aspire.

ARTICLE ***199*** [183] *[Article III-287 (ex Article 183 TEC)]*
Association shall have the following objectives:
1. Member States shall apply to their trade with the countries and territories the same treatment as they accord each other pursuant to ***the Treaties***.

2. Each country or territory shall apply to its trade with Member States and with the other countries and territories the same treatment as that which it applies to the European State with which it has special relations.

3. The Member States shall contribute to the investments required for the progressive development of these countries and territories.

4. For investments financed by the **Union**, participation in tenders and supplies shall be open on equal terms to all natural and legal persons who are nationals of a Member State or of one of the countries and territories.

5. In relations between Member States and the countries and territories the right of establishment of nationals and companies or firms shall be regulated in accordance with the provisions and procedures laid down in the Chapter relating to the right of establishment and on a non-discriminatory basis, subject to any special provisions laid down pursuant to Article ***203***.

ARTICLE ***200*** [184] *[Article III-288 (ex Article 184 TEC)]*
1. Customs duties on imports into the Member States of goods originating in the countries and territories shall be prohibited in conformity with the prohibition of customs duties between Member States in Accordance with the provisions of ***the Treaties***.

2. Customs duties on imports into each country or territory from Member States or from the other countries or territories shall be prohibited in accordance with the provisions of Article ***30***.

3. The countries and territories may, however, levy customs duties which meet the needs of their development and industrialisation or produce revenue for their budget.
The duties referred to in the preceding sub-paragraph may not exceed the level of those imposed on imports of products from the Member State with which each country or territory has special relations.

4. Paragraph 2 shall not apply to countries and territories which, by reason of the particular international obligations by which they are bound, already apply a non-discriminatory customs tariff.

5. The introduction of or any change in customs duties imposed on goods imported into the countries and territories shall not, either in law or in fact, give rise to any direct or indirect discrimination between imports from the various Member States.

ARTICLE ***201*** [185] *[Article III-289 (ex Article 185 TEC)]*
If the level of the duties applicable to goods from a third country on entry into a country or territory is liable, when the provisions of Article ***200(1)*** have been applied, to cause deflections of trade to the detriment of any Member State, the latter may request the Commission to propose to the other Member States the measures needed to remedy the situation.

ARTICLE ***202*** [186] *[Article III-290 (ex Article 186 TEC)]*
Subject to the provisions relating to public health, public security or public policy, freedom of movement within Member States for workers from the countries and territories, and within the countries and territories for workers from Member States, shall be **regulated by acts adopted in accordance with *Article 203***.

ARTICLE ***203*** [187] *[Article III-291 (ex Article 187 TEC)]*
The Council, acting unanimously **on a proposal from the Commission** , shall, on the basis of the experience acquired under the association of the countries and territories with the ***Union*** and of the principles set out in ***the Treaties***, lay down provisions as regards the detailed rules and the procedure for the association of the countries and territories with the ***Union***. ***Where the provisions in question are adopted by the Council in accordance with a special legislative procedure, it shall act unanimously on a proposal from the Commission and after consulting the European Parliament.***

ARTICLE ***204*** [188] *[Article III-286(1) (ex Article 188 TEC)]*
The provisions of Articles ***198*** to ***203*** shall apply to Greenland, subject to the specific provisions for Greenland set out in the Protocol on special arrangements for Greenland, annexed to ***the Treaties***.

PART FIVE

EXTERNAL ACTION BY THE UNION

TITLE I

GENERAL PROVISONS ON THE UNION'S EXTERNAL ACTION

ARTICLE 205 [188A] *[Article III-292(1) (ex Article 3(2) and Article 11 TEU)]*
The Union's action on the international scene, *pursuant to this Part,* shall be guided by the principles, *pursue the objectives and be conducted in accordance with the general provisions laid down in Chapter 1 of Title V of the Treaty on European Union.*

TITLE *II*

COMMON COMMERCIAL POLICY

ARTICLE ***206*** [188B] *[Article taken from 2004 IGC – Article III-314 (ex Article 131 TEC)]*
By establishing a customs **in accordance with *Articles 28 to 32*, the Union shall** contribute, in the common interest, to the harmonious development of world trade, the progressive abolition of restrictions on international trade **and on foreign direct investment,** and the lowering of customs **and other** barriers.
[BMDF Note: Article moved from Article 131 TEC]

ARTICLE *207* [188C] *[Article III-315 (ex Article 133 TEC)]*
1. The common commercial policy shall be based on uniform principles, particularly in regard to changes in tariff rates, the conclusion of tariff and trade agreements **relating to trade in goods and services, and the commercial aspects of intellectual property, foreign direct investment**, the achievement of uniformity in measures of liberalisation, export policy and measures to protect trade such as those to be taken in the event of dumping or subsidies. **The common commercial policy shall be conducted in the context of the principles and objectives of the Union's external action**.
The European Parliament and the Council, acting by means of regulations in accordance with the ordinary legislative procedure, shall adopt **the measures defining the framework** for implementing the common commercial policy.

3. Where agreements with one or more **third countries** or international organisations need to be negotiated, ***Article 218*** **shall apply, subject to the special provisions of this Article**.
The Commission shall make recommendations to the Council, which shall authorise **it** to open the necessary negotiations. The Council and the Commission shall be responsible for ensuring that the agreements negotiated are compatible with internal **Union** policies and rules.
The Commission shall conduct these negotiations in consultation with a special committee appointed by the Council to assist the Commission in this task and within the framework of such directives as the Council may issue to it. The Commission shall report regularly to the special committee on the progress of negotiations.

4. **For the negotiation and conclusion of the agreements referred to in paragraph 3**, the Council shall act by a qualified majority.
For the negotiation and conclusion of agreements in the fields of trade in services and the commercial aspects of intellectual property, as well as foreign direct investment, the Council shall act unanimously where such agreements include provisions for which unanimity is required for the adoption of internal rules.
The Council shall also act unanimously for the negotiation and conclusion of agreements:
(a) in the field of trade in cultural and audiovisual services, where these agreements risk prejudicing the Union's cultural and linguistic diversity;
(b) in the field of trade in social, education and health services, where these agreements risk seriously disturbing the national organisation of such services and prejudicing the responsibility of Member States to deliver them.

5. The negotiation and conclusion of international agreements in the field of transport shall be **subject to** ***Title V of Part Three and to Article 218***.

6. The exercise of the competences conferred by this Article in the field of the common commercial policy shall not affect the delimitation of competences between the Union and the Member States, and shall not lead to harmonisation of legislative or regulatory provisions of the Member States insofar as the *Treaties* exclude such harmonisation.
[BMDF Note: Article moved from Article 133 TEC]

TITLE III

CO-OPERATION WITH THIRD COUNTRIES AND HUMANITARIAN AID

CHAPTER 1

DEVELOPMENT CO-OPERATION

ARTICLE *208* [188D] *[Article III-316 (ex Article 177 TEC)]*
1. Union policy in the field of development co-operation shall be conducted within the framework of the principles and objectives of the Union's external action. The Union's development co-operation policy and that of the Member States shall complement and reinforce each other.
Union development co-operation policy shall have as its primary objective the reduction and, in the long term, the eradication of poverty. The Union shall take account of the objectives of

development co-operation in the policies that it implements which are likely to affect developing countries.

2. The ***Union*** and the Member States shall comply with the commitments and take account of the objectives they have approved in the context of the United Nations and other competent international organisations.
[BMDF Note: Article moved from Article 177 TEC]

ARTICLE ***209*** [188E] *[Article III-317 (ex Article 179 TEC)]*
1. ***The European Parliament and*** the Council, acting in accordance with the ***ordinary legislative procedure***, shall adopt the measures necessary **for the implementation of development co-operation policy, which may relate to** multiannual **co-operation** programmes **with developing countries or programmes with a thematic approach**.

2. The Union may conclude with third countries and competent international organisations any agreement helping to achieve the objectives referred to in *Article 21 of the Treaty on European Union and Article 208 of this Treaty*.
The first subparagraph shall be without prejudice to Member States' competence to negotiate in international bodies and to conclude agreements.

3. The European Investment Bank shall contribute, under the terms laid down in its Statute, to the implementation of the measures referred to in paragraph 1.

ARTICLE ***210*** [188F] *[Article III-318(1) and (2) (ex Article 180 TEC)]*
1. **In order to promote the complementarity and efficiency of their action,** the **Union** and the Member States shall co-ordinate their policies on development co-operation and shall consult each other on their aid programmes, including in international organisations and during international conferences. They may undertake joint action. Member States shall contribute if necessary to the implementation of **Union** aid programmes.

2. The Commission may take any useful initiative to promote the co-ordination referred to in paragraph 1.
[BMDF Note: Article moved from Article 180 TEC]

ARTICLE ***211*** [188G] *[Article III-318(3) (ex Article 181 TEC)]*
Within their respective spheres of competence, the **Union** and the Member States shall co-operate with third countries and with the competent international organisations.

CHAPTER 2

ECONOMIC, FINANCIAL AND TECHNICAL CO-OPERATION WITH THIRD COUNTRIES

ARTICLE ***212*** [188H] *[Article III-319 (ex Article 181a TEC)]*
1. Without prejudice to the other provisions of ***the Treaties***, and in particular ***Articles 208 to 211***, the ***Union*** shall carry out economic, financial and technical co-operation measures**, including assistance, in particular financial assistance,** with third countries **other than developing countries**. Such measures shall be consistent with the development policy of the **Union and shall be carried out within the framework of the principles and objectives of its external action**. **The Union's operations and those of the Member States shall complement and reinforce each other.**

2. ***The European Parliament and t***he Council, acting ***in accordance with the ordinary legislative procedure***, shall adopt the measures necessary for the implementation of paragraph 1.
3. Within their respective spheres of competence, the **Union** and the Member States shall co-operate with third countries and the competent international organisations. The arrangements for **Union** co-operation may be the subject of agreements between the **Union** and the third parties concerned.
The first sub-paragraph shall be without prejudice to the Member States' competence to negotiate in international bodies and to conclude international agreements.
[BMDF Note: Article moved from Article 181a TEC]

ARTICLE 213 [188I] *[Article III-320 (new article in 2004 IGC)]*
When the situation in a third country requires urgent financial assistance from the Union, the Council shall adopt the necessary decisions on a proposal from the Commission.

CHAPTER 3

HUMANITARIAN AID

ARTICLE 214 [188J] *[Article III-321 (new article in 2004 IGC)]*
1. The Union's operations in the field of humanitarian aid shall be conducted within the framework of the principles and objectives of the external action of the Union. Such operations shall be intended to provide ad hoc assistance and relief and protection for people in third countries who are victims of natural or man-made disasters, in order to meet the humanitarian needs resulting from these different situations. The Union's operations and those of the Member States shall complement and reinforce each other.

2. Humanitarian aid operations shall be conducted in compliance with the principles of international law and with the principles of impartiality, neutrality and non-discrimination.

3. *The European Parliament and the Council, acting in accordance with the ordinary legislative procedure,* shall establish the measures defining the framework within which the Union's humanitarian aid operations shall be implemented.

4. The Union may conclude with third countries and competent international organisations any agreement helping to achieve the objectives referred to in paragraph 1 and in *Article 21 of the Treaty on European Union.*
The first subparagraph shall be without prejudice to Member States' competence to negotiate in international bodies and to conclude agreements.

5. In order to establish a framework for joint contributions from young Europeans to the humanitarian aid operations of the Union, a European Voluntary Humanitarian Aid Corps shall be set up. *The European Parliament and the Council, acting by means of regulations in accordance with the ordinary legislative procedure,* shall determine the rules and procedures for the operation of the Corps.

6. The Commission may take any useful initiative to promote co-ordination between actions of the Union and those of the Member States, in order to enhance the efficiency and complementarity of Union and national humanitarian aid measures.

7. The Union shall ensure that its humanitarian aid operations are co-ordinated and consistent with those of international organisations and bodies, in particular those forming part of the United Nations system.

TITLE IV

RESTRICTIVE MEASURES

ARTICLE 215 [188K] *[Article III-322 (ex Article 301 TEC)]*
1. Where a decision, adopted in accordance with *Chapter 2 of Title V of the Treaty on European Union*, provides for the interruption or reduction, in part or completely, of economic and financial relations with one or more third countries, the Council, acting by a qualified majority on a joint proposal from the *High Representative of the Union for Foreign Affairs and Security Policy* and the Commission, shall adopt the necessary *measures*. It shall inform the European Parliament thereof.

2. **Where a decision adopted in accordance with *Chapter 2 of Title V of the Treaty on European Union* so provides, the Council may adopt restrictive measures under the procedure referred to in paragraph 1 against natural or legal persons and groups or non-State entities.**

3. **The acts referred to in this Article shall include necessary provisions on legal safeguards.**
[BMDF Note: See also Declaration no. 25. Article moved from Article 301 TEC]

TITLE V

INTERNATIONAL AGREEMENTS

ARTICLE 216 [188L] *[Article III-323 (ex Article 24 TEU and Article 300(7) TEC)]*
1. **The Union may conclude an agreement with one or more third countries or international organisations where the *Treaties* so provide or where the conclusion of an agreement is necessary in order to achieve, within the framework of the Union's policies, one of the objectives referred to in the *Treaties*, or is provided for in a legally binding Union act or is likely to affect common rules or alter their scope.**

2. **Agreements concluded by the Union are binding on the institutions of the Union and on its Member States.**

ARTICLE 217 [188M] *[Article III-324 (ex Article 310 TEC)]*
The **Union** may conclude with one or more **third countries** or international organisations agreements establishing an association involving reciprocal rights and obligations, common action and special procedures.

ARTICLE 218 [188N] *[Article III-325 (ex Article III-300 TEC)]*
1. **Without prejudice to the specific provisions laid down in *Article 207*, agreements between the Union and third countries or international organisations shall be negotiated and concluded in accordance with the following procedure.**

2. **The Council shall authorise the opening of negotiations, adopt negotiating directives, authorise the signing of agreements and conclude them.**

3. **The Commission, or the *High Representative of the Union for Foreign Affairs and Security Policy* where the agreement envisaged relates exclusively or principally to the common foreign and security policy, shall submit recommendations to the Council, which shall adopt a decision authorising the opening of negotiations and, depending on the subject of the agreement envisaged, nominating the Union negotiator or head of the Union's negotiating team.**

4. **The Council may address directives to the negotiator and designate a special committee in consultation with which the negotiations must be conducted.**

5. **The Council, on a proposal by the negotiator, shall adopt a decision authorising the signing of the agreement and, if necessary, its provisional application before entry into force.**

6. **The Council, on a proposal by the negotiator, shall adopt a decision concluding the agreement.**
Except where agreements relate exclusively to the common foreign and security policy, the Council shall adopt the decision concluding the agreement:
(a) after obtaining the consent of the European Parliament in the following cases:
- **(i) association agreements;**
- **(ii) Union accession to the European Convention for the Protection of Human Rights and Fundamental Freedoms;**
- **(iii) agreements establishing a specific institutional framework by organising co-operation procedures;**
- **(iv) agreements with important budgetary implications for the Union;**

(v) agreements covering fields to which either the ordinary legislative procedure applies, or the special legislative procedure where consent by the European Parliament is required.

The European Parliament and the Council may, in an urgent situation, agree upon a time-limit for consent.

(b) after consulting the European Parliament in other cases. The European Parliament shall deliver its opinion within a time-limit which the Council may set depending on the urgency of the matter. In the absence of an opinion within that time-limit, the Council may act.

7. When concluding an agreement, the Council may, by way of derogation from paragraphs 5, 6 and 9, authorise the negotiator to approve on the Union's behalf modifications to the agreement where it provides for them to be adopted by a simplified procedure or by a body set up by the agreement. The Council may attach specific conditions to such authorisation.

8. The Council shall act by a qualified majority throughout the procedure.
However, it shall act unanimously when the agreement covers a field for which unanimity is required for the adoption of a Union act as well as for association agreements and the agreements referred to in ***Article 212*** **with the States which are candidates for accession.** ***The Council shall also act unanimously for the agreement on accession of the Union to the European Convention for the Protection of Human Rights and Fundamental Freedoms; the decision concluding this agreement shall enter into force after it has been approved by the Member States in accordance with their respective constitutional requirements.***

9. The Council, on a proposal from the Commission or the ***High Representative of the Union for Foreign Affairs and Security Policy*****, shall adopt a decision suspending application of an agreement and establishing the positions to be adopted on the Union's behalf in a body set up by an agreement, when that body is called upon to adopt acts having legal effects, with the exception of acts supplementing or amending the institutional framework of the agreement.**

10. The European Parliament shall be immediately and fully informed at all stages of the procedure.

11. A Member State, the European Parliament, the Council or the Commission may obtain the opinion of the Court of Justice as to whether an agreement envisaged is compatible with the ***Treaties*****. Where the opinion of the Court of Justice is adverse, the agreement envisaged may not enter into force unless it is amended or the** ***Treaties are*** **revised.**
[BMDF Note: See also Declaration no. 36. Article moved from Article 300 TEC and redrafted in 2004 IGC]

ARTICLE ***219*** [188O] *[Article III-326 (ex Article 111 TEC)]*
1. By way of derogation from ***Article 218***, the Council, **either** on a recommendation from the European Central Bank or **on a recommendation** from the Commission and after consulting the European Central Bank, in an endeavour to reach a consensus consistent with the objective of price stability, **may** conclude formal agreements on an exchange-rate system for the **euro** in relation to currencies **of third States. The Council shall act unanimously after consulting the European Parliament and in accordance with the procedure provided for in paragraph 3.**
The Council may, **either** on a recommendation from the European Central Bank or **on a recommendation** from the Commission, and after consulting the European Central Bank, in an endeavour to reach a consensus consistent with the objective of price stability, adopt, adjust or abandon the central rates of the **euro** within the exchange rate system. The President of the Council shall inform the European Parliament of the adoption, adjustment or abandonment of the central rates **of the euro**.

2. In the absence of an exchange rate system in relation to one or more currencies **of third States** as referred to in paragraph 1, the Council, either on a recommendation from the Commission and after consulting the European Central Bank or on a recommendation from the European Central Bank, may formulate general orientations for exchange rate policy in relation to these currencies. These general orientations shall be without prejudice to the primary objective of the ESCB to maintain price stability.

3. By way of derogation from ***Article 218***, where agreements concerning monetary or foreign exchange regime matters need to be negotiated by the ***Union*** with one or more **third** States or international organisations, the Council, on a recommendation from the Commission and after

consulting the European Central Bank, shall decide the arrangements for the negotiation and for the conclusion of such agreements. These arrangements shall ensure that the ***Union*** expresses a single position. The Commission shall be fully associated with the negotiations.

4. Without prejudice to **Union** competence and **Union** agreements as regards economic and monetary Union, Member States may negotiate in international bodies and conclude international agreements.
[BMDF Note: Article moved from Article 111 TEC. Article does not apply to the UK: Article 139(2)(g) TFEU and Protocol 18(4)].

TITLE VI

THE UNION'S RELATIONS WITH INTERNATIONAL ORGANISATIONS AND THIRD COUNTRIES AND UNION DELEGATIONS

ARTICLE 220 [188P] *[Article III-327 (ex Articles 302, 303 and 304 TEC)]*
1. The Union shall establish all appropriate forms of co-operation with the organs of the United Nations and its specialised agencies, the Council of Europe, the Organisation for Security and Co-operation in Europe and the Organisation for Economic Co-operation and Development. The Union shall also maintain such relations as are appropriate with other international organisations.

2. The *High Representative of the Union for Foreign Affairs and Security Policy* and the Commission shall be instructed to implement this Article.

ARTICLE 221 [188Q] *[Article III-328 (new article in 2004 IGC)]*
1. Union delegations in third countries and at international organisations shall represent the Union.

2. Union delegations shall be placed under the authority of the Union Minister for Foreign Affairs. They shall act in close co-operation with Member States' diplomatic and consular missions.

TITLE VII

SOLIDARITY CLAUSE

ARTICLE 222 [188R] *[Article I-43 and Article III-329 (new Articles in 2004 IGC)]*
1. The Union and its Member States shall act jointly in a spirit of solidarity if a Member State is the object of a terrorist attack or the victim of a natural or man-made disaster. The Union shall mobilise all the instruments at its disposal, including the military resources made available by the Member States, to:
(a) – prevent the terrorist threat in the territory of the Member States;
– protect democratic institutions and the civilian population from any terrorist attack;
– assist a Member State in its territory, at the request of its political authorities, in the event of a terrorist attack;
(b) assist a Member State in its territory, at the request of its political authorities, in the event of a natural or man-made disaster.

***2.* Should a Member State be the object of a terrorist attack or the victim of a natural or man-made disaster, the other Member States shall assist it at the request of its political authorities. To that end, the Member States shall co-ordinate between themselves in the Council.**

3. **The arrangements for the implementation by the Union of the solidarity clause shall be defined by a decision adopted by the Council acting on a joint proposal by the Commission and the *High Representative of the Union for Foreign Affairs and Security Policy.* The Council shall act in accordance with *Article 31(1) of the Treaty on European Union* where this decision has defence implications. The European Parliament shall be informed.**
For the purposes of this paragraph and without prejudice to *Article 240*, the Council shall be assisted by the Political and Security Committee with the support of the structures developed in the context of the common security and defence policy and by the Committee referred to in *Article 71*; the two committees shall, if necessary, submit joint opinions.

4. **The European Council shall regularly assess the threats facing the Union in order to enable the Union and its Member States to take effective action.**
[BMDF Note: See also Declaration no. 37. Article combination of two articles taken from 2004 IGC – paragraph 1 from Article I-43 and paragraphs 2, 3 and 4 from Article III-329]

PART *SIX*

INSTITUTIONAL AND BUDGETARY PROVISIONS

TITLE I

PROVISIONS GOVERNING THE INSTITUTIONS

CHAPTER 1

THE INSTITUTIONS

SECTION 1

THE EUROPEAN PARLIAMENT

[BMDF Note: Article 189 TEC shall be repealed]

ARTICLE ***223*** [190] *[Article III-330 (ex Article 190 TEC)]*
[BMDF Note: Paragraphs 1 to 3 shall be repealed]
1. The European Parliament shall draw up a proposal ***to lay down the provisions necessary for the election of its Members*** by direct universal suffrage in accordance with a uniform procedure in all Member States or in accordance with principles common to all Member States.
The Council, acting unanimously ***in accordance with a special legislative procedure*** after obtaining the assent of the European Parliament, which shall act by a majority of its component members, ***shall*** lay down the appropriate provisions. ***These provisions shall enter into force following their approval by the*** Member States in accordance with their respective constitutional requirements.

2. The European Parliament ***acting by means of regulations on its own initiative in accordance with a special legislative procedure***, after seeking an opinion from the Commission and with the approval of the Council, shall lay down the regulations and general conditions governing the performance of the duties of its Members. All rules or conditions relating to the taxation of current or former Members shall require unanimity within the Council.

ARTICLE ***224*** [191] *[Article III-331 (ex Article 191 TEC)]*
The European Parliament and the Council, acting in accordance with the ***ordinary legislative procedure***, ***by means of regulations,*** shall lay down the regulations governing political parties at European level **referred to in *Article 10(4) of the Treaty on European Union*** and in particular the rules regarding their funding.

ARTICLE *225* [192] *[Article III-332 (ex Article 192 TEC)]*
The European Parliament may, acting by a majority of its **component members**, request the Commission to submit any appropriate proposal on matters on which it considers that a **Union** act is required for the purpose of implementing ***the Treaties***. **If the Commission does not submit a proposal, it shall inform the European Parliament of the reasons.**

ARTICLE *226* [193] *[Article III-333 (ex Article 193 TEC)]*
In the course of its duties, the European Parliament may, at the request of a quarter of its **component members**, set up a temporary Committee of Inquiry to investigate, without prejudice to the powers conferred by ***the Treaties*** on other institutions or bodies, alleged contravention or maladministration in the implementation of **Union** law, except where the alleged facts are being examined before a court and while the case is still subject to legal proceedings.
The temporary Committee of Inquiry shall cease to exist on the submission of its report.
The detailed provisions governing the exercise of the right of inquiry shall be determined by ***the European Parliament, acting by means of regulations on its own initiative in accordance with a special legislative procedure, after obtaining the consent of the Council and the Commission***.

ARTICLE *227* [194] *[Article III-334 (ex Article 194 TEC)]*
Any citizen of the Union, and any natural or legal person residing or having its registered office in a Member State, shall have the right to address, individually or in association with other citizens or persons, a petition to the European Parliament on a matter which comes within the **Union**'s fields of activity and which affects him, her or it directly.

ARTICLE *228* [195] *[Article I-49 and Article III-335 (ex Article 195 TEC)]*
1. **A European** Ombudsman **elected by the European Parliament** ***shall be*** empowered to receive complaints from any citizen of the Union or any natural or legal person residing or having its registered office in a Member State concerning instances of maladministration in the activities of the ***Union institutions, bodies, offices or agencies***, with the exception of the Court of Justice **of the European Union** acting in **its** judicial role. ***He or she shall examine such complaints and report on them.***
In accordance with his duties, the Ombudsman shall conduct inquiries for which he finds grounds, either on his own initiative or on the basis of complaints submitted to him direct or through a Member of the European Parliament, except where the alleged facts are or have been the subject of legal proceedings. Where the Ombudsman establishes an instance of maladministration, he shall refer the matter to the institution concerned, which shall have a period of three months in which to inform him of its views. The Ombudsman shall then forward a report to the European Parliament and the institution, **body, office or agency** concerned. The person lodging the complaint shall be informed of the outcome of such inquiries.
The Ombudsman shall submit an annual report to the European Parliament on the outcome of his inquiries.

2. The Ombudsman shall be **elected** after each election of the European Parliament for the duration of its term of office. The Ombudsman shall be eligible for reappointment.
The Ombudsman may be dismissed by the Court of Justice at the request of the European Parliament if he no longer fulfils the conditions required for the performance of his duties or if he is guilty of serious misconduct.

3. The Ombudsman shall be completely independent in the performance of his duties. In the performance of those duties he shall neither seek nor take instructions from any ***Government***, **institution,** body**, office or agency**. The Ombudsman may not, during his term of office, engage in any other occupation, whether gainful or not.

4. The European Parliament ***acting by means of regulations on its own initiative in accordance with a special legislative procedure*** shall, after seeking an opinion from the Commission and with the approval of the Council, lay down the regulations and general conditions governing the performance of the Ombudsman's duties.
[BMDF Note: Article taken from 2004 IGC – Paragraph 1 from Article I-49, 'The European Ombudsman', paragraphs 2-4 from Article III-335]

ARTICLE ***229*** [196] *[Article III-336 (ex Article 196 TEC)]*
The European Parliament shall hold an annual session. It shall meet, without requiring to be convened, on the second Tuesday in March.
The European Parliament may meet in extraordinary **part-**session at the request of a majority of its Members or at the request of a majority of its **component members** or at the request of the Council or of the Commission.

ARTICLE ***230*** [197] *[Article III-337(1) and (2) (ex Article 197 TEC)]*
The Commission may attend all meetings and shall, at **its** request, be heard.
The Commission shall reply orally or in writing to questions put to it by the European Parliament or by its Members.
The European Council and **t**he Council shall be heard by the European Parliament in accordance with the conditions laid down ***the*** Rules of Procedure ***of the European Council and those of the Council***.

ARTICLE ***231*** [198] *[Article III-338 (ex Article 198 TEC)]*
Save as otherwise provided in ***the Treaties***, the European Parliament shall act by an majority of the votes cast.
The rules of procedure shall determine the quorum.

ARTICLE ***232*** [199] *[Article III-339 (ex Article 199 TEC)]*
The European Parliament shall adopt its Rules of Procedure, acting by a majority of its Members.
The proceedings of the European Parliament shall be published in the manner laid down ***in the treaties and*** in its Rules of Procedure.

ARTICLE ***233*** [200] *[Article III-337(3) (ex Article 200 TEC)]*
The European Parliament shall discuss in open session the annual general report submitted to it by the Commission.

ARTICLE ***234*** [201] *[Article III-340 (ex Article 201 TEC)]*
If a motion of censure on the activities of the Commission is tabled before it, the European Parliament shall not vote thereon until at least three days after the motion has been tabled and only by open vote.
If the motion of censure is carried by a two-thirds majority of the votes cast, representing a majority of the **component m**embers of the European Parliament, the members of the Commission shall resign as a body **and the *High Representative of the Union for Foreign Affairs and Security Policy* shall resign from duties that he or she carries out in the Commission**. They shall **remain in office and** continue to deal with current business until they are replaced in accordance with ***Article 17 of the Treaty on European Union***. In this case, the term of office of the members of the Commission appointed to replace them shall expire on the date on which the term of office of the members of the Commission obliged to resign as a body would have expired.

SECTION 1 a

THE EUROPEAN COUNCIL

ARTICLE 235 [201a] *[Article III-341 (new article in 2004 IGC)]*
1. Where a vote is taken, any member of the European Council may also act on behalf of not more than one other member.
Article 16(4) of the Treaty on European Union and Article 238(2) of this Treaty shall apply to the European Council when it is acting by a qualified majority. Where the European Council decides by vote, its President and the President of the Commission shall not take part in the vote.
Abstentions by members present in person or represented shall not prevent the adoption by the European Council of acts which require unanimity.

2. The President of the European Parliament may be invited to be heard by the European Council.

3. The European Council shall act by a simple majority for procedural questions and for the adoption of its Rules of Procedure.

4. The European Council shall be assisted by the General Secretariat of the Council.

ARTICLE 236 [201b] *[New Article in Treaty of Lisbon, expanded from Article I-24(1) (new Paragraph in 2004 IGC) and (7)]*
The European Council shall adopt by a qualified majority:
(a) a decision establishing the list of Council configurations other than those referred to in the second and third subparagraphs of Article 16(6) of the Treaty on European Union;
(b) a decision on the Presidency of Council configurations, other than that of Foreign Affairs, in accordance with Article 16(9) of the Treaty on European Union.

SECTION 2

THE COUNCIL

[BMDF Note: Article 202 TEC shall be repealed and replaced by Articles 290 and 291 TFEU]

[BMDF Note: Article 203 TEC shall be repealed]

ARTICLE ***237*** [204] *[Article III-342(ex Article 204 TEC)]*
The Council shall meet when convened by its President on his own initiative or at the request of one of its members or of the Commission.

ARTICLE ***238*** [205] *[Article III-343 (ex Article 205 TEC)]*
1. **Where it is required to act by a simple majority, the Council shall act by a majority of its component members.**

2. By way of derogation from Article 16(4) of the Treaty on European Union, as from 1 November 2014 and subject to the provisions laid down in the Protocol on transitional provisions, where the Council does not act on a proposal from the Commission or from the High Representative of the Union for Foreign Affairs and Security Policy, the qualified majority shall be defined as at least 72% of the members of the Council, representing Member States comprising at least 65% of the population of the Union. *[BMDF Note: See also Protocol no. 10 and Declaration no. 7]*

3. As from 1 November 2014 and subject to the provisions laid down in the Protocol on transitional provisions, in cases where, under the Treaties, not all the members of the Council participate in voting, a qualified majority shall be defined as follows:
(a) A qualified majority shall be defined as at least 55% of the members of the Council representing the participating Member States, comprising at least 65% of the population of these States.
A blocking minority must include at least the minimum number of Council members representing more than 35% of the population of the participating Member States, plus one member, failing which the qualified majority shall be deemed attained.
(b) By way of derogation from point (a), where the Council does not act on a proposal from the Commission or from the High Representative of the Union for Foreign Affairs and Security Policy, the qualified majority shall be defined as at least 72% of the members of the Council representing the participating Member States, comprising at least 65% of the population of these States.
[BMDF Note: Paragraph taken from draft Constitution, Article I-25]

4. Abstentions by Members present in person or represented shall not prevent the adoption by the Council of acts which require unanimity.

ARTICLE ***239*** [206] *[Article III-343(1) (ex Article 206 TEC)]*
Where a vote is taken, any member of the Council may also act on behalf of not more than one other member.

ARTICLE ***240*** [207] *[Article III-344 (ex Article 207 TEC)]*
1. A committee consisting of the Permanent Representatives **of the Governments** of the Member States shall be responsible for preparing the work of the Council and for carrying out the tasks assigned

to it by the **latter**. The Committee may adopt procedural decisions in cases provided for in the Council's Rules of Procedure.

2. The Council shall be assisted by a General Secretariat, under the responsibility of a Secretary-General, **appointed by the Council**.
The Council shall decide on the organisation of the General Secretariat **by a simple majority**.

3. The Council shall **act by a simple majority regarding procedural matters and for the adoption of** its Rules of Procedure.

ARTICLE ***241*** [208] *[Article III-345 (ex Article 208 TEC)]*
The Council, ***acting*** **by a simple majority** may request the Commission to undertake any studies the Council considers desirable for the attainment of the common objectives, and to submit to it any appropriate proposals. **If the Commission does not submit a proposal, it shall inform the Council of the reasons.**

ARTICLE ***242*** [209] *[Article III-346 (ex Article 209 TEC)]*
The Council***, acting by a simple majority*** shall, after ***consulting*** the Commission, determine the rules governing the committees provided for in ***the Treaties***.

ARTICLE ***243*** [210] *[Article III-400(1)(a) and(c) (ex Article 210 TEC)]*
The Council shall determine the salaries, allowances and pensions of **the President of the European Council,** the President of the Commission, ***the High Representative of the Union for Foreign Affairs and Security Policy*****, the members of the Commission,** the Presidents, **members** and Registrars of the Court of Justice **of the European Union and the Secretary-General of the Council**. It shall also determine any payment to be made instead of remuneration.

SECTION 3

THE COMMISSION

[BMDF Note: Article 211 TEC shall be repealed]

ARTICLE 244 [211a] *[Article I-26(6) (ex Article 211a TEC)]*
In accordance with Article 17(5) of the Treaty on European Union, the members of the Commission shall be chosen on the basis of a system of rotation established unanimously by the European Council and on the basis of the following principles:
(a) Member States shall be treated on a strictly equal footing as regards determination of the sequence of, and the time spent by, their nationals as members of the Commission; consequently, the difference between the total number of terms of office held by nationals of any given pair of Member States may never be more than one;
(b) subject to point (a), each successive Commission shall be so composed as to reflect satisfactorily the demographic and geographical range of all the Member States.

[BMDF Note: Article 212 TEC moved to Article 249 TFEU, Paragraph 2]

ARTICLE ***245*** [213] *[Article III-347 (ex Article 213 TEC)]*
The Members of the Commission shall refrain from any action incompatible with their duties. Member States shall respect their independence and shall not seek to influence them in the performance of their tasks.
The Members of the Commission may not, during their term of office, engage in any other occupation, whether gainful or not. When entering upon their duties they shall give a solemn undertaking that, both during and after their term of office, they will respect the obligations arising therefrom and in particular their duty to behave with integrity and discretion as regards the acceptance, after they have ceased to hold office, of certain appointments or benefits. In the event of any breach of these obligations, the Court of Justice may, on application by the Council, **acting by a simple majority** or the Commission, rule that the Member concerned be, according to the circumstances, either compulsorily retired in accordance with Article ***247*** or deprived of his right to a pension or other benefits in its stead.

[BMDF Note: Article 214 TEC shall be repealed]

ARTICLE ***246*** [215] *[Article III-348 (ex Article 215 TEC)]*
Apart from normal replacement, or death, the duties of a Member of the Commission shall end when he resigns or is compulsorily retired.
A vacancy caused by resignation, compulsory retirement or death shall be filled for the remainder of the Member's term of office by a new Member **of the same nationality** appointed by the Council, **by common accord with the President of the Commission, after consulting the European Parliament and in accordance with the criteria set out in *the second subparagraph of Article 17(3) of the Treaty on European Union***.
The Council may, acting unanimously **on a proposal from the President of the Commission**, decide that such a vacancy need not be filled**, in particular when the remainder of the member's term of office is short**.
In the event of resignation, compulsory retirement or death, the President shall be replaced for the remainder of his term of office. The procedure laid down in ***Article 17(7), first subparagraph, of the Treaty on European Union*** shall be applicable for the replacement of the President.
In the event of resignation, compulsory retirement or death, *the High Representative of the Union for Foreign Affairs and Security Policy* shall be replaced, for the remainder of his or her term of office, in accordance with *Article 18(1) of the Treaty on European Union.*
In the case of the resignation of all the members of the Commission, they shall remain in office and continue to deal with current business until they have been replaced, for the remainder of their term of office, in accordance with *Article 17 of the Treaty on European Union.*

ARTICLE ***247*** [216] *[Article III-349 (ex Article 216 TEC)]*
If any Member of the Commission no longer fulfils the conditions required for the performance of his duties or if he has been guilty of serious misconduct, the Court of Justice may, on application by the Council, **acting by a simple majority** or the Commission, compulsorily retire him.

ARTICLE ***248*** [217] *[Article III-350 (ex Article 217 TEC)]*
Without prejudice to *Article 18(4) of the Treaty on European Union*, the responsibilities incumbent upon the Commission shall be structured and allocated among its Members by its President**, in accordance with *Article 17(6) of that Treaty***. The President may reshuffle the allocation of those responsibilities during the Commission's term of office. The Members of the Commission shall carry out the duties devolved upon them by the President under his authority.

ARTICLE ***249*** [218] *[Article III-352 (ex Article 218 TEC)]*
1. The Commission shall adopt its rules of procedure so as to ensure that both it and its departments operate. It shall ensure that these rules are published.

2. The Commission shall publish annually, not later than one month before the opening of the session of the European Parliament, a general report on the activities of the **Union.**
[BMDF Note: Paragraph 1 deleted by the Treaty of Lisbon. Paragraph 2 moved from Article 212 TEC]

ARTICLE ***250*** [219] *[Article III-351 (ex Article 219 TEC)]*
The Commission shall act by a majority of **its members**.
Its Rules of Procedure shall determine the quorum.

SECTION 4

THE COURT OF JUSTICE **OF THE EUROPEAN UNION**

[BMDF Note: Article 220 TEC shall be repealed]

ARTICLE ***251*** [221] *[Article III-353 (ex Article 221 TEC)]*
The Court of Justice shall sit in chambers or in a Grand Chamber, in accordance with the rules laid down for that purpose in the Statute of the Court of Justice **of the European Union**.
When provided for in the Statute, the Court of Justice may also sit as a full Court.

ARTICLE *252* [222] *[Article III-354 (ex Article 222 TEC)]*
The Court of Justice shall be assisted by eight Advocates-General. Should the Court of Justice so request, the Council, acting unanimously, may increase the number of Advocates-General.
It shall be the duty of the Advocate-General, acting with complete impartiality and independence, to make, in open court, reasoned submissions on cases which, in accordance with the Statute of the Court of Justice **of the European Union**, require his involvement.
[BMDF Note: See also Declaration no. 38]

ARTICLE *253* [223] *[Article III-355 (ex Article 223 TEC)]*
The Judges and Advocates-General of the Court of Justice shall be chosen from persons whose independence is beyond doubt and who possess the qualifications required for appointment to the highest judicial offices in their respective countries or who are jurisconsults of recognised competence; they shall be appointed by common accord of the governments of the Member States for a term of six years**, after consultation of the panel provided for in *Article 255***.
Every three years there shall be a partial replacement of the Judges and Advocates-General, in accordance with the conditions laid down in the Statute of the Court of Justice **of the European Union**.
The Judges shall elect the President of the Court of Justice from among their number for a term of three years. He may be re-elected.
Retiring Judges and Advocates-General may be reappointed.
The Court of Justice shall appoint its Registrar and lay down the rules governing his service.
The Court of Justice shall establish its Rules of Procedure. Those Rules shall require the approval of the Council.

ARTICLE *254* [224] *[Article III-356 (ex Article 224 TEC)]*
The number of Judges **of the General Court** shall be determined by the Statute of the Court of Justice **of the European Union**. The Statute may provide for the **General Court** to be assisted by Advocates-General.
The members of the **General Court** shall be chosen from persons whose independence is beyond doubt and who possess the ability required for appointment to high judicial office. They shall be appointed by common accord of the governments of the Member States for a term of six years **after consultation of the panel provided for in *Article 255***. The membership shall be partially renewed every three years. Retiring members shall be eligible for reappointment.
The Judges shall elect the President of the **General Court** from among their number for a term of three years. He may be re-elected.
The **General Court** shall establish its Rules of Procedure in agreement with the Court of Justice. Those Rules shall require the approval of the Council,.
Unless the Statute of the Court of Justice ***of the European Union*** provides otherwise, the provisions of ***the Treaties*** relating to the Court of Justice shall apply to the **General Court**.

ARTICLE 255 [224a] *[Article III-357 (new Article in 2004 IGC)]*
A panel shall be set up in order to give an opinion on candidates' suitability to perform the duties of Judge and Advocate-General of the Court of Justice and the General Court before the governments of the Member States make the appointments referred to in *Articles 253 and 254.*
The panel shall comprise seven persons chosen from among former members of the Court of Justice and the General Court, members of national supreme courts and lawyers of recognised competence, one of whom shall be proposed by the European Parliament. The Council shall adopt a decision establishing the panel's operating rules and a decision appointing its members. It shall act on the initiative of the President of the Court of Justice.

ARTICLE *256* [225] *[Article III-358 (ex Article 225 TEC)]*
1. The **General Court** shall have jurisdiction to hear and determine at first instance actions or proceedings referred to in Articles ***263, 265, 268, 270*** and ***272***, with the exception of those assigned to a **specialised court set up under *Article 257*** and those reserved in the Statute for the Court of Justice **of the European Union**. The Statute may provide for the **General Court** to have jurisdiction for other classes of action or proceeding.
Decisions given by the **General Court** under this paragraph may be subject to a right of appeal to the Court of Justice on points of law only, under the conditions and within the limits laid down by the Statute.

2. The **General Court** shall have jurisdiction to hear and determine actions or proceedings brought against decisions of the **specialised courts**.
Decisions given by the **General Court** under this paragraph may exceptionally be subject to review by the Court of Justice, under the conditions and within the limits laid down by the Statute, where there is a serious risk of the unity or consistency of **Union** law being affected.

3. The **General Court** shall have jurisdiction to hear and determine questions referred for a preliminary ruling under Article ***267***, in specific areas laid down by the Statute.
Where the **General Court** considers that the case requires a decision of principle likely to affect the unity or consistency of **Union** law, it may refer the case to the Court of Justice for a ruling.
Decisions given by the **General Court** on questions referred for a preliminary ruling may exceptionally be subject to review by the Court of Justice, under the conditions and within the limits laid down by the Statute, where there is a serious risk of the unity or consistency of **Union** law being affected.

ARTICLE ***257*** [225a] *[Article III-359 (ex Article 225a TEC)]*
The European Parliament and the Council, acting ***in accordance with the ordinary legislative procedure***, may **establish specialised courts attached to the General Court** to hear and determine at first instance certain classes of action or proceeding brought in specific areas. **The *European Parliament and the Council shall act by means of regulations* either on a proposal from the Commission after consultation of the Court of Justice or at the request of the Court of Justice after consultation of the Commission.**
The ***regulation*** establishing a **specialised court** shall lay down the rules on the organisation of the **court** and the extent of the jurisdiction conferred upon it.
Decisions given by **specialised courts** may be subject to a right of appeal on points of law only or, when provided for in the ***regulation*** establishing the **specialised court**, a right of appeal also on matters of fact, before the **General Court**.
The members of the **specialised courts** shall be chosen from persons whose independence is beyond doubt and who possess the ability required for appointment to judicial office. They shall be appointed by the Council, acting unanimously.
The **specialised courts** shall establish their Rules of Procedure in agreement with the Court of Justice. Those Rules shall require the approval of the Council.
Unless the ***regulation*** establishing the **specialised court** provides otherwise, the provisions of ***the Treaties*** relating to the Court of Justice **of the European Union** and the provisions of the Statute of the Court of Justice **of the European Union** shall apply to the **specialised courts**. **Title I of the Statute and Article 64 thereof shall in any case apply to the specialised courts.**

ARTICLE ***258*** [226] *[Article III-360 (ex Article 226 TEC)]*
If the Commission considers that a Member State has failed to fulfil an obligation under ***the Treaties***, it shall deliver a reasoned opinion on the matter after giving the State concerned the opportunity to submit its observations.
If the State concerned does not comply with the opinion within the period laid down by the Commission, the latter may bring the matter before the Court of Justice **of the European Union**.

ARTICLE ***259*** [227] *[Article III-361 (ex Article 227 TEC)]*
A Member State which considers that another Member State has failed to fulfil an obligation under ***the Treaties*** may bring the matter before the Court of Justice **of the European Union**.
Before a Member State brings an action against another Member State for an alleged infringement of an obligation under ***the Treaties***, it shall bring the matter before the Commission.
The Commission shall deliver a reasoned opinion after each of the States concerned has been given the opportunity to submit its own case and its observations on the other party's case both orally and in writing.
If the Commission has not delivered an opinion within three months of the date on which the matter was brought before it, the absence of such opinion shall not prevent the matter from being brought before the Court.

ARTICLE ***260*** [228] *[Article III-362 (ex Article 228 TEC)]*
1. If the Court of Justice **of the European Union** finds that a Member State has failed to fulfil an obligation under ***the Treaties***, the State shall be required to take the necessary measures to comply with the judgment of the Court.

2. **If the Commission considers that the Member State concerned has not taken the necessary measures to comply with judgment *of the Court*, it may bring the case before the Court after giving that State the opportunity to submit its observations. It shall specify the amount of the lump sum or penalty payment to be paid by the Member State concerned which it considers appropriate in the circumstances.**
If the Court finds that the Member State concerned has not complied with its judgment it may impose a lump sum or penalty payment on it.
This procedure shall be without prejudice to Article ***259***.

3. When the Commission brings a case before the Court of Justice of the European Union pursuant to *Article 258* on the grounds that the Member State concerned has failed to fulfil its obligation to notify measures transposing a *directive adopted under a legislative procedure*, it may, when it deems appropriate, specify the amount of the lump sum or penalty payment to be paid by the Member State concerned which it considers appropriate in the circumstances.
If the Court finds that there is an infringement it may impose a lump sum or penalty payment on the Member State concerned not exceeding the amount specified by the Commission. The payment obligation shall take effect on the date set by the Court in its judgment.

ARTICLE ***261*** [229] *[Article III-363 (ex Article 229 TEC)]*
Regulations adopted jointly by the European Parliament and the Council, and by the Council, pursuant to the provisions of ***the Treaties***, may give the Court of Justice **of the European Union** unlimited jurisdiction with regard to the penalties provided for in such regulations.

ARTICLE ***262*** [229a] *[Article III-364 (ex Article 229a TEC)]*
Without prejudice to the other provisions of ***the Treaties***, the Council, acting unanimously ***in accordance with a special legislative procedure*** and after consulting the European Parliament, may adopt provisions to confer jurisdiction, to the extent that it shall determine, on the Court of Justice **of the European Union** in disputes relating to the application of acts adopted on the basis of ***the Treaties*** which create **European intellectual** property rights. The Council shall recommend those provisions to the Member States for adoption in accordance with their respective constitutional requirements.

ARTICLE ***263*** [230] *[Article III-365 (ex Article 230 TEC)]*
The Court of Justice **of the European Union** shall review the legality of ***legislative*** acts, of acts of the Council, of the Commission and of the European Central Bank, other than recommendations and opinions, and of acts of the European Parliament **and of the European Council** intended to produce legal effects *vis-à-vis* third parties. **It shall also review the legality of acts of bodies, offices or agencies of the Union intended to produce legal effects *vis-à-vis* third parties.**
It shall for this purpose have jurisdiction in actions brought by a Member State, the European Parliament, the Council or the Commission on grounds of lack of competence, infringement of an essential procedural requirement, infringement of ***the Treaties*** or of any rule of law relating to its application, or misuse of powers.
The Court shall have jurisdiction under the same conditions in actions brought by the Court of Auditors, by the European Central Bank and **by the Committee of the Regions** for the purpose of protecting their prerogatives.
Any natural or legal person may, under the conditions **laid down in *the first and second paragraphs***, institute proceedings against **an act** addressed to that person or **which** is of direct and individual concern to ***them*, and against a regulatory act which is of direct concern to *them* and does not entail implementing measures.**
Acts setting up bodies, offices and agencies of the Union may lay down specific conditions and arrangements concerning actions brought by natural or legal persons against acts of these bodies, offices or agencies intended to produce legal effects in relation to them.
The proceedings provided for in this Article shall be instituted within two months of the publication of the measure, or of its notification to the plaintiff, or, in the absence thereof, of the day on which it came to the knowledge of the latter, as the case may be.

ARTICLE ***264*** [231] *[Article III-366 (ex Article 231 TEC)]*
If the action is well founded, the Court of Justice **of the European Union** shall declare the act concerned to be void.
However, the Court shall, if it considers this necessary, state which of the effects of the **act** which it has declared void shall be considered as definitive.

ARTICLE *265* [232] *[Article III-367 (ex Article 232 TEC)]*
Should the European Parliament, **the European Council,** the Council, the Commission **or the European Central Bank**, in infringement of ***the Treaties***, fail to act, the Member States and the other institutions of the ***Union*** may bring an action before the Court of Justice **of the European Union** to have the infringement established. **This Article shall apply, under the same conditions, to bodies, offices and agencies of the Union which fail to act.**
The action shall be admissible only if the institution concerned has first been called upon to act. If, within two months of being so called upon, the institution concerned has not defined its position, the action may be brought within a further period of two months.
Any natural or legal person may, under the conditions laid down in the preceding paragraphs, complain to the Court of Justice **of the European Union** that an institution**, body, office or agency** of the ***Union*** has failed to address to that person any act other than a recommendation or an opinion.

ARTICLE *266* [233] *[Article III-368 (ex Article 233 TEC)]*
The institution**, body, office or agency** whose act has been declared void or whose failure to act has been declared contrary to ***the Treaties*** shall be required to take the necessary measures to comply with the judgment of the Court of Justice **of the European Union**.
This obligation shall not affect any obligation which may result from the application of the second paragraph of Article ***340***.

ARTICLE *267* [234] *[Article III-369 (ex Article 234 TEC)]*
The Court of Justice **of the European Union** shall have jurisdiction to give preliminary rulings concerning:
(a) the interpretation of ***the Treaties***;
(b) the validity and interpretation of acts of the institutions**, bodies, offices or agencies** of the ***Union***.
Where such a question is raised before any court or tribunal of a Member State, that court or tribunal may, if it considers that a decision on the question is necessary to enable it to give judgment, request the Court to give a ruling thereon.
Where any such question is raised in a case pending before a court or tribunal of a Member State against whose decisions there is no judicial remedy under national law, that court or tribunal shall bring the matter before the Court.
If such a question is raised in a case pending before a court or tribunal of a Member State with regard to a person in custody, the Court *of Justice of the European Union* shall act with the minimum of delay.

ARTICLE *268* [235] *[Article III-370 (ex Article 235 TEC)]*
The Court of Justice **of the European Union** shall have jurisdiction in disputes relating to compensation for damage provided for in the second **and third** paragraphs of Article ***340***.

ARTICLE ***269*** [235a] *[Article III-371 (ex Article 46(e) TEU)]*
The Court of Justice shall have jurisdiction to decide on the legality of an act adopted by the European Council or by the Council pursuant to *Article 7 of the Treaty on European Union* solely at the request of the Member State concerned by a determination of the European Council or of the Council and in respect solely of the procedural stipulations contained in that Article.
Such a request must be made within one month from the date of such determination. The Court shall rule within one month from the date of the request.
[BMDF Note: Article 7 TEU concerns suspension of certain rights of a Member State.]

ARTICLE *270* [236] *[Article III-372 (ex Article 236 TEC)]*
The Court of Justice **of the European Union** shall have jurisdiction in any dispute between the ***Union*** and its servants within the limits and under the conditions laid down in the Staff Regulations **of Officials and** the Conditions of Employment **of other servants of the Union**.

ARTICLE *271* [237] *[Article III-373 (ex Article 237 TEC)]*
The Court of Justice **of the European Union** shall, within the limits hereinafter laid down, have jurisdiction in disputes concerning:
(a) the fulfilment by Member States of obligations under the Statute of the European Investment Bank. In this connection, the Board of Directors of the Bank shall enjoy the powers conferred upon the Commission by Article ***258***;

(b) measures adopted by the Board of Governors of the European Investment Bank. In this connection, any Member State, the Commission or the Board of Directors of the Bank may institute proceedings under the conditions laid down in Article ***263***;
(c) measures adopted by the Board of Directors of the European Investment Bank. Proceedings against such measures may be instituted only by Member States or by the Commission, under the conditions laid down in Article ***263***, and solely on the grounds of non-compliance with the procedure provided for in Article 21(2), (5), (6) and (7) of the Statute of the Bank;
(d) the fulfilment by national central banks of obligations under ***the Treaties*** and the Statute of the ESCB ***and of the ECB***. In this connection the powers of the **Governing** Council of the European Central Bank in respect of national central banks shall be the same as those conferred upon the Commission in respect of Member States by Article ***258***. If the Court of Justice finds that a national central bank has failed to fulfil an obligation under ***the Treaties***, that bank shall be required to take the necessary measures to comply with the judgment of the Court.

ARTICLE *272* [238] *[Article III-374 (ex Article 238 TEC)]*
The Court of Justice **of the European Union** shall have jurisdiction to give judgment pursuant to any arbitration clause contained in a contract concluded by or on behalf of the **Union**, whether that contract be governed by public or private law.

ARTICLE *273* [239] *[Article III-375(3) (ex Article 239 TEC)]*
The Court of Justice shall have jurisdiction in any dispute between Member States which relates to the subject matter of ***the Treaties*** if the dispute is submitted to it under a special agreement between the parties.

ARTICLE *274* [240] *[Article III-375(1) (ex Article 240 TEC)]*
Save where jurisdiction is conferred on the Court of Justice **of the European Union** by ***the Treaties***, disputes to which the **Union** is a party shall not on that ground be excluded from the jurisdiction of the courts or tribunals of the Member States.

ARTICLE *275* [240a] *[Article III-376 (new Article in 2004 IGC)]*
The Court of Justice of the European Union shall not have jurisdiction with respect to *the provisions relating to the common foreign and security policy nor with respect to acts adopted on the basis of those provisions.*
However, the Court shall have jurisdiction to monitor compliance with *Article 40 of the Treaty on European Union* and to rule on proceedings, brought in accordance with the conditions laid down in *Article 263 of this Treaty*, reviewing the legality of decisions providing for restrictive measures against natural or legal persons adopted by the Council on the basis of Chapter 2 of Title V *of the Treaty on European Union.*

ARTICLE *276* [240b] *[Article III-377(ex Article 35(5) TEU)]*
In exercising its powers regarding the provisions of *Chapters 4 and 5 of Title IV of Part Three* relating to the area of freedom, security and justice, the Court of Justice **of the European Union** shall have no jurisdiction to review the validity or proportionality of operations carried out by the police or other law-enforcement services of a Member State or the exercise of the responsibilities incumbent upon Member States with regard to the maintenance of law and order and the safeguarding of internal security**.**

ARTICLE *277* [241] *[Article III-378 (ex Article 241 TEC)]*
Notwithstanding the expiry of the period laid down in Article ***263***, **fifth paragraph**, any party may, in proceedings in which **an act of general application** adopted **by an institution, body, office or agency of the Union** is at issue, plead the grounds specified in Article ***263, second paragraph,*** in order to invoke before the Court of Justice **of the European Union** the inapplicability of that **act**.

ARTICLE *278* [242] *[Article III-379(1) (ex Article 242 TEC)]*
Actions brought before the Court of Justice **of the European Union** shall not have suspensory effect. The Court may, however, if it considers that circumstances so require, order that application of the contested act be suspended.

ARTICLE ***279*** [243] *[Article III-379(2) (ex Article 243 TEC)]*
The Court of Justice **of the European Union** may in any cases before it prescribe any necessary interim measures.

ARTICLE ***280*** [244] *[Article III-380 (ex Article 244 TEC)]*
The judgments of the Court of Justice **of the European Union** shall be enforceable under the conditions laid down in Article ***299***.

ARTICLE ***281*** [245] *[Article III-381 (ex Article 245 TEC)]*
The Statute of the Court of Justice **of the European Union** shall be laid down in a separate Protocol. ***The European Parliament and t***he Council, acting ***in accordance with the ordinary legislative procedure***, may amend the provisions of the Statute, with the exception of Title I **and Article 64.** ***The European Parliament and the Council shall act*** **either at the request of the Court of Justice and after consultation of the Commission, or on a proposal from the Commission and after consultation of the Court of Justice**.

SECTION 4 a

THE EUROPEAN CENTRAL BANK

ARTICLE 282 [245a] *[Article I-30 The European Central Bank (ex Articles 8, 105 and 107 TEC)]*
1. The European Central Bank, together with the national central banks, shall constitute the European System of Central Banks *(ESCB)*. The European Central Bank, together with the national central banks of the Member States whose currency is the euro, which constitute the Eurosystem, shall conduct the monetary policy of the Union.

2. The *ESCB* shall be governed by the decision-making bodies of the European Central Bank. The primary objective of the *ESCB* shall be to maintain price stability. Without prejudice to that objective, it shall support the general economic policies in the Union in order to contribute to the achievement of the latter's objectives.

3. The European Central Bank shall have legal personality. It alone may authorise the issue of the euro. It shall be independent in the exercise of its powers and in the management of its finances. Union institutions, bodies, offices and agencies and the governments of the Member States shall respect that independence.

4. The European Central Bank shall adopt such measures as are necessary to carry out its tasks in accordance with *Articles 127 to 133* and *Article 138*, and with the conditions laid down in the Statute of the ESCB and of the ECB. In accordance with these same Articles, those Member States whose currency is not the euro, and their central banks, shall retain their powers in monetary matters.

5. Within the areas falling within its responsibilities, the European Central Bank shall be consulted on all proposed Union acts, and all proposals for regulation at national level, and may give an opinion.

ARTICLE ***283*** [245b] *[Article III-382 (ex Article 112 TEC)]*
1. The Governing Council of the European Central Bank shall comprise the members of the Executive Board of the European Central Bank and the Governors of the national central banks **of the Member States *whose currency is the euro.***
[Paragraph does not apply to the UK: Article 5, Protocol 25]

2. The Executive Board shall comprise the President, the Vice-President and four other members. The President, the Vice-President and the other members of the Executive Board shall be appointed **by the European Council, acting by a qualified majority,** from among persons of recognised standing and professional experience in monetary or banking matters, on a recommendation from the Council, after it has consulted the European Parliament and the Governing Council of the European Central Bank.
Their term of office shall be eight years and shall not be renewable.

Only nationals of Member States may be members of the Executive Board.
[BMDF Note: Article moved from Article 112 TEC. Article does not apply to the UK, Protocol 18(4)]

ARTICLE ***284*** [245c] *[Article III-383 (ex Article 113 TEC)]*
1. The President of the Council and a member of the Commission may participate, without having the right to vote, in meetings of the Governing Council of the European Central Bank.
The President of the Council may submit a motion for deliberation to the Governing Council of the European Central Bank.

2. The President of the European Central Bank shall be invited to participate in Council meetings when the Council is discussing matters relating to the objectives and tasks of the ESCB.

3. The European Central Bank shall address an annual report on the activities of the ESCB and on the monetary policy of both the previous and current year to the European Parliament, the Council and the Commission, and also to the European Council. The President of the European Central Bank shall present this report to the Council and to the European Parliament, which may hold a general debate on that basis.
The President of the European Central Bank and the other members of the Executive Board may, at the request of the European Parliament or on their own initiative, be heard by the competent Committees of the European Parliament.
[BMDF Note: Article moved from Article 113 TEC]

SECTION 5

THE COURT OF AUDITORS

ARTICLE ***285*** [246] *[Article I-31 'The Court of Auditors' (ex Articles 246 and 247 TEC)]*
The Court of Auditors shall carry out the **Union's** audit.
It shall consist of one national of each Member State. Its members shall be completely independent in the performance of their duties, in the Union's general interest.

ARTICLE ***286*** [247] *[Article III-385 (Ex Article 247 TEC)]*
1. The Members of the Court of Auditors shall be chosen from among persons who belong or have belonged in their respective **States** to external audit bodies or who are especially qualified for this office. Their independence must be beyond doubt.

2. The Members of the Court of Auditors shall be appointed for a term of six years. The Council, after consulting the European Parliament, shall adopt the list of Members drawn up in accordance with the proposals made by each Member State. The term of office of the Members of the Court of Auditors shall be renewable.
They shall elect the President of the Court of Auditors from among their number for a term of three years. The President may be re-elected.

3. In the performance of these duties, **the Members of the Court of Auditors** shall neither seek nor take instructions from any government or from any other body. They shall refrain from any action incompatible with their duties.

4. The Members of the Court of Auditors may not, during their term of office, engage in any other occupation, whether gainful or not. When entering upon their duties they shall give a solemn undertaking that, both during and after their term of office, they will respect the obligations arising therefrom and in particular their duty to behave with integrity and discretion as regards the acceptance, after they have ceased to hold office, of certain appointments or benefits.

5. Apart from normal replacement, or death, the duties of a Member of the Court of Auditors shall end when he resigns, or is compulsorily retired by a ruling of the Court of Justice pursuant to paragraph 7.
The vacancy thus caused shall be filled for the remainder of the Member's term of office.
Save in the case of compulsory retirement, Members of the Court of Auditors shall remain in office until they have been replaced.

6. A Member of the Court of Auditors may be deprived of his office or of his right to a pension or other benefits in its stead only if the Court of Justice, at the request of the Court of Auditors, finds that he no longer fulfils the requisite conditions or meets the obligations arising from his office.

7. The Council, shall determine the conditions of employment of the President and the Members of the Court of Auditors and in particular their salaries, allowances and pensions. It shall also, by the same majority, determine any payment to be made instead of remuneration.

8. The provisions of the Protocol on the Privileges and Immunities of the European **Union** applicable to the judges of the Court of Justice ***of the European Union*** shall also apply to the Members of the Court of Auditors.

ARTICLE ***287*** [248] *[Article III-384 (ex Article 248 TEC)]*

1. The Court of Auditors shall examine the accounts of all revenue and expenditure of the **Union**. It shall also examine the accounts of all revenue and expenditure of all bodies**, offices or agencies** set up by the **Union** insofar as the relevant constituent instrument does not preclude such examination.
The Court of Auditors shall provide the European Parliament and the Council with a statement of assurance as to the reliability of the accounts and the legality and regularity of the underlying transactions which shall be published in the *Official Journal of the European Union*. This statement may be supplemented by specific assessments for each major area of **Union** activity.

2. The Court of Auditors shall examine whether all revenue has been received and all expenditure incurred in a lawful and regular manner and whether the financial management has been sound. In doing so, it shall report in particular on any cases of irregularity.
The audit of revenue shall be carried out on the basis both of the amounts established as due and the amounts actually paid to the **Union**.
The audit of expenditure shall be carried out on the basis both of commitments undertaken and payments made.
These audits may be carried out before the closure of accounts for the financial year in question.

3. The audit shall be based on records and, if necessary, performed on the spot in the other institutions of the ***Union***, on the premises of any body**, office or agency** which manages revenue or expenditure on behalf of the **Union** and in the Member States, including on the premises of any natural or legal person in receipt of payments from the budget. In the Member States the audit shall be carried out in liaison with national audit bodies or, if these do not have the necessary powers, with the competent national departments. The Court of Auditors and the national audit bodies of the Member States shall co-operate in a spirit of trust while maintaining their independence. These bodies or departments shall inform the Court of Auditors whether they intend to take part in the audit.
The other institutions of the ***Union***, any bodies**, offices or agencies** managing revenue or expenditure on behalf of the **Union**, any natural or legal person in receipt of payments from the budget, and the national audit bodies or, if these do not have the necessary powers, the competent national departments, shall forward to the Court of Auditors, at its request, any document or information necessary to carry out its task.
In respect of the European Investment Bank's activity in managing **Union** expenditure and revenue, the Court's rights of access to information held by the Bank shall be governed by an agreement between the Court, the Bank and the Commission. In the absence of an agreement, the Court shall nevertheless have access to information necessary for the audit of ***Union*** expenditure and revenue managed by the Bank.

4. The Court of Auditors shall draw up an annual report after the close of each financial year. It shall be forwarded to the other institutions of the ***Union*** and shall be published, together with the replies of these institutions to the observations of the Court of Auditors, in the *Official Journal of the European Union*.
The Court of Auditors may also, at any time, submit observations, particularly in the form of special reports, on specific questions and deliver opinions at the request of one of the other institutions of the ***Union***.
It shall adopt its annual reports, special reports or opinions by a majority of its Members. However, it may establish internal chambers in order to adopt certain categories of reports or opinions under the conditions laid down by its Rules of Procedure.
It shall assist the European Parliament and the Council in exercising their powers of control over the implementation of the budget.

The Court of Auditors shall draw up its Rules of Procedure. Those rules shall require the approval of the Council.

CHAPTER 2

LEGAL ACTS OF THE UNION, ADOPTION PROCEDURES AND OTHER PROVISIONS

SECTION 1

THE LEGAL ACTS OF THE UNION

ARTICLE ***288*** [249] *[Article I-33 (ex Article 249 TEC)]*
To exercise the Union's competences, the institutions shall *adopt regulations, directives, recommendations and opinions.*
A regulation shall have general application. It shall be binding in its entirety and directly applicable in all Member States.
A directive shall be binding, as to the result to be achieved, upon each Member State to which it is addressed, but shall leave to the national authorities the choice of form and methods.
A decision shall be binding in its entirety. **A decision which specifies those to whom it is addressed shall be binding only on them.**
Recommendations and opinions shall have no binding force.

ARTICLE 289 [249A] *[Article I-34 'Legislative acts' (new Article in 2004 IGC)]*
1. ***The ordinary legislative procedure shall consist in the joint adoption by the European Parliament and the Council of a regulation, directive or decision on a proposal from the Commission. This procedure is defined in Article 294.***

2. ***In the specific cases provided for by the Treaties, the adoption of a regulation, directive or decision by the European Parliament* with the participation of the Council, or by the latter with the participation of the European Parliament, *shall constitute a special legislative procedure.***

3. Legal acts adopted by legislative procedure shall constitute legislative acts.

4. **In the specific cases provided for *by the Treaties, legislative acts* may be adopted on the initiative of a group of Member States or of the European Parliament, on a recommendation from the European Central Bank or at the request of the Court of Justice or the European Investment Bank.**

ARTICLE 290 [249B] *[Article I-36 'Delegated European regulations' (new Article in 2004 IGC, redrafted and expanded from Article 202 TEC)]*
1. ***A legislative act*** **may delegate to the Commission the power to adopt *non-legislative acts* to supplement or amend certain non-essential elements of the *legislative act.***
The objectives, content, scope and duration of the delegation of power shall be explicitly defined in the *legislative acts.* The essential elements of an area shall be reserved for the *legislative act* and accordingly shall not be the subject of a delegation of power.

2. ***Legislative acts*** **shall explicitly lay down the conditions to which the delegation is subject; these conditions may be as follows:**
(a) the European Parliament or the Council may decide to revoke the delegation;
(b) the delegated *act* may enter into force only if no objection has been expressed by the European Parliament or the Council within a period set by the *legislative act.*
For the purposes of (a) and (b), the European Parliament shall act by a majority of its component members, and the Council by a qualified majority.

3. The adjective "delegated" shall be inserted in the title of delegated acts.
[BMDF Note: See also Declaration no. 39]

ARTICLE 291 [249C] *[Article I-37 'Implementing Acts' (new Article in 2004 IGC, part ex Article 202 TEC)]*

1. Member States shall adopt all measures of national law necessary to implement legally binding Union acts.

2. Where uniform conditions for implementing legally binding Union acts are needed, those acts shall confer implementing powers on the Commission, or, in duly justified specific cases and in the cases provided for in *Articles 24 and 26 of the Treaty on European Union*, on the Council.

3. For the purposes of paragraph 2, *the European Parliament and the Council, acting by means of regulations in accordance with the ordinary legislative procedure,* shall lay down in advance the rules and general principles concerning mechanisms for control by Member States of the Commission's exercise of implementing powers. *(Paragraph ex Article 202 TEC)*

4. The word "implementing" shall be inserted in the title of implementing acts.

ARTICLE 292 [249D] *[Article I-35 'Non-legislative acts' (new Article in 2004 IGC)]*

The Council shall adopt recommendations. It shall act on a proposal from the Commission in all cases where *the Treaties* provide that it shall adopt acts on a proposal from the Commission. It shall act unanimously in those areas in which unanimity is required for the adoption of a Union act. The Commission, and the European Central Bank in the specific cases provided for in *the Treaties*, shall adopt recommendations.

SECTION 2

PROCEDURES FOR THE ADOPTION OF ACTS AND OTHER PROVISIONS

ARTICLE ***293*** [250] *[Article III-395 (ex Article 250 TEC)]*

1. Where, in pursuance of ***the Treaties***, the Council acts on a proposal from the Commission, ***the Council* may amend that proposal only by acting unanimously, except in the cases referred to in *paragraphs 10 and 13 of Article 294, in Articles 310, 312 and 314 and in the second paragraph of Article 315.***

2. As long as the Council has not acted, the Commission may alter its proposal at any time during the procedures leading to the adoption of a **Union** act.

ARTICLE ***294*** [251] *[Article III-396 (ex Article 251 TEC)]*

1. Where reference is made in ***the Treaties*** to ***the ordinary legislative procedure*** for the adoption of an act, the following procedure shall apply.

2. The Commission shall submit a proposal to the European Parliament and the Council.

First reading

3. The European Parliament shall adopt its position at first reading and communicate it to the Council.

4. If the Council approves the European Parliament's position, the act concerned shall be adopted in the wording which corresponds to the position of the European Parliament.

5. If the Council does not approve the European Parliament's position, it shall adopt its position at first reading and communicate it to the European Parliament.

6. The Council shall inform the European Parliament fully of the reasons which led it to adopt its position at first reading. The Commission shall inform the European Parliament fully of its position.

Second reading

7. If, within three months of such communication, the European Parliament:
(a) approves the Council's position at first reading or has not taken a decision, the act concerned shall be deemed to have been adopted in the wording which corresponds to the position of the Council;
(b) rejects, by a majority of its component members, the Council's position at first reading, the proposed act shall be deemed not to have been adopted;
(c) proposes, by a majority of its component members, amendments to the Council's position at first reading, the text thus amended shall be forwarded to the Council and to the Commission, which shall deliver an opinion on those amendments.

8. If, within three months of receiving the European Parliament's amendments, the Council, acting by a qualified majority:
(a) approves all those amendments, the act in question shall be deemed to have been adopted;
(b) does not approve all the amendments, the President of the Council, in agreement with the President of the European Parliament, shall within six weeks convene a meeting of the Conciliation Committee.

9. The Council shall act unanimously on the amendments on which the Commission has delivered a negative opinion.

Conciliation

10. The Conciliation Committee, which shall be composed of the members of the Council or their representatives and an equal number of members representing the European Parliament, shall have the task of reaching agreement on a joint text, by a qualified majority of the members of the Council or their representatives and by a majority of the members representing the European Parliament within six weeks of its being convened, on the basis of the positions of the European Parliament and the Council at second reading.

11. The Commission shall take part in the Conciliation Committee's proceedings and shall take all necessary initiatives with a view to reconciling the positions of the European Parliament and the Council.

12. If, within six weeks of its being convened, the Conciliation Committee does not approve the joint text, the proposed act shall be deemed not to have been adopted.

Third reading

13. If, within that period, the Conciliation Committee approves a joint text, the European Parliament, acting by a majority of the votes cast, and the Council, acting by a qualified majority, shall each have a period of six weeks from that approval in which to adopt the act in question in accordance with the joint text. If they fail to do so, the proposed act shall be deemed not to have been adopted.

14. The periods of three months and six weeks referred to in this Article shall be extended by a maximum of one month and two weeks respectively at the initiative of the European Parliament or the Council.

Special provisions

15. Where, in the cases provided for in the *Treaties*, a *legislative act* is submitted to the ordinary legislative procedure on the initiative of a group of Member States, on a recommendation by the European Central Bank, or at the request of the Court of Justice, paragraph 2, the second sentence of paragraph 6, and paragraph 9 shall not apply.
In such cases, the European Parliament and the Council shall communicate the proposed act to the Commission with their positions at first and second readings. The European Parliament or the Council may request the opinion of the Commission throughout the procedure, which the Commission may also deliver on its own initiative. It may also, if it deems it necessary, take part in the Conciliation Committee in accordance with paragraph 11.

[BMDF Note: Article 252 TEC shall be repealed]

ARTICLE 295 [252a] *[Article III-397 (ex Article 218(1) TEC and new provision in 2004 IGC)]*
The European Parliament, the Council and the Commission shall consult each other and by common agreement make arrangements for their co-operation. To that end, they may, in compliance with the *Treaties*, conclude inter-institutional agreements which may be of a binding nature.

ARTICLE ***296*** [253] *[Article I-38 'Principles common to the Union's legal acts' (ex Article 253 TEC)]*
Where the *Treaties* do not specify the type of act to be adopted, the institutions shall select it on a case-by-case basis, in compliance with the applicable procedures and with the principle of proportionality.
Legal acts shall state the reasons on which they are based and shall refer to any proposals, initiatives, recommendations, requests or opinions required by the Treaties.
When considering draft legislative acts, the European Parliament and the Council shall refrain from adopting acts not provided for by the relevant legislative procedure in the area in question.

ARTICLE ***297*** [254] *[Article I-39 'Publication and entry in force' (ex Article 254 TEC)]*
1. ***Legislative acts*** adopted ***under the ordinary legislative procedure*** shall be signed by the President of the European Parliament and by the President of the Council.
***Legislative acts adopted under a special legislative procedure* shall be signed by the President of the institution which adopted them.**
Legislative acts shall be published in the *Official Journal of the European Union*. They shall enter into force on the date specified in them or, in the absence thereof, on the twentieth day following that of their publication.

2. ***Non-legislative acts adopted in the form of regulations, directives or decisions, when the latter* do not specify to whom they are addressed, shall be signed by the President of the institution which adopted them.**
Regulations ***and directives*** which are addressed to all Member States, ***as well as decisions which* do not specify to whom they are addressed**, shall be published in the *Official Journal of the European Union*. They shall enter into force on the date specified in them or, in the absence thereof, on the twentieth day following that of their publication.
Other directives, and decisions ***which specify to whom they are addressed***, shall be notified to those to whom they are addressed and shall take effect upon such notification.

ARTICLE 298 [254a] *[Article III-398 (new Article in 2004 IGC)]*
1. In carrying out their missions, the institutions, bodies, offices and agencies of the Union shall have the support of an open, efficient and independent European administration.

2. In compliance with the Staff Regulations and the Conditions of Employment adopted on the basis of *Article 336, the European Parliament and the Council, acting by means of regulations in accordance with the ordinary legislative procedure*, shall establish provisions to that end.

[BMDF Note: Article 255 TEC moved to Article 15 TFEU]

ARTICLE ***299*** [256] *[Article III-401 (ex Article 256 TEC)]*
Acts of the Council or of the Commission **or of the European Central Bank** which impose a pecuniary obligation on persons other than States, shall be enforceable.
Enforcement shall be governed by the rules of civil procedure in force in the State in the territory of which it is carried out. The order for its enforcement shall be appended to the decision, without other formality than verification of the authenticity of the decision, by the national authority which the Government of each Member State shall designate for this purpose and shall make known to the Commission and to the Court of Justice **of the European Union**.
When these formalities have been completed on application by the party concerned, the latter may proceed to enforcement in accordance with the national law, by bringing the matter directly before the competent authority.
Enforcement may be suspended only by a decision of the Court. However, the courts of the country concerned shall have jurisdiction over complaints that enforcement is being carried out in an irregular manner.

CHAPTER 3

THE UNION'S ADVISORY BODIES

ARTICLE 300 [256a] *[Article I-32 'The Union's advisory bodies' (ex Article 7 TEC and Articles 257 - 265 TEC)]*
1. The European Parliament, the Council and the Commission shall be assisted by an Economic and Social Committee and a Committee of the Regions, exercising advisory functions.

2. **The Economic and Social Committee shall consist of representatives of organisations of employers, of the employed, and of other parties representative of civil society, notably in socio-economic, civic, professional and cultural areas.**

3. **The Committee of the Regions shall consist of representatives of regional and local bodies who either hold a regional or local authority electoral mandate or are politically accountable to an elected assembly.**

4. The members of the Economic and Social Committee and the Committee of the Regions shall not be bound by any mandatory instructions. They shall be completely independent in the performance of their duties, in the Union's general interest.

5. The rules referred to in paragraphs 2 and 3 governing the nature of their composition shall be reviewed at regular intervals by the Council to take account of economic, social and demographic developments within the Union. The Council, on a proposal from the Commission, shall adopt decisions to that end.

SECTION 1

THE ECONOMIC AND SOCIAL COMMITTEE

[BMDF Note: Article 257 TEC shall be repealed]

ARTICLE ***301*** [258] *[Article III-389 (ex Article 258 TEC)]*
The number of members of the Economic and Social Committee shall not exceed 350.
The Council, acting unanimously on a proposal from the Commission, shall adopt a decision determining the Committee's composition.
The Council, shall determine the allowances of members of the Committee.

ARTICLE ***302*** [259] *[Article III-390 (ex Article 259 TEC)]*
1. The members of the Committee shall be appointed for **five** years. The Council, shall adopt the list of members drawn up in accordance with the proposals made by each Member State. The term of office of the members of the Committee shall be renewable.

2. The Council shall **act after** consult**ing** the Commission. It may obtain the opinion of European bodies which are representative of the various economic and social sectors to which the **Union's** activities are of concern.

ARTICLE ***303*** [260] *[Article III-391 (ex Article 260 TEC)]*
The Committee shall elect its chairman and officers from among its members for a term of two **and a half** years.
It shall adopt its Rules of Procedure.
The Committee shall be convened by its chairman at the request **of the European Parliament,** of the Council or of the Commission. It may also meet on its own initiative.

[BMDF Note: Article 261 TEC shall repealed by the Treaty of Lisbon]

ARTICLE ***304*** [262] *[Article III-392 (ex Article 262 TEC)]*
The Committee **shall** be consulted **by the European Parliament,** by the Council or by the Commission where ***the Treaties*** so provide. The Committee may be consulted by these institutions in all cases in

which they consider it appropriate. It may issue an opinion on its own initiative in cases in which it considers such action appropriate.
The European Parliament, the Council or the Commission shall, if it considers it necessary, set the Committee, for the submission of its opinion, a time-limit which may not be less than one month from the date on which the chairman receives notification to this effect. Upon expiry of the time-limit, the absence of an opinion shall not prevent further action.
The opinion of the Committee, together with a record of the proceedings, shall be forwarded **to the European Parliament,** to the Council and to the Commission.

SECTION 1

THE COMMITTEE OF THE REGIONS

ARTICLE ***305*** [263] *[Article III-386 (ex Article 263 TEC)]*
The number of members of the Committee of the Regions shall not exceed 350.
The Council, acting unanimously on a proposal from the Commission, shall adopt a decision determining the Committee's composition.
The members of the Committee and an equal number of alternate members shall be appointed for **five** years,. Their term of office shall be renewable. The Council, shall adopt the list of members and alternate members drawn up in accordance with the proposals made by each Member State. When the mandate referred to in ***Article 300(2),*** on the basis of which they were proposed comes to an end, the term of office of members of the Committee shall terminate automatically and they shall then be replaced for the remainder of the said term of office in accordance with the same procedure. No member of the Committee shall at the same time be a Member of the European Parliament.

ARTICLE ***306*** [264] *[Article III-387 (ex Article 264 TEC)]*
The Committee of the Regions shall elect its chairman and officers from among its members for a term of two **and a half** years.
It shall adopt its Rules of Procedure.
The Committee shall be convened by its chairman at the request **of the European Parliament,** of the Council or of the Commission. It may also meet on its own initiative.

ARTICLE ***307*** [265] *[Article III-388 (ex Article 265 TEC)]*
The Committee of the Regions shall be consulted **by the European Parliament,** by the Council or by the Commission where ***the Treaties*** so provide and in all other cases, in particular those which concern cross-border co-operation, in which one of these institutions considers it appropriate.
The European Parliament, the Council or the Commission shall, if it considers it necessary, set the Committee, for the submission of its opinion, a time-limit which may not be less than one month from the date on which the chairman receives notification to this effect. Upon expiry of the time-limit, the absence of an opinion shall not prevent further action.
Where the Economic and Social Committee is consulted pursuant to Article ***304***, the Committee of the Regions shall be informed **by the European Parliament,** by the Council or the Commission of the request for an opinion. Where it considers that specific regional interests are involved, the Committee of the Regions may issue an opinion on the matter.
It may issue an opinion on its own initiative in cases in which it considers such action appropriate.
The opinion of the Committee, together with a record of the proceedings, shall be forwarded **to the European Parliament,** to the Council and to the Commission.

CHAPTER *4*

EUROPEAN INVESTMENT BANK

ARTICLE ***308*** [266] *[Article III-393 (ex Article 266 TEC)]*
The European Investment Bank shall have legal personality.
The members of the European Investment Bank shall be the Member States.
The Statute of the European Investment Bank is laid down in a Protocol annexed to ***the Treaties***. The Council acting unanimously ***in accordance with a special legislative procedure***, at the request of the European Investment Bank and after consulting the European Parliament and the Commission, or **on a**

proposal from the Commission and after consulting the European Parliament and the European Investment Bank, may amend the Statute of the Bank.

ARTICLE ***309*** [267] *[Article III-394 (ex Article 267 TEC)]*
The task of the European Investment Bank shall be to contribute, by having recourse to the capital market and utilising its own resources, to the balanced and steady development of the **internal** market in the interest of the ***Union***. For this purpose the Bank shall, operating on a non-profit-making basis, grant loans and give guarantees which facilitate the financing of the following projects in all sectors of the economy:
(a) projects for developing less-developed regions;
(b) projects for modernising or developing undertakings or for developing fresh activities called for by the establishment **or functioning** of the **internal** market, where these projects are of such a size or nature that they cannot be entirely financed by the various means available in the individual Member States;
(c) projects of common interest to several Member States which are of such a size or nature that they cannot be entirely financed by the various means available in the individual Member States.
In carrying out its task, the Bank shall facilitate the financing of investment programmes in conjunction with assistance from the structural Funds and other **Union** financial instruments.

TITLE II

FINANCIAL PROVISIONS

ARTICLE ***310*** [268] *[Article I-53 (ex Articles 268 – 280 TEC) and Article I-56 (ex Article 272 TEC)*
1. All items of revenue and expenditure of the ***Union*** be included in estimates to be drawn up for each financial year and shall be shown in the budget.
The Union's annual budget shall be established by the European Parliament and the Council in accordance with Article 314.
The revenue and expenditure shown in the budget shall be in balance.

2. The expenditure shown in the budget shall be authorised for the annual budgetary period in accordance with the *regulation* referred to in *Article 322*.

3. The implementation of expenditure shown in the budget shall require the prior adoption of a legally binding Union act providing a legal basis for its action and for the implementation of the corresponding expenditure in accordance with the *regulation* referred to in *Article 322*, except in cases for which that law provides.

4. With a view to maintaining budgetary discipline, the Union shall not adopt any act which is likely to have appreciable implications for the budget without providing an assurance that the expenditure arising from such an act *is capable of being financed within the limit of the* Union's own resources and in compliance with the multiannual financial framework referred to in Article 312.

5. The budget shall be implemented in accordance with the principle of sound financial management. Member States shall co-operate with the Union to ensure that the appropriations entered in the budget are used in accordance with this principle.

6. The Union and the Member States, in accordance with *Article 325*, shall counter fraud and any other illegal activities affecting the financial interests of the Union.
[BMDF Note: Article taken from 2004 IGC – Article I-53 'Budgetary and financial principles' (ex Articles 268 – 280 TEC) and Article I-56 'the Union's budget' (ex Article 272 TEC) (for paragraph 1, subparagraph 2)]

CHAPTER 1

THE UNION'S OWN RESOURCES

ARTICLE *311* [269] *[Article I-54 'the Union's own resources' (ex Article 269 TEC)]*
The Union shall provide itself with the means necessary to attain its objectives and carry through its policies.
Without prejudice to other revenue, the budget shall be financed wholly from own resources.
The Council, acting ***in accordance with a special legislative procedure, shall unanimously*** and after consulting the European Parliament ***adopt a decision laying*** down **the** provisions relating to the system of own resources of the **Union. In this context it may establish new categories of own resources or abolish an existing category. That *decision* shall not enter into force until it is approved by** the Member States in accordance with their respective constitutional requirements.
***The Council, acting by means of regulations in accordance with a special legislative procedure,* shall lay down implementing measures of the Union's own resources system insofar as this is provided for in the *regulation* adopted on the basis of the *first paragraph.* The Council shall act after obtaining the consent of the European Parliament.**

[BMDF Note: Article 270 TEC shall be moved to Article 310(4) TFEU]

CHAPTER 2

THE MULTIANNUAL FINANCIAL FRAMEWORK

ARTICLE 312 [270a] *[Paragraphs 1and 2 from Article I-55 and Paragraphs 1, 3, 4 and 5 from Article III-402 (new Articles in 2004 IGC)]*
1. The multiannual financial framework shall ensure that Union expenditure develops in an orderly manner and within the limits of its own resources.
***It* shall be established for a period of at least five years.**
The annual budget of the Union shall comply with the multiannual financial framework.

2. *The Council, acting in accordance with a special legislative procedure, shall adopt a regulation laying* down the multiannual financial framework. The Council shall act unanimously after obtaining the consent of the European Parliament, which shall be given by a majority of its component members.
The European Council may, unanimously, adopt a decision authorising the Council to act by a qualified majority when adopting the *regulation* referred to in the *first paragraph.*

3. The financial framework shall determine the amounts of the annual ceilings on commitment appropriations by category of expenditure and of the annual ceiling on payment appropriations. The categories of expenditure, limited in number, shall correspond to the Union's major sectors of activity.
The financial framework shall lay down any other provisions required for the annual budgetary procedure to run smoothly.

4. Where no *Council act* determining a new financial framework has been adopted by the end of the previous financial framework, the ceilings and other provisions corresponding to the last year of that framework shall be extended until such time as that act is adopted.

5. Throughout the procedure leading to the adoption of the financial framework, the European Parliament, the Council and the Commission shall take any measure necessary to facilitate *its adoption.*
[BMDF Note: See also Declaration no. 59]

CHAPTER 3

THE UNION'S ANNUAL BUDGET

ARTICLE 313 [270b] *[Article III-403 (ex Article 272(1) TEC)]*
1. The financial year shall run from 1 January to 31 December.
[BMDF Note: Article moved from Article 272(1) TEC]

[BMDF Note: Article 271 TEC moved to Article 316 TFEU]

ARTICLE ***314*** [272] *[Article I-56 'The Union's budget' and Article III-404 (ex Article 272 TEC)]*
The European Parliament and the Council, acting in accordance with a special legislative procedure, **shall establish the Union's annual budget in accordance with the following provisions:**

1. ***With the exception of the European Central Bank, e***ach institution shall, before 1 July, draw up estimates of its expenditure **for the following financial year**. The Commission shall consolidate these estimates in a draft budget which may contain different estimates.
The draft budget shall contain an estimate of revenue and an estimate of expenditure.

2. The Commission shall **submit a proposal containing the** draft budget **to the European Parliament and to** the Council not later than 1 September of the year preceding that in which the budget is to be implemented.
The Commission may amend the draft budget during the procedure until such time as the Conciliation Committee, referred to in paragraph 5, is convened.

3. The Council shall adopt its position on the draft budget and forward it to the European Parliament not later than 1 October of the year preceding that in which the budget is to be implemented. The Council shall inform the European Parliament in full of the reasons which led it to adopt its position.

4. If, within forty-two days of such communication, the European Parliament:
(a) approves the position of the Council, the budget shall be adopted;
(b) has not taken a decision, the budget shall be deemed to have been adopted;
(c) adopts amendments by a majority of its component members, the amended draft shall be forwarded to the Council and to the Commission. The President of the European Parliament, in agreement with the President of the Council, shall immediately convene a meeting of the Conciliation Committee. However, if within ten days of the draft being forwarded the Council informs the European Parliament that it has approved all its amendments, the Conciliation Committee shall not meet.

5. The Conciliation Committee, which shall be composed of the members of the Council or their representatives and an equal number of members representing the European Parliament, shall have the task of reaching agreement on a joint text, by a qualified majority of the members of the Council or their representatives and by a majority of the representatives of the European Parliament within twenty-one days of its being convened, on the basis of the positions of the European Parliament and the Council.
The Commission shall take part in the Conciliation Committee's proceedings and shall take all the necessary initiatives with a view to reconciling the positions of the European Parliament and the Council.

6. If, within the twenty-one days referred to in paragraph 5, the Conciliation Committee agrees on a joint text, the European Parliament and the Council shall each have a period of fourteen days from the date of that agreement in which to approve the joint text.

7. If, within the period of fourteen days referred to in paragraph 6:
(a) the European Parliament and the Council both approve the joint text or fail to take a decision, ***or if one of these institutions approves the joint text while the other one fails to take a decision,*** **the budget shall be deemed to be definitively adopted in accordance with the joint text, or**

(b) **the European Parliament, acting by a majority of its component members, and the Council both reject the joint text, or if one of these institutions rejects the joint text while the other one fails to take a decision, a new draft budget shall be submitted by the Commission, or**

(c) **the European Parliament, acting by a majority of its component members, rejects the joint text while the Council approves it, a new draft budget shall be submitted by the Commission, or**

(d) **the European Parliament approves the joint text whilst the Council rejects it, the European Parliament may, within fourteen days from the date of the rejection by the Council and acting by a majority of its component members and three-fifths of the votes cast, decide to confirm all or some of the amendments referred to in paragraph 4(c). Where a European Parliament amendment is not confirmed, the position agreed in the Conciliation Committee on the budget heading which is the subject of the amendment shall be retained. The budget shall be deemed to be definitively adopted on this basis.**

8. If, within the twenty-one days referred to in paragraph 5, the Conciliation Committee does not agree on a joint text, a new draft budget shall be submitted by the Commission.

9. When the procedure provided for in this Article has been completed, the President of the European Parliament shall declare that the budget has been **definitely** adopted.

10. Each institution shall exercise the powers conferred upon it by this Article **in compliance with the *Treaties*** and **the** acts adopted in accordance **thereunder, with** particular **regard** to the **Union's** own resources and the balance between revenue and expenditure.

ARTICLE ***315*** [273] *[Article III-405 (ex Article 273 TEC)]*
If at the beginning of a financial year, the budget has not yet been **definitively adopted**, a sum equivalent to not more than one-twelfth of the budget appropriations for the preceding financial year may be spent each month in respect of any chapter of the budget in accordance with the provisions of the Regulations made pursuant to Article ***322***; **that sum shall not, however, exceed one twelfth of the appropriations provided for in the same chapter of the draft budget.**
The Council **on a proposal from the Commission,** may, provided that the other conditions laid down in the first sub-paragraph are observed, authorise expenditure in excess of one-twelfth **in accordance with the *Regulations made pursuant to Article 322.* The Council shall forward the decision immediately to the European Parliament.**
The decision referred to in the second sub-paragraph shall lay down the necessary measures relating to resources to ensure application of this **Article in accordance with the *acts referred to in Article 311.***
It shall enter into force thirty days following its adoption if the European Parliament, acting by a majority of its component members, has not decided to reduce this expenditure within that time-limit.

ARTICLE ***316*** [273a] *[Article III-406 (ex Article 271 TEC)]*
In accordance with conditions to be laid down pursuant to Article ***322***, any appropriations, other than those relating to staff expenditure, that are unexpended at the end of the financial year may be carried forward to the next financial year only.
Appropriations shall be classified under different chapters grouping items of expenditure according to their nature or purpose and sub-divided in accordance with the regulations made pursuant to Article ***322***.
The expenditure of the European Parliament, **the European Council and** the Council, the Commission and the Court of Justice **of the European Union** shall be set out in separate parts of the budget, without prejudice to special arrangements for certain common items of expenditure.

CHAPTER 4

IMPLEMENTATION OF THE BUDGET AND DISCHARGE

ARTICLE ***317*** [274] *[Article III-407 (ex Article 274 TEC)]*
The Commission shall implement the budget **in co-operation with the Member States**, in accordance with the provisions of the regulations made pursuant to Article ***322***, on its own responsibility and within the limits of the appropriations, having regard to the principles of sound financial management. Member

States shall co-operate with the Commission to ensure that the appropriations are used in accordance with the principles of sound financial management.
The regulations ***shall lay down*** **the control and audit obligations of the Member States in the implementation of the budget and the resulting responsibilities.** ***They*** shall lay down **the responsibilities and** detailed rules for each institution concerning its part in effecting its own expenditure.
Within the budget, the Commission may, subject to the limits and conditions laid down in the regulations made pursuant to Article ***322***, transfer appropriations from one chapter to another or from one sub-division to another.

ARTICLE ***318*** [275] *[Article III-408 (ex Article 285 TEC)]*
The Commission shall submit annually **to the European Parliament and** to the Council the accounts of the preceding financial year relating to the implementation of the budget. The Commission shall also forward to them a financial statement of the assets and liabilities of the ***Union***.
The Commission shall also submit to the European Parliament and to the Council an evaluation report on the Union's finances based on the results achieved, in particular in relation to the indications given by the European Parliament and the Council pursuant to *Article 319*.

ARTICLE ***319*** [276] *[Article III-409 (ex Article 276 TEC)]*
1. The European Parliament, acting on a recommendation from the Council which shall act, shall give a discharge to the Commission in respect of the implementation of the budget. To this end, the Council and the European Parliament in turn shall examine the accounts**,** the financial statement **and the evaluation report** referred to in Article ***318***, the annual report by the Court of Auditors together with the replies of the institutions under audit to the observations of the Court of Auditors, the statement of assurance referred to in Article ***287(1)***, second sub-paragraph and any relevant special reports by the Court of Auditors.

2. Before giving a discharge to the Commission, or for any other purpose in connection with the exercise of its powers over the implementation of the budget, the European Parliament may ask to hear the Commission give evidence with regard to the execution of expenditure or the operation of financial control systems. The Commission shall submit any necessary information to the European Parliament at the latter's request.

3. The Commission shall take all appropriate steps to act on the observations in the decisions giving discharge and on other observations by the European Parliament relating to the execution of expenditure, as well as on comments accompanying the recommendations on discharge adopted by the Council.
At the request of the European Parliament or the Council, the Commission shall report on the measures taken in the light of these observations and comments and in particular on the instructions given to the departments which are responsible for the implementation of the budget. These reports shall also be forwarded to the Court of Auditors.

CHAPTER 5

COMMON PROVISIONS

ARTICLE ***320*** [277] *[Article III-410 (ex Article 277 TEC)]*
The multiannual financial framework and the annual budget shall be drawn up in euro.

ARTICLE ***321*** [278] *[Article III-411 (ex Article 278 TEC)]*
The Commission may, provided it notifies the competent authorities of the Member States concerned, transfer into the currency of one of the Member States its holdings in the currency of another Member State, to the extent necessary to enable them to be used for purposes which come within the scope of ***the Treaties***. The Commission shall as far as possible avoid making such transfers if it possesses cash or liquid assets in the currencies which it needs.
The Commission shall deal with each Member State through the authority designated by the State concerned. In carrying out financial operations the Commission shall employ the services of the bank of issue of the Member State concerned or of any other financial institution approved by that State.

ARTICLE *322* [279] *[Article III-412 (ex Article 279 TEC)]*
1. ***The European Parliament and t***he Council, acting ***in accordance with the ordinary legislative procedure, and after consulting*** the Court of Auditors, shall ***adopt by means of regulations***:
(a) **the financial rules which determine** in particular the procedure to be adopted for establishing and implementing the budget and for presenting and auditing accounts;
(b) **rules providing for checks on** the responsibility of financial **actors, in particular** authorising officers and accounting officers.

2. The Council, acting on a proposal from the Commission and after consulting the European Parliament and the Court of Auditors, shall determine the methods and procedure whereby the budget revenue provided under the arrangements relating to the ***Union***'s own resources shall be made available to the Commission, and determine the measures to be applied, if need be, to meet cash requirements.

ARTICLE 323 [279a] *Article III-413 (new Article in 2004 IGC)]*
The European Parliament, the Council and the Commission shall ensure that the financial means are made available to allow the Union to fulfil its legal obligations in respect of third parties.

ARTICLE 324 [279b] *[Article III-414 (new Article in 2004 IGC)]*
Regular meetings between the Presidents of the European Parliament, the Council and the Commission shall be convened, on the initiative of the Commission, under the budgetary procedures referred to in this Chapter. The Presidents shall take all the necessary steps to promote consultation and the reconciliation of the positions of the institutions over which they preside in order to facilitate the implementation of this *Title*.

CHAPTER 6

COMBATING FRAUD

ARTICLE *325* [280] *[Article III-415 (ex Article 280 TEC)]*
1. The **Union** and the Member States shall counter fraud and any other illegal activities affecting the financial interests of the ***Union*** through measures to be taken in accordance with this Article, which shall act as a deterrent and be such as to afford effective protection in the Member States**, and in all the Union's institutions, bodies, offices and agencies**.

2. Member States shall take the same measures to counter fraud affecting the financial interests of the ***Union*** as they take to counter fraud affecting their own financial interests.

3. Without prejudice to other provisions of ***the Treaties***, the Member States shall co-ordinate their action aimed at protecting the financial interests of the ***Union*** against fraud. To this end they shall organise, together with the Commission, close and regular co-operation between the competent authorities.

4. The Council, acting in accordance with the procedure referred to in Article ***294***, after consulting the Court of Auditors, shall adopt the necessary measures in the fields of the prevention of and fight against fraud affecting the financial interests of the ***Union*** with a view to affording effective and equivalent protection in the Member States **and in all the Union's institutions, bodies, offices and agencies**.

5. The Commission, in co-operation with Member States, shall each year submit to the Council and to the European Parliament a report on the measures taken for the implementation of this Article.

TITLE III

PROVISIONS ON ENHANCED CO-OPERATION

[BMDF Note: new Articles 326 to 334, together with Article 20 TEU replace current Articles 27a to 27e, Articles 40 to 40b and Articles 43 to 45 of the Treaty on European Union and Articles 11 and 11a of the Treaty establishing the European Community. The text of the new articles is drawn from the draft Constitution]

ARTICLE 326 [280A] *[Article III-416 (ex Article 43(e) TEU)]*
Any enhanced co-operation shall comply with the *Treaties* and the law of the Union.
Such co-operation shall not undermine the internal market or economic, social and territorial cohesion. It shall not constitute a barrier to or discrimination in trade between Member States, nor shall it distort competition between them.

ARTICLE 327 [280B] *[Article III-417 (ex Articles 43(h) and 44(2) TEU)]*
Any enhanced co-operation shall respect the competences, rights and obligations of those Member States which do not participate in it. Those Member States shall not impede its implementation by the participating Member States.

ARTICLE 328 [280C] *[Article III-418 (ex Article 43b TEU and new provisions in 2004 IGC)]*
1. When enhanced co-operation is being established, it shall be open to all Member States, subject to compliance with any conditions of participation laid down by the authorising decision. It shall also be open to them at any other time, subject to compliance with the acts already adopted within that framework, in addition to any such conditions.
The Commission and the Member States participating in enhanced co-operation shall ensure that they promote participation by as many Member States as possible.

2. The Commission and, where appropriate, the *High Representative of the Union for Foreign Affairs and Security Policy* shall keep the European Parliament and the Council regularly informed regarding developments in enhanced co-operation.

ARTICLE 329 [280D] *[Article III-419 (ex Article 27c TEU)]*
1. Member States which wish to establish enhanced co-operation between themselves in one of the areas covered by the *Treaties*, with the exception of fields of exclusive competence and the common foreign and security policy, shall address a request to the Commission, specifying the scope and objectives of the enhanced co-operation proposed. The Commission may submit a proposal to the Council to that effect. In the event of the Commission not submitting a proposal, it shall inform the Member States concerned of the reasons for not doing so.
Authorisation to proceed with enhanced co-operation *referred to in the first subparagraph* shall be granted by the Council, on a proposal from the Commission and after obtaining the consent of the European Parliament.

2. The request of the Member States which wish to establish enhanced co-operation between themselves within the framework of the common foreign and security policy shall be addressed to the Council. It shall be forwarded to the *High Representative of the Union for Foreign Affairs and Security Policy*, who shall give an opinion on whether the enhanced co-operation proposed is consistent with the Union's common foreign and security policy, and to the Commission, which shall give its opinion in particular on whether the enhanced co-operation proposed is consistent with other Union policies. It shall also be forwarded to the European Parliament for information.
Authorisation to proceed with enhanced co-operation shall be granted by a decision of the Council acting unanimously.
[BMDF Note: See also Declaration no. 40]

ARTICLE 330 [280E] *[Article I-44(3) 'Enhanced co-operation' (ex Article 44 TEU)]*
All members of the Council may participate in its deliberations, but only members of the Council representing the Member States participating in enhanced co-operation shall take part in the vote.
Unanimity shall be constituted by the votes of the representatives of the participating Member States only.

A qualified majority shall be defined in accordance with Article 238(3).

ARTICLE 331 [280F] *[Article III-420 (ex Article 11a TEC and Article 27e TEU)]*

1. Any Member State which wishes to participate in enhanced co-operation in progress in one of the areas referred to in *Article 329(1)* shall notify its intention to the Council and the Commission.

The Commission shall, within four months of the date of receipt of the notification, confirm the participation of the Member State concerned. It shall note where necessary that the conditions of participation have been fulfilled and shall adopt any transitional measures necessary with regard to the application of the acts already adopted within the framework of enhanced co-operation.

However, if the Commission considers that the conditions of participation have not been fulfilled, it shall indicate the arrangements to be adopted to fulfil those conditions and shall set a deadline for re-examining the request. On the expiry of that deadline, it shall re-examine the request, in accordance with the procedure set out in the second subparagraph. If the Commission considers that the conditions of participation have still not been met, the Member State concerned may refer the matter to the Council, which shall decide on the request. The Council shall act in accordance with *Article 330*. It may also adopt the transitional measures referred to in the second subparagraph on a proposal from the Commission.

2. Any Member State which wishes to participate in enhanced co-operation in progress in the framework of the common foreign and security policy shall notify its intention to the Council, the *High Representative of the Union for Foreign Affairs and Security Policy* and the Commission.

The Council shall confirm the participation of the Member State concerned, after consulting the *High Representative of the Union for Foreign Affairs and Security Policy* and after noting, where necessary, that the conditions of participation have been fulfilled. The Council, on a proposal from the *High Representative*, may also adopt any transitional measures necessary with regard to the application of the acts already adopted within the framework of enhanced co-operation. However, if the Council considers that the conditions of participation have not been fulfilled, it shall indicate the arrangements to be adopted to fulfil those conditions and shall set a deadline for re-examining the request for participation.

For the purposes of this paragraph, the Council shall act unanimously and in accordance with *Article 330*.

ARTICLE 332 [280G] *[Article III-421 (ex Article 44a TEU)]*

Expenditure resulting from implementation of enhanced co-operation, other than administrative costs entailed for the institutions, shall be borne by the participating Member States, unless all members of the Council, acting unanimously after consulting the European Parliament, decide otherwise.

ARTICLE 333 [280H] *[Article III-422 (new Article in 2004 IGC)]*

1. Where a provision of the *Treaties* which may be applied in the context of enhanced co-operation stipulates that the Council shall act unanimously, the Council, acting unanimously in accordance with the arrangements laid down in *Article 330*, may adopt a decision stipulating that it will act by a qualified majority.

2. Where a provision of the *Treaties* which may be applied in the context of enhanced co-operation stipulates that the Council shall adopt *acts* under a special legislative procedure, the Council, acting unanimously in accordance with the arrangements laid down in *Article 330*, may adopt a decision stipulating that it will act under the ordinary legislative procedure. The Council shall act after consulting the European Parliament.

3. Paragraphs 1 and 2 shall not apply to decisions having military or defence implications.

ARTICLE 334 [280I] *[Article III-423 (ex Article 45 TEU)]*

The Council and the Commission shall ensure the consistency of activities undertaken in the context of enhanced co-operation and the consistency of such activities with the policies of the Union, and shall co-operate to that end.

PART *SEVEN*

GENERAL AND FINAL PROVISIONS

[BMDF Note: Article 281 TEC shall be repealed]

ARTICLE ***335*** [282] *[Article III-426 (ex Article 282 TEC)]*
In each of the Member States, the **Union** shall enjoy the most extensive legal capacity accorded to legal persons under their laws; it may, in particular, acquire or dispose of movable and immovable property and may be a party to legal proceedings. To this end, the **Union** shall be represented by the Commission. **However, the Union shall be represented by each of the institutions, by virtue of their administrative autonomy, in matters relating to their respective operation.**

ARTICLE ***336*** [283] *[Article III-427 (ex Article 283 TEC)]*
The European Parliament and the Council shall, acting ***by means of regulations in accordance with the ordinary legislative procedure*** on a proposal from the Commission and after consulting the other institutions concerned, lay down the Staff Regulations of officials of the European **Union** and the Conditions of Employment of other servants of **the Union**.

ARTICLE ***337*** [284] *[Article III-428 (ex Article 284 TEC)]*
The Commission may, within the limits and under conditions laid down by the Council***, acting by a simple majority*** in accordance with the provisions of ***the Treaties***, collect any information and carry out any checks required for the performance of the tasks entrusted to it.

ARTICLE ***338*** [285] *[Article III-429 (ex Article 285 TEC)]*
1. Without prejudice to Article 5 of the Protocol on the Statute of the European System of Central Banks and of the European Central Bank, ***the European Parliament and*** the Council, acting in accordance with the ***ordinary legislative procedure***, shall adopt measures for the production of statistics where necessary for the performance of the activities of the ***Union***.

2. The production of ***Union*** statistics shall conform to impartiality, reliability, objectivity, scientific independence, cost-effectiveness and statistical confidentiality; it shall not entail excessive burdens on economic operators.

[BMDF Note: Article 286 TEC shall be repealed and replaced by Article 16 TFEU]

ARTICLE ***339*** [287] *[Article III-430 (ex Article 287 TEC)]*
The members of the institutions of the ***Union***, the members of committees, and the officials and other servants of the **Union** shall be required, even after their duties have ceased, not to disclose information of the kind covered by the obligation of professional secrecy, in particular information about undertakings, their business relations or their cost components.

ARTICLE ***340*** [288] *[Article III-431 (ex Article 288 TEC)]*
The contractual liability of the ***Union*** shall be governed by the law applicable to the contract in question.
In the case of non-contractual liability, the ***Union*** shall, in accordance with the general principles common to the laws of the Member States, make good any damage caused by its institutions or by its servants in the performance of their duties.
Notwithstanding the second paragraph, the European Central Bank shall, in accordance with the general principles common to the laws of the Member States, make good any damage caused by it or by its servants in the performance of their duties.
The personal liability of its servants towards the ***Union*** shall be governed by the provisions laid down in their Staff Regulations or in the Conditions of Employment applicable to them.

ARTICLE ***341*** [289] *[Article III-432 (ex Article 289 TEC)]*
The seat of the institutions of the ***Union*** shall be determined by common accord of the Governments of the Member States.

ARTICLE *342* [290] *[Article III-433 (ex Article 290 TEC)]*
The rules governing the languages of the institutions of the ***Union*** shall, without prejudice to the provisions contained in the **Statute** of the Court of Justice **of the European Union**, be determined by the Council, acting unanimously ***by means of regulations***.

ARTICLE *343* [291] *{Article III-434 (ex Article 291 TEC)]*
The **Union** shall enjoy in the territories of the Member States such privileges and immunities as are necessary for the performance of their tasks, under the conditions laid down in the Protocol of 8 April 1965 on the privileges and immunities of the European **Union**. The same shall apply to the European Central Bank and the European Investment Bank.

ARTICLE *344* [292] *[Article III-375(2) (ex Article 292 TEC)]*
Member States undertake not to submit a dispute concerning the interpretation of ***the Treaties*** to any method of settlement other than those provided for therein.

[BMDF Note: Article 293 TEC shall be repealed]

[BMDF Note: Article 294 TEC moved to Article 55 TFEU]

ARTICLE *345* [295] *[Article III-425 (ex Article 295 TEC)]*
The Treaties shall in no way prejudice the rules in Member States governing the system of property ownership.

ARTICLE *346* [296] *[Article III-436 (ex Article 296 TEC)]*
1. The provisions of ***the Treaties*** shall not preclude the application of the following rules:
(a) No Member State shall be obliged to supply information the disclosure of which it considers contrary to the essential interests of its security;
(b) Any Member State may take such measures as it considers necessary for the protection of the essential interests of its security which are connected with the production of or trade in arms, munitions and war material; such measures shall not adversely affect the conditions of competition in the **internal** market regarding products which are not intended for specifically military purposes.

2. The Council may, acting unanimously on a proposal from the Commission, make changes to the list which it drew up on 15 April 1958, of the products to which the provisions of paragraph 1(b) apply.

ARTICLE *347* [297] [*Article III-131 (ex Article 297 TEC)]*
Member States shall consult each other with a view to taking together the steps needed to prevent the functioning of the **internal** market being affected by measures which a Member State may be called upon to take in the event of serious internal disturbances affecting the maintenance of law and order, in the event of war, serious international tension constituting a threat of war, or in order to carry out obligations it has accepted for the purpose of maintaining peace and international security.

ARTICLE *348* [298] *[Article III-132 (ex Article 298 TEC)]*
If measures taken in the circumstances referred to in Articles **346** and *347* have the effect of distorting the conditions of competition in the **internal** market, the Commission shall, together with the State concerned, examine how these measures can be adjusted to the rules laid down in ***the Treaties***.
By way of derogation from the procedure laid down in Articles ***258*** and ***259***, the Commission or any Member State may bring the matter directly before the Court of Justice if it considers that another Member State is making improper use of the powers provided for in Articles ***346*** and ***347***. The Court of Justice shall give its ruling *in camera.*

ARTICLE *349* [299] *[Article III-424 (ex Article 299 TEC)]*
Taking account of the structural social and economic situation of **Guadeloupe, French Guiana, Martinique, Réunion, *Saint Barthélemy, Saint Martin,*** the Azores, Madeira and the Canary Islands, which is compounded by their remoteness, insularity, small size, difficult topography and climate, economic dependence on a few products, the permanence and combination of which severely restrain their development, the Council, on a proposal from the Commission and after consulting the European Parliament, shall adopt specific measures aimed, in particular, at laying down the conditions of application of the ***Treaties*** to those regions, including common policies. ***Where the specific measures***

***in question are adopted by the Council in accordance with a special legislative procedure*, it shall *also* act *on a proposal from the Commission and* after consulting the European Parliament.**
The acts referred to in the first paragraph concern in particular areas such as customs and trade policies, fiscal policy, free zones, agriculture and fisheries policies, conditions for supply of raw materials and essential consumer goods, State aids and conditions of access to structural funds and to horizontal ***Union*** programmes.
The Council shall adopt the measures referred to in the **first** sub-paragraph taking into account the special characteristics and constraints of the outermost regions without undermining the integrity and the coherence of the ***Union*** legal order, including the internal market and common policies.

[BMDF Note: Article 300 TEC moved to Article 218 TFEU]

[BMDF Note: Article 301 TEC moved to Article 215 TFEU]

[BMDF Note: Article 302 TEC moved to Article 220 TFEU]

[BMDF Note: Article 303 TEC moved to Article 220 TFEU]

[BMDF Note: Article 304 TEC moved to Article 220 TFEU]

[BMDF Note: Article 305 TEC shall be repealed]

ARTICLE ***350*** [306] *['Regional Unions', Article IV-441 (ex Article 306 TEC)]*
The provisions of ***the Treaties*** shall not preclude the existence or completion of regional unions between Belgium and Luxembourg, or between Belgium, Luxembourg and the Netherlands, to the extent that the objectives of these regional unions are not attained by application of ***the Treaties***.

ARTICLE ***351*** [307] *[Article III-435 (ex Article 307 TEC)]*
The rights and obligations arising from agreements concluded before 1 January 1958 or, for acceding States, before the date of their accession, between one or more Member States on the one hand, and one or more third countries on the other, shall not be affected by the provisions of ***the Treaties***.
To the extent that such agreements are not compatible with ***the Treaties***, that Member State or States concerned shall take all appropriate steps to eliminate the incompatibilities established. Member States shall, where necessary, assist each other to this end and shall, where appropriate, adopt a common attitude.
In applying the agreements referred to in the first paragraph, Member States shall take into account the fact that the advantages accorded under ***the Treaties*** by each Member State form an integral part of the establishment of the ***Union*** and are thereby inseparably linked with the creation of common institutions, the conferring of powers upon them and the granting of the same advantages by all the other Member States.

ARTICLE ***352*** [308] *['Flexibility clause', Article I-18 (ex Article 308 TEC)]*
1. If action by the **Union** should prove necessary, **within the framework of the policies defined *by the Treaties*,** to attain one of the objectives **set out in the *Treaties*, *and the Treaties have*** not provided the necessary powers, the Council**, acting unanimously on a proposal from the Commission and after obtaining the consent of the European Parliament,** shall, **adopt** the appropriate measures. ***Where the measures in question are adopted by the Council in accordance with a special legislative procedure, it shall also act unanimously on a proposal from the Commission and after obtaining the consent of the European Parliament.***
[BMDF Note: the last paragraph was added in the second draft of the Reform Treaty, 5 October 2007]

2. Using the procedure for monitoring the subsidiarity principle referred to in *Article 5(3) of the Treaty on European Union*, the Commission shall draw national Parliaments' attention to proposals based on this Article.

3. Measures based on this Article shall not entail harmonisation of Member States' laws or regulations in cases where the *Treaties* exclude such harmonisation.

4. ***This Article cannot serve as a basis for attaining objectives pertaining to the common foreign and security policy and any acts adopted pursuant to this Article shall respect the limits set out in Article 40, second paragraph, of the Treaty on European Union.***
[BMDF Note: See also Declarations no. 41 and 42]

ARTICLE 353 [308a] *[New Article in Treaty of Lisbon; BMDF notes in italics to show references]*
Article 48 of the Treaty on European Union shall not apply to the following Articles:
- ***311, third and fourth paragraphs,*** *(own resources)*
- ***312(2), first sub-paragraph,*** *(multiannual financial framework)*
- ***352,*** *(flexibility)* ***and***
- ***354.*** *(membership of the Union)*

[BMDF Note: This Article relates to Article 48 TEU, revision procedures of the Treaties under the ordinary and simplified revision procedures.]

ARTICLE *354* [309] *['Suspension of certain rights resulting from Union membership', Article I-59(5) and(6) (ex Article 7 TEU)]*
For the purposes of *Article 7 of the Treaty on European Union on the suspension of certain rights resulting from Union membership*, the member of the European Council or of the Council representing the Member State in question shall not take part in the vote and the Member State in question shall not be counted in the calculation of the one third or four fifths of Member States referred to in paragraphs 1 and 2 *of that Article.* Abstentions by members present in person or represented shall not prevent the adoption of decisions referred to in paragraph 2 *of that Article.*
For the adoption of the decisions referred to in paragraphs 3 and 4 *of Article 7 of the Treaty on European Union,* a qualified majority shall be defined *in accordance with Article 238(3)(b) of this Treaty.*
Where, following a decision to suspend voting rights adopted pursuant to paragraph 3 *of Article 7 of the Treaty on European Union,* the Council acts by a qualified majority on the basis of a provision of the *Treaties,* that qualified majority shall be defined *in accordance with Article 238(3)(b) of this Treaty,* or, where the Council acts on a proposal from the Commission or from the *High Representative of the Union for Foreign Affairs and Security Policy, in accordance with Article 238(3)(a).*
For the purposes of *Article 7 of the Treaty on European Union,* the European Parliament shall act by a two-thirds majority of the votes cast, representing the majority of its component members.
[BMDF Note: Article taken from 2004 IGC - Article I-59(5) and(6) 'Suspension of certain rights resulting from Union membership']

[BMDF Note: Article 310 TEC moved to Article 217 TFEU]

[BMDF Note: Article 311 TEC shall be repealed]

ARTICLE 355 [311a] *['Scope', Article IV-440, paragraphs 2 - 7 (ex Article 299 TEC)]*
In addition to the provisions of Article 49 C of the Treaty on European Union relating to the territorial scope of the Treaties, the following provisions shall apply:
1. The provisions of ***the Treaties*** shall apply to **Guadeloupe, French Guiana, Martinique, Réunion, *Saint Barthélemy, Saint Martin,*** the Azores, Madeira and the Canary Islands **in accordance with *Article 349*.**

2. The special arrangements for association set out in Part Four shall apply to the overseas countries and territories listed in Annex II to ***the Treaties***.
The Treaties shall not apply to those overseas countries and territories having special relations with the United Kingdom of Great Britain and Northern Ireland which are not included in the afore-mentioned list.

3. The provisions of ***the Treaties*** shall apply to the European territories for whose external relations a Member State is responsible.

4. The provisions of ***the Treaties*** shall apply to the Åland Islands in accordance with the provisions set out in Protocol No. 2 to the Act concerning the conditions of accession of the Republic of Austria, the Republic of Finland and the Kingdom of Sweden.

5. Notwithstanding ***Article 52 of the Treaty on European Union and paragraphs 1 to 4 of this Article***:
(a) ***the Treaties*** shall not apply to the Faeroe Islands;
(b) ***the Treaties*** shall not apply to the Sovereign Base Areas of the United Kingdom of Great Britain and Northern Ireland in Cyprus;
(c) ***the Treaties*** shall apply to the Channel Islands and the Isle of Man only to the extent necessary to ensure the implementation of the arrangements for those islands set out in the Treaty concerning the accession of new Member States to the European Economic Community and to the European Atomic Energy Community signed on 22 January 1972.

6. The European Council may, on the initiative of the Member State concerned, adopt a decision amending the status, with regard to the Union, of a Danish, French or Netherlands country or territory referred to in paragraphs *1 and 2*. The European Council shall act unanimously after consulting the Commission.
[BMDF Note: See also Declarations nos. 43 and 60. Paragraphs 2 (renumbered 1) and 3 to 6 (renumbered 2 to 5) from Article 299 TEC]

ARTICLE ***356*** [312] *['Duration', Article IV-446 (ex Articles 51 TEU and 312 TEC)]*
This Treaty is concluded for an unlimited period.

ARTICLE ***357*** [313] *['Ratification and entry into force', Article IV-447 (ex Articles 52 TEU and 313 TEC)]*
This Treaty shall be ratified by the High Contracting Parties in accordance with their respective constitutional requirements.
The instruments of ratification shall be deposited with the Government of the Italian Republic.
This Treaty shall enter into force on the first day of the month following the deposit of the instrument of ratification by the last signatory State to take this step. If, however, such deposit is made less than fifteen days before the beginning of the following month, this Treaty shall not enter into force until the first day of the second month after the date of such deposit.

ARTICLE 358 [313a] *['Authentic texts and translations', Article IV-448 (ex Articles 53 TEU and 314 TEC)]*
The provisions of Article 53 of the Treaty on European Union shall apply to this Treaty.
[BMDF Note: Text of Article IV-448 shown in Article 40 TEU]

[BMDF Note: Article 314 TEC shall be repealed]

IN WITNESS WHEREOF, the Plenipotentiaries have signed this Treaty.

Done in Rome, this twenty-fifth day of March in the year one thousand nine hundred and fifty seven.

[*BMDF Note: For each Member State, the names and the signatures of the Plenipotentiaries follow here.*]

ANNEXES TO THE TREATY

ANNEX I

LIST
referred to in Article 38(3) of
the Treaty *on the Functioning of the European Union*

1	2
Number in the Brussels nomenclature	Description of products
CHAPTER 1	Live animals
CHAPTER 2	Meat and edible meat offal
CHAPTER 3	Fish, crustaceans and molluscs
CHAPTER 4	Dairy produce; birds' eggs; natural honey
CHAPTER 5 05.04	
	Guts, bladders and stomachs of animals (other than fish), whole and pieces thereof
05.15	Animal products not elsewhere specified or included; dead animals of Chapter 1 or Chapter 3, unfit for human consumption
CHAPTER 6	Live trees and other plants; bulbs, roots and the like; cut flowers and ornamental foliage
CHAPTER 7	Edible vegetables and certain roots and tubers
CHAPTER 8	Edible fruit and nuts; peel of melons or citrus fruit
CHAPTER 9	Coffee, tea and spices, excluding maté (heading No 09.03)
CHAPTER 10	Cereals
CHAPTER 11	Products of the milling industry; malt and starches; gluten; inulin
CHAPTER 12	Oil seeds and oleaginous fruit; miscellaneous grains, seeds and fruit; industrial and medical plants; straw and fodder
CHAPTER 13	
ex 13.03	Pectin
CHAPTER 15	
15.01	Lard and other rendered pig fat; rendered poultry fat
15.02	Unrendered fats of bovine cattle, sheep or goats; tallow (including 'premier jus') produced from those fats
15.03	Lard stearin, oleostearin and tallow stearin; lard oil, oleo-oil and tallow oil, not emulsified or mixed or prepared in any way
15.04	Fats and oil, of fish and marine mammals, whether or not refined
15.07	Fixed vegetable oils, fluid or solid, crude, refined or purified
15.12	Animal or vegetable fats and oils, hydrogenated, whether or not refined, but not further prepared
15.13	Margarine, imitation lard and other prepared edible fats
15.17	Residues resulting from the treatment of fatty substances or animal or vegetable waxes
CHAPTER 16	Preparations of meat, of fish, of crustaceans or molluscs
CHAPTER 17	
17.01	Beet sugar and cane sugar, solid
17.02	Other sugars; sugar syrups; artificial honey (whether or not mixed with natural honey); caramel
17.03	Molasses, whether or not decolourised
17.05 (*)	Flavoured or coloured sugars, syrups and molasses, but not including fruit juices containing added sugar in any proportion

(*) Heading added by Article 1 of Regulation No 7a of the Council of the European Economic Community, of 18 December 1959 (OJ No 7, 30. 1. 1961, p. 71 - Special edition (English edition) 1959-1962, p. 68).

1	2
Number in the Brussels nomenclature	Description of products
CHAPTER 18	
18.01	Cocoa beans, whole or broken, raw or roasted
18.02	Cocoa shells, husks, skins and waste
CHAPTER 20	Preparations of vegetables, fruit or other parts of plants
CHAPTER 22	
22.04	Grape must, in fermentation or with fermentation arrested otherwise than by the addition of alcohol
22.05	Wine of fresh grapes; grape must with fermentation arrested by the addition of alcohol
22.07	Other fermented beverages (for example, cider, perry and mead)
ex 22.08 (*) ex 22.09 (*)	Ethyl alcohol or neutral spirits, whether or not denatured, of any strength, obtained from agricultural products listed in Annex I to the Treaty, excluding liqueurs and other spirituous beverages and compound alcoholic preparations (known as 'concentrated extracts') for the manufacture of beverages
22.10 (*)	Vinegar and substitutes for vinegar
CHAPTER 23	Residues and waste from the food industries; prepared animal fodder
CHAPTER 24	
24.01	Unmanufactured tobacco, tobacco refuse
CHAPTER 45	
45.01	Natural cork, unworked, crushed, granulated or ground; waste cork
CHAPTER 54 54.01	Flax, raw or processed but not spun; flax tow and waste (including pulled or garnetted rags)
CHAPTER 57 57.01	True hemp (*Cannabis sativa*), raw or processed but not spun; tow and waste of true hemp (including pulled or garnetted rags or ropes)

(*) Heading added by Article 1 of Regulation No 7a of the Council of the European Economic Community, of 18 December 1959 (OJ No 7, 30. 1. 1961, p. 71 - Special edition (English edition) 1959-1962, p. 68).

ANNEX II

OVERSEAS COUNTRIES AND TERRITORIES

to which the provisions of Part Four of the Treaty *on the Functioning of the European Union* apply

[BMDF Note: This relates in particular to Articles 198 and 355(2) TFEU]

— Greenland,
— New Caledonia and Dependencies,
— French Polynesia,
— French Southern and Antarctic Territories,
— Wallis and Futuna Islands,
— Mayotte,
— Saint Pierre and Miquelon,
— Aruba,
— Netherlands Antilles:
 — Bonaire,
 — Curaçao,
 — Saba,
 — Sint Eustatius,
 — Sint Maarten.
— Anguilla,
— Cayman Islands,
— Falkland Islands,
— South Georgia and the South Sandwich Islands,
— Montserrat,
— Pitcairn,
— Saint Helena and Dependencies,
— British Antarctic Territory,
— British Indian Ocean Territory,
— Turks and Caicos Islands,
— British Virgin Islands,
— Bermuda.

PROTOCOLS

ANNEXED TO THE TREATY ON EUROPEAN UNION AND TO THE TREATY ON THE FUNCTIONING OF THE EUROPEAN UNION

BMDF notes are shown in brackets and in italics after some of the protocol titles, to give an indication of the subject matter.

A. Protocols to be annexed to the Treaty on European Union, to the Treaty on the Functioning of the European Union and, where applicable, to the Treaty establishing the European Atomic Energy Community

1. **Protocol on the role of national parliaments in the European Union** 129
2. **Protocol on the application of the principles of subsidiarity and proportionality** 131
3. **Protocol on the Euro Group** 133
4. **Protocol on permanent structured co-operation established by *Article 42*** [28A] ***of the Treaty on European Union*** 133
5. **Protocol relating to *Article 6(2) of the Treaty on European Union* on the accession of the Union to the European Convention on Human Rights and fundamental freedoms** 135
6. ***Protocol on the Internal Market and Competition*** 136
7. ***Protocol on the application of the Charter of Fundamental Rights to Poland and to the United Kingdom*** 136
8. ***Protocol on the exercise of shared competence*** 137
9. ***Protocol on services of general interest*** 137
10. ***Protocol on the decision of the Council relating to the implementation of Article 16(4)*** [9C(4)] ***of the Treaty on European Union and Article 238(2)*** [205(2)] ***of the Treaty on the Functioning of the European Union between 1 November 2014 and 31 March 2017 on the one hand, and as from 1 April 2017 on the other*** 138
11. **Protocol on transitional provisions** 138

Protocols already in force and amended by Protocol no.1 annexed to the Treaty of Lisbon

12. Protocol on the Statute of the Court of Justice of the European Union 143
13. Protocol on the Statute of the European System of Central Banks and of the European Central Bank 156
14. Protocol on the Statute of the European Investment Bank 168
15. Protocol on the location of the seats of the institutions and of certain bodies, offices, agencies and departments of the European Union
16. Protocol on the privileges and immunities of the European Union 176
17. Protocol on the convergence criteria 180
18. Protocol on certain provisions relating to the United Kingdom of Great Britain and Northern Ireland (*Economic and Monetary Union*) 181
19. Protocol on certain provisions relating to Denmark (*Economic and Monetary Union*) 183

20. Protocol on the Schengen *acquis* integrated into the framework of the European Union 183

21. Protocol on the application of certain aspects of Article ***26*** [22a] of the Treaty on the Functioning of the European Union to the United Kingdom and to Ireland (*border checks and travel arrangements*) 185

22. Protocol on the position of the United Kingdom and Ireland on policies in respect of the area of freedom, security and justice 186

23. Protocol on the position of Denmark 188

24. Protocol on asylum for nationals of Member States 192

25. Protocol on economic, social and territorial cohesion 193

26. Protocol on the excessive deficit procedure 194

27. Protocol on France (*Pacific Financial Community franc system*) 195

28. Protocol on external relations of the Member States with regard to the crossing of external borders 195

29. Protocol on Article ***42*** [28A] of the Treaty on European Union (*enhanced co-operation with the WEU*) 195

30. Protocol on the system of public broadcasting in the Member States 196

31. Protocol concerning imports into the European Union of petroleum products refined in the Netherlands Antilles 196

32. Protocol concerning Article ***157*** [141] of the Treaty on the Functioning of the European Union (*the 'Barber Protocol' on pensions funds*) 198

33. Protocol on special arrangements for Greenland 198

34. Protocol on Article 40.3.3 of the Constitution of Ireland 199

35. Protocol on the financial consequences of the expiry of the Treaty establishing the European Coal and Steel Community and on the Research Fund for Coal and Steel 199

36. Protocol on Denmark (*certain tasks of the National Bank of Denmark*) 200

37. Protocol on the acquisition of property in Denmark 200

B. Protocols to be annexed to the Treaty of Lisbon

1. Protocol amending the Protocols annexed to Treaty on European Union, to the Treaty establishing the European Community and/or the Treaty establishing the European Atomic Energy Community 201

2. **Protocol amending the Treaty establishing the European Atomic Energy Community** 205

* * *

Protocols repealed by the Treaty of Lisbon 206

* * * * * *

PROTOCOLS

A. PROTOCOLS TO BE ANNEXED TO THE TREATY ON EUROPEAN UNION, TO THE TREATY ON THE FUNCTIONING OF THE EUROPEAN UNION AND, WHERE APPLICABLE, TO THE TREATY ESTABLISHING THE EUROPEAN ATOMIC ENERGY COMMUNITY

1. PROTOCOL ON THE ROLE OF NATIONAL PARLIAMENTS IN THE EUROPEAN UNION

THE HIGH CONTRACTING PARTIES,

RECALLING that the way in which national Parliaments scrutinise their governments in relation to the activities of the Union is a matter for the particular constitutional organisation and practice of each Member State;

DESIRING to encourage greater involvement of national Parliaments in the activities of the European Union and to enhance their ability to express their views on draft legislative acts *of the Union* as well as on other matters which may be of particular interest to them,

HAVE AGREED UPON the following provisions, which shall be annexed to the *Treaty on European Union, to the Treaty on the Functioning of the European Union* and to the Treaty establishing the European Atomic Energy Community:

TITLE I

INFORMATION FOR NATIONAL PARLIAMENTS

ARTICLE 1
Commission consultation documents (green and white papers and communications) shall be forwarded directly by the Commission to national Parliaments upon publication. The Commission shall also forward the annual legislative programme as well as any other instrument of legislative planning or policy to national Parliaments, at the same time as to the European Parliament and the Council.

ARTICLE 2
Draft legislative acts sent to the European Parliament and to the Council shall be forwarded to national Parliaments.
For the purposes of this Protocol, "draft legislative acts" shall mean proposals from the Commission, initiatives from a group of Member States, initiatives from the European Parliament, requests from the Court of Justice, recommendations from the European Central Bank and requests from the European Investment Bank for the adoption of a legislative act.
Draft legislative acts originating from the Commission shall be forwarded to national Parliaments directly by the Commission, at the same time as to the European Parliament and the Council.
Draft legislative acts originating from the European Parliament shall be forwarded to national Parliaments directly by the European Parliament.
Draft legislative acts originating from a group of Member States, the Court of Justice, the European Central Bank or the European Investment Bank shall be forwarded to national Parliaments by the Council.

ARTICLE 3
National Parliaments may send to the Presidents of the European Parliament, the Council and the Commission a reasoned opinion on whether a draft legislative act complies with the principle of subsidiarity, in accordance with the procedure laid down in the Protocol on the application of the principles of subsidiarity and proportionality.

If the draft legislative act originates from a group of Member States, the President of the Council shall forward the reasoned opinion or opinions to the governments of those Member States.
If the draft legislative act originates from the Court of Justice, the European Central Bank or the European Investment Bank, the President of the Council shall forward the reasoned opinion or opinions to the institution or body concerned.

ARTICLE 4
A*n eight*-week period shall elapse between a draft legislative act being made available to national Parliaments in the official languages of the Union and the date when it is placed on a provisional agenda for the Council for its adoption or for adoption of a position under a legislative procedure. Exceptions shall be possible in cases of urgency, the reasons for which shall be stated in the act or position of the Council. Save in urgent cases for which due reasons have been given, no agreement may be reached on a draft legislative act during those *eight* weeks. Save in urgent cases for which due reasons have been given, a ten-day period shall elapse between the placing of a draft legislative act on the provisional agenda for the Council and the adoption of a position.

ARTICLE 5
The agendas for and the outcome of meetings of the Council, including the minutes of meetings where the Council is deliberating on draft legislative acts, shall be forwarded directly to national Parliaments, at the same time as to Member States' governments.

ARTICLE 6
When the European Council intends to make use of *Article 48(7) of the Treaty on European Union*, national Parliaments shall be informed of the initiative of the European Council at least six months before any European decision is adopted.

ARTICLE 7
The Court of Auditors shall forward its annual report to national Parliaments, for information, at the same time as to the European Parliament and to the Council.

ARTICLE 8
Where the national Parliamentary system is not unicameral, Articles 1 to 7 shall apply to the component chambers.

TITLE II

INTER-PARLIAMENTARY CO-OPERATION

ARTICLE 9
The European Parliament and national Parliaments shall together determine the organisation and promotion of effective and regular inter-parliamentary co-operation within the Union.

ARTICLE 10
A conference of Parliamentary Committees for Union Affairs may submit any contribution it deems appropriate for the attention of the European Parliament, the Council and the Commission. That conference shall in addition promote the exchange of information and best practice between national Parliaments and the European Parliament, including their special committees. It may also organise inter-parliamentary conferences on specific topics, in particular to debate matters of common foreign and security policy, including common security and defence policy. Contributions from the conference shall not bind national Parliaments and shall not prejudge their positions.
[BMDF Note: This protocol is taken from the draft Constitutional Treaty, replacing the protocol introduced in the Treaty of Amsterdam]

2. PROTOCOL ON THE APPLICATION OF THE PRINCIPLES OF SUBSIDIARITY AND PROPORTIONALITY

THE HIGH CONTRACTING PARTIES,

WISHING to ensure that decisions are taken as closely as possible to the citizens of the Union;

RESOLVED to establish the conditions for the application of the principles of subsidiarity and proportionality, as laid down in *Article 5 of the Treaty on European Union*, and to establish a system for monitoring the application of those principles,

HAVE AGREED UPON the following provisions, which shall be annexed to the *Treaty on European Union and to the Treaty on the Functioning of the European Union*:

ARTICLE 1

Each institution shall ensure constant respect for the principles of subsidiarity and proportionality, as laid down in *Article 5 of the Treaty on European Union.*

ARTICLE 2

Before proposing legislative acts, the Commission shall consult widely. Such consultations shall, where appropriate, take into account the regional and local dimension of the action envisaged. In cases of exceptional urgency, the Commission shall not conduct such consultations. It shall give reasons for its decision in its proposal.

ARTICLE 3

For the purposes of this Protocol, "draft legislative acts" shall mean proposals from the Commission, initiatives from a group of Member States, initiatives from the European Parliament, requests from the Court of Justice, recommendations from the European Central Bank and requests from the European Investment Bank for the adoption of a ~~European~~ legislative act.

ARTICLE 4

The Commission shall forward its draft legislative acts and its amended drafts to national Parliaments at the same time as to the Union legislator.

The European Parliament shall forward its draft legislative acts and its amended drafts to national Parliaments.

The Council shall forward draft legislative acts originating from a group of Member States, the Court of Justice, the European Central Bank or the European Investment Bank and amended drafts to national Parliaments.

Upon adoption, legislative resolutions of the European Parliament and positions of the Council shall be forwarded by them to national Parliaments.

ARTICLE 5

Draft legislative acts shall be justified with regard to the principles of subsidiarity and proportionality. Any draft legislative act should contain a detailed statement making it possible to appraise compliance with the principles of subsidiarity and proportionality. This statement should contain some assessment of the proposal's financial impact and, in the case of a *directive*, of its implications for the rules to be put in place by Member States, including, where necessary, the regional legislation. The reasons for concluding that a Union objective can be better achieved at Union level shall be substantiated by qualitative and, wherever possible, quantitative indicators. Draft legislative acts shall take account of the need for any burden, whether financial or administrative, falling upon the Union, national governments, regional or local authorities, economic operators and citizens, to be minimised and commensurate with the objective to be achieved.

ARTICLE 6

Any national Parliament or any chamber of a national Parliament may, within *eight* weeks from the date of transmission of a draft legislative act, send to the Presidents of the European Parliament, the Council and the Commission a reasoned opinion stating why it considers that the draft in question does not comply with the principle of subsidiarity. It will be for each national

Parliament or each chamber of a national Parliament to consult, where appropriate, regional parliaments with legislative powers.
If the draft legislative act originates from a group of Member States, the President of the Council shall forward the opinion to the governments of those Member States.
If the draft legislative act originates from the Court of Justice, the European Central Bank or the European Investment Bank, the President of the Council shall forward the opinion to the institution or body concerned.

ARTICLE 7
1. **The European Parliament, the Council and the Commission, and, where appropriate, the group of Member States, the Court of Justice, the European Central Bank or the European Investment Bank, if the draft legislative act originates from them, shall take account of the reasoned opinions issued by national Parliaments or by a chamber of a national Parliament.**
Each national Parliament shall have two votes, shared out on the basis of the national Parliamentary system. In the case of a bicameral Parliamentary system, each of the two chambers shall have one vote.

2. **Where reasoned opinions on a draft legislative act's non-compliance with the principle of subsidiarity represent at least one third of all the votes allocated to the national Parliaments in accordance with the second** ***sub*****paragraph** ***of paragraph 1,*** **the draft must be reviewed. This threshold shall be a quarter in the case of a draft legislative act submitted on the basis of** ***Article76 of the Treaty on the Functioning of the European Union*** **on the area of freedom, security and justice.**
After such review, the Commission or, where appropriate, the group of Member States, the European Parliament, the Court of Justice, the European Central Bank or the European Investment Bank, if the draft legislative act originates from them, may decide to maintain, amend or withdraw the draft. Reasons must be given for this decision.

3. Furthermore, under the ordinary legislative procedure, where reasoned opinions on the non-compliance of a proposal for a legislative act with the principle of subsidiarity represent at least a simple majority of the votes allocated to the national Parliaments in accordance with the second subparagraph of paragraph 1, the proposal must be reviewed. After such review, the Commission may decide to maintain, amend or withdraw the proposal.
If it chooses to maintain the proposal, the Commission will have, in a reasoned opinion, to justify why it considers that the proposal complies with the principle of subsidiarity. This reasoned opinion, as well as the reasoned opinions of the national Parliaments, will have to be submitted to the Union legislator, for consideration in the procedure:
(a) before concluding the first reading, the legislator (Council and European Parliament) shall consider whether the legislative proposal is compatible with the principle of subsidiarity, taking particular account of the reasons expressed and shared by the majority of national Parliaments as well as the reasoned opinion of the Commission;
(b) if, by a majority of 55% of the members of the Council or a majority of the votes cast in the European Parliament, the legislator is of the opinion that the proposal is not compatible with the principle of subsidiarity, the legislative proposal shall not be given further consideration.

ARTICLE 8
The Court of Justice of the European Union shall have jurisdiction in actions on grounds of infringement of the principle of subsidiarity by a legislative act, brought in accordance with the rules laid down in ***Article 263 of the Treaty on the Functioning of the European Union*** **by Member States, or notified by them in accordance with their legal order on behalf of their national Parliament or a chamber of it.**
In accordance with the rules laid down in the said Article, the Committee of the Regions may also bring such actions against legislative acts for the adoption of which the ***Treaty on the Functioning of the European Union*** **provides that it be consulted.**

ARTICLE 9
The Commission shall submit each year to the European Council, the European Parliament, the Council and national Parliaments a report on the application of *Article 5 of the Treaty on European Union*. This annual report shall also be forwarded to the Committee of the Regions and to the Economic and Social Committee.
[BMDF Note: This protocol is taken from the draft Constitutional Treaty, replacing the protocol introduced in the Treaty of Amsterdam]

3. PROTOCOL ON THE EURO GROUP

THE HIGH CONTRACTING PARTIES,

DESIRING to promote conditions for stronger economic growth in the European Union and, to that end, to develop ever-closer co-ordination of economic policies within the euro area,

CONSCIOUS of the need to lay down special provisions for enhanced dialogue between the Member States whose currency is the euro, pending the euro becoming the currency of all Member States of the Union,

HAVE AGREED upon the following provisions, which are annexed to the *Treaty on European Union and to the Treaty on the Functioning of the European Union*:

ARTICLE 1
The Ministers of the Member States whose currency is the euro shall meet informally. Such meetings shall take place, when necessary, to discuss questions related to the specific responsibilities they share with regard to the single currency. The Commission shall take part in the meetings. The European Central Bank shall be invited to take part in such meetings, which shall be prepared by the representatives of the Ministers with responsibility for finance of the Member States whose currency is the euro and of the Commission.

ARTICLE 2
The Ministers of the Member States whose currency is the euro shall elect a president for two and a half years, by a majority of those Member States.
[BMDF Note: This protocol is taken from the draft Constitutional Treaty]

4. PROTOCOL ON PERMANENT STRUCTURED CO-OPERATION ESTABLISHED BY *ARTICLE 28 A OF THE TREATY ON EUROPEAN UNION*

THE HIGH CONTRACTING PARTIES,

HAVING REGARD TO *Article 42(6) and Article 46 of the Treaty on European Union*,

RECALLING that the Union is pursuing a common foreign and security policy based on the achievement of growing convergence of action by Member States;

RECALLING that the common security and defence policy is an integral part of the common foreign and security policy; that it provides the Union with operational capacity drawing on civil and military assets; that the Union may use such assets in the tasks referred to in *Article 43 of the Treaty on European Union* outside the Union for peace-keeping, conflict prevention and strengthening international security in accordance with the principles of the United Nations Charter; that the performance of these tasks is to be undertaken using capabilities provided by the Member States in accordance with the principle of a single set of forces;

RECALLING that the common security and defence policy of the Union does not prejudice the specific character of the security and defence policy of certain Member States;

RECALLING that the common security and defence policy of the Union respects the obligations under the North Atlantic Treaty of those Member States, which see their common defence realised in the North Atlantic Treaty Organisation, which remains the foundation of the collective defence of its members, and is compatible with the common security and defence policy established within that framework;

CONVINCED that a more assertive Union role in security and defence matters will contribute to the vitality of a renewed Atlantic Alliance, in accordance with the Berlin Plus arrangements;

DETERMINED to ensure that the Union is capable of fully assuming its responsibilities within the international community;

RECOGNISING that the United Nations Organisation may request the Union's assistance for the urgent implementation of missions undertaken under Chapters VI and VII of the United Nations Charter;

RECOGNISING that the strengthening of the security and defence policy will require efforts by Member States in the area of capabilities;

CONSCIOUS that embarking on a new stage in the development of the European security and defence policy involves a determined effort by the Member States concerned;

RECALLING the importance of the *High Representative of the Union for Foreign Affairs and Security Policy* being fully involved in proceedings relating to permanent structured co-operation,

HAVE AGREED UPON the following provisions, which shall be annexed to the *Treaty on European Union and to the Treaty on the Functioning of the European Union*:

ARTICLE 1

The permanent structured co-operation referred to in *Article 42(6) of the Treaty on European Union* shall be open to any Member State which undertakes, from the date of entry into force of the *Treaty of Lisbon*, to:

(a) proceed more intensively to develop its defence capacities through the development of its national contributions and participation, where appropriate, in multinational forces, in the main European equipment programmes, and in the activity of the Agency in the field of defence capabilities development, research, acquisition and armaments (European Defence Agency), and

(b) have the capacity to supply by *2010* at the latest, either at national level or as a component of multinational force groups, targeted combat units for the missions planned, structured at a tactical level as a battle group, with support elements including transport and logistics, capable of carrying out the tasks referred to in *Article 43 of the Treaty on European Union*, within a period of 5 to 30 days, in particular in response to requests from the United Nations Organisation, and which can be sustained for an initial period of 30 days and be extended up to at least 120 days.

ARTICLE 2

To achieve the objectives laid down in Article 1, Member States participating in permanent structured co-operation shall undertake to:

(a) co-operate, as from the entry into force of the *Treaty of Lisbon*, with a view to achieving approved objectives concerning the level of investment expenditure on defence equipment, and regularly review these objectives, in the light of the security environment and of the Union's international responsibilities;

(b) bring their defence apparatus into line with each other as far as possible, particularly by harmonising the identification of their military needs, by pooling and, where appropriate, specialising their defence means and capabilities, and by encouraging co-operation in the fields of training and logistics;

(c) take concrete measures to enhance the availability, interoperability, flexibility and deployability of their forces, in particular by identifying common objectives regarding the commitment of forces, including possibly reviewing their national decision-making procedures;

(d) work together to ensure that they take the necessary measures to make good, including through multinational approaches, and without prejudice to undertakings in this regard within the North Atlantic Treaty Organisation, the shortfalls perceived in the framework of the "Capability Development Mechanism";

(e) take part, where appropriate, in the development of major joint or European equipment programmes in the framework of the European Defence Agency.

ARTICLE 3

The European Defence Agency shall contribute to the regular assessment of participating Member States' contributions with regard to capabilities, in particular contributions made in accordance with the criteria to be established *inter alia* on the basis of Article 2, and shall report thereon at least once a year. The assessment may serve as a basis for Council recommendations and European decisions adopted in accordance with *Article 46 of the Treaty on European Union.*

[BMDF Note: This protocol is taken from the draft Constitutional Treaty]

5. PROTOCOL RELATING TO *ARTICLE 6(2) OF THE TREATY ON EUROPEAN UNION* ON THE ACCESSION OF THE UNION TO THE EUROPEAN CONVENTION ON THE PROTECTION OF HUMAN RIGHTS AND FUNDAMENTAL FREEDOMS

THE HIGH CONTRACTING PARTIES

HAVE AGREED on the following provisions, which shall be annexed to the *Treaty on European Union and to the Treaty on the Functioning of the European Union*:

ARTICLE 1

The agreement relating to the accession of the Union to the European Convention on the Protection of Human Rights and Fundamental Freedoms (hereinafter referred to as the "European Convention") provided for in *Article 6(2) of the Treaty on European Union* shall make provision for preserving the specific characteristics of the Union and Union law, in particular with regard to:

(a) the specific arrangements for the Union's possible participation in the control bodies of the European Convention;

(b) the mechanisms necessary to ensure that proceedings by non-Member States and individual applications are correctly addressed to Member States and/or the Union as appropriate.

ARTICLE 2

The agreement referred to in Article 1 shall ensure that accession of the Union shall not affect the competences of the Union or the powers of its institutions. It shall ensure that nothing therein affects the situation of Member States in relation to the European Convention, in particular in relation to the Protocols thereto, measures taken by Member States derogating from the European Convention in accordance with Article 15 thereof and reservations to the European Convention made by Member States in accordance with Article 57 thereof.

ARTICLE 3

Nothing in the agreement referred to in Article 1 shall affect *Article 344 of the Treaty on the Functioning of the European Union.*

[BMDF Note: This protocol is taken from the draft Constitutional Treaty]

6. *PROTOCOL ON THE INTERNAL MARKET AND COMPETITION*

The High Contracting Parties,

CONSIDERING that the internal market as set out in Article 3 of the Treaty on European Union includes a system ensuring that competition is not distorted,

HAVE AGREED that:

to this end, the Union shall, if necessary, take action under the provisions of the Treaties, including under Article 352 of the Treaty on the Functioning of the European Union.

This Protocol shall be annexed to the Treaty on European Union and to the Treaty on the Functioning of the European Union.

7. *PROTOCOL ON THE APPLICATION OF THE CHARTER OF FUNDAMENTAL RIGHTS TO POLAND AND TO THE UNITED KINGDOM*

THE HIGH CONTRACTING PARTIES,

WHEREAS in Article 6 of the Treaty on European Union, the Union recognises the rights, freedoms and principles set out in the Charter of Fundamental Rights;

WHEREAS the Charter is to be applied in strict accordance with the provisions of the aforementioned Article 6 and Title VII of the Charter itself;

WHEREAS the aforementioned Article 6 requires the Charter to be applied and interpreted by the courts of Poland and of the United Kingdom strictly in accordance with the explanations referred to in that Article;

WHEREAS the Charter contains both rights and principles;

WHEREAS the Charter contains both provisions which are civil and political in character and those which are economic and social in character;

WHEREAS the Charter reaffirms the rights, freedoms and principles recognised in the Union and makes those rights more visible, but does not create new rights or principles;

RECALLING the obligations devolving upon Poland and the United Kingdom under the Treaty on European Union, the Treaty on the Functioning of the European Union, and Union law generally;

NOTING the wish of Poland and the United Kingdom to clarify certain aspects of the application of the Charter;

DESIROUS therefore of clarifying the application of the Charter in relation to the laws and administrative action of Poland and of the United Kingdom and of its justiciability within Poland and within the United Kingdom;

REAFFIRMING that references in this Protocol to the operation of specific provisions of the Charter are strictly without prejudice to the operation of other provisions of the Charter;

REAFFIRMING that this Protocol is without prejudice to the application of the Charter to other Member States;

REAFFIRMING that this Protocol is without prejudice to other obligations devolving upon Poland and the United Kingdom under the Treaty on European Union, the Treaty on the Functioning of the European Union, and Union law generally,

HAVE AGREED UPON the following provisions, which shall be annexed to the Treaty on European Union and to the Treaty on the Functioning of the European Union:

ARTICLE 1

1. The Charter does not extend the ability of the Court of Justice of the European Union, or any court or tribunal of Poland or of the United Kingdom, to find that the laws, regulations or administrative provisions, practices or action of Poland or of the United Kingdom are inconsistent with the fundamental rights, freedoms and principles that it reaffirms.

2. In particular, and for the avoidance of doubt, nothing in Title IV of the Charter creates justiciable rights applicable to Poland or the United Kingdom except in so far as Poland or the United Kingdom has provided for such rights in its national law.

ARTICLE 2

To the extent that a provision of the Charter refers to national laws and practices, it shall only apply to Poland or the United Kingdom to the extent that the rights or principles that it contains are recognised in the law or practices of Poland or of the United Kingdom.

8. PROTOCOL ON THE EXERCISE OF SHARED COMPETENCE

THE HIGH CONTRACTING PARTIES

HAVE AGREED UPON the following provision, which shall be annexed to the Treaty on European Union and to the Treaty on the Functioning of the European Union:

SOLE ARTICLE

With reference to Article 2 of the Treaty on the Functioning of the European Union on shared competence, when the Union has taken action in a certain area, the scope of this exercise of competence only covers those elements governed by the Union act in question and therefore does not cover the whole area.

9. PROTOCOL ON SERVICES OF GENERAL INTEREST

THE HIGH CONTRACTING PARTIES,

WISHING to emphasise the importance of services of general interest,

HAVE AGREED UPON the following interpretative provisions, which shall be annexed to the Treaty on European Union and to the Treaty on the Functioning of the European Union:

ARTICLE 1

The shared values of the Union in respect of services of general economic interest within the meaning of Article 14 of the Treaty on the Functioning of the European Union include in particular:

- *the essential role and the wide discretion of national, regional and local authorities in providing, commissioning and organising services of general economic interest as closely as possible to the needs of the users;*
- *the diversity between various services of general economic interest and the differences in the needs and preferences of users that may result from different geographical, social or cultural situations;*
- *a high level of quality, safety and affordability, equal treatment and the promotion of universal access and of user rights.*

ARTICLE 2
The provisions of the Treaties do not affect in any way the competence of Member States to provide, commission and organise non-economic services of general interest.

10. PROTOCOL ON THE DECISION OF THE COUNCIL RELATING TO THE IMPLEMENTATION OF ARTICLE 16(4) OF THE TREATY ON EUROPEAN UNION AND ARTICLE 238(2) OF THE TREATY ON THE FUNCTIONING OF THE EUROPEAN UNION BETWEEN 1 NOVEMBER 2014 AND 31 MARCH 2017 ON THE ONE HAND, AND AS FROM 1 APRIL 2017 ON THE OTHER

THE HIGH CONTRACTING PARTIES,

TAKING INTO ACCOUNT the fundamental importance that agreeing on the Decision of the Council relating to the implementation of Article 16(4) of the Treaty on European Union and Article 238(2) of the Treaty on the Functioning of the European Union between 1 November 2014 and 31 March 2017 on the one hand, and as from 1 April 2017 on the other (hereinafter "the Decision"), had when approving the Treaty of Lisbon,

HAVE AGREED UPON the following provisions, which shall be annexed to the Treaty on European Union and to the Treaty on the Functioning of the European Union:

SOLE ARTICLE
Before the examination by the Council of any draft which would aim either at amending or abrogating the Decision or any of its provisions, or at modifying indirectly its scope or its meaning through the modification of another legal act of the Union, the European Council shall hold a preliminary deliberation on the said draft, acting by consensus in accordance with Article 15(4) of the Treaty on European Union.
[BMDF Note: Protocol introduced on 19 October 2007 at the Lisbon summit]

11. PROTOCOL ON TRANSITIONAL PROVISIONS

THE HIGH CONTRACTING PARTIES,

WHEREAS, in order to organise the transition from the ***institutional provisions of the Treaties applicable prior to the entry into force of the Treaty of Lisbon to the provisions contained in that Treaty***, it is necessary to lay down transitional provisions,

HAVE AGREED UPON the following provisions, which shall be annexed to the ***Treaty on European Union, to the Treaty on the Functioning of the European Union*** and to the Treaty establishing the European Atomic Energy Community:

ARTICLE 1
In this Protocol, the words "the Treaties" shall mean the Treaty on European Union, the Treaty on the Functioning of the European Union and the Treaty establishing the European Atomic Energy Community.
[BMDF Note: Article 1 was added in the revision of the draft Reform Treaty dated 5 October 2007, and the numbering of the remaining Articles was changed as a result]

TITLE I

PROVISIONS CONCERNING THE EUROPEAN PARLIAMENT

ARTICLE **2**

In accordance with ***Article 14(2) of the Treaty on European Union***, the European Council shall adopt a decision determining the composition of the European Parliament ***in good time before*** the 2009 European Parliament elections.

Until the end of the 2004-2009 parliamentary term, the composition and the number of representatives elected to the European Parliament shall remain the same as on the date of the entry into force of ***the Treaty of Lisbon.***

TITLE II

PROVISIONS CONCERNING THE QUALIFIED MAJORITY

ARTICLE **3**

1. ***In accordance with Article 16(4) of the Treaty on European Union, the provisions of that paragraph and of Article 238(2) of the Treaty on the Functioning of the European Union relating*** **to** the definition of the qualified majority in the European Council and the Council shall take effect on 1 November ***2014.***

2. Between 1 November 2014 and 31 March 2017, when an act is to be adopted by qualified majority, a member of the Council may request that it be adopted in accordance with the qualified majority as defined in paragraph 3. In that case, paragraph 3 shall apply.

3. Until 31 October 2014, the following provisions shall remain in force, without prejudice to the second subparagraph of Article 235(1) of the Treaty on the Functioning of the European Union.

For acts of the European Council and of the Council requiring a qualified majority, members' votes shall be weighted as follows:

Belgium	12	Luxembourg	4
Bulgaria	10	Hungary	12
Czech Republic	12	Malta	3
Denmark	7	Netherlands	13
Germany	29	Austria	10
Estonia	4	Poland	27
Ireland	7	Portugal	12
Greece	12	Romania	14
Spain	27	Slovenia	4
France	29	Slovakia	7
Italy	29	Finland	7
Cyprus	4	Sweden	10
Latvia	4	United Kingdom	29
Lithuania	7		

Acts shall be adopted if there are at least ***255*** votes in favour representing a majority of the members where, under the ***Treaties***, they must be adopted on a proposal from the Commission. In other cases decisions shall be adopted if there are at least ***255*** votes in favour representing at least two thirds of the members.

A member of the European Council or the Council may request that, where an act is adopted by the European Council or the Council by a qualified majority, a check is made to ensure that the Member States comprising the qualified majority represent at least 62% of the total population of the Union. If that proves not to be the case, the act shall not be adopted.

4. Until 31 October ***2014***, the qualified majority shall, in cases where not all the members of the Council participate in voting, namely in the cases ***where reference is made to the qualified majority as defined in Article 238(3) of the Treaty on the Functioning of the European Union***, be defined as the same proportion of the weighted votes and the same proportion of the number of the Council members and, if appropriate, the same percentage of the population of the Member States concerned as laid down in paragraph ***3 of this Article***.

TITLE III

PROVISIONS CONCERNING THE CONFIGURATIONS OF THE COUNCIL

ARTICLE *4*
Until the entry into force of the decision referred to in ***the first subparagraph of Article 16(6) of the Treaty on European Union***, the Council may meet in the configurations laid down in ***the second and third subparagraphs of that paragraph*** and in the other configurations on the list established by a decision of the General Affairs Council, acting by a simple majority.

TITLE **IV**

PROVISIONS CONCERNING THE COMMISSION, INCLUDING THE ***HIGH REPRESENTATIVE OF THE UNION FOR FOREIGN AFFAIRS AND SECURITY POLICY***

ARTICLE *5*
The members of the Commission in office on the date of entry into force of the ***Treaty of Lisbon*** shall remain in office until the end of their term of office. However, on the day of the appointment of the ***High Representative of the Union for Foreign Affairs and Security Policy***, the term of office of the member having the same nationality as the ***High Representative*** shall end.

TITLE *V*

PROVISIONS CONCERNING THE SECRETARY-GENERAL OF THE COUNCIL, HIGH REPRESENTATIVE FOR THE COMMON FOREIGN AND SECURITY POLICY, AND THE DEPUTY SECRETARY-GENERAL OF THE COUNCIL

ARTICLE *6*
The terms of office of the Secretary-General of the Council, High Representative for the common foreign and security policy, and the Deputy Secretary-General of the Council shall end on the date of entry into force of the ***Treaty of Lisbon***. The Council shall appoint a Secretary-General in conformity with ***Article 240(2) of the Treaty on the Functioning of the European Union***.

TITLE *VI*

PROVISIONS CONCERNING ADVISORY BODIES

ARTICLE *7*
Until entry into force of the European decision referred to in ***Article 301 of the Treaty on the Functioning of the European Union***, the allocation of members of the Committee of the Regions shall be as follows:

Belgium	12	Luxembourg	6
Bulgaria	12	Hungary	12
Czech Republic	12	Malta	5
Denmark	9	Netherlands	12
Germany	24	Austria	12
Estonia	7	Poland	21
Ireland	9	Portugal	12
Greece	12	Romania	15
Spain	21	Slovenia	7
France	24	Slovakia	9
Italy	24	Finland	9
Cyprus	6	Sweden	12
Latvia	7	United Kingdom	24
Lithuania	9		

ARTICLE *8*
Until entry into force of the European decision referred to in ***Article 305 of the Treaty on the Functioning of the European Union***, the allocation of members of the Economic and Social Committee shall be as follows:

Belgium	12	Luxembourg	6
Bulgaria	12	Hungary	12
Czech Republic	12	Malta	5
Denmark	9	Netherlands	12
Germany	24	Austria	12
Estonia	7	Poland	21
Ireland	9	Portugal	12
Greece	12	Romania	15
Spain	21	Slovenia	7
France	24	Slovakia	9
Italy	24	Finland	9
Cyprus	6	Sweden	12
Latvia	7	United Kingdom	24
Lithuania	9		

TITLE VII

TRANSITIONAL PROVISIONS CONCERNING ACTS ADOPTED ON THE BASIS OF TITLES V AND VI OF THE TREATY ON EUROPEAN UNION PRIOR TO THE ENTRY INTO FORCE OF THE TREATY OF LISBON

ARTICLE 9
The legal effects of the acts of the institutions, bodies, offices and agencies of the Union adopted on the basis of Titles V and VI of the Treaty on European Union prior to the entry into force of the Treaty of Lisbon shall be preserved until those acts are repealed, annulled or amended in implementation of the Treaties. The same shall apply to agreements concluded between Member States on the basis of the Treaty on European Union.

ARTICLE 10

1. As a transitional measure, and with respect to acts of the Union in the field of police co-operation and judicial co-operation in criminal matters which have been adopted before the entry into force of the Treaty of Lisbon, the powers of the institutions shall be the following at the date of entry into force of that Treaty: the powers of the Commission under Article 258 of the Treaty on the Functioning of the European Union shall not be applicable and the powers of the Court of Justice of the European Union under Title VI of the Treaty on European Union, in the version in force before the entry into force of the Treaty of Lisbon, shall remain the same, including where they have been accepted under Article 35(2) of the said Treaty on European Union.

2. The amendment of an act referred to in paragraph 1 shall entail the applicability of the powers of the institutions referred to in that paragraph as set out in the Treaties with respect to the amended act for those Member States to which that amended act shall apply.

3. In any case, the transitional measure mentioned in paragraph 1 shall cease to have effect five years after the date of entry into force of the Treaty of Lisbon.

4. At the latest six months before the expiry of the transitional period referred to in paragraph 3, the United Kingdom may notify to the Council that it does not accept, with respect to the acts referred to in paragraph 1, the powers of the institutions referred to in paragraph 1 as set out in the Treaties. In case the United Kingdom has made that notification, all acts referred to in paragraph 1 shall cease to apply to it as from the date of expiry of the transitional period referred to in paragraph 3. This subparagraph shall not apply with respect to the amended acts which are applicable to the United Kingdom as referred to in paragraph 2.
The Council, acting by a qualified majority on a proposal from the Commission, shall determine the necessary consequential and transitional arrangements. The United Kingdom shall not participate in the adoption of this decision. A qualified majority of the Council shall be defined in accordance with Article 238(3)(a) of the Treaty on the Functioning of the European Union.
The Council, acting by a qualified majority on a proposal from the Commission, may also adopt a decision determining that the United Kingdom shall bear the direct financial consequences, if any, necessarily and unavoidably incurred as a result of the cessation of its participation in those acts.

5. The United Kingdom may, at any time afterwards, notify the Council of its wish to participate in acts which have ceased to apply to it pursuant to paragraph 4, first subparagraph. In that case, the relevant provisions of the Protocol on the Schengen acquis integrated into the framework of the European Union or of the Protocol on the position of the United Kingdom and Ireland in respect of the area of freedom, security and justice, as the case may be, shall apply. The powers of the institutions with regard to those acts shall be those set out in the Treaties. When acting under the relevant Protocols, the Union institutions and the United Kingdom shall seek to re-establish the widest possible measure of participation of the United Kingdom in the acquis of the Union in the area of freedom, security and justice without seriously affecting the practical operability of the various parts thereof, while respecting their coherence.
[BMDF Note: Article 10 was added in the revision of the draft Reform Treaty dated 5 October 2007]
[BMDF Note: This Protocol is taken from the draft Constitutional Treaty]
[BMDF Note: See also Declaration no. 50]

BMDF Note: The following protocols are brought forward from the previous treaties and amended by Protocol no. 1 attached to the Treaty of Lisbon, the 'Protocol amending the protocols annexed to the Treaty on European Union, to the Treaty establishing the European Community and/or to the Treaty establishing the European Atomic Energy Community'. The order of these protocols has been taken from the order in that Protocol.

12. PROTOCOL ON THE STATUTE OF THE COURT OF JUSTICE *OF THE EUROPEAN UNION*

THE HIGH CONTRACTING PARTIES

DESIRING to lay down the Statute of the Court of Justice **of the European Union** provided for in Article ***281*** of ***the Treaty on the Functioning of the European Union*** and in Article 160 of the Treaty establishing the European Atomic Energy Community,

HAVE AGREED upon the following provisions, which shall be annexed to the Treaty on European Union, the Treaty ***on the Functioning of the European Union*** and the Treaty establishing the European Atomic Energy Community:

ARTICLE 1

The Court of Justice **of the European Union** shall be constituted and shall function in accordance with the provisions of ***the Treaties***, of the Treaty establishing the European Atomic Energy Community (EAEC Treaty) and of this Statute.

TITLE I

JUDGES AND ADVOCATES-GENERAL

ARTICLE 2

Before taking up his duties each Judge shall, **before the Court of Justice sitting** in open court, take an oath to perform his duties impartially and conscientiously and to preserve the secrecy of the deliberations of the Court.

ARTICLE 3

The Judges shall be immune from legal proceedings. After they have ceased to hold office, they shall continue to enjoy immunity in respect of acts performed by them in their official capacity, including words spoken or written.

The Court **of Justice**, sitting as a full Court, may waive the immunity. **If the decision concerns a member of the General Court or of a specialised court, the Court shall decide after consulting the court concerned.**

Where immunity has been waived and criminal proceedings are instituted against a Judge, he shall be tried, in any of the Member States, only by the court competent to judge the members of the highest national judiciary.

Articles 12 to 15 and Article 18 of the Protocol on the privileges and immunities of the European **Union** shall apply to the Judges, Advocates-General, Registrar and Assistant Rapporteurs of the Court **of Justice of the European Union**, without prejudice to the provisions relating to immunity from legal proceedings of Judges which are set out in the preceding paragraphs.

ARTICLE 4

The Judges may not hold any political or administrative office.

They may not engage in any occupation, whether gainful or not, unless exemption is exceptionally granted by the Council **acting by a simple majority**.

When taking up their duties, they shall give a solemn undertaking that, both during and after their term of office, they will respect the obligations arising therefrom, in particular the duty to behave with integrity and discretion as regards the acceptance, after they have ceased to hold office, of certain appointments or benefits.

Any doubt on this point shall be settled by decision of the Court **of Justice**. **If the decision concerns a member of the General Court or of a specialised court, the Court shall decide after consulting the court concerned.**

ARTICLE 5
Apart from normal replacement, or death, the duties of a Judge shall end when he resigns.
Where a Judge resigns, his letter of resignation shall be addressed to the President of the Court **of Justice** for transmission to the President of the Council. Upon this notification a vacancy shall arise on the bench.
Save where Article 6 applies, a Judge shall continue to hold office until his successor takes up his duties.

ARTICLE 6
A Judge may be deprived of his office or of his right to a pension or other benefits in its stead only if, in the unanimous opinion of the Judges and Advocates-General of the Court **of Justice**, he no longer fulfils the requisite conditions or meets the obligations arising from his office. The Judge concerned shall not take part in any such deliberations. **If the person concerned is a member of the General Court or of a specialised court, the Court shall decide after consulting the court concerned.**
The Registrar of the Court shall communicate the decision of the Court to the President of the European Parliament and to the President of the Commission and shall notify it to the President of the Council.
In the case of a decision depriving a Judge of his office, a vacancy shall arise on the bench upon this latter notification.

ARTICLE 7
A Judge who is to replace a member of the Court whose term of office has not expired shall be appointed for the remainder of his predecessor's term.

ARTICLE 8
The provisions of Articles 2 to 7 shall apply to the Advocates-General.

TITLE II

ORGANISATION **OF THE COURT OF JUSTICE**

ARTICLE 9
When, every three years, the Judges are partially replaced, fourteen and thirteen Judges shall be replaced alternately.
When, every three years, the Advocates-General are partially replaced, four Advocates-General shall be replaced on each occasion.
[BMDF Note: Article, paragraph 1, amended by the Act of Accession of Bulgaria and Romania, from thirteen and twelve Judges to fourteen and thirteen Judges.]

ARTICLE 10
The Registrar shall take an oath before the Court **of Justice** to perform his duties impartially and conscientiously and to preserve the secrecy of the deliberations of the Court **of Justice**.

ARTICLE 11
The Court **of Justice** shall arrange for replacement of the Registrar on occasions when he is prevented from attending the Court **of Justice**.

ARTICLE 12
Officials and other servants shall be attached to the Court **of Justice** to enable it to function. They shall be responsible to the Registrar under the authority of the President.

ARTICLE 13
At the request of the Court, **the European Parliament and** the Council may, acting **in accordance with the ordinary legislative procedure**, provide for the appointment of Assistant Rapporteurs and lay down the rules governing their service. The Assistant Rapporteurs may be required, under conditions laid down in the Rules of Procedure, to participate in preparatory inquiries in cases pending before the Court **of Justice** and to co-operate with the Judge who acts as Rapporteur.

The Assistant Rapporteurs shall be chosen from persons whose independence is beyond doubt and who possess the necessary legal qualifications; they shall be appointed by the Council **acting by a simple majority**. They shall take an oath before the Court **of Justice** to perform their duties impartially and conscientiously and to preserve the secrecy of the deliberations of the Court **of Justice**.

ARTICLE 14
The Judges, the Advocates-General and the Registrar shall be required to reside at the place where the Court **of Justice** has its seat.

ARTICLE 15
The Court **of Justice** shall remain permanently in session. The duration of the judicial vacations shall be determined by the Court **of Justice** with due regard to the needs of its business.

ARTICLE 16
The Court **of Justice** shall form chambers consisting of three and five Judges. The Judges shall elect the Presidents of the chambers from among their number. The Presidents of the chambers of five Judges shall be elected for three years. They may be re-elected once.
The Grand Chamber shall consist of eleven Judges. It shall be presided over by the President of the Court. The Presidents of the chambers of five Judges and other Judges appointed in accordance with the conditions laid down in the Rules of Procedure shall also form part of the Grand Chamber.
The Court shall sit in a Grand Chamber when a Member State or an institution of the **Union** that is party to the proceedings so requests.
The Court shall sit as a full Court where cases are brought before it pursuant to Article ***228(2),*** Article ***245(2),*** Article ***247*** or Article ***286(7)*** of the ***Treaty on the Functioning of the European Union***.
Moreover, where it considers that a case before it is of exceptional importance, the Court may decide, after hearing the Advocate-General, to refer the case to the full Court.

ARTICLE 17
Decisions of the Court **of Justice** shall be valid only when an uneven number of its members is sitting in the deliberations.
Decisions of the chambers consisting of either three or five Judges shall be valid only if they are taken by three Judges.
Decisions of the Grand Chamber shall be valid only if nine Judges are sitting.
Decisions of the full Court shall be valid only if eleven Judges are sitting.
In the event of one of the Judges of a chamber being prevented from attending, a Judge of another chamber may be called upon to sit in accordance with conditions laid down in the Rules of Procedure.

ARTICLE 18
No Judge or Advocate-General may take part in the disposal of any case in which he has previously taken part as agent or adviser or has acted for one of the parties, or in which he has been called upon to pronounce as a member of a court or tribunal, of a commission of inquiry or in any other capacity.
If, for some special reason, any Judge or Advocate-General considers that he should not take part in the judgment or examination of a particular case, he shall so inform the President. If, for some special reason, the President considers that any Judge or Advocate-General should not sit or make submissions in a particular case, he shall notify him accordingly.
Any difficulty arising as to the application of this Article shall be settled by decision of the Court **of Justice**.
A party may not apply for a change in the composition of the Court or of one of its chambers on the grounds of either the nationality of a Judge or the absence from the Court or from the chamber of a Judge of the nationality of that party.

TITLE III

PROCEDURE **BEFORE THE COURT OF JUSTICE**

ARTICLE 19
The Member States and the institutions of the **Union** shall be represented before the Court **of Justice** by an agent appointed for each case; the agent may be assisted by an adviser or by a lawyer.

The States, other than the Member States, which are parties to the Agreement on the European Economic Area and also the EFTA Surveillance Authority referred to in that Agreement shall be represented in same manner.
Other parties must be represented by a lawyer.
Only a lawyer authorised to practise before a court of a Member State or of another State which is a party to the Agreement on the European Economic Area may represent or assist a party before the Court.
Such agents, advisers and lawyers shall, when they appear before the Court, enjoy the rights and immunities necessary to the independent exercise of their duties, under conditions laid down in the Rules of Procedure.
As regards such advisers and lawyers who appear before it, the Court shall have the powers normally accorded to courts of law, under conditions laid down in the Rules of Procedure.
University teachers being nationals of a Member State whose law accords them a right of audience shall have the same rights before the Court as are accorded by this Article to lawyers.

ARTICLE 20
The procedure before the Court **of Justice** shall consist of two parts: written and oral.
The written procedure shall consist of the communication to the parties and to the institutions of the **Union** whose decisions are in dispute, of applications, statements of case, defences and observations, and of replies, if any, as well as of all papers and documents in support or of certified copies of them.
Communications shall be made by the Registrar in the order and within the time laid down in the Rules of Procedure.
The oral procedure shall consist of the reading of the report presented by a Judge acting as Rapporteur, the hearing by the Court of agents, advisers and lawyers and of the submissions of the Advocate-General, as well as the hearing, if any, of witnesses and experts.
Where it considers that the case raises no new point of law, the Court may decide, after hearing the Advocate-General, that the case shall be determined without a submission from the Advocate-General.

ARTICLE 21
A case shall be brought before the Court **of Justice** by a written application addressed to the Registrar.
The application shall contain the applicant's name and permanent address and the description of the signatory, the name of the party or names of the parties against whom the application is made, the subject-matter of the dispute, the form of order sought and a brief statement of the pleas in law on which the application is based.
The application shall be accompanied, where appropriate, by the measure the annulment of which is sought or, in the circumstances referred to in Article ***265*** of the ***Treaty on the Functioning of the European Union***, by documentary evidence of the date on which an institution was, in accordance with those Articles, requested to act. If the documents are not submitted with the application, the Registrar shall ask the party concerned to produce them within a reasonable period, but in that event the rights of the party shall not lapse even if such documents are produced after the time-limit for bringing proceedings.

ARTICLE 22
A case governed by Article 18 of the EAEC Treaty shall be brought before the Court **of Justice** by an appeal addressed to the Registrar. The appeal shall contain the name and permanent address of the applicant and the description of the signatory, a reference to the decision against which the appeal is brought, the names of the respondents, the subject-matter of the dispute, the submissions and a brief statement of the grounds on which the appeal is based.
The appeal shall be accompanied by a certified copy of the decision of the Arbitration Committee which is contested.
If the Court rejects the appeal, the decision of the Arbitration Committee shall become final.
If the Court annuls the decision of the Arbitration Committee, the matter may be re-opened, where appropriate, on the initiative of one of the parties in the case, before the Arbitration Committee. The latter shall conform to any decisions on points of law given by the Court.

ARTICLE 23
In the cases governed, by Article ***267*** of the ***Treaty*** **on the Functioning of the European Union**, the decision of the court or tribunal of a Member State which suspends its proceedings and refers a case to the Court **of Justice** shall be notified to the Court **of Justice** by the court or tribunal concerned. The decision shall then be notified by the Registrar of the Court **of Justice** to the parties, to the Member

States and to the Commission, and **to the institution, body, office or agency which adopted the act the validity or interpretation of which is in dispute**.
Within two months of this notification, the parties, the Member States, the Commission and, where appropriate, **the institution, body, office or agency which adopted the act the validity or interpretation of which is in dispute**, shall be entitled to submit statements of case or written observations to the Court.
In the cases governed by Article ***267*** of the ***Treaty on the Functioning of the European Union***, the decision of the national court or tribunal shall, moreover, be notified by the Registrar of the Court to the States, other than the Member States, which are parties to the Agreement on the European Economic Area and also to the EFTA Surveillance Authority referred to in that Agreement which may, within two months of notification, where one of the fields of application of that Agreement is concerned, submit statements of case or written observations to the Court.

ARTICLE 24
The Court **of Justice** may require the parties to produce all documents and to supply all information which the Court considers desirable. Formal note shall be taken of any refusal.
The Court may also require the Member States and institutions**, bodies, offices and agencies** not being parties to the case to supply all information which the Court considers necessary for the proceedings.

ARTICLE 25
The Court **of Justice** may at any time entrust any individual, body, authority, committee or other organisation it chooses with the task of giving an expert opinion.

ARTICLE 26
Witnesses may be heard under conditions laid down in the Rules of Procedure.

ARTICLE 27
With respect to defaulting witnesses the Court **of Justice** shall have the powers generally granted to courts and tribunals and may impose pecuniary penalties under conditions laid down in the Rules of Procedure.

ARTICLE 28
Witnesses and experts may be heard on oath taken in the form laid down in the Rules of Procedure or in the manner laid down by the law of the country of the witness or expert.

ARTICLE 29
The Court **of Justice** may order that a witness or expert be heard by the judicial authority of his place of permanent residence.
The order shall be sent for implementation to the competent judicial authority under conditions laid down in the Rules of Procedure. The documents drawn up in compliance with the letters rogatory shall be returned to the Court under the same conditions.
The Court shall defray the expenses, without prejudice to the right to charge them, where appropriate, to the parties.

ARTICLE 30
A Member State shall treat any violation of an oath by a witness or expert in the same manner as if the offence had been committed before one of its courts with jurisdiction in civil proceedings. At the instance of the Court **of Justice**, the Member State concerned shall prosecute the offender before its competent court.

ARTICLE 31
The hearing in court shall be public, unless the Court **of Justice**, of its own motion or on application by the parties, decides otherwise for serious reasons.

ARTICLE 32
During the hearings the Court **of Justice** may examine the experts, the witnesses and the parties themselves. The latter, however, may address the Court **of Justice** only through their representatives.

ARTICLE 33
Minutes shall be made of each hearing and signed by the President and the Registrar.

ARTICLE 34
The case list shall be established by the President.

ARTICLE 35
The deliberations of the Court **of Justice** shall be and shall remain secret.

ARTICLE 36
Judgments shall state the reasons on which they are based. They shall contain the names of the Judges who took part in the deliberations.

ARTICLE 37
Judgments shall be signed by the President and the Registrar. They shall be read in open court.

ARTICLE 38
The Court **of Justice** shall adjudicate upon costs.

ARTICLE 39
The President of the Court **of Justice** may, by way of summary procedure, which may, in so far as necessary, differ from some of the rules contained in this Statute and which shall be laid down in the Rules of Procedure, adjudicate upon applications to suspend execution, as provided for in Article ***278*** of the ***Treaty on the Functioning of the European Union*** and Article 157 of the EAEC Treaty, or to prescribe interim measures in pursuance of Article ***279*** of the ***Treaty on the Functioning of the European Union***, or to suspend enforcement in accordance with the fourth paragraph of Article ***299*** of the ***Treaty on the Functioning of the European Union*** or the third paragraph of Article 164 of the EAEC Treaty.
Should the President be prevented from attending, his place shall be taken by another Judge under conditions laid down in the Rules of Procedure.
The ruling of the President or of the Judge replacing him shall be provisional and shall in no way prejudice the decision of the Court **of Justice** on the substance of the case.

ARTICLE 40
Member States and institutions of the **Union** may intervene in cases before the Court **of Justice**.
The same right shall be open **to the bodies, offices and agencies of the Union and** to any other person **which can establish** an interest in the result of **a** case submitted to the Court **of Justice. Natural or legal persons shall not intervene** in cases between Member States, between institutions of the **Union** or between Member States and institutions of the **Union**.
Without prejudice to the second paragraph, the States, other than the Member States, which are parties to the Agreement on the European Economic Area, and also the EFTA Surveillance Authority referred to in that Agreement, may intervene in cases before the Court **of Justice** where one of the fields of application that Agreement is concerned.
An application to intervene shall be limited to supporting the form of order sought by one of the parties.

ARTICLE 41
Where the defending party, after having been duly summoned, fails to file written submissions in defence, judgment shall be given against that party by default. An objection may be lodged against the judgment within one month of it being notified. The objection shall not have the effect of staying enforcement of the judgment by default unless the Court **of Justice** decides otherwise.

ARTICLE 42
Member States, institutions**, bodies, offices and agencies** of the **Union** and any other natural or legal persons may, in cases and under conditions to be determined by the Rules of Procedure, institute third-party proceedings to contest a judgment rendered without their being heard, where the judgment is prejudicial to their rights.

ARTICLE 43
If the meaning or scope of a judgment is in doubt, the Court **of Justice** shall construe it on application by any party or any institution of the **Union** establishing an interest therein.

ARTICLE 44
An application for revision of a judgment may be made to the Court **of Justice** only on discovery of a fact which is of such a nature as to be a decisive factor, and which, when the judgment was given, was unknown to the Court **of Justice** and to the party claiming the revision.
The revision shall be opened by a judgment of the Court expressly recording the existence of a new fact, recognising that it is of such a character as to lay the case open to revision and declaring the application admissible on this ground.
No application for revision may be made after the lapse of 10 years from the date of the judgment.

ARTICLE 45
Periods of grace based on considerations of distance shall be determined by the Rules of Procedure.
No right shall be prejudiced in consequence of the expiry of a time-limit if the party concerned proves the existence of unforeseeable circumstances or of *force majeure*.

ARTICLE 46
Proceedings against the **Union** in matters arising from non-contractual liability shall be barred after a period of five years from the occurrence of the event giving rise thereto. The period of limitation shall be interrupted if proceedings are instituted before the Court **of Justice** or if prior to such proceedings an application is made by the aggrieved party to the relevant institution of the **Union**. In the latter event the proceedings must be instituted within the period of two months provided for in Article ***263*** of the ***Treaty on the Functioning of the European Union***; the provisions of the second paragraph of Article ***265*** of the ***Treaty on the Functioning of the European Union***, shall apply where appropriate.
This Article shall also apply to proceedings against the European Central Bank regarding non-contractual liability.

TITLE IV

GENERAL COURT

ARTICLE 47
The first paragraph of Article 9, Articles 14 and 15, the first, second, fourth and fifth paragraphs of Article 17 and Article 18 shall apply to the **General Court** and its members.
The fourth paragraph of Article 3 and Articles 10, 11 and 14 shall apply to the Registrar of the **General Court** *mutatis mutandis.*

ARTICLE 48
The **General Court** shall consist of **twenty-seven** Judges.
[BMDF Note: Article amended by the Act of Accession of Bulgaria and Romania, from twenty-five judges.]

ARTICLE 49
The members of the **General Court** may be called upon to perform the task of an Advocate-General.
It shall be the duty of the Advocate-General, acting with complete impartiality and independence, to make, in open court, reasoned submissions on certain cases brought before the **General Court** in order to assist the **General Court** in the performance of its task.
The criteria for selecting such cases, as well as the procedures for designating the Advocates-General, shall be laid down in the Rules of Procedure of the **General Court**.
A member called upon to perform the task of Advocate-General in a case may not take part in the judgment of the case.

ARTICLE 50
The **General Court** shall sit in chambers of three or five Judges. The Judges shall elect the Presidents of the chambers from among their number. The Presidents of the chambers of five Judges shall be elected for three years. They may be re-elected once.
The composition of the chambers and the assignment of cases to them shall be governed by the Rules of Procedure. In certain cases governed by the Rules of Procedure, the **General Court** may sit as a full court or be constituted by a single Judge.
The Rules of Procedure may also provide that the **General Court** may sit in a Grand Chamber in cases and under the conditions specified therein.

ARTICLE 51
By way of derogation from the rule laid down in Article ***256(1)*** of the ***Treaty on the Functioning of the European Union***, jurisdiction shall be reserved to the Court of Justice in the actions referred to in Articles ***263*** and ***265*** of the ***Treaty on the Functioning of the European Union*** when they are brought by a Member State:

(a) against an act of or failure to act by the European Parliament or the Council, or by those institutions acting jointly, except for:
   - decisions taken by the Council under the third subparagraph of Article ***108(2)*** of the ***Treaty on the Functioning of the European Union***;
   - acts of the Council adopted pursuant to a Council regulation concerning measures to protect trade within the meaning of Article ***207*** of the ***Treaty on the Functioning of the European Union***;
   - acts of the Council by which it exercises implementing powers in accordance with the ***second paragraph of Article 288 of the Treaty on the Functioning of the European Union***;

(b) against an act of or failure to act by the Commission under ***the first paragraph of Article 333 of the Treaty on the Functioning of the European Union***.

Jurisdiction shall also be reserved to the Court of Justice in the actions referred to in the same articles when they are brought by an institution of the **Union** against an act of or failure to act by the European Parliament, the Council, both those institutions acting jointly, the Commission, or brought by an institution of the **Union** against an act of or failure to act by the European Central Bank.

ARTICLE 52
The President of the Court of Justice and the President of the **General Court** shall determine, by common accord, the conditions under which officials and other servants attached to the Court of Justice shall render their services to the **General Court** to enable it to function. Certain officials or other servants shall be responsible to the Registrar of the **General Court** under the authority of the President of the **General Court**.

ARTICLE 53
The procedure before the **General Court** shall be governed by Title III.
Such further and more detailed provisions as may be necessary shall be laid down in its Rules of Procedure. The Rules of Procedure may derogate from the fourth paragraph of Article 40 and from Article 41 in order to take account of the specific features of litigation in the field of intellectual property.
Notwithstanding the fourth paragraph of Article 20, the Advocate-General may make his reasoned submissions in writing.

ARTICLE 54
Where an application or other procedural document addressed to the **General Court** is lodged by mistake with the Registrar of the Court of Justice, it shall be transmitted immediately by that Registrar to the Registrar of the **General Court**; likewise, where an application or other procedural document addressed to the Court of Justice is lodged by mistake with the Registrar of the **General Court**, it shall be transmitted immediately by that Registrar to the Registrar of the Court of Justice.
Where the **General Court** finds that it does not have jurisdiction to hear and determine an action in respect of which the Court of Justice has jurisdiction, it shall refer that action to the Court of Justice; likewise, where the Court of Justice finds that an action falls within the jurisdiction of the **General Court**, it shall refer that action to the **General Court**, whereupon that Court may not decline jurisdiction.
Where the Court of Justice and the **General Court** are seised of cases in which the same relief is sought, the same issue of interpretation is raised or the validity of the same act is called in question, the **General Court** may, after hearing the parties, stay the proceedings before it until such time as the Court of Justice shall have delivered judgment. Where applications are made for the same act to be declared void, the **General Court** may also decline jurisdiction in order that the Court of Justice may rule on such applications. In the cases referred to in this paragraph, the Court of Justice may also decide to stay the proceedings before it; in that event, the proceedings before the **General Court** shall continue.

ARTICLE 55
Final decisions of the **General Court**, decisions disposing of the substantive issues in part only or disposing of a procedural issue concerning a plea of lack of competence or inadmissibility, shall be

notified by the Registrar of the **General Court** to all parties as well as all Member States and the institutions of the **Union** even if they did not intervene in the case before the **General Court**.

ARTICLE 56
An appeal may be brought before the Court of Justice, within two months of the notification of the decision appealed against, against final decisions of the **General Court** and decisions of that Court disposing of the substantive issues in part only or disposing of a procedural issue concerning a plea of lack of competence or inadmissibility.
Such an appeal may be brought by any party which has been unsuccessful, in whole or in part, in its submissions. However, interveners other than the Member States and the institutions of the **Union** may bring such an appeal only where the decision of the **General Court** directly affects them.
With the exception of cases relating to disputes between the **Union** and **its** servants, an appeal may also be brought by Member States and institutions of the **Union** which did not intervene in the proceedings before the **General Court**. Such Member States and institutions shall be in the same position as Member States or institutions which intervened at first instance.

ARTICLE 57
Any person whose application to intervene has been dismissed by the **General Court** may appeal to the Court of Justice within two weeks from the notification of the decision dismissing the application.
The parties to the proceedings may appeal to the Court of Justice against any decision of the **General Court** made pursuant to Article ***278*** or Article ***279*** or the fourth paragraph of Article ***299*** of the ***Treaty on the Functioning of the European Union*** or Article 157 or the third paragraph of Article 164 of the EAEC Treaty within two months from their notification.
The appeal referred to in the first two paragraphs of this Article shall be heard and determined under the procedure referred to in Article 39.

ARTICLE 58
An appeal to the Court of Justice shall be limited to points of law. It shall lie on the grounds of lack of competence of the **General Court**, a breach of procedure before it which adversely affects the interests of the appellant as well as the infringement of Community law by the **General Court**.
No appeal shall lie regarding only the amount of the costs or the party ordered to pay them.

ARTICLE 59
Where an appeal is brought against a decision of the **General Court**, the procedure before the Court of Justice shall consist of a written part and an oral part. In accordance with conditions laid down in the Rules of Procedure, the Court of Justice, having heard the Advocate-General and the parties, may dispense with the oral procedure.

ARTICLE 60
Without prejudice to Articles ***278*** and ***279*** of the ***Treaty on the Functioning of the European Union*** or **Article 157** of the EAEC Treaty, an appeal shall not have suspensory effect.
By way of derogation from Article ***280*** of the ***Treaty on the Functioning of the European Union***, decisions of the **General Court** declaring a regulation to be void shall take effect only as from the date of expiry of the period referred to in the first paragraph of Article 56 of this Statute or, if an appeal shall have been brought within that period, as from the date of dismissal of the appeal, without prejudice, however, to the right of a party to apply to the Court of Justice, pursuant to Articles ***278*** and ***279*** of the ***Treaty on the Functioning of the European Union*** or **Article 157** of the EAEC Treaty, for the suspension of the effects of the regulation which has been declared void or for the prescription of any other interim measure.

ARTICLE 61
If the appeal is well founded, the Court of Justice shall quash the decision of the **General Court**. It may itself give final judgment in the matter, where the state of the proceedings so permits, or refer the case back to the **General Court** for judgment.
Where a case is referred back to the **General Court**, that Court shall be bound by the decision of the Court of Justice on points of law.
When an appeal brought by a Member State or an institution of the **Union**, which did not intervene in the proceedings before the **General Court**, is well founded, the Court of Justice may, if it considers this necessary, state which of the effects of the decision of the **General Court** which has been quashed shall be considered as definitive in respect of the parties to the litigation.

ARTICLE 62
In the cases provided for in Article ***256***(2) and (3) of the ***Treaty on the Functioning of the European Union***, where the First Advocate-General considers that there is a serious risk of the unity or consistency of **Union** law being affected, he may propose that the Court of Justice review the decision of the **General Court**.
The proposal must be made within one month of delivery of the decision by the **General Court**. Within one month of receiving the proposal made by the First Advocate-General, the Court of Justice shall decide whether or not the decision should be reviewed.

ARTICLE 62 a
The Court of Justice shall give a ruling on the questions which are subject to review by means of an urgent procedure on the basis of the file forwarded to it by the **General Court**.
Those referred to in Article 23 of this Statute and, in the cases provided for in Article ***256***(2) of the ***Treaty on the Functioning of the European Union***, the parties to the proceedings before the **General Court** shall be entitled to lodge statements or written observations with the Court of Justice relating to questions which are subject to review within a period prescribed for that purpose.
The Court of Justice may decide to open the oral procedure before giving a ruling.

ARTICLE 62 b
In the cases provided for in Article ***256***(2) of the ***Treaty on the Functioning of the European Union***, without prejudice to Articles ***278*** and ***279*** of the ***Treaty on the Functioning of the European Union***, proposals for review and decisions to open the review procedure shall not have suspensory effect. If the Court of Justice finds that the decision of the **General Court** affects the unity or consistency of **Union** law, it shall refer the case back to the **General Court** which shall be bound by the points of law decided by the Court of Justice; the Court of Justice may state which of the effects of the decision of the **General Court** are to be considered as definitive in respect of the parties to the litigation. If, however, having regard to the result of the review, the outcome of the proceedings flows from the findings of fact on which the decision of the **General Court** was based, the Court of Justice shall give final judgment.
In the cases provided for in Article ***256***(3) of the ***Treaty on the Functioning of the European Union***, in the absence of proposals for review or decisions to open the review procedure, the answer(s) given by the **General Court** to the questions submitted to it shall take effect upon expiry of the periods prescribed for that purpose in the second paragraph of Article 62. Should a review procedure be opened, the answer(s) subject to review shall take effect following that procedure, unless the Court of Justice decides otherwise. If the Court of Justice finds that the decision of the **General Court** affects the unity or consistency of **Union** law, the answer given by the Court of Justice to the questions subject to review shall be substituted for that given by the **General Court**.

TITLE IVa

SPECIALISED COURTS

ARTICLE 62 c
The provisions relating to the jurisdiction, composition, organisation and procedure of the **specialised courts** established under Article ***257*** of the ***Treaty on the Functioning of the European Union*** are set out in an Annex to this Statute.

TITLE V

FINAL PROVISIONS

ARTICLE 63
The Rules of Procedure of the Court of Justice and of the **General Court** shall contain any provisions necessary for applying and, where required, supplementing this Statute.

ARTICLE 64
The rules governing the language arrangements applicable at the Court of Justice of the European Union shall be laid down by a regulation of the Council acting unanimously. This regulation shall be adopted either at the request of the Court of Justice and after consultation of the Commission and the European Parliament, or on a proposal from the Commission and after consultation of the Court of Justice and of the European Parliament.

Until those rules have been adopted, the provisions of the Rules of Procedure of the Court of Justice and of the Rules of Procedure of the **General Court** governing language arrangements shall continue to apply. **By way of derogation from *Articles 253 and 254 of the Treaty on the Functioning of the European Union*,** those provisions may only be amended or repealed **with the unanimous consent of the Council**.

ANNEX I

THE EUROPEAN UNION CIVIL SERVICE TRIBUNAL

ARTICLE 1
The European Union Civil Service Tribunal (hereafter the Civil Service Tribunal) shall exercise at first instance jurisdiction in disputes between the **Union** and their servants referred to in Article ***270*** of the ***Treaty on the Functioning of the European Union***, including disputes between all bodies or agencies and their servants in respect of which jurisdiction is conferred on the Court of Justice **of the European Union**.

ARTICLE 2
The Civil Service Tribunal shall consist of seven judges. Should the Court of Justice so request, the Council, acting by a qualified majority, may increase the number of judges.
The judges shall be appointed for a period of six years. Retiring judges may be reappointed.
Any vacancy shall be filled by the appointment of a new judge for a period of six years.

ARTICLE 3
1. The judges shall be appointed by the Council, acting in accordance with the fourth paragraph of Article ***257*** of the ***Treaty on the Functioning of the European Union***, after consulting the committee provided for by this Article. When appointing judges, the Council shall ensure a balanced composition of the **Civil Service** Tribunal on as broad a geographical basis as possible from among nationals of the Member States and with respect to the national legal systems represented.

2. Any person who is a Union citizen and fulfils the conditions laid down in the fourth paragraph of Article ***257*** of the ***Treaty on the Functioning of the European Union*** may submit an application. The Council, acting on a recommendation from the Court **of Justice**, shall determine the conditions and the arrangements governing the submission and processing of such applications.

3. A committee shall be set up comprising seven persons chosen from among former members of the Court of Justice and the **General Court** and lawyers of recognised competence. The committee's membership and operating rules shall be determined by the Council, acting on a recommendation by the President of the Court of Justice.

4. The committee shall give an opinion on candidates' suitability to perform the duties of judge at the Civil Service Tribunal. The committee shall append to its opinion a list of candidates having the most suitable high-level experience. Such list shall contain the names of at least twice as many candidates as there are judges to be appointed by the Council.

ARTICLE 4
1. The judges shall elect the President of the Civil Service Tribunal from among their number for a term of three years. He may be re-elected.

2. The Civil Service Tribunal shall sit in chambers of three judges. It may, in certain cases determined by its rules of procedure, sit in full court or in a chamber of five judges or of a single judge.

3. The President of the Civil Service Tribunal shall preside over the full court and the chamber of five judges. The Presidents of the chambers of three judges shall be designated as provided in paragraph 1. If the President of the Civil Service Tribunal is assigned to a chamber of three judges, he shall preside over that chamber.

4. The jurisdiction of and quorum for the full court as well as the composition of the chambers and the assignment of cases to them shall be governed by the rules of procedure.

ARTICLE 5
Articles 2 to 6, 14, 15, the first, second and fifth paragraphs of Article 17, and Article 18 of the Statute of the Court of Justice **of the European Union** shall apply to the Civil Service Tribunal and its members.
The oath referred to in Article 2 of the Statute shall be taken before the Court of Justice, and the decisions referred to in Articles 3, 4 and 6 thereof shall be adopted by the Court of Justice after consulting the Civil Service Tribunal.

ARTICLE 6
1. The Civil Service Tribunal shall be supported by the departments of the Court of Justice and of the **General Court**. The President of the Court of Justice or, in appropriate cases, the President of the **General Court**, shall determine by common accord with the President of the Civil Service Tribunal the conditions under which officials and other servants attached to the Court of Justice or the **General Court** shall render their services to the Civil Service Tribunal to enable it to function. Certain officials or other servants shall be responsible to the Registrar of the Civil Service Tribunal under the authority of the President of that Tribunal.

2. The Civil Service Tribunal shall appoint its Registrar and lay down the rules governing his service. The fourth paragraph of Article 3 and Articles 10, 11 and 14 of the Statute of the Court of Justice **of the European Union** shall apply to the Registrar of the Tribunal.

ARTICLE 7
1. The procedure before the Civil Service Tribunal shall be governed by Title III of the Statute of the Court of Justice **of the European Union**, with the exception of Articles 22 and 23. Such further and more detailed provisions as may be necessary shall be laid down in the rules of procedure.

2. The provisions concerning the **General Court's** language arrangements shall apply to the Civil Service Tribunal.

3. The written stage of the procedure shall comprise the presentation of the application and of the statement of defence, unless the Civil Service Tribunal decides that a second exchange of written pleadings is necessary. Where there is such second exchange, the Civil Service Tribunal may, with the agreement of the parties, decide to proceed to judgment without an oral procedure.

4. At all stages of the procedure, including the time when the application is filed, the Civil Service Tribunal may examine the possibilities of an amicable settlement of the dispute and may try to facilitate such settlement.

5. The Civil Service Tribunal shall rule on the costs of a case. Subject to the specific provisions of the Rules of Procedure, the unsuccessful party shall be ordered to pay the costs should the court so decide.

ARTICLE 8
1. Where an application or other procedural document addressed to the Civil Service Tribunal is lodged by mistake with the Registrar of the Court of Justice or **General Court**, it shall be transmitted immediately by that Registrar to the Registrar of the Civil Service Tribunal. Likewise, where an application or other procedural document addressed to the Court of Justice or to the **General Court** is lodged by mistake with the Registrar of the Civil Service Tribunal, it shall be transmitted immediately by that Registrar to the Registrar of the Court of Justice or **General Court**.

2. Where the Civil Service Tribunal finds that it does not have jurisdiction to hear and determine an action in respect of which the Court of Justice or the **General Court** has jurisdiction, it shall refer that action to the Court of Justice or to the **General Court**. Likewise, where the Court of Justice or the **General Court** finds that an action falls within the jurisdiction of the Civil Service Tribunal, the Court seised shall refer that action to the Civil Service Tribunal, whereupon that Tribunal may not decline jurisdiction.

3. Where the Civil Service Tribunal and the **General Court** are seised of cases in which the same issue of interpretation is raised or the validity of the same act is called in question, the Civil Service Tribunal, after hearing the parties, may stay the proceedings until the judgment of the **General Court** has been delivered.
Where the Civil Service Tribunal and the **General Court** are seised of cases in which the same relief is sought, the Civil Service Tribunal shall decline jurisdiction so that the **General Court** may act on those cases.

ARTICLE 9
An appeal may be brought before the **General Court**, within two months of notification of the decision appealed against, against final decisions of the Civil Service Tribunal and decisions of that Tribunal disposing of the substantive issues in part only or disposing of a procedural issue concerning a plea of lack of jurisdiction or inadmissibility.
Such an appeal may be brought by any party which has been unsuccessful, in whole or in part, in its submissions. However, interveners other than the Member States and the institutions of the **Union** may bring such an appeal only where the decision of the Civil Service Tribunal directly affects them.

ARTICLE 10
1. Any person whose application to intervene has been dismissed by the Civil Service Tribunal may appeal to the **General Court** within two weeks of notification of the decision dismissing the application.

2. The parties to the proceedings may appeal to the **General Court** against any decision of the Civil Service Tribunal made pursuant to Article ***278*** or Article ***279*** or the fourth paragraph of Article ***299*** of the ***Treaty on the Functioning of the European Union*** or Article 157 or the third paragraph of Article 164 of the EAEC Treaty within two months of its notification.

3. The President of the **General Court** may, by way of summary procedure, which may, insofar as necessary, differ from some of the rules contained in this Annex and which shall be laid down in the rules of procedure of the **General Court**, adjudicate upon appeals brought in accordance with paragraphs 1 and 2.

ARTICLE 11
1. An appeal to the **General Court** shall be limited to points of law. It shall lie on the grounds of lack of jurisdiction of the Civil Service Tribunal, a breach of procedure before it which adversely affects the interests of the appellant as well as the infringement of Community law by the Tribunal.

2. No appeal shall lie regarding only the amount of the costs or the party ordered to pay them.

ARTICLE 12
1. Without prejudice to Articles ***278*** and ***279*** of the ***Treaty on the Functioning of the European Union*** or Article 157 of the EAEC Treaty, an appeal before the **General Court** shall not have suspensory effect.

2. Where an appeal is brought against a decision of the Civil Service Tribunal, the procedure before the **General Court** shall consist of a written part and an oral part. In accordance with conditions laid down in the rules of procedure, the **General Court**, having heard the parties, may dispense with the oral procedure.

ARTICLE 13
1. If the appeal is well founded, the **General Court** shall quash the decision of the Civil Service Tribunal and itself give judgment in the matter. It shall refer the case back to the Civil Service Tribunal for judgment where the state of the proceedings does not permit a decision by the Court.

2. Where a case is referred back to the Civil Service Tribunal, the Tribunal shall be bound by the decision of the **General Court** on points of law.

[BMDF Note: this protocol was introduced on 17 April 1957. It was extensively rewritten and replaced by a new protocol on the Court of Justice in the Treaty of Nice and amended by the Treaty of Lisbon, which has included many of the changes introduced by the draft Constitution.]

13. PROTOCOL ON THE STATUTE OF THE EUROPEAN SYSTEM OF CENTRAL BANKS AND OF THE EUROPEAN CENTRAL BANK

THE HIGH CONTRACTING PARTIES,

DESIRING to lay down the Statute of the European System of Central Banks and of the European Central Bank provided for in ***the second paragraph of Article 129 of the Treaty on the Functioning of the European Union***,

HAVE AGREED UPON the following provisions, which shall be annexed to the ***Treaty on European Union and to the Treaty on the Functioning of the European Union***:

CHAPTER I

THE EUROPEAN SYSTEM OF CENTRAL BANKS

ARTICLE 1 *The European System of Central Banks*
In accordance with *Article 282(1) of the Treaty on the Functioning of the European Union*, the European Central Bank (ECB) and the national central banks shall constitute the European System of Central Banks (ESCB). The ECB and the national central banks of those Member States whose currency is the euro shall constitute the Eurosystem.
The ESCB and the ECB shall perform their tasks and carry on their activities in accordance with the provisions of ***these Treaties*** and of this Statute.

CHAPTER II

OBJECTIVES AND TASKS OF THE ESCB

ARTICLE 2 *Objectives*
In accordance with Article ***127(1) and Article 282(2)*** of ***the Treaty on the Functioning of the European Union***, the primary objective of the ESCB shall be to maintain price stability. Without prejudice to the objective of price stability, it shall support the general economic policies in the Community with a view to contributing to the achievement of the objectives of the Community as laid down in Article 2 of ***the Treaty on the Functioning of the European Union***. The ESCB shall act in accordance with the principle of an open market economy with free competition, favouring an efficient allocation of resources, and in compliance with the principles set out in Article 4 of ***the Treaty on the Functioning of the European Union***.

ARTICLE 3 *Tasks*
3.1. In accordance with Article ***127(2)*** of ***the Treaty on the Functioning of the European Union***, the basic tasks to be carried out through the ESCB shall be:
- to define and implement the monetary policy of the Community;
- to conduct foreign exchange operations consistent with the provisions of ***Article 219 of that Treaty***;
- to hold and manage the official foreign reserves of the Member States;
- to promote the smooth operation of payment systems.

3.2. In accordance with Article ***127(3)*** of ***the Treaty on the Functioning of the European Union***, the third indent of Article 3.1 shall be without prejudice to the holding and management by the governments of Member States of foreign exchange working balances.

3.3. In accordance with Article ***127(5)*** of ***the Treaty on the Functioning of the European Union***, the ESCB shall contribute to the smooth conduct of policies pursued by the competent authorities relating to the prudential supervision of credit institutions and the stability of the financial system.
[Article does not apply to the UK: Protocol 20, Article 8]

ARTICLE 4 *Advisory functions*
In accordance with Article ***127(4)*** of ***the Treaty on the Functioning of the European Union***:
(a) the ECB shall be consulted:
- on any proposed Community act in its fields of competence;

- by national authorities regarding any draft legislative provision in its fields of competence, but within the limits and under the conditions set out by the Council in accordance with the procedure laid down in Article 42;

(b) the ECB may submit opinions to the **Union** institutions, bodies**, offices or agencies** or to national authorities on matters in its fields of competence.
[Article does not apply to the UK: Protocol 20, Article 8]

ARTICLE 5 *Collection of statistical information*
5.1. In order to undertake the tasks of the ESCB, the ECB, assisted by the national central banks, shall collect the necessary statistical information either from the competent national authorities or directly from economic agents. For these purposes it shall co-operate with the **Union** institutions, bodies**, offices or agencies** and with the competent authorities of the Member States or third countries and with international organisations.

5.2. The national central banks shall carry out, to the extent possible, the tasks described in Article 5.1.

5.3. The ECB shall contribute to the harmonisation, where necessary, of the rules and practices governing the collection, compilation and distribution of statistics in the areas within its fields of competence.

5.4. The Council, in accordance with the procedure laid down in Article 42, shall define the natural and legal persons subject to reporting requirements, the confidentiality regime and the appropriate provisions for enforcement.

ARTICLE 6 *International co-operation*
6.1. In the field of international co-operation involving the tasks entrusted to the ESCB, the ECB shall decide how the ESCB shall be represented.

6.2. The ECB and, subject to its approval, the national central banks may participate in international monetary institutions.

6.3. Articles 6.1 and 6.2 shall be without prejudice to Article ***138(4)*** of ***the Treaty on the Functioning of the European Union***.
[Article does not apply to the UK: Protocol 20, Article 8]

CHAPTER III

ORGANISATION OF THE ESCB

ARTICLE 7 *Independence*
In accordance with Article ***130*** of ***the Treaty on the Functioning of the European Union***, when exercising the powers and carrying out the tasks and duties conferred upon them by ***the Treaty on the Functioning of the European Union*** and this Statute, neither the ECB, nor a national central bank, nor any member of their decision-making bodies shall seek or take instructions from **Union** institutions, bodies**, offices or agencies**, from any government of a Member State or from any other body. The **Union** institutions, bodies**, offices or agencies** and the governments of the Member States undertake to respect this principle and not to seek to influence the members of the decision-making bodies of the ECB or of the national central banks in the performance of their tasks.
[Article does not apply to the UK: Protocol 20, Article 8]

ARTICLE 8 *General principle*
The ESCB shall be governed by the decision-making bodies of the ECB.

ARTICLE 9 *The European Central Bank*
9.1. The ECB which, in accordance with ***Article 282(3)*** of ***the Treaty on the Functioning of the European Union***, shall have legal personality, shall enjoy in each of the Member States the most extensive legal capacity accorded to legal persons under its law; it may, in particular, acquire or dispose of movable and immovable property and may be a party to legal proceedings.

9.2. The ECB shall ensure that the tasks conferred upon the ESCB under Article ***127(2), (3)*** and ***(5)*** of ***the Treaty on the Functioning of the European Union*** are implemented either by its own activities pursuant to this Statute or through the national central banks pursuant to Articles 12.1 and 14.
[Paragraph does not apply to the UK: Protocol 20, Article 8]

9.3. In accordance with Article ***129(3)*** of ***the Treaty on the Functioning of the European Union***, the decision-making bodies of the ECB shall be the Governing Council and the Executive Board.

ARTICLE 10 *The Governing Council*
10.1. In accordance with Article ***283(l)*** of ***the Treaty on the Functioning of the European Union***, the Governing Council shall comprise the members of the Executive Board of the ECB and the Governors of the national central banks **of the Member States whose currency is the euro**.
[Paragraph does not apply to the UK: Protocol 20, Article 8]

10.2. Each member of the Governing Council shall have one vote. As from the date on which the number of members of the Governing Council exceeds 21, each member of the Executive Board shall have one vote and the number of governors with a voting right shall be 15. The latter voting rights shall be assigned and shall rotate as follows:

- as from the date on which the number of governors exceeds 15, until it reaches 22, the governors shall be allocated to two groups, according to a ranking of the size of the share of their national central bank's Member State in the aggregate gross domestic product at market prices and in the total aggregated balance sheet of the monetary financial institutions of the Member States **whose currency is** the euro. The shares in the aggregate gross domestic product at market prices and in the total aggregated balance sheet of the monetary financial institutions shall be assigned weights of 5/6 and 1/6, respectively. The first group shall be composed of five governors and the second group of the remaining governors. The frequency of voting rights of the governors allocated to the first group shall not be lower than the frequency of voting rights of those of the second group. Subject to the previous sentence, the first group shall be assigned four voting rights and the second group eleven voting rights;
- as from the date on which the number of governors reaches 22, the governors shall be allocated to three groups according to a ranking based on the above criteria. The first group shall be composed of five governors and shall be assigned four voting rights. The second group shall be composed of half of the total number of governors, with any fraction rounded up to the nearest integer, and shall be assigned eight voting rights. The third group shall be composed of the remaining governors and shall be assigned three voting rights;
- within each group, the governors shall have their voting rights for equal amounts of time;
- for the calculation of the shares in the aggregate gross domestic product at market prices Article 29.2 shall apply. The total aggregated balance sheet of the monetary financial institutions shall be calculated in accordance with the statistical framework applying in the European Community at the time of the calculation;
- whenever the aggregate gross domestic product at market prices is adjusted in accordance with Article 29.3, or whenever the number of governors increases, the size and/or composition of the groups shall be adjusted in accordance with the above principles;
- the Governing Council, acting by a two-thirds majority of all its members, with and without a voting right, shall take all measures necessary for the implementation of the above principles and may decide to postpone the start of the rotation system until the date on which the number of governors exceeds 18.

The right to vote shall be exercised in person. By way of derogation from this rule, the Rules of Procedure referred to in Article 12.3 may lay down that members of the Governing Council may cast their vote by means of teleconferencing. These rules shall also provide that a member of the Governing Council who is prevented from attending meetings of the Governing Council for a prolonged period may appoint an alternate as a member of the Governing Council.
The provisions of the previous paragraphs are without prejudice to the voting rights of all members of the Governing Council, with and without a voting right, under Articles 10.3, **40.2 and 40.3**.
Save as otherwise provided for in this Statute, the Governing Council shall act by a simple majority of the members having a voting right. In the event of a tie, the President shall have the casting vote.
In order for the Governing Council to vote, there shall be a quorum of two-thirds of the members having a voting right. If the quorum is not met, the President may convene an extraordinary meeting at which decisions may be taken without regard to the quorum.

10.3. For any decisions to be taken under Articles 28, 29, 30, 32, 33 and 51, the votes in the Governing Council shall be weighted according to the national central banks' shares in the subscribed capital of the ECB. The weights of the votes of the members of the Executive Board shall be zero. A decision requiring a qualified majority shall be adopted if the votes cast in favour represent at least two-thirds of the subscribed capital of the ECB and represent at least half of the shareholders. If a Governor is unable to be present, he may nominate an alternate to cast his weighted vote.
[Paragraph does not apply to the UK: Protocol 20, Article 8]

10.4. The proceedings of the meetings shall be confidential. The Governing Council may decide to make the outcome of its deliberations public.

10.5. The Governing Council shall meet at least ten times a year.

ARTICLE 11 *The Executive Board*
11.1. In accordance with Article ***283(2)(a)*** of ***the Treaty on the Functioning of the European Union***, the Executive Board shall comprise the President, the Vice-President and four other members.
The members shall perform their duties on a full-time basis. No member shall engage in any occupation, whether gainful or not, unless exemption is exceptionally granted by the Governing Council.

11.2. In accordance with Article ***283(2)(b)*** of ***the Treaty on the Functioning of the European Union***, the President, the Vice-President and the other Members of the Executive Board shall be appointed **by the European Council, acting by a qualified majority, from among persons of recognised standing and professional experience in monetary or banking matters**, on a recommendation from the Council after it has consulted the European Parliament and the Governing Council.
Their term of office shall be 8 years and shall not be renewable.
Only nationals of Member States may be members of the Executive Board.
[Paragraph does not apply to the UK: Protocol 20, Article 8]

11.3. The terms and conditions of employment of the members of the Executive Board, in particular their salaries, pensions and other social security benefits shall be the subject of contracts with the ECB and shall be fixed by the Governing Council on a proposal from a Committee comprising three members appointed by the Governing Council and three members appointed by the Council. The members of the Executive Board shall not have the right to vote on matters referred to in this paragraph.

11.4. If a member of the Executive Board no longer fulfils the conditions required for the performance of his duties or if he has been guilty of serious misconduct, the Court of Justice may, on application by the Governing Council or the Executive Board, compulsorily retire him.

11.5. Each member of the Executive Board present in person shall have the right to vote and shall have, for that purpose, one vote. Save as otherwise provided, the Executive Board shall act by a simple majority of the votes cast. In the event of a tie, the President shall have the casting vote. The voting arrangements shall be specified in the Rules of Procedure referred to in Article 12.3.

11.6. The Executive Board shall be responsible for the current business of the ECB.

11.7. Any vacancy on the Executive Board shall be filled by the appointment of a new member in accordance with Article 11.2.

ARTICLE 12 *Responsibilities of the decision-making bodies*
12.1. The Governing Council shall adopt the guidelines and take the decisions necessary to ensure the performance of the tasks entrusted to the ESCB under ***these Treaties*** and this Statute. The Governing Council shall formulate the monetary policy of the **Union** including, as appropriate, decisions relating to intermediate monetary objectives, key interest rates and the supply of reserves in the ESCB, and shall establish the necessary guidelines for their implementation.
The Executive Board shall implement monetary policy in accordance with the guidelines and decisions laid down by the Governing Council. In doing so the Executive Board shall give the necessary instructions to national central banks. In addition the Executive Board may have certain powers delegated to it where the Governing Council so decides.
To the extent deemed possible and appropriate and without prejudice to the provisions of this Article, the ECB shall have recourse to the national central banks to carry out operations which form part of the tasks of the ESCB.
[Paragraph does not apply to the UK: Protocol 20, Article 8]

12.2. The Executive Board shall have responsibility for the preparation of meetings of the Governing Council.

12.3. The Governing Council shall adopt Rules of Procedure which determine the internal organisation of the ECB and its decision-making bodies.

12.4. The Governing Council shall exercise the advisory functions referred to in Article 4.

12.5. The Governing Council shall take the decisions referred to in Article 6.

ARTICLE 13 *The President*
13.1. The President or, in his absence, the Vice-President shall chair the Governing Council and the Executive Board of the ECB.

13.2. Without prejudice to Article 39, the President or his nominee shall represent the ECB externally.

ARTICLE 14 *National central banks*
14.1. In accordance with Article ***131*** of ***the Treaty on the Functioning of the European Union***, each Member State shall ensure that its national legislation, including the statutes of its national central bank, is compatible with ***these Treaties*** and this Statute.

14.2. The statutes of the national central banks shall, in particular, provide that the term of office of a Governor of a national central bank shall be no less than 5 years.
A Governor may be relieved from office only if he no longer fulfils the conditions required for the performance of his duties or if he has been guilty of serious misconduct. A decision to this effect may be referred to the Court of Justice by the Governor concerned or the Governing Council on grounds of infringement of ***these Treaties*** or of any rule of law relating to its application. Such proceedings shall be instituted within two months of the publication of the decision or of its notification to the plaintiff or, in the absence thereof, of the day on which it came to the knowledge of the latter, as the case may be.

14.3. The national central banks are an integral part of the ESCB and shall act in accordance with the guidelines and instructions of the ECB. The Governing Council shall take the necessary steps to ensure compliance with the guidelines and instructions of the ECB, and shall require that any necessary information be given to it.

14.4. National central banks may perform functions other than those specified in this Statute unless the Governing Council finds, by a majority of two-thirds of the votes cast, that these interfere with the objectives and tasks of the ESCB. Such functions shall be performed on the responsibility and liability of national central banks and shall not be regarded as being part of the functions of the ESCB.
[Article does not apply to the UK: Protocol 20, Article 8]

ARTICLE 15 *Reporting commitments*
15.1. The ECB shall draw up and publish reports on the activities of the ESCB at least quarterly.

15.2. A consolidated financial statement of the ESCB shall be published each week.

15.3. In accordance with Article ***294(3)*** of ***the Treaty on the Functioning of the European Union***, the ECB shall address an annual report on the activities of the ESCB and on the monetary policy of both the previous and the current year to the European Parliament, the Council and the Commission, and also to the European Council.

15.4. The reports and statements referred to in this Article shall be made available to interested parties free of charge.

ARTICLE 16 *Bank Notes*
In accordance with Article ***128(1)*** of ***the Treaty on the Functioning of the European Union***, the Governing Council shall have the exclusive right to authorise the issue of **euro** bank notes within the **Union**. The ECB and the national central banks may issue such notes. The bank notes issued by the ECB and the national central banks shall be the only such notes to have the status of legal tender within the **Union**.
The ECB shall respect as far as possible existing practices regarding the issue and design of bank notes.
[Article does not apply to the UK: Protocol 20, Article 8]

CHAPTER IV

MONETARY FUNCTIONS AND OPERATIONS OF THE ESCB

ARTICLE 17 *Accounts with the ECB and the national central banks*
In order to conduct their operations, the ECB and the national central banks may open accounts for credit institutions, public entities and other market participants and accept assets, including book-entry securities, as collateral.

ARTICLE 18 *Open market and credit operations*
18.1. In order to achieve the objectives of the ESCB and to carry out its tasks, the ECB and the national central banks may:

- operate in the financial markets by buying and selling outright (spot and forward) or under repurchase agreement and by lending or borrowing claims and marketable instruments, **euro or other** currencies, as well as precious metals;
- conduct credit operations with credit institutions and other market participants, with lending being based on adequate collateral.

18.2. The ECB shall establish general principles for open market and credit operations carried out by itself or the national central banks, including for the announcement of conditions under which they stand ready to enter into such transactions.
[Article does not apply to the UK: Protocol 20, Article 8]

ARTICLE 19 *Minimum reserves*
19.1. Subject to Article 2, the ECB may require credit institutions established in Member States to hold minimum reserves on accounts with the ECB and national central banks in pursuance of monetary policy objectives. Regulations concerning the calculation and determination of the required minimum reserves may be established by the Governing Council. In cases of non-compliance the ECB shall be entitled to levy penalty interest and to impose other sanctions with comparable effect.

19.2. For the application of this Article, the Council shall, in accordance with the procedure laid down in Article 42, define the basis for minimum reserves and the maximum permissible ratios between those reserves and their basis, as well as the appropriate sanctions in cases of non-compliance.
[Article does not apply to the UK: Protocol 20, Article 8]

ARTICLE 20 *Other instruments of monetary control*
The Governing Council may, by a majority of two-thirds of the votes cast, decide upon the use of such other operational methods of monetary control as it sees it, respecting Article 2.
The Council shall, in accordance with the procedure laid down in Article 42, define the scope of such methods if they impose obligations on third parties.
[Article does not apply to the UK: Protocol 20, Article 8]

ARTICLE 21 *Operations with public entities*
21.1. In accordance with Article ***123*** of ***the Treaty on the Functioning of the European Union***, overdrafts or any other type of credit facility with the ECB or with the national central banks in favour of **Union** institutions**,** bodies**, offices or agencies**, central governments, regional, local or other public authorities, other bodies governed by public law, or public undertakings of Member States shall be prohibited, as shall the purchase directly from them by the ECB or national central banks of debt instruments.

21.2. The ECB and national central banks may act as fiscal agents for the entities referred to in Article 21.1.

21.3. The provisions of this Article shall not apply to publicly-owned credit institutions which, in the context of the supply of reserves by central banks, shall be given the same treatment by national central banks and the ECB as private credit institutions.

ARTICLE 22 *Clearing and payment systems*
The ECB and national central banks may provide facilities, and the ECB may make regulations, to ensure efficient and sound clearing and payment systems within the **Union** and with other countries.
[Article does not apply to the UK: Protocol 20, Article 8]

ARTICLE 23 *External operations*
The ECB and national central banks may:

- establish relations with central banks and financial institutions in other countries and, where appropriate, with international organisations;
- acquire and sell spot and forward all types of foreign exchange assets and precious metals; the term 'foreign exchange asset' shall include securities and all other assets in the currency of any country or units of account and in whatever form held;
- hold and manage the assets referred to in this Article;
- conduct all types of banking transactions in relations with third countries and international organisations, including borrowing and lending operations.

[Article does not apply to the UK: Protocol 20, Article 8]

ARTICLE 24 *Other operations*
In addition to operations arising from their tasks, the ECB and national central banks may enter into operations for their administrative purposes or for their staff.

CHAPTER V

PRUDENTIAL SUPERVISION

ARTICLE 25 *Prudential supervision*
25.1. The ECB may offer advice to and be consulted by the Council, the Commission and the competent authorities of the Member States on the scope and implementation of **Union** legislation relating to the prudential supervision of credit institutions and to the stability of the financial system.

25.2. In accordance with any **regulation** of the Council under Article ***127(6)*** of ***the Treaty on the Functioning of the European Union***, the ECB may perform specific tasks concerning policies relating to the prudential supervision of credit institutions and other financial institutions with the exception of insurance undertakings.

CHAPTER VI

FINANCIAL PROVISIONS OF THE ESCB

ARTICLE 26 *Financial accounts*
26.1. The financial year of the ECB and national central banks shall begin on the first day of January and end on the last day of December.

26.2. The annual accounts of the ECB shall be drawn up by the Executive Board, in accordance with the principles established by the Governing Council. The accounts shall be approved by the Governing Council and shall thereafter be published.

26.3. For analytical and operational purposes, the Executive Board shall draw up a consolidated balance sheet of the ESCB, comprising those assets and liabilities of the national central banks that fall within the ESCB.

26.4. For the application of this Article, the Governing Council shall establish the necessary rules for standardising the accounting and reporting of operations undertaken by the national central banks.
[Article does not apply to the UK: Protocol 25, Article 8]

ARTICLE 27 *Auditing*
27.1. The accounts of the ECB and national central banks shall be audited by independent external auditors recommended by the Governing Council and approved by the Council. The auditors shall have full power to examine all books and accounts of the ECB and national central banks and obtain full information about their transactions.

27.2. The provisions of Article ***287*** of ***the Treaty on the Functioning of the European Union*** shall only apply to an examination of the operational efficiency of the management of the ECB.
[Article does not apply to the UK: Protocol 20, Article 8]

ARTICLE 28 *Capital of the ECB*
28.1. The capital of the ECB shall be **euro** 5,000 million. The capital may be increased by such amounts as may be decided by the Governing Council acting by the qualified majority provided for in Article 10.3, within the limits and under the conditions set by the Council under the procedure laid down in Article 42.

28.2. The national central banks shall be the sole subscribers to and holders of the capital of the ECB. The subscription of capital shall be according to the key established in accordance with Article 29.

28.3. The Governing Council, acting by the qualified majority provided for in Article 10.3, shall determine the extent to which and the form in which the capital shall be paid up.

28.4. Subject to Article 28.5, the shares of the national central banks in the subscribed capital of the ECB may not be transferred, pledged or attached.

28.5. If the key referred to in Article 29 is adjusted, the national central banks shall transfer among themselves capital shares to the extent necessary to ensure that the distribution of capital shares corresponds to the adjusted key. The Governing Council shall determine the terms and conditions of such transfers.

ARTICLE 29 *Key for capital subscription*
29.1. **The key for subscription of the ECB's capital, fixed for the first time in 1998 when the ESCB was established, shall be determined by assigning to each national central bank a weighting in this key equal to the sum of:**
- 50% of the share of its respective Member State in the population of the **Union** in the penultimate year preceding the establishment of the ESCB;
- 50% of the share of its respective Member State in the gross domestic product at market prices of the **Union** as recorded in the last five years preceding the penultimate year before the establishment of the ESCB;

The percentages shall be rounded up to the nearest multiple of **0.0001** percentage points.

29.2. The statistical data to be used for the application of this Article shall be provided by the Commission in accordance with the rules adopted by the Council under the procedure provided for in Article 42.

29.3. The weightings assigned to the national central banks shall be adjusted every five years after the establishment of the ESCB by analogy with the provisions laid down in Article 29.1. The adjusted key shall apply with effect from the first day of the following year.

29.4. The Governing Council shall take all other measures necessary for the application of this Article.

ARTICLE 30 *Transfer of foreign reserve assets to the ECB*
30.1. Without prejudice to Article 28, the ECB shall be provided by the national central banks with foreign reserve assets, other than Member States' currencies, ECUs, IMF reserve positions and SDRs, up to an amount equivalent to **euro** 50,000 million. The Governing Council shall decide upon the proportion to be called up by the ECB following its establishment and the amounts called up at later dates. The ECB shall have the full right to hold and manage the foreign reserves that are transferred to it and to use them for the purposes set out in this Statute.

30.2. The contributions of each national central bank shall be fixed in proportion to its share in the subscribed capital of the ECB.

30.3. Each national central bank shall be credited by the ECB with a claim equivalent to its contribution. The Governing Council shall determine the denomination and remuneration of such claims.

30.4. Further calls of foreign reserve assets beyond the limit set in Article 30.1 may be effected by the ECB, in accordance with Article 30.2, within the limits and under the conditions set by the Council in accordance with the procedure laid down in Article 42.

30.5. The ECB may hold and manage IMF reserve positions and SDRs and provide for the pooling of such assets.

30.6. The Governing Council shall take all other measures necessary for the application of this Article.
[Article does not apply to the UK: Protocol 20, Article 8]

ARTICLE 31 *Foreign reserve assets held by national central banks*
31.1. The national central banks shall be allowed to perform transactions in fulfilment of their obligations towards international organisations in accordance with Article 23.

31.2. All other operations in foreign reserve assets remaining with the national central banks after the transfers referred to in Article 30, and Member States' transactions with their foreign exchange working balances shall, above a certain limit to be established within the framework of Article 31.3, be subject to approval by the ECB in order to ensure consistency with the exchange rate and monetary policies of the **Union**.

31.3. The Governing Council shall issue guidelines with a view to facilitating such operations.
[Article does not apply to the UK: Protocol 20, Article 8]

ARTICLE 32 *Allocation of monetary income of national central banks*
32.1. The income accruing to the national central banks in the performance of the ESCB's monetary policy function (hereinafter referred to as 'monetary income') shall be allocated at the end of each financial year in accordance with the provisions of this Article.

32.2. The amount of each national central bank's monetary income shall be equal to its annual income derived from its assets held against notes in circulation and deposit liabilities to credit institutions. These assets shall be earmarked by national central banks in accordance with guidelines to be established by the Governing Council.

32.3. If, after **introduction of the euro**, the balance sheet structures of the national central banks do not, in the judgment of the Governing Council, permit the application of Article 32.2, the Governing Council, acting by a qualified majority, may decide that, by way of derogation from Article 32.2, monetary income shall be measured according to an alternative method for a period of not more than five years.

32.4. The amount of each national central bank's monetary income shall be reduced by an amount equivalent to any interest paid by that central bank on its deposit liabilities to credit institutions in accordance with Article 19.

The Governing Council may decide that national central banks shall be indemnified against costs incurred in connection with the issue of bank notes or in exceptional circumstances for specific losses arising from monetary policy operations undertaken for the ESCB. Indemnification shall be in a form deemed appropriate in the judgment of the Governing Council; these amounts may be offset against the national central banks' monetary income.

32.5. The sum of the national central banks' income shall be allocated to the national central banks in proportion to their paid-up shares in the capital of the ECB, subject to any decision taken by the Governing Council pursuant to Article 33.2.

32.6. The clearing and settlement of the balances arising from the allocation of monetary income shall be carried out by the ECB in accordance with guidelines established by the Governing Council.

32.7. The Governing Council shall take all other measures necessary for the application of this Article.
[Article does not apply to the UK: Protocol 20, Article 8]

ARTICLE 33 *Allocation of net profits and losses of the ECB*
33.1. The net profit of the ECB shall be transferred in the following order:
(a) an amount to be determined by the Governing Council, which may not exceed 20% of the net profit, shall be transferred to the general reserve fund subject to a limit equal to 100% of the capital;
(b) the remaining net profit shall be distributed to the shareholders of the ECB in proportion to their paid-up shares.

33.2. In the event of a loss incurred by the ECB, the shortfall may be offset against the general reserve fund of the ECB and, if necessary, following a decision by the Governing Council, against the monetary income of the relevant financial year in proportion and up to the amounts allocated to the national central banks in accordance with Article 32.5.
[Article does not apply to the UK: Protocol 20, Article 8]

CHAPTER VII

GENERAL PROVISIONS

ARTICLE 34 *Legal acts*
34.1. In accordance with Article ***132*** of ***the Treaty on the Functioning of the European Union***, the ECB shall:
- make regulations to the extent necessary to implement the tasks defined in Article 3.1, first indent, Articles 19.1, 22 or 25.2 and in cases which shall be laid down in the acts of the Council referred to in Article 42;
- take decisions necessary for carrying out the tasks entrusted to the ESCB under ***these Treaties*** and this Statute;
- make recommendations and deliver opinions.

34.2. The ECB may decide to publish its decisions, recommendations and opinions.

34.3. Within the limits and under the conditions adopted by the Council under the procedure laid down in Article 42, the ECB shall be entitled to impose fines or periodic penalty payments on undertakings for failure to comply with obligations under its regulations and decisions.
[Article does not apply to the UK: Protocol 20, Article 8]

ARTICLE 35 *Judicial control and related matters*
35.1. The acts or omissions of the ECB shall be open to review or interpretation by the Court of Justice **of the European Union** in the cases and under the conditions laid down in ***the Treaty on the Functioning of the European Union***. The ECB may institute proceedings in the cases and under the conditions laid down in ***the Treaty on the Functioning of the European Union***.

35.2. Disputes between the ECB, on the one hand, and its creditors, debtors or any other person, on the other, shall be decided by the competent national courts, save where jurisdiction has been conferred upon the Court of Justice **of the European Union**.

35.3. The ECB shall be subject to the liability regime provided for in Article ***325*** of ***the Treaty on the Functioning of the European Union***. The national central banks shall be liable according to their respective national laws.

35.4. The Court of Justice **of the European Union** shall have jurisdiction to give judgment pursuant to any arbitration clause contained in a contract concluded by or on behalf of the ECB, whether that contract be governed by public or private law.

35.5. A decision of the ECB to bring an action before the Court of Justice **of the European Union** shall be taken by the Governing Council.

35.6. The Court of Justice **of the European Union** shall have jurisdiction in disputes concerning the fulfilment by a national central bank of obligations under ***the Treaties*** **and** this Statute. If the ECB considers that a national central bank has failed to fulfil an obligation under this Statute, it shall deliver a reasoned opinion on the matter after giving the national central bank concerned the opportunity to submit its observations. If the national central bank concerned does not comply with the opinion within the period laid down by the ECB, the latter may bring the matter before the Court of Justice **of the European Union**.

ARTICLE 36 *Staff*
36.1. The Governing Council, on a proposal from the Executive Board, shall lay down the conditions of employment of the staff of the ECB.

36.2. The Court of Justice **of the European Union** shall have jurisdiction in any dispute between the ECB and its servants within the limits and under the conditions laid down in the conditions of employment.

ARTICLE **37** *Professional secrecy*
37.1. Members of the governing bodies and the staff of the ECB and the national central banks shall be required, even after their duties have ceased, not to disclose information of the kind covered by the obligation of professional secrecy.

37.2. Persons having access to data covered by **Union** legislation imposing an obligation of secrecy shall be subject to such legislation.

ARTICLE **38** *Signatories*
The ECB shall be legally committed to third parties by the President or by two members of the Executive Board or by the signatures of two members of the staff of the ECB who have been duly authorised by the President to sign on behalf of the ECB.

ARTICLE **39** *Privileges and immunities*
The ECB shall enjoy in the territories of the Member States such privileges and immunities as are necessary for the performance of its tasks, under the conditions laid down in the Protocol on the Privileges and Immunities of the European **Union**.

CHAPTER VIII

AMENDMENT OF THE STATUTE AND COMPLEMENTARY LEGISLATION

ARTICLE **40** *Simplified amendment procedure*
40.1. In accordance with Article ***129(5)*** of ***the Treaty on the Functioning of the European Union***, Articles 5.1, 5.2, 5.3, 17, 18, 19.1, 22, 23, 24, 26, 32.2, 32.3, 32.4, 32.6, 33.1(a) and 36 of this Statute **may be amended by the European Parliament and the Council, acting in accordance with the ordinary legislative procedure either** on a recommendation from the ECB and after consulting the Commission, or on a proposal from the Commission and after consulting the ECB.

40.2. Article 10.2 may be amended by a decision of the European Council, acting unanimously, either on a recommendation from the European Central Bank and after consulting the European Parliament and the Commission, or on a recommendation from the Commission and after consulting the European Parliament and the European Central Bank. These amendments shall not enter into force until they are approved by the Member States in accordance with their respective constitutional requirements.

40.3. A recommendation made by the ECB under this Article shall require a unanimous decision by the Governing Council.

ARTICLE **41** *Complementary legislation*
In accordance with Article ***129(6)*** of ***the Treaty on the Functioning of the European Union***, the Council, either on a proposal from the Commission and after consulting the European Parliament and the ECB or on a recommendation from the ECB and after consulting the European Parliament and the Commission, shall adopt the provisions referred to in Articles 4, 5.4, 19.2, 20, 28.1, 29.2, 30.4 and 34.3 of this Statute.

CHAPTER IX

TRANSITIONAL AND OTHER PROVISIONS FOR THE ESCB

ARTICLE **42** *General provisions*
42.1. A derogation as referred to in ***Article 139(1) of the Treaty on the Functioning of the European Union*** shall entail that the following Articles of this Statute shall not confer any rights or impose any obligations on the Member State concerned: 3, 6, 9.2, 12.1, 14.3, 16, 18, 19, 20, 22, 23, 26.2, 27, 30, 31, 32, 33, 34, 50 and 52.

42.2. The central banks of Member States with a derogation as specified in ***Article 139(1) of the Treaty on the Functioning of the European Union*** shall retain their powers in the field of monetary policy according to national law.

42.3. In accordance with ***Article 139(4) of the Treaty on the Functioning of the European Union***, 'Member States' shall be read as '**Member States whose currency is the euro**' in the following Articles of this Statute: 3, 11.2, **and** 19.

42.4. 'National central banks' shall be read as 'central banks of **Member States whose currency is the euro**' in the following Articles of this Statute: 9.2, ***10.2***, 10.3, 12.1, 16, 17, 18, 22, 23, 27, 30, 31, 32, 33.2 and 52.

42.5. 'Shareholders' shall be read as 'central banks of **Member States whose currency is the euro**' in Articles 10.3 and 33.1.

42.6. 'Subscribed capital of the ECB' shall be read as 'capital of the ECB subscribed by the central banks of **Member States whose currency is the euro**' in Articles 10.3 and 30.2.

ARTICLE **43** *Transitional tasks of the ECB*
The ECB shall take over **the former tasks of the EMI referred to in *Article 141(2) of the Treaty on the Functioning of the European Union*** which, because of the derogations of one or more Member States, still have to be performed **after the introduction of the euro**.
The ECB shall give advice in the preparations for the abrogation of the derogations specified in ***Article 140 of the Treaty on the Functioning of the European Union***.

ARTICLE **44** *The General Council of the ECB*
44.1. Without prejudice to Article ***129(3)*** of ***the Treaty on the Functioning of the European Union***, the General Council shall be constituted as a third decision-making body of the ECB.

44.2. The General Council shall comprise the President and Vice-President of the ECB and the Governors of the national central banks. The other members of the Executive Board may participate, without having the right to vote, in meetings of the General Council.

44.3. The responsibilities of the General Council are listed in full in Article 47 of this Statute.

ARTICLE **45** *Rules of procedure of the General Council*
45.1. The President or, in his absence, the Vice-President of the ECB shall chair the General Council of the ECB.

45.2. The President of the Council and a member of the Commission may participate, without having the right to vote, in meetings of the General Council.

45.3. The President shall prepare the meetings of the General Council.

45.4. By way of derogation from Article 12.3, the General Council shall adopt its Rules of Procedure.

45.5. The Secretariat of the General Council shall be provided by the ECB.

ARTICLE **46** *Responsibilities of the General Council*
46.1. The General Council shall:
- perform the tasks referred to in Article 44;
- contribute to the advisory functions referred to in Articles 4 and 25.1.

46.2. The General Council shall contribute to:
- the collection of statistical information as referred to in Article 5;
- the reporting activities of the ECB as referred to in Article 15;
- the establishment of the necessary rules for the application of Article 26 as referred to in Article 26.4;
- the taking of all other measures necessary for the application of Article 29 as referred to in Article 29.4;
- the laying down of the conditions of employment of the staff of the ECB as referred to in Article 36.

46.3. The General Council shall contribute to the necessary preparations for irrevocably fixing the exchange rates of the currencies of Member States with a derogation against **the euro**, as referred to in Article ***140(5)*** of ***the Treaty on the Functioning of the European Union***.

46.4. The General Council shall be informed by the President of the ECB of decisions of the Governing Council.

ARTICLE **47** *Transitional provisions for the capital of the ECB*
In accordance with Article 29.1 each national central bank shall be assigned a weighting in the key for subscription of the ECB's capital. By way of derogation from Article 28.3, central banks of Member States with a derogation shall not pay up their subscribed capital unless the General Council, acting by a majority representing at least two-thirds of the subscribed capital of the ECB and at least half of the shareholders, decides that a minimal percentage has to be paid up as a contribution to the operational costs of the ECB.

ARTICLE **48** *Deferred payment of capital, reserves and provisions of the ECB*
48.1 The central bank of a Member State whose derogation has been abrogated shall pay up its subscribed share of the capital of the ECB to the same extent as the central banks of other **Member**

States whose currency is the euro, and shall transfer to the ECB foreign reserve assets in accordance with Article 30.1. The sum to be transferred shall be determined by multiplying the **euro** value at current exchange rates of the foreign reserve assets which have already been transferred to the ECB in accordance with Article 30.1, by the ratio between the number of shares subscribed by the national central bank concerned and the number of shares already paid up by the other national central banks.

48.2. In addition to the payment to be made in accordance with Article 49.1, the central bank concerned shall contribute to the reserves of the ECB, to those provisions equivalent to reserves, and to the amount still to be appropriated to the reserves and provisions corresponding to the balance of the profit and loss account as at 31 December of the year prior to the abrogation of the derogation. The sum to be contributed shall be determined by multiplying the amount of the reserves, as defined above and as stated in the approved balance sheet of the ECB, by the ratio between the number of shares subscribed by the central bank concerned and the number of shares already paid up by the other central banks.

48.3. Upon one or more countries becoming Member States and their respective national central banks becoming part of the ESCB, the subscribed capital of the ECB and the limit on the amount of foreign reserve assets that may be transferred to the ECB shall be automatically increased. The increase shall be determined by multiplying the respective amounts then prevailing by the ratio, within the expanded capital key, between the weighting of the entering national central banks concerned and the weighting of the national central banks already members of the ESCB. Each national central bank's weighting in the capital key shall be calculated by analogy with Article 29.1 and in compliance with Article 29.2.The reference periods to be used for the statistical data shall be identical to those applied for the latest quinquennial adjustment of the weightings under Article 29.3.

ARTICLE **49** *Exchange of bank notes in* ***Union*** *currencies*
Following the irrevocable fixing of exchange rates **in accordance with *Article 139(3) of the Treaty on the Functioning of the European Union***, the Governing Council shall take the necessary measures to ensure that bank notes denominated in currencies with irrevocably fixed exchange rates are exchanged by the national central banks at their respective par values.
[Article does not apply to the UK: Protocol 20, Article 8]

ARTICLE **50** *Applicability of the transitional provisions*
If and as long as there are Member States with a derogation Articles 43 to 48 shall be applicable.
[BMDF Note: This protocol was introduced by the Maastricht Treaty]

14. PROTOCOL ON THE STATUTE OF THE EUROPEAN INVESTMENT BANK

The High Contracting Parties,

DESIRING to lay down the Statute of the European Investment Bank provided for in Article ***308*** of ***the Treaty on the Functioning of the European Union***,

HAVE AGREED UPON the following provisions, which shall be annexed to ***the Treaty on European Union and to the Treaty on the Functioning of the European Union*****:**

ARTICLE 1
The European Investment Bank established by Article ***308*** of ***the Treaty on the Functioning of the European Union*** (hereinafter called the 'Bank') is hereby constituted; it shall perform its functions and carry on its activities in accordance with the provisions of ***the Treaty on the Functioning of the European Union*** and of this Statute.

ARTICLE 2
The task of the Bank shall be that defined in Article ***309*** of ***the Treaty on the Functioning of the European Union***.

ARTICLE 3
In accordance with Article ***308*** of ***the Treaty on the Functioning of the European Union*****, the Bank's members shall be the Member States**.

ARTICLE 4

1. The capital of the Bank shall be **164,808,169,000** euro, subscribed by the Member States as follows:

Germany	26,649,532,500	Czech Republic	**1,258,785,500**
France	26,649,532,500	Hungary	**1,190,868,500**
Italy	26,649,532,500	Ireland	935,070,000
United Kingdom	26,649,532,500	**Romania**	**863,514,500**
Spain	15,989,719,500	Slovakia	**428,490,500**
Belgium	7,387,065,000	Slovenia	**397,815,000**
Netherlands	7,387,065,000	**Bulgaria**	**290,917,500**
Sweden	4,900,585,500	Lithuania	**249,617,500**
Denmark	3,740,283,000	Luxembourg	187,015,500
Austria	3,666,973,500	Cyprus	**183,382,000**
Poland	**3,411,263,500**	Latvia	**152,335,000**
Finland	2,106,816,000	Estonia	**117,640,000**
Greece	2,003,725,500	Malta	**69,804,000**
Portugal	1,291,287,000		

The Member States shall be liable only up to the amount of their share of the capital subscribed and not paid up.

2. The admission of a new member shall entail an increase in the subscribed capital corresponding to the capital brought in by the new member.

3. The Board of Governors may, acting unanimously, decide to increase the subscribed capital.

4. The share of a member in the subscribed capital may not be transferred, pledged or attached.

ARTICLE 5

1. The subscribed capital shall be paid in by Member States to the extent of 5 per cent on average of the amounts laid down in Article 4(1).

2. In the event of an increase in the subscribed capital, the Board of Governors, acting unanimously, shall fix the percentage to be paid up and the arrangements for payment. **Cash payments shall be made exclusively in euro.**

3. The Board of Directors may require payment of the balance of the subscribed capital, to such extent as may be required for the Bank to meet its obligations.
Each Member State shall make this payment in proportion to its share of the subscribed capital.

ARTICLE 6

The Bank shall be directed and managed by a Board of Governors, a Board of Directors and a Management Committee.

ARTICLE 7

1. The Board of Governors shall consist of the Ministers designated by the Member States.

2. The Board of Governors shall lay down general directives for the credit policy of the Bank **in accordance with the Union's objectives**.
The Board of Governors shall ensure that these directives are implemented.

3. The Board of Governors shall in addition:

(a) decide whether to increase the subscribed capital in accordance with Article 4(3) and Article 5(2);

(b) **for the purposes of Article 9(1), determine the principles applicable to financing operations undertaken within the framework of the Bank's task**;

(c) exercise the powers provided in Articles 11 and 13 in respect of the appointment and the compulsory retirement of the members of the Board of Directors and of the Management Committee, and those powers provided in the second sub-paragraph of Article 13(1);

(d) **take decisions in respect of the granting of finance for investment operations to be carried out, in whole or in part, outside the territories of the Member States in accordance with Article 16(1);**

(e) approve the annual report of the Board of Directors;

(f) approve the annual balance sheet and profit and loss account;

(g) exercise the **other** powers and functions **conferred by this Statute**;
(h) approve the rules of procedure of the Bank.

4. Where the framework of ***the Treaty on the Functioning of the European Union*** and this Statute the Board of Governors shall be competent to take, acting unanimously, any decisions concerning the suspension of the operations of the Bank and, should the event arise, its liquidation.

ARTICLE **8**
Save as otherwise provided for in this Statute, decisions of the Board of Governors shall be taken by a majority of its members. This majority must represent at least 50 per cent of the subscribed capital.
A qualified majority shall require eighteen votes in favour and 68% of the subscribed capital.
Abstentions by members present in person or represented shall not prevent the adoption of decisions requiring unanimity.

ARTICLE **9**
1. The Board of Directors shall take decisions in respect of granting finance, in particular in the form of loans and guarantees, and raising loans; it shall fix the interest rates on loans granted and the commission and other charges. It may, on the basis of a decision taken by a qualified majority, delegate some of its functions to the Management Committee. It shall determine the terms and conditions for such delegation and shall supervise its execution.
The Board of Directors shall see that the Bank is properly run; it shall ensure that the Bank is managed in accordance with the provisions of the Treaty and of this Statute and with the general directives laid down by the Board of Governors.
At the end of the financial year the Board of Directors shall submit a report to the Board of Governors and shall publish it when approved.

2. The Board of Directors shall consist of 28 directors and 18 alternate directors.
The directors shall be appointed by the Board of Governors for five years, one nominated by each Member State, and one nominated by the Commission.
The alternate directors shall be appointed by the Board of Governors for five years as shown below:
- two alternates nominated by the Federal Republic of Germany,
- two alternates nominated by the French Republic,
- two alternates nominated by the Italian Republic,
- two alternates nominated by the United Kingdom of Great Britain and Northern Ireland,
- one alternate nominated by common accord of the Kingdom of Spain and the Portuguese Republic,
- one alternate nominated by common accord of the Kingdom of Belgium, the Grand Duchy of Luxembourg and the Kingdom of the Netherlands,
- two alternates nominated by common accord of the Kingdom of Denmark, the Hellenic Republic and Ireland and Romania,
- two alternates nominated by common accord of the Republic of Estonia, the Republic of Latvia, the Republic of Lithuania, the Republic of Austria, the Republic of Finland and the Kingdom of Sweden,
- three alternates nominated by common accord of the Republic of Bulgaria, the Czech Republic, the Republic of Cyprus, the Republic of Hungary, the Republic of Malta, the Republic of Poland, the Republic of Slovenia and the Slovak Republic,
- one alternate nominated by the Commission.

The Board of Directors shall co-opt six non-voting experts: three as members and three as alternates.
The appointments of the directors and the alternates shall be renewable.
The Rules of Procedure shall lay down the arrangements for participating in the meetings of the Board of Directors and the provisions applicable to alternates and co-opted experts.
The President of the Management Committee or, in his absence, one of the Vice-Presidents, shall preside over meetings of the Board of Directors but shall not vote.
Members of the Board of Directors shall be chosen from persons whose independence and competence are beyond doubt; they shall be responsible only to the Bank.

3. A director may be compulsorily retired by the Board of Governors only if he no longer fulfils the conditions required for the performance of his duties; the Board must act by a qualified majority.
If the annual report is not approved, the Board of Directors shall resign.

4. Any vacancy arising as a result of death, voluntary resignation, compulsory retirement or collective resignation shall be filled in accordance with paragraph 2. A member shall be replaced for the remainder of his term of office, save where the entire Board of Directors is being replaced.

5. The Board of Governors shall determine the remuneration of members of the Board of Directors. The Board of Governors shall lay down what activities are incompatible with the duties of a director or an alternate.

ARTICLE **10**

1. Each director shall have one vote on the Board of Directors. He may delegate his vote in all cases, according to procedures to be laid down in the rules of procedure of the Bank.

2. Save as otherwise provided in this Statute, decisions of the Board of Directors shall be taken by at least one third of the members entitled to vote Representing at least fifty per cent of the subscribed capital. A qualified majority shall require eighteen votes in favour and sixty-eight per cent of the subscribed capital. The rules of procedure of the Bank shall lay down the quorum required for the decisions of the Board of Directors to be valid.

ARTICLE **11**

1. The Management Committee shall consist of a President and eight Vice-Presidents appointed for a period of six years by the Board of Governors on a proposal from the Board of Directors. Their appointments shall be renewable.
The Board of Governors, acting unanimously, may vary the number of members on the Management Committee.

2. On a proposal from the Board of Directors adopted by a qualified majority, the Board of Governors may, acting in its turn by a qualified majority, compulsorily retire a member of the Management Committee.

3. The Management Committee shall be responsible for the current business of the Bank, under the authority of the President and the supervision of the Board of Directors.
It shall prepare the decisions of the Board of Directors, in particular decisions on the raising of loans and the granting of **finance, in particular in the form of loans** and guarantees; it shall ensure that these decisions are implemented.

4. The Management Committee shall act by a majority when delivering opinions on proposals for raising loans or granting **finance, in particular in the form of loans** and guarantees.

5. The Board of Governors shall determine the remuneration of members of the Management Committee and shall lay down what activities are incompatible with their duties.

6. The President or, if he is prevented, a Vice-President shall represent the Bank in judicial and other matters.

7. The **staff** of the Bank shall be under the authority of the President. They shall be engaged and discharged by him. In the selection of staff, account shall be taken not only of personal ability and qualifications but also of an equitable representation of nationals of Member States. **The Rules of Procedure shall determine which organ is competent to adopt the provisions applicable to staff.**

8. The Management Committee and the staff of the Bank shall be responsible only to the Bank and shall be completely independent in the performance of their duties.

ARTICLE **12**

1. A Committee consisting of **six** members, appointed on the grounds of their competence by the Board of Governors, **shall verify that the activities of the Bank conform to best banking practice and shall be responsible for the auditing of its accounts.**

2. The Committee referred to in paragraph 1 shall annually ascertain that the operations of the Bank have been conducted and its books kept in a proper manner. To this end, it shall verify that the Bank's operations have been carried out in compliance with the formalities and procedures laid down by this Statute and the Rules of Procedure.

3. The Committee referred to in paragraph 1 shall confirm that the financial statements, as well as any other financial information contained in the annual accounts drawn up by the Board of Directors, give a true and fair view of the financial position of the Bank in respect of its assets and liabilities, and of the results of its operations and its cash flows for the financial year under review.

4. The Rules of Procedure shall specify the qualifications required of the members of the Committee and lay down the terms and conditions for the Committee's activity.

ARTICLE **13**
The Bank shall deal with each Member State through the authority designated by that State. In the conduct of financial operations the Bank shall have recourse to the **national central bank** of the Member State concerned or to other financial institutions approved by that State.

ARTICLE **14**
1. The Bank shall co-operate with all international organisations active in fields similar to its own.

2. The Bank shall seek to establish all appropriate contacts in the interests of co-operation with banking and financial institutions in the countries to which its operations extend.

ARTICLE **15**
At the request of a Member State or of the Commission, or on its own initiative, the Board of Governors shall, in accordance with the same provisions as governed their adoption, interpret or supplement the directives laid down by it under Article 9 of this Statute.

ARTICLE **16**
1. Within the framework of the task set out in Article ***309*** of ***the Treaty on the Functioning of the European Union***, the Bank shall grant **finance, in particular in the form of loans and guarantees** to its members or to private or public undertakings for **investments** to be carried out in the territories of Member States, to the extent that funds are not available from other sources on reasonable terms.
However, by **decision of the Board of Governors, acting by a qualified majorit**y on a proposal from the Board of Directors, the Bank may grant **financing for investment** to be carried out, in whole or in part, outside the territories of Member States.

2. As far as possible, loans shall be granted only on condition that other sources of finance are also used.

3. When granting a loan to an undertaking or to a body other than a Member State, the Bank shall make the loan conditional either on a guarantee from the Member State in whose territory the **investment** will be carried out or on other adequate guarantees**, or on the financial strength of the debtor**.
Furthermore, in accordance with the principles established by the Board of Governors pursuant to Article 7(3)(b), and where the implementation of projects provided for in *Article 309 of the Treaty on the Functioning of the European Union* so requires, the Board of Directors shall, acting by a qualified majority, lay down the terms and conditions of any financing operation presenting a specific risk profile and thus considered to be a special activity.

4. The Bank may guarantee loans contracted by public or private undertakings or other bodies for the purpose of carrying out projects provided for in Article ***309*** of ***the Treaty on the Functioning of the European Union***.

5. The aggregate amount outstanding at any time of loans and guarantees granted by the Bank shall not exceed 250 per cent of its subscribed capital**, reserves, non-allocated provisions and profit and loss account surplus. The latter aggregate amount shall be reduced by an amount equal to the amount subscribed (whether or not paid in) for any equity participation of the Bank.**
The amount of the Bank's disbursed equity participations shall not exceed at any time an amount corresponding to the total of its paid-in subscribed capital, reserves, non-allocated provisions and profit and loss account surplus.
By way of exception, the special activities of the Bank, as decided by the Board of Governors and the Board of Directors in accordance with paragraph 3, will have a specific allocation of reserve.
This paragraph shall also apply to the consolidated accounts of the Bank.

6. The Bank shall protect itself against exchange risks by including in contracts for loans and guarantees such clauses as it considers appropriate

ARTICLE **17**
1. Interest rates on loans to be granted by the Bank and commission **and other charges** shall be adjusted to conditions prevailing on the capital market and shall be calculated in such a way that the income therefrom shall enable the Bank to meet its obligations, to cover its expenses **and risks** and to build up a reserve fund as provided for in Article 24.

2. The Bank shall not grant any reduction in interest rates. Where a reduction in the interest rate appears desirable in view of the nature of the **investment** to be financed, the Member State concerned

or some other agency may grant aid towards the payment of interest to the extent that this is compatible with Article *309* of ***the Treaty on the Functioning of the European Union***.

ARTICLE **18**

In its **financing** operations, the Bank shall observe the following principles:

1. It shall ensure that its funds are employed as rationally as possible in the interests of the **Union**. It may grant loans or guarantees only:
   (a) where, in the case of **investments** by undertakings in the production sector, interest and amortisation payments are covered out of operating profits, or, in **the case of other investments**, either by a commitment entered into by the State in which **the investment is made** or by some other means; and
   (b) where the execution of the **investment** contributes to an increase in economic productivity in general and promotes the attainment of the **internal** market.

2. It shall neither acquire any interest in an undertaking nor assume any responsibility in its management unless this is required to safeguard the rights of the Bank in ensuring recovery of funds lent.
However, in accordance with the principles determined by the Board of Governors pursuant to Article 7(3)(b), and where the implementation of operations provided for in *Article 309 of the Treaty on the Functioning of the European Union* so requires, the Board of Directors shall, acting by a qualified majority, lay down the terms and conditions for taking an equity participation in a commercial undertaking, normally as a complement to a loan or a guarantee, insofar as this is required to finance an investment or programme.

3. It may dispose of its claims on the capital market and may, to this end, require its debtors to issue bonds or other securities.

4. Neither the Bank nor the Member States shall impose conditions requiring funds lent by the Bank to be spent within a specified Member State.

5. The Bank may make its loans conditional on international invitations to tender being arranged.

6. The Bank shall not finance, in whole or in part, any **investment** opposed by the Member State in whose territory it is to be carried out.

7. As a complement to its lending activity, the Bank may provide technical assistance services in accordance with the terms and conditions laid down by the Board of Governors, acting by a qualified majority, and in compliance with this Statute.

ARTICLE **19**

1. Any undertaking or public or private entity may apply directly to the Bank for financing. Applications to the Bank may also be made either through the Commission or through the Member State on whose territory the investment will be carried out.

2. Applications made through the Commission shall be submitted for an opinion to the Member State in whose territory the **investment** will be carried out. Applications made through a Member State shall be submitted to the Commission for an opinion. Applications made direct by an undertaking shall be submitted to the Member State concerned and to the Commission.
The Member State concerned and the Commission shall deliver their opinions within two months. If no reply is received within this period, the Bank may assume that there is no objection to the project in question.

3. The Board of Directors shall rule on **financing operations** submitted to it by the Management Committee.

4. The Management Committee shall examine whether applications for loans or guarantees submitted to it comply with the provisions of this Statute, in particular with **Articles 16 and 18**. Where the Management Committee is in favour of **the financing operation**, it shall submit the **corresponding proposal** to the Board of Directors; the Committee may make its favourable opinion subject to such conditions as it considers essential. Where the Management Committee is against granting the **finance**, it shall submit the relevant documents together with its opinion to the Board of Directors.

5. Where the Management Committee delivers an unfavourable opinion, the Board of Directors may not grant the **finance** concerned unless its decision is unanimous.

6. Where the Commission delivers an unfavourable opinion, the Board of Directors may not grant the **finance** concerned unless its decision is unanimous, the director nominated by the Commission abstaining.

7. Where both the Management Committee and the Commission deliver an unfavourable opinion, the Board of Directors may not grant the **finance**.

8. In the event that a financing operation relating to an approved investment has to be restructured in order to safeguard the Bank's rights and interests, the Management Committee shall take without delay the emergency measures which it deems necessary, subject to immediate reporting thereon to the Board of Directors.

ARTICLE **20**

1. The Bank shall borrow on the capital markets the funds necessary for the performance of its tasks.

2. The Bank may borrow on the capital **markets of the Member States in accordance with the legal provisions applying to those markets.**

The competent authorities **of a Member State with a derogation within the meaning of *Article 139(1) of the Treaty on the Functioning of the European Union* may oppose this** only if there is reason to fear serious disturbances on the capital market of that State.

ARTICLE **21**

1. The Bank may employ any available funds which it does not immediately require to meet its obligations in the following ways:
   (a) it may invest on the money markets;
   (b) it may, subject to the provisions of Article 20(2), buy and sell securities;
   (c) it may carry out any other financial operation linked with its objectives.

2. Without prejudice to the provisions of Article 25, the Bank shall not, in managing its investments, engage in any currency arbitrage not directly required to carry out its lending operations or fulfil commitments arising out of loans raised or guarantees granted by it.

3. The Bank shall, in the fields covered by this Article, act in agreement with the competent authorities or with the **national central bank** of the Member State concerned.

ARTICLE **22**

1. A reserve fund of up to 10 per cent of the subscribed capital shall be built up progressively. If the state of the liabilities of the Bank should so justify, the Board of Directors may decide to set aside additional reserves. Until such time as the reserve fund has been fully built up, it shall be fed by:
   (a) interest received on loans granted by the Bank out of sums to be paid up by the Member States pursuant to Article 5;
   (b) interest received on loans granted by the Bank out of funds derived from repayment of the loans referred to in (a);

to the extent that this income is not required to meet the obligations of the Bank or to cover its expenses.

2. The resources of the reserve fund shall be so invested as to be available at any time to meet the purpose of the fund.

ARTICLE **23**

1. The Bank shall at all times be entitled to transfer its assets in the currency of **a** Member State **whose currency is not the euro** in order to carry out financial operations corresponding to the task set out in Article ***309*** of ***the Treaty on the Functioning of the European Union***, taking into account the provisions of Article 23 of this Statute. The Bank shall, as far as possible, avoid making such transfers if it has cash or liquid assets in the currency required.

2. The Bank may not convert its assets in the currency of a Member State **whose currency is not the euro** into the currency of a third country without the agreement of the Member State concerned.

3. The Bank may freely dispose of that part of its capital which is paid up and of any currency borrowed on markets outside the **Union**.

4. The Member States undertake to make available to the debtors of the Bank the currency needed to repay the capital and pay the interest on loans or commission on guarantees granted by the Bank for **investment** to be carried out in their territory.

ARTICLE **24**
If a Member State fails to meet the obligations of membership arising from this Statute, in particular the obligation to pay its share of the subscribed capital, or to service its borrowings, the granting of loans or guarantees to that Member State or its nationals may be suspended by a decision of the Board of Governors, acting by a qualified majority.
Such decision shall not release either the State or its nationals from their obligations towards the Bank.

ARTICLE **25**
1. If the Board of Governors decides to suspend the operations of the Bank, all its activities shall cease forthwith, except those required to ensure the due realisation, protection and preservation of its assets and the settlement of its liabilities.

2. In the event of liquidation, the Board of Governors shall appoint the liquidators and give them instructions for carrying out the liquidation. **It shall ensure that the rights of the members of staff are safeguarded.**

ARTICLE **26**
1. In each of the Member States, the Bank shall enjoy the most extensive legal capacity accorded to legal persons under their laws; it may, in particular, acquire or dispose of movable or immovable property and may be a party to legal proceedings.

2. The property of the Bank shall be exempt from all forms of requisition or expropriation.

ARTICLE **27**
Disputes between the Bank on the one hand, and its creditors, debtors or any other person on the other, shall be decided by the competent national courts, save where jurisdiction has been conferred on the Court of Justice **of the European Union**. **The Bank may provide for arbitration in any contract.**
The Bank shall have an address for service in each Member State. It may, however, in any contract, specify a particular address for service.
The property and assets of the Bank shall not be liable to attachment or to seizure by way of execution except by decision of a court.

ARTICLE **28**
1. The Board of Governors may, acting unanimously, decide to establish **subsidiaries or other entities**, which shall have legal personality and financial autonomy.

2. The Board of Governors shall establish the **Statutes of the bodies referred to in paragraph 1**. The Statutes shall define, in particular, **their** objectives, structure, capital, membership, **the location of their seat,** financial resources, means of intervention and auditing arrangements, as well as the relationship between the organs of the Bank.

3. The Bank shall be entitled to participate in the management of **these bodies** and contribute to its subscribed capital up to the amount determined by the Board of Governors, acting unanimously.

4. The Protocol on the privileges and immunities of the European **Union** shall apply to the **bodies referred to in paragraph 1 insofar as they are incorporated under Union law**, to the members of its organs in the performance of their duties as such and to its staff**, under the same terms and conditions as those applicable to the Bank**.
Those dividends, capital gains or other forms of revenue stemming from **such bodies** to which the members, other than the European **Union** and the Bank, are entitled, shall however remain subject to the fiscal provisions of the applicable legislation.

5. The Court of Justice **of the European Union** shall, within the limits hereinafter laid down, have jurisdiction in disputes concerning measures adopted by organs of **a body incorporated under Union law**. Proceedings against such measures may be instituted by any member of **such a body** in its capacity as such or by Member States under the conditions laid down in Article ***263*** of ***the Treaty on the Functioning of the European Union***.

6. The Board of Governors may, acting unanimously, decide to admit the staff of bodies incorporated under Union law to joint schemes with the Bank, in compliance with the respective internal procedures.

Done at Rome this twenty-fifth day of March in the year one thousand nine hundred and fifty-seven.
[BMDF Note: This protocol was introduced by the Treaty of Rome.]

15. PROTOCOL ON THE LOCATION OF THE SEATS OF THE INSTITUTIONS AND OF CERTAIN BODIES, *OFFICES, AGENCIES* AND DEPARTMENTS OF THE EUROPEAN UNION

THE REPRESENTATIVES OF THE GOVERNMENTS OF THE MEMBER STATES,

HAVING REGARD to Article ***341*** of the ***Treaty on the Functioning of the European Union*** and Article 189 of the Treaty establishing the European Atomic Energy Community,

RECALLING AND CONFIRMING the Decision of 8 April 1965, and without prejudice to the decisions concerning the seat of future institutions, bodies and departments,

HAVE AGREED UPON the following provisions, which shall be annexed to the Treaty on European Union**, *the Treaty on the Functioning of the European Union* and to the Treaty establishing the European Atomic Energy Community**,

SOLE ARTICLE

(a) The European Parliament shall have its seat in Strasbourg where the 12 periods of monthly plenary sessions, including the budget session, shall be held. The periods of additional plenary sessions shall be held in Brussels. The committees of the European Parliament shall meet in Brussels. The General Secretariat of the European Parliament and its departments shall remain in Luxembourg.

(b) The Council shall have its seat in Brussels. During the months of April, June and October, the Council shall hold its meetings in Luxembourg.

(c) The Commission shall have its seat in Brussels. The departments listed in Articles 7, 8 and 9 of the Decision of 8 April 1965 shall be established in Luxembourg.

(d) The Court of Justice **of the European Union** shall have **its seat** in Luxembourg.

(e) The Court of Auditors shall have its seat in Luxembourg.

(f) The Economic and Social Committee shall have its seat in Brussels.

(g) The Committee of the Regions shall have its seat in Brussels.

(h) The European Investment Bank shall have its seat in Luxembourg.

(i) The European Central Bank shall have **its** seat in Frankfurt.

(j) The European Police Office (Europol) shall have its seat in The Hague.

[BMDF Note: This protocol was introduced by the Treaty of Amsterdam.]

16. PROTOCOL ON THE PRIVILEGES AND IMMUNITIES OF THE EUROPEAN UNION

BMDF Note: This Protocol was originally attached to the Treaty establishing a single Council and a single Commission of the European Communities, signed in Brussels on 8 April 1965. The Treaty, with the exception of this Protocol, was repealed by the Treaty of Amsterdam.

THE HIGH CONTRACTING PARTIES,

CONSIDERING that, in accordance with **Article *343* of the Treaty on the Functioning of the European Union and to Article 191 of the Treaty establishing the European Atomic Energy Community (the EAEC), the European Union and the EAEC** shall enjoy in the territories of the Member States such privileges and immunities as are necessary for the performance of their tasks,

HAVE AGREED upon the following provisions, which shall be annexed to ***the Treaty on European Union, the Treaty on the Functioning of the European Union and the Treaty establishing the European Atomic Energy Community***:

CHAPTER I

PROPERTY, FUNDS, ASSETS AND OPERATIONS OF THE EUROPEAN **UNION**

ARTICLE 1
The premises and buildings of the **Union** shall be inviolable. They shall be exempt from search, requisition, confiscation or expropriation. The property and assets of the **Union** shall not be the subject of any administrative or legal measure of constraint without the authorisation of the Court of Justice.

ARTICLE 2
The archives of the **Union** shall be inviolable.

ARTICLE 3
The **Union**, their assets, revenues and other property shall be exempt from all direct taxes.
The Governments of the Member States shall, wherever possible, take the appropriate measures to remit or refund the amount of indirect taxes or sales taxes included in the price of movable or immovable property, where the **Union** make**s**, for **its** official use, substantial purchases the price of which includes taxes of this kind. These provisions shall not be applied, however, so as to have the effect of distorting competition within the **Union**.
No exemption shall be granted in respect of taxes and dues which amount merely to charges for public utility services.

ARTICLE 4
The **Union** shall be exempt from all customs duties, prohibitions and restrictions on imports and exports in respect of articles intended for **its** official use: articles so imported shall not be disposed of, whether or not in return for payment, in the territory of the country into which they have been imported, except under conditions approved by the Government of that country.
The **Union** shall also be exempt from any customs duties and any prohibitions and restrictions on imports and exports in respect of **its** publications.

CHAPTER II

COMMUNICATIONS AND *LAISSEZ-PASSER*

ARTICLE **5**
For their official communications and the transmission of all their documents, the institutions of the **Union** shall enjoy in the territory of each Member State the treatment accorded by that State to diplomatic missions.
Official correspondence and other official communications of the institutions of the **Union** shall not be subject to censorship.

ARTICLE **6**
Laissez-passer in a form to be prescribed by the Council**, acting by a simple majority**, which shall be recognised as valid travel documents by the authorities of the Member States, may be issued to Members and servants of the institutions of the **Union** by the Presidents of these institutions. These *laissez-passer* shall be issued to officials and other servants under conditions laid down in the Staff Regulations of officials and the Conditions of Employment of other servants of the **Union**.
The Commission may conclude agreements for these *laissez-passer* to be recognised as valid travel documents within the territory of third countries.

CHAPTER III

MEMBERS OF THE EUROPEAN PARLIAMENT

ARTICLE **7**
No administrative or other restriction shall be imposed on the free movement of Members of the European parliament travelling to or from the place of meeting of the European Parliament.
Members of the European Parliament shall, in respect of customs and exchange control, be accorded:
(a) by their own Government, the same facilities as those accorded to senior officials travelling abroad on temporary official missions;

(b) by the Governments of other Member States, the same facilities as those accorded to representatives of foreign Governments on temporary official missions.

ARTICLE **8**
Members of the European Parliament shall not be subject to any form of inquiry, detention or legal proceedings in respect of opinions expressed or votes cast by them in the performance of' their duties.

ARTICLE **9**
During the sessions of the European Parliament, its Members shall enjoy:
(a) in the territory of their own State, the immunities accorded to Members of their Parliament;
(b) in the territory of any other Member State, immunity from any measure of detention and from legal proceedings.
Immunity shall likewise apply to Members while they are travelling to and from the place of meeting of the European Parliament.
Immunity cannot be claimed when a member is found in the act of committing an offence and shall not prevent the European Parliament from exercising its right to waive the immunity of one of its Members.

CHAPTER IV

REPRESENTATIVES OF MEMBER STATES TAKING PART IN THE WORK OF THE INSTITUTIONS OF THE EUROPEAN **UNION**

ARTICLE **10**
Representatives of Member States taking part in the work of the institutions of the **Union**, their advisors and technical experts shall, in the performance of their duties and during their travel to and from the place of meeting, enjoy the customary privileges, immunities and facilities.
This Article shall also apply to Members of the advisory bodies of the **Union**.

CHAPTER V

OFFICIALS AND OTHER SERVANTS OF THE EUROPEAN **UNION**

ARTICLE **11**
In the territory of each Member State and whatever their nationality, officials and other servants of the **Union** shall:

(a) subject to the provisions of the Treaties relating, on the one hand, to the rules on the liability of officials and other servants towards the **Union** and, on the other hand, to the jurisdiction of the Court **of Justice of the European Union** in disputes between the **Union** and their officials and other servants, be immune from legal proceedings in respect of acts performed by them in their official capacity, including their words spoken or written. They shall continue to enjoy this immunity after they have ceased to hold office;

(b) together with their spouses and dependent Members of their families, not be subject to immigration restrictions or to formalities for the registration of aliens;

(c) in respect of currency or exchange regulations, be accorded the same facilities as are customarily accorded to officials of international organisations;

(d) enjoy the right to import free of duty their furniture and effects at the time of first taking up their post in the country concerned, and the right to re-export free of duty their furniture and effects, on termination of their duties in that country, subject in either case to the conditions considered to be necessary by the Government of the country in which this fight is exercised;

(e) have the right to import free of duty a motor car for their personal use, acquired either in the country of their last residence or in the country of which they are nationals on the terms ruling in the home market in that country, and to re-export it free of duty, subject in either case to the conditions considered to be necessary by the Government of the country concerned.

ARTICLE **12**
Officials and other servants of the **Union** shall be liable to a tax for the benefit of the **Union** on salaries, wages and emoluments paid to them by the **Union**, in accordance with the conditions and procedure laid down by **the European Parliament and** the Council, acting **by means of regulations in**

accordance with the ordinary legislative procedure and after consultation of the institutions concerned.
They shall be exempt from national taxes on salaries, wages and emoluments paid by the **Union**.

ARTICLE **13**
In the application of income tax, wealth tax and death duties and in the application of conventions on the avoidance of double taxation concluded between Member States of the **Union**, officials and other servants of the **Union** who, solely by reason of the performance of their duties in the service of the **Union**, establish their residence in the territory of a Member State other than their country of domicile for tax purposes at the time of entering the service of the **Union**, shall be considered, both in the country of their actual residence and in the country of domicile for tax purposes, as having maintained their domicile in the latter country provided that it is a member of the **Union**. This provision shall also apply to a spouse, to the extent that the latter is not separately engaged in a gainful occupation, and to children dependent on and in the care of the persons referred to in this Article.
Movable property belonging to persons referred to in the preceding paragraph and situated in the territory of the country where they are staying shall be exempt from death duties in that country; such property shall for the assessment of such duty, be considered as being in the country of domicile for tax purposes, subject to the rights of third countries and to the possible application of provisions of international conventions on double taxation.
Any domicile acquired solely by reason of the performance of duties in the service of other international organisations shall not be taken into consideration in applying the provisions of this Article.

ARTICLE **14**
The European Parliament and the Council, acting by means of regulations in accordance with the ordinary legislative procedure and after consultation of the institutions concerned, shall lay down the scheme of social security benefits for officials and other servants of the **Union**.

ARTICLE **15**
The European Parliament and the Council, acting by means of regulations in accordance with the ordinary legislative procedure, shall after consulting the other institutions concerned, determine the categories of officials and other servants of the **Union** to whom the provisions of Article 12, the second paragraph of Article 13, and Article 14 shall apply, in whole or in part.
The names, grades and addresses of officials and other servants included in such categories shall be communicated periodically to the Governments of the Member States.

CHAPTER VI

PRIVILEGES AND IMMUNITIES OF MISSIONS OF THIRD COUNTRIES ACCREDITED TO THE EUROPEAN **UNION**

ARTICLE **16**
The Member State in whose territory the **Union** have their seat shall accord the customary diplomatic immunities and privileges to missions of third countries accredited to the **Union**.

CHAPTER VII

GENERAL PROVISIONS

ARTICLE **17**
Privileges, immunities and facilities shall be accorded to officials and other servants of the **Union** solely in the interests of the **Union**.
Each institution of the **Union** shall be required to waive the immunity accorded to an official or other servant wherever that institution considers that the waiver of such immunity is not contrary to the interests of the **Union**.

ARTICLE **18**
The institutions of the **Union** shall, for the purpose of applying this Protocol, co-operate with the responsible authorities of the Member States concerned.

ARTICLE **19**
Articles 12 to 15 and Article 18 shall apply to Members of the Commission.

ARTICLE **20**
Articles 12 to 15 and Article 18 shall apply to the Judges, the Advocates-General, the Registrars and the Assistant Rapporteurs of the Court of Justice **of the European Union**, without prejudice to the provisions of Article 3 of the Protocol on the Statute of the Court of Justice **of the European Union** relating to immunity from legal proceedings of Judges and Advocates-General.

ARTICLE **21**
This Protocol shall also apply to the European Investment Bank, to the Members of its organs, to its staff and to the representatives of the Member States taking part in its activities, without prejudice to the provisions of the Protocol on the Statute of the Bank.
The European Investment Bank shall in addition be exempt from any form of taxation or imposition of a like nature on the occasion of any increase in its capital and from the various formalities which may be connected therewith in the State where the Bank has its seat. Similarly, its dissolution or liquidation shall not give rise to any imposition. Finally, the activities of the Bank and of its organs carried on in accordance with its Statute shall not be subject to any turnover tax.

ARTICLE **22**
This Protocol shall also apply to the European Central Bank, to the Members of its organs and to its staff, without prejudice to the provisions of the Protocol on the Statute of the European System of Central Banks and the European Central Bank.
The European Central Bank shall, in addition, be exempt from any form of taxation or imposition of a like nature on the occasion of any increase in its capital and from the various formalities which may be connected therewith in the State where the bank has its seat. The activities of the Bank and of its organs carried on in accordance with the Statute of the European System of Central Banks and of the European Central Bank shall not be subject to any turnover tax.

IN WITNESS WHEREOF, the undersigned Plenipotentiaries have signed this Protocol

[BMDF Note: This protocol was signed in Brussels on 8 April 1965]

17. PROTOCOL ON THE CONVERGENCE CRITERIA

THE HIGH CONTRACTING PARTIES,

DESIRING to lay down the details of the convergence criteria which shall guide the **Union** in taking decisions **to end the derogations of those Member States with a derogation**, referred to in Article ***140(l)*** of ***the Treaty on the Functioning of the European Union***,

HAVE AGREED upon the following provisions, which shall be annexed to the ***Treaty on European Union and to the Treaty on the Functioning of the European Union***:

ARTICLE 1
The criterion on price stability referred to in the first indent of Article ***140(l)*** of ***the Treaty on the Functioning of the European Union*** shall mean that a Member State has a price performance that is sustainable and an average rate of inflation, observed over a period of one year before the examination, that does not exceed by more than 1½ percentage points that of, at most, the three best performing Member States in terms of price stability. Inflation shall be measured by means of the consumer price index on a comparable basis, taking into account differences in national definitions.

ARTICLE 2
The criterion on the government budgetary position referred to in the second indent of Article ***140(l)*** of **the said** Treaty shall mean that at the time of the examination the Member State is not the subject of a Council decision under Article ***126(6)*** of **the said** Treaty that an excessive deficit exists.

ARTICLE 3
The criterion on participation in the Exchange Rate Mechanism of the European Monetary System referred to in the third indent of Article ***140(l)*** of **the said** Treaty shall mean that a Member State has respected the normal fluctuation margins provided for by the Exchange Rate Mechanism of the European Monetary System without severe tensions for at least the last two years before the examination. In particular, the Member State shall not have devalued its currency's bilateral central rate against **the euro** on its own initiative for the same period.

ARTICLE 4
The criterion on the convergence of interest rates referred to in the fourth indent of Article ***140(l)*** of **the said** Treaty shall mean that, observed over a period of one year before the examination, a Member State has had an average nominal long-term interest rate that does not exceed by more than 2 percentage points that of, at most, the three best performing Member States in terms of price stability. Interest rates shall be measured on the basis of long term government bonds or comparable securities, taking into account differences in national definitions.

ARTICLE 5
The statistical data to be used for the application of this Protocol shall be provided by the Commission.

ARTICLE 6
The Council shall, acting unanimously on a proposal from the Commission and after consulting the European Parliament, the ECB as the case may be, and the **Economic and Financial Committee**, adopt appropriate provisions to lay down the details of the convergence criteria referred to in Article ***140*** of **the said** Treaty, which shall then replace this Protocol.
[BMDF Note: This protocol was introduced by the Maastricht Treaty.]

18. PROTOCOL ON CERTAIN PROVISIONS RELATING TO THE UNITED KINGDOM OF GREAT BRITAIN AND NORTHERN IRELAND

THE HIGH CONTRACTING PARTIES,

RECOGNISING that the United Kingdom shall not be obliged or committed to **adopt the euro** without a separate decision to do so by its government and Parliament,

GIVEN that on 16 October 1996 and 30 October 1997 the United Kingdom government notified the Council of its intention not to participate in the third stage of economic and monetary union,

NOTING the practice of the government of the United Kingdom to fund its borrowing requirement by the sale of debt to the private sector,

HAVE AGREED the following provisions, which shall be annexed to the ***Treaty on European Union and to the Treaty on the Functioning of the European Union***:

1. Unless the United Kingdom notifies the Council that it intends to **adopt the euro**, it shall be under no obligation to do so.

2. **In view of the notice given to the Council by the United Kingdom government on 16 October 1996 and 30 October 1997, Articles 3 to 8 and 10 shall apply to the United Kingdom**.

3. The United Kingdom shall retain its powers in the field of monetary policy according to national law.

4. Articles ***282(2), with the exception of the first and last sentences thereof, 282(5), 119, second paragraph, 126(l), (9)*** **and** ***(11), 127(1)*** **to** ***(5), 128, 130, 131, 132***, **and** ***133, 138, 140(3), 219 and 283*** of ***the Treaty on the Functioning of the European Union*** shall not apply to the United Kingdom. **The same applies to *Article 121(2)* of *this Treaty* as regards the adoption of the parts of the broad economic policy guidelines which concern the euro area generally.** In these provisions references to the **Union** or the Member States shall not include the United Kingdom and references to national central banks shall not include the Bank of England.

5. The United Kingdom shall endeavour to avoid an excessive government deficit.
Articles ***143*** and ***144*** of ***the Treaty on the Functioning of the European Union*** shall continue to apply to the United Kingdom. Articles ***134(4)*** and ***142*** shall apply to the United Kingdom as if it had a derogation.

6. The voting rights of the United Kingdom shall be suspended in respect of acts of the Council referred to in the Articles listed in **paragraph 4 and in the instances referred to in the first subparagraph of *Article 139(4) of the Treaty on the Functioning of the European Union*. For this purpose the second and third subparagraphs of *Article 139(4) of the Treaty* shall apply.**
The United Kingdom shall also have no right to participate in the appointment of the President, the Vice-President and the other members of the Executive Board of the ECB under ***Article 283(2)b*** of **the said** Treaty.

7. Articles, 3, 4, 6, 7, 9.2, 10.1, 10.3, 11.2, 12.1, 14, 16, 18 to 20, 22, 23, 26, 27, 30 to 34, 50 and 52 of the Protocol on the Statute of the European System of Central Banks and of the European Central Bank ('the Statute') shall not apply to the United Kingdom.
In those Articles, references to the **Union** or the Member States shall not include the United Kingdom and references to national central banks or shareholders shall not include the Bank of England.
References in Articles 10.3 and 30.2 of the Statute to 'subscribed capital of the ECB' shall not include capital subscribed by the Bank of England.

8. Article ***141(3)*** of ***the Treaty on the Functioning of the European Union*** and Articles 44 to 48 of the Statute shall have effect, whether or not there is any Member State with a derogation, subject to the following amendments:
(a) References in Article 44 to the tasks of the ECB and the EMI shall include those tasks that still need to be performed in the third stage owing to any decision of the United Kingdom not to **adopt the euro**.
(b) In addition to the tasks referred to in Article 47 the ECB shall also give advice in relation to and contribute to the preparation of any decision of the Council with regard to the United Kingdom taken in accordance with paragraphs 10(a) and 10(c).
(c) The Bank of England shall pay up its subscription to the capital of the ECB as a contribution to its operational costs on the same basis as national central banks of Member States with a derogation.

9. The United Kingdom may notify the Council at any time of its intention to adopt the euro.
In that event:
(a) The United Kingdom shall have the right to **adopt the euro** provided only that it satisfies the necessary conditions. The Council, acting at the request of the United Kingdom and under the conditions and in accordance with the procedure laid down in ***Article 140(1) and (2) of the Treaty on the Functioning of the European Union***, shall decide whether it fulfils the necessary conditions.
(b) The Bank of England shall pay up its subscribed capital, transfer to the ECB foreign reserve assets and contribute to its reserves on the same basis as the national central bank of a Member State whose derogation has been abrogated.
(c) The Council, acting under the conditions and in accordance with the procedure laid down in Article ***141(5)*** of **the said** Treaty, shall take all other necessary decisions to enable the United Kingdom to **adopt the euro**.

If the United Kingdom **adopts the euro** pursuant to the provisions of this protocol, paragraphs 3 to 9 shall cease to have effect.

10. Notwithstanding ***Article 123 of the Treaty on the Functioning of the European Union*** and Article 21.1 of the Statute, the government of the United Kingdom may maintain its 'Ways and Means' facility with the Bank of England if and so long as the United Kingdom does not **adopt the euro**.
[BMDF Note: This protocol was introduced by the Maastricht Treaty.]

19. PROTOCOL ON CERTAIN PROVISIONS RELATING TO DENMARK

THE HIGH CONTRACTING PARTIES,

TAKING INTO ACCOUNT that the Danish Constitution contains provisions which may imply a referendum in Denmark prior to **Denmark renouncing its exemption,**

GIVEN THAT, on 3 November 1993, the Danish Government notified the Council of its intention not to participate in the third stage of economic and monetary union,

HAVE AGREED on the following provisions, which shall be annexed to the ***Treaty on European Union and to the Treaty on the Functioning of the European Union***:

1. **In view of the notice given to the Council by the Danish Government on 3 November 1993, Denmark shall have an exemption**. The effect of the exemption shall be that all Articles and provisions of ***these Treaties*** and the Statute of the ESCB referring to a derogation shall be applicable to Denmark.

2. As for the abrogation of the exemption, the procedure referred to in ***Article 140 of the Treaty on the Functioning of the European Union*** shall only be initiated at the request of Denmark.

3. In the event of abrogation of the exemption status, the provisions of the Protocol shall cease to apply.

[BMDF Note: This protocol was introduced by the Maastricht Treaty.]

20. PROTOCOL *ON* THE SCHENGEN *ACQUIS INTEGRATED* INTO THE FRAMEWORK OF THE EUROPEAN UNION

THE HIGH CONTRACTING PARTIES,

NOTING that the Agreements on the gradual abolition of checks at common borders signed by some Member States of the European Union in Schengen on 14 June 1985 and on 19 June 1990, as well as related agreements and the rules adopted on the basis of these agreements, **have been integrated into the framework of the European Union by the Treaty of Amsterdam of 2 October 1997,**

DESIRING to preserve the Schengen *acquis*, as developed since the entry into force of the Treaty of Amsterdam, and to develop this *acquis* in order to contribute towards achieving the objective of offering citizens of the Union an area of freedom, security and justice without internal borders;

TAKING INTO ACCOUNT the special position of Denmark,

TAKING INTO ACCOUNT the fact that Ireland and the United Kingdom of Great Britain and Northern Ireland **do not participate in all the provisions of the Schengen *acquis***; that provision should, however, be made to allow those Member States to accept **other provisions of this *acquis* in full or in part**;

RECOGNISING that, as a consequence, it is necessary to make use of the provisions of ***the Treaties*** concerning closer co-operation between some Member States,

TAKING INTO ACCOUNT the need to maintain a special relationship with the Republic of Iceland and the Kingdom of Norway, both States **being bound by the provisions of the Nordic passport union, together with the Nordic States which are members of the European Union,**

HAVE AGREED UPON the following provisions, which shall be annexed to the Treaty on European Union and to ***the Treaty on the Functioning of the European Union***:

ARTICLE 1
The Kingdom of Belgium, **the Republic of Bulgaria, the Czech Republic,** the Kingdom of Denmark, **the Federal Republic of Germany, the Republic of Estonia,** the Hellenic Republic, the Kingdom of Spain, the French Republic, the Italian Republic, **the Republic of Cyprus, the Republic of Latvia, the Republic of Lithuania,** the Grand Duchy of Luxembourg, **the Republic of Hungary, the Republic of Malta,** the Kingdom of the Netherlands, the Republic of Austria, **the Republic of Poland,** the Portuguese Republic, **Romania, the Republic of Slovenia, the Slovak Republic**, the Republic of Finland and the Kingdom of Sweden **shall be** authorised to establish closer co-operation among themselves **in areas covered by provisions defined by the Council which constitute** the Schengen acquis. This co-operation shall be conducted within the institutional and legal framework of the European Union and with respect for the relevant provisions of ***the Treaties***.

ARTICLE 2
The Schengen *acquis* shall apply to the Member States referred to in Article 1, without prejudice to Article 3 of the Act of Accession of 16 April 2003 or to Article 4 of the Act of Accession of 25 April 2005. The Council will substitute itself for the Executive Committee established by the Schengen agreements.

ARTICLE 3
The participation of Denmark in the adoption of measures constituting a development of the Schengen *acquis*, as well as the implementation of these measures and their application to Denmark, shall be governed by the relevant provisions of the Protocol on the position of Denmark.

ARTICLE 4
Ireland and the United Kingdom of Great Britain and Northern Ireland, may at any time request to take part in some or all of the provisions of this *acquis*.
The Council shall decide on the request with the unanimity if its members referred to in Article 1 and of the representative of the Government of the State concerned.

ARTICLE 5
1. Proposals and initiatives to build upon the Schengen *acquis* shall be subject to the relevant provisions of the Treaties.
In this context, where either Ireland or the United Kingdom ***has not notified*** the Council in writing within a reasonable period that ***it wishes*** to take part, the authorisation referred to in ***Article 329 of the Treaty on the Functioning of the European Union*** shall be deemed to have been granted to the Members States referred to in Article 1 and to Ireland or the United Kingdom where either of them wishes to take part in the areas of co-operation in question.

2. Where either Ireland or the United Kingdom is deemed to have given notification pursuant to a decision under Article 4, it may nevertheless notify the Council in writing, within 3 months, that it does not wish to take part in such a proposal or initiative. In that case, Ireland or the United Kingdom shall not take part in its adoption. As from the latter notification, the procedure for adopting the measure building upon the Schengen acquis shall be suspended until the end of the procedure set out in paragraphs 3 or 4 or until the notification is withdrawn at any moment during that procedure.

3. For the Member State having made the notification referred to in paragraph 2, any decision taken by the Council pursuant to Article 4 shall, as from the date of entry into force of the proposed measure, cease to apply to the extent considered necessary by the Council and under the conditions to be determined in a decision of the Council acting by a qualified majority on a proposal from the Commission. That decision shall be taken in accordance with the following criteria: the Council shall seek to retain the widest possible measure of participation of the Member State concerned without seriously affecting the practical operability of the various parts of the Schengen acquis, while respecting their coherence. The Commission shall submit its proposal as soon as possible after the notification referred to in paragraph 2. The Council shall, if needed after convening two successive meetings, act within four months of the Commission proposal.

4. If, by the end of the period of four months, the Council has not adopted a decision, a Member State may, without delay, request that the matter be referred to the European Council. In that case, the European Council shall, at its next meeting, acting by a qualified majority on a proposal from the Commission, take a decision in accordance with the criteria referred to in paragraph 3.

5. ***If, by the end of the procedure set out in paragraphs 3 or 4, the Council or, as the case may be, the European Council has not adopted its decision, the suspension of the procedure for adopting the measure building upon the Schengen acquis shall be terminated. If the said measure is subsequently adopted any decision taken by the Council pursuant to Article 4 shall, as from the date of entry into force of that measure, cease to apply for the Member State concerned to the extent and under the conditions decided by the Commission, unless the said Member State has withdrawn its notification referred to in paragraph 2 before the adoption of the measure. The Commission shall act by the date of this adoption. When taking its decision, the Commission shall respect the criteria referred to in paragraph 3.***
[BMDF Note: Paragraphs 2, 3, 4 and 5 introduced by the second draft of the Reform Treaty, dated 5 October2007]

ARTICLE 6
The Republic of Iceland and the Kingdom of Norway shall be associated with the implementation of the Schengen *acquis* and its further development. Appropriate procedures shall be agreed to that effect in an Agreement to be concluded with those States by the Council, acting by the unanimity of its Members mentioned in Article 1. Such Agreement shall include provisions on the contribution of Iceland and Norway to any financial consequences resulting from the implementation of this Protocol.
A separate Agreement shall be concluded with Iceland and Norway by the Council, acting unanimously, for the establishment of rights and obligations between Ireland and the United Kingdom of Great Britain and Northern Ireland on the one hand, and Iceland and Norway on the other, in domains of the Schengen *acquis* which apply to these States.

ARTICLE 7
For the purposes of the negotiations for the admission of new Member States into the European Union, the Schengen *acquis* and further measures taken by the institutions within its scope shall be regarded as an *acquis* which must be accepted in full by all States candidates for admission.
[BMDF Note: The Annex shall be repealed]
[BMDF Note: See also Declarations nos. 44 to 47. This protocol was introduced by the Treaty of Amsterdam.]

21. PROTOCOL ON THE APPLICATION OF CERTAIN ASPECTS OF *ARTICLE 26 OF THE TREATY ON THE FUNCTIONING OF THE EUROPEAN UNION* TO THE UNITED KINGDOM AND TO IRELAND

THE HIGH CONTRACTING PARTIES,

DESIRING to settle certain questions relating to the United Kingdom and Ireland,

HAVING REGARD to the existence for many years of special travel arrangements between the United Kingdom and Ireland,

HAVE AGREED UPON the following provisions, which shall be annexed to the Treaty on European Union ***and to the Treaty on the Functioning of the European Union***:

ARTICLE 1
The United Kingdom shall be entitled, notwithstanding ***Articles 26 and 77 of the Treaty on the Functioning of the European Union***, any other provision of this Treaty or of the Treaty on European Union, any measure adopted under those Treaties, or any international agreement concluded by the **Union** or by the **Union** and its Member States with one or more third States, to exercise at its frontiers with other Member States such controls on persons seeking to enter the United Kingdom as it may consider necessary for the purpose:
(a) of verifying the right to enter the United Kingdom of citizens of **Member States** and of their dependants exercising rights conferred by **Union** law, as well as citizens of other States on whom such rights have been conferred by an agreement to which the United Kingdom is bound; and
(b) of determining whether or not to grant other persons permission to enter the United Kingdom.
Nothing in ***Articles 26 and 77 of the Treaty on the Functioning of the European Union*** or in any other provision of that Treaty or the Treaty on European Union or in any measure adopted under them shall

prejudice the right of the United Kingdom to adopt or exercise any such controls. References to the United Kingdom in this Article shall include territories for whose external relations the United Kingdom is responsible.

ARTICLE 2
The United Kingdom and Ireland may continue to make arrangements between themselves relating to the movement of persons between their territories ("the Common Travel Area"), while fully respecting the rights of persons referred to in Article 1, first paragraph, point (a) of this Protocol. Accordingly, as long as they maintain such arrangements, the provisions of Article 1 of this Protocol shall apply to Ireland with the same terms and conditions as for the United Kingdom. Nothing in ***Articles 26 and 77 of the Treaty on the Functioning of the European Union***, in any other provision of that Treaty or of the Treaty on European Union or in any measure adopted under them, shall affect any such arrangements.

ARTICLE 3
The other Member States shall be entitled to exercise at their frontiers or at any point of entry into their territory such controls on persons seeking to enter their territory from the United Kingdom or any territories whose external relations are under its responsibility for the same purposes stated in Article 1 of this Protocol, or from Ireland as long as the provisions of Article 1 of this Protocol apply to Ireland. Nothing in ***Articles 26 and 77 of the Treaty on the Functioning of the European Union*** or in any other provision of that Treaty or of the Treaty on European Union or in any measure adopted under them shall prejudice the right of the other Member States to adopt or exercise any such controls.
[BMDF Note: This protocol was introduced by the Treaty of Amsterdam.]

22. PROTOCOL ON THE POSITION OF THE UNITED KINGDOM AND IRELAND *IN RESPECT OF THE AREA OF FREEDOM, SECURITY AND JUSTICE*

THE HIGH CONTRACTING PARTIES,

DESIRING to settle certain questions relating to the United Kingdom and Ireland,

HAVING REGARD to the Protocol on the application of certain aspects of Article ***26 of the Treaty on the Functioning of the European Union*** to the United Kingdom and to Ireland,

HAVE AGREED UPON the following provisions, which shall be annexed to the Treaty on European Union ***and to the Treaty on the Functioning of the European Union***:

ARTICLE 1
Subject to Article 3, the United Kingdom and Ireland shall not take part in the adoption by the Council of proposed measures pursuant to Title IV of ***Part Three of the Treaty on the Functioning of the European Union***. The unanimity of the members of the Council, with the exception of the representatives of the governments of the United Kingdom and Ireland, shall be necessary for decisions of the Council which must be adopted unanimously.
For the purposes of this Article, a qualified majority shall be defined in accordance with Article 238(3) of the Treaty on the Functioning of the European Union.
[BMDF Note: the voting procedure in the draft Constitution is shown for information, in bold strikethrough, with the amended text introduced by the Reform Treaty in italics]

ARTICLE 2
In consequence of Article 1 and subject to Articles 3, 4 and 6, none of the provisions of Title IV of ***Part Three of the Treaty on the Functioning of the European Union***, no measure adopted pursuant to that Title, no provision of any international agreement concluded by the **Union** pursuant to that Title, and no decision of the Court of Justice **of the European Union** interpreting any such provision or measure shall be binding upon or applicable in the United Kingdom or Ireland; and no such provision, measure or decision shall in any way affect the competences, rights and obligations of those States; and no such provision, measure or decision shall in any way affect the **Community or Union *acquis*** nor form part of **Union** law as they apply to the United Kingdom or Ireland.

ARTICLE 3

1. The United Kingdom or Ireland may notify the President of the Council in writing, within three months after a proposal or initiative has been presented to the Council pursuant to Title IV of ***Part Three of the Treaty on the Functioning of the European Union***, that it wishes to take part in the adoption and application of any such proposed measure, whereupon that State shall be entitled to do so. By way of derogation from Article ***238(2)*** of the Treaty establishing the European Community, a qualified majority shall be defined as the same proportion of the weighted votes of the members of the Council concerned as laid down in the said Article ***238(2).***

The unanimity of the members of the Council, with the exception of a member which has not made such a notification, shall be necessary for decisions of the Council which must be adopted unanimously. A measure adopted under this paragraph shall be binding upon all Member States which took part in its adoption.

Measures adopted pursuant to Article 70 of the Treaty on the Functioning of the European Union **shall lay down the conditions for the participation of the United Kingdom and Ireland in the evaluations concerning the areas covered by** ***Title IV of Part Three of that Treaty.***

For the purposes of this Article, a qualified majority shall be defined in accordance with Article 238(3) of the Treaty on the Functioning of the European Union.

2. If after a reasonable period of time a measure referred to in paragraph 1 cannot be adopted with the United Kingdom or Ireland taking part, the Council may adopt such measure in accordance with Article 1 without the participation of the United Kingdom or Ireland. In that case Article 2 applies.

[BMDF Note: the voting procedure in the draft Constitution is shown for information, in bold strikethrough, with the amended text introduced by the Reform Treaty in italics]

ARTICLE 4

The United Kingdom or Ireland may at any time after the adoption of a measure by the Council pursuant to Title IV of ***Part Three of the Treaty on the Functioning of the European Union*** notify its intention to the Council and to the Commission that it wishes to accept that measure. In that case, the procedure provided for in ***Article 331(1) of the Treaty on the Functioning of the European Union*** shall apply *mutatis mutandis*.

ARTICLE 4 a

1. The provisions of this Protocol apply for the United Kingdom and Ireland also to measures proposed or adopted pursuant to Title IV of Part III of the Treaty on the Functioning of the European Union amending an existing measure by which they are bound.

2. However, in cases where the Council, acting on a proposal from the Commission, determines that the non-participation of the United Kingdom or Ireland in the amended version of an existing measure makes the application of that measure inoperable for other Member States or the Union, it may urge them to make a notification under Article 3 or 4. For the purposes of Article 3 a further period of two months starts to run as from the date of such determination by the Council.

If at the expiry of that period of two months from the Council's determination the United Kingdom or Ireland has not made a notification under Article 3 or Article 4, the existing measure shall no longer be binding upon or applicable to it, unless the Member State concerned has made a notification under Article 4 before the entry into force of the amending measure. This shall take effect from the date of entry into force of the amending measure or of expiry of the period of two months, whichever is the later.

For the purpose of this paragraph, the Council shall, after a full discussion of the matter, act by a qualified majority of its members representing the Member States participating or having participated in the adoption of the amending measure. A qualified majority of the Council shall be defined in accordance with Article 238(3)(a) of the Treaty on the Functioning of the European Union.

3. The Council, acting by a qualified majority on a proposal from the Commission, may determine that the United Kingdom or Ireland shall bear the direct financial consequences, if any, necessarily and unavoidably incurred as a result of the cessation of its participation in the existing measure.

4. This Article shall be without prejudice to Article 4.

[BMDF Note: Article introduced by the second draft of the Reform Treaty, dated 5 October2007]

ARTICLE 5

A Member State which is not bound by a measure adopted pursuant to Title IV of ***Part Three of the Treaty on the Functioning of the European Union*** shall bear no financial consequences of that measure other than administrative costs entailed for the institutions**, unless all members of the Council, acting unanimously after consulting the European Parliament, decide otherwise**.

ARTICLE 6
Where, in cases referred to in this Protocol, the United Kingdom or Ireland is bound by a measure adopted by the Council pursuant to Title IV of ***Part Three of the Treaty on the Functioning of the European Union***, the relevant provisions of ***the Treaties*** shall apply to that State in relation to that measure.

ARTICLE 6 a
The United Kingdom and Ireland shall not be bound by the rules laid down on the basis of Article 16 of the Treaty on the Functioning of the European Union which relate to the processing of personal data by the Member States when carrying out activities which fall within the scope of Chapter 4 or Chapter 5 of Title IV of Part Three of that Treaty where the United Kingdom and Ireland are not bound by the rules governing the forms of judicial co-operation in criminal matters or police co-operation which require compliance with the provisions laid down on the basis of Article 16.
[BMDF Note: Article introduced by the second draft of the Reform Treaty, dated 5 October2007]

ARTICLE 7
Articles ***3, 4 and 4a*** shall be without prejudice to the Protocol **on** the Schengen *acquis* **integrated** into the framework of the European Union.

ARTICLE 8
Ireland may notify the Council in writing that it no longer wishes to be covered by the terms of this Protocol. In that case, the normal Treaty provisions will apply to Ireland.

ARTICLE 9
With regard to Ireland, this Protocol shall not apply to Article 75 of the Treaty on the Functioning of the European Union.
[BMDF Notes: See also Declaration no. 55. This protocol was introduced by the Treaty of Amsterdam]
[BMDF Note: The title of this Protocol in the draft Constitution was "Protocol on the position of the United Kingdom and Ireland on policies in respect of border controls, asylum and immigration, judicial co-operation in civil matters and on police co-operation']

23. PROTOCOL ON THE POSITION OF DENMARK

THE HIGH CONTRACTING PARTIES,

RECALLING the Decision of the Heads of State or Government, meeting within the European Council at Edinburgh on 12 December 1992, concerning certain problems raised by Denmark on the Treaty on European Union,

HAVING NOTED the position of Denmark with regard to Citizenship, Economic and Monetary Union, Defence Policy and Justice and Home Affairs as laid down in the Edinburgh Decision,

CONSCIOUS of the fact that a continuation under the Treaties of the legal regime originating in the Edinburgh decision will significantly limit Denmark's participation in important areas of co-operation of the Union, and that it would be in the best interest of the Union to ensure the integrity of the *acquis* in the area of freedom, security and justice;

WISHING therefore to establish a legal framework that will provide an option for Denmark to participate in the adoption of measures proposed on the basis of *Title IV of Part Three of the Treaty on the Functioning of the European Union* and welcoming the intention of Denmark to avail itself of this option when possible in accordance with its constitutional requirements;

NOTING that Denmark will not prevent the other Member States from further developing their co-operation with respect to measures not binding on Denmark;

BEARING IN MIND Article 3 of the Protocol **on** the Schengen *acquis* **integrated** into the framework of the European Union,

HAVE AGREED UPON the following provisions, which shall be annexed to the Treaty on European Union ***and to the Treaty on the Functioning of the European Union***:

PART I

ARTICLE 1

Denmark shall not take part in the adoption by the Council of proposed measures pursuant to ***IV of Part Three of the Treaty on the Functioning of the European Union*. For the purposes of this Article, a qualified majority shall be defined in accordance with *Article 238(3) of the Treaty on the Functioning of the European Union*.** The unanimity of the members of the Council, with the exception of the representative of the government of Denmark, shall be necessary for the decisions of the Council which must be adopted unanimously.

ARTICLE 2

None of the provisions of ***Title IV of Part Three of the Treaty on the Functioning of the European Union***, no measure adopted pursuant to that Title, no provision of any international agreement concluded by the **Union** pursuant to that Title, and no decision of the Court of Justice **of the European Union** interpreting any such provision or measure **or any measure amended or amendable pursuant to that Title** shall be binding upon or applicable in Denmark; and no such provision, measure or decision shall in any way affect the competences, rights and obligations of Denmark; and no such provision, measure or decision shall in any way affect the **Community or Union *acquis*** nor form part of **Union** law as they apply to Denmark. **In particular, acts of the Union in the field of police co-operation and judicial co-operation in criminal matters adopted before the entry into force of *the Treaty of Lisbon* which are amended shall continue to be binding upon and applicable to Denmark unchanged.**

ARTICLE 2 a

Article 2 of this Protocol shall also apply in respect of those rules laid down on the basis of *Article 16 of the Treaty on the Functioning of the European Union* which relate to the processing of personal data by the Member States when carrying out activities which fall within the scope of *Chapter 4 or Chapter 5 of Title IV of Part Three of that Treaty*.

ARTICLE 3

Denmark shall bear no financial consequences of measures referred to in Article 1, other than administrative costs entailed for the institutions.

[BMDF Note: Article 4 moved to Article 6]

ARTICLE **4**

1. Denmark shall decide within a period of 6 months after the Council has decided on a proposal or initiative to build upon the Schengen *acquis* **covered by this Part**, whether it will implement this **measure** in its national law. If it decides to do so, this **measure** will create an obligation under international law between Denmark and the other Member States **bound by the measure**.

2. If Denmark decides not to implement a **measure** of the Council as referred to in paragraph 1, the Member States **bound by that measure and Denmark** will consider appropriate measures to be taken.

PART II

ARTICLE **5**

With regard to measures adopted by the Council **pursuant to *Article 13(1), Article 28 A and Articles 43 to 46 of the Treaty on European Union***, Denmark does not participate in the elaboration and the implementation of decisions and actions of the Union which have defence implications. Therefore Denmark shall not participate in their adoption. **Denmark will not prevent the other Member States from further developing their co-operation in this area.** Denmark shall not be obliged to contribute to the financing of operational expenditure arising from such measures**, nor to make military capabilities available to the Union**.

The unanimity of the members of the Council, with the exception of the representative of the government of Denmark, shall be necessary for the acts of the Council which must be adopted unanimously.
For the purposes of this Article, a qualified majority shall be defined in accordance with *Article 238(3) of the Treaty on the Functioning of the European Union.*

PART III

ARTICLE **6**
Articles 1, 2 and 3 shall not apply to measures determining the third countries whose nationals must be in possession of a visa when crossing the external borders of the Member States, or measures relating to a uniform format for visas.
[BMDF Note: Article moved from Article 4]

PART **IV**

ARTICLE 7
At any time Denmark may, in accordance with its constitutional requirements, inform other Member States that it no longer wishes to avail itself of all or part of this Protocol. In that event, Denmark will apply in full all relevant measures then in force taken within the framework of the European Union.

ARTICLE 8
1. At any time and without prejudice to Article 7, Denmark may, in accordance with its constitutional requirements, notify the other Member States that, with effect from the first day of the month following the notification, Part I shall consist of the provisions in the Annex. In that case *Articles 5 to 8* shall be renumbered in consequence.

2. Six months after the date on which the notification referred to in paragraph 1 takes effect all Schengen *acquis* and measures adopted to build upon this *acquis*, which until then have been binding on Denmark as obligations under international law, shall be binding upon Denmark as Union law.

ANNEX

ARTICLE 1
Subject to Article 3, Denmark shall not take part in the adoption by the Council of measures proposed pursuant to *Title IV of Part Three of the Treaty on the Functioning of the European Union.* The unanimity of the members of the Council, with the exception of the representative of the government of Denmark, shall be necessary for the acts of the Council which must be adopted unanimously.
For the purposes of this Article, a qualified majority shall be defined in accordance with *Article 238(3) of the Treaty on the Functioning of the European Union.*

ARTICLE 2
Pursuant to Article 1 and subject to Articles 3, 4 and 6, none of the provisions in *Title IV of Part Three of the Treaty on the Functioning of the European Union*, no measure adopted pursuant to that *Title*, no provision of any international agreements concluded by the Union pursuant to that *Title*, no decision of the Court of Justice of the European Union interpreting any such provision or measure shall be binding upon or applicable in Denmark; and no such provision, measure or decision shall in any way affect the competences, rights and obligations of Denmark; and no such provision, measure or decision shall in any way affect the Community or Union *acquis* nor form part of Union law as they apply to Denmark.

ARTICLE 3
1. Denmark may notify the President of the Council in writing, within three months after a proposal or initiative has been presented to the Council pursuant to *Title IV of Part Three of the*

Treaty on the Functioning of the European Union, that it wishes to take part in the adoption and application of any such proposed measure, whereupon Denmark shall be entitled to do so.

2. If after a reasonable period of time a measure referred to in paragraph 1 cannot be adopted with Denmark taking part, the Council may adopt that measure referred to in paragraph 1 in accordance with Article 1 without the participation of Denmark. In that case Article 2 applies.

ARTICLE 4
Denmark may at any time after the adoption of a measure pursuant to _Title IV of Part Three of the Treaty on the Functioning of the European Union_ notify its intention to the Council and the Commission that it wishes to accept that measure. In that case, the procedure provided for in _Article 331(1) of that Treaty_ shall apply _mutatis mutandis._

ARTICLE 5
1. The provisions of this Protocol apply for Denmark also to measures proposed or adopted pursuant to Title IV of Part III of the Treaty on the Functioning of the European Union amending an existing measure by which it is bound.

2. However, in cases where the Council, acting on a proposal from the Commission, determines that the non-participation of Denmark in the amended version of an existing measure makes the application of that measure inoperable for other Member States or the Union, it may urge it to make a notification under Article 3 or 4. For the purposes of Article 3 a further period of two months starts to run as from the date of such determination by the Council.
If at the expiry of that period of two months from the Council's determination Denmark has not made a notification under Article 3 or Article 4, the existing measure shall no longer be binding upon or applicable to it, unless it has made a notification under Article 4 before the entry into force of the amending measure. This shall take effect from the date of entry into force of the amending measure or of expiry of the period of two months, whichever is the later.
For the purpose of this paragraph, the Council shall, after a full discussion of the matter, act by a qualified majority of its members representing the Member States participating or having participated in the adoption of the amending measure. A qualified majority of the Council shall be defined in accordance with Article 238(3)(a) of the Treaty on the Functioning of the European Union.

3. The Council, acting by a qualified majority on a proposal from the Commission, may determine that Denmark shall bear the direct financial consequences, if any, necessarily and unavoidably incurred as a result of the cessation of its participation in the existing measure.

4. This Article shall be without prejudice to Article 4.

ARTICLE 6
1. Notification pursuant to Article 4 shall be submitted no later than six months after the final adoption of a measure if this measure builds upon the Schengen _acquis_.
If Denmark does not submit a notification in accordance with Articles 3 or 4 regarding a measure building upon the Schengen _acquis_, the Member States bound by that measure and Denmark will consider appropriate measures to be taken.

2. A notification pursuant to Article 3 with respect to a measure building upon the Schengen _acquis_ shall be deemed irrevocably to be a notification pursuant to Article 3 with respect to any further proposal or initiative aiming to build upon that measure to the extent that such proposal or initiative builds upon the Schengen _acquis_.

ARTICLE 7
Denmark shall not be bound by the rules laid down on the basis of Article 16 of the Treaty on the Functioning of the European Union which relate to the processing of personal data by the Member States when carrying out activities which fall within the scope of Chapter 4 or Chapter 5 of Title IV of Part Three of that Treaty where Denmark is not bound by the rules governing the forms of judicial co-operation in criminal matters or police co-operation which require compliance with the provisions laid down on the basis of Article 16.

ARTICLE 8
Where, in cases referred to in this Part, Denmark is bound by a measure adopted by the Council pursuant to *Title IV of Part Three of the Treaty on the Functioning of the European Union*, the relevant provisions of that Treaty shall apply to Denmark in relation to that measure.

ARTICLE 9
Where Denmark is not bound by a measure adopted pursuant to *Title IV of Part Three of the Treaty on the Functioning of the European Union*, it shall bear no financial consequences of that measure other than administrative costs entailed for the institutions unless the Council, acting unanimously after consulting the European Parliament, decides otherwise.
[BMDF Note: This protocol was introduced by the Treaty of Amsterdam.]

24. PROTOCOL ON ASYLUM FOR NATIONALS OF MEMBER STATES OF THE EUROPEAN UNION

THE HIGH CONTRACTING PARTIES,

WHEREAS, in accordance with Article 6(1) of the Treaty on European Union, the Union recognises the rights, freedoms and principles set out in the Charter of Fundamental Rights;

WHEREAS pursuant to Article 6(3) of the Treaty on European Union, fundamental rights, as guaranteed by the European Convention for the Protection of Human Rights and Fundamental Freedoms, constitute part of the Union's law as general principles;

WHEREAS the Court of Justice of the European **Union** has jurisdiction to ensure that in the interpretation and application of ***Article 6(1) and (3)*** of the Treaty on European Union the law is observed by the **Union**;

WHEREAS pursuant to Article 49 of the Treaty on European Union any European State, when applying to become a Member of the Union, must respect the **values** set out in ***Article 2*** of the Treaty on European Union;

BEARING IN MIND that ***Article 7(1) of the Treaty on the European Union*** establishes a mechanism for the suspension of certain rights in the event of a serious and persistent breach by a Member State of those **values**;

RECALLING that each national of a Member State, as a citizen of the Union, enjoys a special status and protection which shall be guaranteed by the Member States in accordance with the provisions of Part Two of the ***Treaty on the Functioning of the European Union***;

BEARING IN MIND that ***the Treaties establish*** an area without internal frontiers and grants every citizen of the Union the right to move and reside freely within the territory of the Member States;

WISHING to prevent that the institution of asylum is resorted to for purposes alien to those for which it is intended;

WHEREAS this Protocol respects the finality and the objectives of the Geneva Convention of 28 July 1951 relating to the status of refugees;

HAVE AGREED UPON the following provisions, which shall be annexed to the ***Treaty on European Union and to the Treaty on the Functioning of the European Union***:

SOLE ARTICLE
Given the level of protection of fundamental rights and freedoms by the Member States of the European Union, Member States shall be regarded as constituting safe countries of origin in respect of each other for all legal and practical purposes in relation to asylum matters. Accordingly, any application for asylum made by a national of a Member State may be taken into consideration or declared admissible for processing by another Member State only in the following cases:

(a) if the Member State of which the applicant is a national proceeds after the entry into force of the Treaty of Amsterdam, availing itself of the provisions of Article 15 of the Convention for the Protection of Human Rights and Fundamental Freedoms, to take measures derogating in its territory from its obligations under that Convention;

(b) if the procedure referred to Article 7(1) of the Treaty on European Union has been initiated and until the Council, **or where appropriate, the European Council,** takes a decision in respect thereof **with regard to the Member State of which the applicant is a national**;

(c) if the Council has adopted a decision in accordance with Article 7(1) of the Treaty on European Union in respect of the Member State of which the applicant is a national or if the European Council has adopted a decision in accordance with Article 7(2) of that Treaty in respect of the Member State of which the applicant is a national;

(d) if a Member State should so decide unilaterally in respect of the application of a national of another Member State; in that case the Council shall be immediately informed; the application shall be dealt with on the basis of the presumption that it is manifestly unfounded without affecting in any way, whatever the cases may be, the decision-making power of the Member State.

[BMDF Note: This protocol was introduced by the Treaty of Amsterdam.]

25. PROTOCOL ON ECONOMIC, SOCIAL *AND TERRITORIAL* COHESION

THE HIGH CONTRACTING PARTIES,

RECALLING that *Article 3 of the Treaty on European Union* includes the objective of promoting economic, social and territorial cohesion and solidarity between Member States and that the said cohesion figures among the areas of shared competence of the Union listed in *Article 4(2)(c) of the Treaty on the Functioning of the European Union*;

RECALLING that the provisions of Part Three, Title XVII, on economic, social **and territorial** cohesion as a whole provide the legal basis for consolidating and further developing the **Union's** action in the field of economic, social **and territorial** cohesion, including the creation of a new fund;

RECALLING that the provisions of *Article 177 of the Treaty on the Functioning of the European Union* envisage setting up a Cohesion Fund;

NOTING that the European Investment Bank is lending large and increasing amounts for the benefit of the poorer regions;

NOTING the desire for greater flexibility in the arrangements for allocations from the Structural Funds;

NOTING the desire for modulation of the levels of **Union** participation in programmes and projects in certain countries;

NOTING the proposal to take greater account of the relative prosperity of Member States in the system of own resources,

REAFFIRM that the promotion of economic, social **and territorial** cohesion is vital to the full development and enduring success of the **Union**;

REAFFIRM their conviction that the Structural Funds should continue to play a considerable part in the achievement of **Union** objectives in the field of cohesion;

REAFFIRM their conviction that the European Investment Bank should continue to devote the majority of its resources to the promotion of economic, social **and territorial** cohesion, and declare their willingness to review the capital needs of the European Investment Bank as soon as this is necessary for that purpose;

AGREE that the Cohesion Fund will provide **Union** financial contributions to projects in the fields of environment and trans-European networks in Member States with a *per capita* GNP of less than 90% of the **Union** average which have a programme leading to the fulfilment of the conditions of economic convergence as set out in Article 104 ***of the Treaty on the Functioning of the European Union***;

DECLARE their intention of allowing a greater margin of flexibility in allocating financing from the Structural Funds to specific needs not covered under the present Structural Funds regulations;

DECLARE their willingness to modulate the levels of **Union** participation in the context of programmes and projects of the Structural Funds, with a view to avoiding excessive increases in budgetary expenditure in the less prosperous Member States;

RECOGNISE the need to monitor regularly the progress made towards achieving economic**,** ~~and~~ social **and territorial** cohesion and state their willingness to study all necessary measures in this respect;

DECLARE their intention of taking greater account of the contributive capacity of individual Member States in the system of own resources, and of examining means of correcting, for the less prosperous Member States, regressive elements existing in the present own resources system;

AGREE to annex this Protocol to ***the Treaty on European Union and to the Treaty on the Functioning of the European Union***.
[BMDF Note: This protocol was introduced by the Maastricht Treaty]

26. PROTOCOL ON THE EXCESSIVE DEFICIT PROCEDURE

THE HIGH CONTRACTING PARTIES,

DESIRING TO lay down the details of the excessive deficit procedure referred to in Article 126 of ***the Treaty on the Functioning of the European Union***,

HAVE AGREED upon the following provisions, which shall be annexed to the ***Treaty on European Union and to the Treaty on the Functioning of the European Union***:

ARTICLE 1
The reference values referred to in Article 126(2) of ***the Treaty on the Functioning of the European Union*** are:
- 3% for the ratio of the planned or actual government deficit to gross domestic product at market prices;
- 60% for the ratio of government debt to gross domestic product at market prices.

ARTICLE 2
In Article ***126*** of **the said** Treaty and in this Protocol:
- government means general government, that is central government, regional or local government and social security funds, to the exclusion of commercial operations, as defined in the European System of Integrated Economic Accounts;
- deficit means net borrowing as defined in the European System of Integrated Economic Accounts;
- investment means gross fixed capital formation as defined in the European System of Integrated Economic Accounts;
- debt means total gross debt at nominal value outstanding at the end of the year and consolidated between and within the sectors of general government as defined in the first indent.

ARTICLE 3
In order to ensure the effectiveness of the excessive deficit procedure, the governments of the Member States shall be responsible under this procedure for the deficits of general government as defined in the first indent of Article 2. The Member States shall ensure that national procedures in the budgetary area enable them to meet their obligations in this area deriving from ***these Treaties***. The Member States shall report their planned and actual deficits and the levels of their debt promptly and regularly to the Commission.

ARTICLE 4
The statistical data to be used for the application of this Protocol shall be provided by the Commission.
(This protocol was introduced by the Maastricht Treaty.)

27. PROTOCOL ON FRANCE

THE HIGH CONTRACTING PARTIES,

DESIRING TO take into account a particular point relating to France,

HAVE AGREED upon the following provisions, which shall be annexed to the ***Treaty on European Union and to the Treaty on the Functioning of the European Union***:

France will keep the privilege of monetary emission in **New Caledonia, French Polynesia and Wallis and Futuna** under the terms established by its national laws, and will be solely entitled to determine the parity of the CFP franc.
[BMDF Note: This protocol was introduced by the Maastricht Treaty and renamed the 'Pacific Community Franc System' in the draft Constitution.]

28. PROTOCOL ON EXTERNAL RELATIONS OF THE MEMBER STATES WITH REGARD TO THE CROSSING OF EXTERNAL BORDERS

THE HIGH CONTRACTING PARTIES,

TAKING INTO ACCOUNT the need of the Member States to ensure effective controls at their external borders, in co-operation with third countries where appropriate,

HAVE AGREED UPON the following provisions, which shall be annexed to the ***Treaty on European Union and to the Treaty on the Functioning of the European Union***:

The provisions on the measures on the crossing of external borders included in ***Article 77(2)(b) of the Treaty on the Functioning of the European Union*** shall be without prejudice to the competence of Member States to negotiate or conclude agreements with third countries as long as they respect **Union** law and other relevant international agreements.
[BMDF Note: This protocol was introduced by the Treaty of Amsterdam.]

29. PROTOCOL ON ARTICLE 42 OF THE TREATY ON EUROPEAN UNION

THE HIGH CONTRACTING PARTIES,

BEARING IN MIND the need to implement fully the provisions of Article ***42(1)***, second sub-paragraph, and (3) of the Treaty on European Union,

BEARING IN MIND that the policy of the Union in accordance with Article ***42*** shall not prejudice the specific character of the security and defence policy of certain Member States and shall respect the obligations of certain Member States, which see their common defence realised in NATO, under the North Atlantic Treaty and be compatible with the common security and defence policy established within that framework,

HAVE AGREED UPON the following provision, which shall be annexed to the Treaty on European Union ***and to the Treaty on the Functioning of the European Union***:

The European Union shall draw up, together with the Western European Union, arrangements for enhanced co-operation between them.
[BMDF Note: This protocol was introduced by the Treaty of Amsterdam.]

30. PROTOCOL ON THE SYSTEM OF PUBLIC SERVICE BROADCASTING IN THE MEMBER STATES

THE HIGH CONTRACTING PARTIES,

CONSIDERING that the system of public broadcasting in the Member States is directly related to the democratic, social and cultural needs of each society and to the need to preserve media pluralism;

HAVE AGREED UPON the following interpretative provisions, which shall be annexed to the ***Treaty on European Union and to the Treaty on the Functioning of the European Union***:

The provisions of ***these Treaties*** shall be without prejudice to the competence of Member States to provide for the funding of public service broadcasting insofar as such funding is granted to broadcasting organisations for the fulfilment of the public service remit as conferred, defined and organised by each Member State, and insofar as such funding does not affect trading conditions and competition in the **Union** to an extent which would be contrary to the common interest, while the realisation of the remit of that public service shall be taken into account.
[BMDF Note: This protocol was introduced by the Treaty of Amsterdam]

31. PROTOCOL CONCERNING IMPORTS INTO THE EUROPEAN UNION OF PETROLEUM PRODUCTS REFINED IN THE NETHERLANDS ANTILLES

THE HIGH CONTRACTING PARTIES,

BEING DESIROUS of giving fuller details about the system of trade applicable to imports into the European **Union** of petroleum products refined in the Netherlands Antilles,

HAVE AGREED on the following provisions to be appended to ***the Treaty on European Union and to the Treaty on the Functioning of the European Union***:

ARTICLE 1
This Protocol is applicable to petroleum products coming under the Brussels Nomenclature numbers 27.10, 27.11, 27.12, ex 27.13 (paraffin wax, petroleum or shale wax and paraffin residues) and 27.14, imported for use in Member States.

ARTICLE 2
Member States shall undertake to grant to petroleum products refined in the Netherlands Antilles the tariff preferences resulting from the association of the latter with the **Union**, under the conditions provided for in this Protocol. These provisions shall hold good whatever may be the rules of origin applied by the Member States.

ARTICLE 3
1. When the Commission, at the request of a Member State or on its own initiative, establishes that imports into the **Union** of petroleum products refined in the Netherlands Antilles under the system provided for in Article 2 above are giving rise to real difficulties on the market of one or more Member States, it shall decide that customs duties on the said imports shall be introduced, increased or re-introduced by the Member States in question, to such an extent and for such a period as may be necessary to meet that situation. The rates of the customs duties thus introduced, increased or re-introduced may not exceed the customs duties applicable to third countries for these same products.

2. The provisions of paragraph 1 can in any case be applied when imports into the **Union** of petroleum products refined in the Netherlands Antilles reach two million metric tonnes a year.

3. The Council shall be informed of decisions taken by the Commission in pursuance of paragraphs 1 and 2, including those directed at rejecting the request of a Member State. The Council shall, at the request of any Member State, assume responsibility for the matter and may at any time amend or revoke them.

ARTICLE 4

1. If a Member State considers that imports of petroleum products refined in the Netherlands Antilles, made either directly or through another Member State under the system provided for in Article 2 above, are giving rise to real difficulties on its market and that immediate action is necessary to meet them, it may on its own initiative decide to apply customs duties to such imports, the rate of which may not exceed those of the customs duties applicable to third countries in respect of the same products. It shall notify its decision to the Commission which shall decide within one month whether the measures taken by the State should be maintained or must be amended or cancelled. The provisions of Article 3(3) shall be applicable to such decision of the Commission.

2. When the quantities of petroleum products refined in the Netherlands Antilles imported either directly or through another Member State, under the system provided for in Article 2 above, into a Member State or States of the EEC exceed during a calendar year the tonnage shown in the Annex to this Protocol, the measures taken in pursuance of paragraph 1 by that or those Member States for the current year shall be considered to be justified; the Commission shall, after assuring itself that the tonnage fixed has been reached, formally record the measures taken. In such a case the other Member States shall abstain from formally placing the matter before the Council.

ARTICLE 5

If the **Union** decides to apply quantitative restrictions to petroleum products, no matter whence they are imported, these restrictions may also be applied to imports of such products from the Netherlands Antilles. In such a case preferential treatment shall be granted to the Netherlands Antilles as compared with third countries.

ARTICLE 6

1. The provisions of Articles 2 to 5 shall be reviewed by the Council, by unanimous decision, after consulting the European Parliament and the Commission, when a common definition of origin for petroleum products from third countries and associated countries is adopted, or when decisions are taken within the framework of a common commercial policy for the products in question or when a common energy policy is established.

2. When such revision is made, however, equivalent preferences must in any case be maintained in favour of the Netherlands Antilles in a suitable form and for a minimum quantity of 2½ million tonnes of petroleum products.

3. The **Union's** commitments in regard to equivalent preferences as mentioned in paragraph 2 of this Article may, if necessary, be broken down country by country taking into account the tonnage indicated in the Annex to this Protocol.

ARTICLE 7

For the implementation of this Protocol, the Commission is responsible for following the pattern of imports into the Member States of petroleum products refined in the Netherlands Antilles. Member States shall communicate to the Commission, which shall see that it is circulated, all useful information to that end in accordance with the administrative conditions recommended by it.

Done at Brussels, the thirteenth day of November, one thousand nine hundred and sixty-two.

ANNEX TO THE PROTOCOL

For the implementation of Article 4(2) of the Protocol concerning imports into the **Union** of petroleum products refined in the Netherlands Antilles, the High Contracting Parties have decided that the quantity of 2 million metric tonnes of petroleum products from the Antilles shall be allocated among the Member States as follows:

Germany	625,000 metric tonnes
Belgo/Luxembourg Economic Union	200,000 metric tonnes
France	75,000 metric tonnes
Italy	100,000 metric tonnes
Netherlands	1,000,000 metric tonnes

32. PROTOCOL CONCERNING ARTICLE 157 OF THE TREATY *ON THE FUNCTIONING OF THE EUROPEAN UNION*

THE HIGH CONTRACTING PARTIES,

HAVE AGREED UPON the following provision, which shall be annexed to ***the Treaty on European Union and to the Treaty on the Functioning of the European Union***:

For the purposes of Article ***157*** of ***the Treaty on the Functioning of the European Union***, benefits under occupational social security schemes shall not be considered as remuneration if and in so far as they are attributable to periods of employment prior to 17 May 1990, except in the case of workers or those claiming under them who have before that date initiated legal proceedings or introduced an equivalent claim under the applicable national law.
[BMDF Note: This protocol was introduced by the Maastricht Treaty]

33. PROTOCOL ON SPECIAL ARRANGEMENTS FOR GREENLAND

THE HIGH CONTRACTING PARTIES,

HAVE AGREED UPON the following provisions, which shall be annexed to the ***Treaty on European Union and to the Treaty on the Functioning of the European Union***:

ARTICLE 1
1. The treatment on import into the **Union** of products subject to the common organisation of the market in fishery products, originating in Greenland, shall, while complying with the mechanisms of the **internal** market organisation, involve exemption from customs duties and charges having equivalent effect and the absence of quantitative restrictions or measures having equivalent effect if the possibilities for access to Greenland fishing zones granted to the **Union** pursuant to an agreement between the **Union** and the authority responsible for Greenland are satisfactory to the **Union**.

2. All measures relating to the import arrangements for such products, including those relating to the adoption of such measures, shall be adopted in accordance with the procedure laid down in Article ***43*** of ***the Treaty on the Functioning of the European Union***.

Done at Brussels on the thirteenth day of March in the year one thousand nine hundred and eighty-four.

34. PROTOCOL *ON ARTICLE 40.3.3 OF THE CONSTITUTION OF IRELAND*

THE HIGH CONTRACTING PARTIES,

HAVE AGREED upon the following provision, which shall be annexed to the Treaty on European Union, ***the Treaty on the Functioning of the European Union*** **and the Treaty establishing the European Atomic Energy Community**:

Nothing in the ***Treaties,*** **or in the Treaty establishing the European Atomic Energy Community**, or in the Treaties or Acts modifying or supplementing those Treaties, shall affect the application in Ireland of Article 40.3.3. of the Constitution of Ireland.
[BMDF Note: This protocol was introduced by the Maastricht Treaty]

Declaration of 1 May 1992

On 1 May 1992, in Guimarães (Portugal), the High Contracting Parties to the Treaty on European Union adopted the following Declaration:

DECLARATION
OF THE HIGH CONTRACTING PARTIES
TO THE TREATY ON EUROPEAN UNION

The High Contracting Parties to the Treaty on European Union signed at Maastricht on the seventh day of February 1992,

Having considered the terms of Protocol No. 6 to the said Treaty on European Union which is annexed to that Treaty and to the Treaties establishing the European Communities,

Hereby give the following legal interpretation:

That it was and is their intention that the Protocol shall not limit freedom to travel between Member States or, in accordance with conditions which may be laid down, in conformity with **Union** law, by Irish legislation, to obtain or make available in Ireland information relating to services lawfully available in Member States.
At the same time the High Contracting Parties solemnly declare that, in the event of a future constitutional amendment in Ireland which concerns the subject matter of Article 40.3.3 of the Constitution of Ireland and which does not conflict with the intention of the High Contracting Parties herein before expressed, they will, following the entry into force of the Treaty on European Union, be favourably disposed to amending the said Protocol so as to extend its application to such constitutional amendment if Ireland so requests.

35. PROTOCOL ON THE FINANCIAL CONSEQUENCES OF THE EXPIRY OF THE ECSC TREATY AND ON THE RESEARCH FUND FOR COAL AND STEEL

THE HIGH CONTRACTING PARTIES,

RECALLING that all assets and liabilities of the European Coal and Steel Community, as they existed on 23 July 2002, were transferred to the European Community on 24 July 2002;

TAKING ACCOUNT of the desire to use these funds for research in sectors related to the coal and steel industry and therefore the necessity to provide for certain special rules in this regard;

HAVE AGREED UPON the following provisions, which shall be annexed to the ***Treaty on European Union and to the Treaty on the Functioning of the European Union***:

ARTICLE 1

1. The net worth of these assets and liabilities, as they appear in the balance sheet of the ECSC of 23 July 2002, subject to any increase or decrease which may occur as a result of the liquidation operations, shall be considered as assets intended for research in the sectors related to the coal and steel industry, referred to as the "ECSC in liquidation". On completion of the liquidation they shall be referred to as the "Assets of the Research Fund for Coal and Steel".

2. The revenue from these assets, referred to as the "Research Fund for Coal and Steel", shall be used exclusively for research, outside the research framework programme, in the sectors related to the coal and steel industry in accordance with the provisions of this Protocol and of acts adopted on the basis hereof.

ARTICLE 2

1. The Council, **acting in accordance with a special legislative procedure** and after **obtaining the content of** the European Parliament, shall adopt all the necessary provisions for the implementation of this Protocol, including essential principles.

2. The Council shall adopt, on a proposal from the Commission and after consulting the European Parliament, measures establishing multi-annual financial guidelines for managing the assets of the Research Fund for Coal and Steel and technical guidelines for the research programme of the Research Fund for Coal and Steel.

ARTICLE 3

Except as otherwise provided in this Protocol and in the acts adopted on the basis hereof, the provisions of ***the Treaties*** shall apply.

[BMDF Note: Article 4 shall be repealed]

[BMDF Note: This Protocol was introduced in the Treaty of Nice]

36. PROTOCOL ON DENMARK

THE HIGH CONTRACTING PARTIES,

DESIRING to settle certain particular problems relating to Denmark,

HAVE AGREED UPON the following provisions, which shall be annexed to the ***Treaty on European Union and to the Treaty on the Functioning of the European Union***:

The provisions of Article 14 of the Protocol on the Statute of the European System of Central Banks and of the European Central Bank shall not affect the right of the National Bank of Denmark to carry out its existing tasks concerning those parts of the Kingdom of Denmark which are not part of the **Union**.
[BMDF Note: This protocol was introduced by the Maastricht Treaty.]

37. PROTOCOL ON THE ACQUISITION OF PROPERTY IN DENMARK

THE HIGH CONTRACTING PARTIES,

DESIRING to settle certain particular problems relating to Denmark,

HAVE AGREED UPON the following provision, which shall be annexed to the ***Treaty on European Union and to the Treaty on the Functioning of the European Union***:

Notwithstanding the provisions of ***these Treaties***, Denmark may maintain the existing legislation on the acquisition of second homes.
[BMDF Note: This protocol was introduced by the Maastricht Treaty]
[BMDF Note: See also Declaration no. 48]

B. PROTOCOLS TO BE ANNEXED TO THE TREATY OF LISBON

BMDF Note: These two Protocols are attached to the Treaty of Lisbon, and not to the main Treaties. The numbering system used for the Article references to the main Treaties follows that of the Treaty of Lisbon. The new numbering system for the consolidated Treaties is shown in the Annex to the Treaty of Lisbon, shown below.

1. PROTOCOL AMENDING THE PROTOCOLS ANNEXED TO THE TREATY ON EUROPEAN UNION, TO THE TREATY ESTABLISHING THE EUROPEAN COMMUNITY AND/OR TO THE TREATY ESTABLISHING THE EUROPEAN ATOMIC ENERGY COMMUNITY

THE HIGH CONTRACTING PARTIES,

DESIRING to amend the Protocols annexed to the Treaty on European Union, to the Treaty establishing the European Community and/or to the Treaty establishing the European Atomic Energy Community, in order to adapt them to the new rules laid down by the Treaty of Lisbon,

HAVE AGREED UPON the following provisions, which shall be annexed to the Treaty of Lisbon:

ARTICLE 1

1) The protocols in force on the date of entry into force of this Treaty and annexed to the Treaty on European Union, to the Treaty establishing the European Community and/or to the Treaty establishing the European Atomic Energy Community shall be amended in accordance with the provisions of this Article.

A. HORIZONTAL AMENDMENTS

[BMDF Note: the horizontal amendments concern changes to the existing protocols and have been consolidated into the text of the protocols and are not reproduced here.]

B. SPECIFIC AMENDMENTS

[BMDF Note: the specific amendments concern changes to the existing protocols and have been consolidated into the text of the protocols and are not reproduced here, except for the provisions relating to the repeal of certain protocols.]

PROTOCOLS REPEALED

9) The following Protocols shall be repealed:

- ***(a) Protocol on Italy (1957);***
- ***(b) Protocol on goods originating in and coming from certain countries and enjoying special treatment when imported into a Member State (1957);***
- ***(c) Protocol on the Statute of the European Monetary Institute (1992);***
- ***(d) Protocol on the transition to the third stage of economic and monetary union (1992);***
- ***(e) Protocol on Portugal (1992);***
- ***(f) Protocol on the role of national parliaments in the European Union (1997), which shall be replaced by a new Protocol with the same title;***
- ***(g) Protocol on the application of the principles of subsidiarity and proportionality (1997), which shall be replaced by a new Protocol with the same title;***
- ***(h) Protocol on protection and welfare of animals (1997), the text of which shall become Article 6b of the Treaty on the Functioning of the European Union;***
- ***(i) Protocol on the enlargement of the European Union (2001);***
- ***(j) Protocol on Article 67 of the Treaty establishing the European Community (2001).***

ARTICLE 2

1. The articles of the Protocol on the Statute of the European System of Central Banks and of the European Central Bank, of the Protocol on the Statute of the European Investment Bank, and of the

Protocol on the privileges and immunities of the European Union, as they are amended by the Treaty of Lisbon, shall be renumbered in accordance with the tables of equivalences set out in the annex to this Protocol. Cross-references to articles of those protocols which appear therein shall be adapted in accordance with the tables.

2. References to recitals of the protocols set out in point 1 of Article 1, or to articles of those protocols, including to paragraphs thereof, as renumbered or rearranged by this Protocol, and which references figure in other protocols or acts of primary legislation shall be adapted in accordance with this Protocol. Such adaptations shall, if necessary, also apply in the event that the provision in question has been repealed.

3. References to recitals and articles, including to paragraphs thereof, of the protocols set out in point 1 of Article 1, as amended by the provisions of this Protocol and which figure in other instruments or acts, shall be understood as references to recitals and articles, including to paragraphs thereof, of those protocols as renumbered or rearranged in accordance with this Protocol.

ANNEX

TABLES OF EQUIVALENCES REFERRED TO IN ARTICLE 2 OF PROTOCOL (No 1) AMENDING THE PROTOCOLS ANNEXED TO THE TREATY ON EUROPEAN UNION, TO THE TREATY ESTABLISHING THE EUROPEAN COMMUNITY AND/OR TO THE TREATY ESTABLISHING THE EUROPEAN ATOMIC ENERGY COMMUNITY.

A. PROTOCOL ON THE STATUTE OF THE EUROPEAN SYSTEM OF CENTRAL BANKS AND OF THE EUROPEAN CENTRAL BANK

Old numbering of the Protocol	*New numbering of the Protocol*
Article 1	*Article 1*
Article 2	*Article 2*
Article 3	*Article 3*
Article 4	*Article 4*
Article 5	*Article 5*
Article 6	*Article 6*
Article 7	*Article 7*
Article 8	*Article 8*
Article 9	*Article 9*
Article 10	*Article 10*
Article 11	*Article 11*
Article 12	*Article 12*
Article 13	*Article 13*
Article 14	*Article 14*
Article 15	*Article 15*
Article 16	*Article 16*
Article 17	*Article 17*
Article 18	*Article 18*
Article 19	*Article 19*
Article 20	*Article 20*
Article 21	*Article 21*
Article 22	*Article 22*
Article 23	*Article 23*
Article 24	*Article 24*

Old numbering of the Protocol	*New numbering of the Protocol*
Article 25	*Article 25*
Article 26	*Article 26*
Article 27	*Article 27*
Article 28	*Article 28*
Article 29	*Article 29*
Article 30	*Article 30*
Article 31	*Article 31*
Article 32	*Article 32*
Article 33	*Article 33*
Article 34	*Article 34*
Article 35	*Article 35*
Article 36	*Article 36*
Article 37 (repealed)	
Article 38	*Article 37*
Article 39	*Article 38*
Article 40	*Article 39*
Article 41	*Article 40*
Article 42	*Article 41*
Article 43	*Article 42*
Article 44	*Article 43*
Article 45	*Article 44*
Article 46	*Article 45*
Article 47	*Article 46*
Article 48	*Article 47*
Article 49	*Article 48*
Article 50 (repealed)	
Article 51 (repealed)	
Article 52	*Article 49*
Article 53	*Article 50*

B. PROTOCOL ON THE STATUTE OF THE EUROPEAN INVESTMENT BANK

Old numbering of the Protocol	*New numbering of the Protocol*
Article 1	*Article 1*
Article 2	*Article 2*
Article 3	*Article 3*
Article 4	*Article 4*
Article 5	*Article 5*
Article 6 (repealed)	
Article 7 (repealed)	
Article 8	*Article 6*
Article 9	*Article 7*
Article 10	*Article 8*
Article 11	*Article 9*
Article 12	*Article 10*
Article 13	*Article 11*
Article 14	*Article 12*
Article 15	*Article 13*
Article 16	*Article 14*

Old numbering of the Protocol	*New numbering of the Protocol*
Article 17	*Article 15*
Article 18	*Article 16*
Article 19	*Article 17*
Article 20	*Article 18*
Article 21	*Article 19*
Article 22	*Article 20*
Article 23	*Article 21*
Article 24	*Article 22*
Article 25	*Article 23*
Article 26	*Article 24*
Article 27	*Article 25*
Article 28	*Article 26*
Article 29	*Article 27*
Article 30	*Article 28*

C. PROTOCOL ON THE PRIVILEGES AND IMMUNITIES OF THE EUROPEAN UNION

Old numbering of the Protocol	*New numbering of the Protocol*
Article 1	*Article 1*
Article 2	*Article 2*
Article 3	*Article 3*
Article 4	*Article 4*
Article 5 (repealed)	
Article 6	*Article 5*
Article 7	*Article 6*
Article 8	*Article 7*
Article 9	*Article 8*
Article 10	*Article 9*
Article 11	*Article 10*
Article 12	*Article 11*
Article 13	*Article 12*
Article 14	*Article 13*
Article 15	*Article 14*
Article 16	*Article 15*
Article 17	*Article 16*
Article 18	*Article 17*
Article 19	*Article 18*
Article 20	*Article 19*
Article 21	*Article 20*
Article 22	*Article 21*
Article 23	*Article 22*

BMDF Note: These tables confirm and clarify the changes to the Articles and the Article numbers introduced in the draft Constitution and brought forward into the Treaty of Lisbon.

2. PROTOCOL AMENDING THE TREATY ESTABLISHING THE EUROPEAN ATOMIC ENERGY COMMUNITY

THE HIGH CONTRACTING PARTIES,

RECALLING the necessity that the provisions of the Treaty establishing the European Atomic Energy Community should continue to have full legal effect;

DESIRING to adapt that Treaty to the new rules laid down by the *Treaty on European Union and of the Treaty on the Functioning of the European Union*, in particular in the institutional and financial fields,

HAVE AGREED UPON the following provisions, which shall be annexed to the *Treaty of Lisbon* and which amend the Treaty establishing the European Atomic Energy Community as follows:

ARTICLE 1
This Protocol shall amend the Treaty establishing the European Atomic Energy Community (hereinafter referred to as the "EAEC Treaty") in its version in force at the time of entry into force of the *Treaty of Lisbon.*

ARTICLE 2
The heading of Title III of the EAEC Treaty "Institutional provisions" shall be replaced by the heading: "Institutional and financial provisions".

ARTICLE 3
The following chapter shall be inserted at the beginning of Title III of the EAEC Treaty:

"CHAPTER I

APPLICATION OF CERTAIN PROVISIONS OF THE *TREATY ON EUROPEAN UNION AND OF THE TREATY ON THE FUNCTIONING OF THE EUROPEAN UNION*

ARTICLE 106a
1. *Article 7, Articles 9 to 9 F, Article 48(2) to (5), and Articles 49 and 49 A of the Treaty on European Union, Article 16 A, Articles 190 to 201b, Articles 204 to 211a, Article 213, Articles 215 to 236, Articles 238, 239 and 240, Articles 241 to 245, Articles 246 to 262, Articles 268 to 277, Articles 279 to 280 and Articles 283, 290 and 292 of the Treaty on the Functioning of the European Union and the Protocol on transitional provisions* shall apply to this Treaty.

2. Within the framework of this Treaty, the references to the Union and to the *"Treaty on European Union", to the "Treaty on the Functioning of the European Union" or to the "Treaties"* in the provisions referred to in paragraph 1 and those in the protocols annexed both to those Treaties and to this Treaty shall be taken, respectively, as references to the European Atomic Energy Community and to this Treaty.

3. The provisions of the *Treaty on the European Union and the Treaty on the Functioning of the European Union* shall not derogate from the provisions of this Treaty."

ARTICLE 4
Chapters I, II and III of Title III of the EAEC Treaty shall be renumbered II, III and IV *respectively.*

ARTICLE 5
Article 3, Articles 107 to 132, Articles 136 to 143, Articles 146 to 156, Articles 158 to 163, Articles 165 to 170, Articles 173 and 173A, Article 175, Articles 177 to 179a, and Articles 180b, 181, 183, 183A, 190 and 204 of the EAEC Treaty shall be repealed.

ARTICLE 6
The heading of Title IV of the EAEC Treaty "Financial provisions" shall be replaced by the heading: "Specific financial provisions".

ARTICLE 7
1. In the third paragraph of Article 38 and the third paragraph of Article 82 of the EAEC Treaty the references to Articles 141 and 142 shall be replaced by references to *Articles 226 and 227 respectively of the Treaty on the Functioning of the European Union.*

2. In Article 171(2) and Article 176(3) of the EAEC Treaty the references to Article 183 shall be replaced by references to *Article 279 of the Treaty on the Functioning of the European Union.*

3. In Article 172(4) of the EAEC Treaty the reference to Article 177(5) shall be replaced by a reference to *Article 272 of the Treaty on the Functioning of the European Union.*

***4.* In the EAEC Treaty the term "Court of Justice" shall be replaced by "Court of Justice of the European Union".**

ARTICLE 8
Article 191 of the EAEC Treaty shall be replaced by the following:

> **"ARTICLE 191**
> **The Community shall enjoy in the territories of the Member States such privileges and immunities as are necessary for the performance of its tasks, under the conditions laid down in the Protocol on the privileges and immunities of the European Union."**

ARTICLE *9*
Article 206 of the EAEC Treaty shall be replaced by the following:

> **"ARTICLE 206**
> **The Community may conclude with one or more States or international organisations agreements establishing an association involving reciprocal rights and obligations, common action and special procedures.**
> **These agreements shall be concluded by the Council, acting unanimously after consulting the European Parliament.**
> **Where such agreements call for amendments to this Treaty, these amendments shall first be adopted in accordance with the procedure laid down in *Article 48(2) to (5) of the Treaty on European Union.*"**

ARTICLE *10*
The revenue and expenditure of the European Atomic Energy Community, except for those of the Supply Agency and Joint Undertakings, shall be shown in the budget of the Union.
[BMDF Note: This protocol is taken from the draft Constitutional Treaty]

* * * * *

PROTOCOLS INTRODUCED BY THE CONSTITUTION NOT IN THE REFORM TREATY

BMDF Note: the Protocols introduced by the Constitutional Treaty but not included in the Treaty of Lisbon are shown below for reference.

Protocol on the Treaties and Acts of Accession of the Kingdom of Denmark, Ireland and the United Kingdom of Great Britain and Northern Ireland, of the Hellenic Republic, of the Kingdom of Spain and the Portuguese Republic, and of the Republic of Austria, the Republic of Finland and the Kingdom of Sweden.

Protocol on the Treaty and the Act of Accession of the Czech Republic, the Republic of Estonia, the Republic of Cyprus, the Republic of Latvia, the Republic of Lithuania, the Republic of Hungary, the Republic of Malta, the Republic of Poland, the Republic of Slovenia and the Slovak Republic.

Protocol on the Acts and Treaties which have supplemented or amended the Treaty establishing the European Community and the Treaty on European Union.

DECLARATIONS OF THE CONFERENCE

The Declarations attached to the Treaty of Lisbon are based on the Declarations from the Constitution and the majority of the Declarations of the Conference were introduced by the Constitution and brought forward to the Treaty of Lisbon.

The titles of the Declarations introduced by the Treaty of Lisbon are in **bold text**.

Amendments made to the text of the Declarations in the Constitution by the Treaty of Lisbon and new Declarations introduced by the Treaty of Lisbon are shown in ***bold italics***.

The Declarations included in the Constitution but not included in the Treaty of Lisbon are shown for reference after the Declarations attached to the Treaty.

Descriptions have been added in brackets to the titles (in italics) by the BMDF to aid the reader in identifying the subject of each Declaration.

The new numbering system has been used both in the titles of the Declarations and in the text (in ***bold italics****) to ease reference to the main text of the Treaties. The numbering used in the Treaty of Lisbon is shown in the titles of the Declarations [in square brackets] for ease of reference to the Final Act of the Treaty of Lisbon.*

A. Declarations concerning provisions of the Treaties 211

(1) Declaration concerning the Charter of Fundamental Rights of the European Union 211

(2) Declaration re Article 6(2) of the Treaty on European Union (*European Convention on Human Rights*) 211

(3) Declaration re Article ***8*** [7a] of the Treaty on the European Union (*Relationship with third countries*) 211

(4) Declaration on the composition of the European Parliament 211

(5) Declaration on the political agreement by the European Council concerning the draft decision on the composition of the European Parliament 211

(6) Declaration re Articles ***15*** [9B] (5) and (6), ***17*** [9D] (6) and (7) and ***18*** [9E] of the Treaty on European Union (*Election of EU Presidencies*) 212

(7) Declaration re Article ***16*** [9C] (4) of the Treaty on European Union and Article ***238*** [205] (2) of the Treaty on the Functioning of the European Union (*Transitional Council voting procedure – Ioannina Compromise*) 212

(8) Declaration on practical measures to be taken upon the entry into force of the Treaty of Lisbon as regards the Presidency of the European Council and of the Foreign Affairs Council 213

(9) Declaration re Article ***16*** [9C] (9) of the Treaty on European Union concerning the European Council decision on the exercise of the Presidency of the Council 214

(10) Declaration re Article ***17*** [9D] of the Treaty on European Union (*Commission procedures*) 214

(11) Declaration re Article ***17*** [9D] (6) and (7) of the Treaty on European Union (*Election of the Commission President*) 215

(12) Declaration on Article *18* [9E] of the Treaty on European Union *(re appointment of the High Representative)* 215

(13)	**Declaration concerning the Common Foreign and Security Policy**	215
(14)	**Declaration concerning the Common Foreign and Security Policy**	215
(15)	Declaration re Article ***27*** [13a] of the Treaty on European Union (*European External Action Service*)	215
(16)	Declaration re Article ***55*** [53] (2) of the Treaty on European Union (*Official languages of the EU*)	216
(17)	**Declaration concerning primacy**	216
(18)	**Declaration in relation to the delimitation of competences**	217
(19)	Declaration re Article ***8*** [3] of the Treaty on the Functioning of the European Union (*Inequality*)	217
(20)	Declaration re Article ***16*** [16B] of the Treaty on the Functioning of the European Union (*Personal data*)	217
(21)	**Declaration on the protection of personal data in the field of police and judicial co-operation in criminal matters**	217
(22)	Declaration re Articles ***48*** [42] and ***79*** [63a] of the Treaty on the Functioning of the European Union (*Social security*)	218
(23)	**Declaration on the second paragraph of Article *48* [42] of the Treaty on the Functioning of the European Union** *(European Council to act by consensus on social security)*	218
(24)	**Declaration concerning the Legal Personality of the European Union**	218
(25)	Declaration re Articles ***75*** [61H] and ***215*** [188K] of the Treaty on the Functioning of the European Union (*Restrictive measures on capital*)	218
(26)	**Declaration on non-participation by a Member State in a measure based on Title IV of Part Three of the Treaty on the Functioning of the European Union** *(re freedom, security and justice)*	218
(27)	Declaration re Article ***85*** [69D] (1) second subparagraph, of the Treaty on the Functioning of the European Union (*Eurojust*)	219
(28)	Declaration re Article ***98*** [78] of the Treaty on the Functioning of the European Union (*Transport in east Germany*)	219
(29)	Declaration re Article ***107*** [87] (2)(c) of the Treaty on the Functioning of the European Union (*State aid in east Germany*)	219
(30)	Declaration re Article ***124*** [104] of the Treaty on the Functioning of the European Union (*Stability and Growth Pact*)	219
(31)	Declaration re Article ***156*** [140] of the Treaty on the Functioning of the European Union (*Co-ordination of Social Policy*)	220
(32)	**Declaration on Article *168* [152] (4)(c) of the Treaty on the Functioning of the European Union** *(safety and human health)*	220
(33)	Declaration re Article ***174*** [158] of the Treaty on the Functioning of the European Union (*Economic, social and territorial cohesion on island regions*)	220
(34)	Declaration re Article ***179*** [163] of the Treaty on the Functioning of the European Union (*Research and technological development*)	220

(35) Declaration re Article ***194*** [176A] of the Treaty on the Functioning of the European Union (*Energy*) 220

(36) Declaration re Article ***218*** [188N] of the Treaty on the Functioning of the European Union concerning the negotiation and conclusion of international agreements by Member States relating to the Area of Freedom, Security and Justice 220

(37) Declaration re Article ***222*** [188R] of the Treaty on the Functioning of the European Union (*Solidarity clause procedures*) 221

(38) Declaration on Article *252* [222] of the Treaty on the Functioning of the European Union on the number of Advocates-General in the Court of Justice 221

(39) Declaration re Article ***290*** [249B] of the Treaty on the Functioning of the European Union (*Lamfalussy procedure - Financial services*) 221

(40) Declaration re Article ***329*** [280D] of the Treaty on the Functioning of the European Union (*Enhanced co-operation*) 221

(41) Declaration on Article *352* [308] of the Treaty on the Functioning of the European Union *(use of flexibility clause in Common Foreign and Security Policy)* 221

(42) Declaration on Article *352* [308] of the Treaty on the Functioning of the European Union *(use of flexibility clause to extend EU competence)* 222

(43) Declaration re Article ***355*** [311a] (6) of the Treaty on the Functioning of the European Union (*Outermost regions*) 222

B. Declarations concerning Protocols annexed to the Treaties **222**

(44) Declaration on Article 5 of the Protocol on the Schengen *acquis* integrated into the framework of the European Union 222

(45) Declaration on Article 5(2) of the Protocol on the Schengen *acquis* integrated into the framework of the European Union 222

(46) Declaration on Article 5(3) of the Protocol on the Schengen *acquis* integrated into the framework of the European Union 223

(47) Declaration on Article 5(3), (4) and (5) of the Protocol on the Schengen *acquis* integrated into the framework of the European Union 223

(48) Declaration concerning the Protocol on the position of Denmark 223

(49) Declaration concerning Italy 223

(50) Declaration on Article 10 of the Protocol on transitional provisions *(voting)* 224

C: Declarations by Member States **225**

(51) Declaration by the Kingdom of Belgium on national parliaments 225

(52) Declaration by the Kingdom of Belgium, the Republic of Bulgaria, the Federal Republic of Germany, the Hellenic Republic, the Kingdom of Spain, the Italian Republic, the Republic of Cyprus, the Republic of Lithuania, the Grand-Duchy of Luxembourg, the Republic of Hungary, the Republic of Malta, the Republic of Austria, the Portuguese Republic, Romania, the Republic of Slovenia and the Slovak Republic on the symbols of the European Union 225

(53) Declaration by the Czech Republic on the Charter of Fundamental Rights of the European Union 225

(54) Declaration by the Federal Republic of Germany, Ireland, the Republic of Hungary, the Republic of Austria and the Republic of Sweden (*revision of the Treaty establishing the European Atomic Energy Community*) 226

(55) Declaration by the Kingdom of Spain and the United Kingdom of Great Britain and Northern Ireland (*Gibraltar*) 226

(56) Declaration by Ireland on Article 3 of the Protocol on the position the United Kingdom and Ireland in respect of the area of freedom, security and justice 226

(57) Declaration by the Italian Republic on the composition of the European Parliament 226

(58) Declaration by the Republic of Latvia, the Republic of Hungary **and the Republic of Malta** on the spelling of the name of the single currency in the Treaties 227

(59) Declaration by the Kingdom of the Netherlands on Article ***312*** [270a] of the Treaty on the Functioning of the European Union 227

(60) Declaration by the Kingdom of the Netherlands on Article ***355*** [311a] of the Treaty on the Functioning of the European Union 227

(61) Declaration by Poland on the Charter of Fundamental Rights of the European Union 227

(62) Declaration by the Republic of Poland concerning the Protocol on the application of the Charter of Fundamental Rights in relation to Poland and the United Kingdom 227

(63) Declaration by the United Kingdom of Great Britain and Northern Ireland on the definition of the term "nationals" 228

(64) Declaration by the United Kingdom of Great Britain and Northern Ireland on the franchise for elections to the European Parliament 228

(65) Declaration by the United Kingdom on Article *75* [61H] of the Treaty on the Functioning of the European Union *(financial sanctions on terrorism)* 228

* * *

Declarations in the Constitution not included in the Treaty of Lisbon 229

* * * * * *

DECLARATIONS

A. DECLARATIONS CONCERNING PROVISIONS OF THE TREATIES

1. DECLARATION CONCERNING THE CHARTER OF FUNDAMENTAL RIGHTS OF THE EUROPEAN UNION

The Charter of Fundamental Rights, which has legally binding force, confirms the fundamental rights guaranteed by the European Convention on Human Rights and Fundamental Freedoms and as they result from the constitutional traditions common to the Member States.
The Charter does not extend the field of application of Union law beyond the powers of the Union or establish any new power or task for the Union, or modify powers and tasks as defined by the Treaties.
[BMDF Note: This is a new Declaration in the Treaty of Lisbon]

2. DECLARATION ON ARTICLE *6(2) OF THE TREATY ON EUROPEAN UNION*

The Conference agrees that the Union's accession to the European Convention on the Protection of Human Rights and Fundamental Freedoms should be arranged in such a way as to preserve the specific features of Union law. In this connection, the Conference notes the existence of a regular dialogue between the Court of Justice of the European Union and the European Court of Human Rights; such dialogue could be reinforced when the Union accedes to that Convention.

3. DECLARATION ON ARTICLE *8* [7a] *OF THE TREATY ON EUROPEAN UNION*

The Union will take into account the particular situation of small-sized countries which maintain specific relations of proximity with it.

4. DECLARATION ON THE COMPOSITION OF THE EUROPEAN PARLIAMENT

The additional seat in the European Parliament will be attributed to Italy.
[BMDF Note: new Declaration in the Treaty of Lisbon, agreed at Lisbon 18 October 2007]

5. DECLARATION ON THE POLITICAL AGREEMENT BY THE EUROPEAN COUNCIL CONCERNING THE DRAFT DECISION ON THE COMPOSITION OF THE EUROPEAN PARLIAMENT

The European Council will give its political agreement on the revised draft Decision on the composition of the European Parliament for the legislative period 2009-2014, based on the proposal from the European Parliament.
[BMDF Note: new Declaration in the Treaty of Lisbon, agreed at Lisbon 18 October 2007]

6. DECLARATION ON ARTICLES *15* [9B] *(5) AND (6), 17* [9D] *(6) AND (7) AND 18* [9E] *OF THE TREATY ON EUROPEAN UNION*

In choosing the persons called upon to hold the offices of President of the European Council, President of the Commission and ***High Representative of the Union for Foreign Affairs and Security Policy***, due account is to be taken of the need to respect the geographical and demographic diversity of the Union and its Member States.

7. DECLARATION ON ARTICLE *16* [9C] *(4) OF THE TREATY ON EUROPEAN UNION AND ARTICLE 238* [205] *(2) OF THE TREATY ON THE FUNCTIONING OF THE EUROPEAN UNION*

The Conference declares that the decision relating to the implementation of ***Article 16(4) of the Treaty on European Union and Article 238(2) of the Treaty on the Functioning of the European Union*** will be adopted by the Council ***on*** the date of the signature of the ***Treaty of Lisbon*** and will enter into force on the day that Treaty enters into force. The draft decision is set out below:

DRAFT DECISION OF THE COUNCIL
RELATING TO THE IMPLEMENTATION OF ARTICLE *16* [9C] ***(4) OF THE TREATY ON EUROPEAN UNION AND ARTICLE 238*** [205] ***(2) OF THE TREATY ON THE FUNCTIONING OF THE EUROPEAN UNION*** BETWEEN 1 NOVEMBER 2014 AND 31 MARCH 2017 ON THE ONE HAND, AND AS FROM 1 APRIL 2017 ON THE OTHER

THE COUNCIL OF THE EUROPEAN UNION,

Whereas:

(1) Provisions should be adopted allowing for a smooth transition from the system for decision-making in the Council by a qualified majority as defined in ***Article 3(3)*** of the Protocol on the transitional provisions, which will continue to apply until 31 October 2014, to the voting system provided for in ***Article 16(4) of the Treaty on European Union and Article 238(2) of the Treaty on the Functioning of the European Union***, which will apply with effect from 1 November 2014, including, during a transitional period until 31 March 2017, specific provisions laid down in ***Article 3(2)*** of that Protocol.

(2) It is recalled that it is the practice of the Council to devote every effort to strengthening the democratic legitimacy of decisions taken by a qualified majority.

HAS DECIDED AS FOLLOWS:

Section 1

Provisions to be applied from 1 November 2014 to 31 March 2017

ARTICLE 1

From 1 November 2014 to 31 March 2017, if members of the Council, representing:

(a) at least three quarters of the population, or

(b) at least three quarters of the number of Member States

necessary to constitute a blocking minority resulting from the application of ***Article 16(4), first subparagraph, of the Treaty on European Union or Article 238(2) of the Treaty on the Functioning of the European Union***, indicate their opposition to the Council adopting an act by a qualified majority, the Council shall discuss the issue.

ARTICLE 2

The Council shall, in the course of these discussions, do all in its power to reach, within a reasonable time and without prejudicing obligatory time limits laid down by Union law, a satisfactory solution to address concerns raised by the members of the Council referred to in Article 1.

ARTICLE 3
To this end, the President of the Council, with the assistance of the Commission and in compliance with the Rules of Procedure of the Council, shall undertake any initiative necessary to facilitate a wider basis of agreement in the Council. The members of the Council shall lend him or her their assistance.

Section 2

Provisions to be applied as from 1 April 2017

ARTICLE 4
As from 1 April 2017, if members of the Council, representing:
(a) at least 55 % of the population, or
(b) at least 55 % of the number of Member States
necessary to constitute a blocking minority resulting from the application of ***Article 16(4), first subparagraph, of the Treaty on European Union or Article 238(2) of the Treaty on the Functioning of the European Union***, indicate their opposition to the Council adopting an act by a qualified majority, the Council shall discuss the issue.

ARTICLE 5
The Council shall, in the course of these discussions, do all in its power to reach, within a reasonable time and without prejudicing obligatory time limits laid down by Union law, a satisfactory solution to address concerns raised by the members of the Council referred to in Article 4.

ARTICLE 6
To this end, the President of the Council, with the assistance of the Commission and in compliance with the Rules of Procedure of the Council, shall undertake any initiative necessary to facilitate a wider basis of agreement in the Council. The members of the Council shall lend him or her their assistance.

Section 3

Entry into force

ARTICLE 7
This Decision shall enter into force on the date of the entry into force of the Treaty of Lisbon.
[BMDF Note: Declaration amended on 19 October 2007 at the Lisbon summit]

8. DECLARATION ON PRACTICAL MEASURES TO BE TAKEN UPON THE ENTRY INTO FORCE OF THE TREATY OF LISBON AS REGARDS THE PRESIDENCY OF THE EUROPEAN COUNCIL AND OF THE FOREIGN AFFAIRS COUNCIL

In the event that the Treaty of Lisbon enters into force later than 1 January 2009, the Conference requests the competent authorities of the Member State holding the six-monthly Presidency of the Council at that time, on the one hand, and the person elected President of the European Council and the person appointed High Representative of the Union for Foreign Affairs and Security Policy, on the other hand, to take the necessary specific measures, in consultation with the following six-monthly Presidency, to allow an efficient handover of the material and organisational aspects of the Presidency of the European Council and of the Foreign Affairs Council.
[BMDF Note: This is a new Declaration in the Treaty of Lisbon]

9. DECLARATION ON ARTICLE *16* [9C] *(9) OF THE TREATY ON EUROPEAN UNION* CONCERNING THE EUROPEAN COUNCIL DECISION ON THE EXERCISE OF THE PRESIDENCY OF THE COUNCIL

The Conference declares that the Council should begin preparing the decision establishing the procedures for implementing the decision on the exercise of the Presidency of the Council as soon as the ***Treaty of Lisbon*** is signed, and should give its political approval within six months. A draft decision of the European Council, which will be adopted on the date of entry into force of the said Treaty, is set out below:

DRAFT DECISION OF THE EUROPEAN COUNCIL
ON THE EXERCISE OF THE PRESIDENCY OF THE COUNCIL

ARTICLE 1

1. The Presidency of the Council, with the exception of the Foreign Affairs configuration, shall be held by pre-established groups of three Member States for a period of 18 months. The groups shall be made up on a basis of equal rotation among the Member States, taking into account their diversity and geographical balance within the Union.

2. Each member of the group shall in turn chair for a six-month period all configurations of the Council, with the exception of the Foreign Affairs configuration. The other members of the group shall assist the Chair in all its responsibilities on the basis of a common programme. Members of the team may decide alternative arrangements among themselves.

ARTICLE 2

The Committee of Permanent Representatives of the Governments of the Member States shall be chaired by a representative of the Member State chairing the General Affairs Council.

The Chair of the Political and Security Committee shall be held by a representative of the Union Minister for Foreign Affairs.

The chair of the preparatory bodies of the various Council configurations, with the exception of the Foreign Affairs configuration, shall fall to the member of the group chairing the relevant configuration, unless decided otherwise in accordance with Article 4.

ARTICLE 3

The General Affairs Council shall ensure consistency and continuity in the work of the different Council configurations in the framework of multiannual programmes in co-operation with the Commission. The Member States holding the Presidency shall take all necessary measures for the organisation and smooth operation of the Council's work, with the assistance of the General Secretariat of the Council.

ARTICLE 4

The Council shall adopt a decision establishing the measures for the implementation of this decision.

10. DECLARATION ON ARTICLE *17* [9D] *OF THE TREATY ON EUROPEAN UNION*

The Conference considers that when the Commission no longer includes nationals of all Member States, the Commission should pay particular attention to the need to ensure full transparency in relations with all Member States. Accordingly, the Commission should liaise closely with all Member States, whether or not they have a national serving as member of the Commission, and in this context pay special attention to the need to share information and consult with all Member States.

The Conference also considers that the Commission should take all the necessary measures to ensure that political, social and economic realities in all Member States, including those which have no national serving as member of the Commission, are fully taken into account. These measures should include ensuring that the position of those Member States is addressed by appropriate organisational arrangements.

11. DECLARATION ON ARTICLE *17* [9D] *(6) AND (7) OF THE TREATY ON EUROPEAN UNION*

The Conference considers that, in accordance with the provisions of ***the Treaties***, the European Parliament and the European Council are jointly responsible for the smooth running of the process leading to the election of the President of the European Commission. Prior to the decision of the European Council, representatives of the European Parliament and of the European Council will thus conduct the necessary consultations in the framework deemed the most appropriate. These consultations will focus on the backgrounds of the candidates for President of the Commission, taking account of the elections to the European Parliament, in accordance with ***the first subparagraph of Article 17(7)***. The arrangements for such consultations may be determined, in due course, by common accord between the European Parliament and the European Council.

12. DECLARATION ON ARTICLE *18* [9E] OF THE TREATY ON EUROPEAN UNION

1. The Conference declares that, in the course of the preparatory work preceding the appointment of the High Representative of the Union for Foreign Affairs and Security Policy which is due to take place on the date of entry into force of the Treaty of Lisbon in accordance with Article 18 of the Treaty on European Union and Article 5 of the Protocol on transitional provisions and whose term of office will be from that date until the end of the term of office of the Commission in office on that date, appropriate contacts will be made with the European Parliament.

2. Furthermore, the Conference recalls that, as regards the High Representative of the Union for Foreign Affairs and Security Policy whose term of office will start in November 2009 at the same time and for the same duration as the next Commission, he or she will be appointed in accordance with the provisions of Articles 17 and 18 of the Treaty on European Union.
[BMDF Note: new Declaration in the Treaty of Lisbon, agreed at Lisbon 18 October 2007]

13. DECLARATION CONCERNING THE COMMON FOREIGN AND SECURITY POLICY

The Conference underlines that the provisions in the Treaty on European Union covering the Common Foreign and Security Policy, including the creation of the office of High Representative of the Union for Foreign Affairs and Security Policy and the establishment of an External Action Service, do not affect the responsibilities of the Member States, as they currently exist, for the formulation and conduct of their foreign policy nor of their national representation in third countries and international organisations.
The Conference also recalls that the provisions governing the Common Security and Defence Policy do not prejudice the specific character of the security and defence policy of the Member States.
It stresses that the European Union and its Member States will remain bound by the provisions of the Charter of the United Nations and, in particular, by the primary responsibility of the Security Council and of its Members for the maintenance of international peace and security.
[BMDF Note: This is a new Declaration in the Treaty of Lisbon]

14. DECLARATION CONCERNING THE COMMON FOREIGN AND SECURITY POLICY

In addition to the specific rules and procedures referred to in paragraph 1 of Article 24 of the Treaty on European Union, the Conference underlines that the provisions covering the Common Foreign and Security Policy including in relation to the High Representative of the Union for Foreign Affairs and Security Policy and the External Action Service will not affect the existing legal basis, responsibilities, and powers of each Member State in relation to the formulation and conduct of its foreign policy, its national diplomatic service, relations with third countries and participation in international organisations, including a Member State's membership of the Security Council of the United Nations.

The Conference also notes that the provisions covering the Common Foreign and Security Policy do not give new powers to the Commission to initiate decisions or increase the role of the European Parliament.
The Conference also recalls that the provisions governing the Common Security and Defence Policy do not prejudice the specific character of the security and defence policy of the Member States.
[BMDF Note: This is a new Declaration in the Treaty of Lisbon]

15. DECLARATION ON ARTICLE *27* [13a] *OF THE TREATY ON EUROPEAN UNION*

The Conference declares that, as soon as the ***Treaty of Lisbon*** is signed, the Secretary-General of the Council, High Representative for the common foreign and security policy, the Commission and the Member States should begin preparatory work on the European External Action Service.

16. DECLARATION ON ARTICLE *55* [53] *(2) OF THE TREATY ON EUROPEAN UNION*

The Conference considers that the possibility of producing translations of the ***Treaties*** in the languages mentioned in ***Article 55(2)*** contributes to fulfilling the objective of respecting the Union's rich cultural and linguistic diversity as set forth in the fourth subparagraph of ***Article 3(3)***. In this context, the Conference confirms the attachment of the Union to the cultural diversity of Europe and the special attention it will continue to pay to these and other languages.
The Conference recommends that those Member States wishing to avail themselves of the possibility recognised in ***Article 55(2)*** communicate to the Council, within six months from the date of the signature of ***the Treaty of Lisbon***, the language or languages into which translations of ***the Treaties*** will be made.

17. DECLARATION CONCERNING PRIMACY

The Conference recalls that, in accordance with well settled case law of the EU Court of Justice, the Treaties and the law adopted by the Union on the basis of the Treaties have primacy over the law of Member States, under the conditions laid down by the said case law.
The Conference has also decided to attach as an Annex to this Final Act the Opinion of the Council Legal Service on the primacy of EC law as set out in 11197/07 (JUR 260):

"Opinion of the Council Legal Service
of 22 June 2007

It results from the case-law of the Court of Justice that primacy of EC law is a cornerstone principle of Community law. According to the Court, this principle is inherent to the specific nature of the European Community. At the time of the first judgment of this established case law (Costa/ENEL, 15 July 1964, Case 6/64[1]) there was no mention of primacy in the treaty. It is still the case today. The fact that the principle of primacy will not be included in the future treaty shall not in any way change the existence of the principle and the existing case-law of the Court of Justice."

1. *Extract from the Judgement in Costa/ENEL*: "It follows (...) that the law stemming from the treaty, an independent source of law, could not, because of its special and original nature, be overridden by domestic legal provisions, however framed, without being deprived of its character as Community law and without the legal basis of the Community itself being called into question."
[BMDF Note: This is a new Declaration in the Treaty of Lisbon]

18. DECLARATION IN RELATION TO THE DELIMITATION OF COMPETENCES

The Conference underlines that, in accordance with the system of division of competences between the Union and the Member States as provided for in the Treaty on European Union and the Treaty on the Functioning of the European Union, competences not conferred upon the Union in the Treaties remain with the Member States.

When the Treaties confer on the Union a competence shared with the Member States in a specific area, the Member States shall exercise their competence to the extent that the Union has not exercised, or has decided to cease exercising, its competence. The latter situation arises when the relevant EU institutions decide to repeal a legislative act, in particular better to ensure constant respect for the principles of subsidiarity and proportionality. The Council may, at the initiative of one or several of its members (representatives of Member States) and in accordance with Article 208 of the Treaty on the Functioning of the European Union, request the Commission to submit proposals for repealing a legislative act. The Conference welcomes the Commission's declaration that it shall devote particular attention to those requests.

Equally, the representatives of the governments of the Member States, meeting in an Intergovernmental Conference, in accordance with the ordinary revision procedure provided for in Article 48(2) to (5) of the Treaty on European Union, may decide to amend the Treaties, including either to increase or to reduce the competences conferred on the Union in the said Treaties.

[BMDF Note: This is a new Declaration in the Treaty of Lisbon. Declaration amended on 19 October 2007 at the Lisbon summit]

19. DECLARATION ON ARTICLE *8* [3] *OF THE TREATY ON THE FUNCTIONING OF THE EUROPEAN UNION*

The Conference agrees that, in its general efforts to eliminate inequalities between women and men, the Union will aim in its different policies to combat all kinds of domestic violence. The Member States should take all necessary measures to prevent and punish these criminal acts and to support and protect the victims.

20. DECLARATION ON ARTICLE *16* [16B] *OF THE TREATY ON THE FUNCTIONING OF THE EUROPEAN UNION*

The Conference declares that, whenever rules on protection of personal data to be adopted on the basis of ***Article 16*** could have direct implications for national security, due account will have to be taken of the specific characteristics of the matter. It recalls that the legislation presently applicable (see in particular Directive 95/46/EC) includes specific derogations in this regard.

21. DECLARATION ON THE PROTECTION OF PERSONAL DATA IN THE FIELD OF POLICE AND JUDICIAL CO-OPERATION IN CRIMINAL MATTERS

The Conference acknowledges that specific rules on the protection of personal data and the free movement of such data in the fields of judicial co-operation in criminal matters and police co-operation based on Article 16 of the Treaty on the Functioning of the European Union may prove necessary because of the specific nature of these fields.

[BMDF Note: This is a new Declaration in the Treaty of Lisbon]

22. DECLARATION ON ARTICLES *48* [42] *AND 79* [63a] *OF THE TREATY ON THE FUNCTIONING OF THE EUROPEAN UNION*

The Conference considers that in the event that a draft ***legislative act*** based on ***Article 82(2)*** would affect ***important*** aspects of the social security system of a Member State, including its scope, cost or financial structure, or would affect the financial balance of that system as set out in ***the second paragraph of Article 48***, the interests of that Member State will be duly taken into account.

23. DECLARATION ON THE SECOND PARAGRAPH OF ARTICLE *48* [42] OF THE TREATY ON THE FUNCTIONING OF THE EUROPEAN UNION

The Conference recalls that in that case, in accordance with Article 15(4), the European Council acts by consensus.
[BMDF Note: This is a new Declaration in the Treaty of Lisbon, concerns social security. The article reference in the text refers to Article 15(4) TEU]

24. DECLARATION CONCERNING THE LEGAL PERSONALITY OF THE EUROPEAN UNION

The Conference confirms that the fact that the European Union has a legal personality will not in any way authorise the Union to legislate or to act beyond the competences conferred upon it by the Member States in the Treaties.
[BMDF Note: This is a new Declaration in the Treaty of Lisbon]

25. DECLARATION ON ARTICLES *75* [61H] *AND 215* [188K] *OF THE TREATY ON THE FUNCTIONING OF THE EUROPEAN UNION*

The Conference recalls that the respect for fundamental rights and freedoms implies, in particular, that proper attention is given to the protection and observance of the due process rights of the individuals or entities concerned. For this purpose and in order to guarantee a thorough judicial review of European decisions subjecting an individual or entity to restrictive measures, such decisions must be based on clear and distinct criteria. These criteria should be tailored to the specifics of each restrictive measure.

26. DECLARATION ON NON-PARTICIPATION BY A MEMBER STATE IN A MEASURE BASED ON TITLE IV OF PART THREE OF THE TREATY ON THE FUNCTIONING OF THE EUROPEAN UNION

The Conference declares that, where a Member State opts not to participate in a measure based on Title IV of Part Three of the Treaty on the Functioning of the European Union, the Council will hold a thorough discussion on the possible implications and effects of that Member State's non-participation in the measure.
In addition, any Member State may ask the Commission to examine the situation on the basis of Article 116 of the Treaty on the Functioning of the European Union.
The above paragraphs are without prejudice to the entitlement of a Member State to refer the matter to the European Council.
[BMDF Note: This is a new Declaration in the Treaty of Lisbon. The Declaration refers to Member States not being involved in matters relating to the Area of Freedom, Security and Justice, in particular the UK. Article 116 concerns actions by the Member States which distort the internal market]

27. DECLARATION ON ARTICLE *85* [69D] (1), SECOND SUBPARAGRAPH *OF THE TREATY ON THE FUNCTIONING OF THE EUROPEAN UNION*

The Conference considers that the ***regulations*** referred to in the second subparagraph of ***Article 85(1) of the Treaty on the Functioning of the European Union*** should take into account national rules and practices relating to the initiation of criminal investigations.

28. DECLARATION ON ARTICLE *98* [78] *OF THE TREATY ON THE FUNCTIONING OF THE EUROPEAN UNION*

The Conference notes that the provisions of ***Article 98*** shall be applied in accordance with the current practice. The terms "such measures are required in order to compensate for the economic disadvantages caused by the division of Germany to the economy of certain areas of the Federal Republic affected by that division" shall be interpreted in accordance with the existing case law of the Court of Justice of the European ***Union***.

29. DECLARATION ON ARTICLE *107* [87] *(2)(c) OF THE TREATY ON THE FUNCTIONING OF THE EUROPEAN UNION*

The Conference notes that ***Article 107(2)(c)*** shall be interpreted in accordance with the existing case law of the Court of Justice of the European ***Union*** regarding the applicability of the provisions to aid granted to certain areas of the Federal Republic of Germany affected by the former division of Germany.

30. DECLARATION ON ARTICLE *126* [104] *OF THE TREATY ON THE FUNCTIONING OF THE EUROPEAN UNION*

With regard to Article ***126***, the Conference confirms that raising growth potential and securing sound budgetary positions are the two pillars of the economic and fiscal policy of the Union and the Member States. The Stability and Growth Pact is an important tool to achieve these goals.

The Conference reaffirms its commitment to the provisions concerning the Stability and Growth Pact as the framework for the co-ordination of budgetary policies in the Member States.

The Conference confirms that a rule-based system is the best guarantee for commitments to be enforced and for all Member States to be treated equally.

Within this framework, the Conference also reaffirms its commitment to the goals of the Lisbon Strategy: job creation, structural reforms, and social cohesion.

The Union aims at achieving balanced economic growth and price stability. Economic and budgetary policies thus need to set the right priorities towards economic reforms, innovation, competitiveness and strengthening of private investment and consumption in phases of weak economic growth. This should be reflected in the orientations of budgetary decisions at the national and Union level in particular through restructuring of public revenue and expenditure while respecting budgetary discipline in accordance with the ***Treaties*** and the Stability and Growth Pact.

Budgetary and economic challenges facing the Member States underline the importance of sound budgetary policy throughout the economic cycle.

The Conference agrees that Member States should use periods of economic recovery actively to consolidate public finances and improve their budgetary positions. The objective is to gradually achieve a budgetary surplus in good times which creates the necessary room to accommodate economic downturns and thus contribute to the long-term sustainability of public finances.

The Member States look forward to possible proposals of the Commission as well as further contributions of Member States with regard to strengthening and clarifying the implementation of the Stability and Growth Pact. The Member States will take all necessary measures to raise the growth potential of their economies. Improved economic policy co-ordination could support this objective. This Declaration does not prejudge the future debate on the Stability and Growth Pact.

31. DECLARATION ON ARTICLE *156* [140] *OF THE TREATY ON THE FUNCTIONING OF THE EUROPEAN UNION*

The Conference confirms that the policies described in ***Article 156*** fall essentially within the competence of the Member States. Measures to provide encouragement and promote co-ordination to be taken at Union level in accordance with this Article shall be of a complementary nature. They shall serve to strengthen co-operation between Member States and not to harmonise national systems. The guarantees and practices existing in each Member State as regards the responsibility of the social partners will not be affected.
This Declaration is without prejudice to the provisions of the ***Treaties*** conferring competence on the Union, including in social matters.

32. DECLARATION ON ARTICLE *168* [152] (4)(c) OF THE TREATY ON THE FUNCTIONING OF THE EUROPEAN UNION

The Conference declares that the measures to be adopted pursuant to Article 168(4)(c) must meet common safety concerns and aim to set high standards of quality where national standards affecting the internal market would otherwise prevent a high level of human health protection being achieved.
[BMDF Note: This is a new Declaration in the Treaty of Lisbon]

33. DECLARATION ON ARTICLE *174* [158] *OF THE TREATY ON THE FUNCTIONING OF THE EUROPEAN UNION*

The Conference considers that the reference in ***Article 174*** to island regions can include island States in their entirety, subject to the necessary criteria being met.

34. DECLARATION ON ARTICLE *179* [163] *OF THE TREATY ON THE FUNCTIONING OF THE EUROPEAN UNION*

The Conference agrees that the Union's action in the area of research and technological development will pay due respect to the fundamental orientations and choices of the research policies of the Member States.

35. DECLARATION ON ARTICLE *194* [176A] *OF THE TREATY ON THE FUNCTIONING OF THE EUROPEAN UNION*

The Conference believes that ***Article 194*** does not affect the right of the Member States to take the necessary measures to ensure their energy supply under the conditions provided for in ***Article 347***.

36. DECLARATION ON ARTICLE *218* [188N] *OF THE TREATY ON THE FUNCTIONING OF THE EUROPEAN UNION* CONCERNING THE NEGOTIATION AND CONCLUSION OF INTERNATIONAL AGREEMENTS BY MEMBER STATES RELATING TO THE AREA OF FREEDOM, SECURITY AND JUSTICE

The Conference confirms that Member States may negotiate and conclude agreements with third countries or international organisations in the areas covered by ***Chapters*** 3, 4 and 5 of ***Title IV of Part Three*** insofar as such agreements comply with Union law.

37. DECLARATION ON ARTICLES *222* [188R] *OF THE TREATY ON THE FUNCTIONING OF THE EUROPEAN UNION*

Without prejudice to the measures adopted by the Union to comply with its solidarity obligation towards a Member State which is the object of a terrorist attack or the victim of natural or man-made disaster, none of the provisions of ***Article 222*** is intended to affect the right of another Member State to choose the most appropriate means to comply with its own solidarity obligation towards that Member State.

38. DECLARATION ON ARTICLE *252* [222] OF THE TREATY ON THE FUNCTIONING OF THE EUROPEAN UNION REGARDING THE NUMBER OF ADVOCATES-GENERAL IN THE COURT OF JUSTICE

The Conference declares that if, in accordance with Article 252, first subparagraph, of the Treaty on the Functioning of the European Union, the Court of Justice requests that the number of Advocates-General be increased by three (eleven instead of eight), the Council will, acting unanimously, agree on such an increase.
In that case, the Conference agrees that Poland will, as it is already the case for Germany, France, Italy, Spain and the United-Kingdom, have a permanent Advocate-General and no longer take part in the rotation system, while the existing rotation system will involve the rotation of five Advocates-General instead of three.
[BMDF Note: new Declaration in the Treaty of Lisbon, agreed at Lisbon 18 October 2007]

39. DECLARATION ON ARTICLE *290* [249B] *OF THE TREATY ON THE FUNCTIONING OF THE EUROPEAN UNION*

The Conference takes note of the Commission's intention to continue to consult experts appointed by the Member States in the preparation of draft delegated acts in the financial services area, in accordance with its established practice.

40. DECLARATION ON ARTICLE *329* [280D] *OF THE TREATY ON THE FUNCTIONING OF THE EUROPEAN UNION*

The Conference declares that Member States may indicate, when they make a request to establish enhanced co-operation, if they intend already at that stage to make use of ***Article 329*** providing for the extension of qualified majority voting or to have recourse to the ordinary legislative procedure.

41. DECLARATION ON ARTICLE *352* [308] OF THE TREATY ON THE FUNCTIONING OF THE EUROPEAN UNION

The Conference declares that the reference in Article 352(1) of the Treaty on the Functioning of the European Union to objectives of the Union refers to the objectives as set out in Article 3(2) and (3) of the Treaty on European Union and to the objectives of Articles 3(5) with respect to external action under Title V of Part Three, of that Treaty. It is therefore excluded that an action based on Article 352 of the Treaty on the Functioning of the European Union would only pursue objectives set out in Article 3(1) of the Treaty on European Union. In this connection, the Conference notes that in accordance with Article 42(1) of the Treaty on European Union, legislative acts may not be adopted in the area of the Common Foreign and Security Policy.
[BMDF Note: This is a new Declaration in the Treaty of Lisbon]

42. DECLARATION ON ARTICLE *352* [308] OF THE TREATY ON THE FUNCTIONING OF THE EUROPEAN UNION

The Conference underlines that, in accordance with the settled case law of the Court of Justice of the European Union, Article 352 of the Treaty on the Functioning of the European Union, being an integral part of an institutional system based on the principle of conferred powers, cannot serve as a basis for widening the scope of Union powers beyond the general framework created by the provisions of the Treaties as a whole and, in particular, by those that define the tasks and the activities of the Union. In any event, this Article cannot be used as a basis for the adoption of provisions whose effect would, in substance, be to amend the Treaties without following the procedure which they provide for that purpose.

[BMDF Note: This is a new Declaration in the Treaty of Lisbon]

43. DECLARATION ON ARTICLE *355* [311a] *(6) OF THE TREATY ON THE FUNCTIONING OF THE EUROPEAN UNION*

The High Contracting Parties agree that the European Council, pursuant to ***Article 355(6)***, will take a European decision leading to the modification of the status of Mayotte with regard to the Union in order to make this territory an outermost region within the meaning of ***Article 355(1) and Article 349***, when the French authorities notify the European Council and the Commission that the evolution currently underway in the internal status of the island so allows.

B. DECLARATIONS CONCERNING PROTOCOLS ANNEXED TO THE TREATIES

44. DECLARATION ON ARTICLE 5 OF THE PROTOCOL ON THE SCHENGEN ACQUIS INTEGRATED INTO THE FRAMEWORK OF THE EUROPEAN UNION

The Conference notes that where a Member State has made a notification under Article 5(2) of the Protocol on the Schengen acquis integrated into the framework of the European Union that it does not wish to take part in a proposal or initiative, that notification may be withdrawn at any moment before the adoption of the measure building upon the Schengen acquis.

[BMDF Note: This is a new Declaration in the Treaty of Lisbon]

45. DECLARATION ON ARTICLE 5(2) OF THE PROTOCOL ON THE SCHENGEN ACQUIS INTEGRATED INTO THE FRAMEWORK OF THE EUROPEAN UNION

The Conference declares that whenever the United Kingdom or Ireland indicates to the Council its intention not to participate in a measure building upon a part of the Schengen acquis in which it participates, the Council will have a full discussion on the possible implications of the non-participation of that Member State in that measure. The discussion within the Council should be conducted in the light of the indications given by the Commission concerning the relationship between the proposal and the Schengen acquis.

[BMDF Note: This is a new Declaration in the Treaty of Lisbon]

46. DECLARATION ON ARTICLE 5(3) OF THE PROTOCOL ON THE SCHENGEN *ACQUIS* INTEGRATED INTO THE FRAMEWORK OF THE EUROPEAN UNION

The Conference recalls that if the Council does not take a decision after a first substantive discussion of the matter, the Commission may present an amended proposal for a further substantive re-examination by the Council within the deadline of 4 months.
[BMDF Note: This is a new Declaration in the Treaty of Lisbon]

47. DECLARATION ON ARTICLE 5(3), (4) AND (5) OF THE PROTOCOL ON THE SCHENGEN *ACQUIS* INTEGRATED INTO THE FRAMEWORK OF THE EUROPEAN UNION

The Conference notes that the conditions to be determined in the decision referred to in paragraphs 3, 4 or 5 of Article 5 of the Protocol on the Schengen acquis integrated into the framework of the European Union may determine that the Member State concerned shall bear the direct financial consequences, if any, necessarily and unavoidably incurred as a result of the cessation of its participation in some or all of the acquis referred to in any decision taken by the Council pursuant to Article 4 of the said Protocol.
[BMDF Note: This is a new Declaration in the Treaty of Lisbon]

48. DECLARATION CONCERNING THE PROTOCOL ON THE POSITION OF DENMARK

The Conference notes that with respect to legal acts to be adopted by the Council acting alone or jointly with the European Parliament and containing provisions applicable to Denmark as well as provisions not applicable to Denmark because they have a legal basis to which Part I of the Protocol on the position of Denmark applies, Denmark declares that it will not use its voting right to prevent the adoption of the provisions which are not applicable to Denmark.
Furthermore, the Conference notes that on the basis of the Declaration by the Conference on ***Article 222***, Denmark declares that Danish participation in actions or legal acts pursuant to ***Article 222*** will take place in accordance with Part I and Part II of the Protocol on the position of Denmark.

49. DECLARATION CONCERNING ITALY

The Conference notes that the Protocol on Italy annexed in 1957 to the Treaty establishing the European Economic Community, as amended upon adoption of the Treaty on European Union, stated that:

"THE HIGH CONTRACTING PARTIES,

DESIRING to settle certain particular problems relating to Italy,

HAVE AGREED upon the following provisions, which shall be annexed to this Treaty:

THE MEMBER STATES OF THE COMMUNITY

TAKE NOTE of the fact that the Italian Government is carrying out a ten-year programme of economic expansion designed to rectify the disequilibria in the structure of the Italian economy, in particular by providing an infrastructure for the less developed areas in Southern Italy and in the Italian islands and by creating new jobs in order to eliminate unemployment;

RECALL that the principles and objectives of this programme of the Italian Government have been considered and approved by organisations for international co-operation of which the Member States are members;

RECOGNISE that it is in their common interest that the objectives of the Italian programme should be attained;

AGREE, in order to facilitate the accomplishment of this task by the Italian Government, to recommend to the institutions of the Community that they should employ all the methods and procedures provided in this Treaty and, in particular, make appropriate use of the resources of the European Investment Bank and the European Social Fund;

ARE OF THE OPINION that the institutions of the Community should, in applying this Treaty, take account of the sustained effort to be made by the Italian economy in the coming years and of the desirability of avoiding dangerous stresses in particular within the balance of payments or the level of employment, which might jeopardise the application of this Treaty in Italy;

RECOGNISE that in the event of Articles 109 H and 109 I being applied it will be necessary to take care that any measures required of the Italian Government do not prejudice the completion of its programme for economic expansion and for raising the standard of living of the population."

50. DECLARATION CONCERNING ARTICLE 10 OF THE PROTOCOL ON TRANSITIONAL PROVISIONS

The Conference invites the European Parliament, the Council and the Commission, within their respective powers, to seek to adopt, in appropriate cases and as far as possible within the five-year period referred to in Article 10(3) of the Protocol on transitional provisions, legal acts amending or replacing the acts referred to in Article 10(1) of that Protocol.

[BMDF Note: This is a new Declaration in the Treaty of Lisbon]

C. DECLARATIONS BY MEMBER STATES

Furthermore, the Conference has noted the declarations listed hereafter and annexed to this Final Act:

51. DECLARATION BY THE KINGDOM OF BELGIUM ON NATIONAL PARLIAMENTS

Belgium wishes to make clear that, in accordance with its constitutional law, not only the Chamber of Representatives and Senate of the Federal Parliament but also the parliamentary assemblies of the Communities and the Regions act, in terms of the competences exercised by the Union, as components of the national parliamentary system or chambers of the national Parliament.

52. DECLARATION BY THE KINGDOM OF BELGIUM, THE REPUBLIC OF BULGARIA, THE FEDERAL REPUBLIC OF GERMANY, THE HELLENIC REPUBLIC, THE KINGDOM OF SPAIN, THE ITALIAN REPUBLIC, THE REPUBLIC OF CYPRUS, THE REPUBLIC OF LITHUANIA, THE GRAND-DUCHY OF LUXEMBOURG, THE REPUBLIC OF HUNGARY, THE REPUBLIC OF MALTA, THE REPUBLIC OF AUSTRIA, THE PORTUGUESE REPUBLIC, ROMANIA, THE REPUBLIC OF SLOVENIA AND THE SLOVAK REPUBLIC ON THE SYMBOLS OF THE EUROPEAN UNION

Belgium, Bulgaria, Germany, Greece, Spain, Italy, Cyprus, Lithuania, Luxemburg, Hungary, Malta, Austria, Portugal, Romania, Slovenia and the Slovak Republic declare that the flag with a circle of twelve golden stars on a blue background, the anthem based on the "Ode to Joy" from the Ninth Symphony by Ludwig van Beethoven, the motto "United in diversity", the euro as the currency of the European Union and Europe Day on 9 May will for them continue as symbols to express the sense of community of the people in the European Union and their allegiance to it.
[BMDF Note: This is a new Declaration in the 3 December 2007 draft of the Treaty of Lisbon]

53. DECLARATION BY THE CZECH REPUBLIC ON THE CHARTER OF FUNDAMENTAL RIGHTS OF THE EUROPEAN UNION

1. The Czech Republic recalls that the provisions of the Charter of Fundamental Rights of the European Union are addressed to the institutions and bodies of the European Union with due regard for the principle of subsidiarity and division of competences between the European Union and its Member States, as reaffirmed in Declaration (No 18) in relation to the delimitation of competences. The Czech Republic stresses that its provisions are addressed to the Member States only when they are implementing Union law, and not when they are adopting and implementing national law independently from Union law.

2. The Czech Republic also emphasises that the Charter does not extend the field of application of Union law and does not establish any new power for the Union. It does not diminish the field of application of national law and does not restrain any current powers of the national authorities in this field.

3. The Czech Republic stresses that, in so far as the Charter recognises fundamental rights and principles as they result from constitutional traditions common to the Member States, those rights and principles are to be interpreted in harmony with those traditions.

4. The Czech Republic further stresses that nothing in the Charter may be interpreted as restricting or adversely affecting human rights and fundamental freedoms as recognised, in their respective field of application, by Union law and by international agreements to which the Union or all the Member States are party, including the European Convention for the Protection of Human Rights and Fundamental Freedoms, and by the Member States' Constitutions.
[BMDF Note: This is a new Declaration in the 3 December 2007 draft of the Treaty of Lisbon]

54. DECLARATION BY THE FEDERAL REPUBLIC OF GERMANY, IRELAND, THE REPUBLIC OF HUNGARY, THE REPUBLIC OF AUSTRIA AND THE KINGDOM OF SWEDEN

Germany, Ireland, Hungary, Austria and Sweden note that the core provisions of the Treaty establishing the European Atomic Energy Community have not been substantially amended since its entry into force and need to be brought up to date. They therefore support the idea of a Conference of the Representatives of the Governments of the Member States, which should be convened as soon as possible.

55. DECLARATION BY THE KINGDOM OF SPAIN AND THE UNITED KINGDOM OF GREAT BRITAIN AND NORTHERN IRELAND

The ***Treaties apply*** to Gibraltar as a European territory for whose external relations a Member State is responsible. This shall not imply changes in the respective positions of the Member States concerned.

56. DECLARATION BY IRELAND ON ARTICLE 3 OF THE PROTOCOL ON THE POSITION OF THE UNITED KINGDOM AND IRELAND IN RESPECT OF THE AREA OF FREEDOM, SECURITY AND JUSTICE

Ireland affirms its commitment to the Union as an area of freedom, security and justice respecting fundamental rights and the different legal systems and traditions of the Member States within which citizens are provided with a high level of safety.
Accordingly, Ireland declares its firm intention to exercise its right under Article 3 of the Protocol on the position of the United Kingdom and Ireland in respect of the area of freedom, security and justice to take part in the adoption of measures pursuant to Title IV of Part Three of the Treaty on the Functioning of the European Union to the maximum extent it deems possible.
Ireland will, in particular, participate to the maximum possible extent in measures in the field of police co-operation.
Furthermore, Ireland recalls that in accordance with Article 8 of the Protocol it may notify the President of the Council in writing that it no longer wishes to be covered by the terms of the Protocol.
Ireland intends to review the operation of these arrangements within three years of the entry into force of the Treaty of Lisbon.
[BMDF Note: This is a new Declaration in the Treaty of Lisbon]

57. DECLARATION BY THE ITALIAN REPUBLIC ON THE COMPOSITION OF THE EUROPEAN PARLIAMENT

Italy notes that, pursuant to Article 8 A (renumbered Article 10) and Article 9 A (renumbered Article 14) of the Treaty on European Union, the European Parliament is to be composed of representatives of the Union's citizens; this representation is to be degressively proportional.
Italy likewise notes that on the basis of Article 8 (renumbered Article 9) of the Treaty on European Union and Article 17 (renumbered Article 20) of the Treaty on the Functioning of the European Union, every national of a Member State is a citizen of the Union.
Italy therefore considers that, without prejudice to the decision on the 2009/2014 legislative period, any decision adopted by the European Council, at the initiative of the European Parliament and with its consent, establishing the composition of the European Parliament, must abide by the principles laid down out in the first subparagraph of Article 9 A(2) (renumbered Article 14).
[BMDF Note: This is a new Declaration in the 3 December 2007 draft of the Treaty of Lisbon]

58. DECLARATION BY THE REPUBLIC OF LATVIA, THE REPUBLIC OF HUNGARY *AND THE REPUBLIC OF MALTA* ON THE SPELLING OF THE NAME OF THE SINGLE CURRENCY IN THE *TREATIES*

Without prejudice to the unified spelling of the name of the single currency of the European Union referred to in the ***Treaties*** as displayed on the banknotes and on the coins, Latvia, Hungary ***and Malta*** declare that the spelling of the name of the single currency, including its derivatives as applied throughout the Latvian, Hungarian ***and Maltese*** text of the ***Treaties***, has no effect on the existing rules of the Latvian, Hungarian ***or Maltese*** languages.

59. DECLARATION BY THE KINGDOM OF THE NETHERLANDS ON ARTICLE *312* [270a] ON THE TREATY ON THE FUNCTIONING OF THE EUROPEAN UNION

The Kingdom of the Netherlands will agree to a decision as referred to in **the second paragraph of** ***Article 312(2) of the Treaty on the Functioning of the European Union*** once a revision of the ***decision*** referred to in ***the third paragraph of Article 311 of that Treaty*** has provided the Netherlands with a satisfactory solution for its excessive negative net payment position vis-à-vis the Union budget.

60. DECLARATION BY THE KINGDOM OF THE NETHERLANDS ON ARTICLE *355* [311a] OF THE TREATY ON THE FUNCTIONING OF THE EUROPEAN UNION

The Kingdom of the Netherlands declares that an initiative for a European decision, as referred to in Article ***355(6)*** aimed at amending the status of the Netherlands Antilles and/or Aruba with regard to the Union, will be submitted only on the basis of a decision taken in conformity with the Charter for the Kingdom of the Netherlands.

61. DECLARATION BY POLAND ON THE CHARTER OF FUNDAMENTAL RIGHTS

The Charter does not affect in any way the right of Member States to legislate in the sphere of public morality, family law, as well as the protection of human dignity and respect for human physical and moral integrity.

[BMDF Note: This is a new Declaration in the Treaty of Lisbon]

62. DECLARATION BY THE REPUBLIC OF POLAND CONCERNING THE PROTOCOL ON THE APPLICATION OF THE CHARTER OF FUNDAMENTAL RIGHTS IN RELATION TO POLAND AND THE UNITED KINGDOM

The Republic of Poland declares that, having regard to the tradition of social movement of "Solidarity" and its significant contribution to the struggle for social and labour rights, it fully respects social and labour rights, as established by European Union law, and in particular those reaffirmed in Title IV of the Charter of Fundamental Rights of the European Union.

[BMDF Note: This is a new Declaration in the Treaty of Lisbon]

63. DECLARATION BY THE UNITED KINGDOM OF GREAT BRITAIN AND NORTHERN IRELAND ON THE DEFINITION OF THE TERM "NATIONALS"

In respect of the ***Treaties*** and the Treaty establishing the European Atomic Energy Community, and in any of the acts deriving from those Treaties or continued in force by those Treaties, the United Kingdom reiterates the Declaration it made on 31 December 1982 on the definition of the term "nationals" with the exception that the reference to "British Dependent Territories Citizens" shall be read as meaning "British overseas territories citizens".

64. DECLARATION BY THE UNITED KINGDOM OF GREAT BRITAIN AND NORTHERN IRELAND ON THE FRANCHISE FOR ELECTIONS TO THE EUROPEAN PARLIAMENT

The United Kingdom notes that ***Article 14 of the Treaty on European Union*** and other provisions of the ***Treaties*** are not intended to change the basis for the franchise for elections to the European Parliament.

65. DECLARATION BY THE UNITED KINGDOM ON ARTICLE *75* [61H] OF THE TREATY ON THE FUNCTIONING OF THE EUROPEAN UNION

The United Kingdom fully supports robust action with regard to adopting financial sanctions designed to prevent and combat terrorism and related activities. Therefore, the United Kingdom declares that it intends to exercise its right under Article 3 of the Protocol on the position of the United Kingdom and Ireland in respect of the area of freedom, security and justice to take part in the adoption of all proposals made under Article 75 of the Treaty on the Functioning of the European Union.
[BMDF Note: This is a new Declaration in the Treaty of Lisbon]

DECLARATIONS IN THE CONSTITUTION *NOT* INCLUDED IN THE TREATY OF LISBON

[BMDF Note: the numbering of these Declarations is from the Constitutional Treaty]

1. **Declaration on Article I-6** (*existing case law of the Court of Justice*)

26. **Declaration on Article III-402(4)**
(*financial framework shall be extended until such time a new law is adopted*)

30. **Declaration on the ratification of the Treaty establishing a Constitution for Europe**

31. **Declaration on the Åland Islands**

32. **Declaration on the Sami People**

33. **Declaration on the Sovereign Base Areas of the United Kingdom of Great Britain and Northern Ireland In Cyprus**

34. **Declaration by the Commission on the Sovereign Base Areas of the United Kingdom of Great Britain and Northern Ireland in Cyprus**

35. **Declaration on the Ignalina nuclear power plant in Lithuania**

36. **Declaration on the transit of persons by land between the Region of Kaliningrad and other parts of the Russian Federation**

37. **Declaration on Unit 1 and Unit 2 of the Bohunice V1 nuclear power plant in Slovakia**

38. **Declaration on Cyprus**

40. **Declaration concerning the Protocol on the transitional provisions relating to the institutions and bodies of the Union**
(*allocation of seats in the European Parliament throughout the 2004-2009 parliamentary term*)

47. **Declaration by the Kingdom of Spain on the definition of the term "nationals"**

ADDITIONAL PAPERS

Page

* **Treaty of Lisbon:**
  - **Text of Treaty of Lisbon** 233
  - **Final Act** 239
  - **Annex: Tables of Equivalences** 243

  The text contains the names of the signatories and the preamble, together with the articles which do not contain the amendments to the Treaties. The Final Act lists the texts agreed in the Treaty. The Annex shows the changes to the numbering of the articles in the Treaties.

* **Charter of Fundamental Rights** 269

  This is the text of the Charter as signed on 12 December 2007 in Strasbourg by the Presidents of the Council, the European Parliament and the Commission. The bold text shows the changes made to the text by the draft Constitution and the Treaty of Lisbon to the text of 7 December 2000. The Charter becomes part of the primary law of the European Union from the date that the Treaty of Lisbon enters into force.

* **Explanations relating to the Charter of Fundamental Rights** 277

  The explanations are not part of the Charter and are not legally binding, but they are intended to enable better understanding and interpretation of the provisions of the Charter. They have also been updated to show the changes made to the text by the draft Constitution and the Treaty of Lisbon to the text of 7 December 2000.

* **Berlin Declaration of 25 March 2007** 291

  The Berlin Declaration marked the 50th anniversary of the signing of the Treaties of Rome and started the process leading to the agreement of the Treaty of Lisbon.

* **Speeches:**
  - **The European Union after the Lisbon Treaty – José Barroso, 4 December 2007** 293
  - **Debate on the informal Council in Lisbon - José Barroso, 23 October 2007** 297
  - **Report on the Lisbon informal Summit - José Sócrates, 23 October 2007** 299

  These three speeches, by the Presidents of the Commission and the Council review the Treaty of Lisbon and their views on the future of the Union.

* **European Parliament Decision on the Charter of Fundamental Rights** 303

  This decision of the European Parliament gives its opinion on the Charter and the mandate to the President of the European Parliament to sign the Charter.

* **European Parliament Resolution on the convening of the IGC** 305

* **Commission Opinion: 'Reforming Europe for the 21st Century'** 309

  These papers by the European Parliament and the Commission give their opinions on the future of the European Union and the issues that should be included in the Treaty of Lisbon.

* **Council Decision on cross-border co-operation (the Prüm Treaty)** 315

The Prüm Treaty concerns cross-border police co-operation and has great relevance to provisions in Justice and Home Affairs; the Council Decision is intended to bring this treaty into Union law.

* **The Laeken Declaration on the future of the European Union, 15 December 2001** 327

The Laeken Declaration lays out the purpose and aspirations for a new European Treaty and is the starting point for the discussions that led tot eh draft Constitution and the Treaty of Lisbon.

* **Tables of Equivalences - Tables from the Constitution to the Treaty on European Union and the Treaty on the Functioning of the European Union** 333

These tables have been prepared by the BMDF to enable the reader to trace articles from the draft Constitution to the two European Treaties as amended by the Treaty of Lisbon. The new numbering system is used that has been introduced by the Treaty of Lisbon, and in the annex to the Treaty.

TREATY OF LISBON AMENDING THE TREATY ON EUROPEAN UNION AND THE TREATY ESTABLISHING THE EUROPEAN COMMUNITY

HIS MAJESTY THE KING OF THE BELGIANS,

THE PRESIDENT OF THE REPUBLIC OF BULGARIA,

THE PRESIDENT OF THE CZECH REPUBLIC,

HER MAJESTY THE QUEEN OF DENMARK,

THE PRESIDENT OF THE FEDERAL REPUBLIC OF GERMANY,

THE PRESIDENT OF THE REPUBLIC OF ESTONIA,

THE PRESIDENT OF IRELAND,

THE PRESIDENT OF THE HELLENIC REPUBLIC,

HIS MAJESTY THE KING OF SPAIN,

THE PRESIDENT OF THE FRENCH REPUBLIC,

THE PRESIDENT OF THE ITALIAN REPUBLIC,

THE PRESIDENT OF THE REPUBLIC OF CYPRUS,

THE PRESIDENT OF THE REPUBLIC OF LATVIA,

THE PRESIDENT OF THE REPUBLIC OF LITHUANIA,

HIS ROYAL HIGHNESS THE GRAND DUKE OF LUXEMBOURG,

THE PRESIDENT OF THE REPUBLIC OF HUNGARY,

THE PRESIDENT OF MALTA,

HER MAJESTY THE QUEEN OF THE NETHERLANDS,

THE FEDERAL PRESIDENT OF THE REPUBLIC OF AUSTRIA,

THE PRESIDENT OF THE REPUBLIC OF POLAND,

THE PRESIDENT OF THE PORTUGUESE REPUBLIC,

THE PRESIDENT OF ROMANIA,

THE PRESIDENT OF THE REPUBLIC OF SLOVENIA,

THE PRESIDENT OF THE SLOVAK REPUBLIC,

THE PRESIDENT OF THE REPUBLIC OF FINLAND,

THE GOVERNMENT OF THE KINGDOM OF SWEDEN,

HER MAJESTY THE QUEEN OF THE UNITED KINGDOM OF GREAT BRITAIN AND NORTHERN IRELAND,

DESIRING to complete the process started by the Treaty of Amsterdam and by the Treaty of Nice with a view to enhancing the efficiency and democratic legitimacy of the Union and to improving the coherence of its action,

HAVE RESOLVED to amend the Treaty on European Union, the Treaty establishing the European Community and the Treaty establishing the European Atomic Energy Community,

and to this end have designated as their Plenipotentiaries:

HIS MAJESTY THE KING OF THE BELGIANS

Guy VERHOFSTADT
Prime Minister

Karel DE GUCHT
Minister for Foreign Affairs

THE PRESIDENT OF THE REPUBLIC OF BULGARIA

Sergei STANISHEV
Prime Minister

Ivailo KALFINE
Deputy Prime Minister and Minister for Foreign Affairs

THE PRESIDENT OF THE CZECH REPUBLIC

Mirek TOPOLÁNEK
Prime Minister

Karel SCHWARZENBERG
Minister for Foreign Affairs

HER MAJESTY THE QUEEN OF DENMARK

Anders Fogh RASMUSSEN
Prime Minister

Per Stig MØLLER
Minister for Foreign Affairs

THE PRESIDENT OF THE FEDERAL REPUBLIC OF GERMANY

Dr Angela MERKEL
Federal Chancellor

Dr Frank-Walter STEINMEIER
Deputy Federal Chancellor and Federal Minister for Foreign Affairs

THE PRESIDENT OF THE REPUBLIC OF ESTONIA

Andrus ANSIP
Prime Minister

Urmas PAET
Minister for Foreign Affairs

THE PRESIDENT OF IRELAND

Bertie AHERN
Taoiseach (Prime Minister)

Dermot AHERN
Minister for Foreign Affairs

THE PRESIDENT OF THE HELLENIC REPUBLIC

Konstantinos KARAMANLIS
Prime Minister

Dora BAKOYANNIS
Minister for Foreign Affairs

HIS MAJESTY THE KING OF SPAIN

José Luis RODRÍGUEZ ZAPATERO
President of the Government

Miguel Ángel MORATINOS CUYAUBÉ
Minister for Foreign Affairs and Co-operation

THE PRESIDENT OF THE FRENCH REPUBLIC

Nicolas SARKOZY
President

François FILLON
Prime Minister

Bernard KOUCHNER
Minister for Foreign and European Affairs

THE PRESIDENT OF THE ITALIAN REPUBLIC

Romano PRODI
President of the Council of Ministers

Massimo D'ALEMA
Vice-President of the Council of Ministers and Minister for Foreign Affairs

THE PRESIDENT OF THE REPUBLIC OF CYPRUS

Tassos PAPADOPOULOS
President

Erato KOZAKOU-MARCOULLIS
Minister for Foreign Affairs

THE PRESIDENT OF THE REPUBLIC OF LATVIA

Valdis ZATLERS
President

Aigars KALVĪTIS
Prime Minister

Māris RIEKSTIŅŠ
Minister for Foreign Affairs

THE PRESIDENT OF THE REPUBLIC OF LITHUANIA

Valdas ADAMKUS
President

Gediminas KIRKILAS
Prime Minister

Petras VAITIEKŪNAS
Minister for Foreign Affairs

HIS ROYAL HIGHNESS THE GRAND DUKE OF LUXEMBOURG

Jean-Claude JUNCKER
Prime Minister, Minister of State

Jean ASSELBORN
Minister for Foreign Affairs and Immigration

THE PRESIDENT OF THE REPUBLIC OF HUNGARY

Ferenc GYURCSÁNY
Prime Minister

Dr Kinga GÖNCZ
Minister for Foreign Affairs

THE PRESIDENT OF MALTA

The Hon. Lawrence GONZI
Prime Minister

The Hon. Michael FRENDO
Minister for Foreign Affairs

HER MAJESTY THE QUEEN OF THE NETHERLANDS

Dr J. P. BALKENENDE
Prime Minister

M. J. M. VERHAGEN
Minister for Foreign Affairs

THE FEDERAL PRESIDENT OF THE REPUBLIC OF AUSTRIA

Dr Alfred GUSENBAUER
Federal Chancellor

Dr Ursula PLASSNIK
Federal Minister for European and International Affairs

THE PRESIDENT OF THE REPUBLIC OF POLAND

Donald TUSK
Prime Minister

Radosław SIKORSKI
Minister for Foreign Affairs

THE PRESIDENT OF THE PORTUGUESE REPUBLIC

José SÓCRATES CARVALHO PINTO DE SOUSA
Prime Minister

Luis Filipe MARQUES AMADO
Minister of State; Minister for Foreign Affairs

THE PRESIDENT OF ROMANIA,

Traian BĂSESCU
President

Calin POPESCU TĂRICEANU
Prime Minister

Adrian CIOROIANU
Minister for Foreign Affairs

THE PRESIDENT OF THE REPUBLIC OF SLOVENIA

Janez JANŠA
President of the Government

Dr Dimitrij RUPEL
Minister for Foreign Affairs

THE PRESIDENT OF THE SLOVAK REPUBLIC

Robert FICO
Prime Minister

Ján KUBIŠ
Minister for Foreign Affairs

THE PRESIDENT OF THE REPUBLIC OF FINLAND

Matti VANHANEN
Prime Minister

Ilkka KANERVA
Minister for Foreign Affairs

THE GOVERNMENT OF THE KINGDOM OF SWEDEN

Fredrik REINFELDT
Prime Minister

Cecilia MALMSTRÖM
Minister for European Affairs

HER MAJESTY THE QUEEN OF THE UNITED KINGDOM OF GREAT BRITAIN AND NORTHERN IRELAND

The Rt Hon. Gordon BROWN
Prime Minister

The Rt Hon. David MILIBAND
Secretary of State for Foreign and Commonwealth Affairs

WHO, having exchanged their full powers, found in good and due form,

HAVE AGREED AS FOLLOWS:

AMENDMENTS TO THE TREATY ON EUROPEAN UNION AND TO THE TREATY ESTABLISHING THE EUROPEAN COMMUNITY

ARTICLE 1
The Treaty on European Union shall be amended in accordance with the provisions of this Article.

[BMDF Note: the paragraphs in this Article amend the text of the Treaty on European Union , they have been incorporated into the consolidated text of the Treaty on European Union and are not shown here]

ARTICLE 2
1. The Treaty establishing the European Community shall be amended in accordance with the provisions of this Article.

2. The title of the Treaty shall be replaced by "Treaty on the Functioning of the European Union".

[BMDF Note: the remaining paragraphs in this Article amend the text of the Treaty establishing the European Community, they have been incorporated into the consolidated text of the Treaty on the Functioning of the European Union and are not shown here]

FINAL PROVISIONS

ARTICLE 3
This Treaty is concluded for an unlimited period.

ARTICLE 4
1. Protocol No. 1 annexed to this Treaty contains the amendments to the Protocols annexed to the Treaty on European Union, to the Treaty establishing the European Community and/or to the Treaty establishing the European Atomic Energy Community.

2. Protocol No. 2 annexed to this Treaty contains the amendments to the Treaty establishing the European Atomic Energy Community.

ARTICLE 5
1. The articles, sections, chapters, titles and parts of the Treaty on European Union and of the Treaty establishing the European Community, as amended by this Treaty, shall be renumbered in accordance with the tables of equivalences set out in the Annex to this Treaty, and which form an integral part of this Treaty.

2. The cross-references to the articles, sections, chapters, titles and parts of the Treaty on European Union and of the Treaty on the Functioning of the European Union, as well as between them, shall be adapted pursuant to paragraph 1 and the references to paragraphs of the said articles as renumbered or re-ordered by the provisions of this Treaty shall be adapted in accordance with those provisions.

References to the articles, sections, chapters, titles and parts of the Treaty on European Union and of the Treaty establishing the European Community contained in the other treaties and acts of primary legislation on which the Union is founded shall be adapted pursuant to paragraph 1 of this Article.
References to recitals of the Treaty on European Union or to paragraphs or articles of the Treaty on European Union or of the Treaty establishing the European Community as renumbered or re-arranged by the provisions of this Treaty shall be adapted pursuant to this latter.
Such adaptations shall, where necessary, also apply in the event that the provision in question has been repealed.

3. The references to the recitals, articles, sections, chapters, titles and parts of the Treaty on European Union and of the Treaty establishing the European Community, as amended by this Treaty, contained in other instruments or acts shall be understood as referring to the recitals, articles, sections, chapters, titles and parts of those Treaties as renumbered pursuant to paragraph 1 and, respectively, to the paragraphs of the said articles, as renumbered or re-arranged by certain provisions of this Treaty.

ARTICLE 6

1. This Treaty shall be ratified by the High Contracting Parties in accordance with their respective constitutional requirements. The instruments of ratification shall be deposited with the Government of the Italian Republic.

2. This Treaty shall enter into force on 1 January 2009, provided that all the instruments of ratification have been deposited, or, failing that, on the first day of the month following the deposit of the instrument of ratification by the last signatory State to take this step.

ARTICLE 7

This Treaty, referred to as the Treaty of Lisbon, drawn up in a single original in the Bulgarian, Czech, Danish, Dutch, English, Estonian, Finnish, French, German, Greek, Hungarian, Irish, Italian, Latvian, Lithuanian, Maltese, Polish, Portuguese, Romanian, Slovak, Slovenian, Spanish and Swedish languages, the texts in each of these languages being equally authentic, shall be deposited in the archives of the Government of the Italian Republic, which will transmit a certified copy to each of the governments of the other signatory States.

IN WITNESS WHEREOF the undersigned Plenipotentiaries have signed this Treaty.

Done at Lisbon on the thirteenth day of December in the year two thousand and seven.

[BMDF Note: For each Member State, the names and the signatures of the Plenipotentiaries follow here; they have not been reproduced for the sake of space]

FINAL ACT

BMDF Note; The numbering system used in the Final Act follows that used in the text of the Treaty of Lisbon; the Tables of Equivalences in the Annex to the Treaty show the article numbering in the treaty and in the new numbering system to be used in the main Treaties.

THE CONFERENCE OF THE REPRESENTATIVES OF THE GOVERNMENTS OF THE MEMBER STATES, convened in Brussels on 23 July 2007 to adopt by common accord the amendments to be made to the Treaty on European Union, the Treaty establishing the European Community, and to the Treaty establishing the European Atomic Energy Community, has adopted the following texts:

I. The Treaty of Lisbon amending the Treaty on European Union and the Treaty establishing the European Community

II. Protocols

A. Protocols annexed to the Treaty on European Union, to the Treaty establishing the European Community, and/or the Treaty establishing the European Atomic Energy Community:

- Protocol on the role of national Parliaments in the European Union
- Protocol on the application of the principles of subsidiarity and proportionality
- Protocol on the Euro Group
- Protocol on permanent structured co-operation established by Article 28 A of the Treaty on European Union
- Protocol relating to Article 6(2) of the Treaty on European Union on the accession of the Union to the European Convention on the Protection of Human Rights and Fundamental Freedoms
- Protocol on the internal market and competition
- Protocol on the application of the Charter of Fundamental Rights of the European Union to Poland and to the United Kingdom
- Protocol on the exercise of shared competence
- Protocol on services of general interest
- Protocol on the Decision of the Council relating to the implementation of Article 9 C(4) of the Treaty on European Union and Article 205(2) of the Treaty on the Functioning of the European Union between 1 November 2014 and 31 March 2017 on the one hand, and as from 1 April 2017 on the other
- Protocol on transitional provisions

B. Protocols annexed to the Treaty of Lisbon

- Protocol No 1 amending the Protocols annexed to the Treaty on European Union, to the Treaty establishing the European Community and/or to the Treaty establishing the European Atomic Energy Community
- Tables of equivalences referred to in Article 2 of Protocol No 1 amending the protocols annexed to the Treaty on European Union, to the Treaty establishing the European Community and/or the Treaty establishing the European Atomic Energy Community
- Protocol No 2 amending the Treaty establishing the European Atomic Energy Community

II. Annexe to the Treaty of Lisbon:

- Tables of equivalences referred to in Article 5 of the Treaty of Lisbon

The Conference has adopted the following declarations annexed to this Final Act.

A. Declarations concerning provisions of the Treaties

1. Declaration concerning the Charter of Fundamental Rights of the European Union
2. Declaration on Article 6(2) of the Treaty on European Union
3. Declaration on Article 7a of the Treaty on European Union
4. Declaration on the composition of the European Parliament
5. Declaration on the political agreement by the European Council concerning the draft Decision on the composition of the European Parliament
6. Declaration on Articles 9 B(5) and (6), Articles 9 D(6) and (7), and Article 9 E of the Treaty on European Union
7. Declaration on Article 9 C(4) of the Treaty on European Union and Article 205(2) of the Treaty on the Functioning of the European Union
8. Declaration on practical measures to be taken upon the entry into force of the Treaty of Lisbon as regards the Presidency of the European Council and of the Foreign Affairs Council
9. Declaration on Article 9 C(9) of the Treaty on European Union concerning the European Council decision on the exercise of the Presidency of the Council
10. Declaration on Article 9 D of the Treaty on European Union
11. Declaration on Article 9 D(6) and (7) of the Treaty on European Union
12. Declaration on Article 9 E of the Treaty on European Union
13. Declaration concerning the common foreign and security policy
14. Declaration concerning the common foreign and security policy
15. Declaration on Article 13a of the Treaty on European Union
16. Declaration on Article 53(2) of the Treaty on European Union
17. Declaration concerning primacy
18. Declaration in relation to the delimitation of competences
19. Declaration on Article 3 of the Treaty on the Functioning of the European Union
20. Declaration on Article 16 B of the Treaty on the Functioning of the European Union
21. Declaration on the protection of personal data in the fields of judicial co-operation in criminal matters and police co-operation
22. Declaration on Articles 42 and 63a of the Treaty on the Functioning of the European Union
23. Declaration on the second paragraph of Article 42 of the Treaty on the Functioning of the European Union
24. Declaration concerning the legal personality of the European Union
25. Declaration on Articles 61 H and 188 K of the Treaty on the Functioning of the European Union
26. Declaration on non-participation by a Member State in a measure based on Title IV of Part Three of the Treaty on the Functioning of the European Union
27. Declaration on Article 69 D(1), second subparagraph, of the Treaty on the Functioning of the European Union

28. Declaration on Article 78 of the Treaty on the Functioning of the European Union
29. Declaration on Article 87(2)(c) of the Treaty on the Functioning of the European Union
30. Declaration on Article 104 of the Treaty on the Functioning of the European Union
31. Declaration on Article 140 of the Treaty on the Functioning of the European Union
32. Declaration on Article 152(4)(c) of the Treaty on the Functioning of the European Union
33. Declaration on Article 158 of the Treaty on the Functioning of the European Union
34. Declaration on Article 163 of the Treaty on the Functioning of the European Union
35. Declaration on Article 176 A of the Treaty on the Functioning of the European Union
36. Declaration on Article 188 N of the Treaty on the Functioning of the European Union concerning the negotiation and conclusion of international agreements by Member States relating to the area of freedom, security and justice
37. Declaration on Article 188 R of the Treaty on the Functioning of the European Union
38. Declaration on Article 222 of the Treaty on the Functioning of the European Union regarding the number of Advocates-General in the Court of Justice
39. Declaration on Article 249 B of the Treaty on the Functioning of the European Union
40. Declaration on Article 280 D of the Treaty on the Functioning of the European Union
41. Declaration on Article 308 of the Treaty on the Functioning of the European Union
42. Declaration on Article 308 of the Treaty on the Functioning of the European Union
43. Declaration on Article 311a(6) of the Treaty on the Functioning of the European Union

B. Declarations concerning Protocols annexed to the Treaties

44. Declaration on Article 5 of the Protocol on the Schengen *acquis* integrated into the framework of the European Union
45. Declaration on Article 5(2) of the Protocol on the Schengen *acquis* integrated into the framework of the European Union
46. Declaration on Article 5(3) of the Protocol on the Schengen *acquis* integrated into the framework of the European Union
47. Declaration on Article 5(3), (4) and (5) of the Protocol on the Schengen *acquis* integrated into the framework of the European Union
48. Declaration concerning the Protocol on the position of Denmark
49. Declaration concerning Italy
50. Declaration concerning Article 10 of the Protocol on transitional provisions

Furthermore, the Conference has noted the declarations listed hereafter and annexed to this Final Act:

51. Declaration by the Kingdom of Belgium on national Parliaments
52. Declaration by the Kingdom of Belgium, the Republic of Bulgaria, the Federal Republic of Germany, the Hellenic Republic, the Kingdom of Spain, the Italian Republic, the Republic of Cyprus, the Republic of Lithuania, the Grand-Duchy of Luxembourg, the Republic of Hungary, the Republic of Malta, the Republic of Austria, the Portuguese Republic, Romania, the Republic of Slovenia, and the Slovak Republic on the symbols of the European Union
53. Declaration by the Czech Republic on the Charter of Fundamental Rights of the European Union
54. Declaration by the Federal Republic of Germany, Ireland, the Republic of Hungary, the Republic of Austria and the Kingdom of Sweden

55. Declaration by the Kingdom of Spain and the United Kingdom of Great Britain and Northern Ireland

56. Declaration by Ireland on Article 3 of the Protocol on the position of the United Kingdom and Ireland in respect of the area of freedom, security and justice

57. Declaration by the Italian Republic on the composition of the European Parliament

58. Declaration by the Republic of Latvia, the Republic of Hungary and the Republic of Malta on the spelling of the name of the single currency in the Treaties

59. Declaration by the Kingdom of the Netherlands on Article 270a of the Treaty on the Functioning of the European Union

60. Declaration by the Kingdom of the Netherlands on Article 311a of the Treaty on the Functioning of the European Union

61. Declaration by the Republic of Poland on the Charter of Fundamental Rights of the European Union

62. Declaration by the Republic of Poland concerning the Protocol on the application of the Charter of Fundamental Rights of the European Union in relation to Poland and the United Kingdom

63. Declaration by the United Kingdom of Great Britain and Northern Ireland on the definition of the term "nationals"

64. Declaration by the United Kingdom of Great Britain and Northern Ireland on the franchise for elections to the European Parliament

65. Declaration by the United Kingdom of Great Britain and Northern Ireland on Article 61 H of the Treaty on the Functioning of the European Union

Done at Lisbon on the thirteenth day of December in the year two thousand and seven

[*BMDF Note: For each Member State, the names and the signatures of the Plenipotentiaries follow here but have not been reproduced.*]

ANNEX

TABLES OF EQUIVALENCES REFERRED TO IN ARTICLE 5 OF THE TREATY OF LISBON

A. Treaty on European Union

Old numbering of the Treaty on European Union	Numbering in the Treaty of Lisbon	New numbering of the Treaty on European Union
TITLE I – COMMON PROVISIONS	TITLE I – COMMON PROVISIONS	TITLE I – COMMON PROVISIONS
Article 1	Article 1	Article 1
	Article 1a	Article 2
Article 2	Article 2	Article 3
Article 3 (repealed)[1]		
	Article 3a	Article 4
	Article 3b[2]	Article 5
Article 4 (repealed)[3]		
Article 5 (repealed)[4]		
Article 6	Article 6	Article 6
Article 7	Article 7	Article 7
	Article 7a	Article 8
TITLE II – PROVISIONS AMENDING THE TREATY ESTABLISHING THE EUROPEAN ECONOMIC COMMUNITY WITH A VIEW TO ESTABLISHING THE EUROPEAN COMMUNITY	TITLE II – PROVISIONS ON DEMOCRATIC PRINCIPLES	TITLE II – PROVISIONS ON DEMOCRATIC PRINCIPLES
Article 8 (repealed)[5]	Article 8	Article 9
	Article 8 A[6]	Article 10
	Article 8 B	Article 11
	Article 8 C	Article 12
TITLE III – PROVISIONS AMENDING THE TREATY ESTABLISHING THE EUROPEAN COAL AND STEEL COMMUNITY	TITLE III – PROVISIONS ON THE INSTITUTIONS	TITLE III – PROVISIONS ON THE INSTITUTIONS
Article 9 (repealed)[7]	Article 9	Article 13
	Article 9 A[8]	Article 14
	Article 9 B[9]	Article 15
	Article 9 C[10]	Article 16

Old numbering of the Treaty on European Union	Numbering in the Treaty of Lisbon	New numbering of the Treaty on European Union
	Article 9 D[11]	Article 17
	Article 9 E	Article 18
	Article 9 F[12]	Article 19
TITLE IV – PROVISIONS AMENDING THE TREATY ESTABLISHING THE EUROPEAN ATOMIC ENERGY COMMUNITY	TITLE IV – PROVISIONS ON ENHANCED CO-OPERATION	TITLE IV – PROVISIONS ON ENHANCED CO-OPERATION
Article 10 (repealed)[13] Articles 27 A to 27 E (replaced) Articles 40 to 40 B (replaced) Articles 43 to 45 (replaced)	Article 10[14]	Article 20
TITLE V – PROVISIONS ON A COMMON FOREIGN AND SECURITY POLICY	TITLE V – GENERAL PROVISIONS ON THE UNION'S EXTERNAL ACTION AND SPECIFIC PROVISIONS ON THE COMMON FOREIGN AND SECURITY POLICY	TITLE V – GENERAL PROVISIONS ON THE UNION'S EXTERNAL ACTION AND SPECIFIC PROVISIONS ON THE COMMON FOREIGN AND SECURITY POLICY
	Chapter 1 – General provisions on the Union's external action	Chapter 1 – General provisions on the Union's external action
	Article 10 A	Article 21
	Article 10 B	Article 22
	Chapter 2 – Specific provisions on the common foreign and security policy	Chapter 2 – Specific provisions on the common foreign and security policy
	Section 1 – Common provisions	Section 1 – Common provisions
	Article 10 C	Article 23
Article 11	Article 11	Article 24
Article 12	Article 12	Article 25
Article 13	Article 13	Article 26
	Article 13a	Article 27
Article 14	Article 14	Article 28
Article 15	Article 15	Article 29
Article 22 (moved)	Article 15a	Article 30
Article 23 (moved)	Article 15b	Article 31
Article 16	Article 16	Article 32
Article 17 (moved)	*Article 28 A*	*Article 42*
Article 18	Article 18	Article 33
Article 19	Article 19	Article 34
Article 20	Article 20	Article 35

Old numbering of the Treaty on European Union	Numbering in the Treaty of Lisbon	New numbering of the Treaty on European Union
Article 21	Article 21	Article 36
Article 22 (moved)	*Article 15a*	*Article 30*
Article 23 (moved)	*Article 15b*	*Article 31*
Article 24	Article 24	Article 37
Article 25	Article 25	Article 38
	Article 25a	Article 39
Article 47 (moved)	Article 25b	Article 40
Article 26 (repealed)		
Article 27 (repealed)		
Article 27 A (replaced)[15]	Article 10	Article 20
Article 27 B (replaced)[15]	Article 10	Article 20
Article 27 C (replaced)[15]	Article 10	Article 20
Article 27 D (replaced)[15]	Article 10	Article 20
Article 27 E (replaced)[15]	Article 10	Article 20
Article 28	Article 28	Article 41
	Section 2 – Provisions on the common security and defence policy	Section 2 – Provisions on the common security and defence policy
Article 17 (moved)	Article 28 A	Article 42
	Article 28 B	Article 43
	Article 28 C	Article 44
	Article 28 D	Article 45
	Article 28 E	Article 46
TITLE VI – PROVISIONS ON POLICE AND JUDICIAL CO-OPERATION IN CRIMINAL MATTERS (repealed)[16]		
Article 29 (replaced)[17]		
Article 30 (replaced)[18]		
Article 31 (replaced)[19]		
Article 32 (replaced)[20]		
Article 33 (replaced)[21]		
Article 34 (repealed)		
Article 35 (repealed)		
Article 36 (replaced)[22]		
Article 37 (repealed)		
Article 38 (repealed)		

Old numbering of the Treaty on European Union	Numbering in the Treaty of Lisbon	New numbering of the Treaty on European Union
Article 39 (repealed)		
Article 40 (replaced)[23]	*Article 10*	*Article 20*
Article 40 A (replaced)[23]	*Article 10*	*Article 20*
Article 40 B (replaced)[23]	*Article 10*	*Article 20*
Article 41 (repealed)		
Article 42 (repealed)		
TITLE VII – PROVISIONS ON ENHANCED CO-OPERATION (replaced)[24]	TITLE IV – PROVISION ON ENHANCED CO-OPERATION	TITLE IV – PROVISION ON ENHANCED CO-OPERATION
Article 43 (replaced)[24]	*Article 10*	*Article 20*
Article 43 A (replaced)[24]	*Article 10*	*Article 20*
Article 43 B (replaced)[24]	*Article 10*	*Article 20*
Article 44 (replaced)[24]	*Article 10*	*Article 20*
Article 44 A (replaced)[24]	*Article 10*	*Article 20*
Article 45 (replaced)[24]	*Article 10*	*Article 20*
TITLE VIII – FINAL PROVISIONS	TITLE VI – FINAL PROVISIONS	TITLE VI – FINAL PROVISIONS
Article 46 (repealed)		
	Article 46a	Article 47
Article 47 (moved)	*Article 25b*	*Article 40*
Article 48	Article 48	Article 48
Article 49	Article 49	Article 49
	Article 49 A	Article 50
	Article 49 B	Article 51
	Article 49 C	Article 52
Article 50 (repealed)		
Article 51	Article 51	Article 53
Article 52	Article 52	Article 54
Article 53	Article 53	Article 55

(1) Replaced, in substance, by Article 2 F (renumbered 7) of the Treaty on the Functioning of the European Union ('TFEU') and by Articles 9(1) and 10 A, paragraph 3, second subparagraph (renumbered 13 and 21) of the Treaty on European Union ('TEU').

(2) Replaces Article 5 of the Treaty establishing the European Community ('TEC').

(3) Replaced, in substance, by Article 9 B (renumbered 15).

(4) Replaced, in substance, by Article 9, paragraph 2 (renumbered 13).

(5) Article 8 TEU, which was in force until the entry into force of the Treaty of Lisbon (hereinafter 'current'), amended the TEC. Those amendments are incorporated into the latter Treaty and Article 8 is repealed. Its number is used to insert a new provision.

(6) Paragraph 4 replaces, in substance, the first subparagraph of Article 191 TEC.

(7) The current Article 9 TEU amended the Treaty establishing the European Coal and Steel Community. This latter expired on 23 July 2002. Article 9 is repealed and the number thereof is used to insert another provision.

(8) — Paragraphs 1 and 2 replace, in substance, Article 189 TEC;
— paragraphs 1 to 3 replace, in substance, paragraphs 1 to 3 of Article 190 TEC;
— paragraph 1 replaces, in substance, the first subparagraph of Article 192 TEC;
— paragraph 4 replaces, in substance, the first subparagraph of Article 197 TEC.

(9) Replaces, in substance, Article 4.

(10) — Paragraph 1 replaces, in substance, the first and second indents of Article 202 TEC;
— paragraphs 2 and 9 replace, in substance, Article 203 TEC;
— paragraphs 4 and 5 replace, in substance, paragraphs 2 and 4 of Article 205 TEC.

(11) — Paragraph 1 replaces, in substance, Article 211 TEC;
— paragraphs 3 and 7 replace, in substance, Article 214 TEC.
— paragraph 6 replaces, in substance, paragraphs 1, 3 and 4 of Article 217 TEC.

(12) — Replaces, in substance, Article 220 TEC.
— the second subparagraph of paragraph 2 replaces, in substance, the first subparagraph of Article 221 TEC.

(13) The current Article 10 TEU amended the Treaty establishing the European Atomic Energy Community. Those amendments are incorporated into the Treaty of Lisbon. Article 10 is repealed and the number thereof is used to insert another provision.

(14) Also replaces Articles 11 and 11a TEC.

(15) The current Articles 27 A to 27 E, on enhanced cooperation, are also replaced by Articles 280 A to 280 I TFEU (renumbered 326 to 334).

(16) The current provisions of Title VI of the TEU, on police and judicial cooperation in criminal matters, are replaced by the provisions of Chapters 1, 5 and 5 of Title IV of Part Three of the TFEU.

(17) Replaced by Article 61 TFEU (renumbered 67).

(18) Replaced by Articles 69 F and 69 G TFEU (renumbered 87 and 88).

(19) Replaced by Articles 69 A, 69 B and 69 D TFEU (renumbered 82, 83 and 85).

(20) Replaced by Article 69 H TFEU (renumbered 89).

(21) Replaced by Article 61 E TFEU (renumbered 72).

(22) Replaced by Article 61 D TFEU (renumbered 71).

(23) The current Articles 40 to 40 B, on enhanced cooperation, are also replaced by Articles 280 A to 280 I TFEU (renumbered 326 to 334).

(24) The current Articles 43 to 45 and Title VII of the TEU, on enhanced cooperation, are also replaced by Articles 280 A to 280 I TFEU (renumbered 326 to 334).

B. Treaty on the Functioning of the European Union

Old numbering of the Treaty establishing the European Community	Numbering in the Treaty of Lisbon	New numbering of the Treaty on the Functioning of the European Union
PART ONE – PRINCIPLES	PART ONE – PRINCIPLES	PART ONE – PRINCIPLES
Article 1 (repealed)		
	Article 1a	Article 1
Article 2 (repealed)[1]		
	Title I – Categories and areas of union competence	Title I – Categories and areas of union competence
	Article 2 A	Article 2
	Article 2 B	Article 3
	Article 2 C	Article 4
	Article 2 D	Article 5
	Article 2 E	Article 6
	Title II – Provisions having general application	Title II – Provisions having general application
	Article 2 F	Article 7
Article 3, paragraph 1 (repealed)[2]		
Article 3, paragraph 2	Article 3	Article 8
Article 4 (moved)	*Article 97b*	*Article 119*
Article 5 (replaced)[3]		
	Article 5a	Article 9
	Article 5b	Article 10
Article 6	Article 6	Article 11
Article 153, paragraph 2 (moved)	Article 6a	Article 12
	Article 6b[4]	Article 13
Article 7 (repealed)[5]		
Article 8 (repealed)[6]		
Article 9 (repealed)		
Article 10 (repealed)[7]		
Article 11 (replaced)[8]	Articles 280 A to 280 I	Articles 326 to 334
Article 11a (replaced)[8]	*Articles 280 A to 280 I*	*Articles 326 to 334*
Article 12 (repealed)	*Article 16 D*	*Article 18*
Article 13 (moved)	*Article 16 E*	*Article 19*
Article 14 (moved)	*Article 22a*	*Article 26*
Article 15 (moved)	*Article 22b*	*Article 27*

Old numbering of the Treaty establishing the European Community	Numbering in the Treaty of Lisbon	New numbering of the Treaty on the Functioning of the European Union
Article 16	Article 16	Article 14
Article 255 (moved)	Article 16 A	Article 15
Article 286 (moved)	Article 16 B	Article 16
	Article 16 C	Article 17
PART TWO – CITIZENSHIP OF THE UNION	PART TWO – NON-DISCRIMINATION AND CITIZENSHIP OF THE UNION	PART TWO – NON-DISCRIMINATION AND CITIZENSHIP OF THE UNION
Article 12 (moved)	Article 16 D	Article 18
Article 13 (moved)	Article 16 E	Article 19
Article 17	Article 17	Article 20
Article 18	Article 18	Article 21
Article 19	Article 19	Article 22
Article 20	Article 20	Article 23
Article 21	Article 21	Article 24
Article 22	Article 22	Article 25
PART THREE – COMMUNITY POLICIES	PART THREE – POLICIES AND INTERNAL ACTIONS OF THE UNION	PART THREE – POLICIES AND INTERNAL ACTIONS OF THE UNION
	Title I – The internal market	Title I – The internal market
Article 14 (moved)	Article 22a	Article 26
Article 15 (moved)	Article 22b	Article 27
Title I – Free movement of goods	Title Ia – Free movement of goods	Title II – Free movement of goods
Article 23	Article 23	Article 28
Article 24	Article 24	Article 29
Chapter 1 – The customs union	Chapter 1 – The customs union	Chapter 1 – The customs union
Article 25	Article 25	Article 30
Article 26	Article 26	Article 31
Article 27	Article 27	Article 32
Part Three, Title X, Customs co-operation (moved)	Chapter 1a – Customs co-operation	Chapter 2 – Customs co-operation
Article 135 (moved)	Article 27a	Article 33
Chapter 2 – Prohibition of quantitative restrictions between Member States	Chapter 2 – Prohibition of quantitative restrictions between Member States	Chapter 3 – Prohibition of quantitative restrictions between Member States
Article 28	Article 28	Article 34
Article 29	Article 29	Article 35
Article 30	Article 30	Article 36

Old numbering of the Treaty establishing the European Community	Numbering in the Treaty of Lisbon	New numbering of the Treaty on the Functioning of the European Union
Article 31	Article 31	Article 37
Title II – Agriculture	Title II – Agriculture and fisheries	Title III – Agriculture and fisheries
Article 32	Article 32	Article 38
Article 33	Article 33	Article 39
Article 34	Article 34	Article 40
Article 35	Article 35	Article 41
Article 36	Article 36	Article 42
Article 37	Article 37	Article 43
Article 38	Article 38	Article 44
Title III – Free movement of persons, services and capital	Title III – Free movement of persons, services and capital	Title IV – Free movement of persons, services and capital
Chapter 1 – Workers	Chapter 1 – Workers	Chapter 1 – Workers
Article 39	Article 39	Article 45
Article 40	Article 40	Article 46
Article 41	Article 41	Article 47
Article 42	Article 42	Article 48
Chapter 2 – Right of establishment	Chapter 2 – Right of establishment	Chapter 2 – Right of establishment
Article 43	Article 43	Article 49
Article 44	Article 44	Article 50
Article 45	Article 45	Article 51
Article 46	Article 46	Article 52
Article 47	Article 47	Article 53
Article 48	Article 48	Article 54
Article 294 (moved)	Article 48a	Article 55
Chapter 3 – Services	Chapter 3 – Services	Chapter 3 – Services
Article 49	Article 49	Article 56
Article 50	Article 50	Article 57
Article 51	Article 51	Article 58
Article 52	Article 52	Article 59
Article 53	Article 53	Article 60
Article 54	Article 54	Article 61
Article 55	Article 55	Article 62

Old numbering of the Treaty establishing the European Community	Numbering in the Treaty of Lisbon	New numbering of the Treaty on the Functioning of the European Union
Chapter 4 – Capital and payments	Chapter 4 – Capital and payments	Chapter 4 – Capital and payments
Article 56	Article 56	Article 63
Article 57	Article 57	Article 64
Article 58	Article 58	Article 65
Article 59	Article 59	Article 66
Article 60 (moved)	*Article 61 H*	*Article 75*
Title IV – Visas, asylum, immigration and other policies related to free movement of persons	Title IV – Area of freedom, security and justice	Title V – Area of freedom, security and justice
	Chapter 1 – General provisions	Chapter 1 – General provisions
Article 61	Article 61[9]	Article 67
	Article 61 A	Article 68
	Article 61 B	Article 69
	Article 61 C	Article 70
	Article 61 D[10]	Article 71
Article 64, paragraph 1 (replaced)	Article 61 E[11]	Article 72
	Article 61 F	Article 73
Article 66 (replaced)	Article 61 G	Article 74
Article 60 (moved)	Article 61 H	Article 75
	Article 61 I	Article 76
	Chapter 2 – Policies on border checks, asylum and immigration	Chapter 2 – Policies on border checks, asylum and immigration
Article 62	Article 62	Article 77
Article 63, points 1 and 2, and Article 64, paragraph 2[12]	Article 63	Article 78
Article 63, points 3 and 4	Article 63a	Article 79
	Article 63b	Article 80
Article 64, paragraph 1 (replaced)	*Article 61 E*	*Article 72*
	Chapter 3 – Judicial co-operation in civil matters	Chapter 3 – Judicial co-operation in civil matters
Article 65	Article 65	Article 81
Article 66 (replaced)	*Article 61 G*	*Article 74*
Article 67 (repealed)		
Article 68 (repealed)		

Old numbering of the Treaty establishing the European Community	Numbering in the Treaty of Lisbon	New numbering of the Treaty on the Functioning of the European Union
Article 69 (repealed)		
	Chapter 4 – Judicial co-operation in criminal matters	Chapter 4 – Judicial co-operation in criminal matters
	Article 69 A[13]	Article 82
	Article 69 B[13]	Article 83
	Article 69 C	Article 84
	Article 69 D[13]	Article 85
	Article 69 E	Article 86
	Chapter 5 - Police co-operation	Chapter 5 – Police co-operation
	Article 69 F[14]	Article 87
	Article 69 G[14]	Article 88
	Article 69 H[15]	Article 89
Title V – Transport	Title V – Transport	Title VI – Transport
Article 70	Article 70	Article 90
Article 71	Article 71	Article 91
Article 72	Article 72	Article 92
Article 73	Article 73	Article 93
Article 74	Article 74	Article 94
Article 75	Article 75	Article 95
Article 76	Article 76	Article 96
Article 77	Article 77	Article 97
Article 78	Article 78	Article 98
Article 79	Article 79	Article 99
Article 80	Article 80	Article 100
Title VI – Common rules on competition, taxation and approximation of laws	Title VI – Common rules on competition, taxation and approximation of laws	Title VII – Common rules on competition, taxation and approximation of laws
Chapter 1 – Rules on competition	Chapter 1 – Rules on competition	Chapter 1 – Rules on competition
Section 1 – Rules applying to undertakings	Section 1 – Rules applying to undertakings	Section 1 – Rules applying to undertakings
Article 81	Article 81	Article 101
Article 82	Article 82	Article 102
Article 83	Article 83	Article 103
Article 84	Article 84	Article 104
Article 85	Article 85	Article 105

Old numbering of the Treaty establishing the European Community	Numbering in the Treaty of Lisbon	New numbering of the Treaty on the Functioning of the European Union
Article 86	Article 86	Article 106
Section 2 – Aids granted by States	Section 2 – Aids granted by States	Section 2 – Aids granted by States
Article 87	Article 87	Article 107
Article 88	Article 88	Article 108
Article 89	Article 89	Article 109
Chapter 2 – Tax provisions	Chapter 2 – Tax provisions	Chapter 2 – Tax provisions
Article 90	Article 90	Article 110
Article 91	Article 91	Article 111
Article 92	Article 92	Article 112
Article 93	Article 93	Article 113
Chapter 3 – Approximation of laws	Chapter 3 – Approximation of laws	Chapter 3 – Approximation of laws
Article 95 (moved)	Article 94	Article 114
Article 94 (moved)	Article 95	Article 115
Article 96	Article 96	Article 116
Article 97	Article 97	Article 117
	Article 97a	Article 118
Title VII – Economic and monetary policy	Title VII – Economic and monetary policy	Title VIII – Economic and monetary policy
Article 4 (moved)	Article 97b	Article 119
Chapter 1 – Economic policy	Chapter 1 – Economic policy	Chapter 1 – Economic policy
Article 98	Article 98	Article 120
Article 99	Article 99	Article 121
Article 100	Article 100	Article 122
Article 101	Article 101	Article 123
Article 102	Article 102	Article 124
Article 103	Article 103	Article 125
Article 104	Article 104	Article 126
Chapter 2 – monetary policy	Chapter 2 – monetary policy	Chapter 2 – monetary policy
Article 105	Article 105	Article 127
Article 106	Article 106	Article 128
Article 107	Article 107	Article 129
Article 108	Article 108	Article 130
Article 109	Article 109	Article 131
Article 110	Article 110	Article 132

Old numbering of the Treaty establishing the European Community	Numbering in the Treaty of Lisbon	New numbering of the Treaty on the Functioning of the European Union
Article 111, paragraphs 1 to 3 and 5 (moved)	*Article 188 O*	*Article 219*
Article 111, paragraph 4 (moved)	*Article 115 C, paragraph 1*	*Article 138*
	Article 111a	Article 133
Chapter 3 – Institutional provisions	Chapter 3 – Institutional provisions	Chapter 3 – Institutional provisions
Article 112 (moved)	Article 245b	Article 283
Article 113 (moved)	Article 245c	Article 294
Article 114	Article 114	Article 134
Article 115	Article 115	Article 135
	Chapter 3a – Provisions specific to Member States whose currency is the euro	Chapter 4 – Provisions specific to Member States whose currency is the euro
	Article 115 A	Article 136
	Article 115 B	Article 137
Article 111, paragraph 4 (moved)	Article 115 C	Article 138
Chapter 4 – Transitional provisions	Chapter 4 – Transitional provisions	Chapter 5 – Transitional provisions
Article 116 (repealed)		
	Article 116a	Article 139
Article 117, paragraph 2, first five indents (moved)	*Article 118a, paragraph 2*	*Article 141, paragraph 2*
Article 117, paragraphs 1, 2, sixth indent, and 3 to 9 (repealed)		
Article 121, paragraph 1 (moved) Article 122, paragraph 2, second sentence (moved) Article 123, paragraph 5 (moved)	Article 117a, first paragraph[16] Article 117a, second paragraph[17] Article 117a, third paragraph[18]	Article 140
Article 118 (repealed)		
Article 123, paragraph 3 (moved) Article 117, paragraph 2, first five indents (moved)	Article 118a, paragraph 1[19] Article 118a, paragraph 2[20]	Article 141
Article 124, paragraph 1 (moved)	Article 118b	Article 142
Article 119	Article 119	Article 143
Article 120	Article 120	Article 144

Old numbering of the Treaty establishing the European Community	Numbering in the Treaty of Lisbon	New numbering of the Treaty on the Functioning of the European Union
Article 121, paragraph 1 (moved)	*Article 117a, paragraph 1*	*Article 140, paragraph 1*
Article 121, paragraphs 2 to 4 (repealed)		
Article 122, paragraphs 1, 2, first sentence, 3, 4, 5 and 6 (repealed)		
Article 122, paragraph 2, second sentence (moved)	*Article 117a, paragraph 2, first subparagraph*	*Article 140, paragraph 2, first subparagraph*
Article 123, paragraphs 1, 2 and 4 (repealed)		
Article 123, paragraph 3 (moved)	*Article 118a, paragraph 1*	*Article 141, paragraph 1*
Article 123, paragraph 5 (moved)	*Article 117a, paragraph 3*	*Article 140, paragraph 3*
Article 124, paragraph 1 (moved)	Article 118b	Article 142
Article 124, paragraph 2 (repealed)		
Title VIII – Employment	Title VIII – Employment	Title IX – Employment
Article 125	Article 125	Article 145
Article 126	Article 126	Article 146
Article 127	Article 127	Article 147
Article 128	Article 128	Article 148
Article 129	Article 129	Article 149
Article 130	Article 130	Article 150
Title IX – Common commercial policy (moved)	Part Five, Title II, common commercial policy	Part Five, Title II, common commercial policy
Article 131 (moved)	Article 188 B	Article 206
Article 132 (repealed)		
Article 133 (moved)	Article 188 C	Article 207
Article 134 (repealed)		
Title X – Customs co-operation (moved)	Part Three, Title II, Chapter 1a, Customs co-operation	Part Three, Title II, Chapter 2, Customs co-operation
Article 135 (moved)	Article 27a	Article 33

Old numbering of the Treaty establishing the European Community	Numbering in the Treaty of Lisbon	New numbering of the Treaty on the Functioning of the European Union
Title XI – Social policy, education, vocational training and youth	Title IX – Social policy	Title X – Social policy
Chapter 1 – social provisions (repealed)		
Article 136	Article 136	Article 151
	Article 136a	Article 152
Article 137	Article 137	Article 153
Article 138	Article 138	Article 154
Article 139	Article 139	Article 155
Article 140	Article 140	Article 156
Article 141	Article 141	Article 157
Article 142	Article 142	Article 158
Article 143	Article 143	Article 159
Article 144	Article 144	Article 160
Article 145	Article 145	Article 161
Chapter 2 – The European Social Fund	Title X – The European Social Fund	Title XI – The European Social Fund
Article 146	Article 146	Article 162
Article 147	Article 147	Article 163
Article 148	Article 148	Article 164
Chapter 3 – Education, vocational training and youth	Title XI – Education, vocational training, youth and sport	Title XII – Education, vocational training, youth and sport
Article 149	Article 149	Article 165
Article 150	Article 150	Article 166
Title XII – Culture	Title XII – Culture	Title XIII – Culture
Article 151	Article 151	Article 167
Title XIII – Public health	Title XIII – Public health	Title XIV – Public health
Article 152	Article 152	Article 168
Title XIV – Consumer protection	Title XIV – Consumer protection	Title XV – Consumer protection
Article 153, paragraphs 1, 3, 4 and 5	Article 153	Article 169
Article 153, paragraph 2 (moved)	*Article 6a*	*Article 12*
Title XV – Trans–European networks	Title XV – Trans–European networks	Title XVI – Trans–European networks
Article 154	Article 154	Article 170

Old numbering of the Treaty establishing the European Community	Numbering in the Treaty of Lisbon	New numbering of the Treaty on the Functioning of the European Union
Article 155	Article 155	Article 171
Article 156	Article 156	Article 172
Title XVI – Industry	Title XVI – Industry	Title XVII – Industry
Article 157	Article 157	Article 173
Title XVII – Economic and social cohesion	Title XVII – Economic, social and territorial cohesion	Title XVIII – Economic, social and territorial cohesion
Article 158	Article 158	Article 174
Article 159	Article 159	Article 175
Article 160	Article 160	Article 176
Article 161	Article 161	Article 177
Article 162	Article 162	Article 178
Title XVIII – Research and technological development	Title XVIII – Research and technological development and space	Title XIX – Research and technological development and space
Article 163	Article 163	Article 179
Article 164	Article 164	Article 180
Article 165	Article 165	Article 181
Article 166	Article 166	Article 182
Article 167	Article 167	Article 183
Article 168	Article 168	Article 184
Article 169	Article 169	Article 185
Article 170	Article 170	Article 186
Article 171	Article 171	Article 187
Article 172	Article 172	Article 188
	Article 172bis	Article 189
Article 173	Article 173	Article 190
Title XIX – Environment	Title XIX – Environment	Title XX – Environment
Article 174	Article 174	Article 191
Article 175	Article 175	Article 192
Article 176	Article 176	Article 193
	Title XX – Energy	Title XXI – Energy
	Article 176 A	Article 194
	Title XXI – Tourism	Title XXII – Tourism
	Article 176 B	Article 195
	Title XXII – Civil protection	Title XXIII – Civil protection
	Article 176 C	Article 196

Old numbering of the Treaty establishing the European Community	Numbering in the Treaty of Lisbon	New numbering of the Treaty on the Functioning of the European Union
	Title XXIII – Administrative co-operation	Title XXIV – Administrative co-operation
	Article 176 D	Article 197
Title XX – Development co-operation (moved)	*Part Five, Title III, Chapter 1, Development co-operation*	*Part Five, Title III, Chapter 1, Development co-operation*
Article 177 (moved)	Article 188 D	Article 208
Article 178 (repealed)[21]		
Article 179 (moved)	Article 188 E	Article 209
Article 180 (moved)	Article 188 F	Article 210
Article 181 (moved)	Article 188 G	Article 211
Title XXI – Economic, financial and technical co-operation with third countries (moved)	Part Five, Title III, Chapter 2, Economic, financial and technical co-operation with third countries	Part Five, Title III, Chapter 2, Economic, financial and technical co-operation with third countries
Article 181a (moved)	Article 188 H	Article 212
PART FOUR – ASSOCIATION OF THE OVERSEAS COUNTRIES AND TERRITORIES	PART FOUR – ASSOCIATION OF THE OVERSEAS COUNTRIES AND TERRITORIES	PART FOUR – ASSOCIATION OF THE OVERSEAS COUNTRIES AND TERRITORIES
Article 182	Article 182	Article 198
Article 183	Article 183	Article 199
Article 184	Article 184	Article 200
Article 185	Article 185	Article 201
Article 186	Article 186	Article 202
Article 187	Article 187	Article 203
Article 188	Article 188	Article 204
	PART FIVE – EXTERNAL ACTION BY THE UNION	PART FIVE – EXTERNAL ACTION BY THE UNION
	Title I – General provisions on the union's external action	Title I – General provisions on the union's external action
	Article 188 A	Article 205
Part Three, Title IX, Common commercial policy (moved)	Title II – Common commercial policy	Title II – Common commercial policy
Article 131 (moved)	Article 188 B	Article 206
Article 133 (moved)	Article 188 C	Article 207

Old numbering of the Treaty establishing the European Community	Numbering in the Treaty of Lisbon	New numbering of the Treaty on the Functioning of the European Union
	Title III – Co-operation with third countries and humanitarian aid	Title III – Co-operation with third countries and humanitarian aid
Part Three, Title XX, Development co-operation (moved)	Chapter 1 – development co-operation	Chapter 1 – development co-operation
Article 177 (moved)	Article 188 D[22]	Article 208
Article 179 (moved)	Article 188 E	Article 209
Article 180 (moved)	Article 188 F	Article 210
Article 181 (moved)	Article 188 G	Article 211
Part Three, Title XXI, Economic, financial and technical co-operation with third countries (moved)	Chapter 2 – Economic, financial and technical co-operation with third countries	Chapter 2 – Economic, financial and technical co-operation with third countries
Article 181a (moved)	Article 188 H	Article 212
	Article 188 I	Article 213
	Chapter 3 – Humanitarian aid	Chapter 3 – Humanitarian aid
	Article 188 J	Article 214
	Title IV – Restrictive measures	Title IV – Restrictive measures
Article 301 (replaced)	Article 188 K	Article 215
	Title V – International agreements	Title V – International agreements
	Article 188 L	Article 216
Article 310 (moved)	Article 188 M	Article 217
Article 300 (replaced)	Article 188 N	Article 218
Article 111, paragraphs 1 to 3 and 5 (moved)	Article 188 O	Article 219
	Title VI – The Union's relations with international organisations and third countries and the Union delegations	Title VI – The Union's relations with international organisations and third countries and the Union delegations
Articles 302 to 304 (replaced)	Article 188 P	Article 220
	Article 188 Q	Article 221
	Title VII – Solidarity clause	Title VII – Solidarity clause
	Article 188 R	Article 222

Old numbering of the Treaty establishing the European Community	Numbering in the Treaty of Lisbon	New numbering of the Treaty on the Functioning of the European Union
PART FIVE – INSTITUTIONS OF THE COMMUNITY	PART SIX – INSTITUTIONAL AND BUDGETARY PROVISIONS	PART SIX – INSTITUTIONAL AND BUDGETARY PROVISIONS
Title I – Institutional provisions	Title I – Institutional provisions	Title I – Institutional provisions
Chapter 1 – The institutions	Chapter 1 – The institutions	Chapter 1 – The institutions
Section 1 – The European Parliament	Section 1 – The European Parliament	Section 1 – The European Parliament
Article 189 (repealed)[23]		
Article 190, paragraphs 1 to 3 (repealed)[24]		
Article 190, paragraphs 4 and 5	Article 190	Article 223
Article 191, first paragraph (repealed)[25]		
Article 191, second paragraph	Article 191	Article 224
Article 192, first paragraph (repealed)[26]		
Article 192, second paragraph	Article 192	Article 225
Article 193	Article 193	Article 226
Article 194	Article 194	Article 227
Article 195	Article 195	Article 228
Article 196	Article 196	Article 229
Article 197, first paragraph (repealed)[27]		
Article 197, second, third and fourth paragraphs	Article 197	Article 230
Article 198	Article 198	Article 231
Article 199	Article 199	Article 232
Article 200	Article 200	Article 233
Article 201	Article 201	Article 234
	Section 1a – The European Council	Section 2 – The European Council
	Article 201a	Article 235
	Article 201b	Article 236
Section 2 – The Council	Section 2 – The Council	Section 3 – The Council
Article 202 (repealed)[28]		
Article 203 (repealed)[29]		
Article 204	Article 204	Article 237
Article 205, paragraphs 2 and 4 (repealed)[30]		
Article 205, paragraphs 1 and 3	Article 205	Article 238
Article 206	Article 206	Article 239

Old numbering of the Treaty establishing the European Community	Numbering in the Treaty of Lisbon	New numbering of the Treaty on the Functioning of the European Union
Article 207	Article 207	Article 240
Article 208	Article 208	Article 241
Article 209	Article 209	Article 242
Article 210	Article 210	Article 243
Section 3 – The Commission	Section 3 – The Commission	Section 4 – The Commission
Article 211 (repealed)[31]		
	Article 211a	Article 244
Article 212 (moved)	*Article 218, paragraph 2*	*Article 249, paragraph 2*
Article 213	Article 213	Article 245
Article 214 (repealed)[32]		
Article 215	Article 215	Article 246
Article 216	Article 216	Article 247
Article 217, paragraphs 1, 3 and 4 (repealed)[33]		
Article 217, paragraph 2	Article 217	Article 248
Article 218, paragraph 1 (repealed)[34]		
Article 218, paragraph 2	Article 218	Article 249
Article 219	Article 219	Article 250
Section 4 – The Court of Justice	Section 4 – The Court of Justice of the European Union	Section 5 – The Court of Justice of the European Union
Article 220 (repealed)[35]		
Article 221, first paragraph (repealed)[36]		
Article 221, second and third paragraphs	Article 221	Article 251
Article 222	Article 222	Article 252
Article 223	Article 223	Article 253
Article 224[37]	Article 224	Article 254
	Article 224a	Article 255
Article 225	Article 225	Article 256
Article 225a	Article 225a	Article 257
Article 226	Article 226	Article 258
Article 227	Article 227	Article 259
Article 228	Article 228	Article 260
Article 229	Article 229	Article 261
Article 229a	Article 229a	Article 262

Old numbering of the Treaty establishing the European Community	Numbering in the Treaty of Lisbon	New numbering of the Treaty on the Functioning of the European Union
Article 230	Article 230	Article 263
Article 231	Article 231	Article 264
Article 232	Article 232	Article 265
Article 233	Article 233	Article 266
Article 234	Article 234	Article 267
Article 235	Article 235	Article 268
	Article 235a	Article 269
Article 236	Article 236	Article 270
Article 237	Article 237	Article 271
Article 238	Article 238	Article 272
Article 239	Article 239	Article 273
Article 240	Article 240	Article 274
	Article 240a	Article 275
	Article 240b	Article 276
Article 241	Article 241	Article 277
Article 242	Article 242	Article 278
Article 243	Article 243	Article 279
Article 244	Article 244	Article 280
Article 245	Article 245	Article 281
	Section 4a – The European Central Bank	Section 6 – The European Central Bank
	Article 245a	Article 282
Article 112 (moved)	Article 245b	Article 283
Article 113 (moved)	Article 245c	Article 284
Section 5 – The Court of Auditors	Section 5 – The Court of Auditors	Section 7 – The Court of Auditors
Article 246	Article 246	Article 285
Article 247	Article 247	Article 286
Article 248	Article 248	Article 287
Chapter 2 – Provisions common to several institutions	Chapter 2 – Legal acts of the Union, adoption procedures and other provisions	Chapter 2 – Legal acts of the Union, adoption procedures and other provisions
	Section 1 – The legal acts of the Union	Section 1 – The legal acts of the Union
Article 249	Article 249	Article 288
	Article 249 A	Article 289

Old numbering of the Treaty establishing the European Community	Numbering in the Treaty of Lisbon	New numbering of the Treaty on the Functioning of the European Union
	Article 249 B[38]	Article 290
	Article 249 C[38]	Article 291
	Article 249 D	Article 292
	Section 2 – Procedures for the adoption of acts and other provisions	Section 2 – Procedures for the adoption of acts and other provisions
Article 250	Article 250	Article 293
Article 251	Article 251	Article 294
Article 252 (repealed)		
	Article 252a	Article 295
Article 253	Article 253	Article 296
Article 254	Article 254	Article 297
	Article 254a	Article 298
Article 255 (moved)	Article 16 A	Article 15
Article 256	Article 256	Article 299
	Chapter 3 – The Union's advisory bodies	Chapter 3 – The Union's advisory bodies
	Article 256a	Article 300
Chapter 3 – The Economic and Social Committee	Section 1 – The Economic and Social Committee	Section 1 – The Economic and Social Committee
Article 257 (repealed)[39]		
Article 258, first, second and fourth paragraphs[40]	Article 258	Article 301
Article 258, third paragraph (repealed)[40]		
Article 259	Article 259	Article 302
Article 260	Article 260	Article 303
Article 261 (repealed)		
Article 262	Article 262	Article 304
Chapter 4 – The Committee of the Regions	Section 2 – The Committee of the Regions	Section 2 – The Committee of the Regions
Article 263, first and fifth paragraphs (repealed)[41]		
Article 263, second to fourth paragraphs	Article 263	Article 305
Article 264	Article 264	Article 306
Article 265	Article 265	Article 307

Old numbering of the Treaty establishing the European Community	Numbering in the Treaty of Lisbon	New numbering of the Treaty on the Functioning of the European Union
Chapter 5 – The European Investment Bank	Chapter 4 – The European Investment Bank	Chapter 4 – The European Investment Bank
Article 266	Article 266	Article 308
Article 267	Article 267	Article 309
Title II – Financial provisions	Title II – Financial provisions	Title II – Financial provisions
Article 268	Article 268	Article 310
	Chapter 1 – The Union's own resources	Chapter 1 – The Union's own resources
Article 269	Article 269	Article 311
Article 270 (repealed)[42]		
	Chapter 2 – The multiannual financial framework	Chapter 2 – The multiannual financial framework
	Article 270a	Article 312
	Chapter 3 – The Union's annual budget	Chapter 3 – The Union's annual budget
Article 272, paragraph 1 (moved)	Article 270b	Article 313
Article 271 (moved)	*Article 273a*	*Article 316*
Article 272, paragraph 1 (moved)	*Article 270b*	*Article 313*
Article 272, paragraphs 2 to 10	Article 272	Article 314
Article 273	Article 273	Article 315
Article 271 (moved)	Article 273a	Article 316
	Chapter 4 – Implementation of the budget and discharge	Chapter 4 – Implementation of the budget and discharge
Article 274	Article 274	Article 317
Article 275	Article 275	Article 318
Article 276	Article 276	Article 319
	Chapter 5 – Common provisions	Chapter 5 – Common provisions
Article 277	Article 277	Article 320
Article 278	Article 278	Article 321
Article 279	Article 279	Article 322
	Article 279a	Article 323
	Article 279b	Article 324
	Chapter 6 – Combating fraud	Chapter 6 – Combating fraud
Article 280	Article 280	Article 325
	Title III – Enhanced co-operation	Title III – Enhanced co-operation
Articles 11 and 11 A (replaced)	Article 280 A[43]	Article 326

Old numbering of the Treaty establishing the European Community	Numbering in the Treaty of Lisbon	New numbering of the Treaty on the Functioning of the European Union
Articles 11 and 11 A (replaced)	Article 280 B[43]	Article 327
Articles 11 and 11 A (replaced)	Article 280 C[43]	Article 328
Articles 11 and 11 A (replaced)	Article 280 D[43]	Article 329
Articles 11 and 11 A (replaced)	Article 280 E[43]	Article 330
Articles 11 and 11 A (replaced)	Article 280 F[43]	Article 331
Articles 11 and 11 A (replaced)	Article 280 G[43]	Article 332
Articles 11 and 11 A (replaced)	Article 280 H[43]	Article 333
Articles 11 and 11 A (replaced)	Article 280 I[43]	Article 334
PART SIX – GENERAL AND FINAL PROVISIONS	PART SEVEN – GENERAL AND FINAL PROVISIONS	PART SEVEN – GENERAL AND FINAL PROVISIONS
Article 281 (repealed)[44]		
Article 282	Article 282	Article 335
Article 283	Article 283	Article 336
Article 284	Article 284	Article 337
Article 285	Article 285	Article 338
Article 286 (replaced)	*Article 16 B*	*Article 16*
Article 287	Article 287	Article 339
Article 288	Article 288	Article 340
Article 289	Article 289	Article 341
Article 290	Article 290	Article 342
Article 291	Article 291	Article 343
Article 292	Article 292	Article 344
Article 293 (repealed)		
Article 294 (moved)	*Article 48a*	*Article 55*
Article 295	Article 295	Article 345
Article 296	Article 296	Article 346
Article 297	Article 297	Article 347
Article 298	Article 298	Article 348
Article 299, paragraph 1 (repealed)[45]		
Article 299, paragraph 2, second, third and fourth subparagraphs	Article 299	Article 349
Article 299, paragraph 2, first subparagraph, and paragraphs 3 to 6 (moved)	*Article 311a*	*Article 355*
Article 300 (replaced)	*Article 188 N*	*Article 218*
Article 301 (replaced)	*Article 188 K*	*Article 215*
Article 302 (replaced)	*Article 188 P*	*Article 220*
Article 303 (replaced)	*Article 188 P*	*Article 220*
Article 304 (replaced)	*Article 188 P*	*Article 220*

Old numbering of the Treaty establishing the European Community	Numbering in the Treaty of Lisbon	New numbering of the Treaty on the Functioning of the European Union
Article 305 (repealed)		
Article 306	Article 306	Article 350
Article 307	Article 307	Article 351
Article 308	Article 308	Article 352
	Article 308a	Article 353
Article 309	Article 309	Article 354
Article 310 (moved)	*Article 188 M*	*Article 217*
Article 311 (repealed)[46]		
Article 299, paragraph 2, first subparagraph, and paragraphs 3 to 6 (moved)	Article 311a	Article 355
Article 312	Article 312	Article 356
Final Provisions		
Article 313	Article 313	Article 357
	Article 313a	Article 358
Article 314 (repealed)[47]		

(1) Replaced, in substance, by Article 2 TEU (renumbered 3).

(2) Replaced, in substance, by Articles 2 B to 2 E TFEU (renumbered 3 to 6).

(3) Replaced, in substance, by Article 3b TEU (renumbered 5).

(4) Insertion of the operative part of the protocol on protection and welfare of animals.

(5) Replaced, in substance, by Article 9 TEU (renumbered 13).

(6) Replaced, in substance, by Article 9 TEU (renumbered 13) and Article 245a, paragraph 1, TFEU (renumbered 282).

(7) Replaced, in substance, by Article 3a, paragraph 3, TEU (renumbered 4).

(8) Also replaced by Article 10 TEU (renumbered 20).

(9) Also replaces the current Article 29 TEU.

(10) Also replaces the current Article 36 TEU.

(11) Also replaces the current Article 33 TEU.

(12) Points 1 and 2 of Article 63 EC are replaced by paragraphs 1 and 2 of Article 63 TFEU, and paragraph 2 of Article 64 is replaced by paragraph 3 of Article 63 TFEU.

(13) Replaces the current Article 31 TEU.

(14) Replaces the current Article 30 TEU.

(15) Replaces the current Article 32 TEU.

(16) Article 117a, paragraph 1, (renumbered 140) takes over the wording of paragraph 1 of Article 121.

(17) Article 117a, paragraph 2, (renumbered 140) takes over the second sentence of paragraph 2 of Article 122.

(18) Article 117a, paragraph 3, (renumbered 140) takes over paragraph 5 of Article 123.

(19) Article 118a, paragraph 1, (renumbered 140) takes over paragraph 3 of Article 123.

(20) Article 118a, paragraph 2, (renumbered 141) takes over the first five indents of paragraph 2 of Article 117.

(21) Replaced, in substance, by the second sentence of the second subparagraph of paragraph 1 of Article 188 D TFEU.

(22) The second sentence of the second subparagraph of paragraph 1 replaces, in substance, Article 178 TEC.

(23) Replaced, in substance, by Article 9 A, paragraphs 1 and 2, TEU (renumbered 14).

(24) Replaced, in substance, by Article 9 A, paragraphs 1 to 3, TEU (renumbered 14).

(25) Replaced, in substance, by Article 8 A, paragraph 4, TEU (renumbered 11).

(26) Replaced, in substance, by Article 9 A, paragraph 1, TEU (renumbered 14).

(27) Replaced, in substance, by Article 9 A, paragraph 4, TEU (renumbered 14).

(28) Replaced, in substance, by Article 9 C, paragraph 1, TEU (renumbered 16) and Articles 249 B and 249 C TFEU (renumbered 290 and 291).

(29) Replaced, in substance, by Article 9 C, paragraphs 2 and 9 TEU (renumbered 16).

(30) Replaced, in substance, by Article 9 C, paragraphs 4 and 5 TEU (renumbered 16).

(31) Replaced, in substance, by Article 9 D, paragraph 1 TEU (renumbered 17).

(32) Replaced, in substance, by Article 9 D, paragraphs 3 and 7 TEU (renumbered 17).

(33) Replaced, in substance, by Article 9 D, paragraph 6, TEU (renumbered 17).

(34) Replaced, in substance, by Article 252a TFEU (renumbered 295).

(35) Replaced, in substance, by Article 9 F TEU (renumbered 19).

(36) Replaced, in substance, by Article 9 F, paragraph 2, first subparagraph, of the TEU (renumbered 19).

(37) The first sentence of the first subparagraph is replaced, in substance, by Article 9 F, paragraph 2, second subparagraph of the TEU (renumbered 19).

(38) Replaces, in substance, the third indent of Article 202 TEC.

(39) Replaced, in substance, by Article 256a, paragraph 2 of the TFEU (renumbered 300).

(40) Replaced, in substance, by Article 256a, paragraph 4 of the TFEU (renumbered 300).

(41) Replaced, in substance, by Article 256a, paragraphs 3 and 4, TFEU (renumbered 300).

(42) Replaced, in substance, by Article 268, paragraph 4, TFEU (renumbered 310).

(43) Also replaces the current Articles 27 A to 27 E, 40 to 40 B, and 43 to 45 TEU.

(44) Replaced, in substance, by Article 49 C TEU (renumbered 52).

(45) Replaced, in substance by Article 49 C TEU (renumbered 52).

(46) Replaced, in substance by Article 49 B TEU (renumbered 51).

(47) Replaced, in substance by Article 53 TEU (renumbered 55).

PROCLAMATION OF THE CHARTER OF FUNDAMENTAL RIGHTS BY THE EUROPEAN PARLIAMENT, THE COUNCIL AND THE COMMISSION

OJ 2007/C 303/01

The European Parliament, the Council and the Commission solemnly proclaim the following text as the Charter of Fundamental Rights of the European Union:

THE CHARTER OF FUNDAMENTAL RIGHTS OF THE UNION

PREAMBLE

The peoples of Europe, in creating an ever closer union among them, are resolved to share a peaceful future based on common values.

Conscious of its spiritual and moral heritage, the Union is founded on the indivisible, universal values of human dignity, freedom, equality and solidarity; it is based on the principles of democracy and the rule of law. It places the individual at the heart of its activities, by establishing the citizenship of the Union and by creating an area of freedom, security and justice.

The Union contributes to the preservation and to the development of these common values while respecting the diversity of the cultures and traditions of the peoples of Europe as well as the national identities of the Member States and the organisation of their public authorities at national, regional and local levels; it seeks to promote balanced and sustainable development and ensures free movement of persons, services, **goods** and capital, and the freedom of establishment.

To this end, it is necessary to strengthen the protection of fundamental rights in the light of changes in society, social progress and scientific and technological developments by making those rights more visible in a Charter.

This Charter reaffirms, with due regard for the powers and tasks of the Union and the principle of subsidiarity, the rights as they result, in particular, from the constitutional traditions and international obligations common to the Member States, the European Convention for the Protection of Human Rights and Fundamental Freedoms, the Social Charters adopted by the Union and by the Council of Europe and the case law of the Court of Justice of the European Union and of the European Court of Human Rights. In this context the Charter will be interpreted by the courts of the Union and the Member States with due regard to the explanations prepared **under the authority** of the Praesidium of the Convention which drafted the Charter **and updated under the responsibility of the Praesidium of the European Convention.** †
Enjoyment of these rights entails responsibilities and duties with regard to other persons, to the human community and to future generations.

The Union therefore recognises the rights, freedoms and principles set out hereafter.

---

† *BMDF Note: In the Text of the Charter in the draft Constitution, amendments were made by the Legal Advisor, as follows*: "IGC Note: The Legal Adviser to the IGC suggests adding this phrase at the end of this sentence, for reasons of legal certainty and transparency, to point out that the explanations mentioned here have been updated on the responsibility of the Praesidium of the European Convention; if this were not done, the existing text would be inaccurate.

"Also, since the text explicitly states that the Charter will be interpreted by the courts of the Union and of the Member States *"with due regard to"* those explanations, it would be legally inconceivable that the text of the explanations should not be available to those courts and to the Union's citizens. The Legal Adviser therefore suggests that they be made universally accessible, by ensuring that they are published in the "C" series of the Official Journal of the European Union."

BMDF Note: The changes made in the draft Constitution have been retained in the Treaty of Lisbon.

TITLE I

DIGNITY

ARTICLE 1 *Human dignity*
Human dignity is inviolable. It must be respected and protected.

ARTICLE 2 *Right to life*
1. Everyone has the right to life.

2. No one shall be condemned to the death penalty, or executed.

ARTICLE 3 *Right to the integrity of the person*
1. Everyone has the right to respect for his or her physical and mental integrity.

2. In the fields of medicine and biology, the following must be respected in particular:
   (a) the free and informed consent of the person concerned, according to the procedures laid down by law;
   (b) the prohibition of eugenic practices, in particular those aiming at the selection of persons;
   (c) the prohibition on making the human body and its parts as such a source of financial gain;
   (d) the prohibition of the reproductive cloning of human beings.

ARTICLE 4 *Prohibition of torture and inhuman or degrading treatment or punishment*
No one shall be subjected to torture or to inhuman or degrading treatment or punishment.

ARTICLE 5 *Prohibition of slavery and forced labour*
1. No one shall be held in slavery or servitude.

2. No one shall be required to perform forced or compulsory labour.

3. Trafficking in human beings is prohibited.

TITLE II

FREEDOMS

ARTICLE 6 *Right to liberty and security*
Everyone has the right to liberty and security of person.

ARTICLE 7 *Respect for private and family life*
Everyone has the right to respect for his or her private and family life, home and communications.

ARTICLE 8 *Protection of personal data*
1. Everyone has the right to the protection of personal data concerning him or her.

2. Such data must be processed fairly for specified purposes and on the basis of the consent of the person concerned or some other legitimate basis laid down by law. Everyone has the right of access to data which has been collected concerning him or her, and the right to have it rectified.

3. Compliance with these rules shall be subject to control by an independent authority.

ARTICLE 9 *Right to marry and right to found a family*
The right to marry and the right to found a family shall be guaranteed in accordance with the national laws governing the exercise of these rights.

ARTICLE 10 *Freedom of thought, conscience and religion*
1. Everyone has the right to freedom of thought, conscience and religion. This right includes freedom to change religion or belief and freedom, either alone or in community with others and in public or in private, to manifest religion or belief, in worship, teaching, practice and observance.

2. The right to conscientious objection is recognised, in accordance with the national laws governing the exercise of this right.

ARTICLE 11 *Freedom of expression and information*

1. Everyone has the right to freedom of expression. This right shall include freedom to hold opinions and to receive and impart information and ideas without interference by public authority and regardless of frontiers.

2. The freedom and pluralism of the media shall be respected.

ARTICLE 12 *Freedom of assembly and of association*

1. Everyone has the right to freedom of peaceful assembly and to freedom of association at all levels, in particular in political, trade union and civic matters, which implies the right of everyone to form and to join trade unions for the protection of his or her interests.

2. Political parties at Union level contribute to expressing the political will of the citizens of the Union.

ARTICLE 13 *Freedom of the arts and sciences*

The arts and scientific research shall be free of constraint. Academic freedom shall be respected.

ARTICLE 14 *Right to education*

1. Everyone has the right to education and to have access to vocational and continuing training.

2. This right includes the possibility to receive free compulsory education.

3. The freedom to found educational establishments with due respect for democratic principles and the right of parents to ensure the education and teaching of their children in conformity with their religious, philosophical and pedagogical convictions shall be respected, in accordance with the national laws governing the exercise of such freedom and right.

ARTICLE 15 *Freedom to choose an occupation and right to engage in work*

1. Everyone has the right to engage in work and to pursue a freely chosen or accepted occupation.

2. Every citizen of the Union has the freedom to seek employment, to work, to exercise the right of establishment and to provide services in any Member State.

3. Nationals of third countries who are authorised to work in the territories of the Member States are entitled to working conditions equivalent to those of citizens of the Union.

ARTICLE 16 *Freedom to conduct a business*

The freedom to conduct a business in accordance with Union law and national laws and practices is recognised.

ARTICLE 17 *Right to property*

1. Everyone has the right to own, use, dispose of and bequeath his or her lawfully acquired possessions. No one may be deprived of his or her possessions, except in the public interest and in the cases and under the conditions provided for by law, subject to fair compensation being paid in good time for their loss. The use of property may be regulated by law insofar as is necessary for the general interest.

2. Intellectual property shall be protected.

ARTICLE 18 *Right to asylum*

The right to asylum shall be guaranteed with due respect for the rules of the Geneva Convention of 28 July 1951 and the Protocol of 31 January 1967 relating to the status of refugees and in accordance with the ***Treaty on European Union and the Treaty on the Functioning of the European Union (hereinafter referred to as "the Treaties").***

ARTICLE 19 *Protection in the event of removal, expulsion or extradition*

1. Collective expulsions are prohibited.

2. No one may be removed, expelled or extradited to a State where there is a serious risk that he or she would be subjected to the death penalty, torture or other inhuman or degrading treatment or punishment.

TITLE III

EQUALITY

ARTICLE 20 *Equality before the law*
Everyone is equal before the law.

ARTICLE 21 *Non-discrimination*
1. Any discrimination based on any ground such as sex, race, colour, ethnic or social origin, genetic features, language, religion or belief, political or any other opinion, membership of a national minority, property, birth, disability, age or sexual orientation shall be prohibited.

2. Within the scope of application of the ***Treaties*** and without prejudice to any of its specific provisions, any discrimination on grounds of nationality shall be prohibited.

ARTICLE 22 *Cultural, religious and linguistic diversity*
The Union shall respect cultural, religious and linguistic diversity.

ARTICLE 23 *Equality between women and men*
Equality between women and men must be ensured in all areas, including employment, work and pay.
The principle of equality shall not prevent the maintenance or adoption of measures providing for specific advantages in favour of the under-represented sex.

ARTICLE 24 *The rights of the child*
1. Children shall have the right to such protection and care as is necessary for their well-being. They may express their views freely. Such views shall be taken into consideration on matters which concern them in accordance with their age and maturity.

2. In all actions relating to children, whether taken by public authorities or private institutions, the child's best interests must be a primary consideration.

3. Every child shall have the right to maintain on a regular basis a personal relationship and direct contact with both his or her parents, unless that is contrary to his or her interests.

ARTICLE 25 *The rights of the elderly*
The Union recognises and respects the rights of the elderly to lead a life of dignity and independence and to participate in social and cultural life.

ARTICLE 26 *Integration of persons with disabilities*
The Union recognises and respects the right of persons with disabilities to benefit from measures designed to ensure their independence, social and occupational integration and participation in the life of the community.

TITLE IV

SOLIDARITY

ARTICLE 27 *Workers' right to information and consultation within the undertaking*
Workers or their representatives must, at the appropriate levels, be guaranteed information and consultation in good time in the cases and under the conditions provided for by Union law and national laws and practices.

ARTICLE 28 *Right of collective bargaining and action*
Workers and employers, or their respective organisations, have, in accordance with Union law and national laws and practices, the right to negotiate and conclude collective agreements at the appropriate levels and, in cases of conflicts of interest, to take collective action to defend their interests, including strike action.

ARTICLE 29 *Right of access to placement services*
Everyone has the right of access to a free placement service.

ARTICLE 30 *Protection in the event of unjustified dismissal*
Every worker has the right to protection against unjustified dismissal, in accordance with Union law and national laws and practices.

ARTICLE 31 *Fair and just working conditions*
1. Every worker has the right to working conditions which respect his or her health, safety and dignity.

2. Every worker has the right to limitation of maximum working hours, to daily and weekly rest periods and to an annual period of paid leave.

ARTICLE 32 *Prohibition of child labour and protection of young people at work*
The employment of children is prohibited. The minimum age of admission to employment may not be lower than the minimum school-leaving age, without prejudice to such rules as may be more favourable to young people and except for limited derogations.
Young people admitted to work must have working conditions appropriate to their age and be protected against economic exploitation and any work likely to harm their safety, health or physical, mental, moral or social development or to interfere with their education.

ARTICLE 33 *Family and professional life*
1. The family shall enjoy legal, economic and social protection.

2. To reconcile family and professional life, everyone shall have the right to protection from dismissal for a reason connected with maternity and the right to paid maternity leave and to parental leave following the birth or adoption of a child.

ARTICLE 34 *Social security and social assistance*
1. The Union recognises and respects the entitlement to social security benefits and social services providing protection in cases such as maternity, illness, industrial accidents, dependency or old age, and in the case of loss of employment, in accordance with the rules laid down by Union law and national laws and practices.

2. Everyone residing and moving legally within the European Union is entitled to social security benefits and social advantages in accordance with Union law and national laws and practices.

3. In order to combat social exclusion and poverty, the Union recognises and respects the right to social and housing assistance so as to ensure a decent existence for all those who lack sufficient resources, in accordance with the rules laid down by Union law and national laws and practices.

ARTICLE 35 *Health care*
Everyone has the right of access to preventive health care and the right to benefit from medical treatment under the conditions established by national laws and practices. A high level of human health protection shall be ensured in the definition and implementation of all ***the*** Union***'s*** policies and activities.

ARTICLE 36 *Access to services of general economic interest*
The Union recognises and respects access to services of general economic interest as provided for in national laws and practices, in accordance with the ***Treaties***, in order to promote the social and territorial cohesion of the Union.

ARTICLE 37 *Environmental protection*
A high level of environmental protection and the improvement of the quality of the environment must be integrated into the policies of the Union and ensured in accordance with the principle of sustainable development.

ARTICLE 38 *Consumer protection*
Union policies shall ensure a high level of consumer protection.

TITLE V

CITIZENS' RIGHTS

ARTICLE 39 *Right to vote and to stand as a candidate at elections to the European Parliament*
1. Every citizen of the Union has the right to vote and to stand as a candidate at elections to the European Parliament in the Member State in which he or she resides, under the same conditions as nationals of that State.

2. Members of the European Parliament shall be elected by direct universal suffrage in a free and secret ballot.

ARTICLE 40 *Right to vote and to stand as a candidate at municipal elections*
Every citizen of the Union has the right to vote and to stand as a candidate at municipal elections in the Member State in which he or she resides under the same conditions as nationals of that State.

ARTICLE 41 *Right to good administration*
1. Every person has the right to have his or her affairs handled impartially, fairly and within a reasonable time by the institutions, bodies, **offices** and agencies of the Union.

2. This right includes:
   (a) the right of every person to be heard, before any individual measure which would affect him or her adversely is taken;
   (b) the right of every person to have access to his or her file, while respecting the legitimate interests of confidentiality and of professional and business secrecy;
   (c) the obligation of the administration to give reasons for its decisions.

3. Every person has the right to have the Union make good any damage caused by its institutions or by its servants in the performance of their duties, in accordance with the general principles common to the laws of the Member States.

4. Every ***citizen*** may write to the Institutions of the Union in one of the languages of the ***Treaties*** and must have an answer in the same language.

ARTICLE 42 *Right of access to documents*
Any citizen of the Union, and any natural or legal person residing or having its registered office in a Member State, has a right of access to documents of the institutions, bodies, **offices** and agencies of the Union, whatever **their medium**.

ARTICLE 43 *European Ombudsman*
Any citizen of the Union and any natural or legal person residing or having its registered office in a Member State has the right to refer to the European Ombudsman cases of maladministration in the activities of the Institutions, bodies, **offices** or agencies of the Union, with the exception of the Court of Justice **of the European Union** acting in **its** judicial role.

ARTICLE 44 *Right to petition*
Any citizen of the Union and any natural or legal person residing or having its registered office in a Member State has the right to petition the European Parliament.

ARTICLE 45 *Freedom of movement and of residence*
1. Every citizen of the Union has the right to move and reside freely within the territory of the Member States.

2. Freedom of movement and residence may be granted, in accordance with the ***Treaties***, to nationals of third countries legally resident in the territory of a Member State.

ARTICLE 46 *Diplomatic and consular protection*
Every citizen of the Union shall, in the territory of a third country in which the Member State of which he or she is a national is not represented, be entitled to protection by the diplomatic or consular authorities of any Member State, on the same conditions as the nationals of that Member State.

TITLE VI

JUSTICE

ARTICLE 47 *Right to an effective remedy and to a fair trial*
Everyone whose rights and freedoms guaranteed by the law of the Union are violated has the right to an effective remedy before a tribunal in compliance with the conditions laid down in this Article.
Everyone is entitled to a fair and public hearing within a reasonable time by an independent and impartial tribunal previously established by law. Everyone shall have the possibility of being advised, defended and represented.
Legal aid shall be made available to those who lack sufficient resources insofar as such aid is necessary to ensure effective access to justice.

ARTICLE 48 *Presumption of innocence and right of defence*
1. Everyone who has been charged shall be presumed innocent until proved guilty according to law.

2. Respect for the rights of the defence of anyone who has been charged shall be guaranteed.

ARTICLE 49 *Principles of legality and proportionality of criminal offences and penalties*
1. No one shall be held guilty of any criminal offence on account of any act or omission which did not constitute a criminal offence under national law or international law at the time when it was committed. Nor shall a heavier penalty be imposed than that which was applicable at the time the criminal offence was committed. If, subsequent to the commission of a criminal offence, the law provides for a lighter penalty, that penalty shall be applicable.

2. This Article shall not prejudice the trial and punishment of any person for any act or omission which, at the time when it was committed, was criminal according to the general principles recognised by the community of nations.

3. The severity of penalties must not be disproportionate to the criminal offence.

ARTICLE 50 *Right not to be tried or punished twice in criminal proceedings for the same criminal offence*
No one shall be liable to be tried or punished again in criminal proceedings for an offence for which he or she has already been finally acquitted or convicted within the Union in accordance with the law.

TITLE VII

GENERAL PROVISIONS GOVERNING THE INTERPRETATION AND APPLICATION OF THE CHARTER

ARTICLE 51 *Field of application*
1. The provisions of this Charter are addressed to the institutions, bodies, **offices** and agencies of the Union with due regard for the principle of subsidiarity and to the Member States only when they are implementing Union law. They shall therefore respect the rights, observe the principles and promote the application thereof in accordance with their respective powers and respecting the limits of the powers of the Union as conferred on it in the ***Treaties***.

2. This Charter does not extend the field of application of Union law beyond the powers of the Union or establish any new power or task for the Union, or modify powers and tasks ***as*** defined in the ***Treaties***.

ARTICLE 52 *Scope and interpretation of rights and principles*
1. Any limitation on the exercise of the rights and freedoms recognised by this Charter must be provided for by law and respect the essence of those rights and freedoms. Subject to the principle of proportionality, limitations may be made only if they are necessary and genuinely meet objectives of general interest recognised by the Union or the need to protect the rights and freedoms of others.

2. Rights recognised by this Charter for which provision is made in ***the Treaties*** shall be exercised under the conditions and within the limits defined by ***those Treaties***.

3. Insofar as this Charter contains rights which correspond to rights guaranteed by the Convention for the Protection of Human Rights and Fundamental Freedoms, the meaning and scope of those rights shall be the same as those laid down by the said Convention. This provision shall not prevent Union law providing more extensive protection.

4. Insofar as this Charter recognises fundamental rights as they result from the constitutional traditions common to the Member States, those rights shall be interpreted in harmony with those traditions.

5. The provisions of this Charter which contain principles may be implemented by legislative and executive acts taken by institutions, bodies, **offices and agencies** of the Union, and by acts of Member States when they are implementing Union law, in the exercise of their respective powers. They shall be judicially cognisable only in the interpretation of such acts and in the ruling on their legality.

6. Full account shall be taken of national laws and practices as specified in this Charter.

7. The explanations drawn up as a way of providing guidance in the interpretation of the Charter of Fundamental Rights *shall* be given due regard by the courts of the Union and of the Member States.

ARTICLE 53 *Level of protection*
Nothing in this Charter shall be interpreted as restricting or adversely affecting human rights and fundamental freedoms as recognised, in their respective fields of application, by Union law and international law and by international agreements to which the Union or all the Member States are party, including the European Convention for the Protection of Human Rights and Fundamental Freedoms, and by the Member States' constitutions.

ARTICLE 54 *Prohibition of abuse of rights*
Nothing in this Charter shall be interpreted as implying any right to engage in any activity or to perform any act aimed at the destruction of any of the rights and freedoms recognised in this Charter or at their limitation to a greater extent than is provided for herein.

* * *

The above text adapts the wording of the Charter proclaimed on 7 December 2000, and will replace it as from the date of entry into force of the Treaty of Lisbon.

Done at Strasbourg on the twelfth day of December in the year two thousand and seven.

For the European Parliament,	***The President, Hans-Gert Pöttering***
For the Council of the European Union,	***The President, José Sócrates***
For the Commission of the European Communities,	***The President, José Manuel Barroso***

EXPLANATIONS RELATING TO THE CHARTER OF FUNDAMENTAL RIGHTS

OJ 2007/C 303/02

These explanations were originally prepared under the authority of the Praesidium of the Convention which drafted the Charter of Fundamental Rights of the European Union. They have been updated under the responsibility of the Praesidium of the European Convention, in the light of the drafting adjustments made to the text of the Charter by that Convention (notably to Articles 51 and 52) and of further developments of Union law. Although they do not as such have the status of law, they are a valuable tool of interpretation intended to clarify the provisions of the Charter.

TITLE I

DIGNITY

ARTICLE 1 *Human dignity - Explanation*

The dignity of the human person is not only a fundamental right in itself but constitutes the real basis of fundamental rights. The 1948 Universal Declaration of Human Rights enshrined human dignity in its preamble: "Whereas recognition of the inherent dignity and of the equal and inalienable rights of all members of the human family is the foundation of freedom, justice and peace in the world." In its judgment of 9 October 2001 in case C-377/98 *Netherlands v. European Parliament and Council*, 2001 ECR 7079, at grounds No 70 - 77, the Court of Justice confirmed that a fundamental right to human dignity is part of Union law.
It results that none of the rights laid down in this Charter may be used to harm the dignity of another person, and that the dignity of the human person is part of the substance of the rights laid down in this Charter. It must therefore be respected, even where a right is restricted.

ARTICLE 2 *Right to life - Explanation*

1. Paragraph 1 of this Article is based on the first sentence of Article 2(1) of the ECHR, which reads as follows:
"1. Everyone's right to life shall be protected by law..."

2. The second sentence of the provision, which referred to the death penalty, was superseded by the entry into force of Article 1 of Protocol No 6 to the ECHR, which reads as follows:
"The death penalty shall be abolished. No-one shall be condemned to such penalty or executed."
Article 2(2) of the Charter is based on that provision.

3. The provisions of Article 2 of the Charter correspond to those of the above Articles of the ECHR and its Protocol. They have the same meaning and the same scope, in accordance with Article 52(3) of the Charter. Therefore, the "negative" definitions appearing in the ECHR must be regarded as also forming part of the Charter:
   (a) Article 2(2) of the ECHR:
   "Deprivation of life shall not be regarded as inflicted in contravention of this article when it results from the use of force which is no more than absolutely necessary:
      (a) in defence of any person from unlawful violence;
      (b) in order to effect a lawful arrest or to prevent the escape of a person lawfully detained;
      (c) in action lawfully taken for the purpose of quelling a riot or insurrection."
   (b) Article 2 of Protocol No 6 to the ECHR:
   "A State may make provision in its law for the death penalty in respect of acts committed in time of war or of imminent threat of war; such penalty shall be applied only in the instances laid down in the law and in accordance with its provisions..."

ARTICLE 3 *Right to the integrity of the person - Explanation*

1. In its judgment of 9 October 2001 in case C-377/98 *Netherlands v. European Parliament and Council*, 2001 ECR 7079, at grounds No 70, 78 - 80, the Court of Justice confirmed that a fundamental right to human integrity is part of Union law and encompasses, in the context of medicine and biology, the free and informed consent of the donor and recipient.

2. The principles of Article 3 of the Charter are already included in the Convention on Human Rights and Biomedicine, adopted by the Council of Europe (ETS 164 and additional protocol ETS 168). The Charter does not set out to depart from those principles, and therefore prohibits only reproductive cloning. It neither authorises nor prohibits other forms of cloning. Thus it does not in any way prevent the legislature from prohibiting other forms of cloning.

3. The reference to eugenic practices, in particular those aiming at the selection of persons, relates to possible situations in which selection programmes are organised and implemented, involving campaigns for sterilisation, forced pregnancy, compulsory ethnic marriage among others, all acts deemed to be international crimes in the Statute of the International Criminal Court adopted in Rome on 17 July 1998 (see its Article 7(1)(g)).

ARTICLE 4 *Prohibition of torture and inhuman or degrading treatment or punishment - Explanation*

The right in Article 4 the right guaranteed by Article 3 of the ECHR, which has the same wording: "No one shall be subjected to torture or to inhuman or degrading treatment or punishment". By virtue of Article 52(3) of the Charter, it therefore has the same meaning and the same scope as the ECHR Article.

ARTICLE 5 *Prohibition of slavery and forced labour - Explanation*

1. The right in Article 5(1) and (2) corresponds to Article 4(1) and (2) of the ECHR, which has the same wording. It therefore has the same meaning and scope as the ECHR Article, by virtue of Article 52(3) of the Charter. Consequently:

- no limitation may legitimately affect the right provided for in paragraph 1;
- in paragraph 2, "forced or compulsory labour" must be understood in the light of the "negative" definitions contained in Article 4(3) of the ECHR:

"For the purpose of this article the term "forced or compulsory labour" shall not include:

(a) any work required to be done in the ordinary course of detention imposed according to the provisions of Article 5 of this Convention or during conditional release from such detention;

(b) any service of a military character or, in case of conscientious objectors in countries where they are recognised, service exacted instead of compulsory military service;

(c) any service exacted in case of an emergency or calamity threatening the life or well-being of the community;

(d) any work or service which forms part of normal civic obligations."

2. Paragraph 3 stems directly from human dignity and takes account of recent developments in organised crime, such as the organisation of lucrative illegal immigration or sexual exploitation networks. The annex to the Europol Convention contains the following definition which refers to trafficking for the purpose of sexual exploitation: "traffic in human beings: means subjection of a person to the real and illegal sway of other persons by using violence or menaces or by abuse of authority or intrigue with a view to the exploitation of prostitution, forms of sexual exploitation and assault of minors or trade in abandoned children". Chapter VI of the Convention implementing the Schengen Agreement, which has been integrated into the Union's *acquis*, in which the United Kingdom and Ireland participate, contains the following wording in Article 27(1) which refers to illegal immigration networks: " The Contracting Parties undertake to impose appropriate penalties on any person who, for financial gain, assists or tries to assist an alien to enter or reside within the territory of one of the Contracting Parties in breach of that Contracting Party's laws on the entry and residence of aliens." On 19 July 2002, the Council adopted a framework decision on combating trafficking in human beings (OJ L 203/1, 1.8.2002, p.1) whose Article 1 defines in detail the offences concerning trafficking in human beings for the purposes of labour exploitation or sexual exploitation, which the Member States must make punishable by virtue of that framework decision.

TITLE II

FREEDOMS

ARTICLE 6 *Right to liberty and security - Explanation*

The rights in Article 6 are the rights guaranteed by Article 5 of the ECHR, and in accordance with Article 52(3) of the Charter, they have the same meaning and scope. Consequently, the limitations which may legitimately be imposed on them may not exceed those permitted by the ECHR, in the wording of Article 5:

"1. Everyone has the right to liberty and security of person. No one shall be deprived of his liberty save in the following cases and in accordance with a procedure prescribed by law:

(a) the lawful detention of a person after conviction by a competent court;

(b) the lawful arrest or detention of a person for non-compliance with the lawful order of a court or in order to secure the fulfilment of any obligation prescribed by law;
(c) the lawful arrest or detention of a person effected for the purpose of bringing him before the competent legal authority on reasonable suspicion of having committed an offence or when it is reasonably considered necessary to prevent his committing an offence or fleeing after having done so;
(d) the detention of a minor by lawful order for the purpose of educational supervision or his lawful detention for the purpose of bringing him before the competent legal authority;
(e) the lawful detention of persons for the prevention of the spreading of infectious diseases, of persons of unsound mind, alcoholics or drug addicts or vagrants;
(f) the lawful arrest or detention of a person to prevent his effecting an unauthorised entry into the country or of a person against whom action is being taken with a view to deportation or extradition.

2. Everyone who is arrested shall be informed promptly, in a language which he understands, of the reasons for his arrest and of any charge against him.

3. Everyone arrested or detained in accordance with the provisions of paragraph 1.c of this article shall be brought promptly before a judge or other officer authorised by law to exercise judicial power and shall be entitled to trial within a reasonable time or to release pending trial. Release may be conditioned by guarantees to appear for trial.

4. Everyone who is deprived of his liberty by arrest or detention shall be entitled to take proceedings by which the lawfulness of his detention shall be decided speedily by a court and his release ordered if the detention is not lawful.

5. Everyone who has been the victim of arrest or detention in contravention of the provisions of this Article shall have an enforceable right to compensation."

The rights enshrined in Article 6 must be respected particularly when the European Parliament and the Council adopt laws and framework laws in the area of judicial co-operation in criminal matters, on the basis of Articles ***82, 83 and 85 of the Treaty on the Functioning of the European Union***, notably to define common minimum provisions as regards the categorisation of offences and punishments and certain aspects of procedural law.

ARTICLE 7 *Respect for private and family life - Explanation*

The rights guaranteed in Article 7 correspond to those guaranteed by Article 8 of the ECHR. To take account of developments in technology the word "correspondence" has been replaced by "communications".
In accordance with Article 52(3), the meaning and scope of this right are the same as those of the corresponding article of the ECHR. Consequently, the limitations which may legitimately be imposed on this right are the same as those allowed by Article 8 of the ECHR:

"1. Everyone has the right to respect for his private and family life, his home and his correspondence.
2. There shall be no interference by a public authority with the exercise of this right except such as is in accordance with the law and is necessary in a democratic society in the interests of national security, public safety or the economic well-being of the country, for the prevention of disorder or crime, for the protection of health or morals, or for the protection of the rights and freedoms of others."

ARTICLE 8 *Protection of personal data - Explanation*

This Article has been based on Article 286 of the Treaty establishing the European Community and Directive 95/46/EC of the European Parliament and of the Council on the protection of individuals with regard to the processing of personal data and on the free movement of such data (OJ L 281, 23.11.1995, p.31) as well as on Article 8 of the ECHR and on the Council of Europe Convention of 28 January 1981 for the Protection of Individuals with regard to Automatic Processing of Personal Data, which has been ratified by all the Member States. Article 286 EC Treaty is now replaced by Article ***16 of the Treaty on the Functioning of the European Union and Article 39 of the Treaty on European Union***. Reference is also made to Regulation No 45/2001 of the European Parliament and of the Council on the protection of individuals with regard to the processing of personal data by the Community institutions and bodies and on the free movement of such data (OJ L 8, 12.1.2001, p.1). The above-mentioned Directive and Regulation contain conditions and limitations for the exercise of the right to the protection of personal data.

ARTICLE 9 *Right to marry and right to found a family - Explanation*

This Article is based on Article 12 of the ECHR, which reads as follows: "Men and women of marriageable age have the right to marry and to found a family according to the national laws governing the exercising of this right." The wording of the Article has been modernised to cover cases in which national legislation recognises arrangements other than marriage for founding a family. This Article neither prohibits nor imposes the granting of the status of marriage to unions between people of the same sex. This right is thus similar to that afforded by the ECHR, but its scope may be wider when national legislation so provides.

ARTICLE 10 *Freedom of thought, conscience and religion - Explanation*

The right guaranteed in paragraph 1 corresponds to the right guaranteed in Article 9 of the ECHR and, in accordance with Article 52(3) of the Charter, has the same meaning and scope. Limitations must therefore respect Article 9(2) of the Convention, which reads as follows: "Freedom to manifest one's religion or beliefs shall be subject only to such limitations as are prescribed by law and are necessary in a democratic society in the interests of public safety, for the protection of public order, health or morals, or for the protection of the rights and freedoms of others."
The right guaranteed in paragraph 2 corresponds to national constitutional traditions and to the development of national legislation on this issue.

ARTICLE 11 *Freedom of expression and information - Explanation*

1. Article 11 corresponds to Article 10 of the European Convention on Human Rights, which reads as follows:

"1. Everyone has the right to freedom of expression. This right shall include freedom to hold opinions and to receive and impart information and ideas without interference by public authority and regardless of frontiers. This Article shall not prevent States from requiring the licensing of broadcasting, television or cinema enterprises.

2. The exercise of these freedoms, since it carries with it duties and responsibilities, may be subject to such formalities, conditions, restrictions or penalties as are prescribed by law and are necessary in a democratic society, in the interests of national security, territorial integrity or public safety, for the prevention of disorder or crime, for the protection of health or morals, for the protection of the reputation or rights of others, for preventing the disclosure of information received in confidence, or for maintaining the authority and impartiality of the judiciary."

Pursuant to Article 52(3) of the Charter, the meaning and scope of this right are the same as those guaranteed by the ECHR. The limitations which may be imposed on it may therefore not exceed those provided for in Article 10(2) of the Convention, without prejudice to any restrictions which competition law of the Union may impose on Member States' right to introduce the licensing arrangements referred to in the third sentence of Article 10(1) of the ECHR.

2. Paragraph 2 of this Article spells out the consequences of paragraph 1 regarding freedom of the media. It is based in particular on Court of Justice case-law regarding television, particularly in case C-288/89 (judgment of 25 July 1991, *Stichting Collectieve Antennevoorziening Gouda and others* [1991] ECR I-4007), and on the Protocol on the system of public broadcasting in the Member States annexed to the EC Treaty and now to the ***Treaties***, and on Council Directive 89/552/EC (particularly its seventeenth recital).

ARTICLE 12 *Freedom of assembly and of association - Explanation*

Paragraph 1 of this Article corresponds to Article 11 of the ECHR, which reads as follows:

"1. Everyone has the right to freedom of peaceful assembly and to freedom of association with others, including the right to form and to join trade unions for the protection of his interests.

2. No restrictions shall be placed on the exercise of these rights other than such as are prescribed by law and are necessary in a democratic society in the interests of national security or public safety, for the prevention of disorder or crime, for the protection of health or morals or for the protection of the rights and freedoms of others. This article shall not prevent the imposition of lawful restrictions on the exercise of these rights by members of the armed forces, of the police or of the administration of the State."

The meaning of the provisions of paragraph 1 ***of this Article 12*** is the same as that of the ECHR, but their scope is wider since they apply at all levels including European level. In accordance with Article 52(3) of the Charter, limitations on that right may not exceed those considered legitimate by virtue of Article 11(2) of the ECHR.

2. This right is also based on Article 11 of the Community Charter of the Fundamental Social Rights of Workers.

3. Paragraph 2 of this Article corresponds to ***Article 10(4) of the Treaty on European Union***.

ARTICLE 13 *Freedom of the arts and sciences - Explanation*

This right is deduced primarily from the right to freedom of thought and expression. It is to be exercised having regard to Article 1 and may be subject to the limitations authorised by Article 10 of the ECHR.

ARTICLE 14 *Right to education - Explanation*

1. This Article is based on the common constitutional traditions of Member States and on Article 2 of the Protocol to the ECHR, which reads as follows:

"No person shall be denied the right to education. In the exercise of any functions which it assumes in relation to education and to teaching, the State shall respect the right of parents to ensure such education and teaching in conformity with their own religious and philosophical convictions."

It was considered useful to extend this article to access to vocational and continuing training (see point 15 of the Community Charter of the Fundamental Social Rights of Workers and Article 10 of the Social Charter) and to add the principle of free compulsory education. As it is worded, the latter principle merely implies that as regards compulsory education, each child has the possibility of attending an establishment which offers free education. It does not require all establishments which provide education or vocational and continuing training, in particular private ones, to be free of charge. Nor does it exclude certain specific forms of education having to be paid for, if the State takes measures to grant financial compensation. Insofar as the Charter applies to the Union, this means that in its training policies the Union must respect free compulsory education, but this does not, of course, create new powers. Regarding the right of parents, it must be interpreted in conjunction with the provisions of Article 24.

2. Freedom to found public or private educational establishments is guaranteed as one of the aspects of freedom to conduct a business but it is limited by respect for democratic principles and is exercised in accordance with the arrangements defined by national legislation.

ARTICLE 15 *Freedom to choose an occupation and right to engage in work - Explanation*

Freedom to choose an occupation, as enshrined in Article 15(1) 1, is recognised in Court of Justice case-law (see *inter alia* judgment of 14 May 1974, Case 4/73 *Nold* [1974] ECR 491, paragraphs 12 to 14 of the grounds; judgment of 13 December 1979, Case 44/79 *Hauer* [1979] ECR 3727; judgment of 8 October 1986, Case 234/85 *Keller* [1986] ECR 2897, paragraph 8 of the grounds).

This paragraph also draws upon Article 1(2) of the European Social Charter, which was signed on 18 October 1961 and has been ratified by all the Member States, and on point 4 of the Community Charter of the Fundamental Social Rights of Workers of 9 December 1989. The expression "working conditions" is to be understood in the sense of ***Article 156 of the Treaty on the Functioning of the European Union***.

Paragraph 2 deals with the three freedoms guaranteed by ***Articles 26, 45, 49 and 56 of the Treaty on the Functioning of the European Union***, namely freedom of movement for workers, freedom of establishment and freedom to provide services.

Paragraph 3 has been based on ***Article 153(1)(g) of the Treaty on the Functioning of the European Union***, and on Article 19(4) of the European Social Charter signed on 18 October 1961 and ratified by all the Member States. Article 52(2) of the Charter is therefore applicable. The question of recruitment of seamen having the nationality of third States for the crews of vessels flying the flag of a Member State of the Union is governed by Union law and national legislation and practice.

ARTICLE 16 *Freedom to conduct a business - Explanation*

This Article is based on Court of Justice case-law which has recognised freedom to exercise an economic or commercial activity (see judgments of 14 May 1974, Case 4/73 *Nold* [1974] ECR 491, paragraph 14 of the grounds, and of 27 September 1979, Case 230-78 *SpA Eridiana and others* [1979] ECR 2749, paragraphs 20 and 31 of the grounds) and freedom of contract (see *inter alia Sukkerfabriken Nykøbing* judgment, Case 151/78 [1979] ECR 1, paragraph 19 of the grounds, and judgment of 5 October 1999, C-240/97 *Spain v. Commission*, [1999] ECR I-6571, paragraph 99 of the grounds) and Article ***119(1) and (3) of the Treaty on the Functioning of the European Union***, which recognises free competition. Of course, this right is to be exercised with respect for Union law and national legislation. It may be subject to the limitations provided for in Article 52(1) of the Charter.

ARTICLE 17 *Right to property - Explanation*

This Article is based on Article 1 of the Protocol to the ECHR:

"Every natural or legal person is entitled to the peaceful enjoyment of his possessions. No one shall be deprived of his possessions except in the public interest and subject to the conditions provided for by law and by the general principles of international law.

The preceding provisions shall not, however, in any way impair the right of a State to enforce such laws as it deems necessary to control the use of property in accordance with the general interest or to secure the payment of taxes or other contributions or penalties."

This is a fundamental right common to all national constitutions. It has been recognised on numerous occasions by the case-law of the Court of Justice, initially in the *Hauer* judgment (13 December 1979, ECR [1979] 3727). The wording has been updated but, in accordance with Article 52(3), the meaning and scope of the right are the same as those of the right guaranteed by the ECHR and the limitations may not exceed those provided for there.

Protection of intellectual property, one aspect of the right of property, is explicitly mentioned in paragraph 2 because of its growing importance and Community secondary legislation. Intellectual property covers not only literary and artistic property but also *inter alia* patent and trademark rights and associated rights. The guarantees laid down in paragraph 1 shall apply as appropriate to intellectual property.

ARTICLE 18 *Right to asylum - Explanation*

The text of the Article has been based on TEC Article 63, now replaced by ***Article 78 of the Treaty on the Functioning of the European Union***, which requires the Union to respect the Geneva Convention on refugees. Reference should be made to the Protocols relating to the United Kingdom and Ireland annexed to the Treaty of Amsterdam and to Denmark to determine the extent to which those Member States implement Union law in this area and the extent to which this Article is applicable to them. This Article is in line with the Protocol on Asylum annexed to the ***Treaties***.

ARTICLE 19 *Protection in the event of removal, expulsion or extradition - Explanation*

Paragraph 1 of this Article has the same meaning and scope as Article 4 of Protocol No 4 to the ECHR concerning collective expulsion. Its purpose is to guarantee that every decision is based on a specific examination and that no single measure can be taken to expel all persons having the nationality of a particular State (see also Article 13 of the Covenant on Civil and Political Rights).

Paragraph 2 incorporates the relevant case-law from the European Court of Human Rights regarding Article 3 of the ECHR (see *Ahmed v. Austria*, judgment of 17 December 1996, [1996] ECR VI-2206 and *Soering*, judgment of 7 July 1989).

TITLE III

EQUALITY

ARTICLE 20 *Equality before the law - Explanation*

This Article corresponds to a general principle of law which is included in all European constitutions and has also been recognised by the Court of Justice as a basic principle of Community law (judgment of 13 November 1984, Case 283/83 *Racke* [1984] ECR 3791, judgment of 17 April 1997, Case 15/95 *EARL* [1997] ECR I–1961, and judgment of 13 April 2000, Case 292/97 *Karlsson* [2000] ECR 2737).

ARTICLE 21 *Non-discrimination - Explanation*

Paragraph 1 draws on Article 13 of the EC Treaty, now replaced by ***Article 19 of the Treaty on the Functioning of the European Union***, Article 14 of the ECHR and Article 11 of the Convention on Human Rights and Biomedicine as regards genetic heritage. Insofar as this corresponds to Article 14 of the ECHR, it applies in compliance with it.

There is no contradiction or incompatibility between paragraph 1 and ***Article 19 of the Treaty on the Functioning of the European Union*** which has a different scope and purpose: ***Article 19*** confers power on the Union to adopt legislative acts, including harmonisation of the Member States' laws and regulations, to combat certain forms of discrimination, listed exhaustively in that Article. Such legislation may cover action of Member State authorities (as well as relations between private individuals) in any area within the limits of the Union's powers. In contrast, the provision in ***Article 21(1)*** does not create any power to enact anti-discrimination laws in these areas of Member State or private action, nor does it lay down a sweeping ban of discrimination in such wide-ranging areas. Instead, it only addresses discriminations by the institutions and bodies of the Union themselves, when exercising powers conferred under ***the Treaties***, and by Member States only when they are implementing Union law. Paragraph 1 therefore does not alter the extent of powers granted under Article ***19*** nor the interpretation given to that Article.

Paragraph 2 corresponds to ***Article 18 of the Treaty on the Functioning of the European Union*** and must be applied in compliance with that Article.

ARTICLE 22 *Cultural, religious and linguistic diversity - Explanation*

This Article has been based on Article 6 of the Treaty on European Union and on Article 151(1) and (4) of the EC Treaty, now replaced by ***Article 167(1) and (4) of the Treaty on the Functioning of the European Union***, concerning culture. Respect for cultural and linguistic diversity is now also laid down in Article 3(3) of the ***Treaty on European Union***. The Article is also inspired by Declaration No 11 to the Final Act of the Amsterdam Treaty on the status of churches and non-confessional organisations, now taken over in ***Article 17 of the Treaty on the Functioning of the European Union***.

ARTICLE 23 *Equality between women and men - Explanation*

The first paragraph has been based on Articles 2 and 3(2) of the EC Treaty, now replaced by ***Article 3 of the Treaty on European Union and Article 8 of the Treaty on the Functioning of the European Union*** which impose the objective of promoting equality between men and women on the Union, and on ***Article 157(1) of the Treaty on the Functioning of the European Union***. It draws on Article 20 of the revised European Social Charter of 3 May 1996 and on point 16 of the Community Charter on the rights of workers.
It is also based on ***Article 157(3) of the Treaty on the Functioning of the European Union***, and Article 2(4) of Council Directive 76/207/EEC on the implementation of the principle of equal treatment for men and women as regards access to employment, vocational training and promotion, and working conditions.
The second paragraph takes over in shorter form ***Article 157(4) of the Treaty on the Functioning of the European Union*** which provides that the principle of equal treatment does not prevent the maintenance or adoption of measures providing for specific advantages in order to make it easier for the under-represented sex to pursue a vocational activity or to prevent or compensate for disadvantages in professional careers. In accordance with Article 52(2), the present paragraph does not amend ***Article 157(4)***.

ARTICLE 24 *The rights of the child - Explanation*

This Article is based on the New York Convention on the Rights of the Child signed on 20 November 1989 and ratified by all the Member States, particularly Articles 3, 9, 12 and 13 thereof.
Paragraph 3 takes account of the fact that, as part of the establishment of an area of freedom, security and justice, Union legislation on civil matters having cross-border implications, for which ***Article 81 of the Treaty on the Functioning of the European Union*** confers power, may include notably visiting rights ensuring that children can maintain on a regular basis a personal and direct contact with both his or her parents.

ARTICLE 25 *The rights of the elderly - Explanation*

This Article draws on Article 23 of the revised European Social Charter and Articles 24 and 25 of the Community Charter of the Fundamental Social Rights of Workers. Of course, participation in social and cultural life also covers participation in political life.

ARTICLE 26 *Integration of persons with disabilities - Explanation*

The principle set out in this Article is based on Article 15 of the European Social Charter and also draws on point 26 of the Community Charter of the Fundamental Social Rights of Workers.

TITLE IV

SOLIDARITY

ARTICLE 27 *Workers' right to information and consultation within the undertaking - Explanation*

This Article appears in the revised European Social Charter (Article 21) and in the Community Charter on the rights of workers (points 17 and 18). It applies under the conditions laid down by Union law and by national laws. The reference to appropriate levels refers to the levels laid down by Union law or by national laws and practices, which might include the European level when Union legislation so provides. There is a considerable Union *acquis* in this field: ***Articles 154 and 155 of the Treaty on the Functioning of the European Union***, and Directives 2002/14/EC (general framework for informing and consulting employees in the European Community), 98/59/EC (collective redundancies), 2001/23/EC (transfers of undertakings) and 94/45/EC (European works councils).

ARTICLE 28 *Right of collective bargaining and action - Explanation*

This Article is based on Article 6 of the European Social Charter and on the Community Charter of the Fundamental Social Rights of Workers (points 12 to 14). The right of collective action was recognised by the European Court of Human Rights as one of the elements of trade union rights laid down by Article 11 of the ECHR. As regards the appropriate levels at which collective negotiation might take place, see the explanation given for the above Article. The modalities and limits for the exercise of collective action, including strike action, come under national laws and practices, including the question of whether it may be carried out in parallel in several Member States.

ARTICLE 29 *Right of access to placement services - Explanation*

This Article is based on Article 1(3) of the European Social Charter and point 13 of the Community Charter of the Fundamental Social Rights of Workers.

ARTICLE 30 *Protection in the event of unjustified dismissal - Explanation*

This Article draws on Article 24 of the revised Social Charter. See also Directive 2001/23/EC on the safeguarding of employees' rights in the event of transfers of undertakings, and Directive 80/987/EEC on the protection of employees in the event of the insolvency of their employer, as amended by Directive 2002/74/EC.

ARTICLE 31 *Fair and just working conditions - Explanation*

1. Paragraph 1 of this Article is based on Directive 89/391/EEC on the introduction of measures to encourage improvements in the safety and health of workers at work. It also draws on Article 3 of the Social Charter and point 19 of the Community Charter on the rights of workers, and, as regards dignity at work, on Article 26 of the revised Social Charter. The expression "working conditions" must be understood in the sense of ***Article 156 of the Treaty on the Functioning of the European Union***.

2. Paragraph 2 is based on Directive 93/104/EC concerning certain aspects of the organisation of working time, Article 2 of the European Social Charter and point 8 of the Community Charter on the rights of workers.

ARTICLE 32 *Prohibition of child labour and protection of young people at work - Explanation*

This Article is based on Directive 94/33/EC on the protection of young people at work, Article 7 of the European Social Charter and points 20 to 23 of the Community Charter of the Fundamental Social Rights of Workers.

ARTICLE 33 *Family and professional life - Explanation*

Article 33(1) is based on Article 16 of the European Social Charter. The second paragraph draws on Council Directive 92/85/EEC on the introduction of measures to encourage improvements in the safety and health at work of pregnant workers and workers who have recently given birth or are breastfeeding and Directive 96/34/EC on the framework agreement on parental leave concluded by UNICE, CEEP and the ETUC. It is also based on Article 8 (protection of maternity) of the European Social Charter and draws on Article 27 (right of workers with family responsibilities to equal opportunities and equal treatment) of the revised Social Charter. "Maternity" covers the period from conception to weaning.

ARTICLE 34 *Social security and social assistance - Explanation*

The principle set out in Article 34(1) is based on ***Articles 153 and 156 of the Treaty on the Functioning of the European Union*** and on Article 12 of the European Social Charter and point 10 of the Community Charter on the rights of workers. The Union must respect it when exercising the powers conferred on it by ***Articles 153 and 156 of the Treaty on the Functioning of the European Union***. The reference to social services relates to cases in which such services have been introduced to provide certain advantages but does not imply that such services must be created where they do not exist. "Maternity" must be understood in the same sense as in the preceding Article.

Paragraph 2 is based on Articles 12(4) and 13(4) of the European Social Charter and point 2 of the Community Charter of the Fundamental Social Rights of Workers and reflects the rules arising from Regulation No 1408/71 and Regulation No 1612/68.

Paragraph 3 draws on Article 13 of the European Social Charter and Articles 30 and 31 of the revised Social Charter and point 10 of the Community Charter. The Union must respect it in the context of policies based on ***Article 153 of the Treaty on the Functioning of the European Union***.

ARTICLE 35 *Health care - Explanation*

The principles set out in this Article are based on Article 152 of the EC Treaty, now replaced by ***Article 168 of the of the Treaty on the Functioning of the European Union***, and on Articles 11 and 13 of the European Social Charter. The second sentence of the Article takes over ***Article 168(1)***.

ARTICLE 36 *Access to services of general economic interest - Explanation*

This Article is fully in line with ***Article 14 of the Treaty on the Functioning of the European Union*** and does not create any new right. It merely sets out the principle of respect by the Union for the access to services of general economic interest as provided for by national provisions, when those provisions are compatible with Union law.

ARTICLE 37 *Environmental protection - Explanation*

The principles set out in this Article have been based on Articles 2, 6 and 174 of the EC Treaty, which have now been replaced by ***Article 3(3) of the Treaty on European Union and Articles 11 and 191 of the Treaty on the Functioning of the European Union***.
It also draws on the provisions of some national constitutions.

ARTICLE 38 *Consumer protection - Explanation*

The principles set out in this Article have been based on ***Article 169 of the Treaty on the Functioning of the European Union***.

TITLE V

CITIZENS' RIGHTS

ARTICLE 39 *Right to vote and to stand as a candidate at elections to the European Parliament - Explanation*

Article 39 applies under the conditions laid down in ***the Treaties***, in accordance with Article 52(2) of the Charter. Article 39(1) corresponds to the right guaranteed in ***Article 20(2) of the Treaty on the Functioning of the European Union*** (cf. also the legal base in ***Article 22 of the Treaty on the Functioning of the European Union*** for the adoption of detailed arrangements for the exercise of that right) and Article 39(2) corresponds to ***Article 14(3) of the Treaty on European Union***. Article 39(2) takes over the basic principles of the electoral system in a democratic State.

ARTICLE 40 *Right to vote and to stand as a candidate at municipal elections - Explanation*

This Article corresponds to the right guaranteed by ***Article 20(2) of the Treaty on the Functioning of the European Union*** (cf. also the legal base in ***Article 20 of the Treaty on the Functioning of the European Union*** for the adoption of detailed arrangements for the exercise of that right). In accordance with Article 52(2) of the Charter, it applies under the conditions set out in these Articles ***in the Treaties***.

ARTICLE 41 *Right to good administration - Explanation*

Article 41 is based on the existence of the Union as subject to the rule of law whose characteristics were developed in the case-law which enshrined *inter alia* good administration as a general principle of law (see *inter alia* Court of Justice judgment of 31 March 1992 in Case C-255/90 P, *Burban* [1992] ECR I-2253, and Court of First Instance judgments of 18 September 1995 in Case T-167/94 *Nölle* [1995] ECR II-2589, and 9 July 1999 in Case T-231/97 *New Europe Consulting and others* [1999] ECR II-2403). The wording for that right in the first two paragraphs results from the case-law (Court of Justice judgment of 15 October 1987 in Case 222/86 *Heylens* [1987] ECR 4097, paragraph 15 of the grounds, judgment of 18 October 1989 in Case 374/87 *Orkem* [1989] ECR 3283, judgment of 21 November 1991 in Case C-269/90 *TU München* [1991] ECR I-5469, and Court of First Instance judgments of 6 December 1994 in Case T-450/93 *Lisrestal* [1994] ECR II-1177, 18 September 1995 in Case T-167/94 *Nölle* [1995] ECR II-2589) and the wording regarding the obligation to give reasons comes from ***Article 296 of the Treaty on the Functioning of the European Union*** (cf. also the legal base in ***Article 298 of the Treaty on the Functioning of the European Union*** for the adoption of legislation in the interest of an open, efficient and independent European administration).
Paragraph 3 reproduces the right now guaranteed by ***Article 340 of the Treaty on the Functioning of the European Union***. Paragraph 4 reproduces the right now guaranteed by ***Articles 20(2)(d) and 25 of the Treaty***

on the Functioning of the European Union. In accordance with Article 52(2) of the Charter, those rights are to be applied under the conditions and within the limits defined by ***the Treaties***.
The right to an effective remedy, which is an important aspect of this question, is guaranteed in Article 47 of this Charter.

ARTICLE 42 *Right of access to documents - Explanation*

The right guaranteed in this Article has been taken over from Article 255 of the EC Treaty, on the basis of which Regulation 1049/2001 has subsequently been adopted. The European Convention has extended this right to documents of institutions, bodies and agencies generally, regardless of their form, see ***Article 15(3) of the Treaty on the Functioning of the European Union***. In accordance with Article 52(2) of the Charter, the right of access to documents is exercised under the conditions and within the limits for which provision is made in ***Article 15(3) of the Treaty on the Functioning of the European Union***.

ARTICLE 43 *European Ombudsman - Explanation*

The right guaranteed in this Article is the right guaranteed by ***Articles 20 and 228 of the Treaty on the Functioning of the European Union***. In accordance with Article 52(2) of the Charter, it applies under the conditions defined in these two Articles.

ARTICLE 44 *Right to petition - Explanation*

The right guaranteed in this Article is the right guaranteed by ***Articles 20 and 227 of the Treaty on the Functioning of the European Union***. In accordance with Article 52(2) of the Charter, it applies under the conditions defined in these two Articles.

ARTICLE 45 *Freedom of movement and of residence - Explanation*

The right guaranteed by paragraph 1 is the right guaranteed by ***Article 20(2)(a) of the Treaty on the Functioning of the European Union*** (cf. also the legal base in ***Article 21***; and the judgement of the Court of Justice of 17 September 2002, C-413/99 *Baumbast*, [2002] ECR I-7091). In accordance with Article 52(2) of the Charter, it applies under the conditions and within the limits defined ***by the Treaties***.
Paragraph 2 refers to the power granted to the Union by ***Articles 77, 78 and 79 of the Treaty on the Functioning of the European Union***. Consequently, the granting of this right depends on the institutions exercising that power.

ARTICLE 46 *Diplomatic and consular protection - Explanation*

The right guaranteed by this Article is the right guaranteed by ***Article 20 of the Treaty on the Functioning of the European Union*** (cf. also the legal base in ***Article 23***). In accordance with Article 52(2) of the Charter, it applies under the conditions defined in these ***two*** Articles.

TITLE VI

JUSTICE

ARTICLE 47 *Right to an effective remedy and to a fair trial- Explanation*

The first paragraph is based on Article 13 of the ECHR:

> "Everyone whose rights and freedoms as set forth in this Convention are violated shall have an effective remedy before a national authority notwithstanding that the violation has been committed by persons acting in an official capacity."

However, in Union law the protection is more extensive since it guarantees the right to an effective remedy before a court. The Court of Justice enshrined that right in its judgment of 15 May 1986 as a general principle of Union law (Case 222/84 *Johnston* [1986] ECR 1651; see also judgment of 15 October 1987, Case 222/86 *Heylens* [1987] ECR 4097 and judgment of 3 December 1992, Case C-97/91 *Borelli* [1992] ECR I-6313). According to the Court, that general principle of Union law also applies to the Member States when they are implementing Union law. The inclusion of this precedent in the Charter has not been intended to change the system of judicial review laid down by ***the Treaties***, and particularly the rules relating to admissibility for direct actions before the Court of Justice of the European Union. The European Convention has considered the Union's system of judicial review including the rules on admissibility, and confirmed them while amending them as to certain aspects, as reflected in ***Articles 251 to 281 of the Treaty on the Functioning of the European Union***, and in particular in ***Article 263***. Article 47 applies to the institutions of the Union and of Member States when they are implementing Union law.
The second paragraph corresponds to Article 6(1) of the ECHR which reads as follows:

"In the determination of his civil rights and obligations or of any criminal charge against him, everyone is entitled to a fair and public hearing within a reasonable time by an independent and impartial tribunal established by law. Judgment shall be pronounced publicly but the press and public may be excluded from all or part of the trial in the interests of morals, public order or national security in a democratic society, where the interests of juveniles or the protection of the private life of the parties so require, or to the extent strictly necessary in the opinion of the court in special circumstances where publicity would prejudice the interests of justice."

In Union law, the right to a fair hearing is not confined to disputes relating to civil law rights and obligations. That is one of the consequences of the fact that the Union is a community based on the rule of law as stated by the Court in Case 294/83, *"Les Verts" v. European Parliament* (judgment of 23 April 1986, [1988] ECR 1339). Nevertheless, in all respects other than their scope, the guarantees afforded by the ECHR apply in a similar way to the Union.

With regard to the third paragraph, it should be noted that in accordance with the case-law of the European Court of Human Rights, provision should be made for legal aid where the absence of such aid would make it impossible to ensure an effective remedy (ECHR Judgment of 9.10.1979, Airey, Series A, Volume 32, 11). There is also a system of legal assistance for cases before the Court of Justice of the European Union.

ARTICLE 48 *Presumption of innocence and right of defence - Explanation*

Article 48 is the same as Article 6(2) and (3) of the ECHR, which reads as follows:

"2. Everyone charged with a criminal offence shall be presumed innocent until proved guilty according to law.

3. Everyone charged with a criminal offence has the following minimum rights:
   (a) to be informed promptly, in a language which he understands and in detail, of the nature and cause of the accusation against him;
   (b) to have adequate time and facilities for the preparation of his defence;
   (c) to defend himself in person or through legal assistance of his own choosing or, if he has not sufficient means to pay for legal assistance, to be given it free when the interests of justice so require;
   (d) to examine or have examined witnesses against him and to obtain the attendance and examination of witnesses on his behalf under the same conditions as witnesses against him;
   (e) to have the free assistance of an interpreter if he cannot understand or speak the language used in court."

In accordance with Article 52(3), this right has the same meaning and scope as the right guaranteed by the ECHR.

ARTICLE 49 *Principles of legality and proportionality of criminal offences and penalties - Explanation*

This Article follows the traditional rule of the non-retroactivity of laws and criminal sanctions. There has been added the rule of the retroactivity of a more lenient penal law, which exists in a number of Member States and which features in Article 15 of the Covenant on Civil and Political Rights.

Article 7 of the ECHR is worded as follows:

"1. No one shall be held guilty of any criminal offence on account of any act or omission which did not constitute a criminal offence under national or international law at the time when it was committed. Nor shall a heavier penalty be imposed than the one that was applicable at the time the criminal offence was committed.

2. This Article shall not prejudice the trial and punishment of any person for any act or omission which, at the time when it was committed, was criminal according to the general principles of law recognised by civilised nations."

In paragraph 2, the reference to "civilised" nations has been deleted; this does not change the meaning of this paragraph, which refers to crimes against humanity in particular. In accordance with Article 52(3), the right guaranteed here therefore has the same meaning and scope as the right guaranteed by the ECHR.

Paragraph 3 states the general principle of proportionality between penalties and criminal offences which is enshrined in the common constitutional traditions of the Member States and in the case-law of the Court of Justice of the Communities.

ARTICLE 50 *Right not to be tried or punished twice in criminal proceedings for the same criminal offence - Explanation*

Article 4 of Protocol No 7 to the ECHR reads as follows:

"1. No one shall be liable to be tried or punished again in criminal proceedings under the jurisdiction of the same State for an offence for which he has already been finally acquitted or convicted in accordance with the law and penal procedure of that State.

2. The provisions of the preceding paragraph shall not prevent the reopening of the case in accordance with the law and the penal procedure of the State concerned, if there is evidence of

new or newly discovered facts, or if there has been a fundamental defect in the previous proceedings, which could affect the outcome of the case.

3. No derogation from this Article shall be made under Article 15 of the Convention."

The "*non bis in idem*" rule applies in Union law (see, among the many precedents, the judgment of 5 May 1966, Cases 18/65 and 35/65, *Gutmann v. Commission* [1966] ECR 103 and a recent case, the decision of the Court of First Instance of 20 April 1999, Joined Cases T-305/94 and others, *Limburgse Vinyl Maatschappij NV v. Commission* [1999] ECR II-931). The rule prohibiting cumulation refers to cumulation of two penalties of the same kind, that is to say criminal law penalties.

In accordance with Article 50, the "*non bis in idem*" rule applies not only within the jurisdiction of one State but also between the jurisdictions of several Member States. That corresponds to the *acquis* in Union law; see Articles 54 to 58 of the Schengen Convention and the judgment of the Court of Justice of 11 February 2003, C-187/01 *Gözütok* ***ECR I-1345***, Article 7 of the Convention on the Protection of the European Communities' Financial Interests and Article 10 of the Convention on the fight against corruption. The very limited exceptions in those Conventions permitting the Member States to derogate from the "*non bis in idem*" rule are covered by the horizontal clause in Article 52(1) of the Charter concerning limitations. As regards the situations referred to by Article 4 of Protocol No 7, namely the application of the principle within the same Member State, the guaranteed right has the same meaning and the same scope as the corresponding right in the ECHR.

TITLE VII

GENERAL PROVISIONS GOVERNING THE INTERPRETATION AND APPLICATION OF THE CHARTER

ARTICLE 51 *Field of application - Explanation*

The aim of Article 51 is to determine the scope of the Charter. It seeks to establish clearly that the Charter applies primarily to the institutions and bodies of the Union, in compliance with the principle of subsidiarity. This provision was drafted in keeping with ***Article 6(2) of the Treaty on European Union***, which required the Union to respect fundamental rights, and with the mandate issued by Cologne European Council. The term "institutions" is enshrined ***in the Treaties***. The expression "bodies, offices and agencies" is commonly used in the ***Treaties*** to refer to all the authorities set up by the ***Treaties*** or by secondary legislation (see, e.g., ***Articles 15 or 16 of the Treaty on the Functioning of the European Union***).

As regards the Member States, it follows unambiguously from the case-law of the Court of Justice that the requirement to respect fundamental rights defined in a Union context is only binding on the Member States when they act in the scope of Union law (judgment of 13 July 1989, Case 5/88 *Wachauf* [1989] ECR 2609; judgment of 18 June 1991, *ERT* [1991] ECR I-2925; judgment of 18 December 1997, C-309/96 *Annibaldi* [1997] ECR I-7493). The Court of Justice confirmed this case-law in the following terms: "In addition, it should be remembered that the requirements flowing from the protection of fundamental rights in the Community legal order are also binding on Member States when they implement Community rules ..." (judgment of 13 April 2000, Case C-292/97, [2000] ECR I-2737, paragraph 37 of the grounds). Of course this rule, as enshrined in this Charter, applies to the central authorities as well as to regional or local bodies, and to public organisations, when they are implementing Union law.

Paragraph 2, together with the second sentence of paragraph 1, confirms that the Charter may not have the effect of extending the competences and tasks which the ***Treaties*** confer on the Union. Explicit mention is made here of the logical consequences of the principle of subsidiarity and of the fact that the Union only has those powers which have been conferred upon it. The fundamental rights as guaranteed in the Union do not have any effect other than in the context of the powers determined by ***the Treaties***. Consequently, an obligation, pursuant to the second sentence of paragraph 1, for the Union's institutions to promote principles laid down in the Charter may arise only within the limits of these same powers.

Paragraph 2 also confirms that the Charter may not have the effect of extending the field of application of Union law beyond the powers of the Union as established in the ***Treaties***. The Court of Justice has already established this rule with respect to the fundamental rights recognised as part of Union law (judgment of 17 February 1998, C-249/96 *Grant*, 1998 ECR I-621, paragraph 45 of the grounds). In accordance with this rule, it goes without saying that the ***reference to*** the Charter ***in Article 6 of the Treaty on European Union*** cannot be understood as extending by itself the range of Member State action considered to be "implementation of Union law" (within the meaning of paragraph 1 and the above-mentioned case-law).

ARTICLE 52 *Scope and interpretation of rights and principles- Explanation*

The purpose of Article 52 is to set the scope of the rights and principles of the Charter, and to lay down rules for their interpretation. Paragraph 1 deals with the arrangements for the limitation of rights. The wording is based on the case-law of the Court of Justice: "... it is well established in the case-law of the Court that restrictions may be imposed on the exercise of fundamental rights, in particular in the context of a common organisation of the market, provided that those restrictions in fact correspond to objectives of general interest pursued by the Community and do not constitute, with regard to the aim pursued, disproportionate and unreasonable interference undermining the very substance of those rights" (judgment of 13 April 2000, Case C-292/97, paragraph 45 of the grounds). The reference to general interests recognised by the Union covers both the objectives mentioned in ***Article 3 of the Treaty on the European Union*** and other interests protected by specific provisions of the ***Treaties*** such as ***Article 4(1) of the Treaty on European Union*** and ***Articles 35(3), 36 and 346 of the Treaty on the Functioning of the European Union***.

Paragraph 2 refers to rights which were already expressly guaranteed in the Treaty establishing the European Community and have been recognised in the Charter, and which are now found in ***the Treaties*** (notably the rights derived from Union citizenship). It clarifies that such rights remain subject to the conditions and limits applicable to the Union law on which they are based, and for which provision is now made in ***the Treaties***. The Charter does not alter the system of rights conferred by the EC Treaty and now taken over by ***the Treaties***.

Paragraph 3 is intended to ensure the necessary consistency between the Charter and the ECHR by establishing the rule that, insofar as the rights in the present Charter also correspond to rights guaranteed by the ECHR, the meaning and scope of those rights, including authorised limitations, are the same as those laid down by the ECHR. This means in particular that the legislator, in laying down limitations to those rights, must comply with the same standards as are fixed by the detailed limitation arrangements laid down in the ECHR, which are thus made applicable for the rights covered by this paragraph, without thereby adversely affecting the autonomy of Union law and of that of the Court of Justice of the European Union.

The reference to the ECHR covers both the Convention and the Protocols to it. The meaning and the scope of the guaranteed rights are determined not only by the text of those instruments, but also by the case-law of the European Court of Human Rights and by the Court of Justice of the European Union. The last sentence of the paragraph is designed to allow the Union to guarantee more extensive protection. In any event, the level of protection afforded by the Charter may never be lower than that guaranteed by the ECHR.

The Charter does not affect the possibilities of Member States to avail themselves of Article 15 ECHR, allowing derogations from ECHR rights in the event of war or of other public dangers threatening the life of the nation, when they take action in the areas of national defence in the event of war and of the maintenance of law and order, in accordance with their responsibilities recognised in ***Article 4(1) of the Treaty on European Union and in Articles 72 and 347 of the Treaty on the Functioning of the European Union***.

The list of rights which may at the present stage, without precluding developments in the law, legislation and the Treaties, be regarded as corresponding to rights in the ECHR within the meaning of the present paragraph is given hereafter. It does not include rights additional to those in the ECHR.

1. Articles of the Charter where both the meaning and the scope are the same as the corresponding Articles of the ECHR:

- Article 2 corresponds to Article 2 of the ECHR
- Article 4 corresponds to Article 3 of the ECHR
- Article 5(1) and (2) correspond to Article 4 of the ECHR
- Article 6 corresponds to Article 5 of the ECHR
- Article 7 corresponds to Article 8 of the ECHR
- Article 10(1) corresponds to Article 9 of the ECHR
- Article 11 corresponds to Article 10 of the ECHR without prejudice to any restrictions which Union law may impose on Member States' right to introduce the licensing arrangements referred to in the third sentence of Article 10(1) of the ECHR
- Article 17 corresponds to Article 1 of the Protocol to the ECHR
- Article 19(1) corresponds to Article 4 of Protocol No 4
- Article 19(2) corresponds to Article 3 of the ECHR as interpreted by the European Court of Human Rights
- Article 48 corresponds to Article 6(2) and (3) of the ECHR
- Article 49(1) (with the exception of the last sentence) and (2) correspond to Article 7 of the ECHR

2. Articles where the meaning is the same as the corresponding Articles of the ECHR, but where the scope is wider:

- Article 9 covers the same field as Article 12 of the ECHR, but its scope may be extended to other forms of marriage if these are established by national legislation
- Article 12(1) corresponds to Article 11 of the ECHR, but its scope is extended to European Union level
- Article 14(1) corresponds to Article 2 of the Protocol to the ECHR, but its scope is extended to cover access to vocational and continuing training
- Article 14(3) corresponds to Article 2 of the Protocol to the ECHR as regards the rights of parents
- Article 47(2) and (3) correspond to Article 6(1) of the ECHR, but the limitation to the determination of civil rights and obligations or criminal charges does not apply as regards Union law and its implementation

- Article 50 corresponds to Article 4 of Protocol No 7 to the ECHR, but its scope is extended to European Union level between the Courts of the Member States.
- Finally, citizens of the European Union may not be considered as aliens in the scope of the application of Union law, because of the prohibition of any discrimination on grounds of nationality. The limitations provided for by Article 16 of the ECHR as regards the rights of aliens therefore do not apply to them in this context.

The rule of interpretation contained in paragraph 4 has been based on the wording of ***Article 6(3) of the Treaty on European Union*** and takes due account of the approach to common constitutional traditions followed by the Court of Justice (e.g., judgment of 13 December 1979, Case 44/79 *Hauer* [1979] ECR 3727; judgment of 18 May 1982, Case 155/79, *AM&S* [1982] ECR 1575). Under that rule, rather than following a rigid approach of "a lowest common denominator", the Charter rights concerned should be interpreted in a way offering a high standard of protection which is adequate for the law of the Union and in harmony with the common constitutional traditions.

Paragraph 5 clarifies the distinction between "rights" and "principles" set out in the Charter. According to that distinction, subjective rights shall be respected, whereas principles shall be observed (Article 51(1)). Principles may be implemented through legislative or executive acts (adopted by the Union in accordance with its powers, and by the Member States only when they implement Union law); accordingly, they become significant for the Courts only when such acts are interpreted or reviewed. They do not however give rise to direct claims for positive action by the Union's institutions or Member States authorities. This is consistent both with case-law of the Court of Justice (c.f. notably case-law on the "precautionary principle" in ***Article 191(2) of the Treaty on the Functioning of the European Union***: judgment of the CFI of 11 September 2002, T-13/99, *Pfizer vs. Council*, with numerous references to earlier case-law; and a series of judgments on Article 33 (ex-39) on the principles of agricultural law, e.g. judgment of the Court of Justice Case 265/85, *Van den Berg* [1987] ECR 1155: scrutiny of the principle of market stabilisation and of reasonable expectations) and with the approach of the Member States' constitutional systems to "principles" particularly in the field of social law. For illustration, examples for principles recognised in the Charter include e.g. Articles 25, 26 and 37. In some cases, an Article of the Charter may contain both elements of a right and of a principle, e.g. Articles 23, 33 and 34.

Paragraph 6 refers to the various Articles in the Charter which, in the spirit of subsidiarity, make reference to national laws and practices.

ARTICLE 53 *Level of protection - Explanation*

This provision is intended to maintain the level of protection currently afforded within their respective scope by Union law, national law and international law. Owing to its importance, mention is made of the ECHR.

ARTICLE 54 Prohibition of abuse of rights - Explanation

This Article corresponds to Article 17 of the ECHR:

> "Nothing in this Convention may be interpreted as implying for any State, group or person any right to engage in any activity or perform any act aimed at the destruction of any of the rights and freedoms set forth herein or at their limitation to a greater extent than is provided for in the Convention."

DECLARATION
on the occasion of the 50th anniversary of the signature of the Treaties of Rome

25 March 2007

For centuries Europe has been an idea, holding out hope of peace and understanding. That hope has been fulfilled. European unification has made peace and prosperity possible. It has brought about a sense of community and overcome differences. Each Member State has helped to unite Europe and to strengthen democracy and the rule of law. Thanks to the yearning for freedom of the peoples of central and eastern Europe the unnatural division of Europe is now consigned to the past. European integration shows that we have learnt the painful lessons of a history marked by bloody conflict. Today we live together as was never possible before.

We, the citizens of the European Union, have united for the better.

I.

In the European Union, we are turning our common ideals into reality: for us, the individual is paramount. His dignity is inviolable. His rights are inalienable. Women and men enjoy equal rights.

We are striving for peace and freedom, for democracy and the rule of law, for mutual respect and shared responsibility, for prosperity and security, for tolerance and participation, for justice and solidarity.

We have a unique way of living and working together in the European Union. This is expressed through the democratic interaction of the Member States and the European institutions. The European Union is founded on equal rights and mutually supportive co-operation. This enables us to strike a fair balance between Member States' interests.

We preserve in the European Union the identities and diverse traditions of its Member States.
We are enriched by open borders and a lively variety of languages, cultures and regions. There are many goals which we cannot achieve on our own, but only in concert. Tasks are shared between the European Union, the Member States and their regions and local authorities.

II.

We are facing major challenges which do not stop at national borders. The European Union is our response to these challenges. Only together can we continue to preserve our ideal of European society in future for the good of all European Union citizens. This European model combines economic success and social responsibility. The common market and the euro make us strong. We can thus shape the increasing interdependence of the global economy and ever-growing competition on international markets according to our values. Europe's wealth lies in the knowledge and ability of its people; that is the key to growth, employment and social cohesion.

We will fight terrorism, organised crime and illegal immigration together. We stand up for liberties and civil rights also in the struggle against those who oppose them. Racism and xenophobia must never again be given any rein.

We are committed to the peaceful resolution of conflicts in the world and to ensuring that people do not become victims of war, terrorism and violence. The European Union wants to promote freedom and development in the world. We want to drive back poverty, hunger and disease. We want to continue to take a leading role in that fight.

We intend jointly to lead the way in energy policy and climate protection and make our contribution to averting the global threat of climate change.

III.

The European Union will continue to thrive both on openness and on the will of its Member States to consolidate the Union's internal development. The European Union will continue to promote democracy, stability and prosperity beyond its borders.

With European unification a dream of earlier generations has become a reality. Our history reminds us that we must protect this for the good of future generations. For that reason we must always renew the political shape of Europe in keeping with the times. That is why today, 50 years after the signing of the Treaties of Rome, we are united in our aim of placing the European Union on a renewed common basis before the European Parliament elections in 2009.

For we know that Europe is our common future.

Done at Berlin on the twenty-fifth day of March in the year two thousand and seven.

For the European Parliament	The President, Hans-Gert Pöttering
For the Council of the European Union	The President, Angela Merkel
For the Commission of the European Communities	The President, José Manuel Barroso

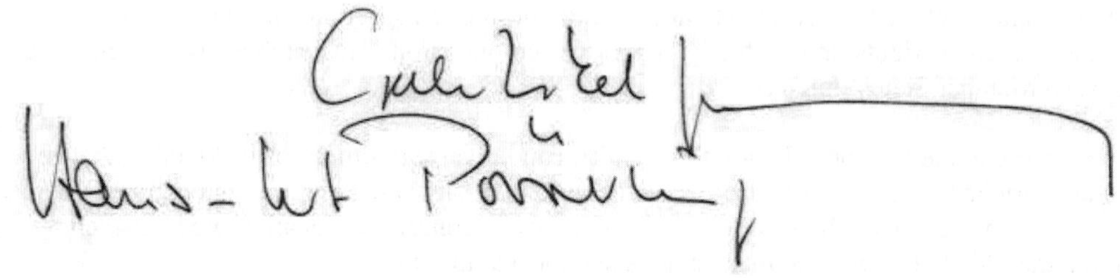

"THE EUROPEAN UNION AFTER THE LISBON TREATY"

JOSÉ MANUEL DURÃO BARROSO

PRESIDENT OF THE EUROPEAN COMMISSION

4TH JOINT PARLIAMENTARY MEETING ON THE FUTURE OF EUROPE

BRUSSELS, 4 DECEMBER 2007

SPEECH/07/793

Six months ago, here, in the European Parliament, during the 3rd Joint Parliamentary Meeting on the Future of Europe, I discussed how a Reform Treaty would bring real progress to the European Union. That was just one week before the June European Council, and I expressed my hope that European leaders would arrive at an agreement. In particular, I said that a new Treaty should reinforce the Union's capacity to act, its democratic nature and its cohesion in external affairs: in short, to make the Union better placed to shape globalization.

We know now that, thanks to the leadership of the German Presidency, the June European Council agreed on a detailed and comprehensive mandate. Then, the Portuguese Presidency carried the torch of success, through a skilfully oriented IGC, to the Lisbon Informal Council, in October. Next Thursday, we will sign the Treaty of Lisbon, and leave behind us six years of discussions, hesitations and some set backs on institutional issues.

As many others, I feel somehow frustrated with the number of opt-outs. However, as I have said before, the opt-outs are the price that we pay for progress and for an ambitious Reform Treaty. Respect for European diversity often means institutional compromises. The crucial point is that, despite our differences, the Union remains united in its fundamental values and its fundamental goals.

For 2008, the successful ratification of the Treaty of Lisbon should be one of our overriding priorities. It is important to explain to European citizens how the Reform Treaty will improve the Union's capacity to act, will better protect their interests and will deliver results. The Commission is ready to work in partnership with other European Institutions and with Member States to communicate the Treaty of Lisbon to European citizens.

In particular, I would like to make a special appeal to all national parliaments to engage in explaining what the Treaty of Lisbon does for our citizens. 'Europe' is not 'Brussels'. You are also 'Europe'. The Treaty will have profound and positive implications for your electorates. It also brings more competences to national parliaments, and rightly so, as the Commission always defended. But this brings more responsibility. It is now the moment to actively support the Treaty.

Let me discuss, today, in more detail two progresses introduced by the Lisbon Treaty: a more democratic Union, and a more cohesive Union in external affairs.

A More Democratic European Union

The Treaty of Lisbon will reinforce the democratic nature of the European Union.

First, thanks to the efforts of the European Parliament, supported by the Commission, the Treaty of Lisbon introduces a clear definition of what European citizenship means. Europeans will benefit from such a clarification.

Second, the Treaty of Lisbon also gives legal force to the Charter of Fundamental Rights, which will strengthen the Union's legal system of checks and balances. Next week in Strasbourg, together with

President Pottering and Prime Minister Socrates, we will proclaim the Charter before the signature of the Reform Treaty. The solemn dignity of the Charter will thus be properly recognised by the three European political institutions.

Third, the Treaty of Lisbon increases the rights of national parliaments, which will reinforce accountability and help us all to guarantee the respect for the principle of subsidiarity. The Treaty will allow national parliaments to give a reasoned opinion on whether a draft legislative act complies with the principle of subsidiarity. The Commission will then review or re-examine its proposal in light of the concerns expressed by national parliaments.

Without questioning the right of initiative of the Commission and the institutional balance of the Union, the Treaty of Lisbon recognises the important political role of national parliaments. Over recent years, we have also been working to develop a deeper policy dialogue with national parliaments. I hope this process will be further developed in the future.

Finally, the European Parliament will have a greater role in the legislative process of the Union. With the Treaty of Lisbon, the vast majority of European laws will be adopted jointly by the European Parliament and by the Council. Under the new provisions, the European Parliament also elects the President of the Commission on a proposal from the European Council and approves the composition of the College of the Commission, chosen by the designated President.

As a result of the deepening of Union's democracy, the Commission reinforces its political nature. The increased political responsibility of the Commission goes hand in hand with the growth of the competences of the European Parliament and of the national parliaments. The Commission is ready to play its full part in the new democratic system of the Union and to consolidate its role as agenda-settler and as the catalyst for the direction of European policy.

More democracy means also that the European Union will be more and more the arena for European political and ideological debates. And this will enrich the Union's political life and European politics in general. It is, however, crucial to turn these debates into consensual policies that represent the general European interest. In other words, we need a permanent exercise in finding the right political balance:

- the balance between the European interest and national interests;
- the balance between social justice and economic competitiveness;
- the balance between openness and protection.

To find the right balance is the task of the Commission and the Treaty of Lisbon will reinforce its legitimacy to do that job.

The Interest of an Enlarged European Union in a 'Global World'

During the first five decades of its history, European construction achieved great results. Europeans built legitimate ways to resolve their political, cultural and ideological differences in a peaceful way and to promote common values and economic and social prosperity. To preserve and to improve what we achieved during the last fifty years, we need to influence and to shape the world around us.

Together, the European Union and Member States can achieve results that they could never dream of on their own. Working in close cooperation with our main partners, namely the countries that share the common values of freedom and democracy, we are in a position to decisively shape globalization.

United, the European Union and Member States are stronger and in a much better condition to tackle the challenges of the globalised world: to create and to maintain a just world order, to address climate change and global poverty, to guarantee energy security, to fight terrorism and organised crime, to deal with mass migration, and to succeed in a more competitive economic environment.

Common challenges require common solutions. The task for the coming decades is how to use the power and the capacities we built during the last half century to promote our values and interests at the global level.

At the same time, global order will benefit from the European experience.

- The world needs the European method of putting together different national practices,
- The world needs the European principles of open societies and open economies,
- The world needs the European way of linking the imperative of freedom to the idea of solidarity and justice,
- The world needs the European priority in tackling climate change and promoting sustainable development with respect for our planet.

By promoting its values and its interests, the Union not only delivers to its citizens but also helps the world to be a better place.

This is why, for the Commission, it is crucial to defend and to promote the European interest in the age of globalization. 'Offensive openness' is the key idea to protect the European interest without falling into a protectionist agenda: openness without naiveté, but with an activist stance that calls on partners to respond in a reciprocal way. An open European Union in an open world has been at the heart of our policy agenda, and will continue to be a top priority. The Treaty of Lisbon will be a step forward to achieve this.

Only the right institutions and policies can give Europe the capacity to act. We cannot face successfully the 21st Century globalisation with the institutions of the 20th Century. With the Treaty of Lisbon, the European Union will strengthen its political, its strategic and its economic voice in diplomatic, security, defence, trade and development issues.

The new Treaty will turn the European Union into a full external political actor by giving the Union legal personality. In particular, the Treaty establishes common principles and objectives for the EU's external action in all its aspects, including the external aspects of internal policies. Thus, the consistency between the different areas of external action and between these areas and the Union's internal policies will be substantially reinforced.

In more specific areas,

- the Treaty of Lisbon will update the Petersberg Tasks to contribute to combating terrorism;
- It will allow the emergence of a true common European defence;
- It will introduce a mutual defence clause and a solidarity clause, including energy security;
- It will strengthen development policy and humanitarian aid.

In short, the Treaty of Lisbon will reinforce the Union's cohesion, coherence and effectiveness in external affairs. As such, it will improve the Union's capacity to pursue one of its central tasks: to shape globalization.

* * *

"DEBATE ON THE INFORMAL COUNCIL IN LISBON"

José Manuel Durão Barroso

President of the European Commission

Speech to the European Parliament

Strasbourg, 23 October 2007

SPEECH/07/649

The Informal European Council in Lisbon was the Council of a unified European Union. We overcame a period of six years discussing institutional issues and put our divisions behind us. We now have the Treaty of Lisbon, which will be signed on the 13th of December. I wish to pay tribute and applaud the work of the Portuguese Presidency, in particular the leadership of the Portuguese Prime Minister.

At this special moment, I also wish to express my gratitude to the German Presidency, who so skilfully steered the mandate that led to the Lisbon Treaty.

Let me also salute the European Parliament for your commitment during the IGC. Throughout this process, the European Parliament showed a strong political will to resolve the institutional issue, while being determined to reinforce European democracy. The collaboration between the Parliament and the Commission was exemplary and contributed to some of the most important advances of the new Treaty.

The Treaty of Lisbon is the Treaty of a large Europe. It is the first time in the history of European integration that states, which were once divided by a totalitarian curtain, together negotiate and reach an agreement on a common European Treaty. It is appropriate to remind us all today that our journey started precisely with the Berlin Declaration, which celebrated not only the fiftieth anniversary of the Rome Treaty but also the emergence of a free and reunited Europe.

Let me recall today some of the predictions we have heard during the last two years. In 2005, after the negative referenda, we heard people saying that a European Union of 25 and then 27 would never agree on a Treaty, whatever its content. There were far too many different national interests to allow the Union to reach a consensus.

In 2007, critics said that Member States would never agree on a mandate.

Then, they said that the mandate from the June European Council would never be respected.

On my way to Lisbon, last week, I still heard some saying that it would be very, very difficult to reach an agreement and that delegations had even booked hotels until Sunday morning.

Well, the fact is that 27 Member States reached a consensus, respected a mandate and agreed on a Treaty. And all of this on Thursday night after dinner.

The success of Lisbon tells us that the European Union is much tougher than it looks, with a strong ability to recover from setbacks. Today, the European Union is alive and delivering.

The Commission is very happy with the results of the IGC. First, the "two nonnegotiable conditions" set by the Commission were fully respected. On the one hand, the Lisbon Treaty has clearly advanced from the current status quo. I always said that the Commission could not accept a solution less ambitious that the Nice Treaty. In fact, we wanted as much progress as possible. On the other hand, we fought hard to keep the competences of the Commission intact. And there were certain attempts to reduce and to weaken those competences. Let me be clear: there is no European integration without strong European Institutions.

The Treaty of Lisbon will reinforce the democratic nature of the European Union. **First**, thanks to the efforts of the European Parliament, there is now a clear definition of what European citizenship means.

Second, The Reform Treaty also gives legal force to the Charter of Fundamental Rights, which will be a central part of the system of checks and balances in our Union of law. Together with President Pottering and Prime Minister Socrates, we will proclaim the Charter before the signature of the Reform Treaty. The solemn dignity of the Charter will thus be properly recognised, here in this Parliament.

Third, the European Parliament will have a greater role in the legislative process of the Union.

The **fourth** democratic advance introduced by the Reform Treaty regards the rights of national parliaments, which will reinforce the principles of accountability and subsidiarity.

But the central feature of the democratic nature of the Union remains the European Parliament. One of the things that I most enjoy when I am in Strasbourg is to listen to all those political leaders and public figures, from all over the world, addressing this plenary on their aspirations to democracy and their strong beliefs in freedom and in individual rights. This is really one of the vocations of the European Parliament: a house for the voices of freedom in this world. And I think it is something that should make all Europeans proud. When we hear those voices, we also realize what we have achieved in Europe. Because once we also had people in European cities marching for the same rights. We should be very proud to live in a continent where all enjoy fundamental rights. And we will say it, together, when we approve the Reform Treaty and the Charter of Fundamental Rights.

The European Union faces many challenges, both internal and external, and our citizens want results. The Treaty of Lisbon will turn a new page in our ability to deliver and will reinforce our capacity to act. In particular, the Treaty will introduce substantial advances in the area of justice and home affairs.

The Reform Treaty will also reinforce the Union's cohesion in external affairs. Our internal prosperity, our freedom, and our security depend on the capacity of the European Union to act decisively at the global level. With the Reform Treaty, Europe will have the conditions and the instruments to shape globalization. We cannot miss this opportunity.

I know that some committed Europeans are not happy with the number of opt-outs. Myself and the Commission, we would also have preferred to avoid them. However, diversity is a central feature of the European Union and sometimes it requires political and institutional compromises. I prefer to have specific opt-outs for specific countries than to be forced to lower the level of overall ambition of the Treaty. The crucial point is that, despite our diversity, we remain united regarding fundamental goals, fundamental values and fundamental principles.

We have now many tasks ahead. Economic reform, growth and jobs, the reinforcement of social justice, our focus on innovation, our package on energy and climate change, our programme for justice, freedom and security. We need to keep proving that we are not engaged in institutional navel-gazing, and show that we are dealing with the real issues facing Europe.

In this regard, in Lisbon, we also discussed the great issue for the European Union of the 21st Century: to promote the European interest in the age of globalization. Our discussion was the natural complement to concluding the Reform Treaty. We had a very positive debate, the paper presented by the Commission, based on the concept of "European Interest", was fully endorsed, and it was decided to work on a "Declaration on Globalization" for the December European Council, to show that tackling globalization is a common thread in much of European Union's work today. The Heads of State and Government welcomed the concept of 5th freedom: freedom of circulation of researchers and ideas, a cornerstone of our response to globalization. This is particularly important as we are engaged in crucial debates about Galileo and prepare to implement the European Institute of Technology.

As this Commission has argued all along: institutional reform and delivery of results, side-by-side. As the Commission said in 2006, the twin-track approach as the way out for the institutional stalemate.

In Lisbon, we achieved a strategic objective: we all agreed on a Reform Treaty. Now, it is crucially important to achieve a further goal: the ratification of the Lisbon Treaty before the European elections of 2009. I believe there is indeed a new political confidence in Europe. The last polls demonstrate the highest support for the Union since 1994. The political climate is right to move ahead.

The IGC and the Lisbon Informal Council demonstrated that when European Institutions and Member States co-operate, we are able to solve even what seem to be the most complicated problems. I wish that the spirit of Lisbon, which brought us a consensus on a new Treaty, will inspire the European Union in the year to come towards a successful ratification process. We need it for a strong Union that delivers results for citizens.

* * * * *

REPORT ON THE LISBON INFORMAL SUMMIT AND THE FINAL SESSION OF THE INTERGOVERNMENTAL CONFERENCE

José Sócrates, President of the European Council Speech to the European Parliament

23 October 2007

Mr President,

Mr President of the European Commission,

Members,

You will allow my first words to be spoken in memory of my friend. In memory of the MEP, Fausto Correia, who died a few days ago at an early age. His death was a great loss to the European Parliament, and in particular to the Portuguese Socialist Party.

Fausto Correia was a man of great political and human qualities. He was an intelligent politician, well prepared and always committed to European ideas. But it is his human qualities of generosity, companionship and tolerance that I would like to recall now. After all, these are the qualities that give meaning to a life in politics.

For me, his death is a personal loss, the loss of an old friend who shared many moments of my political life and who will be greatly missed.

When I stood before this Plenary three months ago to present the programme of the Portuguese Presidency, I referred clearly to what the main challenge - the top priority - of the Portuguese Presidency would be: to draw up and reach an agreement on a new Reforming Treaty, bringing to an end six years of deadlock in the European Union's institutional debate.

It is therefore with great satisfaction that I have come here today to the European Parliament to present you the agreement reached by the Intergovernmental Conference on 18 October. The agreement that will give birth to the new Lisbon Treaty. The Treaty that will be signed on 13 December in the city whose name it will bear.

The Portuguese Presidency began with the task of transforming the mandate we were given by the German Presidency - and let me stress its clarity and precision - into a new Treaty.

The agreement we have reached is confirmation of the wisdom of the method and calendar defined at the start of our Presidency. It was necessary - as I told you at the beginning of the Presidency - to take advantage of the June Council so as to try and conclude the Treaty not in December, as many advocated, but in October.

In fact, we made the IGC for the revision of the treaties the fastest in the history of the European Union. We began on 23 July and we finished on 18 October.

When we look at the background to this Treaty it is easier to appreciate the importance of this political decision, of not leaving until the end of the year a task that was in our grasp to finish sooner. Europe needed a rapid agreement and that is what it got. Europe needed a sign of confidence and that is what it got. Europe needed to turn towards the future and that is what it has done.

We got quickly down to work with all the Member States who, without exception, constructively and resolutely sought to overcome the difficulties that still remained and we were able to present a complete text of the Treaty on 3 October which brought us closer to our goal.

The questions that remained for the Lisbon Summit were few, but they were politically difficult. In this context, our strategy was to try for an agreement on the very first day of the Summit. Not only did this seem possible to us, but we would be giving Europe a very important signal. The signal that the European Union can decide quickly, even when decisions we all know are difficult are at stake.

In Lisbon, agreement was reached on the following questions which allowed the final agreement on the Treaty to be sealed:

On the Ioannina clause, the solution involved two levels:

- a declaration on the decision making system in the Council by qualified majority that specifies the actual Ioannina safeguarding mechanism;
- which is complemented by a protocol that requires consensus in the European Council on any attempt to modify or revoke this mechanism.

In so doing we provided guarantees on the Ioannina compromise without affecting the integrity of the decision making process by qualified majority.

A solution also had to be found to the political question on the number of Advocates-General in the Court of Justice. Agreement was reached on a declaration stating that the Council would give its approval to any request from the Court of Justice for the number of Advocates-General to be increased by three from eight to eleven. In this case, Poland would have a permanent Advocate-General and would no longer participate in the rotation system, while the current rotation system would cover five Advocates-General instead of three.

As for the appointment of the Union's High Representative for Foreign Affairs and Security Policy, the agreed declaration foresees that the European Parliament can use suitable contacts to participate in the appointment process even in the very first phase in January 2009.

The Conference also approved a declaration clarifying the delimitation of competences between the Union and the Member States, foreseen in the Treaties.

And, lastly, the issue of the composition of the European Parliament. An amendment was made to Article 9.a of the Treaty of the European Union, defining that the number of members cannot exceed seven hundred and fifty (750), plus the President, maintaining the proportional degressivity of its representation.

Two declarations are added to this amendment:

- one defining that the additional seat in the European Parliament will be attributed to Italy; and
- the other guaranteeing that the European Council will give its political agreement on the composition of the European Parliament, on the basis of the proposal from Parliament itself.

The Council therefore accepted the criteria put forward by Parliament and went ahead with what it considered an acceptable adjustment, with a view to adapting the current framework during the 2009-2014 period.

In addition to these questions I have mentioned, the Portuguese Presidency also took care to include the opt out rules and clauses in the Treaty that were part of the mandate, obviously respecting the positions of the Member States that wanted them whilst taking constant care not to take away from the essence of the community decision process and the overall coherence of the Treaty.

Thus we have a new Treaty. And a good Treaty. A Treaty that resolves the crisis of the past and puts Europe in a position to set its eyes on the future. A Treaty with significant advances of which I highlight just some. This Treaty:

- adopts, with no alteration, the enlargement of the European Parliament's participation in the legislative process, as well as the innovations in the budgetary process, thereby enhancing the Union's democratic legitimacy;
- improves the decision making process, namely by the extension of the vote by qualified majority to the area of freedom, security and justice;
- also on the area of freedom, security and justice, it upholds the legal foundations required for the development of more effective immigration and asylum policies, as well as police and judicial co-ordination against terrorism and organised crime thus strengthening the security of our citizens;
- clearly lists the domains in which the Member States transfer powers to the Union;
- strengthens the supervisory role of the national Parliaments;

But in the set of advances that this Treaty brings, there is one I find particularly gratifying to underline: the Charter of Fundamental Rights which will be proclaimed by the European Union's three institutions on 12 December is explicitly made legally-binding by the Treaty.

To this, I must add the Union's membership to the European Convention for Human Rights and the fact that a solution has been found to the question of the judicial framework of European citizenship, as requested by the representatives of this Parliament.

On the external front, the new institutional framework that the Treaty creates - in particular combining the position of High representative and Vice President of the European Commission for Foreign Affairs - reflects the extent of our ambition: to give Europe a more significant role on the international stage and the means for effective co-operation with our partners.

Negotiations were tough and demanding. But Europe was successful. It achieved the crucial goal: it has a Treaty that affirms European values, that strengthens Europe as a global economic player and that provides its institutions with more effective conditions to fulfil this role.

Europe has left this Summit stronger. Stronger to face up to global questions. Stronger to assume its role in the world. Stronger because it sends a signal of confidence to our economy and to our citizens.

The Treaty of Lisbon now shows a Europe that is prepared, confident, sure of itself. What the Treaty of Lisbon brings is a new Europe fit for the times.

I want to thank the European Parliament. I want to thank its President, Hans-Gert Pöttering and its representatives at the IGC - Elmar Brok (EPP-ED), Enrique Barón-Crespo (PSE) and Andrew Duff (ALDE). On behalf of the Portuguese Presidency, I want to thank you for your excellent collaboration, the constructive suggestion put forward and the dedication so that Europe could reach an agreement and do so quickly.

But I also want to thank the European Commission, and in particular its President, for the help they gave the Presidency throughout this negotiation process.

But it is only right that I should express my profound gratitude to the General Secretariat of the Council and especially to its legal services and to its Director, Jean-Claude Piris. I thank them for their hard work, competence and dedication. They did a magnificent job. Europe is indebted to them.

I would also like to thank all the representatives of the Member States who participated at various levels in the IGC. The Presidency cannot forget the spirit of collaboration, dedication and openness that everyone demonstrated in search of the best solutions.

Allow me now to extend my personal gratitude to Luís Amado, Minister of Foreign Affairs and Lobo Antunes, Secretary of State, and to all the Portuguese diplomats who gave their best for what undoubtedly will be one of the greatest successes of the Portuguese Presidency.

Once their goal of concluding the Treaty in Lisbon was achieved, the Heads of State and of Government were able to dedicate the morning of the second day to debate on the external dimension of the Lisbon Agenda and the response to the challenges of globalisation. It was a good debate in which we benefited from the participation and valuable contribution of the President of the European Parliament. It was a debate looking towards the future.

The President of the European Commission gave an important contribution to the discussion with his communication on 'The European interest: being successful in globalisation', which received great praise from the heads of State and Government.

The debate addressed in particular the financial markets in the light of the recent troubles, and climate change with a view to the Bali Conference.

Among the various conclusions I took from debate, I want to highlight one: Europe has everything it needs - and even the duty in a number of matters - to lead the globalisation process. Be it in the reciprocal opening of markets; in the improved environmental, social and financial standards and of intellectual property; and also in the boosting of strategic co-operation with our international partners.

It is a conclusion that I am proud to say is in keeping with the motto set by the Portuguese Presidency: "A stronger Union for a better world".

Let me make one last reference before I close. It is true that 18 October brought the agreement on the Treaty of Lisbon to a close.

But that very day began with another important agreement. The agreement between the European social partners on the challenges of the labour market. The social partners set a good example of constructive commitment and responsibility. A good example of attention to the need for dialogue and the needs for reforms in the light of a globalised world in constant change.

In political life, moments when we have the opportunity to serve our country and Europe at a critical moment are rare. I feel honoured to have had such an opportunity. I want to thank you for the support that I have always felt from this Parliament.

But the job is not yet finished. There is still much to be done. I want to assure you that the Presidency will continue to work with the same commitment and the same conviction as at the first hour for a stronger European in the service of a better world.

* * * * *

EUROPEAN PARLIAMENT DECISION OF 29 NOVEMBER 2007 ON THE APPROVAL BY THE EUROPEAN PARLIAMENT OF THE CHARTER OF FUNDAMENTAL RIGHTS OF THE EUROPEAN UNION

(2007/2218(ACI)

The European Parliament,

– having regard to the letter from its President of 25 October 2007,

– having regard to the Charter of Fundamental Rights of the European Union signed and proclaimed in Nice on 7 December 2000[1],

– having regard to its decision of 14 November 2000 approving the draft Charter of Fundamental Rights of the European Union[2],

– having regard to its resolution of 23 October 2002 on the impact of the Charter of Fundamental Rights of the European Union and its future status[3],

– having regard to its resolution of 24 September 2003 on the draft Treaty establishing a Constitution for Europe and the European Parliament's opinion on the convening of the Intergovernmental Conference (IGC)[4], in particular paragraph 4 thereof,

– having regard to its resolution of 12 January 2005 on the Treaty establishing a Constitution for Europe[5], in particular paragraph 5, point (a), and paragraph 6 thereof,

– having regard to its resolution of 11 July 2007 on the convening of the Intergovernmental Conference (IGC): The European Parliament's opinion (Article 48 of the EU Treaty)[6], in particular paragraphs 8, 12 and 17 thereof,

– having regard to Article 6, Paragraph 1 of the Treaty on European Union, as revised by the draft Treaty of Lisbon agreed by the 2007 Intergovernmental Conference,

– having regard to Rule 120(1) of its Rules of Procedure,

– having regard to the report of the Committee on Constitutional Affairs (A6-0445/2007),

A. whereas, by confirming the legally binding status of the Charter of Fundamental Rights, the draft Treaty of Lisbon has safeguarded the substance of the major achievement represented by Part II of the Treaty establishing a Constitution for Europe,

B. whereas the European Parliament has already agreed to the adaptations made to the Charter of Fundamental Rights as originally solemnly proclaimed in Nice on 7 December 2000, when, in its above-mentioned resolution of 24 September 2003, it assessed the results of the work of the Convention on the Future of Europe and when, in its above-mentioned resolution of 12 January 2005, it approved the Constitutional Treaty resulting from the work of the 2004 Intergovernmental Conference (IGC),

---

1. OJ C 364, 18.12.2000, p. 1.
2. OJ C 223, 8.8.2001, p. 74 (Duff/Voggenhuber report).
3. OJ C 300 E, 11.12.2003, p. 432 (Duff report).
4. OJ C 77 E, 26.3.2004, p. 255 (Gil-Robles Gil-Delgado/Tsatsos report).
5. OJ C 247 E, 6.10.2005, p. 88 (Corbett/Méndez de Vigo report).
6. Texts Adopted, P6_TA(2007)0328 (Leinen report).

C. whereas, in its above-mentioned resolution of 11 July 2007, in giving its opinion on the convening of the 2007 IGC, it welcomed the fact that the IGC mandate safeguarded the legally binding status of the Charter of Fundamental Rights, while expressing its strong concerns about the Protocol on the application of the Charter of Fundamental Rights of the European Union to Poland and to the United Kingdom, which seeks to limit the justiciability of the Charter in certain Member States,

D. whereas, in paragraph 17 of its above-mentioned resolution of 11 July 2007, it stressed its intention to carefully scrutinise the outcome of the 2007 IGC, when it will give its opinion on the Treaty of Lisbon after the latter has been signed,

1. Approves the Charter of Fundamental Rights of the European Union in the version thereof annexed hereto; [*BMDF Note: Annex not shown, see Charter of Fundamental Rights, shown above*]

2. Gives a mandate to its President to solemnly proclaim the Charter, before the signature of the Treaty of Lisbon, jointly with the President of the Council of the European Union and the President of the Commission, and instructs him to take the necessary steps to have it published in the Official Journal of the European Union;

3. Urges Poland and the United Kingdom to make every effort to arrive, after all, at a consensus on the unrestricted applicability of the Charter;

4. Instructs its President to forward this decision to the President of the Council of the European Union and the President of the Commission, for information.

* * * * *

EUROPEAN PARLIAMENT RESOLUTION OF 11 JULY 2007

ON THE CONVENING OF THE INTERGOVERNMENTAL CONFERENCE: OPINION OF THE EUROPEAN PARLIAMENT (ARTICLE 48 OF THE EU TREATY)

(11222/2007 – C6-0206/2007 – 2007/0808(CNS))

The European Parliament,

– having regard to Article 48(2) of the Treaty on European Union, pursuant to which the Council consulted Parliament (C6-0206/2007),

– having regard to the Treaty on European Union and the Treaty establishing the European Community,

– having regard to the Treaty establishing a Constitution for Europe signed in Rome on 29 October 2004 (hereafter referred to as 'the Constitutional Treaty'),

– having regard to the Charter of Fundamental Rights of the European Union signed and proclaimed in Nice on 7 December 2000,

– having regard to the Laeken Declaration of 15 December 2001 on the future of the Union,

– having regard to the Berlin Declaration of 25 March 2007 on the occasion of the fiftieth anniversary of the signature of the Treaties of Rome,

– having regard to its resolutions of 12 January 2005 on the Treaty establishing a Constitution for Europe[1] and of 7 June 2007 on the roadmap for the Union's constitutional process[2],

– having regard to the resolution of the European Economic and Social Committee of 30 May 2007 on the roadmap for the constitutional process and to the opinion of the Committee of the Regions of 6 June 2007 on relaunching the process of reforming the European Union in anticipation of the European Council of 21 and 22 June 2007,

– having regard to the joint parliamentary meeting on the future of Europe held on 11 and 12 June 2007 in Brussels,

– having regard to the Presidency Conclusions of the European Council held in Brussels on 21 and 22 June 2007 setting out the mandate for the IGC,

– having regard to the report of the Committee on Constitutional Affairs (A6-0279/2007),

Whereas:

A. two years of reflection on the future of Europe have confirmed the need to safeguard and to improve the content of the innovations of the Constitutional Treaty in terms of democracy, efficiency and transparency, in order to ensure the proper functioning of the European Union as well as to enhance the rights of its citizens and its role in the world,

B. this view is broadly shared by the national parliaments of the Member States and the European Parliament, whose representatives worked out the basis for these innovations within the Convention entrusted with drafting the Charter of Fundamental Rights and in the European Convention,

C. the European Council of June 2007 agreed on convening an IGC with a mandate to transform most of the innovations contained in the Constitutional Treaty into amendments to the Treaties in force,

---

1 OJ C 247 E, 6.10.2005, p. 88.
2 Texts adopted, P6_TA(2007)0234.

D. that mandate is very precise and also allows the IGC to quickly agree on the modification of some of the innovations contained in the Constitutional Treaty, without jeopardising its substance;

E. the mandate, however, renounces the ambition of creating a single, constitutional treaty to replace the existing ones, abandons terminology which would give citizens a clear understanding of the nature of the acts of the Union, does not maintain a set of symbols which would make it easier for citizens to identify with the European Union, and includes several opt-outs in certain areas where difficulties have been raised by individual Member States,

F. the mandate does not sufficiently address the new challenges which the Union has been facing since the Constitutional Treaty was signed,

G. the European Parliament, as the only institution of the Union directly elected by the citizens, is duty bound to voice the common interest of the European Union in order to strengthen European construction and the Community method, which, for more than 50 years, have been a source of peace, stability and prosperity,

1. Welcomes the efforts deployed by the German Presidency of the Council to achieve unanimous agreement at the European Council of 21 and 22 June 2007;

2. Takes note of the mandate for the IGC which was agreed by the European Council; welcomes its elaborate precision and the tight timetable for conclusion of the IGC, and calls on the Member States not to retreat from the commitments to which they subscribed in the European Council; expresses a favourable opinion on the convening of the IGC;

3. Regrets, however, that this mandate implies the loss of some important elements that had been agreed during the 2004 IGC, such as the concept of a constitutional treaty, the symbols of the Union, comprehensible names for the legal acts of the Union, a clear statement of the primacy of the law of the Union and the definition of the Union as a Union of citizens and states, and also implies a long delay in the introduction of others;

4. Expresses its concern at the fact that the mandate allows for an increasing number of derogations granted to certain Member States from the implementation of major provisions of the envisaged Treaties that could lead to a weakening of the cohesion of the Union;

5. Regrets that the mandate allows for various drafting changes to the Constitutional Treaty, which give an impression of distrust vis-à-vis the Union and its institutions and thus send a wrong signal to public opinion;

6. Regrets the decreasing European goodwill and political courage of Member State representatives and expresses its concern at the development of attitudes opposed to the European ideals of solidarity and integration;

7. Stresses that the mandate allows for modification of the names of legal acts, but does not provide for any substantial change in their structure or hierarchy, and expresses its intention to closely scrutinise the way in which this will be introduced in the relevant provisions, with a view to guaranteeing political accountability and safeguarding its legislative powers, in particular as regards the scrutiny of delegated acts;

8. Welcomes, nevertheless, the fact that the mandate safeguards much of the substance of the Constitutional Treaty, notably the single legal personality of the Union and the abolition of the 'pillars' structure, the extension of qualified majority voting in the Council and co-decision by Parliament and the Council, the elements of participatory democracy, the legally binding status of the Charter of Fundamental Rights, the enhancement of the coherence of the external action of the Union and the balanced institutional package;

9. Observes that all positive results in terms of strengthening democratic procedures and citizens' rights, extending competences and defining the EU's values and objectives derive exclusively from the work of the European Convention;

10. Welcomes the fact that economic and monetary union is to be recognised in the Treaty on European Union as an objective of the EU;

11. Welcomes the fact that the mandate provides for the introduction of certain new elements into the Treaties, such as the explicit mention of climate change and solidarity in the field of energy;

12. Recalls that the EU has declared itself, both to its own citizens and to the whole world, to be a community of values, that fundamental rights and freedoms form the innermost core of this community of values and that they have been comprehensively expressed in the Charter of Fundamental Rights and recognised by the EU institutions and all the Member States on many occasions; considers, therefore, that if one or more Member States now claim an opt-out from the Charter of Fundamental Rights, this would represent a dramatic setback and cause serious damage to the EU's innermost sense of identity; for this reason, urgently appeals to all Member States once again to make every effort to overcome this internal division and to reach a consensus after all on the complete validity of the Charter;

13. Invites the IGC to conclude its work before the end of 2007, so as to enable the new Treaty to enter into force in good time before the 2009 European elections;

14. Welcomes the strengthening of the modalities of its participation in the IGC at all levels, as agreed by the European Council of June 2007;

15. Reserves its right to make concrete proposals to the IGC on specific items within the scope of the mandate;

16. Will respond in due time to the invitation made by the European Council to deal with the issue of its own composition;

17. Stresses its intention to carefully scrutinise the outcome of the IGC in order to assess whether the reforms agreed during the negotiations comply in a satisfactory way with its interpretation of the mandate;

18. Calls on the Member States and its own representatives to ensure the full transparency of the work done by the IGC, notably by publishing all the documents submitted to it for discussion;

19. Reaffirms its intention to maintain a very close relationship with national parliaments and with civil society during the process of revision of the Treaties;

20. Calls on the IGC to ensure, for reasons of transparency, that the results of its work will also be published in the form of a draft consolidated version of the Treaties;

21. Announces its firm resolve to put forward, after the 2009 elections, new proposals for a further constitutional settlement for the Union, in accordance with the clause on treaty revision[3], since the European Union is a common project that is constantly being renewed;

22. Calls on the EU institutions to put forward specific proposals to involve Union citizens once again in dialogue during the continuation of the constitutional process;

23. Invites its competent committee to consider the possible amendment of its Rules of Procedure so as to lend official character to the European Union flag and anthem chosen in the Constitutional Treaty in its activities and premises;

24. Instructs its President to forward this resolution, constituting its opinion on the convening of the IGC, to the Council, the Commission, the Heads of State or Government and parliaments of the Member States and the European Central Bank.

---

3. See Article IV-443 of the Constitutional Treaty.

REFORMING EUROPE FOR THE 21ST CENTURY

OPINION OF THE EUROPEAN COMMISSION, PURSUANT TO ARTICLE 48 OF THE TREATY ON EUROPEAN UNION, ON THE CONFERENCE OF REPRESENTATIVES OF THE GOVERNMENTS OF THE MEMBER STATES CONVENED TO REVISE THE TREATIES

Brussels, 10.7.2007

COM(2007) 412 final

I. REFORMING EUROPE TOGETHER

Europe has changed, the world has changed. The 21st century brings new challenges and new opportunities. The interaction of economies and peoples worldwide – whether by communication, trade, migration, shared security concerns or cultural exchange – is in constant evolution. In such a globalised world, Europe needs to be competitive to secure economic growth and more and better jobs, in order to achieve an overall sustainable development. Climate change calls for a response that must be both global and local. Demographic change has shifted some of the old certainties about the patterns of how society works. New security threats call for new strategies and policies. In all these areas, Europe needs to be equipped for change. Tomorrow's prosperity requires new skills, new ways of working, and political, economic and social reforms. European society has the creativity and the ability to respond to these challenges. It has a bedrock of core values – freedom, human dignity, solidarity, tolerance, social justice, the rule of law – which have proved their worth. But to preserve and consolidate these values, Europe needs to adapt. It also needs the levers to turn intentions into reality. Member States cannot cope with the challenges of today or of the future on their own: only a collective effort – applied in full respect for subsidiarity – can provide the right response. This is the task of the European Union, and this is why it needs to have the right treaties, the right institutions and the right working methods.

The test for Europe is the delivery of policies which meet the expectations and aspirations of citizens: a vision of a Europe ready to work together to realise a common future.

The European Union is uniquely well placed to find the answers to today's most pressing questions. A Europe of 27 or more Member States gives the opportunity to act on a continental scale and to face up to issues which transcend national boundaries. After fifty years of integration and enlargement, the vision set out by Europe's founding fathers holds as good as ever. Common solutions are often the only viable approach to achieve the right responses for Europe in the globalised world: to modernise the European economy to face new competition, to keep Europe as the forefront of efforts to address climate change worldwide, to secure sustainable energy supplies, to manage migration effectively, to combat terrorism, to help developing countries to fight poverty, and to see European values promoted effectively in the global community. The European Union has the potential to reinforce its policies in all these areas: but that potential must not be held back by outdated ways of working.

To realise its potential, the European Union needs modernisation and reform. Policy provisions need to be updated to reflect the demands of today. The delicate balance of the Union's institutional mix still provides the best combination to bring together Europe's strengths. The "Community method" – and more particularly the European Commission's special role and its right of initiative – is key to the success of the European system. But the instruments used must keep pace with the needs of the enlarged Union. They need to be effective and cohesive, overcoming the inevitable complications of dealing with a diverse Europe of 27 Member States to make a reality of the EU's common vision: institutions and working methods must enjoy streamlined decision-making equal to the fast-moving challenges of today. They also need to be democratic – modern European society rightly demands high standards of accountability, transparency and participation. The legitimacy of the European project must be grounded both in what it does, and how it acts.

* * *

Over the past decade, the European Union has been looking for the right way forward to modernise and to respond better to the concerns and aspirations of its citizens. The Commission has always been an active participant in this process. The Laeken Declaration set out where the EU needed reform. The enlargement of 2004 and 2007 intensified the need for the way the Union works to be updated. The Convention and the Inter-Governmental Conference of 2004 sought to provide an answer in the form of the treaty establishing a Constitution for Europe. The Commission has always strongly supported the Constitutional Treaty as providing the right response to the challenges Europe faces. The Constitutional Treaty, despite being ratified in a majority of Member States, failed to secure unanimous support. The period of reflection helped the Union to find a springboard for a resolution, with the Commission leading the way through the Plan D initiative[1] to spark ideas about how to make the EU more democratic, transparent and effective.

With ratification of the Constitutional Treaty at a standstill, the need to reform Europe's way of working remained as compelling as ever. The European Commission set out to implement a new agenda, which won support at the Hampton Court informal European Council of October 2005 and was pursued in the twin track approach set out in the "Citizens Agenda"[2]. This showed that to address the policy imperatives facing Europe, we need the right tools and the right working methods. The steps laid out towards an institutional settlement – a framework at the European Council in June 2006, the Berlin Declaration in March 2007, and a comprehensive agreement on the elements for reform in June 2007 – have been realised. At the same time, the European Union has confirmed to European citizens its commitment to policy reform from economic growth to job creation, from energy to migration, from climate change to innovation. In all these areas, Europe has delivered results.

As well as celebrating the 50th anniversary of the Treaty of Rome, the Berlin Declaration made a commitment to putting the Union on a new common basis before the European Parliament elections of 2009. After a period of political consultations, the European Council of June 2007 agreed to convene an Inter-Governmental Conference (IGC) in July 2007. A precise mandate was set out detailing the elements of reform. The task of the IGC is to agree the text of a Reform Treaty to "amend the existing Treaties with a view to enhancing the efficiency and democratic legitimacy of the enlarged Union, as well as the coherence of its external action".

The agreement on the mandate confirms the twin track strategy as the right approach for the Union. Europe can best tackle institutional change when the institutions show their commitment to deliver on the political, economic and social imperatives. The Union seeks to serve its citizens, to deliver results to make their lives more prosperous and more secure, and to cement a Europe based on the values on which 50 years of European integration have been built.

II. THE REFORM TREATY

The European Council of June 2007 agreed a precise mandate for the Inter-Governmental Conference. The mandate was the fruit of a carefully crafted compromise. Together with many positive elements, which are to be welcomed, this compromise meant that some of the changes agreed in the 2004 IGC were not retained, and a number of derogations were granted to individual Member States. The disappearance of some elements, including some symbolic ones, as well as changes that reduced the readability of the Treaty text, were necessary parts of a package agreement which could be subscribed to by all Member States. The Commission actively contributed to this compromise by finding solutions which balanced political realism with ambition. Compared with the existing Treaties, the changes proposed will leave the European Union with a sound institutional and political basis to meet the expectations of its citizens.

The proposed Reform Treaty will amend the EU's two core treaties. The result will be a legal framework designed to give the Union the tools it needs to meet the challenges of the future, promoting reform while respecting the strong foundations of the established institutional balance which has served Europe so well over the past fifty years.

---

1. The Commission's contribution to the period of reflection and beyond: Plan D for Democracy, Dialogue and Debate - COM(2005) 494 , 13.10.2005.
2. A Citizens Agenda: Delivering results for Europe - COM(2006) 211, 10.5.2006.

The mandate set out in considerable detail how the Inter-Governmental Conference (IGC) will put together the Reform Treaty. It defines the scope of the IGC, and is the exclusive basis for the IGC, detailing where the innovations agreed at the 2004 IGC will be taken on board and where specific new elements are brought in. As such it gives a clear picture of the two treaties of equal status which will emerge from the process to be presented for ratification.

The mandate provides the right basis for a swift and efficient IGC able to agree a treaty for early ratification. The goal set by the European Council of ensuring ratification before the European Parliament elections in June 2009 is both desirable and realistic. This goal should be met.

The European Council emphasised that during the IGC and during the process of ratification, the EU should reinforce communication with its citizens, providing them with full and comprehensive information and involving them in permanent dialogue. The approach chosen – amending the existing treaties – makes it particularly important to communicate the proposed reforms and their underlying rationale, and to make available as soon as possible an easily accessible and readable text of the Treaties.

A More Democratic and Transparent Europe

With the Reform Treaty, Europe's democratic infrastructure will be refreshed and reinforced. It will offer more open institutions and more opportunities for Europeans to see their voice heard in the work of the Union. A new section of the treaty lays out the principles underlying the Union's democratic accountability.

- The increase of co-decision in around 50 areas will see the European Parliament placed on an equal footing with the Council for the vast bulk of EU legislation. This will include keyareas of policy including freedom, security and justice. The Parliament will also see important new powers over the budget and international agreements.
- National parliaments will have greater opportunities to be involved in the work of the EU while respecting the established roles of the EU institutions. This includes a two-stage procedure to monitor subsidiarity which will allow national parliaments to draw concerns to the attention of the Commission: if a majority share the same concerns about a particular proposal, the Commission, as well as the option to withdraw or amend, may choose to maintain its draft and explain its reasoning for final decision by the European Parliament and the Council of Ministers.
- Citizens and national parliaments will see the decisions taken by their governments at first hand through opening the legislative discussions in the Council of Ministers to the public.
- The Citizens' Initiative will create a possibility for a million citizens from different Member States – out of the Union's population of almost 500 million – to trigger an invitation to the Commission to bring forward a new proposal.
- The relationship between the Member States and the European Union will become clearer with the clear categorisation of competences.
- The Reform Treaty will make clear that Member States remain inside the Union by their own choosing, with a provision recognising that withdrawal from the EU is an option.

A more effective Europe

To turn policy aspirations into effective change for citizens, the EU needs the capacity to act. That requires institutions and working methods which are effective and streamlined. The Community method, the Union's unique mix of institutions, provides the basic structure to enable the interests of different states and peoples in Europe to be married with the interests of the Union as a whole. The Commission attaches particular importance to the primacy of EU law, clearly established in existing case law and recognised in the mandate. It will continue to use its powers in areas such as competition policy to deliver the benefits of the Internal Market to its citizens.

The Reform Treaty would update the Union's institutional system to reflect the need for the enlarged Union to adapt policies to a fast-moving world.

- The Reform Treaty will bring swifter and more consistent decisions to the policy areas of freedom, security and justice. This will mean a step change in Europe's ability to combat terrorism, to tackle crime and human trafficking, and to manage migratory flows. Member States which have decided not to participate in all aspects of freedom, security and justice policies might choose to play a full part in those areas of activity in the future.
- The Union will have an improved ability to act in areas of major priority for today's Union, through new and reinforced legal bases in areas including energy policy, public health and civil protection, and new provisions on climate change, services of general interest, research and technological development, territorial cohesion, commercial policy, space, humanitarian aid, sport, tourism, and administrative co-operation.
- Streamlined procedures for economic governance will enhance co-ordination and facilitate decision-taking in the euro area.
- Qualified majority voting in the Council of Ministers will ensure that common issues can be tackled through common decision-making, fairly reflecting the varying sizes of the EU's Member States. The extension of qualified majority voting to more than 40 new cases will make a reality of EU action in these areas.
- A simplified way of calculating qualified majority voting will strengthen the Council's efficiency and provide a clear balance between the number of Member States and the size of their population, once applied in November 2014.
- Where at least nine Member States would like to take collective action inside the Union framework, they will be able to use enhanced co-operation procedures. In particular, the path to enhanced co-operation is smoothed in the areas of judicial co-operation in criminal matters and police co-operation. Whilst enhanced co-operation can be a way to take the diversity of the enlarged Union into account, it works within the common framework necessary for all Member States.
- The permanent President of the European Council will, in co-operation with the President of the Commission, ensure a better preparation and continuity in the work of the European Council.
- A streamlined Commission, with reinforced authority for its President, will continue to play its central role in EU decision-making and to reflect different parts of the Union through a system of equal rotation.
- A ceiling on the number of MEPs, with a lower and upper limit for any one Member State, will stabilise citizens' representation in the European Parliament.
- Introducing qualified majority voting and co-decision for future reforms to the Union's judicial system will help this system to adapt to the challenges of the future.
- Arrangements for conducting external policy will reflect the existing balance between the Member States and the institutions, while enabling the EU as a whole to better promote and protect European interests and values at the global level.
- Future changes to policies within existing competences, extensions to qualified majority voting and use of co-decision can be agreed without needing to call a new IGC, while preserving the need for unanimous agreement.
- The confusing distinction between the "European Community" and the "European Union" will be brought to an end.

A Europe of rights and values, solidarity and security

The Reform Treaty will reinforce the imperatives of solidarity and security in the Union. These bind together the Union, the Member States and Europe's citizens and encapsulate a Union of mutual support and mutual protection. At the same time, practical steps will be taken in the new Treaty to develop EU action in areas like climate change and health, and give the Union new possibilities to promote greater solidarity and cohesion throughout Europe. The extension of the Union's capacity to act in freedom, security and justice will bring direct benefits in terms of the Union's ability to fight crime and terrorism. The Reform Treaty will also introduce a new emphasis on the rights of individuals as citizens in the Union.

- The Union's values and objectives will be set down more clearly than ever before. They will serve as a point of reference for European citizens, and will encapsulate what Europe has to offer to partners worldwide. They show how the European Union balances different goals for Europe, pursuing sustainable development while promoting political, economic and social objectives.
- The Charter of Fundamental Rights will offer Europeans guarantees with the same legal status as the treaties themselves, bringing together civil, political, economic and social rights which the Union's action must respect. Its provisions will also apply in full to acts of implementation of Union law, even if not in all Member States. The Union will be able to join the unique system of human rights protection established by the European Convention of Human Rights.
- Gaps in judicial protection ensured by the European Court of Justice will be filled to ensure jurisdiction in freedom, security and justice and to improve the individuals' rights of recourse to the Court.
- The new solidarity clause will give force to the obligation of Member States to support each other in the event of terrorist attack, natural or man-made disaster.
- The need for solidarity in the area of energy is given special prominence in the Union's powers to help in case of shortage of supply, as well as emphasising that solidarity is an important aspect of new provisions on energy.
- New provisions on civil protection, humanitarian aid and public health all aim at boosting the Union's ability to respond to threats to the security of European citizens.
- The new horizontal social clause will give prominence to the Union's commitment to employment and social protection, and the role of the regions and the social partners will be confirmed as part of the political, economic and social fabric of the Union.

Europe as an actor on the global stage

One of the particular challenges for the European Union is its ability to harness its economic, political and diplomatic strengths to promote European interests and values worldwide. Globalisation has sharpened the need to address the most pressing issues – sustainable development, competitiveness, climate change, energy, terrorism, migration, the fight against poverty – which link both internal and external policy. Prosperity, freedom and security all depend on Europe's ability to project itself worldwide. This has put the spotlight on the potential for combining the particular assets of all Member States with the collective weight of the Union as a whole, in full respect of the Union's institutional balance. To make a success of external policy, the Union's external policy instruments need to be geared to work together to best effect. The mandate maximises this coherence by ensuring that all external action policies – such as CFSP, trade, enlargement, development, and humanitarian assistance – are on an equal political and legal footing.

The Reform Treaty will develop the Union's capacity to act by bringing together Europe's external policy tools, both in policy development and policy delivery. It will give Europe a clear voice in relations with our partners worldwide, and sharpen the impact and visibility of our message. It will also bring more coherence between the different strands of EU external policy – such as diplomacy, security, trade, development, humanitarian aid, and international negotiations on a range of global issues. This will mean an EU able to play a more responsive and effective part in global affairs.

- Establishing a single legal personality of the Union will strengthen the Union's negotiating power, making it even more effective on the world stage and a more visible partner for third countries and international organisations.
- The new High Representative of the Union for Foreign Affairs and Security Policy/Vice-President of the Commission will increase the impact, the coherence and the visibility of the EU's external action.
- The European External Action Service will provide a structure to support the full range of European external policies – as well as the external dimension of internal policies – in a more effective and coherent way.
- This new architecture for external relations will be married with a respect for the particular interests of Member States by retaining specific decision-making procedures in the area of Common Foreign and Security Policy.

- The European Security and Defence Policy will be brought more clearly into the Union, preserving special decision-making arrangements but also paving the way towards reinforced co-operation amongst a smaller group of Member States.

III. OPINION IN ACCORDANCE WITH ARTICLE 48 OF THE TREATY ON EUROPEAN UNION

The Reform Treaty will underpin some of the most deep-seated aspirations of European citizens. It will reinforce core values; it will clarify key issues; it will reassure persistent concerns. Above all, it will give the Union the capacity to deliver change, to make Europeans more secure and prosperous, to open up their opportunities to shape globalisation.

The European Commission considers that the decisions of the European Council will provide a Reform Treaty to adapt the European Union to the needs of the 21st century. The Commission welcomes the convocation of the Inter-Governmental Conference, gives its full support to the mandate as agreed by the European Council, and is committed to contribute to its success.

Europe needs a Reform Treaty to be agreed and ratified ahead of the June 2009 European elections. It is the responsibility of all participants in the Inter-Governmental Conference to create the conditions for this goal to be met.

* * * * *

Draft COUNCIL DECISION ON THE STEPPING UP OF CROSS-BORDER CO-OPERATION, PARTICULARLY IN COMBATING TERRORISM AND CROSS-BORDER CRIME

COUNCIL DECISION 2007/…/JHA

Brussels, 17 September 2007

11896/07

THE COUNCIL OF THE EUROPEAN UNION,

Having regard to the Treaty on European Union, and in particular Article 30(1)(a) and (b), Article 31(1)(a), Article 32 and Article 34(2)(c) thereof,

Having regard to the initiative of the Kingdom of Belgium, the Republic of Bulgaria, the Federal Republic of Germany, the Kingdom of Spain, the French Republic, the Grand Duchy of Luxembourg, the Kingdom of the Netherlands, the Republic of Austria, the Republic of Slovenia, the Slovak Republic, the Italian Republic, the Republic of Finland, the Portuguese Republic, Romania and the Kingdom of Sweden,

Having regard to the Opinion of the European Parliament,

Whereas:

(1) Following the entry into force of the Treaty between the Kingdom of Belgium, the Federal Republic of Germany, the Kingdom of Spain, the French Republic, the Grand Duchy of Luxembourg, the Kingdom of the Netherlands and the Republic of Austria on the stepping up of cross-border co-operation, particularly in combating terrorism, cross-border crime and illegal migration hereinafter ("Prüm Treaty"), this initiative is submitted, in consultation with the European Commission, in compliance with the provisions of the Treaty on European Union, with the aim of incorporating the substance of the provisions of the Prüm Treaty into the legal framework of the European Union.

(2) The conclusions of the European Council meeting in Tampere in October 1999 confirmed the need for improved exchange of information between the competent authorities of the Member States for the purpose of detecting and investigating offences.

(3) In the Hague Programme for strengthening freedom, security and justice in the European Union of November 2004, the European Council set forth its conviction that for that purpose an innovative approach to the cross-border exchange of law enforcement information was needed.

(4) The European Council accordingly stated that the exchange of such information should comply with the conditions applying to the principle of availability. This means that a law enforcement officer in one Member State of the Union who needs information in order to carry out his duties can obtain it from another Member State and that the law enforcement authorities in the Member State that holds this information will make it available for the declared purpose, taking account of the needs of investigations pending in that Member State.

(5) The European Council set 1 January 2008 as the deadline for achieving this objective in the Hague Programme.

(6) Council Framework Decision 2006/960/JHA of 18 December 2006 on simplifying the exchange of information and intelligence between law enforcement authorities of the Member States of the European Union[1] already lays down rules whereby the Member States' law enforcement authorities may exchange existing information and intelligence expeditiously and effectively for the purpose of carrying out criminal investigations or criminal intelligence operations.

(7) The Hague Programme for strengthening freedom, security and justice states also that full use should be made of new technology and that there should also be reciprocal access to national databases, while stipulating that new centralised European databases should be created only on the basis of studies that have shown their added value.

(8) For effective international co-operation it is of fundamental importance that precise information can be exchanged swiftly and efficiently. The aim is to introduce procedures for promoting fast, efficient and inexpensive means of data exchange. For the joint use of data these procedures should be subject to accountability and incorporate appropriate guarantees as to the accuracy and security of the data during transmission and storage as well as procedures for recording data exchange and restrictions on the use of information exchanged.

(9) These requirements are satisfied by the Prüm Treaty. In order to meet the substantive requirements of the Hague Programme for all Member States within the time-scale set by it, the substance of the essential parts of the Prüm Treaty should become applicable to all Member States.

(10) This Decision therefore contains provisions which are based on the main provisions of the Prüm Treaty and are designed to improve the exchange of information, whereby Member States grant one another access rights to their automated DNA analysis files, automated dactyloscopic identification systems and vehicle registration data. In the case of data from national DNA analysis files and automated dactyloscopic identification systems, a hit/no hit system should enable the searching Member State, in a second step, to request specific related personal data from the Member State administering the file and, where necessary, to request further information through mutual assistance procedures, including those adopted pursuant to Framework Decision 2006/960/JHA.

(11) This would considerably speed up existing procedures enabling Member States to find out whether any other Member State, and if so, which, has the information it needs.

(12) Cross-border data comparison should open up a new dimension in crime fighting. The information obtained by comparing data should open up new investigative approaches for Member States and thus play a crucial role in assisting Member States' law enforcement and judicial authorities.

(13) The rules are based on networking Member States' national databases.

(14) Subject to certain conditions, Member States should be able to supply personal and non-personal data in order to improve the exchange of information with a view to preventing criminal offences and maintaining public order and security in connection with major events with a cross-border dimension.

(15) In the implementation of Article 12, Member States may decide to give priority to combating serious crime bearing in mind the limited technical capacities available for transmitting data.

(16) In addition to improving the exchange of information, there is a need to regulate other forms of closer co-operation between police authorities, in particular by means of joint security operations (e.g. joint patrols).

(17) Closer police and judicial co-operation in criminal matters must go hand in hand with respect for fundamental rights, in particular the right to respect for privacy and to protection of personal data, to be guaranteed by special data protection arrangements, which should be tailored to the specific nature of different forms of data exchange. Such data protection provisions should take particular account of the specific nature of cross-border on-line access to databases. Since, with on-line access, it is not possible for the Member State administering the file to make any prior checks, a system ensuring post hoc monitoring should be in place.

(18) The hit/no hit system provides for a structure of comparing anonymous profiles, where additional personal data is exchanged only after a hit, the supply and receipt of which is governed by national law, including the legal assistance rules. This set-up guarantees an adequate system of data protection, it being understood that the supply of personal data to another Member State requires an adequate level of data protection on the part of the receiving Member States.

(19) Aware of the comprehensive exchange of information and data resulting from closer police and judicial co-operation, this Decision seeks to warrant an appropriate level of data protection. It observes the level of protection designed for the processing of personal data in the Council of Europe Convention of 28 January 1981 for the Protection of Individuals with regard to Automatic Processing of Personal Data, the Additional Protocol of 8 November 2001 to the Convention and the principles of

Recommendation No R (87) 15 of the Council of Europe Regulating the Use of Personal Data in the Police Sector.

(20) The data protection provisions contained in this Decision also include data protection principles which were necessary due to the lack of a Framework Decision on data protection in the Third Pillar. This Framework Decision should be applied to the entire area of police and judicial co-operation in criminal matters under the condition that its level of data protection is not lower than the protection laid down in the Council of Europe Convention for the Protection of Individuals with regard to automatic Processing of Personal Data of 28 January 1981 and its additional Protocol of 8 November 2001 and takes account of Recommendation No R (87) 15 of 17 September 1987 of the Committee of Ministers to Member States regulating the use of personal data in the police sector, also where data are not processed automatically.

(21) Since the objectives of this Decision, in particular the improvement of information exchange in the European Union, cannot be sufficiently achieved by the Member States in isolation owing to the cross-border nature of crime fighting and security issues so that the Member States are obliged to rely on one another in these matters, and can therefore be better achieved at European Union level, the Council may adopt measures in accordance with the principle of subsidiarity as set out in Article 5 of the Treaty establishing the European Community, to which Article 2 of the Treaty on European Union refers. In accordance with the principle of proportionality pursuant to Article 5 of the EC Treaty, this Decision does not go beyond what is necessary to achieve those objectives.

(22) This Decision respects the fundamental rights and observes the principles set out in particular in the Charter of Fundamental Rights of the European Union,

HAS DECIDED AS FOLLOWS:

CHAPTER 1

GENERAL ASPECTS

ARTICLE 1 *Aim and scope*

By means of this Decision, the Member States intend to step up cross-border co-operation in matters covered by Title VI of the Treaty, particularly the exchange of information between authorities responsible for the prevention and investigation of criminal offences. To this end, this Decision contains rules in the following areas:

(a) provisions on the conditions and procedure for the automated transfer of DNA profiles, dactyloscopic data and certain national vehicle registration data (Chapter 2);

(b) provisions on the conditions for the supply of data in connection with major events with a cross-border dimension (Chapter 3);

(c) provisions on the conditions for the supply of information in order to prevent terrorist offences (Chapter 4);

(d) provisions on the conditions and procedure for stepping up cross-border police co-operation through various measures (Chapter 5).

CHAPTER 2

ON-LINE ACCESS AND FOLLOW-UP REQUESTS

SECTION 1

DNA PROFILES

ARTICLE 2 *Establishment of national DNA analysis files*

1. Member States shall open and keep national DNA analysis files for the investigation of criminal offences. Processing of data kept in those files, under this Decision, shall be carried out in accordance with this Decision, in compliance with the national law applicable to the processing.

2. For the purpose of implementing this Decision, the Member States shall ensure the availability of reference data from their national DNA analysis files as referred to in the first sentence of paragraph 1. Reference data shall only include DNA profiles established from the non-coding part of DNA and a reference number. Reference data shall not contain any data from which the data subject can be directly identified.

Reference data which is not attributed to any individual ("unidentified DNA-profiles") shall be recognisable as such.

3. Each Member State shall inform the General Secretariat of the Council of the national DNA analysis files to which Articles 2 to 6 apply and the conditions for automated searching as referred to in Article 3(1) in accordance with Article 36.

ARTICLE 3 *Automated searching of DNA profiles*
1. For the investigation of criminal offences, Member States shall allow other Member States' national contact points as referred to in Article 6, access to the reference data in their DNA analysis files, with the power to conduct automated searches by comparing DNA profiles.
Searches may be conducted only in individual cases and in compliance with the requesting Member State's national law.

2. Should an automated search show that a DNA profile supplied matches DNA profiles entered in the receiving Member State's searched file, the national contact point of the searching Member State shall receive in an automated way the reference data with which a match has been found. If no match can be found, automated notification of this shall be given.

ARTICLE 4 *Automated comparison of DNA profiles*
1. For the investigation of criminal offences, the Member States shall, by mutual consent, via their national contact points, compare the DNA profiles of their unidentified DNA-profiles with all DNA profiles from other national DNA analysis files' reference data. Profiles shall be supplied and compared in automated form. Unidentified DNA profiles shall be supplied for comparison only where provided for under the requesting Member State's national law.

2. Should a Member State, as a result of the comparison referred to in paragraph 1, find that any DNA profiles supplied match any of those in its DNA analysis files, it shall, without delay, supply the other Member State's national contact point with the reference data with which a match has been found.

ARTICLE 5 *Supply of further personal data and other information*
Should the procedures referred to in Articles 3 and 4 show a match between DNA profiles, the supply of further available personal data and other information relating to the reference data shall be governed by the national law, including the legal assistance rules, of the requested Member State.

ARTICLE 6 *National contact point and implementing measures*
1. For the purposes of the supply of data as referred to in Articles 3 and 4, each Member State shall designate a national contact point. The powers of the national contact points shall be governed by the applicable national law.

2. Details of technical arrangements for the procedures set out in Articles 3 and 4 shall be laid down in the implementing measures as referred to in Article 33.

ARTICLE 7 *Collection of cellular material and supply of DNA profiles*
Where, in ongoing investigations or criminal proceedings, there is no DNA profile available for a particular individual present within a requested Member State's territory, the requested Member State shall provide legal assistance by collecting and examining cellular material from that individual and by supplying the DNA profile obtained, if:
(a) the requesting Member State specifies the purpose for which this is required;
(b) the requesting Member State produces an investigation warrant or statement issued by the competent authority, as required under that Member State's law, showing that the requirements for collecting and examining cellular material would be fulfilled if the individual concerned were present within the requesting Member State's territory; and
(c) under the requested Member State's law, the requirements for collecting and examining cellular material and for supplying the DNA profile obtained are fulfilled.

SECTION 2

DACTYLOSCOPIC DATA

ARTICLE 8 *Dactyloscopic data*
For the purpose of implementing this Decision, Member States shall ensure the availability of reference data from the file for the national automated fingerprint identification systems established for the prevention and investigation of criminal offences. Reference data shall only include dactyloscopic data and a reference

number. Reference data shall not contain any data from which the data subject can be directly identified. Reference data which is not attributed to any individual ("unidentified dactyloscopic data") must be recognisable as such.

ARTICLE 9 *Automated searching of dactyloscopic data*

1. For the prevention and investigation of criminal offences, Member States shall allow other Member States' national contact points, as referred to in Article 11, access to the reference data in the automated fingerprint identification systems which they have established for that purpose, with the power to conduct automated searches by comparing dactyloscopic data. Searches may be conducted only in individual cases and in compliance with the requesting Member State's national law.

2. The confirmation of a match of dactyloscopic data with reference data held by the Member State administering the file shall be carried out by the national contact point of the requesting Member State by means of the automated supply of the reference data required for a clear match.

ARTICLE 10 *Supply of further personal data and other information*

Should the procedure referred to in Article 9 show a match between dactyloscopic data, the supply of further available personal data and other information relating to the reference data shall be governed by the national law, including the legal assistance rules, of the requested Member State.

ARTICLE 11 *National contact point and implementing measures*

1. For the purposes of the supply of data as referred to in Article 9, each Member State shall designate a national contact point. The powers of the national contact points shall be governed by the applicable national law.

2. Details of technical arrangements for the procedure set out in Article 9 shall be laid down in the implementing measures as referred to in Article 33.

SECTION 3

VEHICLE REGISTRATION DATA

ARTICLE 12 *Automated searching of vehicle registration data*

1. For the prevention and investigation of criminal offences and in dealing with other offences coming within the jurisdiction of the courts or the public prosecution service in the searching Member State, as well as in maintaining public security, Member States shall allow other Member States' national contact points, as referred to in paragraph 2, access to the following national vehicle registration data, with the power to conduct automated searches in individual cases:

(a) data relating to owners or operators; and

(b) data relating to vehicles.

Searches may be conducted only with a full chassis number or a full registration number.

Searches may be conducted only in compliance with the searching Member State's national law.

2. For the purposes of the supply of data as referred to in paragraph 1, each Member State shall designate a national contact point for incoming requests. The powers of the national contact points shall be governed by the applicable national law. Details of technical arrangements for the procedure shall be laid down in the implementing measures as referred to in Article 33.

CHAPTER 3

MAJOR EVENTS

ARTICLE 13 *Supply of non-personal data*

For the prevention of criminal offences and in maintaining public order and security for major events with a cross-border dimension, in particular for sporting events or European Council meetings, Member States shall, both upon request and of their own accord, in compliance with the supplying Member State's national law, supply one another with any non-personal data required for those purposes.

ARTICLE 14 *Supply of personal data*

1. For the prevention of criminal offences and in maintaining public order and security for major events with a cross-border dimension, in particular for sporting events or European Council meetings, Member States shall, both upon request and of their own accord, supply one another with personal data if any final convictions or other circumstances give reason to believe that the data subjects will commit criminal offences

at the events or pose a threat to public order and security, in so far as the supply of such data is permitted under the supplying Member State's national law.

2. Personal data may be processed only for the purposes laid down in paragraph 1 and for the specified events for which they were supplied. The data supplied must be deleted without delay once the purposes referred to in paragraph 1 have been achieved or can no longer be achieved. The data supplied must in any event be deleted after not more than a year.

ARTICLE 15 *National contact point*
For the purposes of the supply of data as referred to in Articles 13 and 14, each Member State shall designate a national contact point. The powers of the national contact points shall be governed by the applicable national law.

CHAPTER 4

MEASURES TO PREVENT TERRORIST OFFENCES

ARTICLE 16 *Supply of information in order to prevent terrorist offences*
1. For the prevention of terrorist offences, Member States may, in compliance with national law, in individual cases, even without being requested to do so, supply other Member States' national contact points, as referred to in paragraph 3, with the personal data and information specified in paragraph 2, in so far as is necessary because particular circumstances give reason to believe that the data subjects will commit criminal offences as referred to in Articles 1 to 3 of Council Framework Decision 2002/475/JHA of 13 June 2002 on combating terrorism[2].

2. The data to be supplied shall comprise surname, first names, date and place of birth and a description of the circumstances giving rise to the belief referred to in paragraph 1.

3. Each Member State shall designate a national contact point for exchange of information with other Member States' national contact points. The powers of the national contact points shall be governed by the applicable national law.

4. The supplying Member State may, in compliance with national law, impose conditions on the use made of such data and information by the receiving Member State. The receiving Member State shall be bound by any such conditions.

CHAPTER 5

OTHER FORMS OF CO-OPERATION

ARTICLE 17 *Joint operations*
1. In order to step up police co-operation, the competent authorities designated by the Member States may, in maintaining public order and security and preventing criminal offences, introduce joint patrols and other joint operations in which designated officers or other officials ("officers") from other Member States participate in operations within a Member State's territory.

2. Each Member State may, as a host Member State, in compliance with its own national law, and with the seconding Member State's consent, confer executive powers on the seconding Member States' officers involved in joint operations or, in so far as the host Member State's law permits, allow the seconding Member States' officers to exercise their executive powers in accordance with the seconding Member State's law. Such executive powers may be exercised only under the guidance and, as a rule, in the presence of officers from the host Member State. The seconding Member States' officers shall be subject to the host Member State's national law. The host Member State shall assume responsibility for their actions.

3. Seconding Member States' officers involved in joint operations shall be subject to the instructions given by the host Member State's competent authority.

4. Member States shall submit declarations as referred to in Article 36 in which they lay down the practical aspects of co-operation.

ARTICLE 18 *Assistance in connection with mass gatherings disasters and serious accidents*
Member States' competent authorities shall provide one another with mutual assistance, in compliance with national law, in connection with mass gatherings and similar major events, disasters and serious accidents, by seeking to prevent criminal offences and maintain public order and security by:

(a) notifying one another as promptly as possible of such situations with a cross-border impact and exchanging any relevant information;
(b) taking and co-ordinating the necessary policing measures within their territory in situations with a cross-border impact;
(c) as far as possible, dispatching officers, specialists and advisers and supplying equipment, at the request of the Member State within whose territory the situation has arisen.

ARTICLE 19 *Use of arms, ammunition and equipment*
1. Officers from a seconding Member State who are involved in a joint operation within another Member State's territory pursuant to Article 17 or 18 may wear their own national uniforms there. They may carry such arms, ammunition and equipment as they are allowed to under the seconding Member State's national law. The host Member State may prohibit the carrying of particular arms, ammunition or equipment by a seconding Member State's officers.

2. Member States shall submit declarations as referred to in Article 36 in which they list the arms, ammunition and equipment that may be used only in legitimate self-defence or in the defence of others. The host Member State's officer in actual charge of the operation may in individual cases, in compliance with national law, give permission for arms, ammunition and equipment to be used for purposes going beyond those specified in the first sentence.
The use of arms, ammunition and equipment shall be governed by the host Member State's law. The competent authorities shall inform one another of the arms, ammunition and equipment permitted and of the conditions for their use.

3. If officers from a Member State make use of vehicles in action under this Decision within another Member State's territory, they shall be subject to the same road traffic regulations as the host Member State's officers, including as regards right of way and any special privileges.

4. Member States shall submit declarations as referred to in Article 36 in which they lay down the practical aspects of the use of arms, ammunition and equipment.

ARTICLE 20 *Protection and assistance*
Member States shall be required to provide other Member States' officers crossing borders with the same protection and assistance in the course of those officers' duties as for their own officers.

ARTICLE 21 *General rules on civil liability*
1. Where officials of a Member State are operating in another Member State pursuant to Article 17, their Member State shall be liable for any damage caused by them during their operations, in accordance with the law of the Member State in whose territory they are operating.

2. The Member State in whose territory the damage referred to in paragraph 1 was caused shall make good such damage under the conditions applicable to damage caused by its own officials.

3. In the case provided for in paragraph 1, the Member State whose officials have caused damage to any person in the territory of another Member State shall reimburse the latter in full any sums it has paid to the victims or persons entitled on their behalf.

4. Where officials of a Member State are operating in another Member State pursuant to Article 18, the latter Member State shall be liable in accordance with its national law for any damage caused by them during their operations.

5. Where the damage referred to in paragraph 4 results from gross negligence or wilful misconduct, the host Member State may approach the seconding Member State in order to have any sums it has paid to the victims or persons entitled on their behalf reimbursed by the latter.

6. Without prejudice to the exercise of its rights vis-à-vis third parties and with the exception of paragraph 3, each Member State shall refrain, in the case provided for in paragraph 1, from requesting reimbursement of damages it has sustained from another Member State.

ARTICLE 22 *Criminal liability*
Officers operating within another Member State's territory under this Decision, shall be treated in the same way as officers of the host Member State with regard to any criminal offences that might be committed by, or against them, save as otherwise provided in another agreement which is binding on the Member States concerned.

ARTICLE 23 *Employment relationship*
Officers operating within another Member State's territory, under this Decision, shall remain subject to the employment law provisions applicable in their own Member State, particularly as regards disciplinary rules.

CHAPTER 6

GENERAL PROVISIONS ON DATA PROTECTION

ARTICLE 24 *Definitions and scope*
1. For the purposes of this Decision:
(a) "processing of personal data" shall mean any operation or set of operations which is performed upon personal data, whether or not by automatic means, such as collection, recording, organisation, storage, adaptation or alteration, sorting, retrieval, consultation, use, disclosure by supply, dissemination or otherwise making available, alignment, combination, blocking, erasure or destruction of data. Processing within the meaning of this Decision shall also include notification of whether or not a hit exists;
(b) "automated search procedure" shall mean direct access to the automated files of another body where the response to the search procedure is fully automated;
(c) "referencing" shall mean the marking of stored personal data without the aim of limiting their processing in future;
(d) "blocking" shall mean the marking of stored personal data with the aim of limiting their processing in future.

2. The following provisions shall apply to data which are or have been supplied pursuant to this Decision, save as otherwise provided in the preceding Chapters.

ARTICLE 25 *Level of data protection*
1. As regards the processing of personal data which are or have been supplied pursuant to this Decision, each Member State shall guarantee a level of protection of personal data in its national law at least equal to that resulting from the Council of Europe Convention for the Protection of Individuals with regard to Automatic Processing of Personal Data of 28 January 1981 and its Additional Protocol of 8 November 2001 and in doing so, shall take account of Recommendation No R (87) 15 of 17 September 1987 of the Committee of Ministers of the Council of Europe to the Member States regulating the use of personal data in the police sector, also where data are not processed automatically.

2. The supply of personal data provided for under this Decision may not take place until the provisions of this Chapter have been implemented in the national law of the territories of the Member States involved in such supply. The Council shall unanimously decide whether this condition has been met.

3. Paragraph 2 shall not apply to those Member States where the supply of personal data as provided for in this Decision has already started pursuant to the Treaty of 27 May 2005 between the Kingdom of Belgium, the Federal Republic of Germany, the Kingdom of Spain, the French Republic, the Grand Duchy of Luxembourg, the Kingdom of the Netherlands and the Republic of Austria on the stepping up of cross-border co-operation, particularly in combating terrorism, cross-border crime and illegal migration ("Prüm Treaty").

ARTICLE 26 *Purpose*
1. Processing of personal data by the receiving Member State shall be permitted solely for the purposes for which the data have been supplied in accordance with this Decision. Processing for other purposes shall be permitted solely with the prior authorisation of the Member State administering the file and subject only to the national law of the receiving Member State. Such authorisation may be granted provided that processing for such other purposes is permitted under the national law of the Member State administering the file.

2. Processing of data supplied pursuant to Articles 3, 4 and 9 by the searching or comparing Member State shall be permitted solely in order to:
(a) establish whether the compared DNA profiles or dactyloscopic data match;
(b) prepare and submit a police or judicial request for legal assistance in compliance with national law if those data match;
(c) record within the meaning of Article 30.

The Member State administering the file may process the data supplied to it in accordance with Articles 3, 4 and 9 solely where this is necessary for the purposes of comparison, providing automated replies to searches or recording pursuant to Article 30. The supplied data shall be deleted immediately following data comparison or automated replies to searches unless further processing is necessary for the purposes mentioned under points (b) and (c) of the first subparagraph.

3. Data supplied in accordance with Article 12 may be used by the Member State administering the file solely where this is necessary for the purpose of providing automated replies to search procedures or recording as specified in Article 30. The data supplied shall be deleted immediately following automated replies to searches unless further processing is necessary for recording pursuant to Article 30. The searching Member State may use data received in a reply solely for the procedure for which the search was made.

ARTICLE 27 *Competent authorities*
Personal data supplied may be processed only by the authorities, bodies and courts with responsibility for a task in furtherance of the aims mentioned in Article 26. In particular, data may be supplied to other entities only with the prior authorisation of the supplying Member State and in compliance with the law of the receiving Member State.

ARTICLE 28 *Accuracy, current relevance and storage time of data*
1. The Member States shall ensure the accuracy and current relevance of personal data. Should it transpire ex officio or from a notification by the data subject, that incorrect data or data which should not have been supplied have been supplied, this shall be notified without delay to the receiving Member State or Member States. The Member State or Member States concerned shall be obliged to correct or delete the data. Moreover, personal data supplied shall be corrected if they are found to be incorrect. If the receiving body has reason to believe that the supplied data are incorrect or should be deleted the supplying body shall be informed forthwith.

2. Data, the accuracy of which the data subject contests and the accuracy or inaccuracy of which cannot be established shall, in accordance with the national law of the Member States, be marked with a flag at the request of the data subject. If a flag exists, this may be removed subject to the national law of the Member States and only with the permission of the data subject or based on a decision of the competent court or independent data protection authority.

3. Personal data supplied which should not have been supplied or received shall be deleted.
Data which are lawfully supplied and received shall be deleted:

(a) if they are not or no longer necessary for the purpose for which they were supplied; if personal data have been supplied without request, the receiving body shall immediately check if they are necessary for the purposes for which they were supplied;
(b) following the expiry of the maximum period for keeping data laid down in the national law of the supplying Member State where the supplying body informed the receiving body of that maximum period at the time of supplying the data.

Where there is reason to believe that deletion would prejudice the interests of the data subject, the data shall be blocked instead of being deleted in compliance with national law. Blocked data may be supplied or used solely for the purpose which prevented their deletion.

ARTICLE 29 *Technical and organisational measures to ensure data protection and data security*
1. The supplying and receiving bodies shall take steps to ensure that personal data is effectively protected against accidental or unauthorised destruction, accidental loss, unauthorised access, unauthorised or accidental alteration and unauthorised disclosure.

2. The features of the technical specification of the automated search procedure are regulated in the implementing measures as referred to in Article 33 which guarantee that:

(a) state-of-the-art technical measures are taken to ensure data protection and data security, in particular data confidentiality and integrity;
(b) encryption and authorisation procedures recognised by the competent authorities are used when having recourse to generally accessible networks; and (c) the admissibility of searches in accordance with Article 30(2), (4) and (5) can be checked.

ARTICLE 30 *Logging and recording; special rules governing automated and non-automated supply*
1. Each Member State shall guarantee that every non-automated supply and every non-automated receipt of personal data by the body administering the file and by the searching body is logged in order to verify the admissibility of the supply. Logging shall contain the following information:

(a) the reason for the supply;
(b) the data supplied;
(c) the date of the supply; and

(d) the name or reference code of the searching body and of the body administering the file.

2. The following shall apply to automated searches for data based on Articles 3, 9 and 12 and to automated comparison pursuant to Article 4:

(a) only specially authorised officers of the national contact points may carry out automated searches or comparisons. The list of officers authorised to carry out automated searches or comparisons, shall be made available upon request to the supervisory authorities referred to in paragraph 5 and to the other Member States.

(b) each Member State shall ensure that each supply and receipt of personal data by the body administering the file and the searching body is recorded, including notification of whether or not a hit exists. Recording shall include the following information:
   (i) the data supplied;
   (ii) the date and exact time of the supply; and
   (iii) the name or reference code of the searching body and of the body administering the file.

The searching body shall also record the reason for the search or supply as well as an identifier for the official who carried out the search and the official who ordered the search or supply.

3. The recording body shall immediately communicate the recorded data upon request to the competent data protection authorities of the relevant Member State at the latest within four weeks following receipt of the request. Recorded data may be used solely for the following purposes:

(a) monitoring data protection;

(b) ensuring data security.

4. The recorded data shall be protected with suitable measures against inappropriate use and other forms of improper use and shall be kept for two years. After the conservation period the recorded data shall be deleted immediately.

5. Responsibility for legal checks on the supply or receipt of personal data lies with the independent data protection authorities or, as appropriate, the judicial authorities of the respective Member States. Anyone can request these authorities to check the lawfulness of the processing of data in respect of their person in compliance with national law. Independently of such requests, these authorities and the bodies responsible for recording shall carry out random checks on the lawfulness of supply, based on the files involved. The results of such checks shall be kept for inspection for 18 months by the independent data protection authorities. After this period, they shall be immediately deleted. Each data protection authority may be requested by the independent data protection authority of another Member State to exercise its powers in accordance with national law. The independent data protection authorities of the Member States shall perform the inspection tasks necessary for mutual co-operation, in particular by exchanging relevant information.

ARTICLE 31 *Data subjects' rights to information and damages*

1. At the request of the data subject under national law, information shall be supplied in compliance with national law to the data subject upon production of proof of his identity, without unreasonable expense, in general comprehensible terms and without unacceptable delays, on the data processed in respect of his person, the origin of the data, the recipient or groups of recipients, the intended purpose of the processing and, where required by national law, the legal basis for the processing. Moreover, the data subject shall be entitled to have inaccurate data corrected and unlawfully processed data deleted. The Member States shall also ensure that, in the event of violation of his rights in relation to data protection, the data subject shall be able to lodge an effective complaint to an independent court or a tribunal within the meaning of Article 6(1) of the European Convention on Human Rights or an independent supervisory authority within the meaning of Article 28 of Directive 95/46/EC of the European Parliament and of the Council of 24 October 1995 on the protection of individuals with regard to the processing of personal data and on the free movement of such data[3] and that he is given the possibility to claim for damages or to seek another form of legal compensation. The detailed rules for the procedure to assert these rights and the reasons for limiting the right of access shall be governed by the relevant national legal provisions of the Member State where the data subject asserts his rights.

2. Where a body of one Member State has supplied personal data under this Decision, the receiving body of the other Member State cannot use the inaccuracy of the data supplied as grounds to evade its liability vis-à-vis the injured party under national law. If damages are awarded against the receiving body because of its use of inaccurate transfer data, the body which supplied the data shall refund the amount paid in damages to the receiving body in full.

ARTICLE 32 *Information requested by the Member States*

The receiving Member State shall inform the supplying Member State on request of the processing of supplied data and the result obtained.

CHAPTER 7

IMPLEMENTING AND FINAL PROVISIONS

ARTICLE 33 *Implementing measures*
The Council shall adopt measures necessary to implement this Decision at the level of the Union in accordance with the procedure laid down in the second sentence of Article 34(2)(c) of the Treaty.

ARTICLE 34 *Costs*
Each Member State shall bear the operational costs incurred by its own authorities in connection with the application of this Decision. In special cases, the Member States concerned may agree on different arrangements.

ARTICLE 35 *Relationship with other instruments*
1. For the Member States concerned, the relevant provisions of this Decision shall be applied instead of the corresponding provisions contained in the Prüm Treaty. Any other provision of the Prüm Treaty shall remain applicable between the contracting parties of the Prüm Treaty.

2. Without prejudice to their commitments under other acts adopted pursuant to Title VI of the Treaty:
(a) Member States may continue to apply bilateral or multilateral agreements or arrangements on cross-border co-operation which are in force on the date this Decision is adopted in so far as such agreements or arrangements are not incompatible with the objectives of this Decision.
(b) Member States may conclude or bring into force bilateral or multilateral agreements or arrangements on cross-border co-operation after this Decision has entered into force in so far as such agreements or arrangements provide for the objectives of this Decision to be extended or enlarged.

3. The agreements and arrangements referred to in paragraphs 1 and 2 may not affect relations with Member States which are not parties thereto.

4. Within four weeks of this Decision taking effect Member States shall inform the Council and the Commission of existing agreements or arrangements within the meaning of paragraph 2(a) which they wish to continue to apply.

5. Member States shall also inform the Council and the Commission of all new agreements or arrangements within the meaning of paragraph 2(b) within 3 months of their signing or, in the case of instruments which were signed before adoption of this Decision, within three months of their entry into force.

6. Nothing in this Decision shall affect bilateral or multilateral agreements or arrangements between Member States and third States.

7. This Decision shall be without prejudice to existing agreements on legal assistance or mutual recognition of court decisions.

ARTICLE 36 *Implementation and declarations*
1. Member States shall take the necessary measures to comply with the provisions of this Decision within one year of this Decision taking effect, with the exception of the provisions of chapter 2 with respect to which the necessary measures shall be taken within three years of this Decision and the Council Decision on the implementation of this Decision taking effect.

2. Member States shall inform the General Secretariat of the Council and the Commission that they have implemented the obligations imposed on them under this Decision and submit the declarations foreseen by this Decision. When doing so, each Member State may indicate that it will apply immediately this Decision in its relations with those Member States which have given the same notification.

3. Declarations submitted in accordance with paragraph 2 may be amended at any time by means of a declaration submitted to the General Secretariat of the Council. The General Secretariat of the Council shall forward any declarations received to the Member States and the Commission.

4. On the basis of this and other information made available by Member States on request, the Commission shall submit a report to the Council by …[4] on the implementation of this Decision accompanied by such proposals as it deems appropriate for any further development.

ARTICLE 37 *Application*
This Decision shall take effect twenty days following its publication in the Official Journal of the European Union.

Done at

For the Council

The President

---

1. OJ L 386, 29.12.2006, p. 89.

2. OJ L 164, 22.6.2002, p. 3.

3 OJ L 281, 23.11.1995, p. 31. Directive as amended by Regulation (EC) No 1882/2003 (OJ L 284, 31.10.2003, p. 1).

4. OJ please insert date: four years after publication of the OJ plus 20 days.

THE LAEKEN DECLARATION THE FUTURE OF THE EUROPEAN UNION

Laeken, 15 December 2001

SN 273/01

I. EUROPE AT A CROSSROADS

For centuries, peoples and states have taken up arms and waged war to win control of the European continent. The debilitating effects of two bloody wars and the weakening of Europe's position in the world brought a growing realisation that only peace and concerted action could make the dream of a strong, unified Europe come true. In order to banish once and for all the demons of the past, a start was made with a coal and steel community. Other economic activities, such as agriculture, were subsequently added in. A genuine single market was eventually established for goods, persons, services and capital, and a single currency was added in 1999. On 1 January 2002 the euro is to become a day-to-day reality for 300 million European citizens.

The European Union has thus gradually come into being. In the beginning, it was more of an economic and technical collaboration. Twenty years ago, with the first direct elections to the European Parliament, the Community's democratic legitimacy, which until then had lain with the Council alone, was considerably strengthened. Over the last ten years, construction of a political union has begun and cooperation been established on social policy, employment, asylum, immigration, police, justice, foreign policy and a common security and defence policy.

The European Union is a success story. For over half a century now, Europe has been at peace. Along with North America and Japan, the Union forms one of the three most prosperous parts of the world. As a result of mutual solidarity and fair distribution of the benefits of economic development, moreover, the standard of living in the Union's weaker regions has increased enormously and they have made good much of the disadvantage they were at.

Fifty years on, however, the Union stands at a crossroads, a defining moment in its existence. The unification of Europe is near. The Union is about to expand to bring in more than ten new Member States, predominantly Central and Eastern European, thereby finally closing one of the darkest chapters in European history: the Second World War and the ensuing artificial division of Europe. At long last, Europe is on its way to becoming one big family, without bloodshed, a real transformation clearly calling for a different approach from fifty years ago, when six countries first took the lead.

The democratic challenge facing Europe

At the same time, the Union faces twin challenges, one within and the other beyond its borders.

Within the Union, the European institutions must be brought closer to its citizens. Citizens undoubtedly support the Union's broad aims, but they do not always see a connection between those goals and the Union's everyday action. They want the European institutions to be less unwieldy and rigid and, above all, more efficient and open. Many also feel that the Union should involve itself more with their particular concerns, instead of intervening, in every detail, in matters by their nature better left to Member States' and regions' elected representatives. This is even perceived by some as a threat to their identity. More importantly, however, they feel that deals are all too often cut out of their sight and they want better democratic scrutiny.

Europe's new role in a globalised world

Beyond its borders, in turn, the European Union is confronted with a fast-changing, globalised world. Following the fall of the Berlin Wall, it looked briefly as though we would for a long while be living in a stable world order, free from conflict, founded upon human rights. Just a few years later, however, there is no such certainty. The eleventh of September has brought a rude awakening. The opposing forces have not gone away: religious fanaticism, ethnic nationalism, racism and terrorism are on the increase, and regional conflicts, poverty and underdevelopment still provide a constant seedbed for them.

What is Europe's role in this changed world? Does Europe not, now that is finally unified, have a leading role to play in a new world order, that of a power able both to play a stabilising role worldwide and to point the way ahead for many countries and peoples? Europe as the continent of humane values, the Magna Carta, the Bill of Rights, the French Revolution and the fall of the Berlin Wall; the continent of liberty, solidarity and above all diversity, meaning respect for others' languages, cultures and traditions. The European Union's one boundary is democracy and human rights. The Union is open only to countries which uphold basic values such as free elections, respect for minorities and respect for the rule of law.

Now that the Cold War is over and we are living in a globalised, yet also highly fragmented world, Europe needs to shoulder its responsibilities in the governance of globalisation. The role it has to play is that of a power resolutely doing battle against all violence, all terror and all fanaticism, but which also does not turn a blind eye to the world's heartrending injustices. In short, a power wanting to change the course of world affairs in such a way as to benefit not just the rich countries but also the poorest. A power seeking to set globalisation within a moral framework, in other words to anchor it in solidarity and sustainable development.

The expectations of Europe's citizens

The image of a democratic and globally engaged Europe admirably matches citizens' wishes. There have been frequent public calls for a greater EU role in justice and security, action against cross-border crime, control of migration flows and reception of asylum seekers and refugees from far-flung war zones. Citizens also want results in the fields of employment and combating poverty and social exclusion, as well as in the field of economic and social cohesion. They want a common approach on environmental pollution, climate change and food safety, in short, all trans-national issues which they instinctively sense can only be tackled by working together. Just as they also want to see Europe more involved in foreign affairs, security and defence, in other words, greater and better coordinated action to deal with trouble spots in and around Europe and in the rest of the world.

At the same time, citizens also feel that the Union is behaving too bureaucratically in numerous other areas. In coordinating the economic, financial and fiscal environment, the basic issue should continue to be proper operation of the internal market and the single currency, without this jeopardising Member States' individuality. National and regional differences frequently stem from history or tradition. They can be enriching. In other words, what citizens understand by "good governance" is opening up fresh opportunities, not imposing further red tape. What they expect is more results, better responses to practical issues and not a European superstate or European institutions inveigling their way into every nook and cranny of life.

In short, citizens are calling for a clear, open, effective, democratically controlled Community approach, developing a Europe which points the way ahead for the world. An approach that provides concrete results in terms of more jobs, better quality of life, less crime, decent education and better health care. There can be no doubt that this will require Europe to undergo renewal and reform.

II. CHALLENGES AND REFORMS IN A RENEWED UNION

The Union needs to become more democratic, more transparent and more efficient. It also has to resolve three basic challenges: how to bring citizens, and primarily the young, closer to the European design and the European institutions, how to organise politics and the European political area in an enlarged Union and how to develop the Union into a stabilising factor and a model in the new, multi-polar world. In order to address them a number of specific questions need to be put.

A better division and definition of competence in the European Union

Citizens often hold expectations of the European Union that are not always fulfilled. And vice versa - they sometimes have the impression that the Union takes on too much in areas where its involvement is not always essential. Thus the important thing is to clarify, simplify and adjust the division of competence between the Union and the Member States in the light of the new challenges facing the Union. This can lead both to restoring tasks to the Member States and to assigning new missions to the Union, or to the extension of existing powers, while constantly bearing in mind the equality of the Member States and their mutual solidarity.

A first series of questions that needs to be put concerns how the division of competence can be made more transparent. Can we thus make a clearer distinction between three types of competence: the exclusive competence of the Union, the competence of the Member States and the shared competence of the Union and the Member States? At what level is competence exercised in the most efficient way? How is the principle of subsidiarity to be applied here? And should we not make it clear that any powers not assigned by the Treaties to the Union fall within the exclusive sphere of competence of the Member States? And what would be the consequences of this?

The next series of questions should aim, within this new framework and while respecting the "*acquis communautaire*", to determine whether there needs to be any reorganisation of competence. How can citizens' expectations be taken as a guide here? What missions would this produce for the Union? And, vice versa, what tasks could better be left to the Member States? What amendments should be made to the Treaty on the various policies? How, for example, should a more coherent common foreign policy and defence policy be developed? Should the Petersberg tasks be updated? Do we want to adopt a more integrated approach to police and criminal law cooperation? How can economic-policy coordination be stepped up? How can we intensify cooperation in the field of social inclusion, the environment, health and food safety? But then, should not the day-to-day administration and implementation of the Union's policy be left more emphatically to the Member States and, where their constitutions so provide, to the regions? Should they not be provided with guarantees that their spheres of competence will not be affected?

Lastly, there is the question of how to ensure that a redefined division of competence does not lead to a creeping expansion of the competence of the Union or to encroachment upon the exclusive areas of competence of the Member States and, where there is provision for this, regions. How are we to ensure at the same time that the European dynamic does not come to a halt? In the future as well the Union must continue to be able to react to fresh challenges and developments and must be able to explore new policy areas. Should Articles 95 and 308 of the Treaty be reviewed for this purpose in the light of the "*acquis jurisprudentiel*"?

Simplification of the Union's instruments

Who does what is not the only important question; the nature of the Union's action and what instruments it should use are equally important. Successive amendments to the Treaty have on each occasion resulted in a proliferation of instruments, and directives have gradually evolved towards more and more detailed legislation. The key question is therefore whether the Union's various instruments should not be better defined and whether their number should not be reduced.

In other words, should a distinction be introduced between legislative and executive measures? Should the number of legislative instruments be reduced: directly applicable rules, framework legislation and non-enforceable instruments (opinions, recommendations, open coordination)? Is it or is it not desirable to have more frequent recourse to framework legislation, which affords the Member States more room for manoeuvre in achieving policy objectives? For which areas of competence are open coordination and mutual recognition the most appropriate instruments? Is the principle of proportionality to remain the point of departure?

More democracy, transparency and efficiency in the European Union

The European Union derives its legitimacy from the democratic values it projects, the aims it pursues and the powers and instruments it possesses. However, the European project also derives its legitimacy from democratic, transparent and efficient institutions. The national parliaments also contribute towards the legitimacy of the European project. The declaration on the future of the Union, annexed to the Treaty of Nice, stressed the need to examine their role in European integration. More generally, the question arises as to what initiatives we can take to develop a European public area.

The first question is thus how we can increase the democratic legitimacy and transparency of the present institutions, a question which is valid for the three institutions.

How can the authority and efficiency of the European Commission be enhanced? How should the President of the Commission be appointed: by the European Council, by the European Parliament or should he be directly elected by the citizens? Should the role of the European Parliament be strengthened? Should we extend the right of co-decision or not? Should the way in which we elect the members of the European Parliament be reviewed? Should a European electoral constituency be created, or should constituencies continue to be determined nationally? Can the two systems be combined?

Should the role of the Council be strengthened? Should the Council act in the same manner in its legislative and its executive capacities? With a view to greater transparency, should the meetings of the Council, at least in its legislative capacity, be public? Should citizens have more access to Council documents? How, finally, should the balance and reciprocal control between the institutions be ensured?

A second question, which also relates to democratic legitimacy, involves the role of national parliaments. Should they be represented in a new institution, alongside the Council and the European Parliament? Should they have a role in areas of European action in which the European Parliament has no competence? Should they focus on the division of competence between Union and Member States, for example through preliminary checking of compliance with the principle of subsidiarity?

The third question concerns how we can improve the efficiency of decision-making and the workings of the institutions in a Union of some thirty Member States. How could the Union set its objectives and priorities more effectively and ensure better implementation? Is there a need for more decisions by a qualified majority? How is the co-decision procedure between the Council and the European Parliament to be simplified and speeded up? What of the six-monthly rotation of the Presidency of the Union? What is the future role of the European Parliament? What of the future role and structure of the various Council formations? How should the coherence of European foreign policy be enhanced? How is synergy between the High Representative and the competent Commissioner to be reinforced? Should the external representation of the Union in international fora be extended further?

Towards a Constitution for European citizens

The European Union currently has four Treaties. The objectives, powers and policy instruments of the Union are currently spread across those Treaties. If we are to have greater transparency, simplification is essential.

Four sets of questions arise in this connection. The first concerns simplifying the existing Treaties without changing their content. Should the distinction between the Union and the Communities be reviewed? What of the division into three pillars?

Questions then arise as to the possible reorganisation of the Treaties. Should a distinction be made between a basic treaty and the other treaty provisions? Should this distinction involve separating the texts? Could this lead to a distinction between the amendment and ratification procedures for the basic treaty and for the other treaty provisions?

Thought would also have to be given to whether the Charter of Fundamental Rights should be included in the basic treaty and to whether the European Community should accede to the European Convention on Human Rights.

The question ultimately arises as to whether this simplification and reorganisation might not lead in the long run to the adoption of a constitutional text in the Union. What might the basic features of such a constitution be? The values which the Union cherishes, the fundamental rights and obligations of its citizens, the relationship between Member States in the Union?

III. CONVENING OF A CONVENTION ON THE FUTURE OF EUROPE

In order to pave the way for the next Intergovernmental Conference as broadly and openly as possible, the European Council has decided to convene a Convention composed of the main parties involved in the debate on the future of the Union. In the light of the foregoing, it will be the task of that Convention to consider the key issues arising for the Union's future development and try to identify the various possible responses.

The European Council has appointed Mr V. Giscard d'Estaing as Chairman of the Convention and Mr G. Amato and Mr J.L. Dehaene as Vice-Chairmen.

Composition

In addition to its Chairman and Vice-Chairmen, the Convention will be composed of 15 representatives of the Heads of State or Government of the Member States (one from each Member State), 30 members of national parliaments (two from each Member State), 16 members of the European Parliament and two Commission representatives. The accession candidate countries will be fully involved in the Convention's proceedings. They will be represented in the same way as the current Member States (one government representative and two national parliament members) and will be able to take part in the proceedings without, however, being able to prevent any consensus which may emerge among the Member States.

The members of the Convention may only be replaced by alternate members if they are not present. The alternate members will be designated in the same way as full members.

The Praesidium of the Convention will be composed of the Convention Chairman and Vice-Chairmen and nine members drawn from the Convention (the representatives of all the governments holding the Council Presidency during the Convention, two national parliament representatives, two European Parliament representatives and two Commission representatives).

Three representatives of the Economic and Social Committee with three representatives of the European social partners; from the Committee of the Regions: six representatives (to be appointed by the Committee of the Regions from the regions, cities and regions with legislative powers), and the European Ombudsman will be invited to attend as observers. The Presidents of the Court of Justice and of the Court of Auditors may be invited by the Praesidium to address the Convention.

Length of proceedings

The Convention will hold its inaugural meeting on 1 March 2002, when it will appoint its Praesidium and adopt its rules of procedure. Proceedings will be completed after a year, that is to say in time for the Chairman of the Convention to present its outcome to the European Council.

Working methods

The Chairman will pave the way for the opening of the Convention's proceedings by drawing conclusions from the public debate. The Praesidium will serve to lend impetus and will provide the Convention with an initial working basis.

The Praesidium may consult Commission officials and experts of its choice on any technical aspect which it sees fit to look into. It may set up ad hoc working parties.

The Council will be kept informed of the progress of the Convention's proceedings. The Convention Chairman will give an oral progress report at each European Council meeting, thus enabling Heads of State or Government to give their views at the same time.

The Convention will meet in Brussels. The Convention's discussions and all official documents will be in the public domain. The Convention will work in the Union's eleven working languages.

Final document

The Convention will consider the various issues. It will draw up a final document which may comprise either different options, indicating the degree of support which they received, or recommendations if consensus is achieved.

Together with the outcome of national debates on the future of the Union, the final document will provide a starting point for discussions in the Intergovernmental Conference, which will take the ultimate decisions.

Forum

In order for the debate to be broadly based and involve all citizens, a Forum will be opened for organisations representing civil society (the social partners, the business world, non-governmental organisations, academia, etc.). It will take the form of a structured network of organisations receiving regular information on the Convention's proceedings. Their contributions will serve as input into the debate. Such organisations may be heard or consulted on specific topics in accordance with arrangements to be established by the Praesidium.

Secretariat

The Praesidium will be assisted by a Convention Secretariat, to be provided by the General Secretariat of the Council, which may incorporate Commission and European Parliament experts.

* * * * *

BMDF TABLES OF EQUIVALENCES

Tables comparing the numbering in the draft Constitution with the Treaty of Lisbon

The following tables have been prepared by the BMDF to show the comparatives between the numbering system used for the Articles in the Treaty establishing a Constitution for Europe and the new numbering system used for the Treaties introduced by the Treaty of Lisbon and described in the annex attached to the Treaty.

The references to the Treaty of Lisbon are:
TEU – Treaty on European Union
TFEU – Treaty on the Functioning of the European Union

Part I: Text of the Constitution

Constitution	Treaty of Lisbon
Article I-1	Article 1 TEU
Article I-2	Article 2 TEU
Article I-3	Article 3 TEU
Article I-4	Article 18 TFEU
Article I-5	Article 4 TEU
Article I-6	-
Article I-7	Article 47 TEU
Article I-8	-
Article I-9	Article 6 TEU
Article I-10	Article 9 TEU, Articles 20, 24 TFEU
Article I-11	Article 35 TEU
Article I-12	Article 2 TFEU
Article I-13	Article 3 TFEU
Article I-14	Article 4 TFEU
Article I-15	Article 5 TFEU
Article I-16	Article 24 TEU
Article I-17	Article 6 TFEU
Article I-18	Article 352 TFEU
Article I-19	Article 13 TEU
Article I-20	Article 14 TEU
Article I-21	Article 15 TEU
Article I-22	Article 15 TEU
Article I-23	Article 16 TEU
Article I-24	Article 16 TEU and Article 236 TFEU
Article I-25	Article 16 TEU
Article I-26	Article 17 TEU and Article 244 TFEU
Article I-27	Article 17 TEU
Article I-28	Article 18 TEU
Article I-29	Article 19 TEU
Article I-30	Article 282 TFEU
Article I-31	Article 285 TFEU
Article I-32	Article 300 TFEU
Article I-33	Article 288 TFEU
Article I-34	Article 289 TFEU
Article I-35	Article 292 TFEU
Article I-36	Article 290 TFEU
Article I-37	Article 291 TFEU
Article I-38	Article 296 TFEU
Article I-39	Article 297 TFEU
Article I-40	-
Article I-41	Article 42 TEU
Article I-42	Article 70 TFEU
Article I-43	Article 222(1) TFEU
Article I-44	Article 20 TEU and Article 330 TFEU
Article I-45	Article 9 TEU
Article I-46	Article 10 TEU
Article I-47	Article 11 TEU and Article 24 TFEU
Article I-48	Article 152 TFEU
Article I-49	Article 228 TFEU
Article I-50	Article 15 TFEU
Article I-51	Article 39 TEU and Article 16 TFEU
Article I-52	Article 17 TFEU
Article I-53	Article 310 TFEU
Article I-54	Article 311 TFEU
Article I-55	Article 312 TFEU
Article I-56	Article 310, 314 TFEU
Article I-57	Article 8 TEU
Article I-58	Article 49 TEU

Constitution	Treaty of Lisbon
Article I-59	Article 7 TEU, Article 354 TFEU
Article I-60	Article 50 TEU

Part II: Charter of Fundamental Rights

Articles II-61–II-114	Charter of Fundamental Rights

Part III: Policies and Functioning of the Union

Article III-115	Article 7 TFEU
Article III-116	Article 8 TFEU
Article III-117	Article 9 TFEU
Article III-118	Article 10 TFEU
Article III-119	Article 11 TFEU
Article III-120	Article 12 TFEU
Article III-121	Article 13 TFEU
Article III-122	Article 14 TFEU
Article III-123	Article 18 TFEU
Article III-124	Article 19 TFEU
Article III-125	Articles 21, 77 TFEU
Article III-126	Article 22 TFEU
Article III-127	Article 23 TFEU
Article III-128	Article 24 TFEU
Article III-129	Article 25 TFEU
Article III-130	Articles 26-27 TFEU
Article III-131	Article 347 TFEU
Article III-132	Article 348 TFEU
Article III-133	Article 45 TFEU
Article III-134	Article 46 TFEU
Article III-135	Article 47 TFEU
Article III-136	Article 48 TFEU
Article III-137	Article 49 TFEU
Article III-138	Article 50 TFEU
Article III-139	Article 51 TFEU
Article III-140	Article 52 TFEU
Article III-141	Article 53 TFEU
Article III-142	Article 54 TFEU
Article III-143	Article 55 TFEU
Article III-144	Article 56 TFEU
Article III-145	Article 57 TFEU
Article III-146	Article 58 TFEU
Article III-147	Article 59 TFEU
Article III-148	Article 60 TFEU
Article III-149	Article 61 TFEU

Constitution	Treaty of Lisbon
Article III-150	Article 62 TFEU
Article III-151	Articles 28-32 TFEU
Article III-152	Article 33 TFEU
Article III-153	Articles 34-35 TFEU
Article III-154	Article 36 TFEU
Article III-155	Article 37 TFEU
Article III-156	Article 63 TFEU
Article III-157	Article 64 TFEU
Article III-158	Article 65 TFEU
Article III-159	Article 66 TFEU
Article III-160	Article 75 TFEU
Article III-161	Article 101 TFEU
Article III-162	Article 102 TFEU
Article III-163	Article 103 TFEU
Article III-164	Article 104 TFEU
Article III-165	Article 105 TFEU
Article III-166	Article 106 TFEU
Article III-167	Article 107 TFEU
Article III-168	Article 108 TFEU
Article III-169	Article 109 TFEU
Article III-170	Articles 110 - 112 TFEU
Article III-171	Article 113 TFEU
Article III-172	Article 114 TFEU
Article III-173	Article 115 TFEU
Article III-174	Article 116 TFEU
Article III-175	Article 117 TFEU
Article III-176	Article 118 TFEU
Article III-177	Article 119 TFEU
Article III-178	Article 120 TFEU
Article III-179	Article 121 TFEU
Article III-180	Article 122 TFEU
Article III-181	Article 123 TFEU
Article III-182	Article 124 TFEU
Article III-183	Article 125 TFEU
Article III-184	Article 126 TFEU
Article III-185	Article 127 TFEU
Article III-186	Article 128 TFEU
Article III-187	Article 129 TFEU
Article III-188	Article 130 TFEU
Article III-189	Article 131 TFEU
Article III-190	Article 132 TFEU
Article III-191	Article 133 TFEU
Article III-192	Article 134 TFEU
Article III-193	Article 135 TFEU
Article III-194	Article 136 TFEU
Article III-195	Article 137 TFEU

Constitution	Treaty of Lisbon	Constitution	Treaty of Lisbon
Article III-196	Article 138 TFEU	Article III-242	Article 97 TFEU
Article III-197	Article 139 TFEU	Article III-243	Article 98 TFEU
Article III-198	Article 140 TFEU	Article III-244	Article 99 TFEU
Article III-199	Article 141 TFEU	Article III-245	Article 100 TFEU
Article III-200	Article 142 TFEU	Article III-246	Article 170 TFEU
Article III-201	Article 143 TFEU	Article III-247	Articles 171-172 TFEU
Article III-202	Article 144 TFEU	Article III-248	Article 179 TFEU
Article III-203	Article 145 TFEU	Article III-249	Article 180 TFEU
Article III-204	Article 146 TFEU	Article III-250	Article 181 TFEU
Article III-205	Article 147 TFEU	Article III-251	Article 182 TFEU
Article III-206	Article 148 TFEU	Article III-252	Articles 183-186 TFEU, 188 TFEU
Article III-207	Article 149 TFEU		
Article III-208	Article 150 TFEU	Article III-253	Articles 187-188 TFEU
Article III-209	Article 151 TFEU	Article III-254	Article 189 TFEU
Article III-210	Article 153 TFEU	Article III-255	Article 190 TFEU
Article III-211	Article 154 TFEU	Article III-256	Article 194 TFEU
Article III-212	Article 155 TFEU	Article III-257	Article 67 TFEU
Article III-213	Article 156 TFEU	Article III-258	Article 68 TFEU
Article III-214	Article 157 TFEU	Article III-259	Article 69 TFEU
Article III-215	Article 158 TFEU	Article III-260	Article 70 TFEU
Article III-216	Article 159 TFEU	Article III-261	Article 71 TFEU
Article III-217	Article 160 TFEU	Article III-262	Article 72 TFEU
Article III-218	Article 161 TFEU	Article III-263	Article 74 TFEU
Article III-219	Articles 162-164 TFEU	Article III-264	Article 76 TFEU
Article III-220	Article 174 TFEU	Article III-265	Article 77 TFEU
Article III-221	Article 175 TFEU	Article III-266	Article 78 TFEU
Article III-222	Article 176 TFEU	Article III-267	Article 79 TFEU
Article III-223	Article 177 TFEU	Article III-268	Article 80 TFEU
Article III-224	Article 178 TFEU	Article III-269	Article 81 TFEU
Article III-225	Article 38 TFEU	Article III-270	Article 82 TFEU
Article III-226	Article 38 TFEU	Article III-271	Article 83 TFEU
Article III-227	Article 39 TFEU	Article III-272	Article 84 TFEU
Article III-228	Article 40 TFEU	Article III-273	Article 85 TFEU
Article III-229	Article 41 TFEU	Article III-274	Article 86 TFEU
Article III-230	Article 42 TFEU	Article III-275	Article 87 TFEU
Article III-231	Article 43 TFEU	Article III-276	Article 88 TFEU
Article III-232	Article 44 TFEU	Article III-277	Article 89 TFEU
Article III-233	Article 191 TFEU	Article III-278	Article 168 TFEU
Article III-234	Articles 192-193 TFEU	Article III-279	Article 173 TFEU
Article III-235	Article 169 TFEU	Article III-280	Article 167 TFEU
Article III-236	Articles 90, 91 TFEU	Article III-281	Article 195 TFEU
Article III-237	Article 92 TFEU	Article III-282	Article 165 TFEU
Article III-238	Article 93 TFEU	Article III-283	Article 166 TFEU
Article III-239	Article 94 TFEU	Article III-284	Article 196 TFEU
Article III-240	Article 95 TFEU	Article III-285	Article 197 TFEU
Article III-241	Article 96 TFEU	Article III-286	Articles 198, 204 TFEU

Constitution	Treaty of Lisbon
Article III-287	Article 199 TFEU
Article III-288	Article 200 TFEU
Article III-289	Article 201 TFEU
Article III-290	Article 202 TFEU
Article III-291	Article 203 TFEU
Article III-292	Article 21 TEU and Article 205 TFEU
Article III-293	Article 22 TEU
Article III-294	Articles 24 – 25 TEU
Article III-295	Article 26 TEU
Article III-296	Article 27 TEU
Article III-297	Article 28 TEU
Article III-298	Article 29 TEU
Article III-299	Article 30 TEU
Article III-300	Article 31 TEU
Article III-301	Article 32 TEU
Article III-302	Article 33 TEU
Article III-303	Article 37 TEU
Article III-304	Article 36 TEU
Article III-305	Article 34 TEU
Article III-306	Article 35 TEU
Article III-307	Article 38 TEU
Article III-308	Article 40 TEU
Article III-309	Article 43 TEU
Article III-310	Article 44 TEU
Article III-311	Article 45 TEU
Article III-312	Article 46 TEU
Article III-313	Article 41 TEU
Article III-314	Article 206 TFEU
Article III-315	Article 207 TFEU
Article III-316	Article 208 TFEU
Article III-317	Article 209 TFEU
Article III-318	Articles 210, 211 TFEU
Article III-319	Article 212 TFEU
Article III-320	Article 213 TFEU
Article III-321	Article 214 TFEU
Article III-322	Article 215 TFEU
Article III-323	Article 216 TFEU
Article III-324	Article 217 TFEU
Article III-325	Article 218 TFEU
Article III-326	Article 219 TFEU
Article III-327	Article 220 TFEU
Article III-328	Article 221 TFEU
Article III-329	Article 222 TFEU
Article III-330	Article 223 TFEU
Article III-331	Article 224 TFEU

Constitution	Treaty of Lisbon
Article III-332	Article 225 TFEU
Article III-333	Article 226 TFEU
Article III-334	Article 227 TFEU
Article III-335	Article 228 TFEU
Article III-336	Article 229 TFEU
Article III-337	Articles 230, 233 TFEU
Article III-338	Article 231 TFEU
Article III-339	Article 232 TFEU
Article III-340	Article 234 TFEU
Article III-341	Article 235 TFEU
Article III-342	Article 237 TFEU
Article III-343	Articles 238, 239 TFEU
Article III-344	Article 240 TFEU
Article III-345	Article 241 TFEU
Article III-346	Article 242 TFEU
Article III-347	Article 245 TFEU
Article III-348	Article 246 TFEU
Article III-349	Article 247 TFEU
Article III-350	Article 248 TFEU
Article III-351	Article 250 TFEU
Article III-352	Article 249 TFEU
Article III-353	Article 251 TFEU
Article III-354	Article 252 TFEU
Article III-355	Article 253 TFEU
Article III-356	Article 254 TFEU
Article III-357	Article 255 TFEU
Article III-358	Article 256 TFEU
Article III-359	Article 257 TFEU
Article III-360	Article 258 TFEU
Article III-361	Article 259 TFEU
Article III-362	Article 260 TFEU
Article III-363	Article 261 TFEU
Article III-364	Article 262 TFEU
Article III-365	Article 263 TFEU
Article III-366	Article 264 TFEU
Article III-367	Article 265 TFEU
Article III-368	Article 266 TFEU
Article III-369	Article 267 TFEU
Article III-370	Article 268 TFEU
Article III-371	Article 269 TFEU
Article III-372	Article 270 TFEU
Article III-373	Article 271 TFEU
Article III-374	Article 272 TFEU
Article III-375	Articles 273 – 274 and Article 344 TFEU
Article III-376	Article 275 TFEU

Constitution	Treaty of Lisbon
Article III-377	Article 276 TFEU
Article III-378	Article 277 TFEU
Article III-379	Articles 278, 279 TFEU
Article III-380	Article 280 TFEU
Article III-381	Article 281 TFEU
Article III-382	Article 283 TFEU
Article III-383	Article 284 TFEU
Article III-384	Article 287 TFEU
Article III-385	Article 286 TFEU
Article III-386	Article 305 TFEU
Article III-387	Article 306 TFEU
Article III-388	Article 307 TFEU
Article III-389	Article 301 TFEU
Article III-390	Article 302 TFEU
Article III-391	Article 303 TFEU
Article III-392	Article 304 TFEU
Article III-393	Article 308 TFEU
Article III-394	Article 309 TFEU
Article III-395	Article 293 TFEU
Article III-396	Article 294 TFEU
Article III-397	Article 295 TFEU
Article III-398	Article 298 TFEU
Article III-399	Article 15 TFEU
Article III-400	Article 243 TFEU
Article III-401	Article 299 TFEU
Article III-402	Article 312 TFEU
Article III-403	Article 313 TFEU
Article III-404	Article 314 TFEU
Article III-405	Article 315 TFEU
Article III-406	Article 316 TFEU
Article III-407	Article 317 TFEU
Article III-408	Article 318 TFEU
Article III-409	Article 319 TFEU
Article III-410	Article 320 TFEU
Article III-411	Article 321 TFEU
Article III-412	Article 322 TFEU
Article III-413	Article 323 TFEU
Article III-414	Article 324 TFEU
Article III-415	Article 325 TFEU
Article III-416	Article 326 TFEU
Article III-417	Article 327 TFEU
Article III-418	Article 328 TFEU
Article III-419	Article 329 TFEU
Article III-420	Article 331 TFEU
Article III-421	Article 332 TFEU
Article III-422	Article 333 TFEU

Constitution	Treaty of Lisbon
Article III-423	Article 334 TFEU
Article III-424	Article 349 TFEU
Article III-425	Article 345 TFEU
Article III-426	Article 335 TFEU
Article III-427	Article 336 TFEU
Article III-428	Article 337 TFEU
Article III-429	Article 338 TFEU
Article III-430	Article 339 TFEU
Article III-431	Article 340 TFEU
Article III-432	Article 341 TFEU
Article III-433	Article 342 TFEU
Article III-434	Article 343 TFEU
Article III-435	Article 351 TFEU
Article III-436	Article 346 TFEU

Part IV: General and Final Provisions

Article IV-437	-
Article IV-438	-
Article IV-439	-
Article IV-440	Article 52 TEU and Article 355 TFEU
Article IV-441	Article 350 TFEU
Article IV-442	Article 51 TEU
Article IV-443	Article 48 TEU
Article IV-444	Article 48 TEU
Article IV-445	Article 48 TEU
Article IV-446	Article 53 TEU, Article 356 TFEU
Article IV-447	Article 54 TEU, Article 357 TFEU
Article IV-448	Article 55 TEU and Article 358 TFEU

GENERAL INDEX

*The General Index follows the new numbering system introduced by the Treaty of Lisbon. The Index covers the Treaty on European Union (**TEU**) and the Treaty on the Functioning of the European Union (**TFEU**), together with the Protocols and Declarations, and is intended to be a guide to the more important areas.*
*References to the provisions of the Charter of Fundamental Rights (**Charter**) are to the page number of that provision.*
*Protocols (**Prot.**) and Declarations (**Decl.**) have page references.*

		Page
A		
Administrative co-operation	74, 197 TFEU	42, 81
Advisory bodies:		
- Committee of the Regions	300(3), 305 TFEU	108, 109
- Economic and Social Committee	300(2), 301 TFEU	108
- General provisions	300 TFEU	108
Agriculture:		
- General provisions	38 TFEU *et. seq.*	34
- Products covered by the provisions	Annex I	123
Aids granted by Member States	107 TFEU	52
Aims of the Union	3(1) TEU	3
Animal welfare	13 TFEU	28
Areas for supporting, co-ordinating and complementary action	6 TFEU	27
Asylum:		
- Area of freedom, security and justice	67(2) TFEU	41
- Fundamental right	Charter (Art. 18)	271
- Policies on border checks, asylum and immigration	77 - 78 TFEU	42 – 43
Autonomous social dialogue	152 TFEU	67
Authentic texts	55 TEU and 358 TFEU	23, 122
B		
'Bridging' clauses – *see 'passerelle' clauses*		
Broad economic policy guidelines	120 - 121 TFEU	56
Budget:		
- Budgetary and financial Principles	310 TFEU	110
- Budgetary procedure	313 - 316 TFEU	111 -113
- Common foreign and security policy	41 TEU	17
- Implementation of the Budget	317 - 324 TFEU	113 -115
C		
Candidate in municipal and European elections:		
- Detailed arrangements	22 TFEU	31
- Fundamental right	Charter (Art. 39, 40)	274
- General provisions	20(2)(b) and 22 TFEU	30 - 31
Capital and payments	63 TFEU *et. seq.*	40
Categories of competence	2 TFEU	26
Charter of Fundamental Rights:		
- General provisions	6(1) TEU	4
- Charter	Charter	269
- Declarations by the UK, Poland and the Czech Republic	Declarations 1, 53, 61, 62	211, 225 227
- Explanations relating to the Charter	Charter Explanations	277
- Protocol on application to the UK	Protocol 7	136
Checks on persons at borders	67, 77 TFEU	41, 42
Churches and non-confessional organisations	17 TFEU	29
Citizenship of the Union:		
- Fundamental rights	Charter (Art. 39- 46)	274
- General provisions	18 TFEU	30
- Policies	18 to 25 TFEU	30 - 31
Citizens' initiatives	8B TEU, 24 TFEU	5, 31
Civil Protection	196 TFEU	81

		Page
Climate change	191 TFEU	78
Closer co-operation:		
- Competence of the Union	20 TEU	11
- General provisions	20 TEU, 330 TFEU	11, 116
- Procedures	326 to 334 TFEU	116 – 117
- Solidarity	222(1) TFEU	89
Cohesion Fund (economic, social and territorial):		
- General provisions	177 TFEU	76
- Protocol		
Comitology	291 TFEU	105
Commission:		
- Delegated regulations	290 TFEU	104
- General provisions	244 TFEU *et. seq.*	94
- Purpose and structure	17 TEU, 244 TFEU	9, 94
Committees:		
- Committee of Inquiry on Union law	226 TFEU	91
- Committee of the Regions	300, 305 TFEU	108, 109
- Conciliation Committee on legislation	294(10) TFEU	106
- Conciliation Committee on the budget	314(5) TFEU	112
- Economic and Financial Committee	126(4), 134 TFEU	58, 61
- Economic and Social Committee	300, 301 TFEU	108
- Employment Committee	150 TFEU	67
- European Social Fund Committee	163 TFEU	70
- International agreements	207(3), 218(4) TFEU	84, 87
- Parliamentary Committees for Union Affairs	Protocol 1, Art. 10	130
- Permanent Representatives of the Member States (COREPER)	16(7) TEU	9
- Political and Security Committee	38, 43 TEU	17, 19
- Rules governing the committees	242 TFEU	94
- Social Protection Committee	160 TFEU	70
- Standing committee on internal security	71 TFEU	41
- Transport advisory committee	99 TFEU	50
Common Agricultural Policy:		
- Animal welfare	13 TFEU	28
- General provisions	38 TFEU *et seq.*	34
- Shared competence	4(2)(d) TFEU	27
Common commercial policy:		
- Exclusive competence	3(1) TFEU	26
- General provisions	206 to 207 TFEU	83 - 84
- Transitional provisions in EMU	143(1) TFEU	65
Common Fisheries Policy:		
- Animal welfare	13 TFEU	28
- Exclusive competence	3(1)(d) TFEU	26
- General provisions	38, 43(2) TFEU	34, 35
- Shared competence	4(2)(d) TFEU	27
Common Foreign and Security Policy:		
- Closer co-operation between Member States	42(7) TEU	19
- Competence of the Union	2(4) TFEU	26
- Diplomatic and consular missions	35 TEU	16
- Enhanced co-operation	329(2), 331(2) TFEU	116, 117
- Financial provisions	41 TEU	17
- General provisions	21 TEU	12
- NATO	42(2)&(7) TEU	18 - 19
- Political and Security Committee	38 TEU	17
- Permanent structured co-operation	42(6), 46 TEU	19, 20
- Restrictive measures	215 TFEU	86
- Role of Member States	24(3) TEU	13
- Specific provisions for implementation	24(1) TEU	13
- Tasks	42(1)&(5), 43 TEU	18, 19
- Tasks allocated to specific Member States	43 to 44 TEU	19
- High Representative - general	18, 24(1) TEU	10, 13
- High Representative - policy	27 TEU	14
- Voting by Council	28, 31 TEU	14, 15

		Page
Common Security and Defence Policy:		
- Closer co-operation	46 TEU	20
- European Defence Agency	42(3), 45 TEU	18, 19
- General provisions	42, 43 TEU	18, 19
- Permanent structured co-operation	20 TEU	20
- Political and Security Committee	43(2) TEU	19
- Protocol on permanent structured co-operation	Protocol 4	133
- Specific provisions	42 TEU	18
- Union competence	24 TEU	13
- Voting in Council	42(4), 43(2), 46(3) TEU	18, 19, 20
Competences:		
- Categories	2 TFEU	26
- Common Security and Defence Policy	24 TEU	13
- Co-ordination of economic and employment policies	5 TFEU	26
- Enhanced co-operation	20 TEU	11
- Exclusive competences	3 TFEU	26
- Exercise of competences	288 - 299 TFEU	104 – 107
- Extent of competence – legal personality	Declaration 24	218
- Flexibility clause	352 TFEU	120
- Freedom, security and justice	4, 67 TFEU	27, 41
- Fundamental principles	5 TEU	4
- General provisions	2 to 6 TFEU	26 – 27
- Legislative acts	289 TFEU	104
- Member States	4 & 5 TEU	4
- Non-legislative acts (Recommendations)	292 TFEU	105
- Shared competences	4 TFEU	27
- Supporting action	6 TFEU	27
Competition rules:		
- Exclusive competence of the Union	3(1) TFEU	26
- General provisions	101 TFEU *et. seq.*	50
- Commission's role	104(2)(d), 105 TFEU,	51
	106(3) TFEU	52
Conferring of competences	1 TEU	3
Consistency of policy application	7 TFEU	28
Consumer protection:		
- Fundamental right	Charter (Art. 38)	273
- General provisions	4(2)(f), 12, 169 TFEU	27, 28, 73
- Internal market	114(3) TFEU	54
Co-operation between institutions of the Union	295 TFEU	107
Co-operation with regard to internal security	71 TFEU	41
Co-operation with third countries and humanitarian aid:		
- Development co-operation	208 TFEU	84
- Economic, financial and technical co-operation with third countries	212 TFEU	85
- General provisions	8 TEU	5
- Humanitarian aid	214 TFEU	86
Co-ordination of economic policies	2(3), 5 TFEU	26, 27
Co-ordination of policies of Member States	1 TEU, 5 TFEU	3, 27
Copenhagen criteria	2 TEU	3
COREPER (Permanent Representatives of the Member States)	16(7) TEU, 240 TFEU	9, 93
Council configurations	16 TEU, 236 TFEU	8, 93
Council of Europe:		
- Education	165(3) TFEU	71
- Union's relations with international organisations	220 TFEU	89
- Vocational training	166 TFEU	71
Council:		
- Declaration on voting for 2014 to 2017, 2017 onwards	Declaration 7	212
- Detailed provisions	237 TFEU *et. seq.*	93
- General provisions	16 TEU	8
- Protocol on transitional provisions	Protocol 11	138
- Voting - ordinary legislative procedure	16 TEU, 238(2) TFEU,	8, 93
	294 TFEU	105

		Page
Court of Auditors	285 TFEU *et. seq.*	102
Court of First Instance - see General Court		
Court of Justice:		
- Appointments procedure	254 - 255 TFEU	96
- Detailed structure – institutional provisions	251 - 255 TFEU	95 – 96
- Exclusions to jurisdiction - foreign policy	275 TFEU	100
- Exclusions to jurisdiction - freedom, security and justice	276 TFEU	100
- General Court (Court of First Instance)	256 TFEU	96
- General provisions and structure	19 TEU	11
- Jurisdiction	261 - 281 TFEU	99 – 101
- Penalty payments and fines	260 - 261 TFEU	97 – 98
- Specialised courts (judicial panels)	257 TFEU	97
- Preliminary rulings	267 TFEU	99
Crime prevention	84 TFEU	46
Criminal procedure - judicial co-operation	82 TFEU	45
Culture:		
- Fundamental right	Charter (Art. 22)	272
- General provisions	167 TFEU	72
D		
Decisions	288 – 289 TFEU	104
Declarations	-	207
Definition and objectives of the Union	1 to 8 TEU	3 – 5
Delegated European regulations	290 TFEU	104
Democratic life of the Union:		
- Democratic equality	9 TEU	6
- Participatory democracy	11 TEU, 22 & 24 TFEU	6, 31
- Representative democracy	10 TEU	6
- Social partners	152 TFEU	67
Development Fund	175 to 176, 177 TFEU	75 – 76
Diplomatic protection	23 TFEU	31
Directives	288 – 289 TFEU	104
Discrimination:		
- Freedom to provide services	61 TFEU	39
- Fundamental right	Charter (Art. 21)	272
- General policy	10 and 18 TFEU	28, 30
- Nationality	18 TFEU	30
- Workers	45(2) TFEU	36
Duration of the Treaty	53 TEU	23
Duties of citizens	20 TFEU	30
E		
Economic and Financial Committee	134 TFEU	61
Economic and monetary policy:		
- Budgets and deficits of the Member States	126 TFEU	57
- Competence of the Union	2(3) TFEU	26
- Co-ordination	5 TFEU	27
- Economic Policy	120 TFEU *et. seq.*	56
- Exchange-rate mechanism	140, 141, 219 TFEU	63, 64, 88
- Institutional provisions (ECB)	283 - 284 TFEU	101 – 102
- Monetary policy	127 TFEU *et. seq.*	59
- Provisions specific to members of the euro	136 - 138 TFEU	62
- Transitional provisions	139 TFEU *et. seq.*	63
Economic and Monetary Union:		
- General provisions	136 TFEU	62
- International agreements on exchange rates	219 TFEU	88
- Member States outside EMU	139 TFEU	63
- UK opt-out	139(2)TFEU, Prot. 18	63, 181
Economic, financial and technical co-operation with third countries	212 TFEU	85
Economic, social and territorial cohesion:		
- General provisions	174 TFEU *et. seq.*	75
- Protocol	Protocol 25	193

		Page
Education:		
- Fundamental right	169 TFEU,	73
	Charter (Art. 14)	271
- General provisions	165 TFEU	71
Emergency brake provisions:		
- Common foreign and security policy	31(2) TEU	15
- Judicial co-operation in civil matters	81(3) TFEU	44
- Judicial co-operation in criminal matters	82(3), 83(3-4) TFEU	45, 46
- Revision of the Treaties	48(6)&(7) TEU	21 – 22
- Social security	48 TFEU	37
Employment:		
- Competence of the Union	2(3) TFEU	26
- Co-ordination of policy	5(2) TFEU	27
- General provisions	145 TFEU	66
Energy:		
- Declaration	Declaration 35	220
- Difficulties in supply	122 TFEU	57
- Environment	192(2)(c) TFEU	79
- Fiscal policy	194(3) TFEU	80
- General provisions	194 TFEU	80
Enhanced co-operation:		
- Common security and defence policy	329(2) TFEU	116
- Competences of the Union	10 TEU, 330 TFEU	13, 116
- Detailed provisions	326 TFEU *et. seq.*	116
- European Public Prosecutor's Office	86(1) TFEU	47
- General provisions	20 TEU,	11
	326 - 334 TFEU	116 – 117
- Judicial co-operation in criminal matters	83(4) TFEU	46
Environmental protection:		
- Cohesion fund	177 TFEU	76
- Detailed policies	191 TFEU	78
- Fundamental rights	Charter (Art. 37)	273
- General Policies	3(3)TEU, 11 TFEU	3, 28
- Internal market	114(3)-(5) TFEU	54
- Shared competence	4(2)(e) TFEU	27
Equality:		
- Equal pay	157(1) TFEU,	69
	Protocol 32	198
- Fundamental right	Charter (Art. 20, 23)	272
- General provisions	8 TFEU	28
'Escalator' clauses – *see 'passerelle' clauses*		
Establishment of the Union	1 TEU	3
Euratom Treaty	Protocol B2	205
Euro Group:		
- Meetings	137 TFEU, Protocol 3	62, 133
- President	Protocol 3	133
Eurojust:		
- General provisions	85, 86 TFEU	46, 47
- Liaison with Europol	88(2)(b) TFEU	48
European Central Bank (ECB):		
- General provisions	282 TFEU	101
- Institutional provisions	283 - 284 TFEU	101 – 102
- Issue of Euro notes	128 TFEU	60
- Legal personality	282(3) TFEU,	101
	Protocol 13, Art. 9	157
- Monetary Policy	127 to 133 TFEU	59 – 61
- Objective and tasks	127 TFEU	59
- Privileges and immunities	343 TFEU,	119
	Protocol 13, Art. 39	166
- Protocol on privileges and immunities of the EU	Protocol 16, Art. 22	180
- Protocol on the ECB	Protocol 13	156
European Commission	9D TEU, 244 TFEU	10, 94

		Page
European Convention for the Protection of Human Rights:		
- General	6(2) TEU, 218 TFEU	4, 87
- Protocol on accession of the EU	Protocol 5	135
European Council:		
- General	15 TEU	8
- European Public Prosecutor's Office	86(1) TFEU	47
European Council President	15(6) TEU	8
European Court of Justice	19 TEU	11
European Defence Agency	42(3), 45 TEU	18, 19
European External Action Service:		
- General	27(3) TEU	14
- Declaration	Declaration 15	216
European Investment Bank (EIB):		
- General provisions	308 - 309 TFEU	109 – 110
- Legal personality	308 TFEU	109
- Privileges and immunities	343 TFEU,	119
	Protocol 14, Art. 28(4)	175
- Protocol on the EIB	Protocol no.14	168
- Protocol on privileges and immunities	Protocol 16, Art. 21	179
- Subsidiaries and other entities – legal personality	Protocol 14, Art. 28	175
European Judicial Network	85(1)(c) TFEU	46
European Monetary Co-operation Fund	141(2) TFEU	64
European Monetary Institute	141(2) TFEU	64
European Ombudsman	228 TFEU	91
European Parliament:		
- General	14 TEU, 223 TFEU	7, 90
- Protocol on transitional provisions	Protocol 11	138
European Public Prosecutor's Office	86 TFEU	47
European Regional Development Fund	175 to 176, 178 TFEU	75 – 76
European Social Fund	162 – 164 TFEU	70
European System of Central Banks (ESCB):		
- Composition	129 TFEU	60
- Objective and tasks	127 TFEU	59
- Protocol on the ESCB	Protocol 13	156
European Voluntary Humanitarian Aid Corps	214(5) TFEU	86
Europol	88 TFEU	48
'Ever-closer Union'	Preamble 13th Rec. TEU	2
	1 TEU	3
	Charter, preamble	269
Exchange rate controls	66, 143(2)(b) TFEU	40, 65
Exchange-Rate Mechanism	140-142, 219 TFEU	63 - 64
		88
Exclusive Competences	3 TFEU	26
Exercise of Union competence	2, 340 TFEU *et. seq.*	26, 104
External Action:		
- Principles and Objectives	21 TEU, 205 TFEU	12, 83
- Strategic Interests	22 TEU	12
- High Representative for Foreign Affairs	18, 22(2) TEU	10, 12
External Action Service:		
- Declaration	Declaration 15	215
- General	27(3) TEU	14
External Representation of the Union:		
- Commission	17(1) TEU, 244 TFEU	9, 94
- European Council - common foreign and security policy	15(2) TEU	8
- High Representative for Foreign Affairs	34(1) TEU	16

F

Finances of the Union	310 to 314 TFEU	110 – 112
Financial framework	312 TFEU	111
Fines	260, 299 TFEU	97, 107
Fisheries	3(1)(d), 38 TFEU	26, 34
Flexibility Clause - competences	352 TFEU	120

		Page
Foreign Affairs:		
- Common Foreign and Defence Policy	24 TEU	13
- European External Action Service	Declaration 15	216
- Foreign Affairs Council	16(6) TEU, 236 TFEU	8, 93
- High Representative for Foreign Affairs	18 TEU	10
Fraud:		
- Anti-fraud Office	317 TFEU	113
- General provisions	325 TFEU	115
Freedom, Security and Justice:		
- Administrative co-operation	74 - 76 TFEU	42
- Court of Justice - extent of competence	276 TFEU	100
- Definition of area	67 TFEU	41
- Eurojust	85 TFEU	46
- European Public Prosecutor's Office	86 TFEU	47
- Europol	88 TFEU	48
- Evaluation mechanisms	70 TFEU	41
- Judicial co-operation in civil matters	81 TFEU	44
- Judicial co-operation in criminal matters	82 TFEU	45
- Measures concerning law and order and internal security	4(2) TEU, 71 TFEU	4, 41
- Member States' role	73 TFEU	42
- Operational co-operation	71 TFEU	41
- Police co-operation	87 TFEU	47
- Policies on border checks, asylum and immigration	77 TFEU	42
- Right of initiative	76 TFEU	42
- Role of European Council	68 TFEU	41
- Role of national parliaments	69 – 70 TFEU	41
- Shared competence	4(2)(j) TFEU	27
Free movement of goods	28 TFEU *et. seq.*	32
Free movement of persons, capital and services:		
- Capital and payments	63 - 66 TFEU	40
- Fundamental freedoms	18 TFEU	30
- Provision of services	56 - 62 TFEU	39
- Right of establishment	49 - 55 TFEU	37 – 38
- Workers	45 - 48 TFEU	36 – 37
Fundamental Rights:		
- General provisions	6 TEU, Charter	4, 269
- Protocol on Charter re the UK	Protocol 7	137
G		
General Affairs Council	16(6) TEU, 236 TFEU	8, 93
General and Final Provisions	335 TFEU *et. seq.*	118 – 122
General Court:		
- General provisions and structure	19 TEU	11
- Jurisdiction	256 TFEU	96
- Protocol on the Court of Justice	Protocol 12, Art. 47-62b	149 – 152
General secretariat:		
- European Council	235(4) TFEU	93
- Council	240(2) TFEU	94
Geneva Convention	78(1) TFEU	43
H		
Harmonisation of laws	114 TFEU *et. seq.*	54
Health and safety:		
- Internal Market	114(3) TFEU	54
- Social policy	153(1)(a) TFEU	67
High Representative of the Union for Foreign Affairs and Security Policy:		
- Appointment and resignation	9E TEU, 235, 246 TFEU	11, 92, 95
- Common Foreign and Security Policy	21(3), 22, 23 TEU	12, 13
- Economic and financial aid to third countries	214 TFEU	86
- Enhanced co-operation	328, 329, 331 TFEU	116 - 117
- Foreign Affairs Council	27 TEU	14

		Page
High Representative of the Union for Foreign Affairs and Security Policy (continued):		
- General provisions	18, 27 TEU	10, 14
- International agreements	218, 220 TFEU	87, 89
- Member of European Council	15(2) TEU	8
- Representation of the Union	27(2) TEU	14
- Salary and allowances	243 TFEU	94
- Solidarity Clause	222 TFEU	89
- Special representative	33 TEU	16
- United Nations Security Council	34(2) TEU	16
Humanitarian Aid	214 TFEU	86
I		
Identity cards	77(3) TFEU	42
Industry	173 TFEU	75
Immediate Environment of the Union	8 TEU	5
Immigration:		
- Common immigration policy	81 TFEU	44
- General provisions	67(2) TFEU	41
- '*Non-refoulement*' (non-forcible return of immigrants)	78 TFEU	43
- Union policies	77 TFEU	42
Implementation of the Solidarity Clause	222 TFEU	89
Implementing acts	291 TFEU	105
Immunity:		
- Officials of the Union	Protocol 16, Art. 11	178
- The Union	343 TFEU	119
- Protocol on privileges and immunities of the EU	Protocol 16	176
Infringement of national legal systems:		
- Judicial co-operation in criminal matters	82(2), 83(3) TFEU	45, 46
- Social security systems	48 TFEU	37
Institutions of the Union:		
- Co-operation between the institutions	295 TFEU	107
- Council	16 TEU, 237 TFEU	8, 93
- Court of Auditors	285 - 287 TFEU	102 – 103
- Court of Justice	19 TEU, 251 TFEU	11, 95
- European Central Bank	13 TEU, 282-284 TFEU	7, 101-102
- European Commission	17 TEU, 244 TFEU	9, 94
- European Council	15 TEU, 235 TFEU	8, 92
- European Investment Bank	308 - 309 TFEU	109 - 110
- European Parliament	14 TEU, 223 TFEU	7, 90
- General provisions	13 TEU	7
Intellectual property:		
- Common commercial policy	207(1) TFEU	84
- Court of Justice jurisdiction	262 TFEU	98
Internal market:		
- Approximation of legislation (common provisions)	114 TFEU *et. seq.*	54
- Capital and payments	63 TFEU *et. seq.*	40
- Establishment and functioning	26 TFEU *et. seq.*	32
- Fiscal (tax) provisions	110 - 113 TFEU	53 – 54
- Free movement of goods	28 TFEU *et. seq.*	32
- Free movement of persons and services	45 TFEU *et. seq.*	36
- Rules on competition	101 TFEU et. seq.	50
- State aid	107 - 109 TFEU	52 – 53
Internal policies of the Union:		
- General	26 TFEU *et. seq.*	32
- Revision	48 TEU	21
International agreements:		
- Authorisation of signing	218(5) TFEU	87
- Exclusive competence	3(2) TFEU	27
- General provisions	216 TFEU *et. seq.*	87
- Union negotiator	218(3)-(7) TFEU	87 – 88
- Special committee for negotiations	218(4) TFEU	87

		Page
Ioannina compromise	Declarations 7, 50	212, 224
J		
Judicial co-operation in civil matters	81 TFEU	44
Judicial co-operation in criminal matters:		
- Emergency Brake	82(3), 83(3) TFEU	45, 46
- Enhanced co-operation	83(4) TFEU	46
- Eurojust	85 TFEU	46
- European Public Prosecutor	86 TFEU	47
- General	82 TFEU *et. seq.*	45
L		
Languages	55 TEU	23
Law and Order:		
- Area of freedom, security and justice	71 - 72 TFEU	41 – 42
- Court of Justice – limit of jurisdiction	276 TFEU	100
- General provisions	4(2) TEU	4
- Internal market	347 TFEU	119
Legal Acts of the Union:		
- Entry into force	297 TFEU	107
- General provisions	288 TFEU	104
- Legislative Acts	289 TFEU	104
- Non-legislative Acts	290, 292 TFEU	104, 105
- Principles	296 TFEU	107
- Publication	297 TFEU	107
Legal capacity of the Union	335 TFEU	118
Legal Personality:		
- Declaration on competence	Declaration 24	218
- European Central Bank	Protocol 13, Art. 9.1	157
- European Investment Bank	308 TFEU	109
- The Union	47 TEU	29
Legislative Acts:		
- Directives and Regulations	288 – 289 TFEU	104
- Procedure for adoption	293 – 294 TFEU	105
Legislative Procedure:		
- Ordinary	289 TFEU	104
- Ordinary - description of procedure	294 TFEU	105
- Revision of Treaty	48 TEU	21
- Special	289(2) TFEU	104
Lisbon Strategy	Declaration 30	219
Loyalty:		
- Common Security and Defence Policy	24(3) TEU	13
- Sincere co-operation	4(3) TEU	4
M		
Membership of the Union:		
- Procedure for application	49 TEU	22
- Suspension of rights	354 TFEU	121
- Voluntary withdrawal	50 TEU	22
Multi-annual financial framework:		
- Financial provisions	312 TFEU	111
- General provisions	312 TFEU	111
- Research and technological development	182 TFEU	77
N		
National identity	4(2) TEU	4
National Parliaments:		
- Accession to the Union	49 TEU	22
- Eurojust	12 TEU, 85 TFEU	6, 46
- Europol	12 TEU, 88 TFEU	6, 48
- Freedom, security and justice	69, 70 TFEU	41

		Page
National Parliaments (continued):		
- General flexibility clause	352(2) TFEU	120
- Judicial co-operation in civil matters	81(3) TFEU	44
- Proposals under ordinary legislative procedure	Protocol 1 (Art. 2)	129
- Protocol	Protocol 1	129
- Representative democracy	10(2) TEU	6
- Revision of the Treaties – *Passerelle* clause	48 TEU	21
- Role	12 TEU	6
- Subsidiarity	5(3) TEU,	4
	69, 70 TFEU	41
National security	4(2) TEU	4
NATO	42 TEU, Prots. 4, 29	18, 133, 192
'No Bail-Out' clause (EMU)	125 TFEU	57
Non-Discrimination:		
- Humanitarian aid	214 TFEU	86
- Non-discrimination and citizenship	18 TFEU *et seq.*	30
- On grounds of nationality	18 TFEU	30
- Values of the Union	2 TEU	3
Non-Legislative Acts	290, 292 TFEU	104, 105
Non-refoulement (non-forcible return of immigrants)	78 TFEU	43
O		
Objectives of the Union	3 TEU	3
Official Journal of the European Union	287(1)&(4), 297 TFEU	103, 107
OLAF	317, 325 TFEU	113, 115
Ombudsman	228 TFEU	91
Operations in the territory of another Member State	89 TFEU	48
Opinions	288 TFEU	104
Organisation for Economic Co-operation and Development	220(1) TFEU	89
Organisation for Security and Co-operation in Europe	220(1) TFEU	89
Overseas countries and territories:		
- General provisions	198 to 222 TFEU	82 - 90
- List of countries	Annex II	125
Own resources:		
- General provisions	311 TFEU	111
- Multi-annual financial framework	312 TFEU	111
- New categories of own resources	311 TFEU	111
- Procedure for availability of own resources to Commission	322(2) TFEU	115
- Qualified majority voting (implementing measures)	311 TFEU	111
- UK's rebate	311 TFEU	111
P		
Participatory democracy	11 TEU, 24 TFEU	6, 31
'*Passerelle*' clauses:		
- Common foreign and security policy	31(2) TEU	15
- Declaration on amending the Treaties	Declaration 18	181
- Enhanced co-operation	333 TFEU	117
- Environmental protection	192(2) TFEU	79
- General – revision of Part Three of the TFEU	48(7) TEU	22
- Judicial co-operation in civil matters	81(3) TFEU	44
- Multi-annual financial framework	312(2) TFEU	111
- Social Policy - employment and workers' rights	153(2) TFEU	68
Passports	77 TFEU	42
Penalties and fines:		
- Court of Justice	260 TFEU	97
- Economic policy	126(11) TFEU	58
- Enforcement on individuals	299 TFEU	107
Permanent structured co-operation:		
- Common security and defence policy	18(6), 46 TEU	18, 20
- Protocol	Protocol 4	133
Personal data:		
- Declaration	Declaration 20	217

		Page
Personal data (continued):		
- Fundamental right	16 TFEU, Charter (Art. 8)	29, 270
- General provisions	39 TEU, 16 TFEU	17, 29
'Petersberg' tasks	42(1), 43(1) TEU	18, 19
Police co-operation	87 TFEU	47
Policies and functioning of the Union	7 to 15 TFEU	28 – 29
Policies – methods of implementation	288 TFEU *et seq.*	104
Policies on border checks, asylum and immigration	77 TFEU	42
Political parties at European level:		
- Fundamental right	Charter (Art. 12.2)	271
- General provisions	10(4) TEU	6
- Regulations	224 TFEU	90
Preamble:		
- Charter of Fundamental Rights	-	269
- Treaty on European Union	-	1
- Treaty on the Functioning of the European Union	-	25
Precautionary principle - environment	191(2) TFEU	79
President of the Eurogroup	138(2) TFEU, Protocol 3	62, 133
President of the European Commission	17 TEU, Declaration 11	9, 215
President of the European Council:		
- Declaration (Decision) on election	Declaration 9	214
- General provisions	15 TEU	8
Primacy of Union law	Declaration 17	216
Principles:		
- Conferral	5 TEU	4
- Democratic equality	9 TEU	6
- Mutual recognition of judicial decisions	67(3)-(4), 70 TFEU	41
- *Non-refoulement* (non-forcible return of immigrants)	78(1) TFEU	43
- Participatory democracy	11 TEU, 24 TFEU	6, 31
- Proportionality	5(1)&(4) TEU	4
- Representative democracy	10 TEU	6
- Sincere co-operation	4(3) TEU	4
- Solidarity	222 TFEU	89
- Subsidiarity	5(1)&(3) TEU	4
Principles common to legal acts of the Union	296 TFEU	107
Privileged relations with neighbouring states	8 TEU	5
Privileges and immunities of the Union	343 TFEU	119
Procedure for applying for Union membership	49 TEU	22
Procedure for revision of the Treaty	48 TEU	21
Proportionality:		
- Charter of fundamental rights - Preamble	Charter	269
- Freedom, security and justice	69 TFEU	41
- Freedom, security and justice - limit of jurisdiction of Court of Justice in police operations	276 TFEU	100
- Fundamental right – criminal offences	Charter (Art. 49)	275
- Fundamental right - scope	Charter (Art. 52)	275
- General provisions	5(1), (3), (4) TEU	4
- Principles common to the Union's legal acts	296 TFEU	107
- Protocol	Protocol 2	131
Protection of personal data:		
- Fundamental right	16 TFEU, Charter (Art. 8)	29, 270
- General	39 TEU, 16 TFEU	17, 29
Protocols attached to the Treaty	51 TEU	23
Public health	168 TFEU	72
Public Prosecutor's Office	86 TFEU	47
Publication and entry into force of legal acts	297 TFEU	107

		Page
Q		
Qualified Majority:		
- '*Passerelle*' clause	48 TEU	21
- Declaration	Declaration 7	212
- General provisions	16 TEU, 238 TFEU	8, 93
- Ordinary Legislative procedure	294 TFEU	105
- Protocol on transitional provisions	Protocol 11	138
R		
Race and racism	10, 19, 67(3) TFEU	28, 30, 41
Ratification and entry into force	54 TEU	23
Recommendations	288, 292 TFEU	104, 105
Regional unions	350 TFEU	120
Regions – economic, social & territorial cohesion	174 TFEU, Protocol 25	75, 193
Regional government:		
- General	4 TEU, 123 TFEU	4, 57
- Subsidiarity	5(3) TEU, Protocol 2	4, 131
Regulations	288, 289(2) TFEU	104
Relations with international organisations and third countries and Union delegations	220 - 221 TFEU	89
Relations between the Union and Member States	4 TEU	4
Religion:		
- Animal welfare	13 TFEU	28
- General	17 TFEU	29
Resources (financial) - *see also Own resources*	311 TFEU	111
Restrictive measures on relations with third countries	215 TFEU	86
Revision of the Treaties:		
- General flexibility clause	352 TFEU	120
- Ordinary revision procedure	48 TEU	21
- Simplified revision procedure	48 TEU	21
Right of initiative to introduce proposals for legislation:		
- Commission	17(2) TEU	9
- Common foreign and security policy	22(2), 30 TEU	12, 15
- Freedom, security and justice	76 TFEU	42
Rights of Citizens:		
- Fundamental rights	18 - 25 TFEU,	30 - 31
	Charter (Art. 39 - 46)	274
- General provisions	6 TEU	4
Right to strike	Charter (Art. 28)	272
Rules on competition	101 TFEU *et. seq.*	50
S		
Schengen *acquis*	Prot. 20, Decls. 44 - 47	183, 222
Scope:		
- Charter of Fundamental Rights	Charter (Art.52)	275
- Treaty	52 TEU, 355 TFEU	23, 121
Seat of the Institutions	341 TFEU, Protocol 15	118, 176
Services of general economic interest:		
- Competition	106 TFEU	52
- Fundamental right	Charter (Art. 36)	273
- General provisions	14 TFEU	29
- Protocol	Protocol 9	137
- State aid	107 TFEU	52
- Transport	93 TFEU	49
Shared competences	4 TFEU	27
Sincere co-operation	4(3) TEU	4
Social and territorial cohesion:		
- Declaration on island states	Declaration 33	220
- General provisions	174-175 TFEU	75
Social Policy:		
- Areas and fields included in social policy	153 TFEU	67
- Commission's role in co-ordination	156 TFEU	69

		Page
Social Policy (continued):		
- Declaration	Declaration 31	220
- Equal pay	157 TFEU, Protocol 32	69, 198
- European Social Fund	162 to 164 TFEU	70
- Objectives	151 TFEU	67
- Shared competence	4(2)(b) TFEU	27
- Social partners	153 - 155 TFEU	67 – 69
- Social Protection Committee	160 TFEU	70
Social security:		
- *'Barber Protocol'* on pension funds	Protocol 32	198
- Commission's role in co-ordination	156 TFEU	69
- Documentation	77(3) TFEU	43
- Freedom of movement of workers; 'emergency brake'	48 TFEU	37
- Fundamental right	Charter (Art. 34)	273
- Member States' rights	153(4) TFEU	68
- Social policy	153(1)(c) TFEU	67
Solidarity:		
- Border checks, asylum and immigration	80 TFEU	44
- Common foreign and security policy	24 TEU	13
- Competences	222(1) TFEU	89
- Implementation	222 TFEU	89
- Union's values	3 TEU	3
Space	189 TFEU	78
Sport	165 TFEU	71
State aid	107 to 109 TFEU	52 – 53
Status of churches and non-confessional organisations	17 TFEU	29
Structural funds	175 TFEU	75
Subsidiarity:		
- Area of freedom, security and justice	69 TFEU	41
- Charter of fundamental rights - Preamble and application	Charter (Art. 51)	267, 275
- Flexibility	352(2) TFEU	150
- General provisions	5(1), (3), (4) TEU	4
- Protocol	Protocol 2	131
Suspension of Union membership rights	354 TFEU	121
Sustainable development:		
- General	3(5) TEU	4
- Policies	11 TFEU	28
Symbols of the Union	Declaration 52	225

T

Taxation:		
- Capital and payments	65 TFEU	40
- Customs duties	28 to 32 TFEU	32 – 33
- Energy	194(3) TFEU	80
- Environment	192(2)(a) TFEU	79
- French overseas departments	349 TFEU	119
- General provisions	110 to 113 TFEU	53 – 54
- Harmonisation of laws	114(2), 115 TFEU	54, 55
- Industry and employees	173(3) TFEU	75
- Research and technological development	179(2) TFEU	76
Terrorism:		
- Capital movements and payments	75 TFEU	42
- Common security and defence policy	43 TEU	19
- Europol	88 TFEU	48
- Judicial co-operation	83(1) TFEU	46
- Solidarity clause	222 TFEU	89
Tourism	6, 195 TFEU	27, 80
Trade:		
- Common commercial policy	206 to 207 TFEU	83 – 84
- External action	21(2)(e) TEU	12
- Freedom of establishment	50(2)(a) TFEU	37
- Functioning of the internal market	114(6) TFEU	54

		Page
Trade Unions:		
- Fundamental rights	Charter (Arts. 12, 27, 28)	271, 272
- Social Policy	151 to 164 TFEU	67 – 70
- European Social Fund	162 to 164 TFEU	70
Trans-European networks	170 to 172 TFEU	74
Transitional Provisions	Prot. 11, Decl. 7	138, 212
Transparency of the proceedings of the Union's institutions	15 TFEU	29
Transport	90 TFEU *et seq.*	48
Treaty of Lisbon:		
- Annex – Tables of Equivalences	-	243
- Final Act	-	239
- General provisions	-	233
Tripartite Social Summit for Growth and Employment	152 TFEU	67
U		
Union law - primacy	Declaration 17	216
United Kingdom opt-outs:		
- Area of freedom, security and justice	Protocol 22	186
- Border controls	Protocol 21	185
- Charter of Fundamental Rights	Protocol 7	136
- EMU – single currency	Protocol 18	181
- Schengen *acquis*	Protocol 20	183
- Transitional provisions	Protocol 11	138
United Nations:		
- Development co-operation	208(2) TFEU	84
- External action – general provisions	21 TEU, 205 TFEU	12, 83
- Humanitarian aid	214(7) TFEU	86
- Representation of the Union	34(2) TEU	16
- Union's relations with international organisations	220 TFEU	89
United Nations Charter:		
- Common foreign and security policy	34(2) TEU	16
- External action - general provisions	21(1) TEU	12
- Provisions for implementing the common security and defence policy	42(1), (7) TEU	18 – 19
- Union's objectives	3(5) TEU	4
United Nations Security Council:		
- Common foreign and security policy - Union representation	34(2) TEU	16
- Permanent membership of Member States	34(2) TEU, Decl. 14	16, 215
V		
Values	2 TEU	3
Vocational training	166 TFEU	71
Voluntary withdrawal from the Union	50 TEU	22
Voting:		
- Declaration on transitional provisions	Prot. 11, Decl. 7	138, 212
- Qualified majority	16 TEU, 238 TFEU,	8, 93
	Prot. 10	138
- Qualified majority procedure	294 TFEU	105
Voting in elections:		
- Detailed arrangements	17(2)(b), 22 TFEU	30, 31
- Fundamental right	Charter (Arts. 39, 40)	274
W, X, Y		
Weighting of votes:		
- Declaration on transitional procedures	Declaration 7	212
- European Council	15 TEU, 235 TFEU	8, 92
- European Parliament	14 TEU, Protocol 11	7, 138
- Protocol on transitional provisions	Protocol 11	138
- Council	9C TEU, 238 TFEU	9, 93
Working conditions	153(1)(b) TFEU	67
Xenophobia	67(3) TFEU	41
Youth	165 TFEU	71

(Total pages – 448)

BRITISH MANAGEMENT DATA FOUNDATION

The British Management Data Foundation (BMDF) was formed in 1979. It is non-profit making and limited by guarantee.

It is an independent body supported by a wide range of major British companies and is concerned with matters affecting the performance and global competitiveness of its member companies to whom it gives independent advice and data.

The companies and organisations supporting the BMDF do not have an overall corporate view. They represent many differing interests and viewpoints. This, however, is one of the strengths of the BMDF and enables issues to be considered from a wide perspective.

The aim of all BMDF activities is to achieve a better understanding of current core issues so as to enable more informed decision-making.

Activities include review meetings and the issue of data and information on a wide range of current matters of importance to industry.